# Frommer's

W9-ASV-136

# The Carolinas & Georgia
## 7th Edition

### by Darwin Porter & Danforth Prince

**Here's what the critics say about Frommer's:**

"Amazingly easy to use. Very portable, very complete."
—*Booklist*

"Detailed, accurate, and easy-to-read information for all price ranges."
—*Glamour Magazine*

"Hotel information is close to encyclopedic."
—*Des Moines Sunday Register*

"Frommer's Guides have a way of giving you a real feel for a place."
—*Knight Ridder Newspapers*

WILEY

Wiley Publishing, Inc.

## About the Authors

A team of veteran travel writers, **Darwin Porter** and **Danforth Prince** have produced numerous titles for Frommer's, including best-selling guides to Italy, France, the Caribbean, England, and Germany. Porter, a former bureau chief of the *Miami Herald,* is also a Hollywood biographer. His most recent releases are *The Secret Life of Humphrey Bogart* and *Katharine the Great,* the latter a close-up of the private life of the late Katharine Hepburn. Prince was formerly employed by the Paris bureau of the *New York Times,* and is today president of Blood Moon Productions and other media-related firms.

Published by:

## Wiley Publishing, Inc.

111 River St.
Hoboken, NJ 07030-5774

ISBN 0-7645-7526-0

Editor: Alexis Lipsitz Flippin
Production Editor: M. Faunette Johnston
Cartographer: Elizabeth Puhl
Photo Editor: Richard Fox
Production by Wiley Indianapolis Composition Services

Front cover photo: Magnolia plantation near Charleston, SC
Back cover photo: Fishing at sunrise, Cape Hatteras, NC

For information on our other products and services or to obtain technical support, please contact our Customer Care Department within the U.S. at 800/762-2974, outside the U.S. at 317/572-3993 or fax 317/572-4002.

Wiley also publishes its books in a variety of electronic formats. Some content that appears in print may not be available in electronic formats.

Manufactured in the United States of America

5  4  3  2  1

# Contents

**List of Maps**   viii

**What's New in the Carolinas & Georgia**   1

## 1   The Best of the Carolinas & Georgia   4

**1** The Best Scenic Drives ........5

**2** The Best Family Vacations ......5

**3** The Best Places to Rediscover the Old South .............6

**4** The Best Small Towns .........7

**5** The Best Golf Courses .......7

**6** The Best Beaches ...........8

**7** The Best Luxury Hotels & Resorts .................8

**8** The Best Moderately Priced Hotels .............9

**9** The Best Budget Hotels ......9

**10** The Best Restaurants ........10

## 2   For International Visitors   12

**1** Preparing for Your Trip .......12

**2** Getting to the U.S. ..........16

**3** Getting Around the U.S. ......17

*Fast Facts: For the International Traveler* ..................18

## 3   Planning Your Trip to North Carolina   25

**1** The Regions in Brief .........25

**2** Visitor Information ..........28

**3** Money ....................28

**4** When to Go ...............28

*What Things Cost in Asheville* ...............29

*North Carolina Calendar of Events* .................29

**5** The Active Vacation Planner ...33

**6** Specialized Travel Resources ...36

**7** Getting There .............37

**8** Package Tours ............38

**9** Getting Around ...........38

*Fast Facts: North Carolina* .....39

## 4   The Outer Banks   41

**1** The Outer Banks: From Corolla to Oregon Inlet ...........41

*The Lost Colony* ............48

**2** Cape Hatteras National Seashore .................55

**3** Ocracoke Island ...........57

*Two Cuts to Blackbeard's Neck* ....................58

**4** Cedar Island .............61

## 5  Wilmington & the Southern Banks    63

**1** Wilmington & Cape Fear ......63
  *Side Trip: Bald Head Island* ....73
**2** Beaufort .................74
  *Side Trip: Harkers Island* ......77
**3** Morehead City ...........77
**4** New Bern ...............82
**5** Historic Bath: The State's
  Oldest Town .............85

## 6  The Piedmont    87

**1** Raleigh .................87
**2** Durham .................97
  *Field of Dreams* ...........99
**3** Chapel Hill ..............104
**4** Winston-Salem ...........113
  *The Search for Mayberry* .....115
**5** Charlotte ...............123
  *Finger-Lickin' Down-Home
  Cooking* ................127

## 7  Southern Pines & the Pinehurst Sandhills    130

**1** Pinehurst ................131
  *The Links of Pinehurst* ......133
**2** Southern Pines ...........136

## 8  Asheville & the High Country    139

**1** Enjoying the Great Outdoors
  in the High Country .......139
**2** Asheville ...............141
  *The Greatest Mansion
  in the Mountains* ..........144
**3** Boone .................156
**4** Banner Elk ..............159
**5** Beech Mountain ..........162
**6** Blowing Rock ............164
**7** The Blue Ridge Parkway .....167

## 9  Great Smoky Mountains National Park    169

**1** Cherokee: Gateway to
  the Smokies .............171
  *Unto These Hills* ..........174
**2** The Smokies: Just the Facts ...176
**3** Seeing the Park's Highlights ...178
**4** Sports & Outdoor Pursuits ....179
**5** Camping ................182
**6** Where to Stay ...........183
**7** Where to Dine ...........188

## 10  Planning Your Trip to South Carolina    190

**1** The Regions in Brief .......190
**2** Visitor Information .........193
**3** When to Go .............193
  *South Carolina Calendar
  of Events* ................194
  *What Things Cost
  in Charleston* .............197
**4** The Active Vacation Planner ...198
**5** Specialized Travel
  Resources ..............199
**6** Getting There ............199
**7** Getting Around ..........200
  *Fast Facts: South Carolina* ....201

## 11  Charleston                                                                    202

**1** Orientation . . . . . . . . . . . . .202
  *Neighborhoods in Brief* . . . . . .203
**2** Getting Around . . . . . . . . . .204
  *Fast Facts: Charleston* . . . . . . .205
**3** Where to Stay . . . . . . . . . . . .206
  *Family-Friendly Hotels* . . . . . . .214
**4** Where to Dine . . . . . . . . . . . .215
  *Family-Friendly Restaurants* . . .222
**5** Exploring Charleston . . . . . . .223

  *Frommer's Favorite Charleston
  Experiences* . . . . . . . . . . . . . .229
**6** Organized Tours . . . . . . . . . .231
**7** Beaches & Outdoor Pursuits . . .232
**8** Shopping . . . . . . . . . . . . . . .234
**9** Charleston After Dark . . . . . . .237
**10** A Side Trip to Edisto Island . . .240
**11** Kiawah Island & the Isle
  of Palms . . . . . . . . . . . . . . . .241

## 12  Hilton Head & the Low Country                                                 243

**1** Essentials . . . . . . . . . . . . . . .243
**2** Beaches, Golf, Tennis & Other
  Outdoor Pursuits . . . . . . . . . .245
  *Hilton Head's Wonderful
  Wildlife* . . . . . . . . . . . . . . . . .248

**3** Where to Stay . . . . . . . . . . . .250
**4** Where to Dine . . . . . . . . . . . .255
**5** Hilton Head After Dark . . . . . .259
**6** Side Trip to Beaufort . . . . . . .259

## 13  Myrtle Beach & the Grand Strand                                               263

**1** Essentials . . . . . . . . . . . . . . .265
**2** The Beaches, the Links &
  Beyond . . . . . . . . . . . . . . . . .265
  *Building a Better Bear* . . . . . . .269
**3** Where to Stay . . . . . . . . . . . .270
**4** Where to Dine . . . . . . . . . . . .275

**5** The Grand Strand After Dark . . .279
**6** Murrells Inlet: The Seafood
  Capital of South Carolina . . . .281
**7** Pawleys Island & Litchfield . . .282
**8** Georgetown . . . . . . . . . . . . . .284

## 14  Columbia & the Heartland                                                      288

**1** Columbia . . . . . . . . . . . . . . .288
**2** Side Trips from Columbia . . . .298

**3** Aiken: Thoroughbred
  Country . . . . . . . . . . . . . . . . .301

## 15  Planning Your Trip to Georgia                                                 305

**1** The Regions in Brief . . . . . . . .305
**2** Visitor Information . . . . . . . . .307
  *What Things Cost
  in Atlanta* . . . . . . . . . . . . . . .307
**3** When to Go . . . . . . . . . . . . . .308
  *Georgia Calendar of Events* . . .308

**4** The Active Vacation Planner . . .312
**5** Specialized Travel Resources . . .313
**6** Getting There . . . . . . . . . . . . .314
**7** Getting Around . . . . . . . . . . .315
  *Fast Facts: Georgia* . . . . . . . . .315

## 16  Atlanta    316

**1** Orientation ..............318
   *Neighborhoods in Brief* ......318
**2** Getting Around ...........319
   *Fast Facts: Atlanta* .........321
**3** Where to Stay ............323
**4** Where to Dine ............335
   *Family-Friendly Restaurants* ...344

**5** Attractions ..............347
**6** Especially for Kids .........358
**7** Organized Tours ..........359
**8** Outdoor Pursuits ..........359
**9** Shopping ................361
**10** Atlanta After Dark ........365

## 17  Athens, the Antebellum Trail & Augusta    369

**1** Athens .................369
**2** Madison ................374
**3** Eatonton ................376

**4** Milledgeville .............377
**5** Augusta ................379

## 18  North Georgia    385

**1** The Great Outdoors
   in North Georgia .........385
**2** Chickamauga & Chattanooga
   National Military Park ......386
**3** Adairsville ..............387
   *Will the Real Scarlett O'Hara
   Please Stand Up?* .........389

**4** Tate & Jasper ............389
**5** Dahlonega ...............390
**6** Blairsville ...............392
**7** Alpine Helen .............394
**8** Rabun County ...........398

## 19  Macon & the Southwest    400

**1** Macon ..................400
**2** Callaway Gardens ........405
**3** Warm Springs & FDR's
   Little White House ........408

**4** Plains: Jimmy Carter's
   Hometown ..............410
**5** Thomasville .............414

## 20  Savannah    418

**1** Orientation .............419
   *Neighborhoods in Brief* ......419
**2** Getting Around ..........420
   *Fast Facts: Savannah* .......421
**3** Where to Stay ............421
**4** Where to Dine ............430

**5** Exploring Savannah ........436
   *Martinis in the Cemetery* .....439
**6** Organized Tours ..........441
**7** Outdoor Pursuits .........442
**8** Shopping ................444
**9** Savannah After Dark .......446

## 21  The Golden Isles & the Okefenokee Swamp    450

**1** Sapelo Island . . . . . . . . . . . . .452

**2** Brunswick . . . . . . . . . . . . . . .453

**3** St. Simons Island . . . . . . . . . .455

**4** Little St. Simons Island . . . . . .461

**5** Sea Island . . . . . . . . . . . . . . .462

**6** Jekyll Island . . . . . . . . . . . . . .463

**7** Cumberland Island . . . . . . . . .468

**8** The Okefenokee Swamp . . . . .470

## Appendix: The Carolinas & Georgia in Depth    472

**1** History 101 . . . . . . . . . . . . . .472

*Dateline* . . . . . . . . . . . . . . . .472

**2** Southern Living Today . . . . . . .483

**3** What's Cookin' in Dixie . . . . . .485

## Index    488

North Carolina . . . . . . . . . . .488

South Carolina . . . . . . . . . . .492

Georgia . . . . . . . . . . . . . . . .495

# List of Maps

North Carolina   27

The Outer Banks   43

Wilmington & the Southern
  Banks   64

Wilmington   65

The Research Triangle: Raleigh,
  Durham & Chapel Hill   89

Charlotte   125

Blue Ridge Parkway   140

Asheville   143

Great Smoky Mountains National
  Park   170

South Carolina   191

Charleston Accommodations   207

Charleston Dining   217

Charleston Sights   225

Hilton Head Island   244

Myrtle Beach & the Grand
  Strand   264

Georgia   306

Atlanta at a Glance   317

MARTA Rapid Rail   320

Downtown Atlanta Accommodations
  & Dining   324

Midtown Atlanta Accommodations
  & Dining   328

Buckhead Accommodations &
  Dining   332

Downtown Atlanta Sights   348

Central Atlanta Sights   350

Athens, the Antebellum Trail &
  Augusta   370

Macon & the Southwest   401

Savannah Accommodations   422

Savannah Dining   431

Downtown Savannah Sights   437

The Golden Isles   451

## An Invitation to the Reader

In researching this book, we discovered many wonderful places—hotels, restaurants, shops, and more. We're sure you'll find others. Please tell us about them, so we can share the information with your fellow travelers in upcoming editions. If you were disappointed with a recommendation, we'd love to know that, too. Please write to:

*Frommer's The Carolinas & Georgia,* 7th Edition
Wiley Publishing, Inc. • 111 River St. • Hoboken, NJ 07030-5774

## An Additional Note

Please be advised that travel information is subject to change at any time—and this is especially true of prices. We therefore suggest that you write or call ahead for confirmation when making your travel plans. The authors, editors, and publisher cannot be held responsible for the experiences of readers while traveling. Your safety is important to us, however, so we encourage you to stay alert and be aware of your surroundings. Keep a close eye on cameras, purses, and wallets, all favorite targets of thieves and pickpockets.

## Other Great Guides for Your Trip:

*Frommer's Atlanta*
*Frommer's Portable Charleston*
*Frommer's Portable Savannah*

## Frommer's Star Ratings, Icons & Abbreviations

Every hotel, restaurant, and attraction listing in this guide has been ranked for quality, value, service, amenities, and special features using a **star-rating system.** In country, state, and regional guides, we also rate towns and regions to help you narrow down your choices and budget your time accordingly. Hotels and restaurants are rated on a scale of zero (recommended) to three stars (exceptional). Attractions, shopping, nightlife, towns, and regions are rated according to the following scale: zero stars (recommended), one star (highly recommended), two stars (very highly recommended), and three stars (must-see).

In addition to the star-rating system, we also use **seven feature icons** that point you to the great deals, in-the-know advice, and unique experiences that separate travelers from tourists. Throughout the book, look for:

| | |
|---|---|
| *Finds* | Special finds—those places only insiders know about |
| *Fun Fact* | Fun facts—details that make travelers more informed and their trips more fun |
| *Kids* | Best bets for kids and advice for the whole family |
| *Moments* | Special moments—those experiences that memories are made of |
| *Overrated* | Places or experiences not worth your time or money |
| *Tips* | Insider tips—great ways to save time and money |
| *Value* | Great values—where to get the best deals |

The following **abbreviations** are used for credit cards:

| | | | | | |
|---|---|---|---|---|---|
| AE | American Express | DISC | Discover | V | Visa |
| DC | Diners Club | MC | MasterCard | | |

## Frommers.com

Now that you have the guidebook to a great trip, visit our website at **www.frommers.com** for travel information on more than 3,000 destinations. With features updated regularly, we give you instant access to the most current trip-planning information available. At Frommers.com, you'll also find the best prices on airfares, accommodations, and car rentals—and you can even book travel online through our travel booking partners. At Frommers.com, you'll also find the following:

- Online updates to our most popular guidebooks
- Vacation sweepstakes and contest giveaways
- Newsletter highlighting the hottest travel trends
- Online travel message boards with featured travel discussions

# What's New in the Carolinas & Georgia

The New South is in no way mired in its plantation heritage. In fact, it's one of the fastest-growing and most rapidly changing regions of America. Here's a preview of some recent developments.

## NORTH CAROLINA

**OUTER BANKS** On remote Ocracoke Island, reached by a free car ferry from Hatteras, visitors in the summer of 2004 showed a tendency to desert former old favorites, many of which have become tired and stale, to sample more modern accommodations. Gaining favor is the four-story **Anchorage Inn & Marina,** Highway 12 at Anchorage Marina (© 252/928-1101), which lies near the entrance to Silver Lake Harbor. Its raw bar, affordable guest rooms, and location are packing 'em in. Those on the B&B route have discovered **Cove Bed & Breakfast,** 21 Loop Rd. (© 252/928-4192). Tastefully decorated guest rooms, each with a private balcony, provide true Outer Banks hospitality. See chapter 4.

**WILMINGTON** Generating excitement on the culinary front here is **Prima,** 35 N. Front St. (© 910/763-9545), which has become a favorite of film companies in town making movies. Casual and laid-back, it's known for its good-tasting pastas and Tuscan-style pizza. Local foodies and visitors alike are attracted to the cuisine at **Boca Bay,** 2025 Eastwood Rd. (© 910/256-1887). Its tapas are the best in southeastern North Carolina,

and you can make a meal of them. Ever had lobster cheesecake? See chapter 5.

**THE PIEDMONT** In no part of the South has there been such an explosion of new and exciting restaurants as is currently seen in the Research Triangle cities of Chapel Hill, Durham, and Raleigh. Generating excitement in Raleigh itself is **Enoteca Vin,** 410 Glenwood Ave. (© 919/834-3070), the most stylish wine restaurant in the area, serving international cuisine. In Durham, the buzz centers on **Parizäde,** Irwin Square, 2200 Main St. (© 919/286-9712), the most sophisticated and gastronomically eclectic restaurant in town; and on the Italian restaurant, **Pop's,** 810 W. Peabody St. (© 919/956-7677), the hippest of the hip among newcomers. The best, most appealing, and most formal Italian restaurant in North Carolina is Chapel Hill's **Il Palio,** in the Siena Hotel, 1505 E. Franklin St. (© 919/918-2545). Chef Jim Anile has become one of the rising culinary stars in the region.

In Charlotte, the **NBA Bobcats** played their first season in 2004; the team's new $265-million uptown arena opens in 2005. See chapter 6.

**ASHEVILLE** As a younger crowd moves into the old Southern city of Asheville, cafes and hot new restaurants have opened to cater to the demands of the new denizens. Hip and urban is the **Cafe on the Square,**

1 Biltmore Ave. (© **828/251-5565**), which serves a stylish cuisine that evokes California. The modern **Café Soleil,** 62 N. Lexington Ave. (© **828/ 350-1140**), established by a team of French and Argentine expats, features a top-notch Continental cuisine. **The Frog Bar Deli/The Flying Frog Café,** at the corner of Haywood Street and Battery Park (© **828/254-9411**), is the most culturally diverse cafe and restaurant in town. See chapter 8.

## SOUTH CAROLINA

**CHARLESTON** A soaring new **Cooper River Bridge,** replacing the existing truss bridges that connect Charleston with Mount Pleasant, the Isle of Palms, and Sullivan's Island, should be completed by the time you visit. The bridge will be North America's longest cable-stay span.

The submarine of the Confederacy, *H. L. Hunley,* is now on display at the Warren Lasch Conservation Center, 1250 Supply St. (© **866/866-9938**). Finally located in 1995, the submarine in 1864 had achieved a maritime first by sinking the Yankee ship the *Housatonic.* After that, the submarine and its crew mysteriously vanished.

The opening of one of the top resorts in the Southeast occurred in the summer of 2004, when the $125-million **Sanctuary at Kiawah Island,** 12 Kiawah Beach Dr., on Kiawah Island (© **800/576-1570** or 843/768-2121), began receiving its first guests. The deluxe resort and spa was built along the island's 10 miles of sandy beachfront. Its rooms are some of the most spacious and luxurious of any resort in America. See chapter 11.

**HILTON HEAD** The hot new French restaurant on the island is **Rendez-Vous Café,** 14 Greenwood Dr. (© **843/785-5070**), offering inventive cookery in a bistrolike atmosphere that evokes the south of France. The list of hors d'oeuvres alone is the finest on the island. See chapter 12.

**MYRTLE BEACH** A major shopping center, **Coastal Grand** (© **843/ 839-9100**), opened in 2004 at the intersection of Highway 17 Bypass and Highway 501. This shopping venue has a trio of department stores along with dozens of other retail outlets and specialty shops. See chapter 13.

**COLUMBIA** More and more visitors are discovering **Mr. Friendly's New Southern Cafe,** 2001-A Greene St. (© **803/254-7828**), in the business district. Local food critics have hailed it as one of the finest and most innovative restaurants in the state. It actually started as a cookie and sandwich shop in the 1980s, but only in its present reincarnation is it generating press excitement, including praise from *Wine Spectator.* See chapter 14.

## GEORGIA

**ATLANTA** The famous Swissôtel in Buckhead has now become the **Westin Buckhead Hotel,** 3391 Peachtree Rd. NE (© **888/737-9477** or 404/365-0065). Although big changes may occur at some date in the future, the hint of European flavor that made the hotel so popular in its previous incarnation is still a factor here. Those seeking the flavor of rural Georgia of old should head 32 miles south of Atlanta to the **Serenbe Bed & Breakfast,** 10950 Hutcheson Ferry Rd., Palmetto (© **770/463-2610**), which lies on a 350-acre farmstead. It's a place where you can still hand-feed the cows and chickens, or fish from the lake. It's like entering the Georgia of half a century ago. See chapter 16.

**EATONTON** Lying 75 miles southeast of Atlanta, this little town is the home of Br'er Rabbit and the Uncle Remus tales. It is also known for its antebellum architecture. For those wanting to stay over in this charming place, the **Ezell House Bed and Breakfast,** 300 N. Madison Ave. (© 706/923-0031), opened in summer 2004. Set in a Victorian house from 1887, it has been beautifully restored, its guest rooms spacious, handsomely maintained, and filled with Victoriana. See chapter 17.

**WARM SPRINGS**    In Warm Springs, 65 miles south of Atlanta, where President Franklin D. Roosevelt went to recuperate from his polio at "The Little White House," a new $5-million **FDR Memorial Museum** (© 706/655-5870) opened in 2004. The museum displays FDR memorabilia, including the famous "unfinished portrait" he was sitting for the day he died. See chapter 19.

# 1

# The Best of the Carolinas & Georgia

From steep, sloping mountain forests to lush farmlands that evoke the English countryside, the Carolinas and Georgia offer a landscape as diverse and colorful as the personable demeanor of the region's residents.

The tri-state area has aged gracefully with time, leaving in place an amiable drawl and such culinary traditions as hot buttered grits and fresh boiled peanuts, yet it has also managed to rival its Northern competitors in technology and style. Long burdened with a "Scarlett" reputation cluttered with pickup trucks and good ol' boys, these Southern states now boast bright, neon-lighted cities complete with cutting-edge architecture, high-tech industry, exhilarating sports events, and intricately designed highways—not to mention big-city gridlock.

Still, the Old South lives on, at least in pockets, and some achingly pastoral countryscapes seem to be torn from the pages of such Deep South authors as Tennessee Williams, Eudora Welty, and William Faulkner. But it is in the bosom of the tri-state area, in a setting of old-style graciousness, that the muscular, gleaming New South engine of commerce, industry, and innovation powers on.

Clichés die hard, though, and Hollywood has been reluctant to let go of its love affair with the colorful Old South. Best-selling novels and Academy Award–winning screenplays continue to mine the mystique of a South clad in its own troublesome history. The region has become a big attraction for writers and movie producers lured by superb natural settings, historic ambience, and (in the case of the producers) beneficent right-to-work laws. So many movies have been made in and around Wilmington, North Carolina, that it has been dubbed "Hollywood East."

The South of yore may live on in Hollywood, but the talk today is of the New South, a land characterized less by drawls and "y'alls" and more by a bright, intelligent group of people bringing culture and business to an area that once slept quietly by the cotton gin. These new sons and daughters of the South might invite "y'all to come back now" for a second visit; but they'll suggest that you bring along a checkbook to buy their products (such as a set of high-end furniture manufactured in Lenoir) or that you invest in one of the mega-pharmaceutical research labs that have set up shop in the Research Triangle of North Carolina.

The Carolinas and Georgia are no longer whistling "Dixie" but standing up and making their voices heard in the world marketplace. The voices reflect the diversity of a population that not so long ago faced considerable challenges regarding racial inequality, challenges that Georgia native son Martin Luther King, Jr., so eloquently called upon the nation to meet. One happy result of the efforts to surmount those challenges in recent years has been the reverse migration of many African Americans from the North home to the South.

The New South has other voices, including those of politicos clamoring to fill the shoes and Senate seat of the seemingly immortal but at-long-last expired Strom Thurmond. And of course, there's the dignified, soft-spoken peanut farmer from Plains who became president of the United States and is now an agent of world peace.

The Carolinas and Georgia are major destinations for travelers. Charleston and Savannah are ranked among the top 10 cities in the country in *Condé Nast Traveler*'s Readers' Choice Awards year after year. From the Smoky Mountains to the sun-kissed Atlantic coastline, from the windswept dunes of Kitty Hawk all the way to Georgia's Suwannee River country and Okefenokee Swamp, the tri-state area is attracting visitors by the millions.

Taken as a whole, the North Carolina/South Carolina/Georgia tri-state area is like a country unto itself. It's wildly diverse and packed with places to see and things to do. We've traveled the back roads of the Carolinas and Georgia since we were kids, exploring the Old South and the New South. That's why we feel qualified to bring you our suggestions of the best, with the understanding, of course, that there's always plenty of room for disagreement. Here are our picks for the cream of the crop.

## 1 The Best Scenic Drives

- **The Outer Banks** (North Carolina): If you can get past the overly crowded highways in summer and some tawdry development, prepare yourself for one of the strangest and most beautiful natural geographical areas in North America. To explore this thin slip of land, drive N.C. 12, beginning at Corolla in the north and ending at the Ocracoke lighthouse in the south. Along the way, you'll pass the shifting shoals of Oregon Inlet, Pea Island National Wildlife Refuge, and pristine stretches of beach along Cape Hatteras National Seashore. See chapter 4.
- **The Blue Ridge Parkway** (North Carolina): This is the single most dramatic drive in the tri-state area and one of the grandest drives in

the world. Beginning in Virginia, the parkway winds and twists along mountain crests for some 470 miles. It passes through most of western North Carolina before halting at Great Smoky Mountains National Park near the Tennessee border. See chapter 8.
- **Chattahoochee National Forest** (Georgia): U.S. Route 76 from Ellijay and past Blairsville to Clayton is one of the most scenic routes in Georgia, dating back to the 1920s and 1930s, when the federal government purchased much of the land here. That act alone helped preserve the fading culture of the southern Appalachians, which you can see today as you slowly make your way through this national forest. See chapter 18.

## 2 The Best Family Vacations

- **Great Smoky Mountains National Park** (North Carolina): Sixteen peaks of the southern Appalachians soar skyward to approximately 6,000 feet. We're

attracted not just by the mountains, but also by the surrounding theme parks and activities, ranging from water parks to valley railroads and offering countless opportunities for fun. See chapter 9.

- **Charleston** (South Carolina): If the tri-state area has a town that's designed for families, it's Charleston. The city has been called an 18th-century etching come to life. You can take boat rides to Fort Sumter, where the Civil War began; explore Magnolia Plantation, with its petting zoo and gardens; and visit several family-oriented nature parks, including one at Palmetto Islands. See chapter 11.
- **Hilton Head** (South Carolina): Much more upscale than Myrtle Beach, Hilton Head is filled with broad beaches. You can enjoy myriad activities, such as biking on the beaches; taking a dolphin-watching cruise; and exploring the 605-acre Sea Pines Forest Preserve, a public wilderness tract with walking trails. All major hotels offer summer activity centers for kids. See chapter 12.
- **The Golden Isles** (Georgia): This string of lush, subtropical barrier islands, located south of Savannah near the Florida border, is designed for family fun and adventure. Summer Waves, a 118-acre water park on Jekyll Island, is just one of the many attractions designed with children in mind. Nature still thrives in this setting, including Cumberland Island National Seashore, a 16×3-mile wildlife sanctuary. See chapter 21.

## 3 The Best Places to Rediscover the Old South

- **Beaufort** (North Carolina): Not to be confused with the town of the same name in South Carolina, Beaufort is North Carolina's third-oldest settlement, dating from 1713. Its 200-year-old houses and narrow streets reflect the old way of life. The town is rich in Carolina tradition that predates the Civil War. See chapter 5.
- **Beaufort** (South Carolina): Straight from the screen in *The Big Chill* and *The Prince of Tides,* Beaufort is like a sleepy dream of long ago. Established in 1710, it grew fat from Sea Island cotton. Wealthy owners built lavish antebellum houses that still stand today, luring visitors with their faded charm. See chapter 12.
- **Georgetown** (South Carolina): A town with surprisingly well-preserved pre–Revolutionary War houses and churches, Georgetown invites you to enter a time capsule. In this small enclave of some 11,000 people, more than 50 historic homes still stand, dating back as far as 1737. See chapter 13.
- **Madison** (Georgia): Only an hour's drive east of Atlanta stands today's version of what antebellum travelers called "the wealthiest and most aristocratic village between Charleston and New Orleans." General Sherman was an acquaintance of a local U.S. senator from here, and for old times' sake agreed not to burn down the town. Its oak-lined streets and historic homes still stand. See chapter 17.
- **Savannah** (Georgia): Because General Sherman was talked out of burning it, he gave the city to President Lincoln as a Christmas present instead. No city in all the South has Savannah's peculiar charm. Its very name suggests Spanish moss, hoop skirts, mint juleps on the veranda, *Midnight in the Garden of Good and Evil,* and antebellum architecture. See chapter 20.

## 4 The Best Small Towns

- **Edenton** (North Carolina): Edenton is the quintessential small port town along the Outer Banks. If Colonial-style clapboard is your thing, this is the place to see it. You can wander past well-tended gardens on streets shaded by magnolia and pecan trees. Edenton has been here since 1722, and the National Register of Historic Places long ago gave the town its blessing. See chapter 4.

- **Asheville** (North Carolina): The city might object to such a classification, but it's the "small town" of cities. One of the most desirable places to live in America, Asheville has attracted everybody from the Vanderbilts to the tragic feuding couple F. Scott and Zelda Fitzgerald. With its well-tended blocks and broad, tidy streets, it's the most stylish town of its size in the tri-state area, and locals are determined to keep it that way. See chapter 8.

- **Thomasville** (Georgia): The plantation era never died here, and life still moves at a leisurely pace along Thomasville's shady, tree-lined streets. Over the years, the town's aristocratic elegance has attracted the wintering wealthy, including the Rockefellers and Goodriches. Jacqueline Kennedy fled here to recover from the assassination of her husband. See chapter 19.

- **Macon** (Georgia): In the heart of the state, this sleepy town has a historic core of approximately 50 buildings listed on the National Register of Historic Places. Nearly 600 other structures here have been cited for their architectural significance. Macon long ago decided to let Atlanta race hysterically toward the millennium; it prefers to wander slowly along, content in its appealing charm. See chapter 19.

## 5 The Best Golf Courses

- **The Carolina Hotel Golf Courses** (1 Carolina Vista, Pinehurst, North Carolina): This is the only resort in the South that has seven signature courses. The original architect was the now-legendary Donald Ross. All the great names in golf—including Nelson, Jones, and Hogan—have played these courses. In all, there are 126 holes of golf, with modern holes designed by Tom Fazio and Rees Jones. See p. 132.

- **Pine Needles Lodge** (Southern Pines, North Carolina): This 1927 Donald Ross masterpiece is a challenging par-71 course, attracting golfers of various skills. The course plays to 6,708 yards from the championship tees and has been immaculately restored to its original splendor. See p. 132.

- **Palmetto Dunes Resort** (Hilton Head, South Carolina): This course, designed by George Fazio, is an 18-hole, 6,534-yard, par-70 course named by *Golf Digest* as one of the "75 Best American Resort Courses." It has been cited for its combined "length and keen accuracy." See p. 247.

- **Old South Golf Links** (Bluffton, South Carolina): This 18-hole, 6,772-yard, par-72 course has been recognized as one of the "Top 10 Public Courses" by *Golf Digest*. It has panoramic views and a natural setting that ranges from an oak forest to tidal salt marshes. See p. 247.

- **Sea Island Golf Club** (St. Simons Island, Georgia): Owned by the Cloister, the most exclusive resort in the South, this widely acclaimed golf course lies at the end of the Avenue of Oaks, the site of a former plantation. Opened in 1927, the club consists of several courses, such as the 18-hole Ocean Forest (7,011 yd., par 72). It has been compared favorably to such golfing meccas as St. Andrews in Scotland and Pebble Beach in California. See p. 457.

## 6 The Best Beaches

- **Wrightsville Beach** (6 miles east of Wilmington, North Carolina): It's the widest beach on the Cape Fear coast: Wrightsville's beige sands stretch for a mile along the oceanfront, set against a backdrop of thick vegetation. It gets very crowded in summer, however. See chapter 5.
- **Cape Hatteras National Seashore** (North Carolina): Some 70 miles of relatively unspoiled beaches begin at Whalebone Junction in South Nags Head and stretch down through Hatteras and Ocracoke islands in the south; in fact, Ocracoke's beaches consistently show up on top-ten lists of the nation's finest. Ferocious tides, strong currents, and fickle winds constantly alter the most dramatic beaches along the Eastern Seaboard. See chapter 4.
- **Hilton Head** (South Carolina): *Travel & Leisure* has hailed these beaches as being among the most beautiful in the world, and we concur. The resort-studded island offers 12 miles of white-sand beaches; still others front the Calobogue and Port Royal sounds. The sand is extremely firm, providing a good surface for biking and many beach games. It's also ideal for walking and jogging—against a backdrop of natural dunes, live oaks, palmettos, and tall Carolina pines. See chapter 12.
- **Myrtle Beach & the Grand Strand** (South Carolina): This is the most popular sand strip along the Eastern Seaboard, attracting 12 million visitors a year—more than the state of Hawaii. Sure, it's overdeveloped and maddeningly crowded, but what draws visitors to Myrtle Beach is 10 miles of sand, mostly hard-packed and the color of brown sugar. See chapter 13.

## 7 The Best Luxury Hotels & Resorts

- **Grove Park Inn Resort & Spa** (Asheville, North Carolina; ✆ 800/ 438-5800 or 828/252-2711): The premier resort of the state has sheltered everybody from Thomas Edison to F. Scott Fitzgerald, and the big names still check in. The hotel is continually upgraded, and it is said to be just as grand as it was on the day it opened in 1913. A $14-million full-service spa opened in January 2001. See p. 149.
- **The Sea Pines Resort** (Hilton Head, South Carolina; ✆ 888/ 807-6873 or 843/785-3333): This is the oldest and most famous of the island's resort developments. Set on 4,500 thickly wooded acres, with a total of three golf courses, Sea Pines competes for the summer beach traffic as few resorts in the Caribbean ever could. Its focal point is Harbour Town, which is built around one of the most charming marinas in the Carolinas. Luxurious homes and villas open onto the ocean or golf courses. See p. 254.
- **Ritz-Carlton Buckhead** (Atlanta, Georgia; ✆ 800/241-3333 or 404/237-2700): Often a discreet rendezvous for visiting celebrities, this hotel is the epitome of plushness and luxury. General Sherman wouldn't have burned it; he would have checked in and called for

room service. European style and flair set the grace notes, evoked by Regency and Georgian antiques, white marble floors, and French-crystal chandeliers. Exquisitely decorated bedrooms and one of Atlanta's premier deluxe restaurants add much allure. See p. 330.

- **The Gastonian** (Savannah, Georgia; ℂ **800/322-6603** or 912/232-2869): Two 19th-century stone town houses have been turned into a gem of a hotel. Empire furnishings, Persian rugs, working fireplaces, brass headboards, and canopied beds adorn the lushly decorated bedrooms. Antiques, Oriental rugs, fresh flowers in profusion, glowing fires, and even classical music create a welcoming, cozy ambience. Staying at the Gastonian is like living in a wealthy friend's private mansion. See p. 424.

- **The Cloister** (Sea Island, Georgia; ℂ **800/732-4752** or 912/638-3611): This hotel has been called the grande dame of all Southern resorts. A clubby place, The Cloister means formal dinners by night, and outdoor activities by day that range from the best tennis in Georgia to riding, fishing, and swimming (at the beach or in two inviting pools). It's a class act. See p. 462.

## 8 The Best Moderately Priced Hotels

- **Cedar Crest Inn** (Asheville, North Carolina; ℂ **800/252-0310** or 828/252-1389): The city is famed for its B&Bs—the finest in North Carolina—and this one rates at the top. A Queen Anne–style mansion built in 1894, Cedar Crest Inn is rich in Victorian trappings, including a captain's walk, projecting turrets, and various architectural follies. See p. 148.

- **Anchorage Inn** (Charleston, South Carolina; ℂ **800/421-2952** or 843/723-8300): Converted from an antebellum cotton warehouse, this inn, with its mock-Tudor facade, is a bastion of charm and grace, with canopied beds and individually decorated bedrooms. See p. 212.

- **Ansley Inn** (Atlanta, Georgia; ℂ **800/446-5416** or 404/872-9000): A stately yellow-brick Tudor mansion in the prestigious neighborhood of Ansley Park has been reincarnated as a small-scale European inn. From its English Chippendale furnishings to its Venetian chandeliers, it offers first-rate accommodations at affordable prices. See p. 327.

- **17 Hundred 90** (Savannah, Georgia; ℂ **877/468-1200** or 912/238-1200): Like a house in 18th-century New England, this is the oldest inn in Savannah. It's even said to be haunted. The Colonial trappings of this place have won many a devotee, some of whom wouldn't stay anywhere else when they visit Savannah. See p. 429.

## 9 The Best Budget Hotels

- **Governor Eden Inn** (Edenton, North Carolina; ℂ **866/872-5608**): Located in one of the most historic towns along North Carolina's Outer Banks, this charmer is one of the better B&Bs in the area, close to the historic core. Built in 1906 in the neoclassical style, with large white columns and a wraparound veranda, it is the epitome of Southern antebellum style. See p. 49.

- **Old Reynolds Mansion** (Asheville, North Carolina; ℂ **800/709-0496** or 828/254-0496): This antebellum brick house, one of the few left in Asheville, was rescued from the bulldozer and is now a three-story inn. Listed on the National Register of Historic Places, the B&B offers the most inviting budget-priced rooms in the city. See p. 151.

- **The Greenleaf Inn at Camden** (Camden, South Carolina; © 800/437-5874 or 803/425-1806): Situated in the heart of historic Camden, The Greenleaf is the coziest and most comfortable choice in town. A part of the inn dates from 1805, and it's filled with Victorian furnishings. It's also one of the finest dining choices in Camden, even if you're not a guest. See p. 299.

- **Sugar Magnolia** (Atlanta, Georgia; © 404/222-0226): Situated

in a historic district, this 1892 Victorian house of considerable charm rents individually styled and commodious guest rooms with Southern style and flair, each unit suitable to house a colonel in the Confederate army. The staircase alone is worthy of an entrance by Miss Scarlett. See p. 331.

- **Plains Bed and Breakfast Inn** (Plains, Georgia; © 229/824-7252): In Jimmy Carter's hometown, this is a stylish B&B built by a Baptist preacher in 1910. It's just two doors away from a service station where the former president's brother, Billy, often held press conferences. Miss Lillian and her husband were said to have conceived the future president in one of the tasteful and comfortably furnished upstairs bedrooms. See p. 411.

## 10 The Best Restaurants

- **Horizons Restaurant** (in the Grove Park Inn Resort & Spa, Asheville, North Carolina; © 800/438-5800): This is the most formal restaurant in western North Carolina, as befits its location in the city's grandest resort. Horizons is consistently rated among the top restaurants in the nation. Patrons are served an excellent array of Continental dishes—including brook trout, bouillabaisse, and medallions of venison—prepared from the freshest ingredients on the market. See p. 153.

- **Anson** (Charleston, South Carolina; © 843/577-0551): Hip, stylish, and upscale, this is a favorite dining room of discriminating Charlestonians, who flock here for Low Country dishes with an original, modern twist. Anson compares with top-notch restaurants in New York and San Francisco, and offers the best service in

the city. Try the fried cornmeal oysters with potato cakes or the cashew-crusted grouper with champagne sauce. See p. 216.

- **Charlie's L'Etoile Verte** (Hilton Head, South Carolina; © 843/785-9277): Like a whimsical Parisian bistro, this elegant yet unpretentious establishment packs them in every night in an area that has more restaurants than customers. The reason is the food. The cuisine borrows freely from almost everywhere. See p. 256.

- **Pano & Paul's** (Atlanta, Georgia; © 404/261-3662): Its place already secure in the dining hall of fame, this Buckhead eatery combines the best of Continental selections with American produce, and the results have won it a following not only in Atlanta, but also throughout the Southeast. Patrons receive impeccable service while dining in a setting of

Victorian opulence. The broiled dry-aged sirloin steak and the roast double beef filet are the best in town. See p. 343.

- **The Lady & Sons** (Savannah, Georgia; © **912/233-2600**): Launched with $200 in 1989, this restaurant has become one of the finest in eastern Georgia, turning out a Southern cuisine of taste and refinement. The buffets are reason enough to visit. And wait until you try Paula Deen's chicken pot-pie. See p. 432.

# 2

# For International Visitors

This chapter provides some specifics on getting to the United States as economically and effortlessly as possible, plus it gives helpful information on how things are done in the Southeast, from mailing a postcard to making a long-distance telephone call. For more information, see the "Planning Your Trip" chapters for each state: chapter 3 for North Carolina, chapter 10 for South Carolina, and chapter 15 for Georgia.

## 1 Preparing for Your Trip

If you're going to Atlanta, contact the **Atlanta Convention & Visitors Bureau (ACVB),** 233 Peachtree St. NE, Suite 100, Atlanta, GA 30303 (© **404/222-6688** or 404/521-6600; www.atlanta.com), and ask for the *International Visitors Guide* for international tourists, which is available in five languages (2–3 weeks' delivery).

### ENTRY REQUIREMENTS

Check at any U.S. embassy or consulate for current information and requirements. You can also obtain a visa application and other information online at the **U.S. State Department** website, **www.travel.state.gov.**

**VISAS** The U.S. State Department has a **Visa Waiver Program** allowing citizens of certain countries to enter the United States without a visa for stays of up to 90 days. At press time these included Andorra, Australia, Austria, Belgium, Brunei, Denmark, Finland, France, Germany, Iceland, Ireland, Italy, Japan, Liechtenstein, Luxembourg, Monaco, The Netherlands, New Zealand, Norway, Portugal, San Marino, Singapore, Slovenia, Spain, Sweden, Switzerland, the United Kingdom, and Uruguay. Citizens of these countries need only a valid passport and a round-trip air or cruise ticket in

their possession upon arrival. If they first enter the United States, they may also visit Mexico, Canada, Bermuda, and/or the Caribbean islands and return to the United States without a visa. Further information is available from any U.S. embassy or consulate. *Note:* This list can change at any time. Always check visa requirements well in advance. Canadian citizens may enter the United States without visas; they need only proof of residence.

Citizens of all other countries must have (1) a valid passport that expires at least 6 months later than the scheduled end of their visit to the United States; and (2) a tourist visa, which may be obtained without charge from any U.S. consulate.

**To obtain a visa,** the traveler must submit a completed application form (either in person or by mail) with a 1½-inch square photo, and must demonstrate binding ties to a residence abroad. Usually you can obtain a visa at once or within 24 hours, but it may take longer during the summer rush June through August. If you cannot go in person, contact the nearest U.S. embassy or consulate for directions on applying by mail. Your travel agent or airline office may also be able to provide you with a visa application and instructions. The U.S. consulate or embassy that issues your visa will determine whether you will be issued a multiple- or single-entry visa and any restrictions regarding the length of your stay.

**British subjects** can obtain up-to-date passport and visa information by calling the **U.S. Embassy Visa Information Line** (© 9055/44-546) or the **London Passport Office** (© 0870/521-0410 for recorded information), or they can find the visa information on the U.S. Embassy Great Britain website (www.passport.gov.uk).

**Irish** citizens can obtain up-to-date passport and visa information through the **Embassy of USA Dublin,** 42 Elgin Rd., Dublin 4, Ireland (© 353/1-668-8777); or by checking the visa website at www.dublin.usembassy.gov/passports/passportforms.htm.

**Australian** citizens can obtain up-to-date visa information by contacting the **U.S. Embassy Canberra,** Moonah Place, Yarralumla, ACT 2600 (© 02/6214-5600); or by checking the U.S. Diplomatic Mission's website at http://usembassy-australia.state.gov/consular.

Citizens of **New Zealand** can obtain up-to-date passport and visa information by calling the **U.S. Embassy New Zealand,** 29 Fitzherbert Terrace, Thorndon, Wellington, New Zealand (© 644/462-6000); or by going to the website (http://usembassy.org.nz).

## MEDICAL REQUIREMENTS

Unless you're arriving from an area known to be suffering from an **epidemic** (particularly cholera or yellow fever), inoculations or vaccinations are not required for entry into the United States. If you have a medical condition that requires **syringe-administered medications,** carry a valid, signed prescription from your physician—the Federal Aviation Administration (FAA) no longer allows airline passengers to pack syringes in their carry-on baggage without documented proof of medical need. If you have a disease that requires treatment with **narcotics,** you should also carry documented proof with you—smuggling narcotics aboard a plane is a serious offense that carries severe penalties in the U.S.

For **HIV-positive visitors,** requirements for entering the United States are somewhat vague and change frequently. According to the latest publication of *HIV and Immigrants: A Manual for AIDS Service Providers,* the Immigration and Naturalization Service (INS) doesn't require a medical exam for entry into the United States, but INS officials may stop individuals because they look sick or because they are carrying AIDS/HIV medicine.

If an HIV-positive noncitizen applies for a nonimmigrant visa, the question on the application regarding communicable diseases is tricky no matter which way it's answered. If the applicant checks "No," INS may deny the visa on the grounds that the applicant committed fraud. If the applicant checks "Yes" or if INS suspects the person is HIV-positive, it will deny the visa unless the applicant asks for a special waiver for visitors. This waiver is for people visiting the United States for a short time, to attend a conference, for instance, to visit close relatives, or to receive medical treatment. It can be a confusing situation. For up-to-the-minute information, contact **AIDSinfo** (© 800/448-0440 or 301/519-0459 outside the U.S.; www.aidsinfo.nih.gov) or the **Gay Men's Health Crisis** (© 212/367-1000: www.gmhc.org).

## CUSTOMS REQUIREMENTS

Every visitor who is 21 or older may bring in the following items free of duty: 1 liter of wine or hard liquor, 200 cigarettes *or* 50 cigars (but no cigars from Cuba) *or* 2 pounds of smoking tobacco, and $400 worth of gifts. An additional 100 cigars are allowed under your gift exemption. These exemptions are offered to travelers who spend at least 72 hours in the United States and who have not claimed them within the preceding 6 months. It's forbidden to bring into the country foodstuffs (particularly cheese, fruit, cooked meats, and canned goods) or plants (vegetables, seeds, tropical plants, and so on). International tourists may bring in or take out up to $10,000 in U.S. or foreign currency with no formalities; larger sums must be declared to Customs upon entering or leaving the country.

## INSURANCE

The United States has no national health-care system. Because the cost of medical care is extremely high, we strongly advise that every traveler secure health-insurance coverage before setting out. You may want to take out a comprehensive travel policy that covers (for a relatively low premium) sickness or injury costs (medical, surgical, and hospital); loss or theft of your baggage; trip-cancellation costs; guarantee of bail, in case you're arrested; and costs associated with accidents, repatriation, or death.

Packages such as "Europ Assistance Worldwide Services" in Europe are sold by automobile clubs and travel agencies at attractive rates. **Travel Assistance International** (TAI; ✆ **800/ 821-2828** or 202/331-1609; www. travelassistance.com) is the agent for Europ Assistance Worldwide Services, Inc., so holders of this company's policies can contact TAI for assistance while they are in the United States.

Canadians should check with their provincial-health-scheme offices or call **Health Canada** (✆ **613/783-4400;** www.gov.on.ca) to find out the extent of their coverage, as well as what documentation and receipts they must take home in case they are treated in the United States.

British travelers might try **Columbus Travel Insurance, Ltd.** (✆ **020/ 7375-0011;** www.columbusdirect.net).

## MONEY

**CURRENCY & EXCHANGE**    The U.S. monetary system has a decimal base. One American **dollar** ($1) = 100 **cents** (100¢).

Dollar bills commonly come in $1 (a "buck"), $5, $10, and $20 denominations. There are also $2 bills (seldom encountered), $50 bills, and $100 bills. The latter two denominations are usually not welcome as payment for small purchases and are not accepted in taxis or at subway ticket booths.

There are six denominations of coins: 1¢ (one cent, or a "penny"), 5¢ (five cents, or a "nickel"), 10¢ (ten cents, or a "dime"), 25¢ (twenty-five cents, or a "quarter"), and two rare coins: 50¢ (fifty cents, or a "half dollar") and the $1 pieces (the Susan B. Anthony coin; the newer, gold Sacagawea coin; and, prized by collectors, the rare, older silver dollar).

*Note:* The "currency-exchange bureaus" that are so common in Europe are rare even at airports in the United States and nonexistent outside major cities. Try to avoid having to change foreign money or traveler's checks that are not denominated in U.S. dollars at small-town banks or even at branch banks in big cities. In fact, leave any currency other than U.S. dollars at home; it may prove to be more of a nuisance to you than it's worth.

**ATMs**    It's getting easier all the time to use your ATM card to access your bank account from home while you're on the road. Check with your bank at home to be sure your ATM card and PIN will work in U.S. ATMs.

**TRAVELER'S CHECKS**    Some people prefer to carry traveler's checks for that extra security. Traveler's checks denominated in U.S. dollars are readily accepted at most hotels, motels, restaurants, and large stores. But the best place to change traveler's checks is at a

## Fingerprinting Visitors

At this time, US-VISIT requires that most foreign visitors traveling to the U.S. on a visa have their two index fingers scanned and a digital photograph (PDF) taken to verify their identity at the port of entry. Visas are required for most students, business travelers (depending on their length of stay), and millions of other visitors, regardless of where they live. US-VISIT is part of a continuum of security measures that begins overseas, when a person applies for a visa to travel to the United States, and continues on through entry and exit at U.S. air and seaports and, eventually, at land border crossings. The US-VISIT program is designed to enhance the security of U.S. citizens and visitors by verifying the identities of visitors with visas.

bank in a large city or town. Do not bring traveler's checks that are denominated in other currencies.

**CREDIT & CHARGE CARDS**
The method of payment most widely used is credit and charge cards, including Visa (BarclayCard in Britain), MasterCard (EuroCard in Europe, Access in Britain, Chargex in Canada), American Express, Diners Club, and Discover. You can save yourself trouble by using so-called "plastic money" rather than cash or traveler's checks in most hotels, motels, restaurants, and retail stores. (A growing number of food and liquor stores now accept credit/charge cards.) You must have a credit or charge card to rent a car. You can also use the card as proof of identity (it often carries more weight than a passport), or as a "cash card" enabling you to withdraw money from banks and ATMs that accept it.

## SAFETY
**GENERAL** Although tourist areas are generally safe in the South, crime exists everywhere, and U.S. urban areas tend to be less safe than those in western Europe or Japan. Visitors should always stay alert. This is particularly true of large U.S. cities, especially Atlanta. Parts of Savannah, Charleston, and Charlotte can be unsafe at night. It is wise to ask the city or area's tourist office if you're in doubt about which neighborhoods are safe.

Avoid deserted areas at night. Don't go into any city park at night unless there's an event that attracts crowds. Generally speaking, you can feel safe in areas where there are many people and many open establishments.

Remember also that hotels are open to the public, and in a large hotel, security may not be able to screen everyone who enters. Always lock your room door. Don't assume that once you're inside your hotel, you are automatically safe and no longer need to be aware of your surroundings.

Georgia and the Carolinas are among the safest places in the Southeast, especially in the small towns and villages. Resort areas such as Myrtle Beach attract more crime, of course. But on a per-capita basis, Georgia and the Carolinas have far less crime than does Florida, to the south.

**DRIVING** Foreign driver's licenses are mostly recognized in the U.S., although you may want to get an international driver's license if your home license is not written in English. Question your car-rental agency about personal safety, or ask for a brochure of traveler-safety tips when you pick up your car. Obtain from the agency written directions or a map with the route marked in red, showing you how to get to your destination. If possible, arrive and depart during daylight hours.

If you drive off a highway into a doubtful neighborhood, leave the area as quickly as possible. If you have an accident, even on the highway, stay in your car with the doors locked until you assess the situation or until the police arrive. If you are bumped from behind on the street, or if you are involved in a minor accident with no injuries and the situation appears to be suspicious, motion to the other driver to follow you to a police station or a lighted area where there are people and telephones. *Never* get out of your car in such a situation.

If you see someone on the road who indicates a need for help, *don't stop.* Take note of the location, drive on to a well-lighted area, and telephone the police by dialing ☎ **911.**

Park in well-lighted, well-traveled areas, if possible. Always keep your car doors locked, whether the car is attended or unattended. Look around before you get out of your car, and never leave any packages or valuables in sight. If someone attempts to rob you or steal your car, do *not* try to resist the thief or carjacker; report the incident to the police department immediately.

Also, make sure that you have enough gasoline in your tank to reach your intended destination, so that you're not forced to look for a service station in an unfamiliar and possibly unsafe neighborhood, especially at night.

## 2 Getting to the U.S.

Atlanta serves as the gateway to the South for most passengers from overseas. From there, connections can be made to destinations in the Carolinas, including such cities as Charleston and Charlotte.

**British Airways** (☎ **800/AIR-WAYS** in the U.S. or 08457/733-377 in the U.K.; www.britishairways.com) flies nonstop every day from London's Gatwick airport to Atlanta (trip time: 7½ hr.). Flights depart London daily at noon, arriving in Atlanta at 4:15pm (local time). The British Airways flight returns from Atlanta every evening at 6:15pm (Atlanta time), arriving at Gatwick at 7:25am (Greenwich Mean Time). Citizens of Ireland can make this connection to Atlanta by flying to London.

Flying to Atlanta from 23 European cities, **Delta** (☎ **800/221-1212;** www.delta.com) offers daily nonstop flights to Atlanta from Barcelona, Frankfurt, London, Madrid, Manchester, Munich, Paris, Shannon, and Zurich.

**KLM** (☎ **800/447-4747** in the U.S. or 020/4747-747 in Amsterdam; www.klm.nl) has direct service 4 days a week from Amsterdam.

For passengers flying from Australia or New Zealand, either British Airways or **Qantas** (☎ **800/227-4500;** www.qantasusa.com) goes from Sydney to London in 24 hours, where a connecting flight on British Airways can be made into Atlanta (see the British Airways paragraph, above).

**Air Canada** (☎ **888/422-7533;** www.aircanada.ca) has four nonstop flights a day from Toronto to Atlanta (flight time: 2¼ hr.). Air Canada also has one nonstop flight from Montreal to Atlanta (flight time: 2½ hr.). Most passengers from Vancouver go first to Toronto or Montreal to make these connections. In some rare instances, passengers from Vancouver can be routed via Chicago into Atlanta.

Travelers from overseas can take advantage of the **APEX (advance-purchase excursion)** fares offered by all the major international carriers.

The visitor arriving by air, no matter what his or her port of entry, should cultivate patience and resignation before setting foot on U.S. soil. Getting through Immigration Control may take as long as 2 hours on some days, especially during summer weekends.

Add the time that it takes to clear Customs, and you'll see that you should make very generous allowances for delays in planning connections between international and domestic flights—an average of 2 to 3 hours, at least.

By contrast, travelers arriving by car or by rail from Canada will find the border-crossing formalities to be streamlined practically to the vanishing point. Air travelers from Canada, Bermuda, and some places in the Caribbean can sometimes go through Customs and Immigration much more quickly at the point of departure.

## 3 Getting Around the U.S.

**BY PLANE**   The **Visit USA** air pass is offered by several airlines: **American Airlines** (© 800/433-7300; www.aa.com), **Continental** (© 800/525-0280; www.continental.com), **Northwest** (© 800/225-2525; www.nwa.com), **America West Airlines** (© 800/235-9292; www.americawest.com), and **United** (© 800/864-8331; www.united.com). This pass is sold only through airline and travel agents outside the United States. Usually, you must also purchase an inbound international flight from a foreign country, including Canada. The price of each leg of this all-encompassing ticket can vary widely. Regardless of the individual parameters, this system is the best, easiest, and fastest way to see large stretches of the United States, including the Southeast, at a reasonable price. You should obtain information well in advance from your travel agent or from the office of the airline concerned, because the conditions attached to these discount tickets can be changed without notice.

**BY CAR**   The United States is a car culture—that's for sure—and the most cost-effective, convenient, and comfortable way to travel through the country is to drive. The interstate highway system—high-speed, limited-access roadways—connects cities and towns all over the country, and there's also an extensive network of federal, state, and local highways and roads. Travel by car gives visitors the freedom to make—and alter—their itineraries to suit their own needs and interests. Driving also offers the possibility of visiting some off-the-beaten-path locations that cannot be reached easily by public transportation.

Another convenience of traveling by car is the easy access to inexpensive motels at interstate-highway offramps. Such motels are almost always cheaper than hotels and motels in downtown areas. Remember that almost none of the smaller American cities offer any kind of comprehensive local in-city transportation system. This is especially true in the South.

The **American Automobile Association (AAA)** can provide you with an International Driving Permit that validates your foreign license. You may be able to join the AAA even if you're not a member of a reciprocal club. To inquire, call © **800/AAA-HELP.** In addition, some automobile rental agencies provide these services.

**BY TRAIN**   Long-distance trains in the United States are operated by **Amtrak** (© **800/872-7245;** www.amtrak.com), the national passenger rail-service corporation. International travelers can buy a 15- or 30-day **USA Rail Pass.** In 2004, off-peak fares (Sept 5–May 31) for 15 days of unlimited travel nationwide were $295 for adults and $148 for children; for 30 days of unlimited travel around the U.S., $385 for adults and $193 for children. International and domestic visitors can buy a **North America Railpass,** which is good for 30 days of unlimited travel on Amtrak. The pass is available through many foreign travel agents and at any staffed Amtrak office, but it must include travel in both North America and Canada. Prices in 2004 were $495 for off-peak travel and $699 for peak travel (June 1–Oct 15). Reservations are generally required and should be made for each part of your trip as early as possible. Amtrak also offers an **Air/Rail Travel Plan** that allows you to travel both by train and plane; for information, call ⓒ **800/321-8684.**

Visitors should be aware of the limitations of long-distance rail travel in the United States. With a few notable exceptions (such as the Northeast Corridor line between Boston and Washington, D.C.), service is rarely up to European standards. Delays are common, routes are limited and often infrequently served, and fares are rarely significantly lower than discount airfares. Long-distance train travel should be approached with caution.

**BY BUS** Generally, the cheapest way to travel in the United States—especially for short hops between cities—is by bus. **Greyhound** (ⓒ **800/231-2222;** www.greyhound.com), the sole nationwide bus line, offers an **Ameripass** for unlimited travel anywhere in the continental United States. In 2004, an adult 7-day pass cost $192; a 15-day pass, $288; a 30-day pass, $384; and a 60-day pass, $536. Children, students, and seniors receive discounted fares. Reductions are offered for round-trip purchases and, in some cases, for tickets purchased more than 3 weeks in advance. Bus travel in the United States can be both slow and uncomfortable, however, so this option is not for everyone.

---

## FAST FACTS: For the International Traveler

*Accommodations* It's always a good idea to make hotel reservations as soon as you know the dates of your travel. To make a reservation, you'll usually need to leave a deposit of one night's payment. Some of the major hotels listed in this book maintain overseas reservation networks and can be booked either directly or through travel agents. In the United States, major downtown hotels, which cater primarily to business travelers, commonly offer weekend discounts of as much as 50% to entice vacationers to fill the empty hotel rooms. Resorts and hotels near tourist attractions tend to have higher rates on weekends.

*Automobile Organizations* Auto clubs can supply maps, suggested routes, guidebooks, accident and bail-bond insurance, and emergency road service. The major auto club in the United States, with 983 offices nationwide, is the **American Automobile Association (AAA)**, 1000 AAA Dr., Heathrow, FL 32746-5063 (ⓒ **800/AAA-HELP;** www.aaa.com). Membership costs $45 to $55, but some foreign auto clubs have reciprocal arrangements with AAA, and members enjoy its services at no charge. If you belong to an auto club in your home country, inquire about AAA reciprocity before you leave. AAA can provide you with an **International Driving Permit** that validates your foreign license. In addition, some automobile rental agencies now provide these services, so you should inquire about their availability when you rent your car.

*Automobile Rentals* To rent a car, you need a major credit or charge card and a valid driver's license. Sometimes, a passport or an international driver's license is also required if your driver's license is in a language other than English. You usually need to be at least 25 years of age, although some companies do rent to younger people (they may add a daily surcharge). Be sure to return your car with the same amount of gasoline that you started out with, because rental companies charge excessive prices for gas. Keep in mind that a separate motorcycle driver's license is required in most states.

*Business Hours* The following are general open hours; specific establishments may vary. **Banks:** Monday to Friday from 9am to 3pm (some are also open Sat 9am–noon). You usually have 24-hour access to the automated teller machines (ATMs) at most banks and other outlets. **Offices:** Monday to Friday from 9am to 5pm. **Stores:** Monday to Saturday from 10am to 6pm, and some also on Sunday from noon to 5pm. Malls usually stay open until 9pm Monday to Saturday, and department stores are usually open until 9pm at least 1 day a week.

*Climate* See "When to Go," in chapter 3 for North Carolina, chapter 10 for South Carolina, and chapter 15 for Georgia.

*Currency* See the "Money" section of "Preparing for Your Trip," earlier in this chapter.

*Currency Exchange* You'll find currency-exchange services in major airports that have international service. Elsewhere, these services may be quite difficult to come by, although some major hotels will exchange currency if you're a registered guest.

*Drinking Laws* You must be at least 21 to consume alcoholic beverages.

*Electricity* The United States uses 110–120 volts AC, 60 cycles, compared with 220–240 volts AC, 50 cycles, in most of Europe. In addition to a 110-volt transformer, small appliances of non-American manufacture, such as hair dryers and shavers, require a plug adapter with two flat parallel pins.

*Embassies & Consulates* All embassies are located in Washington, D.C.; some consulates are located in major U.S. cities; and most nations have a mission to the United Nations in New York City.

Listed here are the embassies and some consulates of the major English-speaking countries. Travelers from other countries can obtain telephone numbers for their embassies and consulates by calling the "information" number for Washington, D.C. (© **202/555-1212**).

The embassy of **Australia** is at 1601 Massachusetts Ave. NW, Washington, DC 20036 (© **202/797-3000**; www.austemb.org). There are Australian consulates in Chicago, Honolulu, Houston, Los Angeles, New York, and San Francisco.

The embassy of **Canada** is at 501 Pennsylvania Ave. NW, Washington, DC 20001 (© **202/682-1740**; www.canadianembassy.org). There is a Canadian consulate in Atlanta at 1175 Peachtree St., Atlanta, GA 30309 (© **404/532-2000**); a second in Raleigh at 3737 Glenwood Ave., Suite 100, Raleigh, NC 27612 (© **919/573-1808**). Other Canadian consulates are in Buffalo (New York), Chicago, Dallas, Denver, Detroit, Houston, Los Angeles, Miami, Minneapolis, New York, San Diego, San Francisco, San Jose, and Seattle.

The embassy of **Ireland** is at 2234 Massachusetts Ave. NW, Washington, DC 20008 (© **202/462-3939**; www.irelandemb.org). There are Irish consulates in Boston, Chicago, New York, and San Francisco.

The embassy of **New Zealand** is at 37 Observatory Circle NW, Washington, DC 20008 (✆ **202/328-4800**; www.nzemb.org). The New Zealand consulates in the United States are in Los Angeles and New York.

The embassy of the **United Kingdom** is at 3100 Massachusetts Ave. NW, Washington, DC 20008 (✆ **202/588-6500**; www.britainusa.com). There's a British consulate in Atlanta at 245 Peachtree Center Ave., Marquis One Tower, Suite 2700, Atlanta, GA 30303 (✆ **404/954-7706**); other British consulates are in Boston, Chicago, Houston, Los Angeles, New York, San Francisco, and Seattle.

The embassy for **South Africa** is at 3051 Massachusetts Ave. NW, Washington, DC 2008 (✆ **202/232-4400**; www.saembassy.org).

Other countries that have consulates in Atlanta include **France,** at 3475 Piedmont Rd. NE, Suite 1840, Atlanta, GA 30305 (✆ **404/495-1660**); **Germany,** at Marquis Two Tower, Suite 901, 285 Peachtree Center Ave. NE, Atlanta, GA 30303-1221 (✆ **404/659-4760**); and **Japan,** Suite 2000, 100 Colony Sq. at 1175 Peachtree St. NE, Atlanta, GA 30361 (✆ **404/240-4300**). For complete information, contact the Atlanta Chamber of Commerce, International Department, P.O. Box 1740, Atlanta, GA 30301 (✆ **404/880-9000**).

*Emergencies* Dial ✆ **911** to report a fire, call the police, or get an ambulance. This is a nationwide toll-free call (no coins are required at a public telephone).

If theft or an accident has left you stranded, check the local telephone directory to find an office of the **Traveler's Aid Society,** a nationwide, not-for-profit social-service organization that is geared to helping travelers in distress. If you're in trouble, seek it out.

In Atlanta, the **Georgia Council for International Visitors,** 34 Peachtree St., Suite 1200, Atlanta, GA 30303 (✆ **404/832-5560**), can provide a wide variety of help to international visitors in more than 42 languages.

*Gasoline (Petrol)* One U.S. gallon equals 3.8 liters, whereas 1.2 U.S. gallons equals 1 imperial gallon. You'll notice that several variously named grades (and price levels) of gasoline are available at most gas stations. The unleaded fuels with the highest octane rating are the most expensive; most rental cars take the least expensive "regular" unleaded. Often, the price is lower if you pay in cash instead of by credit card. Many gas stations offer lower-priced self-service gas pumps; some gas stations, particularly at night, are all self-service.

*Holidays* On the following legal national holidays, banks, government offices, post offices, and many stores, restaurants, and museums are closed: January 1 (New Year's Day), the third Monday in January (Martin Luther King, Jr., Day), the third Monday in February (Presidents' Day), the last Monday in May (Memorial Day), July 4th (Independence Day), the first Monday after the first Sunday in September (Labor Day), the second Monday in October (Columbus Day), November 11 (Veterans Day), the fourth Thursday in November (Thanksgiving Day), and December 25 (Christmas). The Tuesday following the first Monday in November is Election Day and is a legal holiday in presidential-election years.

*Legal Aid* The international visitor will rarely become involved with the American legal system. If you are stopped for a minor infraction (such as speeding on the highway), never attempt to pay the fine directly to the police officer; you may wind up being accused of the much more serious charge of attempted bribery. Pay fines by mail. (You can also pay them directly into the hands of the clerk of the court.) If you're accused of a more serious offense, it's wise to say and do nothing before consulting a lawyer. Under U.S. law, an arrested person is allowed one telephone call to a party of his or her choice. Call your embassy or consulate.

*Mail* If you want to receive mail during your vacation, and you aren't sure what your address will be, your mail can be sent in your name, c/o **General Delivery (Poste Restante),** to the main post office of the city or region where you expect to be. The addressee must pick up mail in person and produce proof of identity (driver's license, credit or charge card, passport, and so on).

Domestic **postage rates** are 23¢ for a postcard and 37¢ for a letter. For overseas mail, a first-class letter (up to .5 oz.) is 60¢ (46¢ to either Canada or Mexico); a first-class postcard costs 60¢ (40¢ to Canada and Mexico); and a preprinted postal aerogramme costs 70¢.

Generally located at busy intersections, **mailboxes** are blue, with a blue eagle logo and the designation U.S. POSTAL SERVICE. If your mail is addressed to a U.S. destination, don't forget to add the five- (or nine-) digit **postal code,** or ZIP (Zone Improvement Plan) Code, after the two-letter abbreviation of the state (GA for Georgia, NC for North Carolina, SC for South Carolina, and so on).

*Measures* The traditional American system of measures is still used in the United States, although many products now carry both U.S. and metric measures. In general, 1 foot equals about 30.48 centimeters; 1 mile about 1.609 kilometers. A pint equals .47 liter; 1 quart (2 pt.) .94 liter; 1 gallon (4 qt.) 3.79 liters. An ounce equals 28.35 grams, and 1 pound (16 oz.) equals .45 kilograms.

Temperature is measured in degrees Fahrenheit: 0° Celsius equals 32° Fahrenheit.

*Medical Emergencies* To call an ambulance, dial ℭ **911** from any phone. No coins are needed.

*Newspapers & Magazines* National newspapers include the *New York Times, USA Today,* and the *Wall Street Journal.* National newsweeklies include *Newsweek, Time,* and *U.S. News & World Report.* In large cities, most newsstands offer a small selection of the most popular foreign periodicals and newspapers, such as *The Economist, Le Monde,* and *Der Spiegel.* For information on leading state newspapers, see the "Fast Facts" sections for each state in chapters 3, 10, and 15.

*Radio & Television* Audiovisual media, with four coast-to-coast networks (ABC, CBS, NBC, and Fox), plus the Public Broadcasting System (PBS) and Cable News Network (CNN), play a major part in American life. In big cities, viewers have a choice of about a dozen channels (including the UHF channels), most of them transmitting 24 hours a day, not counting the pay-TV channels that show recent movies or sports events. All options are usually indicated on your hotel TV set.

You'll also find a wide choice of local radio stations, both AM and FM. Stations broadcast particular kinds of talk shows and/or music (classical, country, jazz, pop, or gospel, for example), punctuated by news broad-casts and frequent commercials. You'll usually find the affiliates of the National Public Radio system at the bottom of the radio dial, broadcast-ing in-depth news programs as well as talk shows and other eclectic pro-gramming. In smaller towns and communities, local radio and TV stations have a more limited broadcast range.

*Safety* See "Safety" in "Preparing for Your Trip," earlier in this chapter.

*Taxes* The United States has no VAT (value-added tax) or other indirect tax at the national level. Every state, and each county and city in it, is allowed to levy its own local nonrefundable tax on purchases (including hotels, restaurant bills, airline tickets, and so on) and services. Taxes are already included in the price of certain services, such as public trans-portation, cab fares, telephone calls, and gasoline. The amount of sales tax varies from about 4% to 12%, depending on the state and city, so when you're making major purchases (such as photographic equipment, clothing, or stereo components), it can be a significant part of the cost.

The state sales tax is 7% in Georgia, 7.5% in North Carolina, and 6% in South Carolina. Many municipalities also tack on a sometimes hefty accommodations tax (room or occupancy tax) to your hotel bill. Counties have the option of adding an extra .5% to 3% use tax.

*Telephone, Telegraph, Telex & Fax* The telephone system in the United States is run by private corporations, so rates, especially for long-distance service and operator-assisted calls, can vary widely—even on calls made from public telephones. Local calls in the BellSouth area of Georgia, South Carolina, and North Carolina cost 35¢.

Generally, hotel surcharges on long-distance and local calls are astro-nomical. You're usually better off calling collect, using a telephone charge card, or using **public pay telephones,** which you'll find clearly marked in most public buildings and private establishments as well as on the street. Outside metropolitan areas, public telephones are more diffi-cult to find. Stores and gas stations are your best bet.

Most **long-distance and international calls** can be dialed directly from any phone. (Stock up on quarters and dimes if you're calling from a pay phone, or use a telephone charge card.) For calls to Canada and other parts of the United States, dial 1, followed by the area code and the seven-digit number. For international calls, dial 011, followed by the country code (such as 61 for Australia, 353 for the Republic of Ireland, 64 for New Zealand, and 44 for the United Kingdom), the city code (for example, 020 for London and 0121 for Birmingham), and the telephone number of the person you want to call.

All calls to area codes 800, 877, and 888 are toll-free. Calls to numbers in area codes 700 and 900 (chat lines, bulletin boards, "dating" services, and so on) can be very expensive, however. These calls usually carry a charge of 95¢ to $3 or more per minute, and they sometimes have mini-mum charges that can run as high as $15 or more.

For **reversed-charge (collect) calls** and for **person-to-person calls,** dial 0 (zero, *not* the letter "O"), followed by the area code and number you want. An operator will then come on the line, and you should specify that you are calling collect, person-to-person, or both. If your operator-assisted call is international, ask for the overseas operator.

For **local directory assistance** ("information"), dial ✆ 411; for **long-distance information,** dial 1, followed by the appropriate area code and 555-1212.

Like the telephone system, **telegraph** and **telex** services are provided by private corporations such as ITT, MCI, and, above all, Western Union. You can take your telegram to the nearest Western Union office (there are hundreds across the country) or dictate it over the phone (toll-free call: ✆ **800/325-6000**). You can also telegraph money (using a major credit or charge card) or have it telegraphed to you very quickly over the Western Union system. (This service can be very expensive, however. The service charge can run as high as 15%–25% of the amount sent.) If you find yourself out of money, a wire service provided by American Express can help you tap willing friends and family for emergency funds. Through **MONEYGRAM,** 7501 W. Mansfield, Lakewood, CO 80235 (✆ **800/926-9400**), money can be sent around the world in 12 to 24 minutes.

Many hotels have **fax** machines available for guest use (be sure to ask about the charge to use it), and many hotel rooms are even wired for guests' fax machines. Almost all shops that make photocopies offer fax services as well.

*Telephone Directory*  There are two kinds of telephone directories. The general directory is the so-called **White Pages,** in which private and business subscribers are listed in alphabetical order. The inside front cover lists the emergency numbers for police, fire, and ambulance, and other vital numbers (the Coast Guard, poison-control center, crime-victims' hot line, and so on). The first few pages are devoted to community-service numbers, as well as a guide to long-distance and international calling, complete with country codes and area codes.

The second directory, printed on yellow paper (hence its name, **Yellow Pages**), lists all local services, businesses, and industries by type of activity, with an index at the back. The listings include automobile repairs by make of car, drugstores (pharmacies) by geographical location, restaurants by type of cuisine and geographical location, bookstores by special subject and/or language, places of worship by religious denomination, and other information that the tourist might otherwise not readily find. The Yellow Pages often include city plans or detailed area maps, as well as zip codes and public-transportation routes.

*Time*  The United States is divided into six time zones. From east to west, these zones are Eastern Standard Time (EST), Central Standard Time (CST), Mountain Standard Time (MST), Pacific Standard Time (PST), Alaska Standard Time (AST), and Hawaii Standard Time (HST). Always keep the changing time zones in mind if you are traveling (or even telephoning) over long distances in the United States. Noon in New York City (EST), for example, is 11am in Chicago (CST), 10am in Phoenix (MST), 9am in Los Angeles (PST), 8am in Anchorage (AST), and 7am in Honolulu (HST).

Georgia and the Carolinas observe Eastern Standard Time. **Daylight saving time** is in effect from the first Sunday in April through the last Saturday in October (actually, the change is made at 2am on Sun), except in

Arizona, Hawaii, part of Indiana, and Puerto Rico. Daylight saving time moves the clock 1 hour ahead of standard time. (Americans use the adage "spring ahead, fall back" to remember which way to change their clocks and watches.)

*Tipping* This is part of the American way of life, on the principle that you must expect to pay for any service that you get. (Many service personnel receive little direct salary and must depend on tips for their income.) Service charges are generally not included in restaurant checks or hotel bills. Here are some rules of thumb:

In **hotels,** tip bellhops $1 per piece of luggage, and tip the chamber staff $1 per day. Tip the doorman or concierge only if he or she provides some specific service, such as calling a cab for you or obtaining difficult-to-get theater tickets.

In **restaurants, bars,** and **nightclubs,** tip the service staff 15% of the check; tip bartenders 10% to 15%; tip checkroom attendants $1 per garment; and tip valet-parking attendants $1 per vehicle. Tip the doorman only if he provides some specific service, such as calling a cab for you. Tipping is not expected in cafeterias and fast-food restaurants.

Tip **cab drivers** 15% of the fare.

As for **other service personnel,** tip porters at airports or railroad stations $1 per piece of luggage, and tip hairdressers and barbers 15% to 20%.

You are not expected to tip gas-station attendants or ushers in cinemas or theaters.

# 3

# Planning Your Trip to North Carolina

In the pages that follow, we've compiled everything that you need to know to handle the practical details on planning your trip: airlines, a calendar of events, visitor information, and more.

## 1 The Regions in Brief

**THE HIGH COUNTRY** The **Blue Ridge Parkway** seems to touch the sky as it traces the jutting peaks and rising plateaus of the North Carolina mountains. Set in the splendor of these hills are the mountain folk, who strive to retain their lifestyle despite the headaches and traffic caused by tourists taking in the sights along the parkway.

The peak time for entering the parkway is May through October, when hotel accommodations are plentiful and visitor facilities are open. Fall is when the landscape is at its best. The natural foliage of the mountain evergreens is magically enhanced by a brisk palette of reds, yellows, oranges, and golds. Although winter rates are appealing, cold-weather conditions may make roads inaccessible. As though the mountains were not inspiring enough, North Carolina also offers other sites filled with natural splendor.

You can create your own script for this 470-mile drive—called the "Most Scenic Highway in America"—by entering at the southern end of Shenandoah National Park near the Virginia border. The slow drive that follows the road's sharp curves and narrow straightaways is full of serendipitous discoveries, from fresh-grown apples sold at stands along the roadside to rustic "junk" stores.

The rolling pasturelands of the Blue Ridge's northern access lie in Allegheny and Ashe counties, picture-perfect with grazing cows and lichen-covered split-rail fences. As you approach Watauga, Avery, and Mitchell counties, the mountains seem to rise like images in a fast-paced video game. **Grandfather Mountain** is the site of a staggering engineering feat: a roadway that swings treacherously 1,243 feet around the curve of craggy mountain. With down-home eateries, inns, panoramic views of misty blue mountains, and hiking trails spread along the length of the parkway, plus the highest peak in the eastern United States at **Mount Mitchell State Park** (6,684 ft.), you'll be amazed by the sights you'll see along the road, in spite of the traffic.

There are ways to avoid crowds and traffic even during the peak season. Park rangers suggest that you drive the parkway Monday through Friday, when the roads are less congested. Avoid Sunday afternoon altogether, and be adventurous: Go off the beaten track. Numerous side roads run parallel to the parkway or branch off from it. Visitor centers furnish detailed maps, but rangers recommend that you get specific instructions before venturing out onto one of these roads.

Plan on spending at least 2 days in the **Cherokee** area. Although the town is a little touristy, a smattering of intimate hideaways is concealed along the back roads of Great Smoky Mountains National Park near Cherokee.

Set just off the Blue Ridge Parkway, about 40 miles east of Cherokee, is **Asheville,** a stunning small city worthy of a 3-day stay, with attractions such as the Biltmore Estate, the Thomas Wolfe Memorial, and the Folk Art Center.

**THE PIEDMONT**  After you visit the mountains, head east to **Winston-Salem,** our favorite Piedmont City. The former seat of the powerful Reynolds tobacco fortune, Winston-Salem is also home to Old Salem, a restored 18th-and 19th-century village settled by German-speaking Moravians, and Wake Forest University.

Another component of the Piedmont is the **Raleigh/Durham/Chapel Hill area,** often referred to as the Research Triangle. This area has attracted all sorts of high-tech industry to the state—no wonder, because three of the premier universities in the South (Duke, the University of North Carolina, and North Carolina State) are located here, within a stone's throw of one another. The proximity of Duke to UNC has given rise to perhaps the greatest rivalry in college-basketball history—although State's consistently competitive hoops program can never be counted out of the equation. Chapel Hill is the charming college town, Durham the up-and-coming hot spot, and Raleigh the bustling state capital.

The largest city in the Piedmont is **Charlotte.** Surprisingly cosmopolitan and set amid rolling hills, this fast-paced city rivals Orlando or Birmingham and dismisses the down-home label. It's a major banking center and transportation hub, and its diversified manufacturing capabilities include machinery, textiles, metals, and food products. Charlotte has also been transformed into a big-time sports town: The state's first pro football team, the Carolina Panthers, continues to draw fans to its state-of-the-art open-air "retro" stadium.

**THE COAST**  A trip through North Carolina wouldn't be complete without sticking your toes in the brisk Atlantic. The largest city on the coast is **Wilmington,** although much of North Carolina's shoreline remains much less developed than the frenetic scene along South Carolina's beaches. In spite of the slowpoke summer traffic, **Nags Head** especially has a little something for every family member, from a rustic fishing pier to nearby video arcades. It also offers some of the finest seafood restaurants on the East Coast, many in modest settings. Local specialties include Hatteras-style clam chowder, crab cakes, and deep-fried hush puppies. Surprisingly, Nags Head lacks one thing that most of its rival resorts do have: high-rise condos. Instead, towering overhead is Jockey's Ridge, a giant sand dune that forms the tallest *medano* (large, isolated hill of sand) in the East. Climb to the top of the mile-long dune for outstanding views of the ocean and sound.

Another wonderful spot is **Ocracoke Island,** a 45-minute ride across the waters of Pamlico Sound. A free ferry departs Hatteras village every 30 minutes, beginning daily at 5am. Disembark at the north-end ferry visitor station, and head for the village of Ocracoke while enjoying the expanses of wild dunes and forests of cedar and pine. The beaches leading into

# North Carolina

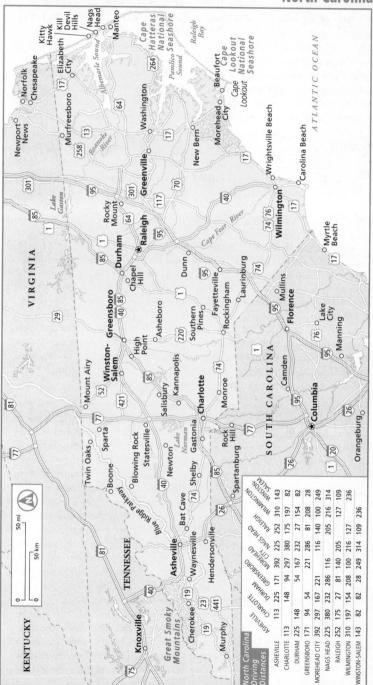

| North Carolina Driving Distances | ASHEVILLE | CHARLOTTE | DURHAM | GREENSBORO | MOREHEAD CITY | NAGS HEAD | RALEIGH | WILMINGTON | WINSTON-SALEM |
|---|---|---|---|---|---|---|---|---|---|
| ASHEVILLE | | 113 | 225 | 171 | 392 | 225 | 252 | 310 | 143 |
| CHARLOTTE | 113 | | 148 | 94 | 297 | 380 | 175 | 197 | 82 |
| DURHAM | 225 | 148 | | 54 | 167 | 232 | 27 | 154 | 82 |
| GREENSBORO | 171 | 94 | 54 | | 221 | 286 | 81 | 208 | 28 |
| MOREHEAD CITY | 392 | 297 | 167 | 221 | | 116 | 140 | 100 | 249 |
| NAGS HEAD | 225 | 380 | 232 | 286 | 116 | | 205 | 216 | 314 |
| RALEIGH | 252 | 175 | 27 | 81 | 140 | 205 | | 127 | 109 |
| WILMINGTON | 310 | 197 | 154 | 208 | 100 | 216 | 127 | | 236 |
| WINSTON-SALEM | 143 | 82 | 82 | 28 | 249 | 314 | 109 | 236 | |

Ocracoke Village are some of the best on the East Coast.

Much of the island is a National Seashore area where large development is prohibited. While this is a place where you still can go into the post office barefoot to check your mail, it's not the sleepy little backwater it was even 10 years ago. The town of Ocracoke has ceded to the demands of tourism, building several multistory hotels around Silver Lake; restaurants; and shops selling the requisite beach hammocks, taffy, T-shirts, and souvenirs. In the summer, the tourist crush can be overwhelming; visit in the fall, when you'll see the island at its best, a real North Carolina charmer.

## 2  Visitor Information

For information, contact the **North Carolina Division of Tourism, Film and Sports Development,** 300 N. Wilmington St., Raleigh, NC 27626-2825 (© **800/VISIT-NC** or 919/733-4171; www.visitnc.com). Excellent visitor centers at the state borders on most major highways can also furnish detailed tourist information.

## 3  Money

In addition to checking the details in this section, international visitors should see "Preparing for Your Trip," in chapter 2.

It's getting easier all the time to access your bank account while you're on the road. You won't have any problem finding ATMs connected to the major national networks, both in small towns and large cities. For specific locations of **Cirrus** machines, call © **800/424-7787;** for the **PLUS** network, dial © **800/843-7587.**

American Express offices are open Monday to Friday from 8:30am to 5pm. See "Fast Facts: North Carolina," later in this chapter, for the main office location.

## 4  When to Go

For the most part, North Carolina's climate is moderate, with average winter temperatures in the 60s along the southern coast and in the low 40s inland. Summer temperatures can rise to the high 90s in the state's interior, accompanied by some serious humidity. If you're in the mountains or on the shore, temperatures can be cooled by breezes to the mid-60s or high 70s.

So if you're thinking about a summer vacation in North Carolina, we don't advise heading for the Piedmont, where all that miserable heat and humidity hangs heavy. But you can escape to Boone, which has an average temperature of 69°F (21°C). It's warm enough during the day to swim or hike, but you'll want a light blanket to sleep under at night. The Outer Banks is another great destination in summer; bring your beach gear, and enjoy the breezes.

In late September or early October, fall colors are brilliant here. During this time, thousands of monarch butterflies cluster in the mountains near Asheville, around Wagon Road Gap on the Blue Ridge Parkway, as part of their annual migration to South America. Don't miss it! (But be prepared for incredible crowds along the parkway.)

Spring is also a spectacular time to visit. In March and April, the state bursts into bloom, with azaleas in vibrant hues everywhere, rhododendrons in the mountains, and the more delicate pink-and-white dogwood blossoms in the woodlands.

## What Things Cost in Asheville

| | US$ |
|---|---|
| Taxi from the airport to downtown | 30.00 |
| Local phone call | 0.35 |
| Double room at Grove Park Resort (expensive) | 325.00 |
| Double room at Cedar Crest Inn (moderate) | 175.00 |
| Double room at Old Reynolds Mansion Bed & Breakfast (inexpensive) | 120.00 |
| Lunch for one at Charlotte Street Grill and Pub (moderate) | 12.00 |
| Lunch for one at New French Bar (inexpensive) | 8.00 |
| Dinner for one, without wine, at Blue Ridge Dining Room (expensive) | 60.00 |
| Dinner for one, without wine, at the Marketplace (moderate) | 25.00 |
| Dinner for one, without wine, at Charlotte Street Grill (inexpensive) | 18.00 |
| Bottle of beer | 4.00 |
| Coca-Cola | 1.00 |
| Roll of 35mm 200-speed film, 36 exposures | 4.00 |
| Movie ticket | 7.50 |
| Ticket to the Asheville Symphony | 20.00–125.00 |
| Adult admission to the Biltmore Estate | 39.00 |

## Raleigh Average Temperatures & Rainfall

| | Jan | Feb | Mar | Apr | May | June | July | Aug | Sept | Oct | Nov | Dec |
|---|---|---|---|---|---|---|---|---|---|---|---|---|
| High (°F) | 50 | 52 | 61 | 72 | 78 | 85 | 88 | 87 | 81 | 71 | 61 | 52 |
| High (°C) | 10 | 11 | 16 | 22 | 26 | 29 | 31 | 31 | 27 | 22 | 16 | 11 |
| Low (°F) | 29 | 30 | 37 | 46 | 55 | 62 | 67 | 66 | 60 | 47 | 38 | 31 |
| Low (°C) | –2 | –1 | 3 | 8 | 13 | 17 | 19 | 19 | 16 | 8 | 3 | –1 |
| Rain (in.) | 3.5 | 3.7 | 3.8 | 2.6 | 3.9 | 3.7 | 4.0 | 4.0 | 3.2 | 2.9 | 3.0 | 3.2 |

## Asheville Average Temperatures & Rainfall

| | Jan | Feb | Mar | Apr | May | June | July | Aug | Sept | Oct | Nov | Dec |
|---|---|---|---|---|---|---|---|---|---|---|---|---|
| High (°F) | 49 | 51 | 57 | 68 | 76 | 83 | 85 | 84 | 79 | 69 | 57 | 50 |
| High (°C) | 9 | 11 | 14 | 20 | 24 | 28 | 29 | 29 | 26 | 21 | 14 | 10 |
| Low (°F) | 30 | 30 | 36 | 44 | 52 | 60 | 64 | 63 | 57 | 46 | 36 | 30 |
| Low (°C) | –1 | –1 | 2 | 7 | 11 | 16 | 18 | 17 | 14 | 8 | 2 | –1 |
| Rain (in.) | 3.2 | 3.0 | 3.7 | 3.2 | 2.9 | 3.5 | 4.3 | 3.6 | 2.8 | 2.5 | 2.2 | 2.9 |

# NORTH CAROLINA CALENDAR OF EVENTS

## January

**African American Arts Festival,** Greensboro. Many cultural and artistic events highlight the achievements of the state's African-American population. Call ⓒ **336/333-6885** or visit www.uac greensboro.org. Early January to April.

## February

**Home, Garden and Flower Show,** Raleigh. You can find everything from roses to garden fountains to furniture in this vast display in the Raleigh Convention Center, which attracts serious gardeners from all over the South. Call ⓒ **919/ 831-6011** or visit www.raleigh convention.com. Late February.

**Duke University Jazz Series,** Durham. Formerly known as the NC International Jazz Festival, this event is in its 20th year. Internationally renowned jazz musicians are featured at various locations throughout the city. Call ⓒ **919/ 660-3300** or go to www.duke.edu/ music. Throughout the year.

## March

**Annual Star Fiddlers Convention,** Biscoe. This memorable event features performances by virtuoso bluegrass fiddlers from all over the South. Call ⓒ **910/895-9057.** First weekend in March.

## April

**Festival of Flowers,** Biltmore Estate, Asheville. The festival celebrates a century of elegance at the Biltmore Estate. The gardens are brilliant with color for your viewing. Call ⓒ **800/543-2961** or go to www.biltmore.com. Early April to mid-May.

**North Carolina Azalea Festival,** Wilmington. A parade, entertainment, and home and garden tours are all included in this annual festival. Call ⓒ **910/794-4650** or visit www.ncazaleafestival.org. Early April.

**Spring Historic Homes and Gardens Tour,** New Bern. Tour Tryon Palace and other area homes, gardens, and historic sites. Call ⓒ **252/ 633-6448.** First weekend in April.

**Full Frame Documentary Film Festival,** the Carolina Theatre, Durham. Largest festival of its kind in North America, this event (formerly the DoubleTake Documentary Film Festival) has been hailed for its creative programming and exhibition of films rarely seen on screen. Call ⓒ **919/687-4100** or

visit www.fullframefest.org. 2005 festival: April 7 to April 10.

**Stoneybrook Steeplechase,** Southern Pines. This event features horse races and tailgate parties. Call ⓒ **800/346-5362** or go to www.five pointshorsepark.com. April (varies). Call for exact date.

**Spring Garden Tour,** Winston-Salem. Each spring in historic Old Salem, people gather from everywhere to celebrate spring with a tour of the city's 18th-century gardens. Call ⓒ **888/653-7253** or visit www.oldsalem.org. Mid-April.

**Easter Sunrise Service,** Winston-Salem. Thousands of people come to see this Moravian religious service in "God's Acres," the cemetery where the early settlers are buried. Call ⓒ **336/722-6171.** Easter Sunday.

## May

**CityFest Live!,** Charlotte. Live bands provide entertainment at this 3-day music festival while folks stroll through the streets of the Uptown Entertainment District, buying snacks from food vendors and checking out the arts and crafts. Go to www.cityfestlive.com. Three days in early May.

**Ole Time Fiddlers & Bluegrass Festival,** Union Grove. Traditional musicians and the fans who love bluegrass make a yearly pilgrimage to what may be the most renowned fiddling competition in the country. PBS made an award-winning documentary on the festival. Call ⓒ **704/539-4417** or visit www. fiddlersgrove.com. Memorial Day weekend.

**Coca-Cola 600,** Charlotte. This action-packed race, which is part of the NASCAR Winston Cup Series, takes place at Lowe's Motor Speedway. Enjoy the Food Lion Speed Street, 3 days of race-related festivities on Tryon Street in Charlotte; over 400,000 people showed up in 2004. Call © **704/455-6814** or go to www.600festival.com. End of May.

## June

**American Dance Festival,** Durham. Considered to be the largest and most prestigious modern-dance event in the world, the festival has been held on the Duke University campus since 1978. Call © **919/684-6402** or go to www.american dancefestival.org. Early June to late July.

**Herb Day,** Durham. See displays of traditional herb remedies and recipes from the mid–19th century. There are herbs from an on-site garden, herbal crafts, and food available for purchase. Call © **919/477-5498.** First Saturday in June.

*The Lost Colony,* Roanoke Island. Paul Green's moving drama is presented in the Waterside Theater Monday through Saturday at 8:30pm. It's the country's oldest outdoor drama, running since 1937. All seats are reserved; contact the Waterside Theater (© **866/468-7630;** www.thelostcolony.org) for Visa or MasterCard bookings. Tickets cost $16 for adults; $15 for seniors, military personnel, and people who have disabilities; and $8 for children 11 and under. Early June to late August.

**Hillsborough Hog Day,** Hillsborough. Featured attractions include barbecue, potbellied-pig contests, entertainment, crafts, and a vintage car show. Call © **919/732-8156** or visit www.hogdays.com. Mid-June.

**National Hollerin' Contest,** Spivey's Corner. Immortalized by a visit from Charles Kuralt at its 1969 inaugural, this event celebrates hollerin' as a traditional form of communication. Drawing visitors from all over the country, the contest swells Spivey's Corner's usual population of 49. Call © **910/567-2600** or go to www.hollerincontest.com. Third Saturday in June.

## July

**Shindig on the Green,** Asheville. At the City/County Plaza (College and Spruce sts.), you'll find mountain musicians and dancers having an old-fashioned wingding. The event is free and lots of fun. For details, go to www.exploreasheville. com/music.htm. Every Saturday night from early July to August (except the first Sat in Aug).

**Grandfather Mountain Highland Games and Gathering of the Scottish Clans,** Linville. The event is complete with Scottish dance, music, and athletic competitions. Call © **828/733-1333** or go to www.gmhg.org. Early July.

**Festival of the Arts,** Brevard. This weeklong festival features a children's exhibit, creative and performing arts, and food, in venues throughout the city. Call © **828/884-2787.** Early July.

**Coon Dog Day,** Saluda. For more than 30 years, coon hunters and nature lovers have gathered for dog trials, arts and crafts shows, a parade, a pancake breakfast, a treeing contest, barbecue, bluegrass and Southern folk concerts, and a square dance. It's truly folkloric Carolina. Call © **828/749-2581** or visit www.saluda.com. Saturday following the Fourth of July.

**Folkmoot USA (North Carolina International Folk Festival),** Waynesville and Maggie Valley. Folkmoot USA provides international music and dance, plus good old-fashioned North Carolina mountain music. Call © **877/365-5872** or 828/452-2997; or visit www.folk moot.com. Late July.

**National Black Theatre Festival,** Winston-Salem. This festival includes performances, workshops, and seminars at various theaters around the city, produced and hosted by the city's own North Carolina Black Repertory Co. Call ⓒ **336/723-7907** or go to www. nbtf.org. Late July to early August. Held biannually in odd years.

**Bele Chere,** Asheville. Billed as the "largest outdoor street festival in the Southeast," this music, arts, and food festival has big-name bands and "Taste of Asheville" samplings from local restaurants. Contact the Department of Parks and Recreation (ⓒ **828/259-5800;** www. belechere.com). July 29 to July 31, 2005.

### August

**Mountain Dance & Folk Festival,** Asheville. At the Civic Center on Haywood Street, the fiddlers, banjo pickers, dulcimer players, ballad singers, and clog dancers don't call it quits until nobody is interested in one more dance. This is the oldest such festival in the country, and you're encouraged to join in. For details, go to www.exploreasheville. com/music.htm. First weekend in August.

**Brevard Music Festival,** Brevard. For more than half a century, this has been one of the major open-air events in western North Carolina, featuring opera, classic music, pops, and jazz. The center for information is at 100 Probart St. (ⓒ **888/ 384-8682** or 828/862-2105; www. brevardmusic.org). First week in August.

### September

**North Carolina Apple Festival,** Hendersonville. Bring your favorite apple-pie recipe, and enjoy music, crafts, games, and a cooking contest. Call ⓒ **828/697-4557** or go to www.ncapplefestival.org. Labor Day weekend.

**Festival in the Park,** Charlotte. A celebration of regional arts and crafts, with entertainment and good food as bonuses. Call ⓒ **704/338- 1060** or visit www.festivalinthe park.net. Six days in mid-September.

**Mayberry Days,** Mount Airy. A celebration of *The Andy Griffith Show,* with entertainment, a golf tournament, walking tours, and a pig pickin'. Call ⓒ **800/286-6193** or visit www.surryarts.org. Last weekend in September.

**SAS Championship,** Cary. This $1.8-million Senior PGA Tour championship is drawing such well-known golfers as Tom Kite and Fuzzy Zoeller as it approaches its fifth tournament year. Call ⓒ **800/5317- PGA** or go to www.saschampionship. com. Mid-September.

### October

**MUMfest,** New Bern. Swiss Bear Downtown Development Corp. hosts a street festival loaded with food, fun, arts and crafts, and tours. Call ⓒ **252/638-5782** or visit www.mumfest.com. Early October.

**North Carolina State Fair,** Raleigh. This traditional gathering draws crowds from all over. Call ⓒ **919/ 733-7400** or visit www.ncstate fair.org. Mid-October.

**Chrysler Classic of Greensboro,** Greensboro. Some 275,000 fans come to the galleries of Forest Oaks Country Club to watch the pros compete for the $1.5-million purse of this nationally televised tournament, one of the richest on the PGA tour. Call ⓒ **888/397-3100** or 336/379-1570; or visit www.ggcc. com. Mid-October.

### November

**Christmas at the Biltmore Estate,** Asheville. The Biltmore Estate becomes a winter wonderland long before Christmas. Enjoy Christmas lights, trees, decorations, and music.

Call ℂ **800/624-1575** or 828/225-1333; or go to www.biltmore.com. November 6 to January 4.

## December

**Festival of Lights,** Tanglewood Park, Winston-Salem. For 9 weeks, more than 750,000 lights are presented in more than five dozen displays. Enjoy storybook themes. Call ℂ **336/778-6300** or visit www.tanglewoodpark.org. Mid-November to early January.

**Old Salem Christmas and Candle Teas,** Winston-Salem. A re-creation of Yuletide as it was celebrated 200 years ago in Old Salem. Enjoy making candles, tasting Moravian sugar cakes, and touring the 1788 Gemeinhaus by candlelight. Call ℂ **336/722-6171** or visit www.home-moravian.org. First 2 weeks in December.

**Holiday Festival, Raleigh.** The city hosts the Holiday Festival at the North Carolina Museum of Art. It's an old-fashioned Yuletide celebration. Call ℂ **919/839-6262** or visit www.ncartmuseum.org. Early December.

## 5 The Active Vacation Planner

North Carolina presents an incredible array of landscapes and recreational offerings. The beaches are outstanding, and they're never as crowded as those on South Carolina's Grand Strand. Broad stretches of white sand offer waves to challenge the most skillful surfer, and quiet, family-oriented seaside resorts can be found on both the Outer Banks and along the southern "Crystal Coast." Fishing, boating, water-skiing, and even hang gliding from gigantic dunes are all part of the fun up and down the coast.

The opposite end of the state holds the Great Smoky Mountains, which offer some of the most spectacular scenery in the Southeast—not to mention ample opportunities for hiking, fly-fishing, white-water rafting, and camping. And if your game is golf or tennis, North Carolina's got plenty to keep you entertained.

## ACTIVITIES A TO Z

**BICYCLING**   Miles of back roads and lots of flat terrain (except in the mountains) make North Carolina an ideal venue for bikers.

Those who like biking by the beach can head for the Outer Banks. It's best to begin in Corolla, where a separate bike path parallels N.C. 12 for many miles south.

The gently sloping Piedmont, with its hard-packed surfaces, is also good road-biking country. The tourist office in Winston-Salem can provide maps of the Piedmont's most scenic bike tours through the historic Bethabara and Tanglewood parks. Outside Charlotte, McAlpine Creek Park has a 2-mile trail for bikers. The nearly deserted lanes and sleepy hamlets of Pinehurst and Southern Pines are our favorite spots.

For mountain bikers, the Asheville Convention and Visitors Bureau supplies a list of outfitters that also provide trail maps. Regrettably, the scenic Blue Ridge Parkway has no lanes for bikers, who are forced to ride single-file along the side of the two-lane highway. Helmets and kneepads are required, and white lights and reflectors are necessary to go through some two dozen dark-as-night tunnels. Fog is also a frequent occurrence. Weekends, any holiday, and the traffic-clogged months of May and October, are the worst times to bike the Blue Ridge.

For bicycle route maps, contact the **North Carolina Department of Transportation's Bicycle Program,** P.O. Box 25201, Raleigh, NC 27611 (ℂ **919/733-2804**). Bikers can also get a free 50-page catalog from **Backroads** (ℂ **800/462-2848;** www.backroads.com), a reliable firm based in Berkeley, California, that offers organized bike tours to the Georgia islands, among others; or **VBT** (© **800/245-3868;** www.vbt.com), which offers deluxe bicycle vacations, such as a tour of the North Carolina coast.

**BIRDING**   The Outer Banks traditionally draws birders, especially those who are interested in seasonal migrations. Cape Lookout National Seashore is the most remote state beach and a nesting area for the piping plover. On Cape Fear, birders head for Sunset Beach. Here, on the west end, they can wade across Mad Inlet at low tide to reach Bird Island, which is Valhalla for all bird-watchers. In this isolated place, herons, egrets, osprey, and an array of other beautiful birds come to feed and nest.

**CAMPING**   Campers can find very good facilities throughout North Carolina, with fees ranging from $15 to $20 per night. RV hookups, however, are available only at selected sites. For details, contact the **Division of Parks and Recreation,** Department of the Environment, Health and Natural Resources, P.O. Box 27687, Raleigh, NC 27611 (© **919/733-4181;** www. ncsparks.net). The excellent "Official North Carolina Highway Map and Guide to Points of Interest" also has extensive information about national and state parks and forests.

**Great Smoky Mountains,** named for the smoky blue haze that crowns their tops, run for more than 70 miles, picking up where the Blue Ridge Parkway ends. The 520,000-acre park lies half in North Carolina and half in Tennessee. It shelters bears, deer, wild turkeys, and grouse, among other forms of wildlife. Summer brings an ever-changing kaleidoscope of color from flowering plants. Within the park boundaries are no fewer than 130 native species of trees in 180,000 acres of virgin forest.

Camping is best along the 70 miles of the Appalachian Trail, which follows the ridge that forms the North Carolina–Tennessee border. Be warned, however, that reservations are required between mid-May and October. Contact **National Park Reservation Service,** P.O. Box 1600, Cumberland, MD 21501 (© **800/365-2267;** http:// reservations.nps.gov).

**FISHING**   From fly-fishing to deep-sea or light-tackle fishing, the **Outer Banks** provide some of the best opportunities for anglers in the United States. You can catch channel bass in the spring; whiting, flounder, and Spanish mackerel during the summer; and small bluefish in autumn. Pompano run from spring until the beginning of winter. Big bluefish are hunted almost year-round. Unless you want to go deep-sea fishing, you won't need a boat along the 300 miles of coastline, studded with jetties and piers; some 25% of all Atlantic piers are in North Carolina. Some piers are better known than others: Nags Head for flounder, bluefish, mullet, and striped bass; and Ocracoke Island for sea mullet, bluefish, and pompano. Pursuers of big amberjack and tarpon head for the piers along the Bogue Banks in the Neuse River region.

The lakes, rivers, and streams of the mountains are the second major venue for fishermen, especially for those who seek trout, muskies, catfish, and small- and largemouth bass. The best places for fishing include the Linville River, the Toe River and its tributaries, the Globe section of the Johns River Gorge, and Howard's Creek (north of Boone). Local tourist offices can supply complete details. For trout fanciers, the lakes and streams of the Blue Ridge are ideal. Trout fishermen are also drawn to the Great Smoky Mountains, with hundreds of miles of streams and creeks that are home to smallmouth bass, rock bass, and brown and rainbow trout. (It's illegal to catch brook trout.) Rangers at the visitor centers provide guidelines, and you can buy Don Kirk's *Smoky Mountains Trout Fishing Guide* if you plan to do serious angling there.

Most hardware and general stores supply fishing licenses, which are required for all freshwater fishermen 16 or older ($15 in state; $30 out of state). With the license comes a list of rules and state laws, especially regarding fish size.

**GOLF**   North Carolina is one of the best states for golf in the nation. Southern Pines and the Pinehurst Sandhills (see chapter 7) are called the Golf Capital of the World—with good reason. Some 35 golf courses fill these sandhills, which have attracted most of the greatest names in the sport. The Pinehurst Hotel and Resort—the only resort with seven signature courses—is legendary. Equally good are the Pine Needles Lodge and the Club at Longleaf.

Golfing isn't confined to the Sandhills region, however. Charlotte is mad for the highly publicized Scottish-style Charlotte Golf Links at Charlotte. The Raleigh-Durham area is filled with master courses, including the one at Duke University designed by Robert Trent Jones.

The best course in the mountains is at Asheville's Grove Park Inn. Yet another high-elevation golfing destination lies in the town of Blowing Rock, a summer haven for golf-loving coastal dwellers who prefer golfing in the much cooler environs of the mountains. Good golfing is also possible on the coast. Cape Fear, near Wilmington, has the most courses, including a George Cobb masterpiece with ocean views at Bald Head Island. Consult the regional chapters that follow for further details.

**HIKING & BACKPACKING**   The best place for hiking and backpacking in the entire state is Great Smoky Mountains National Park, where

you'll find approximately 800 miles of trails. The guide *Walks and Hikes* lists more than 60 of these trails (the best ones) and is available at the visitor centers. Another good source for hiking and backpacking information is the **Great Smoky Mountains Natural History Association,** 416 Cherry St., Gatlinburg, TN 37738 (© **865/436-0120;** www.smokiesstore.org). For the best hiking in North Carolina, you can also contact the **Sierra Club** (© **415/977-5500;** www.sierraclub.org); and the **Appalachian Mountain Club,** 5 Joy St., Boston, MA 02108 (© **617/523-0636;** www.outdoors.org).

**HORSEBACK RIDING**   North Carolina's southern mountains, linked by U.S. 64 south of Asheville, were once the home of the Cherokee, who didn't have horses. But the residents nowadays surely do. Dozens upon dozens of trails offer some of the best riding in the state. Trails are cut through both Nantahala National Forest and Pisgah National Forest. If you'd like to drive down from Asheville for an equestrian day, call the best of the stables: either **Pisgah Forest Stables,** U.S. 276 North, Pisgah Forest (© **828/883-8258**); or **Earthshine Mountain Lodge,** Golden Road, Lake Toxaway (© **828/862-4207;** www.earthshinemtnlodge.com).

**HUNTING**   Deer hunting is a passionate pastime for many Southerners. The mating habits and short gestation season of deer count for an overwhelming annual explosion of the deer population. If you're a hunting enthusiast, you already understand the conservation and preservation tenets of the sport. For information, contact the **Department of Environment and Natural Resources,** 512 Salisbury St., P.O. Box 27687, Raleigh, NC 27611 (© **919/733-4984;** www.enr.state.nc.us).

**RAFTING**   The best rafting in the state is in Great Smoky Mountains National Park. Indeed, this white-water country along the Nantahala River offers some of the best rafting in the United States. If you're a beginner, you can take a rafting course at the **Nantahala Outdoor Center,** U.S. 19/74 (✆ **800/232-7238;** www.noc.com), located 13 miles west of Bryson City, Tennessee. It offers 1- to 7-day courses. The best outfit to call if you already know how to raft is **Rafting in the Smokies** (✆ **800/776-7238;** www. raftinginthesmokies.com), which rafts both the Pigeon and Nantahala rivers.

**SKIING**   For the best skiing in the tri-state area, head for the High Country of North Carolina, where the mountains range from 4,000 to 5,500 feet. Appalachian Ski Mountain, Ski Beech, Hawksnest Golf and Ski Resort, and Sugar Mountain Resort offer snow-laden slopes for both beginners and advanced skiers. The major resorts are close together, and you can easily resort-hop until you find the winter conditions that are suitable for you. Beginners should try the easier slopes of Sugar Mountain. Ski Beech is the highest ski area in

eastern North America; the vertical drop is only 830 feet, but it's straight down, so it's only for daredevils. Hawksnest has two short beginner runs, and Appalachian Ski Mountain attracts the family trade and beginners. All ski areas are open for night runs. For more information about skiing the North Carolina mountains, get in touch with **High Country Host,** 1700 Blowing Rock Rd., Boone, NC 28607 (✆ **828/264-1299;** www.high countryhost.com).

**TENNIS**   The Piedmont has the greatest number of public courts, including 20 in the Winston-Salem area alone. All the cities, big and small, in North Carolina have courts, as do all the major resorts. Most courts in the High Country are outdoors, so you'll want to restrict your playing to spring through autumn. True tennis buffs find it just too windy along the Outer Banks, and games there are often restricted to indoor courts. On the southern Banks, it's a different matter, with mild winters making for fine year-round playing.

## 6 Specialized Travel Resources

**TRAVELERS WITH DISABILITIES**   Many hotels and restaurants in North Carolina now provide easy access, and some display the international wheelchair symbol in their brochures. It's always a good idea to call before you book to find out just what the situation is.

Many agencies provide advance data to help you plan your trip. One such agency is **Travel Information Service,** Industrial Rehab Program, 1200 W. Tabor Rd., Philadelphia, PA 19141 (✆ **215/456-9603** or 215/456-9602 for TTY). It answers questions on various destinations and also offers discounts on videos, publications, and programs that it sponsors. For a free copy of *Air Transportation of Handicapped Persons,* published by the U.S. Department of Transportation,

write for Free Advisory Circular No. AC12032, Distribution Unit, U.S. Department of Transportation, Publications Division, M-4332, Washington, DC 20590.

**Amtrak,** with 24 hours' notice, will provide porter service, special seating, and a deep discount (✆ **800/USA-RAIL;** www.amtrak.com).

The U.S. National Park Service offers a **Golden Access Passport** that gives free lifetime entrance to all properties administered by the National Park Service—national parks, monuments, historic sites, recreation areas, and national wildlife refuges—for persons who are visually impaired or permanently disabled, regardless of age. You may pick up a Golden Access Passport at any NPS entrance fee area by showing proof of medically determined disability and eligibility for receiving benefits under federal law. Besides free entry, the Golden Access Passport also offers a 50% discount on federal-use fees charged for such facilities as camping, swimming, parking, boat launching, and tours. For more information, go to www.nps.gov/fees_passes.htm or call © **888/467-2757.**

**GAY & LESBIAN TRAVELERS** In **Charlotte,** the **Gay Visitor Information Line** (© **704/535-6277**) is open daily from 6:30 to 9:30pm. Throughout the rest of the day, information on gay resources can be directed to the helpful staff at **White Rabbit Books & Things,** 1401 Central Ave., Charlotte, NC 28205 (© **704/377-4067;** www.whiterabbitbooks.com).

**Raleigh** offers the **Gay and Lesbian Helpline** (© **919/821-0055**). An equally helpful source of information about gay and lesbian issues is **White Rabbit Books & Things,** 309 W. Martin St., Raleigh, NC 27601 (© **919/856-1429;** www.whiterabbit books.com).

**SENIOR TRAVEL** Nearly all major U.S. hotel and motel chains now offer seniors a discount, so ask for the reduction *when you make the reservation;* there may be restrictions during peak days. Then be sure to carry proof of your age (driver's license, passport, and so on) when you check in. Among the chains that offer the best discounts are **Marriott Hotels** (© **800/228-9290**) for those 62 and older; and **La Quinta Inns** (© **800/531-5900**) for ages 55 and older.

You can save sightseeing dollars if you're 62 or older by picking up a **Golden Age Passport** from any federally operated park, recreation area, or monument.

**Elderhostel,** 11 de Lafayette, Boston, MA 02111 (© **877/426-8056** or 978/323-4141; www.elder hostel.org), provides stimulating vacations at moderate prices for those over 55, with a balanced mix of learning, field trips, and free time for sightseeing.

One organization for seniors offers a wide variety of travel benefits: **AARP,** 601 E St. NW, Washington, DC 20049 (© **202/434-AARP;** www.aarp.org).

## 7 Getting There

**BY PLANE** Delta (© **800/221-1212;** www.delta.com) and **US Airways** (© **800/428-4322;** www.usair ways.com) serve the largest number of North Carolina destinations from out of state, although not all flights are direct. **American Airlines** (© **800/433-7300;** www.aa.com), **Continental Airlines** (© **800/525-0280;** www. continental.com), and **United Airlines** (© **800/241-6522;** www.ual. com) also have direct flights to many North Carolina cities. Although good regional airports exist, the Raleigh-Durham and Charlotte airports are the major hubs, offering connecting flights to most major U.S. destinations.

**BY CAR** From Virginia and South Carolina, you can enter North Carolina on either I-95 or I-85. I-27 and I-77 also lead in from South Carolina. The main Tennessee entry is I-40. All major border points have helpful welcome centers, some with cookout facilities and playground equipment in a parklike setting.

**BY TRAIN** North Carolina is on **Amtrak**'s New York–Miami and New York–Tampa runs, with stops in Raleigh, Hamlet, Southern Pines, Rocky Mount, and Fayetteville. The New York–Washington–New Orleans route of the *Crescent* stops in Greensboro, High Point, Salisbury, Charlotte, and Gastonia. Be sure to check for excursion fares or seasonal specials. For reservations and fare information, call © **800/USA-RAIL** or go to www.amtrak.com. Ask about the money-saving **All Aboard America** regional fares or any other current fare specials. Amtrak also offers attractive rail/drive vacation packages in the Carolinas and Georgia.

**BY BUS** Greyhound/Carolina Trailways (© **800/231-2222;** www.greyhound.com) has good direct service to major cities in North Carolina, with connections to almost any destination. An advance purchase is the best way to get the best fare. Special fares and programs are offered for purchases ranging from 3 days in advance to 30 days in advance, the latter offering substantial savings from normal fares. Call for information and schedules, or contact the Greyhound depot in your area.

## 8 Package Tours

Tour companies offer package tours that include the Carolinas and Georgia. Most tours include airport transfers, admission to tour attractions, meals, and accommodations. Be sure to ask whether your tour is included under the USOTA consumer-protection guarantee (in case of bankruptcy or insolvency).

**Adventure Depot,** 200 Yellow Mountain Rd., lies in Cullowhee (© **800/903-4401;** www.adventuredepot.net) and offers the state's most diversified cross-section of activities, including white-water kayaking, canoe tours, llama trekking, horseback riding, biking tours, and fly-fishing, among other adventures. Most packages are 2 days and 2 nights with one more day of optional adventures; longer packages are also available. The town of Cullowhee lies in the Blue Ridge Mountains 4 miles off Route 64 and 8 miles from the town of Cashiers.

**Barrier Island Kayaks** (© **252/393-6457;** wwwbarrierislandkayaks.com) offers instruction and guided day trips to the barrier islands of the Outer Banks of North Carolina. Visit such destinations as Bear Island and Cape Lookout. Day-trip prices range from $30 to $75. Daily equipment rental for outdoors enthusiasts is an additional charge.

**Nearly Perfect Tours** (© **704/481-9415;** www.nearlyperfecttours.com) is a western North Carolina mountain tour company specializing in custom tours of the Blue Ridge Mountains. The company will design a tour to fit your interests—whether history, music, mountain culture, architecture, or old general stores. It also offers a North Carolina wineries tour in the Charlotte area. Full-day tours are priced at a rate of $200 daily, and tours have five or less participants.

The region's leading tour operator, **Mid Atlantic Tour & Receptive Services** (© **800/769-5912** or 540/665-1939; www.midatlantictours.com), features all-inclusive customized individual group tours. Tours usually begin at 3 days and 2 nights. Destinations include the Outer Banks, Old Salem, and the western mountains.

## 9 Getting Around

**BY CAR** North Carolina's 76,000 miles of toll-free, well-maintained highways and some state roads have rest areas with picnic tables and outdoor cooking facilities. Write **Travel and Tourism NC,** Department of Commerce, 430 N. Salisbury St., Raleigh, NC 27611, for the "Official North Carolina Highway Map and Guide to Points of Interest," which is one of the easiest maps to use; it's also filled with tourist information.

Before leaving home, it's a good idea to join the **American Automobile Association (AAA),** 1000 AAA Dr., Heathrow, FL 32746-5063

(© **800/222-4357** or 407/444-7000; fax 407/444-4247). For a very small fee, AAA provides a wide variety of services, including trip planning, accommodations and restaurant directories, and a 24-hour toll-free telephone number set up exclusively to deal with members' road emergencies (© **800/AAA-HELP**; www.aaa.com).

North Carolina has a seat-belt law that requires all front-seat passengers to wear seat belts. The state also has a child-restraint law that requires children 3 years old and younger to be secured in a child safety seat. Children 3 to 16 years old must ride in a safety seat or use a car seat belt.

Leading car-rental firms are represented in North Carolina's major cities and airports. For reservations and rate information, contact the following: **Avis** (© **800/331-1212**; www.avis.com), **Budget** (© **800/527-0700**; www.budget.com), **Hertz** (© **800/654-3131**; www.hertz.com), and

**Thrifty Car Rental** (© **800/367-2277**; www.thrifty.com).

**BY PLANE US Airways** (© **800/428-4322**; www.usairways.com) and **Delta** (© **800/221-1212**; www.delta.com) have several in-state connecting flights between cities such as Raleigh, Charlotte, Asheville, Wilmington, New Bern, Greensboro, Winston-Salem, Jacksonville, and Fayetteville.

**BY FERRY** North Carolina has a system of auto ferries that ply the coastal sounds and rivers; most are toll-free, but the longer trips charge a fee. You can cross Currituck Sound from Currituck to Knotts Island, Hatteras Inlet, and Pamlico River at Bayview, and Neuse River at Minnesott Beach. To get an up-to-date printed ferry schedule, contact the Director, Ferry Division, Room 120, Maritime Building, 113 Arendell St., Morehead City, NC 28557 (© **252/726-6446**; fax 252/726-2903; www.ncferry.org).

## FAST FACTS: North Carolina

*American Express* The main American Express Travel Agency is at 4735 Sharon Rd., Charlotte (© 800/508-0274).

*Car Rentals* See "Getting Around," above.

*Driving Rules* See "Getting Around," above.

*Drugstores* The most popular drugstore chains are Eckerd, CVS/Pharmacy, and Rite Aid. Although none of these chains offers 24-hour service, Eckerd does have stores in the larger cities that remain open until midnight.

*Emergencies* Dial © 911 for police, medical, and other emergency services. Travelers Aid can also be helpful; check local telephone directories.

*Liquor Laws* You must be 21 to order any alcoholic beverage. Beer and wine are sold in grocery stores, but all liquor is sold through local government-controlled package stores, which are commonly called ABC (Alcoholic Beverage Control Commission) stores. The availability of mixed drinks in bars is determined by each county.

*Newspapers & Magazines* The state's major dailies are the *News & Observer* (Raleigh) and the *Charlotte Observer* (Charlotte). There are also local papers in Asheville, Durham, Fayetteville, Greensboro, and Winston-Salem. The *North Carolina Folklore Journal* is available by subscription. (Contact the North Carolina Folklore Society, Department of English,

Appalachian State University, Boone, NC 28608, for publication schedule and subscription rates.)

*Pets* Many hotels and motels accept pets for a small fee, and some provide kennel service. Pets can be taken into car-accessible campgrounds in Great Smoky Mountains National Park, but they are not allowed on the trails in the backcountry.

*Police* Call ℂ **911** (no coin required).

*Taxes* North Carolina has a 7.5% sales tax and tacks on a 6% accommodations tax (room or occupancy tax) to your hotel bill. Counties also have the option of adding an extra .5% to 3% use tax.

*Time Zone* North Carolina observes Eastern Standard Time and goes on daylight saving time from April to October.

# The Outer Banks

**4**

They're maddeningly overcrowded in the summer, and development has been rampant over the last 20 years, but the Outer Banks of North Carolina are unlike anything else along the East Coast. The infamous pirate Blackbeard met his end here, and this is the place where the Lost Colony mysteriously disappeared. On these shores, Virginia Dare was born, and centuries later, Wilbur and Orville Wright learned to fly. The Outer Banks once enjoyed a dubious reputation as "the graveyard of the Atlantic," and to this day, you'll see the many lighthouses that stood vigil over centuries of shipwrecks. You can even see the actual shipwrecks—at several places along the shore the rusted bones of schooners and cargo ships are mired in the breakers. The East Coast's tallest lighthouse is at Cape Hatteras, and the oldest is at Ocracoke Island. Sand dunes tower over long stretches of undeveloped national seashore, and you can hop a ferry to explore islands where the residents (descended from the Elizabethans) say *hoigh toids* instead of *high tides* and call tourists "comers 'n' goers."

Both the size of fish and the diversity of species have put the Outer Banks on the map as one of the hottest fishing spots in the world. The 80-mile-long Pamlico Sound is a vast estuarine breeding ground for most of the fish caught off the coast, and the Gulf Stream lies just 12 miles offshore—the closest that this fish-laden current comes to land this side of Florida. The water teems with tuna and such trophy fish as blue marlin, white marlin, and sailfish.

Constant winds—the same ones that brought the Wright brothers here in the early 1900s—blow across the Outer Banks, bringing with them invigorating sea air. The area is a recreational playground, with 800 square miles of accessible water. Wind, water, and temperature conditions are right for ideal sailing from early spring until late autumn. And, as any windsurfer can tell you, the best conditions for sailboarding on the East Coast are along the Banks—in particular, at a place called Canadian Hole, on Hatteras Island.

## 1 The Outer Banks: From Corolla to Oregon Inlet

Nags Head: 234 miles N of Wilmington

The bony finger of land that separates the Atlantic Ocean from the sounds and estuaries of North Carolina's coast actually begins near the Virginia border. But much of the northern Banks is only accessible by four-wheel-drive, and residents need a permit to access the area from Virginia. Highway 12, which runs the length of the Outer Banks to Ocracoke, begins near the town of Corolla, not so long ago a sleepy little coastal village with little more than a lighthouse and wild horses. Today it's the Corolla of super-size beach "cottages," shops, and roads. And the number of wild horses, alas, is so greatly diminished that they have become an endangered species.

To the south of Corolla are the largely residential towns of Sanderling, Duck, and Southern Shores, oceanside communities that, like Corolla, have been utterly transformed by development in the last 20 years. Duck, in particular, has gone from a one-stoplight town to a manicured community with multimillion-dollar homes tucked discreetly into dense thickets of island shrub.

Indeed, development has been brisk in the other barrier-island communities, located south of Duck but north of Oregon Inlet—Kitty Hawk, Kill Devil Hills, Nags Head, Manteo, and Wanchese. But blessedly, there remain miles and miles of fine, sparkling beaches, good eats, plenty of family entertainment, and wonderful opportunities for water-based recreation.

## ESSENTIALS

**GETTING THERE**    The 16-mile, four-lane Chesapeake Expressway linking Virginia and North Carolina makes it easier to reach the Outer Banks. The motorway links Interstate 64 in Chesapeake, Virginia, to North Carolina and the Outer Banks. The 5.2-mile-long **Virginia Dare Memorial Bridge,** the longest bridge in the state, opened in August 2002, providing a much-needed alternative transportation link between the mainland and the barrier islands. The other routes are: from Raleigh, via U.S. 64; and from Wilmington, via the Cedar Island ferry (see "Cedar Island," later in this chapter). N.C. 12 (also called Virginia Dare Trail or the Beach Rd. from Kitty Hawk to Whalebone Junction) runs the length of the Outer Banks, from Ocracoke to Corolla. The four-lane U.S. 158 Bypass runs from Kitty Hawk to Whalebone Junction.

The nearest airport to Nags Head is 80 miles northwest in Norfolk, Virginia. **Norfolk International Airport** (℅ **757/857-3351;** www.norfolkairport.com) is served by **American Airlines** (℅ **800/433-7300;** www.aa.com), **Continental Airlines** (℅ **800/525-0280;** www. continental.com), **Delta** (℅ **800/221-1212;** www.delta.com), **US Airways** (℅ **800/428-4322;** www.usairways.com), **United Airlines** (℅ **800/864-8331;** www.united.com), **Northwest Airlines** (℅ **800/225-2524;** www.nwa.com), **Southwest Airlines** (℅ **800/435-9792;** www.iflysa.com), and **Independence Air** (℅ **800/FLY-FLY;** www.flyi.com).

**VISITOR INFORMATION**    Contact the **Outer Banks Visitors Bureau,** 704 S. Hwy. 64/264, Manteo, NC 27954 (℅ **877/0BX-4FUN** [629-4386]; www.outer banks.org), for information about accommodations and outdoor activities. The bureau is open Monday to Friday from 8am to 6pm, and Saturday to Sunday 10am to 4pm.

**SPECIAL EVENTS**    On Roanoke Island, where it all happened, Paul Green's moving drama *The Lost Colony* ★★ is presented in the Waterside Theater from June to late August, Monday to Saturday at 8:30pm. It's the country's oldest outdoor drama, running since 1937. All seats are reserved. Contact the **Waterside Theater,** 1409 National Park Dr., Manteo, NC 27954 (℅ **866/468-7630** or 252/473-3414; www.thelostcolony.org) for Visa or MasterCard bookings. Tickets cost $16 for adults, $15 for seniors, and $8 for children 11 and under.

In Kill Devil Hills, on December 12 to December 17, 2003, the **First Flight Centennial** (www.firstflightcentennial.org) held a celebration of the Wright brothers' 1903 aeronautical feat, featuring a re-creation of the original flight in what is being touted as the only accurate reproduction of the *Wright Flyer.* If you didn't make the celebration, you can browse the First Flight Centennial Photo Album or order the Official First Flight Centennial Video (check the website).

# The Outer Banks

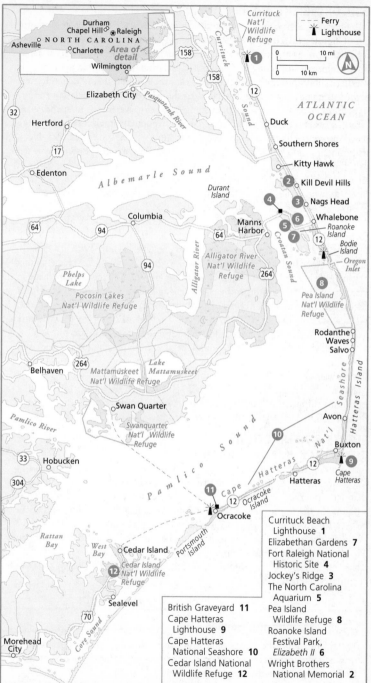

British Graveyard **11**
Cape Hatteras
  Lighthouse **9**
Cape Hatteras
  National Seashore **10**
Cedar Island National
  Wildlife Refuge **12**

Currituck Beach
  Lighthouse **1**
Elizabethan Gardens **7**
Fort Raleigh National
  Historic Site **4**
Jockey's Ridge **3**
The North Carolina
  Aquarium **5**
Pea Island
  Wildlife Refuge **8**
Roanoke Island
  Festival Park,
  *Elizabeth II* **6**
Wright Brothers
  National Memorial **2**

## EXPLORING THE AREA

**Nags Head** ⊛ is the largest resort in the Outer Banks area. Its odd name, according to local legend, comes from the practice of wily old land pirates who used to hang lanterns from the necks of ponies and parade them along the dunes at night to lure unsuspecting ships onto shoals. When the ships ran aground, the waiting robbers promptly stripped their cargoes. Another theory holds that the town was named for the highest point of the Isles of Scilly, which was the last sight English colonists had of their homeland. However it got its name, Nags Head has been one of North Carolina's most popular beach resorts for more than a century. The town is crowded in the summer; roadsides are chockablock with modern motels, restaurants, and watersports stores; and erosion has taken its toll on the once-grand beaches in recent years. Still, it has a certain barefoot charm, and the many handsome old wooden homes from the late 19th century—known as the "Unpainted Aristocracy"—hearken back to the time when the town was an idyllic seaside retreat.

The highest sand dune on the East Coast, Jockey's Ridge, is the focal point of **Jockey's Ridge State Park** (entrance on Carolista Dr., at milepost 12 off U.S. 158 Bypass; ✆ 252/441-7132; www.jockeysridgestatepark.com). With its smooth, sandy, 138-foot-high slopes and reliable winds, this is one of the best hang-gliding destinations in the United States. You can get in a high-flying spirit perhaps in memory of the Wright Brothers by taking a hang-gliding lesson from **Kitty Hawk Kites,** near the park visitor center. This is the world's largest hang-gliding school. For reservations, call ✆ **877/359-8447** or 252/441-4124; or go to www.kitty hawk.com. Beginning, intermediate, and advanced instruction are provided. A self-guided trail, stretching for 1.5 miles, begins at the parking lot and goes over the dunes and back. If you don't want to get sand in your shoes, you can take a shorter walk along a 360-foot boardwalk.

Just north of Nags Head is **Kill Devil Hills** (named for a particularly potent rum once shipped from here), where the Wright brothers made their historic first air flight back in 1903 (see "Wright Brothers National Memorial," below).

## SIGHTS & ATTRACTIONS
### CURRITUCK BEACH LIGHTHOUSE

At Corolla, one of the three working lighthouses on the Outer Banks stands 158 feet above the dunes. It flashed its first beacon on December 1, 1875, filling in that dark spot on the coast between Bodie Island in the south and Cape Henry, Virginia, in the north. Before construction of this lighthouse, whose beam can be seen for 18 miles, many ships foundered in the 80-mile "Sea of Darkness." Weather permitting, the lighthouse can be climbed daily Easter through Thanksgiving from 10am to 6pm for $6 ($3 per person for group tours with advance reservations). For information, call ✆ **252/453-8152** or go to www. currituckbeachlight.com.

---

⌒**Tips**  **Escaping the Hordes**

The traffic along the Outer Banks can be maddening in summer. Avoid gridlock by arriving or leaving on days other than Saturday and Sunday, when the weekly rentals begin and end.

---

## WRIGHT BROTHERS NATIONAL MEMORIAL

The Wright Brothers National Memorial (milepost 8, U.S. 158 Bypass, Kill Devil Hills; © 252/441-7430; www.nps.gov/wrbr) is open to the public for $3 per adult for a 7-day entrance pass or $10 for an annual pass. Children 16 and under are free and seniors 62 and older are free with a valid Golden Age passport. Both the hangar and Orville and Wilbur's living quarters have been restored, and the visitor center has a replica of the first airplane. Exhibits tell the story of the brothers who came here from their Dayton, Ohio, bicycle business to turn their dream into reality. The memorial is open daily from 9am to 6pm (9am–5pm in winter). A park ranger gives two tours at 11am and 3pm year-round.

## MANTEO & ROANOKE ISLAND

From Whalebone Junction, U.S. 64/264 leads to Roanoke Island and the pastoral village of Manteo, with docks, restaurants, and shops along Shallowbag Bay. Four miles west, you'll reach **Fort Raleigh National Historic Site,** where the fort from 1585 is but a mound of dirt. But the beauty of the landscaped park is reason enough to visit. The **visitor center** (© 252/473-5772; www.nps.gov/fora) is a first stop; a museum and an audiovisual program acquaint visitors with the park's story. The site is open daily from 9am to 5pm (until 6pm in summer). There is no admission charge.

Many people visit Roanoke Island to see a performance of *The Lost Colony* at the Waterside Theater (see "Special Events," in the "Essentials" section, above). The nearby 10½-acre **Elizabethan Gardens,** 1411 National Park Dr., Manteo (© 252/473-3234; www.elizabethangardens.org), as well as the Tudor-style auxiliary buildings, remind us that this area was the first connection between Elizabethan England and what was to become the United States of America. The sumptuous gardens are open from the second week in March to November 30, charging $6 adults, $5 seniors, $4 children 6 to 18, and free for children 5 and under. It's open January daily 10am to 4pm (closed New Year's Day); February daily 10am to 4pm; March daily 9am to 5pm; April and May daily 9am to 6pm; June to August Monday to Saturday 9am to 6pm and Sunday 9am to 7pm; September and October daily 9am to 6pm; November daily 9am to 5pm (closed Thanksgiving Day); and December daily 10am to 4pm (closed Christmas Eve and Christmas Day).

**The North Carolina Aquarium** ⭐, off Highway 64/264, Airport Road, north end of Roanoke Island (© 252/473-3493; www.ncaquariums.com), has expanded to twice its former size. Home to the state's largest ocean tank, the aquarium features hundreds of animals found in North Carolina waters that include rivers, marshes, and sounds. A wooden path takes visitors through a sky-lit atrium complete with towering trees, creeks, and streams. In the natural habitat are creatures of the marsh, including alligators, frogs, turtles, and otters. Bluefish, drum, pinfish, eels, and other sea creatures are exhibited in the Saltwater Gallery. In the Discovery Gallery, a favorite with children, skates, rays, crabs, sea stars, urchins, and other invertebrates can be handled. The centerpiece is the 285,000-gallon ocean tank housing the skeletal remains of the USS *Monitor* shipwreck. Large sharks and sea turtles combine to make this exhibit realistic and spectacular. Hours are daily from 9am to 5pm, costing adults $7, seniors and active military $6, and children (6–17) $5; 5 and under enter free. It is closed Thanksgiving Day, Christmas Day, and New Year's Day.

Visitors journey to Manteo to see the 27-acre **Roanoke Island Festival Park,** which features the *Elizabeth II* (© **252/473-1144;** www.roanokeisland.com), moored across from the renovated waterfront. This 69-foot-long three-masted bark, a composite design of 16th-century ships, was built in 1984 with private funds for the 400th anniversary of the 1584 and 1587 Roanoke voyages. From mid-June to late August, Tuesday to Saturday, living-history interpreters portray colonists and mariners. The site is open February 14 to March 31 daily 10am to 5pm; April 1 to June 14 daily 10am to 6pm; June 15 to August 15 daily 10am to 7pm; August 16 to October 31 daily 10am to 6pm; November 1 to December 31 daily 10am to 5pm (closed Dec 24–26); it's closed on major holidays. Admission is $8 for adults and seniors, and $5 for students (6–17); children 5 and under are admitted free.

## SIDE TRIP: EDENTON, COLONIAL WATERFRONT TOWN

About 1½ hours away from Nags Head, a later phase of U.S. history is preserved at **Edenton** ⟨⟩, an atmospheric old town whose streets are lined with homes built by the planters and merchants who settled along the Albemarle Sound. The women of Edenton held their own "tea party" in 1774—one of the first recorded instances of American women taking political action. Take U.S. 64, turn right at N.C. 37, and then turn left when you reach N.C. 32.

Visit the **Historic Edenton Visitor Center** at 108 N. Broad St. (signs are posted throughout the town; © **252/482-2637;** www.ah.dcr.state.nc.us/sections/hs/iredell/iredell.htm), to view a free 14-minute slide show and purchase a historic-district map. The center is open April to October, Monday to Saturday from 9am to 5pm and on Sunday from 1 to 5pm; November to March, Monday to Saturday from 10am to 4pm and on Sunday from 1 to 4pm. Guided tours of five historic buildings—the 1767 Chowan County Courthouse, the 1758 Cupola House, the 1780s Barker House, the 1800/1827 James Iredell House State Historic Site, and the restored St. Paul's Episcopal Church—can be booked here for $7 for adults, $3.50 for students under 18, $15 per family, free for preschool children. From April to October, tours are Monday to Saturday from 10:30am to 1pm, and on Sunday at 1:30pm; off-season, Monday to Saturday from 10:30am to 3pm, and on Sunday at 1:30pm. Expect an increase in entrance fees for 2005.

## BEACHES & OUTDOOR PURSUITS

**BEACHES**    The coterie of northern-bank beaches include those at Kitty Hawk, Kill Devil Hills, and Nags Head, all of which lie along the Beach Road (N.C. 12). Ferocious tides, strong currents, and fickle, constantly changing winds alter the beach scene from day to day on the Outer Banks, and that wide beach you see today may be narrower tomorrow. Water temperatures in summer average in the 70s, sometimes at the low point. Still, on a glorious July day, the cool, clean seawater and fresh salt air riding the constant winds make beachgoing a fine, invigorating experience.

Signs direct you to the various small (and too-often-inadequate) parking lots in the vicinity of the dunes. Toilets, showers, bathhouses, and picnic shelters line some 70 miles of beaches here, many at public beach-access parking lots.

**FISHING**    **Nags Head Fishing Pier,** milepost 12, Beach Road, Nags Head (© **252/441-5141;** www.nagsheadpier.com), has its devotees, who rent rod and reel for $6 per day. The pier itself is open to fishermen for $8 adults, $4 children, and $1.50 sightseers. From Memorial Day to Labor Day, the pier is open daily 24 hours; off season, daily 6am to midnight.

---

**Tips  Beach Safety**

The very conditions that make beachgoing so pleasant here can make ocean swimming hazardous at times, with strong riptides and undertows. All beach areas have roving lifeguards and supervisors, but hours and locations are subject to change without notice. Caution flags are flown if swimming is not advised. A red warning flag means that swimming is prohibited; take heed of these warnings even if the water doesn't look particularly rough. Non-swimmers are advised to wear some sort of flotation device and should not go out past the breakers without other swimmers around. Finally, if you see lightning or hear thunder, leave the beach for safe shelter immediately.

---

**GOLF**    A popular course is **Nags Head Golf Links,** 5615 S. Seachase Dr., Nags Head (✆ **252/441-8073;** www.nagsheadgolflinks.com), with an 18-hole, 6,126-yard, par-71 course that's open daily 7am to 6pm. Greens fees, including the use of a mandatory cart, start at $110. Reservations are required. Professional instruction is available for $45 for 45 minutes or $120 for a series of lessons. Clubs rent for $35. At the clubhouse, you'll find a restaurant and a pro shop.

**Ocean Edge Golf Course,** Frisco (✆ **252/995-4100**), has a 9-hole, par-30 course, open daily from 7am to 6pm. Tee-time reservations are requested and can be made at the pro shop. Greens fees, including the use of a mandatory cart, cost $40 for 18 holes, $30 for 9 holes. Club rental is $8 per round. Ocean Edge lies 50 miles outside Nags Head. Leave Nags Head on Highway 12 west, going to Whalebone Junction, where you continue on Highway 12 west through the communities of Rodanthe, Salvo, and Buxton into Frisco.

**NATURE WALKS**    **Nags Head Woods Preserve** (✆ **252/441-2525**), 701 W. Ocean Acres Dr., off U.S. 158, milepost 9.5, is a fine example of a mid-Atlantic maritime forest. The seashore includes 640 acres of protected wetlands, dunes, and hardwood forest, and is a National Natural Landmark.

At **Jockey's Ridge State Park,** milepost 12 on U.S. 158 (✆ **252/441-7430;** www.jockeysridgestatepark.com), you'll find the East Coast's highest sand-dune formation. This 400-acre park makes you feel that you're traversing the Sahara, with its self-guided nature trail through sifting sands and blowing winds. Park at the northern rim of the park.

**WATERSPORTS**    **Kitty Hawk Watersports Sailing Site,** Bypass Highway, milepost 16, Nags Head (✆ **252/441-2756;** www.kittyhawksports.com), offers watersports equipment. Windsurfers especially flock here, renting equipment for $25 per hour, $45 per half-day, or $75 for a full day. WaveRunners cost $85 for a full hour. You can rent kayaks, for $22 to $35 per half-day, for a trip along the waterways. Toilets and picnic facilities are on-site, and the center is open daily from 9am to 6pm.

**Windsurfing Hatteras,** N.C. Hwy. 12, Avon (✆ **866/995-6644** or 252/995-5000; www.windsurfinghatteras.com), rents a wide range of watersports equipment. Twenty-four-hour kayak rentals range from $25 to $30; surfboards rent for $15 for a day, $40 a week; windsurfing gear is available for 24-hour rental at $40 for the board alone or $65 for a full rig. In addition, a 2-hour introductory windsurfing class is offered for $49.

## The Lost Colony

Roanoke Island, between the Outer Banks and the mainland, is where Sir Walter Raleigh's colony of more than 100 men, women, and children settled in 1585 in what was to be England's first permanent New World foothold. Virginia Dare—granddaughter of the little band's governor, John White—was born that year, the first child of English parents to be born in America. When White sailed back to England on the ships that brought the settlers, it was his intention to return within the year. Instead, because of political events in England, White wasn't able to get back to Roanoke until 1590. What he found on his return was a mystery. The rudimentary houses that he had helped build were all dismantled, and the entire area was enclosed by a high palisade that he later described as "very fortlike." At the entrance, crude letters on a post from which the bark had been peeled spelled out the word CROATOAN.

Because White didn't find the prearranged distress signal—a cross—and no evidence suggested violence, his conclusion was that those he'd left on Roanoke Island had joined the friendly Croatoan tribe. An unhappy chain of circumstances, however, forced him to set sail for England before a search could be made. Despite all sorts of theories about the colony's fate, no link was ever established between the "lost" colonists and the Native Americans. Recent analysis of tree rings has indicated that the colonists may have suffered horrific drought conditions, but no clue has been unearthed revealing exactly what did happen.

The **Fort Raleigh National Historic Site** at Roanoke was named in 1941, and its visitor center tells the colony's story in exhibits and film. Paul Green's symphonic drama *The Lost Colony* brings the events to life in the amphitheater at the edge of Roanoke Sound.

## WHERE TO STAY

Although the beaches are lined with cottage rentals, many of them are spoken for on a year-to-year basis, so it's essential to make reservations well in advance. If you'd like to settle down for a week or more, your best bet is to write the **Outer Banks Visitors Bureau** (see "Essentials," earlier in this section). It is also worth noting that a good number of national motel chains, along with numerous independently owned lodges, are dotted along the coastline and can provide adequate accommodations if you're traveling without reservations.

Nags Head, Kill Devil Hills, and Kitty Hawk are so close together that you can choose your accommodations by style and facilities rather than by location. Duck, about 18 miles north of Nags Head, is the site of an exceptional seaside hotel that's well worth the short drive.

Another option is **camping.** For information on private campgrounds, contact the Outer Banks Visitors Bureau (see "Essentials," earlier in this section).

### IN DUCK

**Advice 5¢** ⚡ *Finds*    As an alternative to the more expensive Sanderling, this B&B lies in the heart of Duck, close to shops and restaurants. It's a small, casual place but a choice one. It's located in the tranquil neighborhood of Sea Pines between the ocean and Currituck Sound. Dating from 1995, Advice 5¢ is thoroughly modernized, with spacious and well-furnished guest rooms, most with private bathrooms with tub and shower plus sun decks. One room has a shower (no tub), and the one suite features a Jacuzzi-style bathtub. There's a pool at Sea Pines and a tennis court, plus a private walkway from Sea Pines to a good beach. The breakfast goodies are "baked from scratch." All rooms are nonsmoking.

111 Scarborough Lane, Duck, NC 27949. ℂ **800/ADVICE-5** or 252/255-1050. www.advice5.com/contactAD. htm. 5 units. $135–$175 double; $155–$205 suite. MC, V. No children 15 and under. **Amenities:** Breakfast room. *In room:* TV (in some), dataport.

**The Sanderling** ★★★   Composed of a complex of three large, beach-house-style buildings, with a separate annex containing two restaurants and bar (and another restaurant across the street), this resort and spa was established in 1985 in a location 25 miles north of Nags Head. It is one of the most affluent and eco-sensitive pockets of posh in the Outer Banks, and one of the three great resorts of the entire state. Standing at the narrowest point of the archipelago, on a manicured set of lawns close to the 3,400-acre Pine Island National Audubon Sanctuary, it features a postmodern design that emulates an 18th-century plantation house, complete with weathered shingle siding and wraparound verandas. Don't come here expecting a wild and raucous time in the South—the allure is calm, sedate, and soothing, all within a sand-and-sea-colored enclave that contains more Carolina pinewood trim than virtually any other recently built hotel in the country. Accommodations are filled with deep carpets, deep upholsteries, and an almost overwhelming sense of serenity. In addition to suites, four oceanfront villas have three to four bedrooms each, with such luxurious features as a covered garage and outdoor showers. Public areas contain majestic spiraling staircases, blazing fireplaces, and what's reputed to be $2 million worth of bird and animal sculptures by a locally famous artist named Granger McKoy.

The **Lifesaving Station** restaurant is recommended separately in "Where to Dine," below. The new restaurant, the **Left Bank,** which opened in summer 2002, is decidedly more formal and a grand departure from the barefoot Outer Banks way of dining. Whether it finds its customer base, only time will tell, but the French-inspired American menu is seriously ambitious (foie gras, don't you know), the waitstaff is savvy and attentive, and it's been handsomely designed. Which is to say, don't go if your ticker can't handle sticker shock. And for gee-whiz theatrical moments, you can't beat sunset, when the restaurant curtains rise dramatically to reveal the soft greens of the marsh grass and the pink hues of the sky melting on the sound waters.

1461 Duck Rd., Duck, NC 27949. ℂ **800/701-4111** or 252/261-4111. Fax 252/261-1638. www.sanderling inn.com. 88 units. May 11–Oct 19 $254–$402 double, $325–$593 suite, from $795 villa; off season $132–$318 double, $193–$516 suite, from $450 villa. Additional person $50. Rates include continental breakfast. AE, DC, DISC, MC, V. Take N.C. 12 about 5 miles north of Duck. **Amenities:** 2 restaurants; 2 bars; 2 pools (indoor); fitness center; health spa; Jacuzzi; sauna; room service; massage; laundry service; rooms for those w/limited mobility. *In room:* A/C, TV, minibar, kitchenette, coffeemaker, hair dryer, safe, iron/ironing board.

## IN EDENTON

**Governor Eden Inn** ★ *Value*   Open year-round, this is one of the better little B&Bs in the area. Within an easy walk of the Edenton Historic District, this 1906-vintage building has large white columns and a wraparound veranda in Southern antebellum style. Many antiques are located throughout the inn. All rooms are well maintained, each with a private bathroom with a shower unit. A telephone is set aside downstairs for the use of guests. Breakfast is a choice of nutritious selections or a full country spread with all the trimmings. All rooms are nonsmoking.

304 N. Broad St., Edenton, NC 27932. © **866/872-5608** or 252/482-2072. Fax 252/482-3613. www.governor edeninn.com. 4 units. $85–$90 double. Rates include breakfast. MC, V. **Amenities:** Breakfast room; library. In room: A/C, TV.

**The Lords Proprietors' Inn** ⭐⭐    The premier inn in Edenton, The Lords Proprietors' offers 20 rooms in three buildings. Set on 1½ acres, each of the buildings has a Victorian parlor filled with antiques. Many guests prefer the Pack House, a converted tobacco barn from a mid-19th-century plantation. The green house with white trim houses eight rooms in its two stories; accommodations include a choice of king- or queen-size beds or twins. The White Bond House, a redbrick Victorian building with equally desirable rooms, was built in 1901; and a third building, the Satterfield House, dates from 1801. The latter houses one suite upstairs and one suite downstairs. All units contain well-kept bathrooms, most of which have tub/shower combinations. Dinner is formal and served in the **Whedbee House,** where a four-course fixed-price menu costs $54. There is also an a la carte menu. *Note:* Children 10 and under are not encouraged to dine here. Pool privileges are available nearby.

300 N. Broad St., Edenton, NC 27932. © **888/394-6622** or 252/482-3641. Fax 252/482-2432. www.edenton inn.com. 20 units. $155–$190 double; $260 suite. Rates include full breakfast. AE, DISC, MC, V. **Amenities:** Restaurant; bar; nonsmoking rooms. In room: A/C, TV, dataport, coffeemaker, hair dryer, iron/ironing board.

**Trestle House Inn** ⭐ (Finds)    Overlooking a pond and lake fed by the Albemarle Sound, the Trestle House Inn was built in 1972 as a 7-acre retreat, surrounded on three sides by water and on the fourth side by an 88-acre wildlife refuge that's ideal for bikers, birders, canoeists, and fishermen. Host Peter L. Bogus has maintained the true tradition of the retreat since he became the innkeeper in 1996. The interior is highlighted by massive beams of California redwood and cedar. Before they became part of the Trestle House Inn, the beams were actual train trestles for the Southern Railway Company. The rooms—Osprey, Cormorant, Mallard, Heron, and Egret—are named for the grand birds that can be viewed from the windows of the respective units. Spacious and furnished with antiques, the rooms contain twin beds or two double beds, or a queen- or king-size bed. Each unit has a well-kept bathroom with a tub/shower combination or just a shower. The management can arrange day trips and tours in either Edenton or the Outer Banks. Smoking is not allowed, and pets are not welcome. The inn has a room for guests' use, containing a library, a television and VCR, and a telephone.

632 Soundside Rd., Edenton, NC 27932. © **800/645-8466** or 252/482-2282. Fax 252/482-7003. www.trestle house.com. 5 units. $95–$125 double. Additional person $15 per day. Rates include full gourmet breakfast. AE, DISC, MC, V. **Amenities:** Breakfast room; lounge. In room: A/C, no phone.

## IN KILL DEVIL HILLS

**The Cypress House Inn** ⭐    This historic B&B dates from the 1940s when it was first constructed as a hunting and fishing lodge on the Outer Banks. An aura of the Outer Banks "as it used to be" is still preserved here, as evoked by its soft cypress tongue-and-groove paneled walls and ceilings. Guests gather around the fireplace in the public lounge. The midsize guest rooms have an old-fashioned feel with white ruffled curtains, ceiling fans, and cheery but comfortable furnishings along with private-shower bathrooms. A large wraparound porch is just right for absorbing those seascapes. A hearty home-baked breakfast and afternoon tea are served in the dining room. All rooms are nonsmoking.

500 N. Virginia Dare Trail, Kill Devil Hills, NC 27948. © **800/554-2764** or 252/441-6127. Fax 252/441-2009. www.cypresshouseinn.com. 7 units. $75–$150 double. AE, DISC, MC, V. No children 13 or under. **Amenities:** Breakfast room; lounge. In room: A/C, TV, hair dryer, no phone.

## IN MANTEO

**Roanoke Island Inn**    Nestled in one of the most spectacular gardens in town, this inn is a white-sided clapboard house whose core dates to the 1860s. Each of several subsequent generations has added on to the core to create the rambling, graciously appointed Colonial Revival home you'll see today. In 1992, a hip and urbanized new generation of family members, headed by John Wilson, added big-city gloss to the place with a sophisticated array of *trompe l'oeil* murals in an Italian Renaissance theme, adding greatly to the establishment's sense of cutting-edge allure. Guest rooms are stately, even imperial, in their appointments, with glowing hardwoods, louvered or Venetian blinds, and many concessions to the 18th-century aesthetic of the Outer Banks. All units have well-kept bathrooms, most of which have tub/shower combinations. Breakfast is the only meal served.

305 Fernando St., P.O. Box 970, Manteo, NC 27954. ℰ 877/473-5511 or 252/473-5511. Fax 252/473-1019. www.roanokeislandinn.com. 8 units. $118–$178 double; $148–$208 suite. Rates include breakfast. AE, MC, V. **Amenities:** Breakfast room; lounge; nonsmoking rooms. *In room:* A/C, TV, dataport.

**Scarborough House Inn**    We like this place because it does much to recapture some of the feel of old-time Roanoke Island. Each unit is filled with antiques, including netting draped over four-poster beds, and a beautifully maintained private bathroom with tub and shower. Each is also stocked for a continental breakfast. For many, the most desirable rental is the cottage loft with a whirlpool. The owners, Phil and Sally Scarborough, are islanders whose roots in the Outer Banks go back centuries, with ancestors who were boat builders, fishermen, and craftsmen. Practically the whole Scarborough family at one time or another has appeared in the long-running stage drama, *The Lost Colony.* Living here is comfortable and laid-back, with rocking chairs on the porch. Gleaming pine floors and local artifacts add to the allure. Children are only permitted in the guesthouse.

323 Fernando St., P.O. Box 1310, Manteo, NC 27954. ℰ 252/473-3849. www.scarboroughhouseinn.com. 5 units. Double: high season $80, low season $50. Cottage: high season $125, low season $110. Guesthouse 1 bedroom with kitchen: high season $150, low season $125. Guesthouse 1 bedroom no kitchen: high season $125, low season $100. Rates include continental breakfast. MC, V. **Amenities:** Breakfast in room; nonsmoking rooms. *In room:* A/C, TV, fridge, coffeemaker, hair dryer, iron/ironing board, microwave.

**The Tranquil House Inn** 🌟🌟    This inn's major competition is the Sanderling at Duck (see "In Duck," above), which we actually prefer, but this is our second choice on the Outer Banks. A weather-beaten three-story structure, this waterfront resort is like one of those old seaboard inns that could have been part of 19th-century Manteo, yet it dates from 1988. Rear porches face the water, boats bob at anchor in the marina, and an entranceway opens onto the charming historic core of Manteo. The entire structure is sheathed in weather-beaten cedar shingles. Guest rooms are spacious and furnished with reproductions of antiques. Rooms also have well-lighted desks, wheelchair access, and well-kept bathrooms with tub/shower combinations. Wine and cheese are served each evening from 5 to 6pm. Bikes are available for guests during daylight hours.

The hotel's 1587 Restaurant offers not only excellent Continental and *cuisine moderne* dishes but also a water view. See "Where to Dine," below.

405 Queen Elizabeth St. (P.O. Box 2045), Manteo, NC 27954. ℰ 800/458-7069 or 252/473-1404. Fax 252/473-1526. www.tranquilinn.com. 25 units. Memorial Day to Labor Day $159–$169 double, $199 suite; off season $99–$119 double, $119 suite. Rates include continental breakfast. AE, DISC, MC, V. Take U.S. 158 south to Whalebone Junction in South Nags Head, then U.S. 64/264 6 miles west to Manteo. The inn is on the harborfront. (Turn right at the 1st traffic light onto Sir Walter Raleigh St.) **Amenities:** Restaurant; bar; limited room service; nonsmoking rooms; rooms for those w/limited mobility. *In room:* A/C, TV, dataport, hair dryer.

**The White Doe Inn** ★★   In 1898 this was the family home of the Meekins family, but today it welcomes those visitors to the Outer Banks who appreciate its old-fashioned style and down-home friendliness. The wraparound porch, on which you are likely to meet fellow guests absorbing the breezes, sets the tone of the place. Its Queen Anne architecture is so appreciated that many nonguests pause to photograph it. The innkeepers welcome you into one of their accommodations, called "bedchambers" here. The rooms are furnished with antiques or reproductions and often have century-old architectural features. Gas fireplaces evoke a return to yesterday, but modern amenities are here, too, including whirlpools and private bathrooms with showers and claw-foot tubs. A delicious three-course Southern-style breakfast is the highlight of the day around here. Children 11 and under are not welcome.

319 Sir Walter Raleigh St., Manteo, NC 27954. © **800/473-6091** or 252/473-9851. Fax 252/473-4708. www. whitedoeinn.com. 8 units. Summer $165–$240 double; off-season $140–$220 double. MC, V. Children over 12 welcomed. **Amenities:** Breakfast room; bikes; afternoon tea, evening sherry. In room: A/C, CD players, hair dryer, wi-fi.

## IN NAGS HEAD

**Cahoons Cottages**   There's very little that evokes the era of modern tourism in this cluster of simple cottages. Low-slung, weather-beaten, and separated from the surf only by a sand dune held tenuously together with fragile scrub grasses, these cottages were built in stages between 1948 and 1968, in a postwar kind of unpretentiousness that many jaded travelers find endearing. Modern building codes long ago prevented equivalent structures from being constructed directly on the dunes, so if you opt for a stay here, consider it a retro-charming kind of holiday that hasn't been very prevalent since the early 1960s. Clientele at this place tends to return year after year, and ever since its hardworking owner, Renée Calhoun, was elected twice as the town's mayor, the place has become a lot more visible. Expect not a smidgeon of grandeur, because that definitely isn't the style at a place that's awash with sun-bleached wooden porches, faux-wood paneling, and battered but comfy furniture. What you'll get instead is the Outer Banks of long ago, complete with its earthiness, ironies, and wry humor. There's no restaurant on-site and very few extras other than the beach and the sense of extended families and friends checking in for long, lazy sojourns. Of the 11 cottages, 2 are efficiencies and one is a bungalow. Each unit has its own kitchen and 2, 3, or 4 bedrooms.

7213 S. Virginia Dare Trail, milepost 16.5, Nags Head, NC 27959. © **252/441-5358.** Fax 252/441-1734. www. cahoonscottages.com. 11 cottages. Summer $525–$1,000 cottage per week; off-season $350–$650 cottage per week. DISC, MC, V. In room: A/C, TV, dataport, kitchens or kitchenettes.

**The First Colony Inn** ★★   This impressive three-story inn near the ocean was constructed in 1932 and has a wraparound veranda with rocking chairs. It was built without the help of an architect, which might explain why the veranda is almost as big as the interior space. Owned by Alan Lawrence and his family, it has received a four-diamond AAA rating, is listed on the National Register of Historic Places, and is the finest inn in the area. The interior is furnished with reproductions of turn-of-the-20th-century items. Units with sitting areas are also available. All units have well-kept bathrooms, most of which have tub/shower combinations. Grills and picnic tables are on hand for guests' use on the 4½-acre grounds, and a private access leads across the highway to the beach, known for its sea breezes and seemingly endless gentle dunes.

6720 S. Virginia Dare Trail, Nags Head, NC 27959. © **800/368-9390** or 252/441-2343. Fax 252/441-9234. www.firstcolonyinn.com. 26 units. May 24–Sept 1 $170–$295 double; Mar 28–May 23 and Sept 2–Nov 2

$125–$230 double; Nov 3–Mar 27 $80–$180 double. Rates include breakfast and afternoon tea. AE, DC, DISC, MC, V. **Amenities:** Bar; outdoor pool; picnic tables; grills; business services; limited room service; non-smoking rooms; rooms for those w/limited mobility. *In room:* A/C, TV, dataport, kitchenette, hair dryer, iron/ironing board, safe.

**The Nags Head Inn** ✦  Don't let the word "inn" mislead you. This is a thoroughly modern and well-kept hotel, one of the best in the area. Right on the oceanfront, it offers fairly luxurious and spacious rooms, with private balconies opening onto the view. Each unit comes with a well-maintained, private tiled bathroom and a tub/shower combination. Not part of a chain in a sea of Best Westerns, the inn is independently owned and nestled on 450 feet of sand dunes, beach, and well-kept lawns and gardens. One of its finest amenities is a heated oceanfront indoor pool along with a large spa and sun deck. The staff is also among the most helpful in the area.

4701 S. Virginia Dare Trail, Nags Head, NC 27959. ✆ **800/327-8881** or 252/441-0454. Fax 252/441-0454. www.nagsheadinn.com. 100 units. Late May to Labor Day $124–$205 double. Children over 12 $10 extra; free for children in parent's room under 12. Off-season discounts. AE, DISC, MC, V. **Amenities:** Indoor pool; spa; nonsmoking rooms; rooms for those w/limited mobility. *In room:* A/C, TV, dataport, fridge, hair dryer.

# WHERE TO DINE
## IN DUCK

**The Lifesaving Station** ✦ COASTAL/SEAFOOD   Although it's one of two premier dining enclaves in the most upscale and exclusive resort in the Outer Banks, there's something refreshingly simple, even spartan-looking about this place. Much of it derives from its origins in 1879 as a government-funded rescue station, when lifeguards and mariners set out from here to rescue crew and passengers from ships foundering on the region's notoriously treacherous shoals. Look for memorabilia that's associated with a heroic rescue 20 years later of the barkentine *Priscilla* that earned the site national attention. A brass bell from the original rescue station is prominently displayed. Top-quality ingredients go into the masterful dishes where sauces or other adornments never overpower the natural flavors. The chef likes to cook in the New South style, suggesting a lighter cuisine. A signature chowder is made with corn, scallions, and shrimp, and you might also enjoy crispy tempura-battered fish and oysters with a tangy rémoulade. Daily seafood and pasta specials are featured. Save room for that divine chocolate raspberry crème brûlée. The **Swan** bar on the second floor is accurate to its original role as a rescue station, whose severe dignity evokes an antique schoolhouse.

In the Sanderling Inn Resort and Spa, 1461 Duck Rd. ✆ **252/261-4111.** www.sanderlinginn.com. Reservations recommended. Main courses $6–$15 lunch, $14–$30 dinner. AE, DC, DISC, MC, V. Daily 7:30am–2pm and 5–9:30pm.

## IN KILL DEVIL HILLS

**Quagmires Oceanfront Bar & Restaurant** SEAFOOD/MEXICAN   Of the only two oceanfront dining options in Nags Head and Kill Devil Hills, this is the most consistently popular. It's housed in the shingle-sided and sprawling wooden structure that for many years was the Croatan Inn, built in stages between 1928 and 1932, before the introduction of building codes that prohibited construction on fragile dunes close to the sea. The dining rooms and bars, as well as the panoramic crow's nest bar on the second floor, reek of Jazz Age nostalgia. Menu items include a succulent version of crab cakes, a zesty shrimp Diablo, shrimp and crabmeat enchiladas, steaks and burgers, and a selection of fresh grilled fish, your best bet.

1315 N. Virginia Dare Trail, milepost 7.5. ℂ **252/441-9188.** www.quags.com. Reservations not accepted. Lunch platters $5–$8; dinner main courses $11–$18. DISC, MC, V. Daily 11:30am–10pm. Bar daily 11:30am–2am.

## IN MANTEO

**1587 Restaurant** 🚖🚖 AMERICAN    This restaurant offers the best creative cuisine along the Outer Banks. A nautical flair makes everyone feel as if he or she has just stepped off one of the expensive boats bobbing at anchor in the nearby marina. Preface your meal with a drink at the convivial bar, where a bar-top sheathed in polished copper reflects the faces and voices of many of the town's amicable locals. Good food and service await you here, and the menu is more sophisticated than most in the area. Menu items are more "fussed over" than what you're likely to find at many nearby competitors. The best examples include sesame-seared sea scallops with a soy-and-wasabi-flavored cream sauce, or skewered tiger shrimp in a sweet pepper broth. Main courses might include pork chops stuffed with sourdough breadcrumbs and summer sausages. Expect a sense of relaxed chic and elegant food in a subtly lit, nautically inspired setting.

In the Tranquil House Inn, 405 Queen Elizabeth St. ℂ **252/473-1404.** www.1587.com. Reservations recommended. Main courses $19–$26. AE, MC, V. Daily 5–9pm.

**Queen Anne's Revenge** 🚖 ★ *Kids* SEAFOOD    The seafood here is so good that locals return time after time and can't wait to tell visitors about the place. Most of the fish is caught in local waters. The captain's platter, a dull, overfried dish when presented in other joints, is quite delectable here; it's served with shrimp, the catch of the day, scallops, and crabmeat, along with vegetables and a salad. Your shrimp dinner can be fried or broiled, and both shrimp and crab are sautéed and served over a bed of homemade fettuccine. Signature dishes include bouillabaisse and Wanchese chowder. Children's plates are also available. The decor is elegant, with white linen tablecloths and paintings of seascapes. The restaurant is licensed only for beer and wine. Surrounded by island pines, it has a garden as well.

1064 Old Wharf Rd. at Wanchese. ℂ **252/473-5466.** www.queenannesrevenge.com. Reservations recommended. Main courses $15–$25. AE, DC, DISC, MC, V. Daily 5–9pm.

## IN NAGS HEAD

**Fishermen's Wharf** 🚖 SEAFOOD    At the south end of Roanoke Island, overlooking the harbor, this restaurant serves the freshest seafood around. It also has a connected retail seafood market. Founded in 1974, it started out serving about 50 diners per day; today, that number has grown to about 500. Lunch sandwiches range from fresh local fish filet (try it!) to a crab-cake delight, everything served with coleslaw and hush puppies. Dinners are more elaborate, including a gargantuan seafood platter with just about everything. Other menu items might include (depending on what's in the larder on the day of your arrival) Miss Maude's crab cakes, a "big" seafood platter, fresh-caught tuna, local flounder, sea scallops, and various preparations of shrimp. Virtually anything you order here can be fried, broiled, or blackened, according to your wishes.

Roanoke Island, N.C. 345, Wanchese. ℂ **252/473-5205.** Lunch platters $4.95–$12; dinner main courses $11–$25. DC, DISC, MC, V. Mon–Sat 11am–9pm.

**Sam & Omie's** SEAFOOD    A father-son partnership established this eatery in the 1930s as a spot where fishermen could get a rib-sticking breakfast before heading out onto the high seas. Today, it's a deliberately downscale, endlessly raffish place that has attracted most of North Carolina's leading, and most notorious, politicians—as well as locals who like the quintessentially funky Outer

Banks vibe. There's a convivial bar area where old salts and young beauties alike mingle, and a series of pinewood banquettes where copious portions of well-prepared seafood are always in demand. Come here for hefty doses of local color, a sense of folksy authenticity, and food items that include marinated tuna steaks served either as a platter or as a sandwich, she-crab soup, fried locally caught oysters, crab cakes, and burgers. This is an early-to-bed kind of place. The last food order is accepted here at 10pm, and the bar closes shortly thereafter.

7228 S. Virginia Dare Trail, milepost 16.5. ⓒ 252/441-7366. Reservations not accepted. Breakfast $3.95–$6.95; main courses $4.95–$10 lunch, $11–$21 dinner. DISC, MC, V. Mon–Sat 9am–10pm; Sun 9am–9pm. Closed Thanksgiving–Mar 1.

## 2 Cape Hatteras National Seashore ⭑⭑

From Whalebone Junction in South Nags Head, Cape Hatteras National Seashore stretches 70 miles south down the Outer Banks barrier islands. The drive along N.C. 12 (about 4½ hr.) takes you through a wildlife refuge and pleasant villages, past miles of sandy beaches untainted by commercial development, and on to Buxton and the Cape Hatteras Lighthouse, the tallest on the coast. Since 1870, the light has been a beacon for ships passing through these treacherous waters, which have claimed more than 1,500 victims by means of foul weather, strong rip currents, and shifting shoals. This is where the ironclad Union gunboat *Monitor* went down during a storm in December 1862.

From the little village of Hatteras, a car ferry crosses to **Ocracoke Island,** where more than 5,000 acres, including 16 miles of beach, are preserved by the National Park Service for recreation. From the southern end of the island, you can take a ferry across the vast, shallow Pamlico Sound to **Cedar Island.**

The National Seashore is best explored on an all-day trip, or on several half-day trips from a Nags Head base. Give yourself plenty of time for swimming, fishing, or just walking along the sand and for visiting the newly moved Cape Hatteras Lighthouse. It's an informal, barefoot kind of place—you can easily beach-hop from one shimmering beach to another; just pull into any of the many beach-access parking lots, cross a small boardwalk over dunes of sea oats, and plop yourself in the tawny sand or race to the surf. Then have lunch (a crab-cake sandwich, perhaps, and a bowl of Hatteras-style clam chowder) and get to know the local people who call this necklace of sand home. The hardy "Bankers" can recount tales of heroism at sea and tell you about the ghostly light that bobs over Teach's (Blackbeard's) Hole, as well as the wild ponies that have roamed Ocracoke Island for more than 400 years—all in a lilting accent that some people say harks back to Devon, England, home base of a band of shipwrecked sailors who came ashore here and stayed.

**VISITOR INFORMATION**    You can get more information at one of the following national park facilities: the **Bodie Island Visitor Center** (Bodie Island Lighthouse, 6½ miles south of Whalebone Junction; ⓒ **252/441-5711;** daily 9am–6pm in summer, 9am–5pm all other times); or the **Hatteras Island Visitor Center** (Cape Hatteras Lighthouse, Buxton; ⓒ **252/995-4474;** daily 9am–6pm in summer, 9am–5pm all other times). Contact the **Superintendent, Cape Hatteras National Seashore,** Rte. 1, Box 675, Manteo, NC 27954, for information about accommodations and outdoor activities.

## EXPLORING THE AREA

Turn left off N.C. 12 about 8 miles south of U.S. 158 to reach **Coquina Beach,** which offers bath shelters, lifeguards (mid-June to Labor Day), picnic shelters, and beach walks guided by National Park Service naturalists. Back on N.C. 12, to the southwest you will soon see the 156-foot-tall black-and-white striped **Bodie Island Lighthouse,** in operation since 1872.

Two miles south, the **Herbert C. Bonner Bridge** cuts an elegant swath over the waters of Oregon Inlet; look down to see anglers wrestling with puppy drum on the spits of sand beneath the bridge. Across Oregon Inlet, the 5,834 acres of **Pea Island Wildlife Refuge** (© 252/473-1131; www.peaisland.fws.gov), on Hatteras Island (the northern part, south of Bonner Bridge), attracts birders from all over the country to see the snow geese in winter and the wading shore and upland birds in summer. Some 265 species of birds winter here. There's a parking area and raised platforms. The wildlife refuge, 10 miles south of Nags Head, is open daily 9am to 4pm; admission is free.

All along N.C. 12, you'll see places to pull off and park to reach the beaches, which are hidden from view by huge protective sand dunes. *Note:* Don't try to park anywhere else; the sands are very soft, and it's easy to get stuck.

*Warning:* Whether you're camping or just stopping at beaches where there are no lifeguards, you should always keep in mind that tides and currents along the Outer Banks are *very* strong, and ocean swimming can be dangerous at times.

When you get to Buxton, turn left off N.C. 12 to see the famed **Cape Hatteras Lighthouse** (www.nps.gov/caha). The lighthouse was reopened to the public in 2000 following a massive relocation effort, which moved the lighthouse back 2,900 feet to save it from toppling into the encroaching sea. Its rotating duplex beacon has a 1,000-watt, 250,000-candlepower lamp on each side and is visible for 20 miles. Admission is free; the lighthouse is open from early April until mid-October 9am to 6pm.

The village of **Hatteras** ✮ exists now, as it has from the 1700s, as a fishing center, with large commercial and sport fleets operating from its docks and marinas. In the spring and fall, boats bring in catches of sea trout, king and Spanish mackerel, red drum, and striped bass. In summer, most of the action is offshore, where blue marlin and other billfish are in plentiful supply. If you're interested in doing some fishing yourself, the Outer Banks Chamber of Commerce can supply a list of charter boats and fishing information. Even if you don't fish, it's fun to watch the boats come in between 4 and 6pm.

## OUTDOOR PURSUITS

**Hatteras Island Fishing Pier,** 24251 Atlantic Ave., Rodanthe (© **252/987-2323;** www.hatterasislandresort.com/pier.html), stretches 653 feet into the Atlantic, charging $6 for fishing or $1 for sightseeing. Fishermen can rent rod and reel from the bait shop for $7.50 per day, plus a refundable $30 deposit. Live and artificial bait are available, along with the necessary tackle. At the beach end of the pier is a restaurant, plus toilets, a motel, and cottages for rent. The pier is open daily from 7am to 11pm.

Windsurfers flock to the area—and especially to a spot called **Canadian Hole,** so named for its popularity among Canadian windsurfers. The best place to hook up with this sport is the **Hatteras Island Surf Shop,** N.C. 12, Waves (© **252/ 987-2296**), open Monday to Saturday from 9am to 6pm and on Sunday from 10am to 6pm. Windsurfing equipment goes for $35 per half-day or $55 per full day. Surfboards cost $20 to $25 per day, and boogie boards rent for $8.

## WHERE TO STAY

**Cape Hatteras Bed & Breakfast** ✮ *(Finds)* Situated in the village of Buxton, directly north of Hatteras, this relatively unknown inn lies down a quiet lane just a stone's throw from the beach. Two miles south of the East Coast windsurfing site of Canadian Hole, this welcoming and thoroughly modernized house has an array of amenities. Each guest room is handsomely maintained, containing a private bathroom with shower and a private entrance. Oddly, the rooms are named after famous hurricanes that have brought destruction to the Outer Banks—talk about paying homage to the enemy. It's a casual place, with guests meeting and exchanging tips on the sun deck or in one of the beach chairs. There are also outdoor showers for your return from the beach. The owners are proud of their Hatteras-style breakfast—fit fortification for the day.

46223 Old Lighthouse Rd., P.O. Box 490, Buxton, NC 27920. ℂ/fax **800/252-3316.** 10 units. $119–$139 double. Rates include full breakfast. MC, V. **Amenities:** Dining room; lounge. *In room:* A/C, TV, no phone.

## WHERE TO DINE

**Austin Creek Grill** ⭐ CONTEMPORARY CAROLINA    This is still the hottest restaurant in Hatteras Landing. Situated in a colony of faux-Colonial buildings that's adjacent to the piers where cars line up for the ferryboats, it looks like a postmodern interpretation of a turn-of-the-20th-century boathouse, brightly painted in tones of yellow and blue. Views of the sea and the nearby marina are enhanced by its position directly above the water, rising on foundations that were sunk directly into the seabed. Dinner items are quite elaborate, and include well-prepared spinach salads garnished with Maytag blue cheese, caramelized pecans, and warm bacon vinaigrette; macadamia-coated shrimp with the salsa of the day; crab cakes with tarragon-flavored béarnaise sauce; and island seafood cassoulet with sausage and a medley of shellfish.

Hatteras Landing. ℂ **252/986-1511.** Dinner main courses $19–$29. AE, DISC, MC, V. Memorial Day to Labor Day daily 5–9pm; off-season Tues–Sat 5–9pm.

**The Channel Bass** SEAFOOD    The nautical decor comes as no surprise; neither does the seafood menu at this family-owned place. The clam chowder will have you calling for seconds. In fact, all the seafood is fresh and cooked to perfection. The menu is semi a la carte, and portions are so ample that the steamed sampler appetizer (oysters, clams, and shrimp) could well do you as a full meal. Specialties are fresh local fish, fried or broiled, and crab imperial. Everything comes with those tasty cornmeal fritters known as hush puppies.

N.C. 12, Hatteras. ℂ **252/986-2250.** Reservations accepted only for parties of 8 or more. Main courses $15–$23. DISC, MC, V. Apr–Nov Wed–Sat and Mon 5–10pm. Take N.C. 12 to 12 miles south of lighthouse.

## 3 Ocracoke Island ⭐⭐

From Hatteras, a free car ferry crosses the inlet to **Ocracoke Island** in 40 minutes; during the peak summer tourist season, the waiting line may be long, so you'll need to get there early to get a place.

Ocracoke has shown up on maps as far back as the late 1500s, when Sir Walter Raleigh's Roanoke Island party landed here. It's rumored to have been the last headquarters of Blackbeard, who died here. The wily pirate, after years of terrorizing merchant ships along the Atlantic coast, made his peace with the British Crown in 1712 and received a full pardon from the king. Soon thereafter, however, he came out of retirement and resumed preying on ships from the Caribbean to the Virginia capes, working hand in glove with the colonial governor, Charles Eden, and Colonial Secretary Tobias Knight.

When Ocracoke Island was isolated from the mainland and few visitors came by boat, as many as 1,000 wild ponies roamed its dunes. Where they came from—shipwrecks, early Spanish explorers, or English settlers—is uncertain.

Eventually, as more and more people traveled to and from the island, many ponies were rounded up and shipped to the mainland. The remnants of the herd (about two dozen) now live at the **Ocracoke Pony Pens,** a range 7 miles north of Ocracoke village, where the National Park Service looks after them.

## Two Cuts to Blackbeard's Neck

The British expected their American colonies to produce *profits*—as in having the colonists grow the raw materials that factories in Great Britain would use to produce the goods, which the colonists in turn would buy at inflated prices. To make sure that this happened, Parliament enacted a series of import duties designed to keep cheaper goods made elsewhere out of its colonies. The tax levies, which later fomented revolutionary sentiment, helped bring about the so-called Golden Age of Piracy between 1689 and 1718. What better way to get duty-free goods than through smuggling? And who better to do it than the pirates who stole the loot in the first place?

Edward "Blackbeard" Teach and others began by roaming the Caribbean, legally plundering French and Spanish ships during Queen Anne's War from 1701 to 1713. But they kept at their trade after the war so, in 1718, the British navy chased them out of the area. Blackbeard relocated to the tangled web of islands and shifting shoals along the North Carolina coast. Teach's cheap smuggled goods were welcomed, and some colonial officials—including Gov. Charles Eden, for whom Edenton is named—were suspected of helping him make a little money.

But the folks down in South Carolina felt differently, because they were now the pirates' prime targets. When Blackbeard struck Charleston in June 1718, looting merchant ships at anchor and taking hostages for ransom, the South Carolinians had had enough. Over the next 2 months, South Carolinians caught and hanged another 20 pirates. Rhett didn't find Blackbeard, but two Royal Navy sloops from Virginia under Lt. Robert Maynard did—off Ocracoke Island at dawn on November 22, 1718. Blackbeard and half his crew of 18 were killed during fierce hand-to-hand combat. The survivors were taken to Virginia and executed.

The incident was reported in the *Boston News-Letter:* "One of Maynard's men, being a Highlander, ingaged [sic] Teach with his broadsword, who gave Teach a cut of the Neck, Teach saying well done, Lad, the Highlander reply'd, if it be not well done, I'll do it better, and with that he gave him a second stroke, which cut off his head, laying it flat on his shoulder."

Maynard sailed back to Virginia with Blackbeard's head hanging from his ship's rigging, as if to warn all pirates that their golden age was over. And it was. Still, tales persist to this day of treasure stashed away along the coast of North Carolina, but none has ever been found; it's likely that Blackbeard sold his spoils quickly and squandered the proceeds.

In a quiet little corner of Ocracoke Island, you'll find a bit of England: the **British Graveyard,** where four British seamen were buried after their bodies washed ashore when the HMS *Bedfordshire* was torpedoed by a German submarine in 1942. The graveyard is leased by the British government but is lovingly tended by townspeople.

Ocracoke village has seen some changes since World War II, when the U.S. Navy dredged out Silver Lake Harbor (still called "Cockle Creek" by many natives) and built a base here. They also brought the first public telephones and paved roads. In spite of the invasion of 20th-century improvements and the influx of tourist-oriented businesses, Ocracoke is essentially what it has always been: a fishing village whose manners and speech reflect its 17th-century ancestry.

## WHERE TO STAY

**The Anchorage Inn & Marina**   This four-story hotel, completely modern and up to date, lies near the entrance to Silver Lake Harbor. It's an island favorite, mainly because of its good-size, comfortably furnished rooms, which open onto some of Ocracoke's best views. The sunsets over Pamlico Sound, of course, are better the higher up your room. We prefer the fourth-floor rooms with balconies because of the views and nonsmoking policy. An elevator services all floors. Boaters and fishermen are fond of this place because of its easy access to the harbor. The hotel also operates a dockside cafe adjacent to its swimming pool at the marina, and grills and picnic tables are placed outside for do-it-yourself cooks. Even if you're not a guest, consider stopping in at the Anchorage's raw bar, which offers fresh local clams, oysters, shrimp, and the catch of the day.

Hwy. 12 at Anchorage Marina, Ocracoke, NC 27960. ℭ **252/928-1101.** Fax 252/928-6322. www.the anchorageinn.com. 35 units. Summer $119–$129 double, $195 suite; low season $79–$89 double, $109 suite. Rates include continental breakfast. AE, DISC, MC, V. Pets allowed. **Amenities:** Cafe at Marina; outdoor pool; full-service marina; fishing trips; bike rentals; small boat rentals; scooter rentals; playground. *In room:* A/C, TV, dataport, kitchenette (full kitchens in suites), coffeemaker, hair dryer.

**Cove Bed & Breakfast**   A stay here is like being in a private home. Each of the tastefully decorated guest rooms or suites has an immaculate private bathroom. Guests meet fellow guests while sitting on the screened-in porch, or else they can enjoy their own private balcony. The day begins with one of the most scrumptious breakfasts on the island. With such names as Dolphin or Sandpiper, the midsize to spacious guest rooms are comfortably furnished, often with four-poster beds. Suites have whirlpool tub/showers. Jim and Mary Ellen Piland welcome guests from all over America and treat them to true Outer Banks hospitality.

21 Loop Rd., Ocracoke, NC 27960. ℭ **252/928-4192.** Fax 252/928-6260. www.thecovebb.com. 6 units. $105–$155 double; $155–$205 suite. Rates include continental breakfast and wine reception. MC, V. Children under 15 not welcome. **Amenities:** Bikes; kayaks; nonsmoking rooms. *In room:* A/C, TV, hair dryer, no phone.

**The Ocracoke Harbor Inn**   Built in 1998, this three-story hotel is one of the most up-to-date, comfortable, and inviting inns on the island. Its front guest rooms open onto Silver Lake Harbor, and guests often sit out on the porches to take in the views. Private decks here allow you to take in the sunset as well, perhaps with a cocktail. The waterfront deck is where continental breakfast can be enjoyed as the Ocracoke fishermen depart in their boats for the day. Guest rooms, small to midsize, are attractively furnished in a kind of Caribbean style, and there are seven suites, each offering a separate bedroom and a queen-size sleeper in the living room. Special features of the suites are kitchenettes and

Jacuzzis. The hosts also offer boat docking and a patio deck with charcoal and gas grills if you want to try your hand at a North Carolina barbecue.

135 Silver Lake Rd., Ocracoke, NC 27960. © **888/456-1998** or 252/928-5731. Fax 252/928-6260. www. ocracokeharborinn.com. 23 units. Summer $98–$135 double, $150–$200 suite; spring/fall $75–$125 double, $140–$190 suite; winter $50 double, $99 suite. Additional person $10. Rates include continental breakfast. AE, DISC, MC, V. **Amenities:** Restaurant; fitness center; boat docking; boat rental; bike rental; business center; coin-operated laundry. *In room:* A/C, TV, dataport, fridge, coffeemaker, hair dryer, iron/ironing board.

**The Thurston House Inn** ★ *Value*    For some 75 years, this cedar-shake cottage (ca. 1920s) was the home of native guide Capt. Thurston Gaskill, who took visitors into the wilds of Ocracoke and surrounds on fishing and hunting expeditions. Today, it is a sun-filled B&B run by Captain Thurston's granddaughter, Marlene Mathews, and her husband, Randal, who in 1999 constructed a new addition next to the original inn. The owners may greet you in bare feet, but they don't believe you have to rough it to enjoy Ocracoke; the rooms are state-of-the-art B&B, with queen- or king-size beds, feather comforters, spacious private bathrooms with showers, and an elegant, understated feel. The inn lies just off the town's main road in a grove of oak trees and flowering shrubs; you can breakfast in the shade on one of the cottage porches.

Hwy. 12, Ocracoke Island, NC 27960. © **252/928-6037.** www.thurstonhouseinn.com. 6 units. $90–$129 double. Rates include expanded continental breakfast. AE, DISC, MC, V. No children under 12 allowed. Airport pickups available. *In room:* A/C, TV.

## WHERE TO DINE

For your luncheon needs, **Cat Ridge Deli,** Lighthouse Road (© **252/928-DELI**), is your best gourmet takeout. Located in Albert Styron's General Store and listed on the National Register of Historic Places, the establishment has been operating since 1920, making it one of the oldest places on Ocracoke Island. The best sandwiches on the island are made here, costing $5 to $7. The deli specializes in Thai food and great meatball sandwiches. You can purchase cheese, coffee beans, North Carolina foods, beer, gifts, bulk spices, and natural foods here as well. It's open from 10:30am to 6:30pm.

**Back Porch** ★★ SEAFOOD/AMERICAN    For Ocracoke's finest cuisine, head here. Offering something more ambitious than other restaurants listed here, Back Porch emphasizes fresh local seafood, and is a great favorite among islanders. Tables are set on an elegant screened-in porch or in the air-conditioned dining room. All the dishes have a down-home flavor. Fish is done plain or else "tarted up" with interesting combos like Vietnamese lime sauce, pineapple salsa, or balsamic brown butter. The sumptuous Back Porch seafood platter is justifiably a favorite, and includes baked fish, sautéed shrimp, and a deep-fried crab beignet. On our last visit we dug into the grilled yellowfin tuna, which came with a surprising and successful addition—a sesame scallion vinaigrette. Black beans and rice accompanied the dish. The scrumptious desserts—a calories-be-damned selection—and the fresh breads are baked daily in their kitchen.

110 Back Rd. © **252/928-6401.** Reservations not required. Main courses $14–$22. MC, V. Daily 5–9pm.

**Café Atlantic** SEAFOOD    Serving mainly satisfied customers since 1989, this cafe/restaurant 2 miles north of Ocracoke harbor attracts those seeking some tasty Carolina seafood. Set on two floors, it is a homey place that does a good family business and offers fine service. In general, the seafood is fresh and each dish well prepared. Those with large appetites can opt for the grilled seafood platter, with tuna, shrimp, scallops, mussels, and clams. The baked

## Moments  The Ghost Town of the Outer Banks

Before the Civil War, **Portsmouth** ⚓ was a thriving little community of some 700 souls. It proudly boasted the first maritime hospital and the first lifesaving station. But when Jefferson Davis ordered that Confederate troops be stationed here during the Civil War, Portsmouth's fate was sealed. Union forces bombarded the island, and most residents fled elsewhere. After the war, the shoaling in of Portsmouth inlet and the coming of the steamboat drove away its final business—the island's harbor was too small for the steamboat.

The National Park Service today maintains the quaint buildings still standing, including a church, a general store, and a lifesaving station, but it's a ghost town. From Ocracoke village you can take two daily, guided tours on all-terrain vehicles (ATVs) offered by **Portsmouth Island ATV Excursions** (✆ **252/928-4484**; www.portsmouthislandatvs.com), costing $75 per person, six-person maximum per trip (reservations are recommended). Service is from April 1 until the end of November. Do-it-yourselfers can go less expensively by taking one of the Portsmouth Island boat tours, costing $20 for a half-day for adults and $10 for children 6 to 12. Reservations must be made 1 day in advance. Once at Portsmouth, swimming, fishing, shelling, and bird-watching are diversions.

---

grouper is a savory treat, cooked under a Parmesan crust. The fried crab cakes are the best in the area. Don't miss the homemade desserts.

Rte. 12 at the northern edge of Ocracoke village. ✆ 252/928-4861. Reservations recommended. Main courses $12–$20. AE, DISC, MC, V. Daily 5–9pm; Sun 11am–2pm. Closed Nov–Feb.

**Howard's Pub and Raw Bar Restaurant** SEAFOOD/AMERICAN   There's more lore associated with this place, and a greater sense of community among its devoted fans, than any other restaurant on Ocracoke Island. Set inside an imposing but weather-beaten building that's the first major business you'll see after heading south from the Hatteras Ferry landing, it occupies the site of what flourished briefly in the 1850s as a pub (Howard's) before it sank into the sands of this reputedly haunted island. Inside the mostly wooden interior, you'll find a cheerful staff that's proud of the establishment's self-sufficiency—thanks to their own generators, they've provided sustenance to famished locals even in the aftermath of hurricanes. Menu items focus on burgers, steaks, fresh oysters and shellfish, barbecued ribs, grilled fish, Maine lobster, and massive amounts of shrimp.

Local ordinances restrict the serving of hard liquor by the glass, so as a means of compensating, Howard's stocks the largest selection of beer—more than 200 kinds—on the Outer Banks. The bar is the single most popular rendezvous point on the island, serving drinks and good cheer every night.

Hwy. 12. ✆ 252/928-4441. www.howardspub.com. Salads and sandwiches $7–$10; main courses $11–$19. DC, DISC, MC, V. Daily 11am–2am.

## 4 Cedar Island

You can get to North Carolina's more southerly beaches in leisurely fashion by taking the car ferry from Ocracoke to Cedar Island. You'll need to make a reservation for the 2¼-hour trip over the calm, sparkling waters of the Pamlico

Sound. Take along a picnic lunch, and don't be surprised to see dolphins cavorting alongside the boat. Call to reserve space on one of the scheduled sailings. To sail from Cedar Island, call © **252/225-3551;** to sail from Ocracoke, call © **252/928-3841.** (East of the Mississippi, you can call Cedar Island at © **800/856-0343** or Ocracoke at © **800/345-1665.**) *Reservations are not honored if your car is not in the loading zone at least 30 minutes before departure time.* The fare is $15 per car and occupants, $3 per bicycle and rider, and $1 for pedestrians. For a complete list of ferries, schedules, and fares, contact the **Ferry Division,** Department of Transportation, 113 Arendell St., Morehead City, NC 28557 (© **252/726-6446;** www.ncferry.org).

On the island, you can explore the **Cedar Island National Wildlife Refuge** (© **252/926-4021;** www.mattamuskeet.fws.gov/cedarisland), a feeding ground for migratory waterfowl. Since 1964, this refuge has taken in 11,000 acres of irregularly flooded and brackish marsh, with such plants as saltmeadow hay, needlerush, and salt-marsh cord grass. The land is a winter habitat for thousands of ducks and a nesting habitat for Colonial water birds. Endangered species such as the American alligator and the brown pelican find a safe haven here.

### WHERE TO STAY & DINE

**Driftwood Motel & Restaurant** (Value    Simple yet cozy, these accommodations are a 3-minute walk from the beach. For the budget-minded traveler, it's a good bet. The lobby is located on the second floor, above the first-floor gift shop, which has items in the expected nautical theme. Rooms are motel-traditional, and the biggest amenity is the price. All units have well-kept bathrooms with tub/shower combinations. The motel also maintains a restaurant, serving lunch from 11am to 2:30pm and dinner nightly from 5 to 9pm. The fare is adequate, with enough seafood and Continental dishes to satisfy everyone in your party. Try the cream of crab soup, the fried oysters, or such homemade desserts as lemon meringue pie. Barbecue is also a popular item here.

3575 N. Cedar Island, NC 28520. © **252/225-4861.** Fax 252/225-1113. www.clis.com/deg. 37 units. $60 double. Rates include continental breakfast. Children $10 extra. AE, DISC, MC, V. **Amenities:** Restaurant; bar. *In room:* A/C, TV.

# 5

# Wilmington & the Southern Banks

The southern banks are dominated by the town of Wilmington, which boasts some 200 restored city blocks, forming one of the largest such districts in the National Register of Historic Places. Wilmington is the gateway to the Cape Fear coast, which, in spite of its ominous-sounding name, is filled with azalea gardens and sun-dappled plantation houses.

Base yourself in historic old Beaufort, Morehead City, or in a cottage along the string of beaches from Atlantic Beach to Emerald Isle, to sun and swim in the ocean or visit New Bern and other area attractions; or in Wilmington, to see plantations and gardens, Fort Fisher, and fine beaches.

If you're thinking about camping, you will find campgrounds throughout the region. But you should know in advance that they're flat and sandy, with no shade, and that you'll need tent stakes longer than you'd normally use. Also, no hookups are provided. Sites are available on a first-come, first-served basis, and the maximum stay is 14 days from mid-April to September 10. For private campgrounds in the area, which do have hookups, call the tourist offices listed.

## 1 Wilmington ★ & Cape Fear ★

123 miles SE of Raleigh

As the chief port of North Carolina, Wilmington is a major retail, trade, and manufacturing center, but tourism is looming larger than ever in its economy. Known first as New Carthage, and then as New Liverpool, New Town, and Newton, this city was given its present name in 1739 in honor of the earl of Wilmington. Technically, it isn't even on the coast; it's inland a bit, at the junction of the Cape Fear River's northeast and northwest branches. Despite the treacherous shoals that guarded the mouth of Cape Fear when explorers first arrived in 1524, upriver Wilmington developed into an important port for goods shipped to and from Europe during colonial days.

The city's history is evident in the old residential section of town, on the grounds of Orton Plantation, in the excavated foundations of Brunswick Town houses, and in the blockade-runner relics at Fort Fisher. Boasting one of the largest districts listed in the National Register of Historic Places, Wilmington is known for its preservation efforts, which are reflected in the grandeur of its restored antebellum, Victorian, Georgian, and Italianate homes.

During both World Wars, Wilmington was a major port for naval supplies. Today, the river is busier than ever with industrial shipping. In recent years, a thriving new industry has developed: filmmaking. Ever since 1983, when Dino De Laurentiis came here to film *Firestarter,* Wilmington has been a major site for the movie industry, hosting the production of more than 400 movie features,

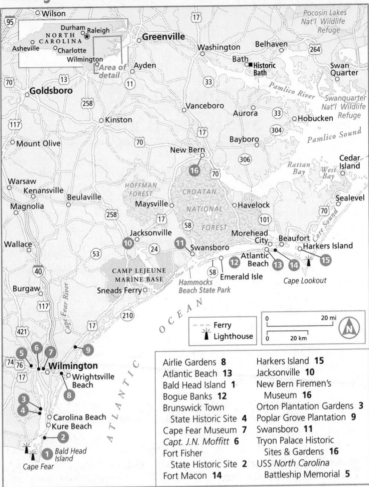

Airlie Gardens **8**
Atlantic Beach **13**
Bald Head Island **1**
Bogue Banks **12**
Brunswick Town
  State Historic Site **4**
Cape Fear Museum **7**
*Capt. J.N. Moffitt* **6**
Fort Fisher
  State Historic Site **2**
Fort Macon **14**
Harkers Island **15**
Jacksonville **10**
New Bern Firemen's
  Museum **16**
Orton Plantation Gardens **3**
Poplar Grove Plantation **9**
Swansboro **11**
Tryon Palace Historic
  Sites & Gardens **16**
USS *North Carolina*
  Battleship Memorial **5**

miniseries, and TV movies. In fact, according to a survey by the International Association of Film Commissioners, Wilmington generated more film revenue than any U.S. city except Los Angeles and New York—giving rise to its nickname "Hollywood East." Among the films made in Wilmington are *Divine Secrets of the Ya-Ya Sisterhood, Forrest Gump, I Know What You Did Last Summer, Sleeping with the Enemy, Titus, Waking Ned Devine, Before Night Falls,* and *Bread and Tulips;* the TV series *One Tree Hill* is filmed on location here.

## ESSENTIALS
**GETTING THERE**   You can reach Wilmington via I-40, U.S. 117, and U.S. 421 from the northwest; U.S. 74/76 from the west; and U.S. 17 from the northeast and south.

   **Wilmington International Airport,** 1740 Airport Blvd. (© **910/341-4125**), lies half a mile from the center of town. Taxis meet arriving planes. The airport is

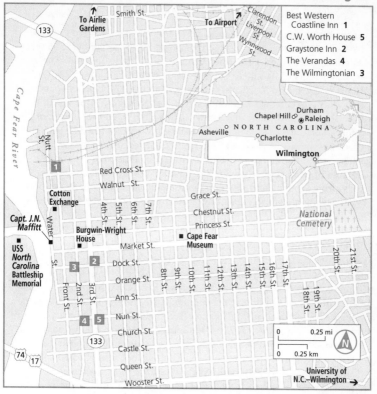

Best Western
    Coastline Inn **1**
C.W. Worth House **5**
Graystone Inn **2**
The Verandas **4**
The Wilmingtonian **3**

host to the following major and commuter airlines: **US Airways** (© **800/428-4322;** www.usairways.com); and **A.S.A. Delta Connection to Atlanta** (© **800/282-3424;** www.delta.com).

**VISITOR INFORMATION**  The **Cape Fear Coast Convention and Visitors Bureau,** 24 N. 3rd St., Wilmington, NC 28401 (© **800/222-4757** or 910/341-4030; www.cape-fear.nc.us), offers free brochures on the many attractions and accommodations of the Cape Fear Coast. The efficient staff can provide a self-guided walking-tour map of historic Wilmington and background details on other area attractions. The center is open Monday to Friday from 8:30am to 5pm, on Saturday from 9am to 4pm, and on Sunday from 1 to 4pm.

**SPECIAL EVENTS**  The **North Carolina Azalea Festival** (www.ncazalea festival.org), held in early April, is the city's most-frequented event. City gardens burst into bloom, and the festivities include garden tours, beauty pageants, and a parade. The dogwoods get almost as much attention as the azaleas. Call © **910/794-4650** for more details.

## SEEING THE SIGHTS
### IN TOWN

To get an overview of the historic Wilmington waterfront, hop aboard the **_Henrietta III_** ✪ (© **800/676-0162** or 910/343-1611; www.cfrboats.com), which at

## Lights, Camera, Action!

As the movie industry continues to operate in the city, the more the business of making movies draws tourists itching to pay a few bucks to see where films are made. **EUE/Screen Gems Studios,** headed by Frank Capra, Jr., offers tours of its studio, the largest full-service film lot outside California (1223 N. 23rd St.). If you're coming from U.S. 17/74, go straight on Dawson Street and take a left onto 17th Street; follow the airport signs to the corner of 23rd Street and Martin Luther King Jr. Parkway. For more information, directions, and group reservations, call 📞 **910/343-3433** or check the website at www.euescreengems.com. Because this is a *working* studio, and not set up as a tourist attraction, tours may be canceled because of production schedules. The hour-long tours are at noon on Saturday from September to May, and Saturday and Sunday at noon and 2pm from Memorial Day to Labor Day. Tickets cost $12 adults, $5 children under 12.

press time was temporarily departing from the Riverwalk beside the Hilton Riverside hotel (call for the latest info) for a 5-mile loop of the Cape Fear River. The 45-minute narrated cruise skirts the busy harbor, passes the Cotton Exchange and the Riverfront Park, and stops at the dock for passengers who want to disembark to tour the battleship USS *North Carolina* (see "Sights Nearby," below). The season runs from May 1 to mid-December. Tours depart daily at 11am and 3pm. The charge is $8, reduced to $4 for children 12 and under. It also offers murder-mystery cruises, evening party cruises, and nature cruises, among others.

**Cotton Exchange** (📞 **910/343-9896**), an in-town shopping center, is in the old exchange building, which has 2-foot-thick brick walls and hurricane rods. The small shops and restaurants are a delight, and the wrought-iron lanterns and benches add to the setting's charm. It's right on the riverfront, and an ample parking deck is just next door. All shops are open Monday to Saturday 10am to 5:30pm (restaurants are open evenings), although some shops are also open Sunday 1 to 5pm.

In Historic Wilmington—the old residential area bounded roughly by Nun, Princess, Front, and 4th streets—the **Burgwin-Wright House,** 224 Market St. (📞 **910/762-0570**), was constructed in 1771 and used by Cornwallis as his headquarters in 1781. The Colonial town house was built over an abandoned city jail. You can tour the interior Tuesday to Saturday 10am to 4pm. Adults pay $7; children 12 and under pay $3; children 5 and under are admitted free.

**Airlie Gardens**   Once the plantation home of a wealthy rice planter, these 67-acre Gilded Age gardens are surrounded by huge lawns, serene lakes, and wooded gardens that hold just about every kind of azalea in existence. The blooms are at their height in the early spring, but even when they're faded, this is a lovely spot. U.S. 76. 📞 **910/798-7700**. www.airliegardens.org. Admission $8 adults, $1 children under 12. Tues–Thurs and Sat 9am–5pm; Fri 9am–7pm; Sun 11am–5pm. Take U.S. 76 toward beach and look for signpost.

**Cape Fear Museum**   This museum showcases the history, science, and culture of the lower Cape Fear region from prehistoric times until the present. Noteworthy are Civil War artifacts and dioramas of the Battle of Fort Fisher and the Wilmington waterfront from around 1863. Children will be interested in a discovery gallery and various hands-on activities.

814 Market St. ✆ 910/341-4350. www.capefearmuseum.com. Admission $5 adults, $4 seniors and college students, $1 children under 17. Memorial Day to Labor Day Mon–Sat 9am–5pm, Sun 1–5pm; off-season Tues–Sat 9am–5pm; Sun 1–5pm.

## SIGHTS NEARBY

**USS *North Carolina* Battleship Memorial**    The USS *North Carolina* was commissioned in 1941 and is permanently berthed here as a memorial to the state's World War II dead. You can tour most of the ship, and the Exhibit Hall houses a "through their eyes" exhibit focusing on recollections of the battleship's former crew. The ship is still painted in its 1944–45 camouflage. A visitor center offers a large gift shop and snack bar.

Eagle Island. ✆ 910/251-5797. www.battleshipnc.com. Admission $9 adults, $8 seniors, $4.50 children 6–11, free for children 5 and under. May 16–Sept 15 daily 8am–8pm; off season daily 8am–5pm. On Cape Fear River across from the historic district at junction of Hwy. 17/74/76/421. Easily accessible from I-95 or I-40.

**Poplar Grove Plantation**    This restored Greek Revival manor house and estate date from 1850. The outbuildings include a smokehouse, tenant house, and old kitchen. Attractions include demonstrations by a basket weaver, a fabric weaver, and a blacksmith.

10200 U.S. 17. ✆ 910/686-9518. www.poplargrove.com. Admission $7 adults, $6 seniors, $3 children 6–15. Mon–Sat 9am–5pm; Sun noon–5pm. Take U.S. 17 9 miles northeast of Wilmington.

**Fort Fisher State Historic Site** ★    One of the Confederacy's largest and most technically advanced forts, Fort Fisher was the last stronghold of the Confederate army. Following the defeats at Savannah and Mobile, Confederate Gen. Robert E. Lee depended solely on Fort Fisher for supplies. President Lincoln recognized that to end the war, Fort Fisher would have to be taken. After withstanding two of the heaviest naval bombardments of the Civil War, the fort finally fell to Union forces in what was the largest land-sea battle in U.S. history until World War II. The unconditional Confederate surrender came only 3 months after the fall of Fort Fisher. The visitor center exhibits artifacts of that era, and there's an audiovisual program as well. Costumed tour guides welcome visitors, and living-history events are depicted during the summer.

Kure Beach. ✆ 910/458-5538. Free admission. Apr–Oct Mon–Sat 9am–5pm, Sun 1–5pm; Nov–Mar Tues–Sat 10am–4pm, Sun 1–4pm. Follow U.S. 421 south to Kure Beach.

**Orton Plantation Gardens** ★ *(Finds)*    The Orton House, dating from 1725, was built by Roger Moore, known as "The King" in this area because of his imperious manner. The house is in the typical Tara style, and although it's a near-perfect example of antebellum architecture, it's privately occupied and can be admired only from the garden paths. Visitors flock to see the gardens, which begin blooming in late winter and reach their height in spring, when camellias, azaleas, pansies, and flowering trees burst into bloom. An occasional alligator drops by to visit.

9149 Orton Rd. SE. ✆ 910/371-6851. www.ortongardens.com. Admission $9 adults, $8 seniors, $3 children 6–12. Mar–Aug daily 8am–6pm; Sept–Nov daily 10am–5pm. Take U.S. 17 across the river and turn onto N.C. 133; the gardens are 18 miles south of Wilmington and 10 miles north of Southport.

## BEACHES & OUTDOOR PURSUITS

**BEACHES**    The main summer target is **Wrightsville Beach** ★, 6 miles east of Wilmington on U.S. 74/76—and don't expect to have the beach to yourself during the high season. The island is separated from the mainland by a small drawbridge. A year-round residence for some 3,200 dwellers, Wrightsville Beach, once known only as "The Banks," is the widest beach on the Cape Fear coast, stretching for a mile along the oceanfront, its beige sands set against a backdrop of hearty vegetation such as sea oats. The south end isn't ideal for swimming; you'll find better conditions between the rebuilt Johnnie Mercer Pier and Crystal Pier (patrolled by lifeguards in summer).

Another important spot is at **Carolina Beach State Park** (© 910/458-8206; www.ils.unc.edu/parkproject/visit/cabe/home.html), sprawling across 1,770 acres 10 miles north of Wilmington off U.S. 421. This beach, flanked on one bank by the Cape Fear River and on the other by the Intracoastal Waterway, lies at the northern edge of aptly named Pleasure Island. The significance of the park lies not in the beach—in fact, swimming is not allowed—but in the natural flora, including the rare Venus' flytrap and other insect-eating plants, which abound in the swamp forest. The park has 5 miles of hiking trails. Facilities include toilets, a marina, a picnic area, and a family campground.

At the southern tip of Pleasure Island is the small, family-friendly community of **Kure Beach.** From here, you can see Cape Fear River and the Atlantic Ocean. The white-sand beaches are generally uncrowded, restaurants are informal, and the Kure Beach fishing pier is a magnet for anglers. You can wander through the remains of Fort Fisher (see "Sights Nearby," above).

**FISHING    Batson's Charter Boats,** Carolina Beach (© 910/458-8671), departs from the Carolina Beach Municipal Marina, offering trolling and bottom-fishing charters. The charter boat can accommodate up to six fishers besides the crew. Prices are $360 for 5 hours, $540 for 8 hours, and $690 for 10 hours; rates include rod, reel, and bait.

**GOLF    The Belvedere Country Club,** 2368 Country Club Dr., Hampstead (© 910/270-2703), is one of the best and most popular courses in the Wilmington area, offering a par-72, 6,315-yard, 18-hole course open daily from 7am to 7pm. From Monday to Thursday greens fees are $28 before noon, $22 from noon to 4:30pm, and $12 from 4:30 to 7pm. Friday to Sunday, greens fees are $30 before noon, $25 from noon to 4:30pm, and $12 from 4:30 to 7pm. Clubs can be rented at $10 for 18 holes. Tee-time reservations are requested. Facilities include a clubhouse, a restaurant, and a pro shop. Professional instruction is available at $30 per half-hour.

The club lies 15 miles outside Wilmington. Take U.S. 17 north to Hampstead (about 10 miles), and continue on the same route the final 4½ miles.

**SCUBA/SNORKELING    The best outfitters are **Aquatic Safaris & Divers Emporium,** 5751 Oleander.Dr. (© 910/392-4-FUN); and **Bottom Time Dive Charters,** 6014 Wrightsville Ave. (© 910/397-0181).

## WHERE TO STAY

**Cape Fear Coast Convention and Visitors Bureau** (see "Essentials," above) will do more than just send you its *Accommodations Guide.* If you're in the market for an apartment or cottage for a week or more (a dollar-saving approach that's hard to beat), write well in advance, describing just what you have in mind. The bureau will circulate your requirements in a bulletin that goes to area owners and managers, who will then contact you directly.

Campers can check out the **Camelot Campground,** 7415 Market St., Wilmington, NC 28405 (© 910/686-7705; www.wilmingtonkoa.com), which sits on 43 wooded acres on U.S. 17. Facilities include a pool, recreation room, playground, laundry, and grocery store, and propane gas is available for stoves. Rates range from $20 for tent sites to $28 for full hookups.

**Best Western Coastline Inn**    Next door to the Coast Line Convention Center, this inn was designed to complement the restored historic rail depot that it's named for. The adjacent full-service restaurant actually occupies one of the original railroad buildings, and has a popular bar and periodic live entertainment. The inn's rooms all have good views of the Cape Fear River. Some units, such as the Overlook Suite, afford two river views. All guest rooms have bathrooms with tub/shower combinations.

503 Nutt St., Wilmington, NC 28401. © **800/617-7732** or 910/763-2800. Fax 910/763-2785. www.coastline inn.com. 53 units. Mon–Thurs $89 double, Fri–Sun $129 double; $119–$169 suite year-round. Rates include continental breakfast. AE, DC, DISC, MC, V. **Amenities:** Restaurant; fitness center; room service. *In room:* A/C, TV, dataport, hair dryer.

**C. W. Worth House** ✪ *Finds*    This 1893 Victorian three-story B&B is a real escape from the modern world. The decorative motif matches the Victorian design of the structure, with rooms furnished in 19th-century antiques. One unit, dubbed the Louisiana Room, breaks the mold with an all-French design, bathed in blue and yellow in a style that evokes a New Orleans B&B. All units have well-kept bathrooms mostly with tub/shower combinations. Some accommodations are equipped with dining nooks. The house is completely nonsmoking, and children under 11 are not admitted. A TV is provided in the sitting room, and the house has central air-conditioning.

412 S. 3rd St., Wilmington, NC 28401. © **800/340-8559** or 910/762-8562. Fax 910/763-2173. www.worth house.com. 7 units. $120–$150 double. Each additional person $25. Rates include full breakfast. AE, DISC, MC, V. Free parking. **Amenities:** Breakfast room; lounge. *In room:* A/C, dataport, hair dryer.

**Graystone Inn** ✪✪    This is the grandest of Wilmington's B&B inns. A neo-classical stone mansion from 1905, it offers 12- to 14-foot ceilings and Victorian-period furnishings. It has a large three-story portico and a grand staircase made of hand-carved red oak. A formal dining room, where breakfast is served, the original drawing room and music room, and a library lined with old volumes, take you back in time. All the handsomely furnished accommodations are on the third floor. All units have private bathrooms with showers, and some have claw-foot tubs.

100 S. 3rd St., Wilmington, NC 28401. © **888/763-4773** or 910/763-2000. Fax 910/763-5555. www.graystone inn.com. 7 units. $159–$199 double; $249–$329 suite. Rates include full breakfast. AE, DC, DISC, MC, V. Free parking. Children under 12 not allowed. **Amenities:** Breakfast room; fitness center; laundry service/dry cleaning; nonsmoking rooms; library. *In room:* A/C, TV, dataport, hair dryer.

**The Verandas** ✪    One of the most appealing and fairly priced B&Bs in Wilmington is a stately, white-sided mansion that, with eight units, is one of the largest owner-occupied guesthouses in town. It was built in 1853 by a local merchant, and then transformed into a convent in the 1860s. A century later, the then-dilapidated building was the site of Wilmington's most popular whorehouse before a devastating fire in 1992 reduced its back side to a smoldering ruin. Three years later, former Washington, D.C. residents Dennis Madsen and Charles Pennington embarked on a radical restoration. After it was rebuilt from its studs, with the addition of modern infrastructures and lots of English and American antiques, it has blossomed into an utterly charming, and very personalized, inn. Each unit is a corner room flooded with sunlight and includes a VCR, a marble-sheathed bathroom with a shower and oversize oval tub, and soundproofing. The second-floor rooms are grander than those on the third floor, which are deliberately cozier and less formal. Throughout the inn, the presence of pets and children under 12 is discouraged. A complimentary wine and beer bar appears every afternoon between 5:30 and 6pm. Breakfasts are elaborate affairs featuring dishes that include croissants with smoked salmon and cream cheese dipped in egg custard and dill and then fried in a way that resembles French toast. If you opt for an overnight here, you'll be in good company—many of the actors working on films in Wilmington like to stay here, as do many business travelers to Washington.

202 Nun St., Wilmington, NC 28401. ℂ 910/251-2212. www.verandas.com. 8 units. $150–$200 double. AE, DC, DISC, MC, V. **Amenities:** Breakfast room; nonsmoking rooms. *In room:* A/C, TV, dataport, hair dryer.

**The Wilmingtonian** ⚐⚐  This renovated 1906 commercial building is rightly regarded as the premier inn of Wilmington; actually, it's a glorified B&B in which all the rooms are suites. Accommodations on the second and third floors have balconies, and all suites contain kitchenettes. The two-bedroom suites sleep four guests comfortably, and the special-occasion suite (ideal for a honeymoon) has a fireplace and a whirlpool bath. All rooms have either queen- or king-size beds and well-kept bathrooms with tub/shower combinations. A small library is near the front desk, and an intimate on-site pub offers beer and wine Wednesday to Saturday from 5:30pm to 1am. About a dozen restaurants lie within safe walking distance. The owners also operate an antebellum (ca. 1840s) home with an additional six luxury suites, each with a whirlpool, a wet bar, antique reproduction furniture, and fireplaces.

101 S. 2nd St., Wilmington, NC 28401. ℂ 800/525-0909 or 910/343-1800. Fax 910/251-1149. www.the wilmingtonian.com. 40 units. $130–$159 suite for 2; $219–$239 2-bedroom suite for 4; $159–$179 special-occasion suite for 2; $179–$299 luxury suite. Rates include continental breakfast. AE, DC, DISC, MC, V. Free parking. **Amenities:** Restaurant; bar; limited room service; laundry service/dry cleaning; nonsmoking rooms; 1 room for those w/limited mobility. *In room:* A/C, TV, dataport, hair dryer.

### STAYING ON THE BEACH NEARBY

**Blockade Runner Beach Resort Hotel & Conference Center**  In the middle of Wrightsville Beach, opening onto views of the ocean, this seven-story hotel is far superior to the lackluster string of motels along Lumina Avenue, north and south. Guest rooms are comfortably and attractively furnished, and often have private patios. Normally, a hurricane is a bad occurrence, but the East Restaurant seems to have rebounded from recent hurricanes to become better than ever, luring the former sous-chef of the Harvard Club in Manhattan, Thomas Sullivan. The SeaEscape beach bar offers drinks in a poolside setting, complete with beach volleyball and a new beachfront dining patio.

275 Waynick Blvd. (P.O. Box 555), Wrightsville Beach, NC 28480. ℂ 800/541-1161 or 910/256-2251. Fax 910/ 256-2251. www.blockade-runner.com. 150 units. Mid-June to mid-Sept $179–$249 double; off season $99–$149 double. Children under 12 stay free in parent's room. AE, DC, DISC, MC, V. **Amenities:** Restaurant; 2 bars; lounge; pool; exercise room; Jacuzzi; sauna; limited room service; massage; babysitting, nonsmoking rooms; rooms for those w/limited mobility. *In room:* A/C, TV, dataport, minibar, fridge, coffeemaker, hair dryer, iron.

## WHERE TO DINE

As is true of so many coastal towns, Wilmington's best dining spots are at the beaches or on its fringes, and you'll find more seafood spots (most of them excellent) than you'll have time to sample.

Sooner or later, you're bound to hear the name **Calabash** ⚐, especially if you love seafood. This tiny town of 150 residents, 35 miles south of Wilmington on U.S. 17, is renowned for its bounty of seafood restaurants—about 30 of them within 1 square mile, vying with one another to serve the biggest and best platter of seafood at the lowest price. Calabash restaurants use family recipes handed down from generation to generation; in one recent year, 1.5 million people were served some 668,000 pounds of flounder and 378,000 pounds of shrimp, to say nothing of tons of oysters, scallops, and other fish. Recommendations for specific restaurants?

We make a point of avoiding **Ella's of Calabash,** 1148 River Rd. (© **910/579-6728**), and head instead to a tiny little place across the street called **Calabash Seafood Hut,** 1125 River Rd. (© **910/579-6723**). The line of customers waiting for a table often stretches around the corner—and you'll hear few complaints about the wait. That's because the fried shrimp, fresh fish, and those old standbys, hush puppies, are the best in the area. Portions are really big, and, in the words of one patron, "the sweet tea is to die for." Platters range from $10 to $13. The bigger restaurants along the waterfront are also good. We don't recommend the all-you-can-eat buffets, however; the food tends to get cold and the quality is not up to standard. Better to order fresh from the a la carte menu.

## MODERATE

**Caffè Phoenix** ✦ MEDITERRANEAN    This cafe, 1 block from the water in the center of town, is easily the best bistro in Wilmington. In a renovated and transformed former dry-goods store, it has a light, open, airy decor, with lots of plants. Luncheon choices include homemade soups, freshly prepared salads, pasta, and sandwiches. Dinner becomes more elaborate, featuring delicacies like Chianti tuna. Specials change weekly. Many Wilmington artists dine here, and the place has a gay following.

9 S. Front St. © **910/343-1395.** Main courses $6–$10 lunch (including soup or salad), $10–$25 dinner. AE, DC, DISC, MC, V. Mon–Sat 11:30am–10:30pm (with light fare served 3–5pm); Sun 11am–10pm.

**Deluxe Restaurant** NOUVELLE AMERICAN    Don't underestimate the value of this restaurant's bar as a meeting point for the artistic and the articulate. Lots of musicians and artists are drawn here because of the ambience and the eclectic, vaguely Southwestern decor, which might have been designed by Frank Lloyd Wright on psychedelics. It was established as a coffeehouse in 1995, and expanded into this full-fledged restaurant in 1998. Menu items are imaginative—a welcome change from the catfish and collards that are staples at some of the local competitors. Reflecting a solid technique and a flair for flavor, the chef delights you with such dishes as grilled rack of lamb flavored with hazelnut oil and fresh herbs, or pecan-dusted red grouper layered with prosciutto, sweet basil, and mozzarella. Brunch is always a treat here, with cinnamon-pecan-swirl French toast or applewood-smoked salmon. Sometimes the chef goes far afield for inspiration, as in the Japanese tempura shrimp. Wines are appropriately eclectic, with origins from around the world.

114 Market St. © **910/251-0333.** www.deluxenc.com. Reservations recommended. Main courses $16–$30; Sun brunch $10–$14. AE, DISC, MC, V. Sun–Thurs 5:30–10pm; Fri–Sat 5:30pm–2am; Sun brunch 10:30am–2pm.

**Elijah's** ✦ AMERICAN/SEAFOOD    This is one of the largest and best-established restaurants along Wilmington's historic riverfront. Elijah's occupies a low-slung, wood-sided building that was originally conceived as a maritime museum. It still contains some of its seafaring memorabilia, which looks striking against the rich paneling that sheathes most of the interior. In the evenings, a wraparound bar with views of the river becomes a convivial nightlife venue. On warm nights, head for the huge waterfront terrace, where a bar is rolled on or off the deck, depending on the weather. Lunches here tend to emphasize sandwiches and simple platters that always include a fine version of crab cakes.

Dinners are more elaborate, with classic and well-prepared dishes that include deep-fried calamari, soft-shell crabs, shrimp in a Dijon mustard and garlic sauce, and tender, juicy steaks.

2 Ann St., Chandler's Wharf. ℂ 910/343-1448. www.elijahs.com. Reservations recommended for 8 or more. Main courses $6.95–$8.95 lunch, $15–$24 dinner. AE, DC, DISC, MC, V. Outdoor: Mon–Thurs 11:30am–10pm; Fri–Sun 11:30am–11pm. Indoor: Mon–Thurs 11:30am–3pm and 5–10pm; Fri–Sun 11:30am–3pm and 5–10pm.

**Pilot House** ⭐ LOW COUNTRY/SEAFOOD    Located on the Cape Fear River in the historic restored Craig House, the Pilot House serves some of the best seafood dishes in the Wilmington area. Set within a yellow-painted clapboard house (ca. 1870) immediately adjacent to the Cape Fear River, it was moved to its present site in 1978. This is the Wilmington restaurant that's more attuned to the gourmet allure of Low Country cuisine than any other, offering both classic and nouvelle twists on traditional dishes. More upscale than its neighbor, Elijah's (with which it shares the same owner), the Pilot House seats most of its diners on a sprawling riverfront terrace, with an additional 10 tables in an isolated upstairs garret room that some visitors find romantic and others interpret as an exile to Siberia. Preface your meal with a drink at the cozy nautical-style bar before diving into the specialties, such as shrimp and grits or crunchy catfish, a true Southern delicacy. The seafood platter is the most-ordered dish. One justifiable favorite is the shredded and deep-fried grouper in a sweet-potato crust, accompanied by ravioli in a balsamic vinaigrette sauce. A choice selection of meats is offered, especially prime cuts of beef, and it wouldn't be a Carolina restaurant if it didn't serve pork chops. The Caribbean fudge pie has its fans.

2 Ann St., Chandler's Wharf. ℂ 910/343-0200. www.pilothouserest.com. Reservations recommended. Lunch $7.95–$12; main courses $17–$26. AE, DC, DISC, MC, V. Sun–Thurs 11:30am–10pm; Fri–Sat 11:30am–11pm.

**Prima** ITALIAN    This spot is for your Italian food fix, and it lies in the center of town. Decorated with a frescoed mural, the restaurant also offers an upstairs martini lounge called **Divano.** In casual attire, guests peruse the menu, opting for one of the many good-tasting pastas prepared fresh daily. A clear favorite is the seafood cannelloni in a sherry cream sauce. Others select the Tuscan-style pizza. The desserts here are worth saving room for, especially the coconut sushi (chocolate truffle with coconut and a chocolate caramel sauce).

35 N. Front St. ℂ 910/763-9545. Reservations recommended. Main courses $9–$20. AE, MC, V. Tues–Sun 11:30am–3pm and 5–10pm (until 11pm Sat–Sun).

## INEXPENSIVE

**Boca Bay** SOUTHERN/INTERNATIONAL    The special feature here is a fountainside outdoor covered patio for dining. That and the good food at reasonable prices have put this place on the culinary map of Wilmington. The menu is unusual in that it is so wide ranging and includes an array of tapas, sushi, and sashimi, plus a bevy of delightful main courses. Many guests make their entire order from the tapas selections, including stuffed grape leaves, vodka-cured salmon, Mediterranean hummus, and marinated mushrooms. From the main menu, you can start with the escargots sautéed with wild mushrooms and spinach, or the Cuban barbecued shrimp. We were pleasantly intrigued by the main course of lobster cheesecake with rock shrimp served with a champagne-and-pink-peppercorn sauce. Desserts are appropriately nicknamed "Colossal Confections," and are best exemplified by the hazel truffle cake with hazelnut cream.

2025 Eastwood Rd. © **910/256-1887.** Reservations recommended. Main courses $7.50–$12. AE, DISC, MC, V. Mon–Wed 5–10pm; Thurs–Sat 5–11pm; Sun 9am–2pm and 4–10pm.

**Circa 1922** ★ *Value* SOUTHERN/INTERNATIONAL    One of Wilmington's most affordable restaurants opened in 2000 in a 1920s bank building.

## Side Trip: Bald Head Island

A 45-minute drive southeast from Wilmington on U.S. 17 South, with a left turn onto N.C. 87, takes you to the little town of Southport, the jumping-off point for the passenger ferry to **Bald Head Island** ★. (The terminal is at Indigo Plantation.) You must call ahead to book the ferry (© **910/457-5003**). The day trip costs $15 adults and $8 children 3 to 12; children 2 and under ride free.

Bald Head Island invites nature lovers to visit for much longer than 1 day. There are some 3,000 pristine acres, with 14 miles of sandy beachfront and miles and miles of salt marshes, tidal creeks, and maritime forests. An 18-hole championship golf course and the Village of Bald Head Island—with shops, restaurants, private homes, and condominiums—offer other diversions. Activities on the island include swimming (the island has a pool as well as all those miles of beaches), biking, tennis, golf, canoeing, fishing, birding, and just plain beachcombing.

Still, human intrusion is kept to a minimum. No cars are permitted on the island; transportation is provided by golf carts and jitneys. Sea oats, yucca, beach grasses, live oak, red cedar, palmetto, sabal palms, loblolly pines, and a yellow wildflower called galardia thrive here. Such birds as white ibises, great blue herons, snowy egrets, black ducks, mallards, and pintails frequent the island, and a protected population of loggerhead sea turtles nests here.

If you'd like to stay over, private homes, as well as condominiums, are available as rentals. You can also rent either of two historic cottages that were the homes of lighthouse keepers and their families from 1903 to 1958. All units are tastefully furnished, with full kitchens, TVs, and other modern conveniences, and most rates include the use of one of the electric passenger carts. There is a 3-night minimum stay at the condos and a weekly-only rental for houses. In summer, daily rates range from $250 to $550, with weekly rates going from $1,647 to $13,000. Off season, the daily rate goes from $200 to $550, with weekly rentals costing $1,500 to $13,000. All kinds of package deals are available. For full details and bookings, contact **Bald Head Island**, P.O. Box 3069, Bald Head Island, NC 28461 (© **800/234-1666** or 910/457-5000; www.baldheadisland.com).

One of the best deals here is a stay at **Theodosia's Bed & Breakfast** (© **800/656-1812** or 910/457-6563; www.theodosias.com), which offers eight handsomely furnished guest rooms, each with private bathroom, plus two very private rooms in a carriage house, and another three guest rooms in a cottage. Each has a porch or balcony. The inn is located at the Marina of Harbour Village. Doubles range from $205 to $295 nightly, including a full breakfast. A 2-night minimum stay is required. American Express, Discover, MasterCard, and Visa are accepted.

Inside you'll find a stately, high-ceilinged interior filled with hardwoods and mirrors, and a menu that features tapas, the small-portioned and savory bar food of Spain. The best way to navigate your way through a meal here is to order a medley of the savory dishes to share among your fellow diners. The culinary inspirations range from Asian to Mediterranean. For starters, Prince Edward Sound mussels are delectable in green curry and coconut milk, and the organic greens salad that follows is a winner with additions of fresh pear, sugared walnuts, tempura Gorgonzola, and a shallot vinaigrette. The lobster ravioli is sublime and prepared with a lobster bisque. Sushi and sashimi also adorn the menu, and you can order such main courses as pan-seared scallops served with a smoked oyster fondue. We'd walk a mile for the B-52 cheesecake (layers of Kahlúa and Bailey's cheesecake finished with chocolate Grand Marnier).

8 N. Front St. ✆ 910/762-1922. www.circa1922.com. Reservations recommended. Tapas $7–$14; main courses $10–$12. AE, DC, DISC, MC, V. Sun–Thurs 5–10pm; Fri–Sat 5–11pm. Bar daily 5pm–midnight (till 1–2am Fri–Sat).

## WILMINGTON AFTER DARK

**Hell's Kitchen**   This is the hot spot in town. The bar itself was created from the set used for the now-defunct TV show *Dawson's Creek*. It's a full liquor bar with a wide selection of microbrew suds and draft beer. If you're hungry, you can devour a pub selection of burgers, nachos, wings, and other such fare, with most plates costing less than $7. It's open Monday to Friday 11:30am to 2am and Saturday and Sunday 5pm to 2am. 118 Princess St. ✆ 910/763-4133.

**The Thalian Hall Theater**   If there's a big event being staged in Wilmington, this is likely to be the venue. The restored 1858 theater hosts about 250 events annually. Local theater groups and the symphony also use the theater as their home base for productions. Performances range from live dance to children's dramas performed by local companies. Contact the box office to learn what's happening at the time of your visit. Ticket prices depend on the event. Center box-office hours are noon to 6pm Monday to Friday, 2 to 6pm Saturday and Sunday. 310 Chestnut St. ✆ 800/523-2820 or 910/343-3664. www.thalianhall.com.

**The Water Street Bar & Restaurant**   Folk, reggae, and the blues are featured here. The club often provides open-mic nights for anyone who thinks that he or she has talent. It's more a pub than a nightclub, and it has a full restaurant. The kitchen is open as long as bands are playing. Live music is featured Thursday to Sunday only. The club opens daily at 11am. Closing times vary according to the day of the week: 9pm Monday to Thursday, until midnight Friday to Sunday. 5 S. Water St. ✆ 910/343-0042. Cover only on special occasions (prices vary).

## 2 Beaufort ⬥

35 miles E of New Bern

North Carolina's third-oldest town, **Beaufort** ⬥ (pronounced *bo*-fort) dates back to 1713 and still reflects its early history. Along its narrow streets are two 200-year-old houses, and more than a hundred houses are over a century old. On the last weekend in June, residents open their homes for the annual Old Homes Tour. Beaufort lies on the Taylor Creek waterfront, where a boardwalk with restaurants, shops, and piers offers pleasant strolling.

## ESSENTIALS

**GETTING THERE**   Access is on U.S. 70 just over the Grayden Paul Bridge from Morehead City. From New Bern, take U.S. 70 East.

**VISITOR INFORMATION** The **Beaufort Historical Association,** 130 Turner St. (P.O. Box 1709), Beaufort, NC 28516 (© **252/728-5225;** www. beaufort-nc.com/bha), is open March to November, Monday to Saturday 9am to 5pm; off season, Monday to Saturday 10am to 4pm.

## EXPLORING THE AREA

**Beaufort Historic Site** ⟨ ⟩, in the 100 block of Turner Street, includes the 1767 Joseph Bell House; the 1825 Josiah Bell House; the 1796 Carteret County Courthouse; the 1829 county jail; the 1859 apothecary shop and doctor's office; and the 1778 Samuel Leffers House, home of the town's first schoolmaster. Tours are given Monday to Saturday at 10am, 11:30am, 1pm, and 3pm. Adults pay $6 for the tour; children older than 5 are charged $4. Not included on the tour is the 1732 Rustell House, an art gallery; entry is free of charge.

A block away is the **Old Burying Ground,** dating from 1709 and listed on the National Register of Historic Places. Both self-guided and narrated tours are available. Narrated tours aboard a British double-decker bus are offered on Tuesday, Wednesday, and Thursday at 2:30pm year-round, for $6 per person. You can also purchase a self-guided tour brochure for $1. Call © **252/728-5225** for more information.

From modest beginnings, the **North Carolina Maritime Museum,** 315 Front St. (© **252/728-7317;** www.ah.dcr.state.nc.us/sections/maritime), grew into a $2.2-million complex. It has natural- and maritime-history exhibits, ship models, and shell collections, and it offers intriguing field trips and programs for all ages. The Wooden Boat Show is held here the first weekend in May. Admission is free. The museum is open Monday to Friday from 9am to 5pm, Saturday from 10am to 5pm, and Sunday from 1 to 5pm; it's closed on major holidays.

Divers are attracted to this area because of the many wrecks off the coast. If you want to get into this action, contact **Discovery Diving Co.,** 414 Orange St. (© **252/728-2265;** www.discoverydiving.com), where the staff knows the local waters best. The company offers charter diving tours for prices ranging from $50 to $110 per person, plus use of the company's equipment. Tanks rent for $12 to $18, with regulators going for $6 and weights for $2. Masks and fins are priced at $3 each, and extra amenities (such as cameras and computers) cost around $40 extra. Call ahead for equipment reservations. Tours include one dive at a shipwreck site offshore, one farther offshore, and two dives on the reefs closer to shore.

## WHERE TO STAY

**Beaufort Inn** Katie and Bruce Ethridge have managed to give their historic district inn a historic feel, even though it's of recent vintage. Rooms are tastefully decorated, with lots of homey touches. Some 15 boat slips are provided for guests who arrive by water, and bicycles are available for rent. A scrumptious hot breakfast is served in the dining area (don't miss Katie's breakfast pie, made of sausages, eggs, and cheese), and good restaurants are within walking distance.

101 Ann St., Beaufort, NC 28516. © **800/726-0321** or 252/728-2600. www.beaufort-inn.com. 44 units. June–Sept $119–$169 double; off season $59–$109 double. Additional person $15. Rates include breakfast. AE, DC, DISC, MC, V. **Amenities:** Breakfast room; exercise room; outdoor Jacuzzi; nonsmoking rooms; rooms for those w/limited mobility. *In room:* A/C, TV, hair dryer, iron/ironing board.

**The Cedars By the Sea and Cedars Inn** ⟨ ⟨ Built in 1768 and once the home of a shipbuilder, this antiques-filled house overlooking the river is the most intriguing and comfortable historic inn in Beaufort. Five of its suites come with fireplaces. A whirlpool (honeymoon suite only), private patios, and balconies are offered as well, providing modern comforts in gracious surroundings. All units have neatly kept bathrooms with showers or tub/shower combinations. Overflow guests are accommodated at the equally comfortable Cedars Inn, built in 1851 as the Belcher Fuller House. All rooms are nonsmoking.

301 and 305 Front St., Beaufort, NC 28516. © **252/728-7036.** Fax 252/728-1685. www.cedarsinn.com. 11 units. High season $135 double, $155–$170 suite; low season $125 double, $140–$160 suite. Rates include breakfast. AE, MC, V. **Amenities:** Breakfast room; lounge. *In room:* A/C, TV, hair dryer, no phone.

**Delamar Inn** (★ (Value)    In 1866, immediately following the Civil War, Jacob Gibbie built this home for his expanding family. In time, the family intermarried with the Delamars, for whom the house is now named. This enlarged saltbox-style cottage is fringed with perennial borders and rosebushes. The decor is homelike and cozy, not at all grandiose. Today, Delamar is one of the finest and best-run B&Bs in Beaufort. Both of the inn's two stories have porches with rockers set out. Each guest room has a king-size Jenny Lind bed and a private shower-only bathroom with original claw-foot tub. Only four antiques-furnished guest rooms (each with private bathroom) are offered, so reservations are important in summer.

Mary and F. J. Hurst are the courteous and helpful hosts, who will provide details about sightseeing in the area. They can also make reservations for ferry connections, advise you about nearby golf, or help you board a charter fishing boat. You can borrow their bicycles, beach chairs, umbrellas, coolers, and beach towels. Soft drinks and cookies will be waiting when you return from exploring.

217 Turner St., Beaufort, NC 28516. © **800/349-5823** or 252/728-4300. www.bbonline.com/nc/delamarinn. 3 units. Summer $112–$125 double; off season $88–$106 double. Rates include continental breakfast. MC, V. No children under 10. **Amenities:** Breakfast room; lounge; nonsmoking rooms. *In room:* A/C, no phone.

**Pecan Tree Inn** (★    Named for the two century-old pecan trees that grace the property, the Pecan Tree Inn is housed in a building that was constructed during the mid-1800s. The Victorian porches, turrets, and gingerbread trim that make the house unique were added in 1890. Recent renovations have improved the inn while maintaining its original architectural essence. The rooms and parlor are furnished with a collection of antiques, designed to highlight the use of pine in the construction. Guest rooms feature king-size, queen-size, or twin beds; specify which you want when you make reservations. Each suite contains a Jacuzzi, and its king-size canopied bed evokes the Southern-plantation ambience. All units contain well-kept bathrooms with showers. A 5,500-square-foot English garden in the back features more than 1,000 plants, each labeled to aid the budding botanist.

116 Queen St., Beaufort, NC 28516. © **800/728-7871** or 252/728-6733. www.pecantree.com. 7 units. $90–$160 double; $130–$160 suite. Rates include continental breakfast. AE, DISC, MC, V. Children under 10 not accepted. **Amenities:** Breakfast room; lounge; free bikes; nonsmoking rooms; private gardens. *In room:* A/C, TV, dataport, hair dryer.

## WHERE TO DINE

**Clawson's 1905 Restaurant** AMERICAN    One of downtown Beaufort's most consistently popular restaurants was built in—you guessed it—1905 by a Swedish immigrant who needed a lot of warehousing space for his growing business. The rough-hewn plank, timber, and brick building has been pierced with skylights and gentrified, with every cranny of its labyrinthine interior jam-packed with nostalgia, diners, and drinkers. If you have to wait at the bar for a table, view the experience as a cultural insight into the New South as you rub elbows with boat owners, local hell-raisers, and golf-playing retirees. Lunches are a lot simpler than dinners, consisting of fried oysters, shrimp or scallops, salads,

## Side Trip: Harkers Island

If you're a boat owner, you can tie up across the sound from Beaufort at **Calico Jack's Marina** (✆ 252/728-3575) on Harkers Island. If you don't have a boat, a **ferry** (✆ 800/BY-FERRY; www.ncferry.org) leaves from Calico Jack's for the 35-minute trip to Cape Lookout. The ferry runs between April and December, and the fare is $10 for adults and $6 for children 12 and under. A jitney service between Cape Point and the lighthouse moves visitors from one spot to another. Bring a picnic, insect repellent, and your own water supply. The island's atmosphere is ideal for those who like sailboats, lots of sun, and miles of sandy beaches. It's also a good venue for fishing and beachcombing. The unique diamond-patterned lighthouse has stood here since 1859.

Calico Jack's also takes visitors on four-wheel-drive tours of the island, highlighting its history and pointing out the best spots for shelling. Cost of a 2-hour tour is $10 for adults and $6 for children under age 12. Weather permitting, tours depart daily at 8:15am, 9:15am, and 9:45am.

and overstuffed sandwiches. Dinners feature larger portions and lots of combination platters piled high with ribs and shrimp, steak, pork, and chicken. A specialty is a very large potato stuffed with broccoli, red pepper, onions, and mushrooms, then topped with cheese and sour cream.

425 Front St. ✆ 252/728-2133. http://clawsonsrestaurant.com. Reservations recommended. Lunch sandwiches and platters $5.95–$11; dinner main courses $9.95–$19. DISC, MC, V. Mon–Thurs 11:30am–9pm; Fri–Sat 11:30am–9:30pm.

**The Spouter Inn** SEAFOOD    Waterfront dining and fresh seafood keep this place humming. The atmosphere is casual, even though the tables are lighted by candles in the evening. Popular with both locals and visitors, the restaurant offers lunches with pastas, salads, chowders, and sandwiches. In the evening, more elaborate meals are served, depending largely on the availability of fresh seafood. Continental dishes—rare in this region—are also featured. For dessert, chocolate silk pie, cream cheese lemon pie, or rum cake may appear on the menu.

218 Front St. ✆ 252/728-5190. Reservations recommended for dinner. Main courses $5.95–$12 lunch, $15–$24 dinner. AE, MC, V. Daily 11:30am–2:30pm and 5–9pm.

## 3 Morehead City

147 miles SE of Raleigh; 3 miles W of Beaufort; 45 miles SE of New Bern; 87 miles NE of Wilmington

This has been an important port for oceangoing vessels since 1857 and is the world's largest tobacco-export terminal. Across the Intracoastal Waterway from Beaufort, and the gateway to the Atlantic Beach/Emerald Isle area (see "The Bogue Banks," below), it attracts many fishermen. Both onshore and offshore fishing trips are offered here, and tournaments are held throughout the year. The biggest event is the **Big Rock Blue Marlin Tournament** (✆ 252/247-3575; www.thebigrock.com), staged over 6 days, beginning the second Monday in June. The contest features cash awards. Stroll the little waterfront boardwalk, where boats hired for deep-sea fishing trips clean the day's catch. Or stop in for a platter of fresh shrimp and hush puppies in old-timey seafood restaurants like Captain Bill's and the Sanitary Fish Market (below), both with waterfront dining.

## ESSENTIALS

**GETTING THERE    By Plane**    The closest commuter-flight connection is the airport at New Bern. (See section 4, "New Bern.")

**By Train**    The nearest **Amtrak** stop is at Raleigh on the New York-to-Miami or New York-to-Tampa run. Call ℭ **800/USA-RAIL** or go to www.amtrak.com for schedules and fares.

**By Bus    Greyhound/Trailways** (ℭ **800/229-9424** or 252/726-3029; www.greyhound.com) serves Morehead City. The terminal is at 105 N. 13th St. (ℭ **252/726-3029**). You can get a taxi here if you're heading for a hotel at Atlantic Beach.

**By Car**    Morehead City is about a 45-minute drive on U.S. 70 East from New Bern.

**VISITOR INFORMATION**    For sightseeing and accommodations information, contact the **Carteret County Tourism Bureau,** 3409 Arendell St., Morehead City, NC 28557 (ℭ **800/SUNNY-NC** or 252/726-8148; www.sunnync.com). Hours are Monday to Friday from 9am to 5pm, Saturday and Sunday 9am to 5pm.

## OUTDOOR PURSUITS

Fishing is especially good here—in fact, it's the reason most visitors come to Morehead City. The Gulf Stream brings in blue marlin, tarpon, amberjack, and other prizes, in addition to inshore fish. Gulf Stream fishing is possible April through November. The area has about 80 miles of surf and 400 miles of protected waterways.

A near-perfect day or evening on the water can be enjoyed on the *Carolina Princess,* 604 Evans St., Morehead City (ℭ **800/682-3456** or 252/726-5479; www.carolinaprincess.com). The *Princess* is a trim vessel that accommodates up to 95 passengers and has a snack bar and sun deck. Full-day deep-sea fishing trips cost $70 for adults, $50 for children 12 and under, and $20 for a passenger who goes along just for the ride and doesn't fish. The boat supplies the rod, reel, and bait. Ice can be purchased to take with you.

## WHERE TO STAY

**Best Western Buccaneer Motor Inn**  *(Kids)*    If you're looking for a family-friendly motel, head for this chain motel. It's not the largest in the area, but it's one of the best. Housekeeping is good. The hotel's standard rooms are comfortable and rather tasteful; some have Jacuzzi tubs. All units have well-kept bathrooms with tub/shower combinations. Amenities include free coffee, free local phone calls (with a $10 deposit), and a pool. The **Anchor Inn Restaurant,** with two dining rooms and a lounge, specializes in seafood, Black Angus steaks, prime rib, and homemade desserts.

2806 Arendell St. (Hwy. 70), Morehead City, NC 28557. ℭ **800/682-4982** or 252/726-3115. Fax 252/726-3864. www.bestwestern.com. 91 units. May–Sept Sun–Thurs $85 double, Fri–Sat $115 double; Jan–Mar $47 double. Children under 17 stay free in parent's room. Rates include continental breakfast. AE, DC, DISC, MC, V. **Amenities:** Restaurant; bar; pool. *In room:* A/C, TV, dataport, fridge, hair dryer.

**The Harborlight Guest House**  *★★* *(Finds)*    We much prefer a B&B with some charm and character to any big chain motel when we visit the Carolina coast. Graced with shady palms along the waterfront, this guesthouse is something of a secret, and no signs from the road give it away. The Harborlight is encircled on three sides by water, giving guests good views of the Intracoastal Waterway and Bogue Sound from every guest room; sometimes you can see porpoises feeding in the waters. Each accommodation is a suite with attractive furnishings, expansive windows, and excellent bathrooms with tub and shower. The best units contain two-person whirlpool tubs and/or fireplaces. The most coveted suites are the Beaufort or Emerald rooms. Breakfast is one more good reason to stay here. Perhaps you'll be served filet mignon, rum-laced French toast with honeybee ambrosia, or blueberry crepes.

332 Live Oak Dr., Cape Carteret, NC 28584. 📞 **800/624-8439** or 252/393-6868. Fax 252/393-6868. www. harborlightguesthousenc.com. 7 units. $185–$300 suite. Children older than 16 only. AE, MC, V. **Amenities:** Health club privileges; golf privileges. *In room:* A/C, TV, dataport, fridge, coffeemaker, whirlpool (in some).

## WHERE TO DINE

**Bistro by the Sea** 🌟 ATLANTIC COASTAL   The town's best restaurant occupies a contemporary, stone-sided building set beside Highway 70, near the Hampton Inn, in a commercial neighborhood west of the waterfront. Inside, you'll find a stylish bar where a *trompe l'oeil* mural adorns the edges of a ceiling cupola. Within the dignified dining rooms, you'll be offered savory dishes that include peppercorn-encrusted seared tuna; sautéed salmon scampi with lemon-flavored linguine, shrimp, and a julienne of vegetables; prime rib of beef; and pastas that include cappellini in pesto sauce with fresh-roasted vegetables. There's also an assortment of burgers. Your hosts are Tim Coyne and his wife, Libby Eaton, who began their restaurant career in a beachfront shack in the 1980s, and who eventually expanded into the substantial building you'll see today.

4031 Arendell St. 📞 **253/247-2777**. www.bistro-by-the-sea.com. Reservations recommended for 6 or more. Main courses $6.95–$25. AE, DC, MC, V. Tues–Sat 5–10pm. Closed Jan.

**Captain Bill's Waterfront Restaurant** SEAFOOD   A tradition since the 1940s, this local favorite overlooks the colorful fishing boats on Bogue Sound. With a name like Captain Bill's, the restaurant obviously specializes in seafood, which is very fresh. Locals look forward to the conch stew on Wednesday and Saturday, as well as all-you-can-eat seafood specials on Friday. Prices are a bargain. There's also a good selection of non-finny dishes. The Down East lemon pie is justly celebrated. A children's menu is available.

701 Evans St. 📞 **252/726-2166**. Reservations recommended. Main courses $4.95–$8.95 lunch, $9.50–$25 dinner. MC, V. Sun–Thurs 11am–9pm; Fri–Sat 11am–10pm.

**Mrs. Willis' Restaurant** 🌟 *Value* SOUTHERN   This eatery was founded by "Ma Willis" when she served up platters of barbecue from a one-room garage with the help of some of her six children. Originally, she cooked barbecue, chicken, and homemade pies for takeout, but in time, business demanded that she open a full-fledged restaurant. The restaurant has remained a local tradition, known for its prime ribs and choice charcoaled steaks. The barbecue is highly recommended, as are the Southern-style vegetables. The place is cozy and rather rustic, with a fireplace, background music, and lots of Southern hospitality. In addition to a good wine list, the restaurant has full bar service.

3114 Bridge St. 📞 **252/726-3741**. Reservations accepted in summer. Main courses $5–$25. AE, DISC, MC, V. Sun and Tues–Fri 11am–2pm and 5–9pm; Sat 5–10pm. Closed Christmas week.

**Sanitary Fish Market & Restaurant** SEAFOOD   This 600-seat restaurant started out as 12 stools, a counter, and a kerosene stove in 1938. It became a regional favorite for families over the years as much for its sunny waterside ambience (vintage wood paneling, windows overlooking the sound, faded photos of politicians and beauty queens of old) as for its reliable seafood platters. And lo and behold, after years of abstinence, the place today serves beer and wine. The shrimp salad is a winner, and the hush puppies here are the best around—hot, crisp, and never cloyingly sweet.

501 Evans St. ℂ 252/247-3111. www.sanitaryfishmarket.com. Main courses $5.95–$22 lunch, $8.95–$22 dinner. DISC, MC, V. Daily 11am–9pm. Closed Dec 1–Feb 1.

## THE BOGUE BANKS ⊛

**Atlantic Beach** is the oldest of the resorts on the 28-mile stretch of barrier island known as the Bogue Banks, which includes the vacation centers directly south, **Pine Knoll Shores, Salter Path, Indian Beach,** and **Emerald Isle.** You may also hear the area referred to as "The Crystal Coast" (also encompassing Morehead City and Beaufort to the north; see listings earlier in this chapter). Whatever its moniker, the long, thin island was relatively undeveloped until 1927, when the first bridge was built across Bogue Sound to Morehead City. It's now one of the state's most popular coastal areas, with fishing festivals and tournaments held in early spring and late fall. A south-facing exposure makes the island's weather less volatile and temperatures milder than those found on the northern Outer Banks, and it's virtually a year-round resort. When you begin to feel waterlogged, plenty of sightseeing is within easy reach.

At the tip of Bogue Island sits **Fort Macon,** a restored Civil War landmark that's open to the public at no charge. The jetties (designed by Gen. Robert E. Lee), moats, gun emplacements, and dungeons make it worth the trip. The museum displays weapons, tools, and artifacts. The public beach has bathhouses, a snack bar, and lifeguards. Fort Macon lies 2 miles east of Atlantic Beach off N.C. 58, and is open daily from 9am to 5:30pm. Free guided tours of the fort are offered only in summer at 11am, 1pm, and 3pm. The museum is open in summer from 9am to 5pm. For more information, call ℂ **252/726-3775.**

The **North Carolina Aquarium** at Pine Knoll Shores is undergoing a major expansion and will not reopen until spring 2006 (ℂ **252/247-4003**). When it reopens, it will be three times larger, with a 300,000-gallon Living Shipwreck Ocean Tank featuring the wreckage of the German sub U-352 and a big collection of marine life.

For further information about the Bogue Banks or Crystal Coast area, contact the **Carteret County Tourism Bureau** (ℂ **800/786-6962;** www.sunnync.com).

## WHERE TO STAY & DINE

**The Oceanana Family Resort** *Kids*    This motel at Atlantic Beach proper, directly beside the ocean, offers a free fishing pier for guests. If you want to turn the day's catch into the evening meal, you'll find grills and a supply of charcoal, starter fluid, and even ketchup and mustard out by the pool, as well as picnic tables nearby. For the small fry, there's a playground, and for vacationers of all ages, the biweekly watermelon party out by the pool is a festive occasion. A tropical breakfast, spread under an open poolside pavilion, features more than 15 fresh fruits. A fast-food grill is out by the fishing pier. Every room has a well-maintained bathroom, most with a tub/shower combination, and suites have stoves. You can take portable grills to the lawn area in front of your room (but not on upper-floor decks) and cook dinner right at your door.

700 Fort Macon Rd. (P.O. Box 250), Atlantic Beach, NC 28512. ℂ 252/726-4111. Fax 252/726-4113. www. ncbeach.com/lodgings/ads/old/oceanana.htm. 109 units. July–Sept $95 double, $136 suite; off season $74

double, $108 suite. Rates include breakfast in summer. MC, V. Closed Nov–Mar. **Amenities:** Restaurant; pool; nonsmoking rooms; rooms for those w/limited mobility. *In room:* A/C, TV, dataport.

**Royal Pavillion Resort**    This rather grandly named hotel was expanded. Its main allure is that it faces a thousand feet of broad ocean beach on Salter Path Road. Guest rooms are only standard, but they're clean and well maintained with bathrooms containing tug/shower combinations. This hotel has a restaurant, lounge, free coffee, one indoor heated pool, two outdoor pools, a pool bar, and golf and tennis privileges at nearby facilities.

125 Salter Pass Rd., Pine Knoll Shores (P.O. Box 790), Atlantic Beach, NC 28512. © **800/533-3700** or 252/726-5188. Fax 252/726-9963. www.rpresort.com. 155 units. June to mid-Aug $120–$195 double; mid-Aug to May $115–$175 double. Children 12 and under stay free in parent's room. AE, DISC, MC, V. Go 3 miles west of U.S. 70 on N.C. 58 to Pine Knoll Shores/Salter Path exit. **Amenities:** Restaurant; bar; 3 pools; exercise room; limited room service; nonsmoking rooms; rooms for those w/limited mobility. *In room:* A/C, TV, hair dryer (in some).

## WHERE TO DINE

**The Crab Shack** SEAFOOD    This is everything a Down East seafood "shack" should be: It's a local favorite with an expansive backside view of Bogue Sound and consistently reliable seafood standards. If it's steamed spiced crabs you crave, here's the spot to order up a dozen or two in season. You won't find fancy sauces here: The Crab Shack offers fresh, unadulterated seafood, fried, grilled, or broiled; a solid Hatteras-style clam chowder (broth-based); and state-of-the-art hush puppies. Families love the friendly, casual ambience. The decor is nothing to write home about, and in the summer, you may have to wait in line for a table, but for good and simple, you can't beat it. Beer and wine are available.

Off Hwy. 58 (behind the Methodist Church), Salter Path, NC 28512. © **252/247-3444.** Main courses $5.95–$15 lunch, $9.95–$25 dinner. Open 7 days a week, year-round; hours change seasonally (normally 4–8:30pm)—call for updates.

## SWANSBORO & JACKSONVILLE

Along the coast southwest of Morehead City, the historic waterfront town of **Swansboro** (www.tourswansboro.com), bordering the White Oak River across

---

*Moments*    **A Real-Life Desert Island**

For those who really want to get away from it all, head to **Bear Island** ⚓ by taking Hammocks Beach Road (State Rd. 1511) off Highway 24 in Swansboro to a passenger ferry. You can only reach this uninhabited barrier island, where the pristine beaches are strewn with little more than snow-white sand dollars and the delicate tracings of bird feet, by private boat or by seasonal ferry—and visitation is limited to how many people can cross on the ferry, so you really do feel as if the island is your own. Bear Island is the island portion of **Hammocks Beach State Park,** 1572 Hammocks Beach Rd. (park office: © 910/326-4881; www.ils.unc.edu/parkproject/visit/habe/home.html), a 3-mile-long barrier island dominated by high sand dunes, a maritime forest, and unspoiled beach. Primitive camping is allowed here year-round—except for 3 nights each month during the summer nesting season of endangered loggerhead sea turtles, which come here under the full moon to lay their eggs. The ferry leaves from the Hammocks Beach Road park entrance on the hour on Monday and Tuesday, Memorial Day to Labor Day, and on the half-hour Wednesday to Sunday. Fees are adults $5, seniors and children 6 to 12 $3, and children under 5 free. Call to confirm ferry hours.

from Cape Carteret, is a diminutive charmer, with shops in renovated centuries-old structures and shrimp boats along the harbor. The **Mullet Festival,** held here every fall, draws huge crowds from around the Southeast.

Almost due west of Swansboro, **Jacksonville** sits inland, but only a 20-minute drive from choice beaches. The focal point of the city is the adjacent New River Marine Base, on Highway 24, universally known as **Camp Lejeune** (© **910/451-7433;** www.lejune.usmc.mil/mcb/index.asp). The 159,439-acre reservation is one of the world's most complete amphibious military training centers, and you can obtain a pass to drive through unrestricted parts of the grounds if you present your driver's license and car registration to personnel at the information center (next to the main gate on N.C. 24).

For a true North Carolina coastal seafood experience, drive south of Jacksonville to the little fishing village of **Sneads Ferry,** which is loaded with eateries featuring right-off-the-boat choices steamed, broiled, or fried to perfection. The town hosts the Sneads Ferry Shrimp Festival the second weekend in August. For more information on the Jacksonville area, call the **Greater Jacksonville/Onslow Chamber of Commerce,** 1099 Gum Branch Rd., P.O. Box 765, Jacksonville, NC 28540 (© **910/347-3141;** www.jacksonvilleonline.org). Hours are Monday to Friday 9am to 5pm.

### WHERE TO DINE NEAR SWANSBORO

**The T & W Oyster Bar** SEAFOOD/STEAKS   Looking like a country roadhouse from the outside, this restaurant has an interior with five dining rooms, two of which have fireplaces. There is a simplicity here bordering on sophistication, and if the place could be transported back to the 1950s, the food would be just the same as it is now. The oysters arrive in the fall—your choice, raw or steamed, plucked from the shells as fast as you can eat them—but the year-round seafood selections are good and fresh, including several versions of crabs, both deviled and in cakes. The classic dish for Carolina sea captains is Mr. T's baked flounder with "taters and onions." Sandwiches are also sold.

2382 Hwy. 58, Swansboro. © 252/393-8838. Main courses $8–$17. MC, V. Mon–Sat 5–9pm; Sun noon–9pm.

## 4 New Bern ⊛

87 miles NE of Wilmington

Less than 50 miles inland, on U.S. 70 and U.S. 17, New Bern is the state's oldest town, lying between the Neuse and Trent rivers, where swimming, boating, and both fresh- and saltwater fishing are favorite pastimes. Its historic district merits a visit—it's filled with Georgian, Victorian, and classical-Revival architecture.

### ESSENTIALS

**GETTING THERE**   From Beaufort, take U.S. 70 West to Morehead City, and continue along the same western route straight into New Bern. From Wilmington, head north on U.S. 17 through Jacksonville and directly into New Bern. From Raleigh, go east along U.S. 70 to New Bern.

The recently expanded **Craven Regional Airport,** 1501 Airport Rd., 2 miles outside New Bern (© **252/638-8591;** www.newbernairport.com), is served by **US Airways** (© **800/428-4322**), with connections from major cities in North Carolina. A taxi from the **Cherry Cab Co.** (© **252/447-3101**) will take passengers into the city. A taxi to the center of New Bern from the airport costs approximately $9.

**VISITOR INFORMATION**   The **Craven County Convention and Visitors Bureau,** located at 203 S. Front St. (© **252/637-9400;** www.visitnewbern.com), is open Monday to Friday from 8am to 5pm, on Saturday from 10am to 4pm (8am–5pm in winter), and on Sunday and holidays from 10am to 2pm (10am–4pm in winter). The **New Bern Historical Society,** at 510 Pollack St. (© **252/638-8558;** www.pamlico-nc.com/historicnewbern), is located in the historic 1790 Attmore-Oliver House, which exhibits 18th- and 19th-century furniture and artifacts. Hours are Tuesday through Saturday 1 to 4:30pm, year-round.

**SPECIAL EVENTS**   In the last week of March or first week of April, when the azaleas and dogwoods burst into bloom, New Bern sponsors a **Spring Historic Homes & Gardens Tour.** About 10 historic homes in town are open to the public, and tours also feature churches. Tickets cost $15 to $18 per person. For information, call the Preservation Foundation (© **252/633-6448**) or the New Bern Historical Society (see above).

## EXPLORING THE AREA

For fresh air, New Berners head for **Croatan National Forest** ☆ (© **252/ 638-5628**), southwest of town via U.S. 17 or U.S. 70 East. This unique coastal forest covers 161,000 acres and is riddled with waterways and estuaries. It's the alligator's northernmost habitat. Many insect-eating plants are here, including the Venus' flytrap. Look for it on the *pocosins,* the Native American word for "swamp on a hill." Activities include boating, fishing on the Neuse River, deer hunting, and camping.

In town, more than 180 18th- and 19th-century structures are listed in the National Register of Historic Places. Among the highlights are the following:

**Tryon Palace Historic Sites & Gardens** ☆   This 19-room museum, built from 1767 to 1770 as both the state capitol and the residence of the royal governor, has been authentically restored. Walking through the elegant rooms, it's easy to see why this mansion was once called the most beautiful in America. The main building burned in 1798 and lay in ruins until the restoration from 1952 to 1959. The handsome grounds and gardens surrounding Tyron Palace are designed in 18th-century style.

Two other landmarks in the 13-acre Tryon Palace complex are the **John Wright Stanly House** (1780), a late-Georgian-style mansion with town-house gardens; and the **Dixon-Stevenson House** (1805), noted for its rare Federal antiques. Crafts shows and historical dramas are mounted, and seasonal guided tours are available.

610 Pollock St. © **800/767-1560** or 252/514-4900. www.tryonpalace.org. Combination ticket $15 adults, $6 children (preschool children free with adult). Guided tours Mon–Sat 9am–5pm; Sun 1–5pm. Closed New Year's Day, Thanksgiving, and Dec 24–26.

**New Bern Firemen's Museum**   The original firefighting equipment of New Bern, dating back to the early 19th century, is on display, including an 1884 horse-drawn steamer and leather fire helmets. There's also a Civil War display case.

408 Hancock St. © **252/636-4087.** Admission $5 adults, $2.50 children. Mon–Sat 10am–4pm.

## SHOPPING

**The Birthplace of Pepsi-Cola Store**   The antique storefront that contains this place once functioned as Caleb Bradham's Pharmacy, the site where the entrepreneur invented the formula for Pepsi-Cola in 1898, 13 years after the development of the original formula for Coca-Cola. Today, the site functions as a hybrid store/museum, dispensing nostalgia along with 8-ounce glasses of Pepsi from a replica of an old-time soda fountain for 64¢ each. Also on display are Frisbees and commemorative T-shirts, each lauding Pepsi and/or its claim on the American soul, in one way or another. Subsidized by the Pepsi-Cola Bottling Company of New Bern, serving several counties of eastern North Carolina, the site is open Monday to Saturday, 10am to 6pm. 256 Middle St. (corner of Pollack St.). © 252/636-5898. www.pepsistore.com.

## WHERE TO STAY

**Aerie Inn Bed & Breakfast** ⋆    A block east of Tryon Palace, within walking distance of several restaurants, this gracious inn is among the top two or three in town. It was fully restored and redecorated in 1985. Built in 1882, it has only two floors. Inside, the rooms are furnished with antiques or reproductions from the 1880s and 1890s. All have private bathrooms and are nicely maintained with tub/shower combinations. Breakfasts are country-style, and afternoon refreshments, served in the tearoom, have become a local tradition.

509 Pollock St., New Bern, NC 28562. © 800/849-5553 or 252/636-5553. Fax 252/514-2157. www.aerie inn.com. 7 units. $109–$139 double. Rates include full breakfast and evening wine and hors d'oeuvres. Additional person $20 extra. AE, DISC, MC, V. **Amenities:** Breakfast room; lounge; nonsmoking rooms. *In room:* A/C, TV, dataport, hair dryer, iron/ironing board.

**Harmony House Inn** ⋆    Close to the Aerie—and a worthy competitor in every way—this Greek Revival house from 1850 receives guests on two floors in the historic district. The furnishings are contemporary, however, not antiques, and the attractive, well-maintained accommodations have king-size, queen-size, or twin beds. All units have bathrooms with tub/shower combinations. The owner displays her own needlepoint and artwork throughout the house. Guests quickly gravitate to their favorite rockers on the front porch. In the evening, wine is served. The house maintains a two-room suite, which is ideal for families and small traveling groups, consisting of two bedrooms and a living room with a sleeper sofa. In addition, the inn has two other Jacuzzi suites, ideal for honeymoons, anniversaries, or any other romantic getaway.

215 Pollock St., New Bern, NC 28560. © 800/636-3113 or 252/636-3810. www.harmonyhouseinn.com. 10 units. $100–$119 double; $150–$160 suite. Rates include full breakfast. Additional person $20 extra. DISC, MC, V. **Amenities:** Breakfast room; lounge; nonsmoking rooms. *In room:* A/C, TV, dataport.

**Meadows Inn B&B**    On the same street as the Aerie and Harmony House, the 1848 Meadows Inn is almost comparable in rating and ambience. This Greek Revival–style home is furnished with antiques and period reproductions. All units contain well-kept bathrooms with tub/shower combinations. Several restaurants are within walking distance.

212 Pollock St., New Bern, NC 28560. © 877/551-1776 or 252/634-1776. Fax 252/634-1776. www.meadows inn-nc.com. 8 units. $110–$120 double; $160 suite. Rates include full breakfast. Additional person $20 extra. Children 6 and under stay free in parent's room at discretion of management. AE, MC, V. **Amenities:** Breakfast room; lounge; nonsmoking rooms. *In room:* A/C, TV, hair dryer.

## WHERE TO DINE

**Captain Ratty's** AMERICAN/LOW COUNTRY    One of New Bern's most popular restaurants occupies a brick structure (ca. 1897) that functioned throughout most local residents' memory as a pharmacy. Its owners, who know virtually everyone in town, define the place as a tavern in the Carolinas style, and print a calendar of events advertising the evenings when oysters, for example, will sell for only 50¢ each. Live music is presented every Thursday, Friday, and

Saturday from 7 to 10pm. The menu includes such dishes as platters of king crab legs; New York–style strip steak (served with or without shrimp); mussels in a white-wine sauce; any of several other kinds of shellfish and fresh fish; and daily specials. It's hardly haute cuisine, but the food is fresh and crowd-pleasing.

202 Middle St. ℂ 252/633-2088. www.captainrattys.com. Reservations recommended. Sandwiches and salads $5.75–$8.95; main courses $17–$29. AE, MC, V. Mon–Thurs 11am–10pm; Fri–Sat 11am–11pm.

**The Chelsea: A Restaurant & Publick House** AMERICAN/FUSION Engaging and popular, this bar and bistro serves simple, well-prepared food that's offered in a brick-lined setting on wooden tables in a turn-of-the-20th-century pharmacy owned by the inventor of Pepsi-Cola, Caleb Bradham. Many customers like to linger at the bar, but for those interested in an actual meal, menu items include such dishes as Black Strap tenderloin of pork (with Dijon mustard and herbs); crab cakes; shrimp Sonoma; Thai-style red curried seafood; and potato-crusted salmon. The food here has more of a cutting edge and modern twist than that found at its nearby competitors. Among the sandwiches is a turkey/cranberry relish sandwich served on Italian flatbread.

335 Middle St. ℂ 252/637-5469. Reservations recommended for 5 or more. Lunch sandwiches and salads $5.95–$8.95; dinner main courses $12–$20. AE, DISC, MC, V. Mon–Thurs 11am–9pm; Fri–Sat 11am–10pm.

**Henderson House** ★★ CONTINENTAL    New Bern's leading restaurant has a devoted following. First, the setting is intriguing; this 1790 structure is listed on the National Register of Historic Places. It's all quite elegant, with crystal chandeliers, linen tablecloths and napkins, antiques, silver place settings, and lush draperies. But it's the food that keeps regulars coming back. First-rate ingredients are used in such dishes as shrimp amandine; roast duck with a zesty plum sauce; and crabmeat Norfolk, chock-full of crab. Guests enjoy full bar service, and appetizers and desserts are made fresh daily. No smoking.

216 Pollock St. ℂ 252/637-4784. Reservations recommended. Main courses $18–$28. MC, V. Tues–Sat 6–9pm. Closed major holidays.

## 5 Historic Bath: The State's Oldest Town ★★

10 miles E of Washington

This tiny historic hamlet on the Pamlico River is the oldest incorporated town in North Carolina. A well-known explorer and surveyor, John Lawson, laid out the original town back in 1706, with Bath's dozen or so settlers allocating a site for a marketplace, a courthouse, and a church, of course. Its most famous citizen was Blackbeard, who married and settled here for a "gentlemanly life," which he found so boring he abandoned it all, including his woman, to return to his life of piracy.

**GETTING THERE**    Bath is reached by heading north of New Bern (see above) on Route 17, until you come to the intersection with Route 264 going east. At the intersection with Route 92, continue east into Bath.

If you have the time, you can also get to Bath by taking the toll-free **Aurora/Bayview auto ferry** (www.ncferry.org) north on Route 306 over the Pamlico Sound leaving from the sleepy little town of Aurora, home to the gigantic PCS Phosphate Mine. Over the years, the phosphate mines have produced a rich trove of ancient marine fossils (such as giant prehistoric shark's teeth) from the time when this area was underwater. You can see the collection at the **Aurora Fossil Museum,** 400 Main St., Aurora, NC (ℂ 252/322-4238; www.aurora fossilmuseum.com; open Mon–Sat 9am–4:30pm; free admission).

Sailors can easily make a stopover in Bath; it's just 12 miles from the Intracoastal Waterway.

**VISITOR INFORMATION** For more information, stop at the **Historic Bath Visitor Center,** on 207 Carteret St. (© **252/923-3971;** www.beaufort-county. com/Bath/bath.html; open Apr 1–Oct 31 Mon–Sat 9am–5pm, Sun 1–5pm; Nov– Mar Tues–Sat 10am–4pm, Sun 1–4pm), and view an orientation film, get a street map, or sign up for a guided walking tour. Self-guided tours are also available.

From March 2005 to March 2006, the town will celebrate its **Tricentennial** (1705–2005) with ongoing celebrations, outdoor dramas, military reenactments, a gala ball, and a visit by the Archbishop of Canterbury. For a schedule of events, contact the **Historic Bath Tricentennial Celebration Committee** at © **252/923-3971** or go to www.historicbathnc.com.

## EXPLORING THE AREA

Armed with a map, set out on a self-guided tour to take in the major houses of historic interest. These include a town museum in the 1790 **Van Der Veer House,** right out the back door of the visitor center; the 1751 **Palmer-Marsh House,** reached along an oyster-shell walkway; and **Harding's Landing,** accessed by going across Main Street.

From Harding's Landing, head south on Main Street to the corner of Craven Street, where you come to **Glebe House.** Several notable citizens of Bath have occupied this building (ca. 1835), which can only be viewed from the outside.

Beside the Glebe House on Craven Street is Bath's grandest landmark, **St. Thomas Church,** built between 1734 and 1762. It's the oldest church in the state.

One more block along Main leads to the 1830 **Bonner House,** the best example of North Carolina coastal architecture in Bath. It's characterized by spacious porches in front and back. An early-20th-century general store, **Swindell's Store,** on Main Street, is still in operation.

A $1 fee is charged for admission to either the Palmer-Marsh House or the Bonner House (sold at the visitor center).

## WHERE TO STAY & DINE

If you fall in love with the picturesque nostalgia of Bath, as many visitors do, the town now has a B&B. **The Inn on Bath Creek,** 116 S. Main St. (© **252/923-9571;** www.innonbathcreek.com), looks as if it's been around a long time. But innkeepers Mark and Kae Penner-Howell, tired of finding an old house to restore, built a new one, albeit in the style of the older historic homes in town. Each guest room is tastefully and comfortably decorated, with its own private bathroom (with shower). All rooms are based on double occupancy, and prices include a full breakfast featuring fresh fruit. Rates are $90 a night. MasterCard, Visa, and Discover cards are accepted. You can putter around town on one of the B&B's bikes or take a sailboat onto the river from the town dock.

For eating (it's not called dining here), there's that old standby, the accurately named **Old Town Country Kitchen,** 436 Carteret St. (© **252/923-1840**). It serves up the best grub in town against a backdrop of seascapes, anchors on the wall, and handcrafted models of pirate ships. During the week, locals file in here for such Southern fare as fried pork chops and fresh collard greens. Fried shrimp is also a house specialty. On the weekend, seafood dominates the menu, including the house special: fresh fried oysters served with hush puppies. Main courses range from $6 to $14 (Tues–Sat 6am–8pm, Sun–Mon 6am–2pm; debit cards only).

# The Piedmont

**N**owhere in the South do old and new come together quite so dramatically as in North Carolina's Piedmont, which lies between the coastal plains and the mountains. The contrast is especially marked in cities such as Winston-Salem, where the mammoth tobacco industry is represented by R. J. Reynolds and where the Stroh Brewery produces millions of barrels of beer each year, while across town, the streets and buildings of Old Salem have been restored to reflect the life of the Moravians who planned the community in 1753.

The landscape here—red-clay hills, tobacco fields, and peach orchards—is as varied as the region's industry and agriculture.

The Piedmont is the home of the vaunted Research Triangle, a multidisciplinary scientific institute founded in 1958 by Duke University in Durham, the University of North Carolina in Chapel Hill, and North Carolina State University in Raleigh. The region boasts a wealth of other educational institutions, including Wake Forest University in Winston-Salem, and Shaw University in Raleigh, founded in 1865 and the oldest historically black university in the South.

The Piedmont is very much the New South, and its residents won't hesitate to brag a bit about the economic miracle that's transformed the area in the past 3 decades. They're especially proud of their big-time sports scene. (College basketball is practically a religion in these parts.) But the cities of the Piedmont haven't lost their manners, and a leisurely pace of life persists in the midst of all the growth and change. Travelers will see that streets lined with gorgeous homes and blooming dogwoods haven't been lost in the name of progress. And outside the cities, there's a lot waiting to be discovered, including some of the nation's greatest championship golf courses.

## 1 Raleigh ✦

143 miles NE of Charlotte

State government has been Raleigh's principal business since 1792, when it became North Carolina's capital. Just before the Civil War, the city was the setting of the fiery legislative debate that led to North Carolina's secession from the Union in 1861. Raleigh endured Union occupation by General Sherman in 1865, and during Reconstruction saw the west wing of its imposing Grecian Doric capitol building turned into a rowdy barroom by "carpetbagger" and "scalawag" legislators, its steps permanently nicked from whiskey barrels rolling in and out of the building.

Today, the 5-acre square fronting the capitol is the focal point for a cluster of state office buildings in the heart of the city. From it radiate wide boulevards and tree-shaded residential streets. Downtown Raleigh has been transformed by an attractive pedestrian mall where trees, fountains, and statuary create a shopping oasis. No fewer than six college campuses dot the city's streets, with wide lawns and impressive brick buildings. The oldest, St. Mary's College, was founded in 1842. The big name in town, though, is North Carolina State University, and cheering for the Wolfpack in basketball or football is more than just an idle pastime. New suburbs and gigantic shopping centers dominate the outskirts of Raleigh, characterized by nicely designed homes blending into a landscape that retains much of its original wooded character.

All this, plus the abundance of good accommodations, makes Raleigh a fine base from which to explore the Research Triangle area. Both Chapel Hill and Durham are within easy reach for day trips, and after a day of sightseeing, the capital city offers a good variety of entertainment options, from college bars to supper-club shows.

## ESSENTIALS

**GETTING THERE** U.S. 64 and U.S. 70 run east and west from Raleigh; U.S. 1 runs north and south, joining I-85, which runs northeast and is joined by I-40 to the west and I-95 to the east. U.S. 401 also runs northeast and southwest. The AAA is represented by the **Carolina Motor Club,** 2301 Blue Ridge Rd., Raleigh, NC 27607 (② **919/832-0543;** www.aaa.carolinas.com).

The Raleigh/Durham International Airport is about 15 miles west of Raleigh, just off I-40. Major airlines serving the airport from out-of-state destinations include **Air Tran** (② 800/825-8538; www.airtran.com), **American Airlines** (② 800/433-7300; www.aa.com), **Continental Airlines** (② 800/525-0280; www.continental.com), **Delta** (② 800/221-1212; www.delta.com), **Northwest Airlines** (② 800/225-2525; www.nwa.com), **United Airlines** (② 800/241-6522; www.ual.com), and **US Airways** (② 800/428-4322; www.usairways.com).

**Amtrak** (② **800/USA-RAIL;** www.amtrak.com) provides rail service to and from New York and Washington, D.C., to the north, and to and from Florida to the south, with one train daily from each direction.

**VISITOR INFORMATION** Contact the **Greater Raleigh Convention and Visitors Bureau,** 421 Fayetteville St. Mall, Suite 1505, Raleigh, NC 27601-1755 (② **800/849-8499** or 919/834-5900; www.raleighcvb.org). Hours are Monday to Friday 8:30am to 5pm. **Capital Area Visitor Center** (in the lobby of the North Carolina Museum of History), 5 E. Edenton St. (② **919/807-7950;** www.visitraleigh.com), provides information about the state-government complex, local attractions, and historic sites; bus-route brochures are available. The center is open Monday to Friday 8am to 5pm, Saturday 10am to 4pm, and Sunday 1 to 3pm.

**SPECIAL EVENTS** In mid-February, the **Home and Garden Show** draws serious gardeners from all over the South; call ② **919/831-6011** for details. In mid-October, the **North Carolina State Fair** (www.ncstatefair.com) also draws crowds from all over with its livestock competitions, culinary bake-offs, and cornpone charm. The fairgrounds are located 5 miles west of town on I-440 and then 1 mile west on N.C. 54. For exact dates, call ② **919/733-2145.** In early December, the city hosts an old-fashioned **Holiday Festival** at the North Carolina Museum of Art (② **919/839-6262;** www.ncartmuseum.org).

## EXPLORING THE CAPITOL & ENVIRONS

For the best possible tour of the capital city, make the **Capital Area Visitor Center** your first stop. The staff starts you off with an orientation film, arms you with brochures, and coordinates walking or driving tours. Most of the attractions listed in this section are within easy walking distance of the state capitol.

# The Research Triangle: Raleigh, Durham & Chapel Hill

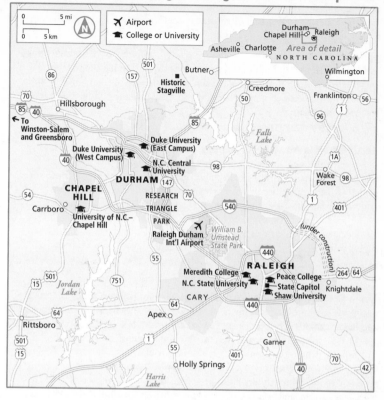

## The State Capitol ★

This stately Greek Revival structure (constructed 1833–40) is a National Historic Landmark. All state business was conducted here until 1888. The building now contains the offices of the governor and lieutenant governor, as well as restored legislative chambers. Beneath the awe-inspiring 97-foot copper dome is a duplicate of Antonio Canova's marble statue of George Washington dressed as a Roman general. The capitol takes about 30 to 45 minutes to tour. Reservations are necessary for guided tours. Call the capitol for additional information and times.

Capitol Sq. ℂ **919/733-4994**. www.ah.dcr.state.nc.us/sections/capitol. Free admission. Mon–Fri 8am–5pm; Sat 10am–4pm.

## North Carolina Museum of Natural Sciences ★ (Kids)

The state's oldest museums has found a bigger and better home, situated between the capitol and the legislature building. The museum's Exhibit Hall daily presents a variety of programs to the public, often featuring live animals. Exhibits focus on North Carolina's geology and geography, notably its plant and animal life. One of the biggest draws is "Willo," the world's only dinosaur with a fossilized heart. Among the big bones is *Acrocanthosaurus,* a spiny-lizard-type dinosaur, the only skeleton of its type in the world. The museum has one of America's greatest displays of whale skeletons as well. The Naturalist Center has a collection of specimens ranging from mammals to reptiles, fossils to minerals, and more. Kids take special delight in the Discovery Room, with its hands-on discovery boxes.

11 W. Jones St. ⓒ **919/733-7450**. www.naturalsciences.org. Free admission, but donations accepted. Extra charges for special exhibits. Mon–Sat 9am–5pm; Sun noon–5pm. Open until 9pm the 1st Fri of every month. Closed Thanksgiving, 2 days at Christmas, and New Year's Day.

**State Legislative Building**    Allow about 30 minutes to go through this striking contemporary building, designed by Edward Durrell Stone. But take longer if you happen to be here when the legislature is in session. You'll be able to watch the proceedings and perhaps even spot a young, post-millennium Jesse Helms in the making.

16 W. Jones St. ⓒ **919/733-7928**. Free admission. Mon–Fri 8am–5pm; Sat 9am–5pm; Sun 1–5pm.

**North Carolina Museum of History**    The state's long and colorful history comes alive through innovative exhibits and programs in this state-of-the-art facility. It's all here, beginning with the Roanoke Island colonists to the present, including the contributions to the state by women and African Americans. The state, which was initially reluctant to enter what it called "a rich man's war and a poor man's fight," lost more native sons in battle than any other state in the Confederacy. The folklife gallery showcases the state's cultural and crafts heritage, exhibiting music, pottery, baskets, and textiles.

5 E. Edenton St. ⓒ **919/715-0200**. http://ncmuseumofhistory.org. Free admission. Tues–Sat 9am–5pm; Sun noon–5pm.

**North Carolina Museum of Art** 🎯    This museum houses a major collection of European paintings, plus American, 20th-century, ancient, African, Oceanic, and Judaic exhibits. The permanent collection—with works by Raphael, Rubens, van Dyck, Monet, Homer, and Wyeth—is complemented by a program of 12 to 15 special exhibitions annually. A special feature of the museum is the Virginia Camp Smith 17th-century Flemish *Kunstkamer,* a re-creation of a Flemish style "art room" with exhibits illustrating both decorative and fine arts. There's wheelchair access, and you can plan to have lunch in the **Blue Ridge Museum Restaurant** (ⓒ **919/833-3548**), open Wednesday to Saturday 11:30am to 2pm and Sunday 10:30am to 2:30pm.

2110 Blue Ridge Rd. ⓒ **919/839-6262**. http://ncartmuseum.org. Free admission (a charge may apply for special exhibits). Wed–Sat 9am–5pm; Sun 10am–5pm.

## OUTDOOR PURSUITS

Raleigh's **parks** and recreational facilities have won awards. In all, there are 3,904 acres of parkland and 1,332 acres of water. A greenway system covers 1,297 acres, offering hiking and jogging trails that link many of Raleigh's 141 parks.

One of the major recreational centers is **Lake Wheeler,** 6404 Lake Wheeler Rd. (ⓒ **919/662-5704;** www.raleigh-nc.org/parks&rec/wheeler), comprising 60 acres of parkland and 600 acres of lake, 5 miles southwest of Raleigh. Activities include sailing, rowing, kayaking, canoeing, and fishing. In summer, open-air concerts are $5. Hours are daily sunrise to sunset.

**William B. Umstead State Park,** 8801 Glenwood Ave. (ⓒ **919/571-4170;** www.ils.unc.edu/parkproject/visit/wium/home.html), is actually two parks, including Crabtree and Reedy Creek, comprising a total acreage of 5,439. We prefer Crabtree; it has better facilities and a big lake where you can rent boats for $5 to $10 and go fishing ($20 deposit). It also has a visitor center and picnic tables. Biking trails riddle the park, as do hiking trails.

The best golf is at the **Cheviot Hills Golf Course,** 6 miles north on U.S. 1 at 7301 Capital Blvd. (ⓒ **919/876-9920**), an 18-hole championship golf course with Bermuda bent greens. Greens fees range from $16 to $25, and the course is open Monday to Friday 8am to dusk, on Saturday 7am to dusk, and on Sunday 8am to dusk. Cart rentals are $12 per person.

Raleigh also has about 24 miles of greenway for **bikers.** For trail maps, call the **Raleigh Parks and Recreation Center** (© **919/890-3285**).

The best **camping** is at **Raven Rock State Park,** 3009 Raven Rock Rd. at Lillington (© **910/893-4888;** www.ils.unc.edu/parkproject/visit/raro); and at **Falls Lake State Recreational Area,** 3304 Creedmoor Rd., 12 miles via N.C. 50 (© **919/676-1027;** www.ils.unc.edu/parkproject/visit/fala). Call for information, which varies seasonally.

Raleigh has at least 112 **tennis** courts in its city parks. For information about one near you, call © **919/872-4129.**

## SHOPPING

Raleigh, with its population of up-and-coming financiers, computer experts, and yuppies, is known for an elegant array of home decorating stores, many of them specializing in antiques. A dense cluster of antiques stores lies along Fairview Road in the suburban neighborhood known as "Five Points" because of its intersection of five different streets. One of the most appealing is **Regency Antiques and Fine Art Gallery,** 2006 Fairview Rd., Five Points (© **919/835-2646**), which focuses on mid-19th- to mid-20th-century American, English, and European antiques and paintings. A nearby competitor loaded with French and English antiques, many of a higher quality than those available from less upscale competitors, is **Acquisitions, Ltd.,** 2003 Fairview Rd. (© **919/755-1110**).

**Peché du Chocolat,** 305 S. Blount St. (© **919/754-1112;** www.peche chocolat.com), is the finest chocolate shop in Raleigh, a tastefully upscale, European-style venue for confections that derive from Belgium, Italy, France, Turkey, and Lebanon. Many of the chocolates are artfully wrapped, come in differing degrees of darkness, and are often deliciously studded with delicacies like hazelnuts, pistachios, and candied fruits.

## WHERE TO STAY
### EXPENSIVE

**Raleigh Marriott Crabtree Valley** ⋇    Located 10 minutes northwest of the city center and 7 miles from the airport, this is Raleigh's leading hotel. It lacks some of the charm of the Oakwood Inn (see below) but is professional in every way and caters to a large business clientele. The city's largest hotel, it rises six floors, offering well-furnished guest rooms and large bathrooms with tub/ shower combinations. The most luxurious and expensive rooms are on the concierge level.

4500 Marriott Dr. (U.S. 70 W. opposite the Crabtree Valley Mall), Raleigh, NC 27612. © **888/236-2427** or 919/781-7000. Fax 919/781-3059. www.marriott.com. 371 units. Sun–Thurs $169–$189 double, Fri–Sat $89–$109 double; $275–$600 suite. Children 17 and under stay free in parent's room. AE, DC, DISC, MC, V. Free parking. **Amenities:** Restaurant; bar; 2 pools (1 indoor, 1 outdoor); fitness center; Jacuzzi; business center; laundry service/dry cleaning; nonsmoking rooms; rooms for those w/limited mobility. *In room:* A/C, TV, dataport, coffeemaker, hair dryer, safe, iron/ironing board.

**Sheraton Capital Center Hotel Raleigh** ⋇    A 17-story redbrick skyscraper that factored prominently into an urban renewal of downtown Raleigh when it was built in 1982, this is the biggest, most visible, most consistently occupied, and most appealing large hotel in the city center. Guests have included celebrities from Al Gore to a gaggle of rock and rap stars. The uniformed staff here is polite and well-versed in the layout of Raleigh. The hotel has a coffee-shop-inspired restaurant within the glass-roofed atrium, a lobby level covered with either travertine marble or flagstones, soaring redbrick arches, and comfortable, conservatively contemporary midsize guest rooms. The hotel is directly connected, through a covered passageway, to the city's convention facilities.

421 S. Salisbury St., Raleigh, NC 27601. ℂ **800/325-3535** or 919/834-9900. Fax 919/833-1217. www.sheraton. com. 355 units. Sun–Thurs $155–$169, Fri–Sun $79–$139. $10 supplement for "concierge level" rooms. $250–$500 suite any day of the week. Parking $8. AE, DC, DISC, MC, V. **Amenities:** Restaurant; bar; cappuccino and espresso bar; health club and exercise room; indoor pool; room service (7am–11:30pm); babysitting; laundry service/dry cleaning; nonsmoking rooms; concierge level with deluxe amenities and accessories; rooms for those w/limited mobility. *In room:* A/C, TV, dataport, minibar.

## MODERATE

**The Oakwood Inn** ★★ *Finds*   Raleigh has no shortage of hotels, motor hotels, and motels, but it has almost no inns. The Oakwood fills the vacuum; it's an inn of charm and character. Built in 1871, the Victorian building lies in the historic district, and guests can stroll to attractions downtown. A wraparound porch evokes the best of Southern architecture in the 19th century. Leaded glass and mahogany and walnut furniture re-create a long-gone era, as do the well-kept bathrooms with showers and claw-foot tubs. The inn, listed on the National Register of Historic Places, serves the best breakfast in the area.

411 N. Bloodworth St., Raleigh, NC 27604. ℂ **800/267-9712** or 919/832-9712. Fax 919/836-9263. www. oakwoodinnbb.com. 6 units. $115–$185 double. Rates include full breakfast. AE, DC, DISC, MC, V. Free parking. **Amenities:** Breakfast room; nearby fitness center; lounge; nonsmoking rooms. *In room:* A/C, TV, dataport, hair dryer, fireplace.

## WHERE TO DINE
### EXPENSIVE

**Bloomsbury Bistro** ★ FRENCH/INTERNATIONAL   ]At Five Points, in the center of the city, chef John Toler offers a delightful cuisine that features a seasonal menu adjusted every 6 weeks to take advantage of what's fresh in the markets. For some, the decor evokes a country club, and the waitstaff is among the most helpful, polished, and, yes, friendliest in the Triangle. The selections include both old favorites and innovative new ones. "Look what they'd done to gazpacho!" one of our party exclaimed, and it was a compliment: The chef took a tried-and-true dish and served it chilled with a scoop of mild jalapeño-spiked lime sorbet, grilled tiger shrimp, and a fresh basil and kalamata oil. Another appetizer with a touch of exoticism is the pan-fried barbecued duck livers over a celery-root and Granny Smith–apple coleslaw with fried pecans and blue cheese dressing. For a main course, we found perfection in the grilled jumbo sea scallops glazed in hoisin sauce over a chilled salad of jasmine rice and wok-seared calamari in a spicy sweet-and-sour cashew sauce. Luscious desserts feature the likes of deep-dish crème brûlée topped with Grand Marnier–spiked strawberries Romanoff and served with a zesty biscotti.

509 W. Whitaker Mill Rd. ℂ **919/834-9011.** www.bloomsburybistro.com. Reservations recommended. Main courses $17–$26. AE, DC, MC, V. Mon–Sat 5:30–10pm.

**Enoteca Vin** ★ INTERNATIONAL   This popular spot has a hot young chef and sizzling press—it was prominently featured in *Food & Wine* magazine in October 2004. The most stylish wine restaurant in Raleigh occupies one of the Glenwood South district's least impressive buildings—a redbrick structure that once held Pine State Creamery. Inside an angular and minimalist dining room focused around display cases of food, the chef concocts a cuisine designed to bring out the flavors of the foods and wines featured, albeit with a European consciousness that has people thinking they've landed in Spain, France, or even a cosmopolitan corner of Denmark. The menu changes frequently but might include red curry and coconut soup with fresh cilantro and black tiger shrimp; porcini-roasted rib roast of pork with morel mushrooms, polenta, and asparagus; and a sophisticated array of European cheeses, selling for around $14 for a well-selected platter. Desserts might include hot chocolate cake with roasted banana ice cream, accompanied by any of several kinds of unusual herbal teas, including Egyptian chamomile.

410 Glenwood Ave. (℃) **919/834-3070.** www.enotecavin.com. Reservations recommended. Main courses $24–$30. AE, MC, V. Tues–Sat 5:30–10:30pm; Sun 11am–2:30pm and 5:30–10:30pm. Late-night menu Fri–Sat only, 11pm–1am.

## Second Empire Restaurant and Tavern ★ INTERNATIONAL   The historically important landmark that contains these two restaurants is one of the most visible antique houses in downtown Raleigh. Originally built in 1879 in the French-inspired Second Empire style, it devotes most of its architectural glamour to the restaurant, and a somewhat folksier and less formal venue to its (less expensive) tavern. Frankly, we feel a bit more comfortable in the tavern (the restaurant, at its worst, can be a wee bit pompous). Among the restaurant's well-prepared menu items are a warm polenta and grilled pork tenderloin salad; steamed local clams studded with chunks of spicy sausage; grilled Alaska salmon; and grilled strip loin of Angus beef. The food in the tavern is less expensive and less fussed-over, and includes fried calamari; "pulled chicken" pasta; meatloaf with curry-flavored mashed potatoes; and seafood paella.

330 Hillsborough St. (℃) **919/829-3663.** www.second-empire.com. Reservations recommended. Main courses in restaurant $25–$35; main courses in tavern $10–$18. AE, DC, MC, V. Restaurant Mon–Sat 5:30–9:30pm; tavern Mon–Sat 4:30–10pm.

## Sullivan's Steakhouse ★ STEAKS   This is the best, most posh, and most upscale steakhouse in Raleigh—the kind of classy, hard-drinking, and indulgent grill room where Sinatra and his Rat Pack might have felt very much at home. Opulent and full of machismo, with an open-to-view kitchen and lots of exposed brick, it emulates a Chicago-style steakhouse with a speakeasy aura. A resident butcher trims the steaks artfully, and a bar area (which some guests enjoy even more than the restaurant) near the entrance is for whiling away time before your table is ready. Here live jazz begins every evening at 5:30pm. Past guests have included Senator John Edwards as well as local sports coaches and players. Steaks come in two-fisted portions of rib-eye, filet, porterhouse, and New York strip. Lamb, veal, chicken, and a selection of fish (ahi tuna steak and tequila-and-lime-flavored shrimp) are also available.

414 Glenwood Ave. (℃) **919/833-2888.** Reservations recommended. Main courses $23–$29. AE, DC, MC, V. Mon–Sat 5:30–11pm; Sun 5–10pm.

## MODERATE

**The Duck & Dumpling** ASIAN   Our favorite Asian restaurant in Raleigh has the kind of glossy, minimalist decor that evokes an upscale neighborhood in Hong Kong—a cocoon of burnished teak and cherrywood. Reasonably priced and charmingly unpretentious, it has a large and accommodating bar near its entrance and a sophisticated array of martinis, some made with sake. The chef is likely to pay a personal visit to your table during the course of your meal, asking how, for example, you like the deep-fried pork-and-shrimp dumplings, the spring rolls, the steamed filet of sea bass with ginger, the lamb chops cooked with curried coconut milk, or the "lion's head" meatball stuffed with scallops and served in a clay pot with baby bok choy.

Moore Sq., 222 Blount St. ⓒ 919/838-0085. Reservations recommended. Main courses $7.95–$12 lunch, $17–$21 dinner. AE, DC, MC, V. Mon–Fri 11:30am–2:30pm; Tues–Thurs 5–10pm; Fri–Sat 5–11pm.

**Fins Restaurant** ⭐ *Finds* CALIFORNIA/ASIAN    The sublime cuisine served at this sophisticated spot in North Raleigh has been called "Cal Asian." The setting is chic, with tables placed in the main dining area or else on raised wooden platforms. An attractive crowd can be spotted at the granite-topped bar, which is separated from the main dining tables by a glass aquarium and panels of frosted glass.

The chefs' technique is impeccably sharp and precise. Recent examples of their prowess in the kitchen include Alaskan king crab cake with a light avocado crust or a pan-seared foie gras served with an almost overripe mango, a lush offering. It was a joy to devour the crisp snapper prepared with a tangy glaze and served with a sauce of roasted cashews. Duck breast is succulently braised with honey and flavored with star anise, and halibut is tantalizingly served like a spring roll with an apricot-flavored mustard glaze. The chef's dessert specialty is a trio of crème brûlées in different flavors, each served in a sake cup.

7713 Lead Mine Rd., State 39. ⓒ 919/847-4119. Reservations recommended. Main courses $18–$26. AE, DISC, MC, V. Mon–Sat 5:45–9:30pm.

**Margaux's** ⭐ INTERNATIONAL    Its strip-mall setting belies the serene and elegant enclave inside. A big aquarium looms in the background, and wooden dividers break up the space and ensure privacy. On an upper level, the bartender makes the best martinis in the capital. Seafood and steak are the specialties, but the chefs roam the globe for inspiration and are particularly strong in Pacific Rim culinary influences. A special feature is the live music presented on Friday.

On our most recent visit, our party plowed through the menu in a quest for new taste sensations, and we weren't disappointed. Quite the contrary. We enjoyed such delights as Shanghai pork wontons with Napa slaw and a sesame hoisin drizzle; crab nachos with white cheddar cheese guacamole and tomato cream; and corn-fried oysters with a creamy bacon tartar sauce. Carolina cookery isn't ignored either: Try the chopped pork on a buttermilk pancake with a tomato

---

### Where Highbrow Meets Biscuits & Grits

Raleigh has its share of posh cosmopolitan dining spots, but a defiantly down-home restaurant in the City Market is still packing 'em in. **Big Ed's City Market Restaurant,** 229 Wolfe St. (ⓒ **919/836-9909**), remains stubbornly old-fashioned despite the encroaching gentrification that surrounds it. Its allegiance to old-time country tradition has endeared it to hundreds of local residents, who crowd in every day for much more than just breakfast and lunch: Some social commentators have likened this place to a deep cultural immersion into Hillbilly Chic. Breakfast platters cost $4 to $7.50 each, and come with grits and red-eyed peas flavored with ham hocks. Don't even think of showing up here on a Sunday, or after 2pm. The folksy-looking dining room evokes a cross between a church bazaar and a grange, all of it layered with nostalgic mementos from the rural South of old. It's open Monday to Friday 7am to 2pm, and Saturday 7am till noon. No credit cards are accepted.

barbecue sauce. There's even a Tuscan-roasted suckling pig with grilled vegetables au jus.

8111 Creedmoor Rd. in Brennan Station. (© **919/846-9846.** www.margauxsrestaurant.com. Main courses $17–$20. AE, DISC, MC, V. Mon–Wed 5:30–10pm; Thurs–Fri 11:30am–1:30pm and 5:30–10pm; Sat 5:30–10pm; Sun 5–9pm.

**Mo's Diner** SOUTHERN    The owners of this popular restaurant are known for their sense of humor and good food. Despite a location on an uninspired street corner in downtown Raleigh, in a blue-sided cottage adjacent to the homeless shelter, it's one of the most sought-after dining spots in town. You'll eat behind lace curtains in an appealingly cluttered warren of small, parlorlike rooms that evoke the home of someone's genteel Southern grandmother. Menu items change with the inspiration of the chef, but might include baked oysters with fresh spinach and bacon-flavored hollandaise; sautéed chicken livers with Madeira sauce; grilled pork tenderloin with caramelized onions and balsamic vinegar; and seared tenderloin of beef with mashed potatoes and port-wine sauce.

306 E. Hargett St. (© **919/856-0980.** Reservations recommended. Main courses $13–$25. AE, DISC, MC, V. Tues–Sat 5:30–10pm.

## INEXPENSIVE

**Carolina Ale House** AMERICAN    This is both a munch-down eatery and a place to occupy your late nights. The design of this good-time bar is a sort of hybrid, the marriage of an Alaskan timber baron's mansion and a Victorian sawmill—sprawling, high-ceilinged, beer-stained, and woodsy. Expect a state of creative cacophony that gets louder as the evening progresses, thanks to about 25 TV screens (some of them jumbo-size). Draft beer costs $2 to $4.25 per mug. Monday features enormous platters of shrimp for around $10 per platter, and the rest of the week the culinary norm involves quesadillas, sandwiches, burgers, pastas, salads, grilled steaks, and seafood.

4512 Falls of Neuse Rd. (© **919/431-0001.** Reservations not necessary. Sandwiches, burgers, salads, pastas, and platters $6.50–$14. AE, DC, MC, V. Daily 11am–2am.

**Clyde Cooper's Barbecue** ⊛ BARBECUE    Since 1938, this old-timer has been *the* place in Raleigh for barbecue. Even if you think you prefer the Texas stuff, Cooper's will convert you. Prices are reasonable, and portions are generous. The chef slow-cooks only top-grade pork shoulders until they're so tender they practically melt. They're then mixed with a zesty barbecue sauce good enough to be bottled. For dessert, try the super-moist carrot cake.

109 E. Davie St. (1 block east of the mall). (© **919/832-7614.** Reservations not accepted. Dinner $4.25–$8. No credit cards. Mon–Sat 10am–6pm.

**NoFo** INTERNATIONAL    When this likable restaurant and its crowded-with-novelties gift emporium opened here, in what was originally conceived in the 1950s as a member of the Piggly-Wiggly grocery store chain, a team of designers added decorative touches such as a spectacular glass chandelier from Murano. Menu items are savory, flavorful, and popular, including shrimp and grits; Thai-style chicken wraps; shrimp-studded BLT sandwiches; grilled chicken salads; and a nightly blue plate special that, on the night of our visit, included sautéed chicken breasts with country-ham gravy. Come here for a sense of fun and whimsy and artfully offhanded cuisine.

2014 Fairview Rd., Five Points. (© **919/821-1240.** Reservations recommended only at dinner, Fri–Sat. Breakfast and brunch platters, and lunch sandwiches and salads $6.50–$8.50; dinner main courses $9.75–$14. AE, DC, MC, V. Mon–Fri 8am–9pm; Sat–Sun 10am–10pm.

## The Most Historic Hot Dogs in North Carolina

The most famous hot dogs in Carolina are dispensed from one of the state's smallest storefronts, and if you weren't seeking it out, you might simply pass it by. The **Roast Grill** was established in 1940 by members of the Salikis family, who had just arrived in Raleigh as new immigrants from Greece. During its tenure at this address, the Roast Grill's hot dogs have been sampled by every politician in North Carolina, including the formidable right-winger Jesse Helms, whose picture and written thank-you letter is one of several such pieces of nostalgia decorating the grill walls. Today, the likable owner is George Poniros, grandson of the founders who, like his forebears, imports his hot dogs from Michigan, serves them on thin sheets of waxed paper, and outlaws ketchup as antithetical to the proper flavor of the hot dog. (Chili, mustard, and cheese sauce are still well-accepted garnishes, however.) Other than hot dogs, which cost $1.75 each, no other food items are served, with the exception of desserts, priced at $1.25 to $2.50 each. The joint contains only two or three tiny tables for seating, plus a half-dozen seats at the luncheonette-style countertop. The Roast Grill—Hot Weiners is located at 7 S. West St., Raleigh (© **919/832-8292**; www.roastgrill.com). It's open Monday to Saturday 11am to 4pm and accepts cash only.

## RALEIGH AFTER DARK

The elegantly renovated **Memorial Auditorium,** 1 E. South St. (© **919/831-6011**), is the home of the North Carolina Symphony Orchestra and the North Carolina Theatre. The orchestra gives around 50 performances annually in Raleigh; Gerhardt Zimmermann is music director and conductor. Critics have hailed the North Carolina Theatre as "the best it gets this side of Broadway." It specializes in large-scale Broadway musicals such as *Hello, Dolly!* under the direction of the artistic director, Tony-nominated actor/director Terrence V. Mann. This is the state's only resident professional musical theater. The box office is open Monday to Friday 10am to 5pm.

**Berkeley Cafe**   This is a blues bar with a back deck. In addition to blues, you're likely to hear everything from folk rock to R&B. Open Wednesday to Saturday from 8pm to 2am, and for lunch Tuesday to Friday from 11am to 3pm. 217 W. Martin St. © **919/821-0777.** Cover varies, depending on the band.

**Flex**   Set within a dank and somewhat claustrophobic cellar, and painted mostly black, this is the most visible and popular gay bar in Raleigh. Many of its patrons drive for miles from the rural hamlets throughout the Piedmont for access, especially on Friday and Saturday nights. Beginning at midnight every Thursday, there's a "Trailer Park Prize Night" where all of the *artistes* are in drag, and where many members of the crowd are nubile young women, presumably fed up with their own heterosexual mating games, and who scream and giggle appropriately. Thursday to Sunday, the club charges a cover of between $2 and $4 per person, depending on the venue. Open Monday to Saturday 5pm to 2:30am and Sunday 2pm to 2am. 2 S. West St. © **919/832-8855.**

**The Pour House**   This is perhaps the most popular bar in the Triangle area. Set on two different levels, it offers live music and pool games. Entertainment might be a jam band, a group of local musicians, or a popular touring act. Bartenders offer 30 quality draft beers, with pints ranging in price from $3.50 to

$4.25. Each band decides what to charge at the door. The house doesn't add to the cover, and the musicians get all the money. Where there is a cover, it's about $5. *Tip:* The bouncer doesn't get here until around 10pm; so go early and get in free. Open Thursday to Saturday 5pm to 2am, and Sunday to Wednesday 8pm to 2am. 224 S. Blount St. ℂ **919/821-1120.**

**Rí Rá**    Designers for this pub scoured Ireland for a quintet of 19th- or early-20th-century bars, which they disassembled and laboriously reassembled within four separate areas of Rí Rá. (Its name, incidentally, translates from the Gaelic as "King of Good Times.") You'll find yourself in either a replica of an Irish cottage in County Kerry, a shop bar (one of the oldest known forms of bars in Ireland, combining sales of hardware with alcohol), or at least three other wood-paneled hideaways whose quirky eccentricities evoke James Joyce, the Irish rebellion, and the great potato famine. The pub-grub-style menu includes Irish potato cakes and Irish potato and leek soup. Open Monday to Saturday 11:30am to 10pm, with the bar remaining open from 11:30am to 2am. On Sunday, hours are 11:30am to 8pm, with the bar closing at midnight. 126 N. West St. ℂ **919/833-5555.**

## 2 Durham ✪

23 miles W of Raleigh

In the late 1860s, Washington Duke left the Confederate army and walked 137 miles back to his farm in Durham, where he took up life again as a tobacco farmer. That first year, he started grinding and packaging the crop to sell in small packets. In 1880, he decided that there was a future in cigarettes—then a new idea—and, along with his three sons, set to work to manufacture them on a small scale. By 1890, the family had formed the American Tobacco Company, and a legendary American manufacturing empire was under way.

Durham, a small village when Duke returned, blossomed into an industrial city, taking its commercial life from the "golden weed." And it still does. From September until the end of December, tobacco warehouses ring with the chants of auctioneers moving from one batch of the cured tobacco to the next, followed by buyers who indicate their bids with nods or hand signals.

Even Duke University, the cultural heart of Durham, owes its life's breath to tobacco. Duke was quiet little Trinity College until national and international prominence came with a Duke family endowment of $40 million in 1924. Along with a change in name, the university gained a new West Campus, complete with massive Gothic structures of stone, flagstone walks, and box hedges. Its medical center is one of the most highly respected in the world.

## ESSENTIALS

**GETTING THERE**    Durham is reached from the east via U.S. 70 and I-40 to N.C. 147, from the north via I-85, from the west via I-40/85 to I-85, and from the south via U.S. 15/501 joining I-40 to N.C. 147. The AAA office in Durham is the **Carolina Motor Club,** 3909 University Dr., Durham, NC 27717 (ℂ **919/489-3306**).

For service to Raleigh/Durham International Airport, see "Essentials," under "Raleigh," earlier in this chapter. **Amtrak** (ℂ **800/USA-RAIL;** www.amtrak.com) has a station on Pettegrew Street (ℂ **919/872-7245**).

**VISITOR INFORMATION**    Contact the **Durham Convention & Visitor Bureau,** 101 E. Morgan St., Durham, NC 27701 (ℂ **800/446-8604** or 919/687-0288; www.durham-nc.com), which can supply local bus-route information.

**SPECIAL EVENTS** Beginning in mid-June and lasting for the first 3 weeks in July, the **American Dance Festival** showcases modern dance on the campus of Duke University. Sometimes as many as 17 dance companies participate, and both national and international works have premiered. For information and tickets, call © **919/684-4444** or go to www.americandancefestival.org.

## EXPLORING THE TOWN & UNIVERSITY

**Duke Homestead State Historic Site** ★ The Duke homestead, where Washington Duke opened his first tobacco factory in a rickety one-room barn, is today a National Historic Landmark. As a Confederate soldier, Duke learned about the Union soldiers' love of Bright Leaf tobacco, and he returned home to begin the humble enterprise that would one day establish North Carolina as the heart of a worldwide tobacco empire. The homestead has been called a "living museum of tobacco history," and the early farming techniques and manufacturing processes used in the production of tobacco are demonstrated. (Don't mention cancer around here.) A color film, *Carolina Bright,* serves as an orientation to the site.

2828 Duke Homestead Rd. © 919/477-5498. www.ah.dcr.state.nc.us/sections/hs/duke/duke.htm. Free admission. Tues–Sat 10am–4pm. Hours may vary. Take the Guess Rd. exit 175 from I-85 and drive ½ mile north.

**Museum of Life and Science** *(Kids)* This museum is especially designed for children, but no matter what your age, you'll love the interactive, high-tech exhibits on the human body, weather, geology, and aerospace. One exhibit displays the Apollo 15 lunar landing module, complete with a sample moon rock. Hands-on exhibits are in the Science Arcade and the Scientific Discovery Room. The 70-acre site also holds a farmyard, Loblolly Park, and a mile-long narrow-gauge railroad charging $2 for a ride.

433 Murray Ave. © 919/220-5429. www.ncmls.org. Admission $9 adults, $8 seniors, $6 children 3–12. Labor Day to Memorial Day Mon–Sat 10am–5pm, Sun noon–5pm. Head north of I-85 off Duke St.

## DUKE UNIVERSITY

The campuses of Duke University (© **919/684-8111;** www.duke.edu) cover more than 1,000 acres on the west side of the city. The **East Campus,** which was the old Trinity College, features Georgian architecture, and its redbrick and limestone buildings border a half-mile-long grassy mall. The East Campus has a certain charm, but it's the **West Campus** (located a short drive away on winding, wooded Campus Dr.) that really steals the show. Its Gothic-style buildings and beautifully landscaped grounds are nothing short of breathtaking.

The highlight of this showplace is the **Duke Chapel** ★ (© **919/684-2572**), reminiscent of England's Canterbury Cathedral. The bell tower of the majestic cruciform chapel rises 210 feet and houses a 50-bell carillon that rings out at the end of each workday and on Sunday. A half-million-dollar Flentrop organ with more than 5,000 pipes (said to be one of the finest in the Western Hemisphere) is in a special oak gallery, its case 40 feet high. Renowned organists perform public recitals on the first Sunday of each month. The long nave, with its ornate screen and carved-oak choir stalls, is lighted in soft shades of red, blue, green, and yellow from 77 stained-glass windows. Visiting hours are 8am to 5pm Monday to Saturday, and there are interdenominational services every Sunday at 11am.

A visit to the West Campus would not be complete without a peek at **Cameron Indoor Stadium,** since 1935 the home of the Duke Blue Devils basketball team. It's an elegant, intimate place in which to scream your lungs out; indeed, the university's rabid fans take pride in its stature as one of the smallest indoor arenas in the nation. Also on the West Campus is the **Duke University Medical Center,** which has gained worldwide fame for its extensive treatment facilities and varied research programs.

To arrange special **guided tours** of the campus and find out more about Duke, call the Admissions Office (© **919/684-3214**) Monday to Friday 9am to 5pm and Saturday 9am to 1pm. We recommend a visit to the **Sarah P. Duke Gardens,** 55 lovely acres on the West Campus that draw more than 200,000 visitors each year. In a valley bordered by a pine forest, the gardens feature a lily pond, stone terraces, a rose garden, a native-plant garden, an Asiatic arboretum, a wisteria-draped pergola, and colorful seasonal plantings. The gardens are open daily from 8am until dark, and admission is free. Free tours of the gardens are available daily from 8am to dusk, and special private tours can be arranged through the Duke Gardens office (© **919/684-3698;** www.hr.duke.edu/dukegardens/dukegardens.html). Private tours last 1½ hours, and the group rate for 10 or fewer people is $50. These tours must be booked 2 weeks in advance.

## WHERE TO STAY

Remember that hotel rates go up during Duke University's graduation ceremonies and for major sporting events.

**Arrowhead Inn** ★★   This inn (ca. 1775) is one of the most highly honored inns in the area, acknowledged by such publications as *USA Today, Southern Living,* and *Food & Wine.* Your hosts, Gloria and Phil Teber, strive to continue the excellence that they have established at this inn. There's a choice of beautifully furnished rooms furnished with king-, queen-, or twin-size beds. All units have bathrooms with tub/shower combinations (five have whirlpools), and seven rooms contain fireplaces. The log cabin is complete with a sleeping loft, sitting

### Field of Dreams

It's true that the real name of the game in these parts is basketball—people take their hoops mighty seriously around here. But thousands of locals and tourists continue to fill the stands each summer as the **Durham Bulls** play a full season in the Class A Carolina League as an affiliate of the Atlanta Braves. The Bulls shot to fame on the shoulders of Kevin Costner catching for hotshot rookie pitcher Tim Robbins in the 1988 flick *Bull Durham.* But if you're in town for a game, don't expect to see the wonderful old-time ballpark where the film was actually shot. In 1995, the Bulls abandoned the old ballpark for snazzy new digs on Magnum Street, designed by the same architects who conceived Camden Yards in Baltimore. By the way, the famous snorting bull in the movie was a mere prop that proved such a hit that it's now a Bulls fixture. And there really *was* a Crash Davis on the team in the 1940s. Other famous alums of the Bulls include Joe Morgan, Mark Lemke, Steve Avery, Ryan Klesko, David Justice, and Rusty Staub. The season runs early April through early September. Unfortunately, tickets are very hard to get. As far in advance as possible, contact the Durham Bulls, 409 Blackwell St., P.O. Box 507, Durham, NC 27702 (© **919/956-2855;** www.dbulls.com).

room with fireplace, and front porch with rocking chairs. The full breakfast is served from 8 to 9am in the dining room, in the "keeping room," or on the patio; the continental breakfast, left out for the earliest and latest risers, is available from 7:30 to 9:30am. There are hammocks outside for your leisure.

106 Mason Rd., Durham, NC 27712. © **800/528-2207** or 919/477-8430. Fax 919/471-9538. www.arrowhead inn.com. 9 units. $130–$275 double; $165–$225 suite; $275 2-room log cabin. Rates include full or continental breakfast. AE, DC, DISC, MC, V. **Amenities:** Restaurant; limited room service; babysitting; laundry service/dry cleaning. *In room:* A/C, TV, dataport, hair dryer.

**Clarion Hotel at Research Triangle Park**   Built in 2002, this is the best and most comfortable of the many modern hotels that have been built in the past dozen or so years on the rural outskirts of Durham. Expect a modern, well-maintained building painted a shade of pale coral, rising from a rural, rather isolated spot that's convenient (if you have a car) to the businesses of the Research Triangle Park. Rooms are modern, well-maintained, and comfortable, and although the neighborhood has few, if any, real diversions, the many business travelers who check in find it restful and easy to get to.

4912 S. Miami Blvd., Durham, NC 27709. © **919/474-9800.** Fax 919/474-9803. www.clarionhotelrtp.com. 81 units. $109–$119 double. AE, DC, MC, V. From downtown Durham, drive south along the Durham Fwy. (aka 147 South) to Rte. I-40 E, get off at exit 281 (S. Miami Blvd.), and turn left after the exit ramp. **Amenities:** Restaurant; bar; fitness center; complimentary shuttle service to the RDU airport; laundry service/dry cleaning. *In room:* Dataport, fridge, coffeemaker, hair dryer, iron/ironing board, microwave.

**Washington Duke Inn & Golf Club** ★★   On the Duke University campus, about a mile from U.S. 15/501, this is the premier inn of Durham, with an 18-hole golf course designed by Robert Trent Jones. Named for the original tobacco tycoon, it's filled with Duke memorabilia, including Washington Duke's own antique desk. The property is like a castle, with an L-shaped lower wing. Many of the helpful staff members are university students. Although the impressive redbrick mansion is traditional in style, the bedrooms are modern, with big mullioned windows, upholstered chairs, quilted spreads, and either one or two double beds. In 2004 the hotel underwent a massive renovation and is now better than ever.

Naturally, someone had to name the bar **Bull Durham.** The full-service restaurant, **Fairview,** the most comfortable in town, serves an excellent contemporary cuisine and features piano music.

3001 Cameron Blvd., Durham, NC 27706. © **800/443-3853** or 919/490-0999. Fax 919/688-0105. www. washingtondukeinn.com. 246 units. $265–$285 double; $550–$925 suite. AE, DC, DISC, MC, V. Free parking. **Amenities:** Restaurant; bar; indoor pool with outdoor deck; 18-hole golf course; 12 tennis courts; fitness center; limited room service; babysitting; laundry service/dry cleaning. *In room:* A/C, TV, dataport, minibar, hair dryer, safe, iron/ironing board.

## WHERE TO DINE

**Brightleaf Square,** a complex of former warehouses built between 1900 and 1904, has a host of restaurants as well as shopping. You can enjoy a stroll and an ice cream in the courtyards.

### EXPENSIVE

**Four Square** ★★   AMERICAN/INTERNATIONAL   Owners Elizabeth Woodhouse and Shane Ingram, a husband-and-wife team, have taken a Greek Revival mansion and put in place an exceptional restaurant. Constructed in 1908, this Edwardian manse is imbued with such architectural delights as leaded-glass windows. Expect some of the best service in town from the experienced and gracious waitstaff. Many in-the-know guests, if the weather agrees, select a table on the wraparound veranda.

The menu is so pleasing and well prepared that some of the most enthusiastic patrons have acclaimed this the best restaurant in North Carolina. Though we applaud, we don't go that far. Nevertheless, everything we've ordered here has been enjoyable, full of flavor, and made with very fresh-tasting ingredients. There is much imagination in the cookery here.

Our most memorable dish was North Carolina pheasant, glazed with molasses and a chili sauce. Loin of rabbit is wrapped in bacon and stuffed with a sausage flavored with orange and rosemary; the *jus* that accompanies the dish is laced with Southern bourbon. The monkfish platter comes with a curry coconut broth and a dash of kumquats. For dessert? Try the divine Key lime or chocolate caramel bread pudding. All desserts are made on-site.

2701 Chapel Hill Rd. ℂ **919/401-9877.** www.foursquarerestaurant.com. Reservations required. Main courses $19–$31. AE, DC, MC, V. Mon–Thurs 5:30–9:30pm; Fri–Sat 5:30–10pm.

**Magnolia Grill** ★★★ SOUTHERN/INTERNATIONAL/REGIONAL AMERICAN  The grandest dining experience in Durham and one of North Carolina's treasures, the Magnolia Grill, with its peach and dark-green interior, delivers old Southern charm with a degree of urban sophistication inspired not just by the region but by such faraway places as Thailand, Mexico, and the Mediterranean. The attentive staff brings attractive dishes from the kitchen, which produces a menu with many seafood and beef selections. This restaurant, better described as a bistro, evokes an unexpected coastal feel. Start with the wine list, which features more than 130 bottled varieties, 10 to 12 of which are sold by the glass. The menu changes frequently. During a recent visit, we started with the green-tomato soup with crab and country ham, followed by the grilled pork porterhouse with Low Country risotto and crawfish ale. Perhaps the grilled beef served with a roasted corn vinaigrette will tempt you, or the tenderloin of pork with roasted sweet potato woven with fresh broad beans and a cider-barbecue *jus*. A lemon pudding was a perfect complement to our meal. The restaurant bar opens at 5pm for predinner drinks.

1002 9th St. ℂ **919/286-3609.** Reservations recommended. Main courses $19–$27. AE, MC, V. Tues–Thurs 6–9:30pm; Fri–Sat 5–9:30pm. Bar 5–9:30pm. Closed Sun–Mon and major holidays.

**Nana's** ★ NEW AMERICAN   Chef/owner Scott Howell has presided over this local favorite since 1992, after having worked with David Bouley at his renowned New York restaurant Bouley. He has also cooked in Imola, Italy, at San Domenico's; and sous-chefed at Magnolia Grill (see above). The Asheville native combined his culinary experience with a love for Tarheel regional cooking, and the result is fresh and delicious. The menu changes daily; on one evening, the risotto special contained local sweet corn and coastal white shrimp and was topped off with spinach, Smithfield country ham, and scallions. A house-cured salmon gravlax came with a salad of arugula, Bosc pears, spicy almonds, and green-tomato vinaigrette. The restaurant is known for its special wine dinners, and has won *Wine Spectator* magazine's Award of Excellence every year since 1993. The restaurant's pleasant ambience is enhanced by the earth tones and local artists' work on the walls.

2514 University Dr. ℂ **919/493-8545.** www.nanas.citysearch.com. Reservations recommended. Main courses $17–$25. AE, DC, DISC, MC, V. Mon–Sat 5:30–10pm.

## MODERATE

**George's Garage** INTERNATIONAL   This is one of the centerpieces of Durham's "Restaurant Row," a neighborhood centered around the 700 block of Ninth Street that's devoted to eateries in all price categories. George's Garage occupies the redbrick premises of what was originally conceived as a food store, but whose trussed, industrial-style ceilings evoke a glamorized version of an auto repair shop. Come here for one of the widest varieties of food options available under one roof in Durham. An excellent array of sushi, visible inside a glass case, is served with a minimum of fuss at the long bartop area. A conventional liquor bar, decorated with Southern memorabilia, occupies a distant end of the place. And in between are dining tables, an open-to-view kitchen, and a bakery serving very fresh breads, rolls, and pastries. During the lunch hour, the biggest luncheon buffet in Durham sprawls abundantly along one wall of the place (whatever you select costs $6.50 a lb.; the average luncheon weighs about 1½ lb.) In addition to sushi, food items are mostly Southern-style and international preparations. Try grilled Australia-derived rack of lamb marinated in herbs and garlic; grilled pork chops served with sweet potatoes and balsamic apple chutney; blackened mahimahi with a cucumber-flavored yogurt sauce; or a "Calabash Platter" piled high with fried catfish, oysters, jumbo shrimp, scallops, and lemon-flavored risotto. Any of these can be prefaced with fresh oysters, fried calamari, or a flavorful version of New England clam chowder.

737 Ninth St. ⓒ **919/286-4131.** Reservations not necessary. Main courses $9–$23. AE, DC, DISC, MC, V. Market/bakery daily 9am–9pm; self-serve lunch buffets daily 11am–4pm (takeout available till 7pm); restaurant Sun–Thurs 5–10pm (till 11pm Fri–Sat).

**Parizäde** ⋆ INTERNATIONAL    Set on the ground floor of Durham's most visible skyscraper (the Wachovia Building), this is the most sophisticated, flashy, and gastronomically eclectic restaurant in town. The airy, high-ceilinged, and stylish room has already welcomed the likes of Senator John Edwards, Elton John, Dan Quayle (remember him?), the prime minister of Canada, and King Constantine of Greece. Lots of "suits and ties" dine here at lunchtime; a somewhat more relaxed and less work-driven crowd shows up at dinner. Menu items feature a sophisticated array of pastas, including a fine version of linguine with clams. Roasted rack of lamb comes with a hazelnut crust; braised chicken breasts are stuffed with goat cheese, almonds, and sun-dried tomatoes; and a local version of bouillabaisse comes replete with monkfish, calamari, and a saffron-and-fennel–flavored broth, for anyone feeling nostalgic for southern France.

In the Wachovia Building, Irwin Sq., 2200 Main St. ⓒ **919/286-9712.** Reservations recommended. Lunch pizzas, pastas, and platters $5.50–$17; dinner main courses $9–$28. AE, DC, MC, V. Mon–Fri 11:30am–2:30pm; Mon–Thurs 5:30pm–10pm; Fri–Sat 5:30–11pm; Sun 5:30–9pm.

**Pop's** ITALIAN    One of the top-recommended of Durham's crop of hip newcomers is Pop's, a stylish Italian affair that's more glamorous inside than its folksy-retro facade indicates. It's housed in what was originally designed as an industrial laundry, just across the street from the restaurant and shopping compound known as Brightleaf Square. What you'll see is a stylishly minimalist decor of napery-clad dining tables, uniformed waiters (most with a sense of humor), and a wood-burning pizza oven within an open-to-view kitchen. Menu items that have become especially popular with this restaurant's growing corps of local fans include linguine with pancetta ham, sun-dried tomatoes, and corn; roasted eggplant soup; sandwiches stuffed with almonds and mussels; and an award-winning pizza topped with salted eggs, sliced prosciutto, roasted garlic, and olives. A favorite dish that never leaves the menu is Pop's chicken filet "cooked under a brick," a technique that flattens the filet and seals in the juices.

810 W. Peabody St. ⓒ **919/956-7677.** Reservations recommended. Pizzas and meal-size salads $9–$10; main courses $7–$9 lunch, $15–$20 dinner. AE, MC, V. Mon–Fri 11:30am–2pm; Tues–Sat 5:30–10pm; Sun–Mon 5:30–9pm.

## The Makings for a Carolina Picnic

Durham's most sophisticated and awe-inspiring food emporium is **Fowler's,** 112 S. Duke St. (✆ **919/683-2555;** www.fowlersfoodandwine.com), a European-with-a-Southern-accent delicatessen whose array of exotic foods and wines is among the very finest in the South, one that would impress even the most jaded of European palates. At the same time, it retains a friendly, low-key, and unpretentious demeanor that doesn't drive away the grits crowd. You can always haul away well-stuffed deli sandwiches from this place, or consume them at the scattering of cafe tables. Brunch selections, priced at $7 to $9 each, include omelets, roasted vegetable quiche, or an award-winning version of shrimp and grits. A box lunch, suitable for an all-inclusive picnic in its own right, costs $10 per person. Sandwiches go for $6 to $7 each. All meats are smoked on the premises. Fowler's is open Monday to Saturday from 7:30am to 9pm; and Sunday from 9am to 6pm. Hours are subject to change.

### INEXPENSIVE

**Elmo's Diner** AMERICAN    This is the busiest, most popular, and most nostalgia-laden diner in Durham, the ultimate burger joint where endless amounts of coffee are dispensed during exam week, and where a Southern/American menu has many locals recalling their childhoods. Set in what was originally designed as a bakery, and housing a staff that's clad in T-shirts, Elmo's has Naugahyde-covered banquettes and counter stools, spinning ceiling fans, and areas of exposed brick. Expect a simple, all-American menu that incorporates burgers, meatloaf, chicken burritos, salmon cakes, and omelets, as well as "full square meals" that stick to the ribs at affordable prices. Biscuits and gravy accompany virtually any main course you select.

776 Ninth St. ✆ **919/416-3823.** www.elmosdiner.com. Reservations not accepted. Breakfast omelets, salads, sandwiches, platters $6–$9.50 each. Sun–Thurs 6:30am–10pm; Fri–Sat 6:30am–11pm.

**Verde** MEDITERRANEAN    Few restaurants in Durham celebrate with as much zest the original, natural flavors of the mostly Mediterranean ingredients used to create the dishes here. It's one of several restaurants in town that's owned by a sophisticated Iranian, Jay Mehdian, and managed by Greek-born *wunderkind* Giorgios Bakatsias. The setting is high-ceilinged, big-windowed, and artfully postmodern, a room entirely sheathed in a pale but vibrant shade of electric green—an appropriate foil for food that's as ultra-fresh as anything you'll find in the state. Come for an eclectic selection of dishes prepared artfully but sans exotic or heavy sauces—its owners refer to it as "naked food," a concept that goes well with the local heat. A meal here might include a perfectly roasted medley of red peppers served with fresh tomatoes and poached fish (halibut, salmon, or North Carolina grouper) and served on a bed of braised leeks. In addition to lots of vegetarian choices, an especially succulent version of lamb steak is rubbed with lemon and thyme and then "romanced" with olive oil.

2200 W. Main St. ✆ **919/286-9755.** Reservations not necessary. Main courses $8–$15. AE, DC, MC, V. Daily 9am–2am.

## DURHAM AFTER DARK

**The Down Under Pub**    Wooden doors open into a chummy pub with a neighborhood feel, where an interesting cross-section of Durhamites meet. Located in the historic downtown area, The Down Under Pub offers a good selection of beers, from European ales and lagers to American microbrews, and more than decent pub food. Play pool, throw darts or, if you're really parched, belly up to the bar for a beer in yard- or half-yard-size glasses. 802 W. Main St. ℂ **919/682-0039.**

**Satisfaction**    This is one of Durham's most enduringly raucous and sometimes frenetic sports bars. It occupies part of what was built in 1904 as a tobacco warehouse, a structure that was renovated in the mid-1980s into a rustic, heavily timbered shopping and restaurant complex. The woodsy-looking decor is such that you can easily imagine endless pitchers of beer spilled on it. Virtually everybody here makes a fuss over the homemade potato chips, served with ranch dressing. It also serves steak, chicken, or submarine sandwiches, as well as burgers, pastas, and platters. In Bright Leaf Sq., 905 W. Main St. ℂ **919/682-7397.** Mon–Sat 11am–1pm.

## 3 Chapel Hill ⊛

28 miles W of Raleigh; 12 miles SW of Durham

The third point of the Research Triangle area is Chapel Hill, a small city that has managed to hold onto its village atmosphere in spite of the presence of a university that annually enrolls more than 25,000 students. Chapel Hill *is* the University of North Carolina and has been in existence since 1795, when it was the first state university in the country. The 2,000-acre campus holds 125 buildings, ranging from Old East, the oldest state university building in the country (its cornerstone was laid in 1793), to the Morehead Planetarium, which was an astronaut-training center in the early days of the U.S. space program.

Just before the Civil War erupted, the student body was the second largest in the country, after Yale's. Then the fighting started, and most of UNC's undergraduates and faculty left for the battlefield. The school closed down from 1868 to 1875.

The university has consistently been a leader in American education and a center of liberal intellectualism in a generally conservative state. Former Senator Jesse Helms, a right-wing conservative, once asked, "Why build a zoo when we can just put up a fence around Chapel Hill?" Was he referring to the town's distinctly liberal bent or to the wild frat parties at the University of North Carolina? At any rate, Chapel Hill (in spite of Helms) has the highest concentrations of Ph.D.s in the United States. By all means, schedule a visit here, ideally in spring, to see the dogwoods and crepe myrtle burst into bloom. At any time, you can wander past the stately pillared houses of Franklin Street and— surprise—find an espresso outlet on virtually every street corner, just as you can in Seattle.

It is estimated that the residents of Chapel Hill purchase more books per capita than anybody else in North Carolina. They also write them. As one local said, "It's no big deal to pick up the Book Review of the *New York Times* and find your neighbor on the cover." Lee Smith, author of 11 novels about the South, lives in the area, as does Allan Gurganus, author of the prize-winning novel *Oldest Living Confederate Widow Tells All: A Novel.*

### ESSENTIALS
**GETTING THERE**    Chapel Hill is reached from the east by I-40 and I-85, from the west by I-85, from the north by N.C. 57, and from the south by N.C. 54.

The nearest airport is in Raleigh.

**VISITOR INFORMATION**   Information is provided by the **Chapel Hill/Orange County Visitors Bureau,** 501 W. Franklin St., Suite 600 (© **919/ 968-2060;** www.chocvb.org), open Monday to Friday 8:30am to 5pm, and Saturday 10am to 2pm.

## EXPLORING ON & OFF CAMPUS

Your best introduction to the university is a free 1-hour **campus tour** ✫ that leaves from the Morehead Planetarium (the west entrance) on East Franklin Street. For details, contact the UNC Visitors Center located within the Morehead Planetarium (© **919/962-1630**). Hours are 9am to 5pm Monday to Friday.

With the tour or on your own, look for the **Old Well,** once the only source of drinking water for Chapel Hill. It stands in the center of the campus on Cameron Avenue, in a small, templelike enclosure with a dome supported by classic columns. Just east of it is **Old East,** begun in 1793 and the country's oldest state-university building. Across the way stands the "newcomer," **Old West,** built in 1824. **South Main Building** was begun nearby in 1798 and wasn't finished until 1814; in the interim, students lived inside the empty shell in rude huts. At the **Coker Arboretum,** at Cameron Avenue and Raleigh Street, 5 acres are planted with a wide variety of plants. As you walk around the campus, you'll hear popular tunes coming from the 167-foot **Morehead-Patterson Bell Tower,** an Italian Renaissance-style campanile.

**Morehead Planetarium,** on East Franklin Street (© **919/549-6863;** www. moreheadplanetarium.org), was the first planetarium owned by a university, and it was once used as a NASA training center. The star of the permanent scientific exhibits here is a large orrery, showing the simultaneous action of planets revolving around the sun, moons revolving around planets, and planets rotating on their axes. There's also a stargazing theater with a 68-foot dome. Show times vary considerably, so call for the current schedule. Admission to the planetarium is free; for the show, it's $4.75 for adults and $3.75 for seniors, students, and children.

UNC has one of the largest athletic programs in the South. The Tarheels field 26 varsity teams and maintain a 24-hour Carolina Hotline number, providing recorded information about all upcoming sporting events to be held on campus. Information is also available from the Smith Center Ticket Office; call © **800/ 722-4335** or 919/962-2296 Monday to Friday 8am to 5pm. Carolina basketball is followed passionately all over the state ("If God's not a Tarheel, why did he make the sky Carolina blue?"). Former coach and local icon Dean Smith is practically revered on campus; the Smith Center, named in his honor, is referred to as the Dean Dome. Carolina has a long history of recruiting top players; its famous alums include Michael Jordan and James Worthy.

Off-campus, one of the most appealing botanical gardens in the southeast comprises nearly 600 acres of mostly donated land and a vast array of plants that are divided into at least six distinctive categories and habitats. Accessible via laboriously laid out paths and walking trails, the **North Carolina Botanical Garden** ✫✫, Totten Center (© **919/962-0522;** www.ncbg.unc.edu), includes about 2,500 of the 4,700 plant species that are known to be native or naturalized in North and South Carolina, as well as herbs and horticultural plants from around the world. Thanks partly to its supervision by the University of North Carolina, there's no admission charge, and maps that show the garden's walking trails and habitats are distributed free. Allow at least 45 minutes for the simplest overview of this amazingly complex compound of gardens and natural habitats. It's open Monday to Friday year-round 8am to 5pm; Saturday hours are 9am to

5pm; Sunday hours are 1 to 5pm. During daylight saving time, closing on Saturday and Sunday is at 6pm.

## OUTDOOR PURSUITS

You'll find several fine golf courses around Chapel Hill. Public ones include the 18-hole **Cedar Grove Golf Course,** 619 McDade Store Rd., Hillsborough (© **919/732-8397**), with greens fees ranging from $12 to $15. Another good course, also an 18-holer, is **Finley Golf Course,** Finley Golf Course Road, Chapel Hill (© **919/962-2349**), with greens fees ranging from $33 to $77.

Orange County has an abundance of parks, gardens, and recreational facilities for visitors, including such activities as boating, fishing, camping, biking, and picnicking. For more information, call the following numbers and tell the staff which activities you'd like to pursue: **Chapel Hill Parks and Recreation** (© **919/968-2784**), and **Orange County Recreation and Parks** (© **919/732-8181**).

## SHOPPING

Many college towns in the South are noted for their quirky character and artistic penchant, however folksy. Chapel Hill is not without its eclectic beat, and you'll discover shops and boutiques that you would expect to find only in big cities.

**A Southern Season,** in the Eastgate Shopping Center, 1800 E. Franklin St. (© **919/929-7133**), is one of the largest, most up-to-date, sprawling, comprehensive, and interesting large-scale shopping emporiums in North Carolina. Departments include a fabulous array of delicatessen-style gourmet foods-to-go; wines and liqueurs; porcelain and crystal; and gift items, many with a distinctive Southern flair. A particularly appealing subdivision involves gift baskets

### Growing Your Own Endangered Plants

The **North Carolina Botanical Garden,** which is maintained by the horticultural department of the University of North Carolina, is separately described in "Exploring On & Off Campus," above. But what many visitors don't realize is that the staff that maintains the gardens also devotes enormous time and effort to its "conservation through propagation program," wherein rare (and sometimes imperiled) Carolina plants are propagated through seeds and cuttings, and then sold at rock-bottom prices to visitors in the hopes that they'll cultivate them in their own private gardens. Unusual and often rare plants, most of them thriving and healthy, are displayed on the "honor system," whereby cash is deposited into a waterproof box near the display tables without supervision from a sales staff. Credit cards (MasterCard and Visa) are accepted for larger purchases as well, and a staff member or volunteer is usually on hand to explain the origin of the plants and their preferred growing conditions. Potted plants, depending on their rarity and how hard they were to propagate, cost from $3.50 to $15 each, and tend to include species that are more rare and unusual than what you'd have found, say, in a Home Depot garden center. If you love plants, and want a living souvenir of your visit to North Carolina, a selection of plants culled from these gardens would be a brilliant idea. The center is open year-round Monday to Friday 8am to 5pm, Saturday 9am to 5pm, Sunday 1 to 5pm.

that, depending on what you specify, might contain kudzu jelly, Moravian spice cookies, chocolate-covered Carolina pecans, Carolina buttercrunch toffee, Blue Ridge bonbons, all manner of North Carolina honey-cured hams, plus about a thousand different gourmet items imported from Europe. You can even order vacuum-packed North Carolina barbecue here, available in either the western (with a touch of tomato sauce) or eastern North Carolina (with salt, pepper, and vinegar) style.

The **Weathervane,** a restaurant associated with A Southern Season shopping emporium, takes the best of its affiliate's produce and turns it into a sophisticated array of salads and sandwiches priced at $5 to $10, and main courses priced at $13 to $18. Set in a woodsy family-friendly format immediately adjacent to the store, it's open Monday to Saturday from 10am to 3pm, and Monday to Saturday from 5 to 9:30pm (see above for address and phone). American Express, Diners Club, MasterCard, and Visa are accepted.

Well-read Chapel Hill has a large book-buying public, and Franklin Street is the site of most bookstores. **The Bookshop,** 400 W. Franklin St. (© **919/942-5178**), has been a civic monument in Chapel Hill since 1981. This bookshop sells only used books covering (in the words of its owner, Bill Loeser) "everything except textbooks and romance novels." It doesn't seem very large, but its cramped, crowded, and somewhat dingy premises contain some 150,000 books, ranging in price from 50¢ to a rare 1770 edition of Catesby's *History of the Carolinas,* selling recently here for around $40,000.

Immediately across the street, and selling a radically different style and type of book, is Chapel Hill's most visible counterculture bookstore. The **Internationalist Book & Magazine Cooperative,** 405 W. Franklin St. (© **919/942-1740**), is funky, artsy, and the darling of Chapel Hill residents with a slightly leftist bent; it focuses on feminist, gay, lesbian, graphic arts, and poetry tomes.

Some 3 miles east of the center of Chapel Hill stands **Meadowmont Village,** adjacent to Route 54 (eastbound). This upscale multipurpose shopping, residential, office, and dining complex is evocative of the way visitors and locals dine and shop in the New South.

One of the most unique food markets in and around Chapel Hill is the **Weaver Street Market,** 101 E. Weaver St. (© **919/929-0010;** www.weaverstreet market.coop), 1 mile west of Chapel Hill, a rambling but modern warehouselike structure near the center of Carrboro that's piled almost to the rafters with all-organic foodstuffs. You can buy things that are fresh, Carolinian, and healthy here, and you can also purchase the fixings for a picnic lunch. Many locals visit its self-service, buffet-style restaurant, the **Weaver Street Market Café** (same address and phone), where an inexpensive buffet (especially pleasing to vegetarians) is served on picnic tables under soaring oak trees, and where Thursday nights include performances from live jazz bands. Both the market and its restaurant are open daily 8am to 9pm.

## WHERE TO STAY

**The Carolina Inn** ★★    Few other hotels in North Carolina carry as many emotional and loyal associations as this one. Owned (but not operated) by the University of North Carolina, it occupies sprawling redbrick premises that date from 1924 and have been artfully upgraded many times since. Part of its appeal, and fascination, derives from its role as UNC's ambassador of goodwill to the world at large. Consequently, its public areas (an interconnected series of graciously appointed living rooms) reek of a kind of genteel Southern dignity. The fortunes and glamour of this hotel took a big upswing during the 1960s, when its importance as an embodiment of the university became more apparent. You never know who you might spot in the also-recommended hotel dining room: The social, financial, athletic, and academic connections of some of your fellow diners are often awe-inspiring. Guest accommodations are tastefully and conservatively outfitted in 18th- and 19th-century themes, with flower-patterned upholsteries and a restrained and relatively formal dignity that evokes the decor of an upscale private home. Each room has a writing table, two phone lines, and a neatly kept bathroom with a tub/shower combination. Reserve as far as you can in advance here, especially if your visit coincides with any important event on the alumni or athletic calendars of the nearby universities.

211 Pittsboro St., Chapel Hill, NC 27516. (C) **800/962-8519** or 919/933-2001. Fax 919/962-3400. www.carolina inn.com. 184 units. $129–$200 double; $224–$294 suite. AE, DC, DISC, MC, V. Valet parking $7; self-parking $5. **Amenities:** Restaurant (see below); bar; exercise room; room service (6am–11pm); laundry service/dry cleaning. *In room:* A/C, TV, dataport, hair dryer.

**The Sheraton Chapel Hill Hotel** ✪  This is Chapel Hill's leading hotel, although the Fearrington House, on the outskirts (see "Staying Nearby," below), has more character. Parents of university students often stay here. The hotel offers ground-floor rooms with private patios and upper floors with balconies. All units contain well-kept bathrooms with tub/shower combinations. The decor is tasteful and the place is well furnished, but it's somewhat unimaginative. Nevertheless, it's the most reliable choice for good, solid comfort. It offers a central location and nearby golf privileges. The hotel restaurant serves ordinary fare.

1 Europa Dr., Chapel Hill, NC 27517. (C) **919/968-4900**. Fax 919/968-3520. www.sheratonchapelhill.com. 168 units. $149–$219 double; $189–$219 suite. Children 15 and under stay free in parent's room. AE, DC, DISC, MC, V. Free parking. **Amenities:** Restaurant; bar; outdoor pool; fitness center; limited room service; laundry service/dry cleaning; nonsmoking rooms; rooms for those w/limited mobility. *In room:* A/C, TV, dataport, coffeemaker, hair dryer, safe (in some).

**Siena Hotel** ✪✪ *(Finds)*  Much of the charm of this well-groomed and well-managed hotel derives from its refusal to copy the Southern theme that's the norm at many of its competitors. Built in the mid-1980s in a distinguished-looking U-shaped design that evokes a villa in Tuscany, it's the closest thing in North Carolina to the kind of hotel you might have selected for a romantic second honeymoon in the Italian countryside. Inside, a lavish use of russet-colored marble, copies of 19th-century antiques, and reproductions of Italian Renaissance paintings (which line the upstairs hallways) create an ambience that's distinct. The hotel's social centerpiece is a plush-looking bar in the lobby, which prefaces one of the best Italian restaurants in the South, **Il Palio** (see below). Rooms are large and accented with plush, elegant furnishings that include writing desks and comfortably upholstered armchairs for reading, rich (Italian) brocades, and marble-trimmed bathrooms. Expect a well-mannered staff, and a clientele of Duke and UNC parents, business travelers, and local politicians.

1505 E. Franklin St., Chapel Hill, NC 27514. (C) **800/223-7393** or 919/929-4000. Fax 919/968-8527. www. sienahotel.com. 80 units. $185–$195 double; $230–$245 suite. AE, DC, MC, V. Free parking. **Amenities:** Restaurant; bar; complimentary membership at a nearby health club; limited room service; laundry service/dry cleaning; nonsmoking rooms; rooms for those w/limited mobility. *In room:* A/C, TV, dataport, hair dryer.

## STAYING NEARBY

**Fearrington House Country Inn** ✪✪✪  The Fearrington House will tug at your heart . . . and your purse, but you won't be disappointed. This isn't the kind of place that lends itself to children, so leave the kids at home. Created in 1974 in a planned community of gracious town houses surrounding a village center, the 60-acre grounds are meticulously kept, with the rose gardens adding a special burst of color. The guest rooms are just as inviting, with lots of little details: silk or dried flowers, antiques mixed with high-quality reproductions, double ottomans, cathedral ceilings, some seating areas, marble tables, various bed arrangements, and luxuriously appointed bathrooms with tub/shower combinations. Some nice extras at the inn include screened porches, vintage Schwinns ready for your ride around the village, and even fresh flowers in the bathroom.

The restaurant is in a separate white clapboard building with elegant decor, ranging from sunny French country to Laura Ashley styles. Little alcoves make dining an intimate experience. The food is expertly prepared and served. Anticipate such dishes as sautéed soft-shell crayfish in orange Creole butter, or baked striped bass with salmon mousse and citron-infused *fumet* (a concentrated stock). Between courses, you can cleanse your palate with buttermilk sorbet. Another, more traditional restaurant is also available.

2000 Fearrington Village Center (15 min. south of Chapel Hill on U.S. 15/501), Pittsboro, NC 27312. (C) **919/542-2121.** Fax 919/542-4202. www.fearringtonhours.com/countryhotel.asp. 32 units. $220–$450 double. Rates include breakfast and afternoon tea. AE, MC, V. **Amenities:** 2 restaurants; bar; outdoor pool; tennis court; fitness center; 24-hr. room service ($20 per-person fee); babysitting; laundry service/dry cleaning. *In room:* A/C, TV, dataport, hair dryer.

# WHERE TO DINE
## EXPENSIVE

**The Carolina Crossroads** ★★ MODERN SOUTHERN/INTERNATIONAL
This charming, sophisticated restaurant has unofficially evolved into the local university's parlor and living room: a place where trustees and benefactors can be wined and dined, where collegiate sports heroes are celebrated, where the intricacies of academic politics are sometimes hammered into policy, and where the world at large can get a fast, favorable, and extremely hospitable overview of North Carolina's most distinguished academic institution. It's set inside a trio of dining rooms in the also-recommended Carolina Inn, amid Chippendale furniture and Colonial tones of yellow and blue. One frequent diner compared it to "a Southern mansion outfitted, year-round, in its spring clothing." It's supervised by master chef Brian Stapleton (formerly associated with the Ritz-Carlton Hotel chain), whose craftsmanship is artfully tied to the seasons and infused with the best tenets of modern Southern cuisine. Especially tasty starters include a flan of sweet garlic and Maine lobster served with lemon-grass broth and baby fennel; and seared chicken livers with country ham and a ragout of fava beans. Main courses include oven-roasted snapper with shrimp jambalaya; pork *osso buco* with "Mom's greens" and black-eyed peas; and a maple-and-rosemary smoked loin and leg of rabbit served with grilled leeks, "cracklin' bread," and baby Swiss chard.

In the Carolina Inn, 211 Pittsboro St. (C) 919/933-2001. Reservations recommended. Main courses $18–$24; set-price menus without wine $35–$55; set-price menus with wine $50–$80. AE, DC, MC, V. Daily 11am–2pm and 5:30–10pm. Afternoon tea $15 per person (with a $5 supplement for champagne) served Mon–Sat 3–5pm.

**Il Palio** ★★ ITALIAN This culinary landmark is the best, most appealing, and most formal Italian restaurant in North Carolina. Set on the lobby level of the Siena Hotel (see above), a 5-minute drive north of the center of Chapel Hill, it's a showcase for the cuisine of chef Jim Anile, one of the most celebrated culinary stars in the region. Expect a meal based on Tuscan priorities, but with a sophisticated use of ultra-fresh local ingredients. Begin with a medley of marinated octopus and roasted peppers, or a succulent mix of morels in basil, sherry, and goat cheese. Pasta might be garnished with cockles, rapini, and pancetta

ham, or perhaps studded with lobster and laced with saffron sauce. Spicy monkfish and tomato stew comes, bouillabaisse-style, with a sauce that's piquant
enough to please, but not biting enough to offend. Smoked breast of duck with
porcini risotto and roasted apricots is absolutely splendid. About 95% of the
wines offered here are Italian, reasonably priced, and presented with finesse by
one of the best-educated and most articulate wine stewards in the state.

In the Siena Hotel, 1505 E. Franklin St. ☎ 919/918-2545. Reservations recommended. Main courses
$12–$19 lunch, $17–$25 dinner. Set menus $50–$55; set menus with wine $75–$80. AE, DC, MC, V. Daily
11:30am–2pm and 5:30–10pm.

**Lantern Restaurant** ☆ PAN-ASIAN    A local reviewer cited the "nouveau-
funky" attitude here. Against a cool decor of walls the color of green tea and
tables like black coral, this restaurant is like no other in Chapel Hill. A brother-
and-sister act, Brendan and Andrea Reusing, are the guiding lights. Our party
got so intrigued with sharing appetizers that we almost didn't make it to the
main courses. The cuisine is lively, original, and tasteful: The crackling calamari
salad with seasonal greens and a lime miso vinaigrette or the bang-bang chicken
with Szechuan peppers did much to establish this place's well-deserved reputation for fiery flavors. We were enchanted by the steamed grouper with seared
ginger, scallions, and black beans, and also found the 6-hour braised pork worth
the trouble. Ever had "tea and spice" smoked chicken? Try it here. For a luscious
treat, top off a fine evening with a hot, rich chocolate cake with a spicy ginger
ice cream, all fire and ice.

423 W. Franklin St. ☎ 919/969-8846. Reservations not accepted. Main courses $16–$27. MC, V. Mon–Sat
5:30–10pm.

## MODERATE

**Crook's Corner** ☆ SOUTHERN    Behind the rather quirky facade of Crook's
Corner lurks one of Chapel Hill's superb restaurants. The seasonal menu may
include such delights as shrimp and grits with mushrooms, bacon, and scallions;
green Tabasco chicken; or mustard-molasses ribs. Among the side dishes are such
down-home delicacies as fresh collard greens and hoppin' John (black-eyed peas
and rice with scallions, tomato, and cheddar cheese). Waiters review the "War of
Northern Aggression" as they haul out those jalapeño hush puppies along with
the oyster and filet mignon scalawags. The wine-by-the-glass list is excellent. The
walls of the dining room are a continuously changing exhibition of works by
local artists. Seating is limited to 70; there's seating for about 50 more out on
the patio in fair weather. You may have to wait for a table, but it's worth it.

610 W. Franklin St. ☎ 919/929-7643. Reservations recommended. Main courses $13–$25. AE, DC, DISC,
MC, V. Tues–Sat 5:30–10:30pm; Sun 5:30–9pm.

**Elaine's on Franklin** ☆☆ *Finds* REGIONAL AMERICAN    Virginia native
Bret Jennings grew up eating "angel biscuits" (buttermilk biscuits), country ham
with red-eye gravy, and fresh tomato sandwiches. Busboy, waiter, caterer, Jennings worked himself up to the top. After training with two of America's top
chefs, he decided to branch out on his own and create his own culinary style.
On a recent visit to Elaine's, we took delight in such appetizers as "Fire & Ice"—
North Carolina yellowfin tuna seviche with habañeros, coconut milk, lime,
cilantro, and plantain chips—or a soft-poached egg on a ragout of chanterelles
with asparagus and porcini *jus*. For your main course, try the delicious pan-
crisped confit duck leg on truffled creamed corn, morels, local thyme, and
arugula; or try seared North Carolina swordfish with calamari, spicy mustard
greens, and shiitake mushrooms. The pastry chef is so good you'll want to adopt

him after tasting his lemon verbena ice cream with blackberries or his local peach cobbler topped with a cream biscuit and freshly made ginger ice cream.

454 W. Franklin St. ✆ **919/960-2770**. www.elainesonfranklin.com. Reservations required. Main courses $16–$26. AE, DISC, MC, V. Tues–Thurs 6–9:30pm; Fri–Sat 6–10pm.

**Pazzo!** ⭐ *Finds*    Local chef Seth Kingsbury has cooked at some of the great restaurants of North Carolina, including Magnolia Grill, but is now forging ahead in his own spot in the heart of Southern Village. Kingsbury's Italian-inspired cuisine boasts many original flourishes and taste sensations. You can eat in the small dining room or alfresco on the patio overlooking Market Street.

The chef uses fresh ingredients to concoct a finely toned cuisine that delights local foodies. Our party sampled a range of delightful appetizers, such as a fritto misto of shrimp and calamari served with a basil-infused aioli, and crispy oysters over baby spinach and a grilled red-onion salad. When the mains arrived, no one was disappointed, digging into such meticulously prepared dishes as grilled double-cut pork chops over garlicky greens, or pan-seared North Carolina red snapper over a grilled eggplant rollatini with a tomato-saffron sauce. Kingsbury also makes one of the best pizzas in town. For dessert, we're still dreaming of the chocolate hazelnut pound cake with soft cream and a hazelnut praline.

700 Market St., Southern Village. ✆ **919/929-9984**. Reservations recommended. Main courses $12–$18. AE, MC, V. Mon–Thurs 5–10pm; Fri–Sat 5–11pm; Sun 5–9pm.

**Spice Street** ⭐ INTERNATIONAL    This is the biggest, most daring, and most experimental theme restaurant in Chapel Hill. The beneficiary of widespread publicity and huge interest from the local culinary press, it's housed in the sprawling premises of what used to be a local department store on the town's eastern outskirts. Evoking a massive Asian spice market, it might have been pulled, depending on where you are within its premises, from Greece, Egypt, India, or anywhere along the Silk Route of China. There's a lot of razzle-dazzle and showmanship here, with specific areas designated as a delicatessen-style marketplace (with an impressive collection of olives, cheeses, and spices), a separate area devoted to sushi, a large rectangular bar area flooded with sunlight from big windows, a dining area that might remind you of a high-ceilinged Zen temple dotted with candelabra and Buddhist and Hindu effigies, and a separate area devoted to cooking classes and presentations by local celebrity chefs. Menu items derive from Asia (steamed pork dumplings with ponzu sauce; salmon roll tempura), Greece (beef kefta with cucumber and yogurt; "mezzo" platters of olives, hummus, tzadziki, and flatbread), the Middle East (grilled lamb chops with Egyptian-style lentils and yogurt sauce), and the Mediterranean (grilled calf's liver with pancetta ham and caramelized onions).

In the University Mall, 201 S. Estes Dr. ✆ **919/928-8200**. Reservations not necessary. Main courses $6–$14 lunch, $14–$28 dinner. AE, DC, MC, V. Mon–Sat 11:30am–2pm; daily 5–10pm.

## INEXPENSIVE

**Allen & Son** ⭐ BARBECUE/SOUTHERN    This joint is regionally known for its ribs. Just follow the smell of billowing hickory smoke, and you'll land here. Its street address might be called "Porcine Way."

One good ol' boy patron gave us some advice about how he arrives at Allen & Son. "When I hanker for some pig, I head here, but make sure I go in a car that smells like a dead squirrel." With that enigmatic statement, he was gone.

The patrons, even those of whom just got out of church, called the barbecue here "kickass." It's very tender—pulled pork, really, which is torn from the shoulder of the meat by hand. It also has a slightly smoky flavor. As for the

## The Barbecue: A Pig-Pickin' Good Time

Collegiate sports and barbecue are things that elicit huge emotion within North Carolina, and when it comes to barbecue, everyone in the state seems to have a strong opinion. Dyed-in-the-wool Tarheels claim they can, blindfolded, tell where they are within their state based on the degree of spiciness, and redness, of their respective barbecues. Here's a brief primer on what local residents expect when it comes to their favorite football food. Eastern North Carolina, site of the first settlers' landing, and presumably where food preparation techniques are the most closely tied to Elizabethan England, seasons its barbecue only with salt, pepper, and vinegar. The farther west you head within the state, the darker, redder, and smokier the barbecue becomes.

Brunswick stew offered nightly, we've had better. The peach cobbler is one of the most luscious desserts served here. The good ol' boy favorite, however, is peanut butter pie. A love of plastic flowers, checked oilcloth, and "pig art" helps you enjoy the place more.

6203 Millhouse Rd. ℂ **919/942-7576.** Main courses $5–$15. MC, V. Tues–Sat 10am–8pm.

**The Barbecue Joint** *Kids* BARBECUE/SOUTHERN   With its "pig kitsch" decor, this eatery serves up some of the best barbecue in Chapel Hill. Two Carolina boys (even adult men are called "boys" in the South), Jonathan Childres and Damon Lapas, have teamed up to create this family favorite where mama, papa, and all the kids show up for a good tuck-in. First, the barbecue itself: It has a mellow, smoky taste; it's moist and served in "fist-sized" knots of unadulterated pulled pork, with Asian chile sauce resting on the table for extra flavor. Barbecue isn't all you get here. The appetizers are the most imaginative of any so-called barbecue joint in town, including smoked duck quesadillas with roasted chipotle sauce; or the hummus, black bean, and pumpkin-seed dip with homemade tortilla chips. Other main-course delights include grilled wahoo with mango chutney, and a classic Cajun jambalaya, a meal in itself. Few can resist such desserts as the bourbon chocolate pecan pie or the caramelized pecan banana cake.

630 Weaver Dairy Rd. ℂ **919/932-7504.** Reservations recommended. Main courses $3.95–$15. AE, MC, V. Mon–Sat 11am–9pm.

**Mama Dip's Kitchen** *Kids Finds* TRADITIONAL COUNTRY COOKING This simple, first-come, first-served place is a great example of how the South likes to live: at the dinner table. The menu serves up succulent fried chicken, zesty beef or pork barbecue, and lip-smacking fried catfish as its tried-and-true specialties, along with a menu so vast it'll make you wish you had room to eat everything. All the main courses are old-fashioned meat dishes; with them, you can select 2 of the 18 vegetable sides offered each day. Naturally, you get biscuits with everything. The drink of choice, of course, is sweet iced tea. All the vegetables are fresh, and the meat is purchased from the butcher shop down the street. Other good-tasting options include spaghetti, homemade soups, and savory gumbos, along with fresh homemade desserts.

408 W. Rosemary St. ℂ **919/942-5837.** www.mamadips.com. Reservations not accepted. Main courses $6.50–$15. DISC, MC, V. Mon–Sat 8am–10pm; Sun 8am–9pm.

## CHAPEL HILL AFTER DARK

**Arts Center**    The Arts Center presents events Thursday to Sunday for about 50 weeks annually, including regional, national, and international concert tours, plays, and children's programs. Call for information. The box office is open Monday to Friday 10am to 6pm and on Saturday 10am to 4pm. Ticket costs depend on the event. 300-G E. Main St., in Carrboro. © **919/929-2787**. www.artscenterlive.org.

**Cat's Cradle**    This casual, intimate space is still going strong as *the* venue to see the latest bands—rock 'n' roll, alternative, bluegrass, you name it. The talent is often native-bred, and the scheduling is made with an eye to quality musicianship. Chapel Hill is the hometown of big-time picker James Taylor, after all. 300 E. Main St., in Carrboro. © **919/967-9053**. www.catacradle.com. Cover varies.

## 4 Winston-Salem ✦

104 miles W of Raleigh

In 1913, the twin communities of Winston and Salem were incorporated into a single city. Winston, founded in 1849, contributed an industry-based economy, whereas Salem added the emphasis on education and crafts and the sense of order that its Moravian settlers brought from Pennsylvania in 1766. The union has proved to be happy and productive.

Salem (the name comes from the Hebrew word *shalom,* meaning "peace") was the last of three settlements established in the Piedmont by Moravian clergymen and laymen in the early 1750s; the little towns of Bethabara and Bethania came first. The hardworking newcomers were devout people who had fled persecution in Europe and brought to the New World their artisans' skills, a deep love of music and education, and an absolute rejection of violence in any form.

In the 20th century, "progress" encroached on the boundaries of the beautiful old congregational town. But in 1949, an organized restoration effort was begun, and today, more than 30 buildings have been restored, with meticulous attention to authenticity; renovation is still under way on others. Devout the Moravians were, but glum they were not: The bright, cheerful reds and blues and soft greens and yellows in the restored interiors and exteriors replicate the colors they used in those early days. The Moravians' love of good food is also preserved in today's Old Salem, especially at the Old Salem Tavern Dining Room (see "Where to Dine," below), which serves meals in an authentic colonial Moravian setting.

## ESSENTIALS

**GETTING THERE**    I-40 (the East-West Expwy.) is the main approach to Winston-Salem from both east and west; from the north, it's U.S. 311, U.S. 52, and U.S. 158; and from the south it's U.S. 52.

Winston-Salem's **Smith Reynolds International Airport** (© **336/767-6361**) is served by **US Airways Express** (© **800/428-4322;** www.usairways.com). Charlotte is the nearest airport served by all major carriers.

**VISITOR INFORMATION**    The **Convention and Visitors Bureau,** 200 Brookstown Ave., Winston-Salem, NC 27101 (© **866/728-4200** or 336/728-4200; www.visitwinstonsalem.com), can tell you about attractions, accommodations, dining, and local bus transportation. It's open Monday to Saturday from 9am to 5pm, and Sunday 1 to 5pm.

**SPECIAL EVENTS** For a relatively small city, Winston-Salem has quite a calendar of events. If you're interested in attending any of these events, the Convention and Visitors Bureau (see above) will provide complete details. In mid-April, the city's 18th-century gardens in Old Salem are open for the **Spring Garden Tour** (call ✆ **888/653-7253** for details). Every year, there's a traditional Moravian **Easter Sunrise Service.** An old-fashioned **Independence Day Celebration** is held each year at Historic Bethabara. Starting in July is the **National Black Theatre Festival.** Early September brings the **Chili Championship** to Tanglewood Park. Mid-October also brings **Folk Festival IV,** a competition complete with country cooking and entertainment. Beginning in November and running to January 1 is the **Festival of Lights** in Tanglewood Park (✆ **336/778-6300**). And the holiday season wouldn't be complete without the **Old Salem Christmas and Candle Teas** ✿ (✆ **888/653-7253;** www.oldsalem.org), a re-creation of Yuletide as it was celebrated 200 years ago in Old Salem. (You've got to sample that Moravian sugar cake!)

## EXPLORING THE AREA

**Historic Old Salem** ✦✦ One of the leading attractions of North Carolina, this restoration of a Moravian community demonstrates old world skills. The **visitor center** has exhibits that trace the Moravians' journey from Europe to America and finally to North Carolina. Costumed hosts and hostesses will show you around, and you'll see craftspeople in Moravian dress practicing the trades of the original settlement. The center is open Monday to Saturday 8:30am to 5:30pm and Sunday 12:30 to 5:30pm. A comprehensive ticket costs $21 adults, $10 children ages 6 to 16. Children 5 and under are admitted free.

When Moravian boys reached the age of 14, they moved into the **Single Brothers House**—the half-timbered section was built in 1769, and the brick wing in 1786—where they began a 7-year apprenticeship to a master artisan. Academic studies continued as they learned to be gunsmiths, tailors, potters, and shoemakers. Adolescent girls lived in the **Single Sisters House,** diagonally across the town square, where they learned the domestic arts that they would need when marrying time arrived. Young single women still live in this building; it's a dormitory for Salem College. It is not open to visitors.

Be sure to go into the **Tavern,** built in 1784 to replace an earlier one that burned. George Washington spent 2 nights here in 1791 and commented in his diary on the industriousness of the Moravians. The dining room, sleeping rooms, barns, and grounds are not much different now than they were when he stopped by; the cooking utensils in the stone-floored kitchen, with its twin fireplaces, are genuine period artifacts.

You can also visit the **Market-Firehouse** and the **Winkler Bakery,** where breads and cookies are still baked in big wood-burning ovens. Many homes have distinctive signs hanging outside to identify the shops inside. One of our favorites is the **tobacco shop** of Matthew Miksch, a yellow, weather-boarded log cottage with a miniature man hanging at the door clutching tobacco leaves and a snuffbox.

Like the historic district of Williamsburg, Virginia, Old Salem still functions as a living community. Many of the restored homes are private residences, and the young people walking the old streets with such familiarity are no doubt students at Salem College, living a 21st-century campus life in an 18th-century setting.

On the square, the **Home Moravian Church,** which dates from 1800, is the center of the denomination in the South. Visitors are always welcome at services; hundreds show up for the Easter Sunrise service, the Christmas Lovefeast

*Moments* **The Search for Mayberry**

Mayberry, the hometown of Sheriff Andy Taylor on *The Andy Griffith Show,* never existed, of course. But its inspiration is said to be **Mount Airy** (www.visitmayberry.com), lying off U.S. 52 in the Upper Piedmont, to the south of the Virginia/North Carolina border. Andy Griffith was born and raised in this sleepy little town.

The town is an example of television's power to affect tourism. Thousands visit Mount Airy yearly, and the town they see looks very much like the fictional Mayberry of the long-running TV series. Southern oaks border the streets, and "just plain folks" sit out on the verandas, swinging and rocking as though it were still 1902. You expect to see Barney Fife appear at any minute.

**Mayberry Days,** held the last Thursday, Friday, and Saturday of September, draw visitors from all over the country for traditional "pig-pickin's" cooking and pie-eating contests. Call the Mount Airy Arts Council (© **800/286-6193** or 336/786-7998; www.surryarts.org) for information. If you'd like a **walking-tour map** of the town, go to the Mount Airy Chamber of Commerce at 200 N. Main St. (© **800/948-0949** or 336/786-6116), open Monday to Friday from 8:30am to 5pm.

**Mount Airy Visitors Center,** 615 N. Main St. (© **800/576-0231** or 336/789-4636), is open Monday to Saturday from 9am to 5pm and on Sunday from 11am to 4:30pm. It will guide visitors through the town, pointing out the still-standing birthplace of Andy Griffith and local businesses that were the inspiration for places seen in the TV series, including the replica of the old jail (Mon–Fri 8:30am–4:30pm). Call © **336/789-4636** for more information. **Floyd's City Barber Shop** (© **336/786-2346**) is still in operation, and the same barber who used to cut Andy's hair is still in business.

If you'd like to follow in the footsteps of Sheriff Andy, head for the **Snappy Lunch** at 125 N. Main St. (© **336/786-4931**) for a pork-chop sandwich. The old-time lunch counter is a virtual showcase for *The Andy Griffith Show.* Andy himself frequented the place as a boy. The proprietor, Charles Dowell, claims to sell about 1,000 pork-chop sandwiches every week. The sandwiches, costing $3.75 each, are consumed at old school desks. The sandwich is a boneless pork chop between steamy bun halves, covered with mustard. It's served Monday to Saturday from 5:45am to 1:45pm (closes at 1:15pm Thurs and Sat).

(Dec 24), and the New Year's Eve Watch Night service. One block north of the square, the graveyard named God's Acre contains more than 4,000 graves, all marked with nearly identical stones. Princes and paupers are shown the same respect. The cemetery is open at the discretion of the church.

**MESDA** (Museum of Early Southern Decorative Arts) ✿ is one of the most interesting museums in the state, conceived as a showcase of furniture design and decorative arts in the American Southeast during the 18th and early 19th centuries. It originated as the result of the outrage generated at a lecture by the then-president of the Winterthur Museum (Delaware) in 1949, when he implied that nothing of artistic importance was produced south of Baltimore during America's Colonial era. MESDA's collection of southeastern American art and antiques grew up in reaction to his words, and today, the organization functions as a research and documentation center, producing large, four-color volumes on esoteric subjects associated with the decorative arts in the American South.

The best way to enter this museum is by navigating your way through the visitor center for Old Salem, passing over a replica of a mortise-and-tenon-covered bridge leading toward Old Salem, and entering the neo-Palladian entryway (inspired by Thomas Jefferson's Monticello) of MESDA. Its collections are set inside replicas of 32 historically important period rooms, many dismantled from places throughout the South, then reassembled, side by side, in a warehouselike structure originally conceived as a Kroger's grocery store in the 1950s. Each of the rooms represents a different region of the South and is appointed with furniture from its era. Hours are the same as those for the Old Salem visitor center, and a ticket to Old Salem includes access to this museum.

MESDA allows you to tour period rooms and galleries, showcasing the furniture, paintings, textiles, ceramics, silver, and other metalwares made and used in the South through 1820. The museum stands at the southern edge of Old Salem.

Old Salem Rd. ℭ **888/653-7253** or 336/721-7300. www.oldsalem.org. Combination ticket for Old Salem and Museum of Early Southern Decorative Arts $21 adults, $10 children 5–16; admission to Old Salem $10 adults, $8 children; admission to Museum of Early Southern Decorative Arts $10 adults, $6 children. Group rates are available. Mon–Sat 9:30am–4:30pm; Sun 1:30–5pm.

**Reynolda House Museum of American Art** ★  Few other museums carry as rich a mother lode of drama and dysfunction as Reynolda House, a sprawling and richly impractical 64-room bungalow built between 1912 and 1917, during the height of the Jazz Age, as a showcase homestead by tobacco tycoon R. J. Reynolds and his beautiful and charismatic young wife, Katharine. At the time of its construction, it was the centerpiece of what was intended to be a productive country estate of 1,065 acres. But with the early deaths of R. J. and Katharine (in 1918 and 1924, respectively), and in the wake of a scandal associated with the untimely suicide (or was it murder?) of one of their sons in 1922, in which nightclub chanteuse Libby Holman was implicated, the house sank into neglect, acreage was sold off, and radical adjustments were made to its public areas. All of that changed in 1967, when the heirs to the estate reconfigured the house, its artworks, and its furnishings into a museum. In 2004, plans were finalized for a massive expansion of the original premises with the construction of a postmodern, mostly glass-sided, new wing, and Reynolda House, in cooperation with nearby Wake Forest University, embarked on a new and potentially controversial era as one of central North Carolina's most radically innovative museums.

Don't be surprised by the deliberate and sometimes provocative juxtapositions of paintings and sculpture from radically different eras. The museum's permanent collection includes American art from the Colonial era to the present. Charmingly, about 90% of Katharine Reynold's original furnishings from 1917 (many of them purchased from Wanamaker's department store in Philadelphia) have been restored and/or replaced, and these, in contrast with the modern and contemporary art, make for some very interesting museum-watching. If the weather is clement, don't miss a visit to Katharine's formal gardens, to the left of the main house as you face it. They're spectacular.

2250 Reynolda Rd. ℭ **336/725-5325.** www.reynoldahouse.org. Tues–Sat 9:30am–4:30pm; Sun 1:30–4:30pm. $8 adults, $7 seniors, free for students 18 and under, free for college students with ID.

**SECCA (Southeastern Center for Contemporary Art)** ⭐ *(Finds)*    One of the most radical, creative, and innovative museums in North Carolina was established in 1956 within the solid stone walls of the estate that was originally built in 1929 by the James G. Hanes family, an energetic textile mogul and founder of the company best known today for the manufacture of underwear. The original structure, bequeathed by Hanes to SECCA "for the enjoyment of art in a home-like setting," was designed to resemble a much-enlarged version of a stone manor house in the Cotswold district of England. Two massive greenhouse-style enlargements were added in the mid-1970s. This is a showplace for the exposition of avant-garde and cutting-edge contemporary art. One of the strengths (and weaknesses) of this place is its lack of a permanent collection. Everything you'll see here is conceived and constructed only for exhibitions that last up to a maximum of about 3 months.

In the Historic Hanes Estate, 750 Marguerite Dr. ©️ 336/725-1904. www.secca.org. Admission $5 adults, $3 students and seniors, free for children under 17. Tues–Sat 10am–5pm; Sun 2–5pm. 1st Thurs of every month 10am–8pm.

## OUTDOOR PURSUITS

We believe that the best way to get a sense of the early origins of Winston-Salem involves a detour to the 175-acre tract known as **Historic Bethabara Park** ⭐, 2147 Bethabara Rd. (©️ **336/924-8191;** www. bethabarapark.com). Positioned 7½ miles north of Old Salem, and the beneficiary of intensive excavation since the mid-1970s, at which time much of it lay in ruins, it was established in 1753 as the site of the first Moravian settlement in North Carolina. Later, it played an important role in the local politics surrounding the French and Indian War. Fifteen Moravian men came to this part of North Carolina from Bethlehem, Pennsylvania, site of an even earlier Moravian settlement, and quickly built a small agrarian community of log houses, a crudely fortified palisade, a meeting house and church (the stone-sided *Gemeinhaus*), and a medicinal garden (the first well-documented garden of its kind in what later became the United States) whose restored version is one of the highlights of the modern-day park. By 1766, the newer town of Salem was established, and Bethabara (which had originally been envisioned only as a temporary community) gradually sank into obscurity. Today, however, in its restored form, Bethabara illuminates much of the early history of this part of North Carolina. Additionally, the mass of written records, journals, inventories, and maps generated by the early Moravian settlers at Bethabara forms one of the most important bodies of research materials for the study of U.S. Colonial history.

Highlights of the much-restored settlement include a 15-minute video presentation in the visitor center, a guided walking tour of the compound conducted by well-informed volunteers, and access to walking trails that fan out over the surrounding acreage.

Historic Bethabara's buildings, gardens, and visitor center are open Tuesday to Friday 10:30am to 4:30pm, and Saturday and Sunday 1:30 to 4:30pm. Admission costs $2 for adults, $1 for children.

**Tanglewood Park,** U.S. 158 West in Clemmons (©️ **336/778-6370**), is a year-round recreational facility set on some 1,100 acres. You can enjoy golf on two of *Golf Digest*'s top-rated courses, or tennis on one of nine tennis courts, both hard and clay. Stop by the horse stables to ask about trail rides and riding lessons or to arrange a leisurely carriage drive around the park. A nature trail has also been cut through the acreage. The park has two modern, fully equipped children's playgrounds, plus an Olympic-size pool. It's open daily from 7am to dusk. Admission is $2 per car.

## SHOPPING

Winston-Salem offers all types of shopping options, thanks to its dual Southern and Moravian heritage. **Stratford Place,** Stratford Road at I-40 Business (② **336/ 723-2221**), offers a collection of specialty shops and restaurants in one locale.

Winston-Salem has a selection of antiques stores, as do the neighboring cities. Those worth a look include **Oxford Antiques and Gifts,** 2707 Tudor Rd. (② **336/ 723-7080**); and **Reynolda Antique Gallery,** 114-C Reynolda Village (② **336/ 728-2500**). All these shops are open Monday to Saturday 10am to 6pm.

If rare and old used books are your forte, we recommend a stop at **Larry Laster Old and Rare Books,** 2416 Maplewood Ave. (② **336/724-7544**), a great place to make that rare find. Visits are by appointment only and must be made 1 day in advance.

Everything you might ever have associated with the Moravians is available in the cozily claustrophobic premises of the **Moravian Gift Shop,** 614 S. Main St. (② **336/723-6262**), where the folkloric and Christmas traditions of the town's earliest settlers remain alive. Expect an inventory of arts and crafts, beeswax candles, Moravian stars in all shapes and sizes, upscale gift items, and a safe and somewhat stodgy collection of conservative reading material. A nearby competitor with roughly equivalent merchandise is **T. Bagge,** 626 S. Main St. (② **336/ 721-7387**).

**Winkler Bakery,** 529 Main St. in Old Salem (② **336/721-7302**), is known for its domed and wood-fired brick oven in this shop dating back to the turn of the 19th century. Drop in for a bevy of goodies, including old-fashioned and paper-thin Old Salem Moravian ginger, lemon, sugar, and black walnut cookies.

The funky and appealing **Earthbound Arts (Gifts from Nature),** 610 N. Trade St. (② **336/773-1043**), is what you get when you mix a psychedelic-era "head shop" with New Age philosophy, an art gallery, and a dose of hillbilly charm. The result is an emporium of scented soaps that seem to pull you into the nearest bathtub or shower. Also for sale are handcrafted jewelry and scented herbs. Everything on display here shows a great sense of fun and whimsy— always with a North Carolina accent and a strong sense of the state's mountains and hideaway hollers.

**Piedmont Craftsmen** ⁂, 601 N. Trade St. (② **336/725-1516**), is richly inventoried with products from more than 350 craftspersons based throughout central North Carolina, each of whom is required by company charter to pass minimum standards of quality, creativity, and originality. As such, its merchandise is more appealing, and in many cases much more humorous, than that found in competing shops. Much of its creative force derives from its founder and executive director, Tomi Melson, who's famous for her pithy, well-articulated company motto: "No matter what your mamma might have told you, *craftspersons,* not prostitutes, represent the world's oldest profession, and as such, crafts guilds with tightly enforced standards are vital as a means of keeping professional standards high." Come here expecting to be charmed.

Just a 7-mile drive north of Winston-Salem is the town of Germanton, settled in 1790 by German immigrants. It's the home of the **Germanton Art Gallery and Winery,** Highway 8, Germanton (② **800/322-2894** or 336/969-6121; www. germantongallery.com), where you can find originals and prints by many internationally known artists. The gallery is an authorized dealer for art dealers all over the world. The wines are well worth tasting; the climate of the foothills of the Blue Ridge Mountains provides an ideal setting for the French-American hybrid grape

Travel Tip: He who finds the best hotel deal has more to spend on facials involving knobbly vegetables.

Hello, the Roaming Gnome here. I've been nabbed from the garden and taken round the world. The people who took me are so terribly clever. They find the best offerings on Travelocity. For very little cha-ching. And that means I get to be pampered and exfoliated till I'm pink as a bunny's doodah.

travelocity®

1-888-TRAVELOCITY / travelocity.com / America Online Keyword: Travel

**Plan your vacation**

• flights, hotels, car rentals
• cruises & vacation packages
• destination guides
• fare alerts
• go to yahoo.com, click travel

©2003 Yahoo! Inc.

powered by *hp*

to flourish. Allow yourself time for shopping, and bring a credit card. Open Tuesday to Friday 10am to 6pm and Saturday 9am to 5pm.

## WHERE TO STAY

**Adam's Mark Winston Plaza** ★★ The leading hotel of Winston-Salem and one of the state's best, Adam's Mark is located in the heart of the business district and is connected underground to the Benton Convention Center. Consisting of a 17-story and a 9-story building, the complex is like a grand hotel in a major world city. The most expensive rooms are at the luxury-club level on three floors, with a private lounge, complimentary continental breakfast, and concierge. All the guest rooms are tasteful and spacious, and many have panoramic views. Some accommodations open onto balconies that overlook the atrium. All units contain well-kept bathrooms with tub/shower combinations. The **Cherry Street Bar** offers an entertainment cafe. Dine in upscale style at **Trattoria Carolina,** or more casually in the hotel's sports bar, Players.

425 N. Cherry St., Winston-Salem, NC 27101. © **800/444-2326** or 336/725-3500. Fax 336/728-4020. www. adamsmark.com. 603 units. $89–$169 double; from $225 suite. Children 17 and under stay free in parent's room. AE, DC, DISC, MC, V. Parking $6. **Amenities:** Restaurant; 2 bars; indoor pool; fitness center; sauna; 24-hr. room service; laundry service/dry cleaning; nonsmoking rooms; rooms for those w/limited mobility. *In room:* A/C, TV, dataport, coffeemaker, hair dryer, iron/ironing board, safe.

**Augustus T. Zevely Inn** ★★ This 1844 home of Old Salem physician A. T. Zevely was saved from decay in the 1950s by Old Salem, Inc. This group of citizens who preserve historic Moravian structures restored the home into the grandest B&B in Old Salem. A first glimpse of the classic 19th-century brick facade evokes the Old Moravian style. Beautifully furnished in Old South style, it's well maintained, snug, and cozy. The inn is centrally located in the historic district, near many sights, shops, and activities, including golfing, tennis, and boating. The dining room serves 24 comfortably.

Rooms are done in 1800s period style, complete with antique furnishings. All units have well-kept bathrooms, most with tub/shower combinations. Some rooms feature fireplaces, refrigerators, and balconies. When you are making reservations, be sure to be specific about which extras you prefer.

803 S. Main St., Winston-Salem, NC 27101. © **800/928-9299** or 336/748-9299. Fax 336/721-2211. www. winston-salem-inn.com. 13 units. $80–$135 double; $205 suite. Rates include continental breakfast weekdays, full breakfast Sat–Sun. AE, MC, V. Free parking. **Amenities:** Breakfast room; lounge; nonsmoking rooms; rooms for those w/limited mobility. *In room:* A/C, TV, hair dryer.

**The Brookstown Inn** ★★★ The premier inn of Winston-Salem, the Brookstown is housed in an 1837 cotton mill that supplied material for Confederate uniforms. This jewel of a building offers spacious rooms with two double beds, a chest of drawers, an armoire, a loveseat, a desk, chairs, and tables. Most suites have a separate sitting room and garden tub. All units contain well-kept bathrooms with tub/shower combinations. Silk flowers, quilts, baskets, and wooden decoys adorn the parlor areas, decorated in Wedgwood blue, burgundy, gold, and olive. The inn, listed on the National Register of Historic Places, is conveniently near the Old Salem restoration. Another area of the mill, where its boiler was once located, is the site of a visitor center.

200 Brookstown Ave., Winston-Salem, NC 27101. © **800/845-4262** or 336/725-1120. Fax 336/773-0147. www.brookstowninn.com. 71 units. $135 double; $116–$185 suite. Rates include continental breakfast. Children 12 and under stay free in parent's room. AE, DC, DISC, MC, V. Free parking. Take the Cherry St. exit from I-40. **Amenities:** Breakfast room; lounge; fitness center; laundry service/dry cleaning; nonsmoking rooms; rooms for those w/limited mobility. *In room:* A/C, TV, dataport, coffeemaker, hair dryer, iron/ironing board.

**The Summit Street Bed & Breakfast Inns** ★★ *Finds*    This is the most sophisticated, elegant, and adult-oriented B&B in Winston-Salem, the kind that appeals to worldly business travelers and romantic couples. It occupies a pair of elaborately decorated and lavishly restored side-by-side West End Victorian houses, one built in 1895, the other 2 years later. We've rarely seen a bed-and-breakfast that's better accessorized than this one, or one with management as discreet and cooperative. Each house has richly decorated public rooms that look like pages from *Architectural Digest*, and each has lavish and whimsical furnishings that evoke the most charming aspects of the late Victorian Age. All but one of the rooms has a Jacuzzi that's designed for up to two friends at a time, and each has a state-of-the-art stereo system and access to a varied collection of movies. One of the houses has the largest and most up-to-date exercise room we've ever seen in a comparably small hotel, artfully tucked away into what might have originally functioned as a formal parlor. Local entrepreneur Ken Land, a man well-versed in the dining options of Winston-Salem, is your host.

420 and 434 Summit St. at the corner of W. 5th St., Winston-Salem, NC 27101. © **800/301-1887** or 336/777-1887. www.bbinn.com. 9 units. Sun–Thurs $89–$169 double, Fri–Sat $99–$189 double. Free parking. AE, DC, MC, V. **Amenities:** Billiards table; exercise room. *In room:* A/C, TV, Jacuzzi, iron/ironing board.

**Tanglewood Manor House Bed & Breakfast** ★ *Finds*    In Tanglewood Park, part of the former 1,100-acre estate of William Reynolds (the brother of R. J.), this stately former house lies southwest of Winston-Salem in a landscape of Carolina pines and dogwood. The 1859 home has been restored and adapted for the use of guests. All the rooms are spacious and handsomely furnished, like the rooms in an English country house. The tasteful decor is in cranberry and hunter green, with louvered wooden blinds and Austrian swag-style draperies. All units come with bathrooms equipped with tub/shower combinations. The cost of swimming and fishing nearby is included.

4061 Clemmons Rd., Tanglewood Park (P.O. Box 1040), Clemmons, NC 27012. © **336/778-6370.** Fax 336/778-6379. www.forsythe.cc/tanglewood/acom_manorhouse.aspx. 10 units. $86–$150 double. Rates include continental breakfast (manor house only). AE, DC, MC, V. Free parking. **Amenities:** Breakfast room; lounge; outdoor pool; 2 18-hole golf courses; 10 tennis courts; horseback riding; nonsmoking rooms; rooms for those w/limited mobility. *In room:* A/C, TV, fridge, coffeemaker.

## WHERE TO DINE
### IN OLD SALEM

**Old Salem Tavern Dining Room** ★ AMERICAN/CONTINENTAL    Here, as everywhere else in the restored village, authenticity is the keynote. The three ground-floor dining rooms were built in 1816 as an annex to the 1784 Tavern next door. Upstairs is a trio of three additional dining rooms; dining is also available on the rear veranda. In summer only, you can eat under a wisteria arbor in the rear garden. The simple furnishings and colonial-costumed staff provide an appropriate 18th-century ambience. The manager, Ms. Doris Hamilton, works hard to keep original Moravian culinary tenets alive, basing at least some of her recipes (meatloaf fortified with rolled oats; Moravian chicken pie; Moravian gingerbread for dessert; and ample use of apples, fresh lemons, and sauerkraut) on authentic 19th-century recipes. The pumpkin-and-raisin muffins are a specialty. For dessert, there's Moravian gingerbread topped with homemade lemon ice cream.

736 S. Main St. © **336/748-8585.** Reservations recommended for dinner and for lunch for parties of 6 or more. Main courses $6–$9 lunch, $11–$25 dinner. AE, MC, V. Sun–Fri 11:30am–2pm; Sat 11:30am–2:30pm; Mon–Sat 5–9pm (till 9:30pm Fri–Sat).

**Ollie's Bakery** SANDWICHES/PASTRIES   This is Winston-Salem's most popular and sophisticated bakery, chugging out a staggering variety (at least two dozen types) of breads every day, as well as an assortment of pastries, some of which are influenced by the traditions of the Moravians. Although we respect this place for its role as a bakery, we especially value its sandwiches which, when consumed with a steaming cup of coffee, make for a satisfying light lunch. The place originated in the 19th century as a grocery store, and much of that antique sense of fresh-baked wholesomeness remains. You'll find it in the center of historic Salem, opening onto the back side of the city's tourist information office.

300 S. Marshall St. Sandwiches $3–$4 each, loaves of bread and individual portions of pastries $1.95–$3.75. DISC, MC, V. Tues–Fri 7am–5:30pm; Sat 8am–5pm; Sun 8am–4pm.

## IN WINSTON-SALEM
### Expensive

**Ryan's** ✶ CONTINENTAL   This restaurant is every bit the equal of Zevely House (recommended below), with which it's often compared. In a wooded setting overlooking a stream, Ryan's is rustic in decor but has a truly sophisticated Continental menu. Dishes are executed with polished technique. Beef dishes are specialties, as are some excellent seafood creations. The homemade soups are exceptional, and there's a good wine list. It's estimated that you could eat here all the time and always find something new to surprise and delight you. Valet parking is available.

719 Coliseum Dr. ✆ 336/724-6132. www.ryansrestaurant.com. Reservations recommended. Main courses $17–$37. AE, DC, MC, V. Mon–Thurs 5–10pm; Fri–Sat 5–10:30pm. Closed major holidays. Take the Cherry St. exit from I-40 Business.

**The Vineyards** AMERICAN/CONTINENTAL   Katharine Reynolds, the Edwardian Age matriarch who commissioned the construction of this sprawling white-sided outbuilding on her estate, Reynolda, might be surprised to see its present manifestation as a restaurant. But if you're hungry before or after your visit to the nearby art museum, this restaurant is a sensible choice. The decor inside evokes southern France, thanks to beige-and-cream painted furniture, straw-seat chairs, arched doorways, and floors crafted from herringbone patterns of red brick. The food, fussed-over and relatively formal, includes crisp-fried crab cakes with rémoulade sauce; carpaccio of beef with capers and shallots; oysters fried in Pernod and served with spinach in cream sauce; filet steak Reynolda, with sautéed mushrooms, crabmeat, and a lobster-flavored cream sauce; and pan-roasted quail stuffed with wild rice and Cassis sauce. An especially pleasing dessert is an old-fashioned bread pudding garnished with fresh blueberries.

In Reynolda Village, 2250 Reynolds Rd. ✆ 336/748-0269. Reservations recommended. Main courses $11–$16 lunch, $14–$25 dinner. AE, DC, MC, V. Mon–Sat 5–10pm.

**Zevely House** ✶ CONTINENTAL   Antiques and a fireplace decorate this house, which dates back to 1815. It was constructed by Van Neuman Zevely, a Moravian cabinetmaker, and became the center of his plantation. In 1974, the building was hauled to its present site and authentically restored. This restaurant has steadily improved and truly justifies its star rating. The cuisine is creative and accomplished, the sauces are in harmony, and the wine list is well chosen and reasonable in price. Try the potato cakes with sour cream and caviar, or maybe something simple and grandmotherly—chicken potpie, for example. A pork tenderloin is perfectly prepared. Venison and beef filet are often featured, but pan-fried trout is the signature dish. The Moravian-style pumpkin muffins are always a good choice. A fireplace keeps the place snug in winter, although you'll want to retreat to the patio when the weather's fair.

901 W. Fourth St. ✆ **336/725-6666.** www.zevelyhouse.com. Reservations recommended. Main courses $15–$26; Sun brunch $6.25–$13. AE, DC, DISC, MC, V. Tues–Sat 5–9pm; Sun 11am–2pm (brunch).

## Moderate

**The Old Filling Station** CONTEMPORARY AMERICAN    Whenever a Carolina TV station wants to include a local restaurant in one of its "reality TV" programs, complete with spotlights and a sound crew, they tend to schedule it here at this hip and trendy spot. Don't expect anything even vaguely related to a gas station, since most of its architectural remnants were ripped out long ago. There's a walled-in and partially covered dining terrace, plus an interior that's partially devoted to an animated bar where you're likely to find a high percentage of the city's available and nubile young women. Menu items are well-prepared and based on a creative interpretation of modern American cuisine. Examples include deep-fried wontons stuffed with crabmeat, cream cheese, and scallions; Jamaican-style jerk chicken quesadillas; pizzas (an ongoing favorite comes with spicy Thai-style chicken); a succulent version of fried filet of chicken with pancetta ham, tomatoes, and spinach; filet steak with bacon and Gorgonzola sauce; and Carolina shrimp and grits served with Cajun-style andouille sausage and hominy cakes. A fine dessert is bourbon-laced pecan pie with chocolate sauce.

871 W. Fourth St. ✆ **336/724-7600.** Reservations recommended for tables inside, not accepted for outdoor dining on the patio. Pizzas, salads, and sandwiches $7.95–$8.95; pastas and main courses $13–$23. AE, DC, MC, V. Daily 11:30am–3pm and 5:30–10pm.

## Inexpensive

**Cat's Corner Café** (*Kids*) AMERICAN    Positioned in the geographical center of Winston-Salem's business district, this is the most appealing and least pretentious sandwich joint and cafe in town. It evokes a California-inspired oasis of wholesomeness and informality that's incongruously set into a high-ceilinged commercial space on the ground floor of one of the town's largest office buildings. Tables are set under the open sky of West Fourth Street, with additional seating inside the public space of the anonymous-looking shopping arcade. We prefer the luncheonette-style counter that faces the busy kitchen, out of which emerges some of the tastiest sandwiches we've ever had. The entire menu consists of salads, burgers, and sandwiches, examples of which include fried green tomatoes with bacon, lettuce, and red tomatoes; blackened catfish with Cajun-flavored mayo; and Caesar salads garnished with strips of grilled chicken.

411 W. Fourth St. ✆ **336/722-9911.** Reservations not accepted. Salads, sandwiches, and platters $5–$7. MC, V. Mon–Fri 11am–3pm; Thurs–Sat 5–10pm; Sun (brunch) 10:30am–2:30pm.

# WINSTON-SALEM AFTER DARK

**Club Odyssey**    This is the most visible gay bar in the region. Located 6 miles from Old Salem, in a small-scale shopping center beside a busy traffic artery, it includes two bar areas (only one of which is open whenever the place isn't busy), a pool table (where older patrons sporting just a whiff of leather tend to congregate), and a dance floor. It's open nightly 9pm to 2:30pm, but the place is never really crowded except on Friday and Saturday nights after around 10pm. Be prepared to show your ID at the door. 4019A Country Club Rd. ✆ **336/774-7071.** Cover $2–$5.

**Ziggy's**    Come here for the best live music in Winston-Salem, performed in a battered building that you can find by following the directions in the club's recorded phone message. There's a different event every night of the week, although the schedule changes frequently. The setting is a cramped, once-private house 3 miles north of the town center (near the campus of Wake Forest University) and ringed by the largest deck in town. The club was designed to allow sightlines directly to the stage. The club has hosted such live acts as Elastica, Loud Lucy, and Hootie & The Blowfish (before they went platinum). It's open Monday to Saturday from 9pm to 2am. 433 Baity St. ⓒ 336/748-1064. www.ziggy rock.com. Cover (sometimes) $5–$20.

## 5 Charlotte

143 miles SW of Raleigh; 91 miles S of Winston-Salem

In the past decade or so, Charlotte has been sprouting skyscrapers, including the 40-story, trapezoidal steel-and-glass tower of the Bank of America Plaza and the stunning 46-story Hearst Tower, which was completed in 2002. The city has attracted and taken to heart a professional football team—the Carolina Panthers—that was good enough to get to the Super Bowl in 2004 and nearly pull off an upset against the favorite, the New England Patriots. Suburban districts have mushroomed, with landscaped housing developments and enormous shopping malls springing up in every direction. This is the New South, built squarely on the foundation of the Old South.

The largest city in the Piedmont, Charlotte was named for George III's wife, Queen Charlotte. Evidently, however, its residents didn't take their royal affiliation too seriously. When Lord Cornwallis occupied the town briefly in 1780, he was so annoyed by patriot activities that he called it a "hornet's nest," a name that has been proudly incorporated into the city seal.

Indeed, more than a year before the Declaration of Independence was signed in Philadelphia, the Mecklenburg Declaration, proclaiming independence from Britain, was signed in Charlotte on May 20, 1775. The Captain James Jack monument (211 W. Trade St.) is a memorial to the man who carried the document on horseback to Philadelphia and the Continental Congress. According to Charlotte's citizens, Thomas Jefferson used their declaration as a model for the one that he wrote.

In 1865, Confederate President Jefferson Davis convened his last full cabinet meeting here. After the Confederacy fell and the local boys came home from war, the city set out on a course that eventually led it to a position of industrial leadership in the South. The Catawba River provided water power for the rapid development of manufacturing plants and textile mills. Today, these mills and factories, bowing to foreign competition, have been closing at an alarming rate.

For years, the Charlotte region was also the nation's major gold producer. A branch of the U.S. Mint was located here from 1837 to 1913. The exquisite 1835 mint building, designed by William Strickland, is now part of the Mint Museum, which houses one of the southern Atlantic region's major art collections.

Today, the city is booming, and business is just fine, thank you very much. The banking, insurance, and transportation industries keep feeding the economy. With all this growth, a new generation of Charlotteans is champing at the bit for recognition that their city has hit the big time. There's not much here for the casual tourist, but business travelers are certainly coming to town in droves.

## ESSENTIALS

**GETTING THERE**    North-south routes through Charlotte are I-85 and I-77; I-40, a major east-west highway, crosses I-77 some 40 miles to the north. Contact the AAA through the **Carolina Motor Club,** 9433 Pineville-Matthews Rd., Suite A, Pineville, NC 28134 (ⓒ **704/541-7409**).

Charlotte-Douglas International Airport (© 704/359-4000) is served by American Airlines (© 800/433-7300; www.aa.com); British Airways (© 800/ AIRWAYS; www.britishairways.com); Air Canada (© 888/247-2262; www.air canada.com); Continental Airlines (© 800/525-0280; www.continental.com); Delta, Delta ASA, and Delta Comair (© 800/221-1212; www.delta.com); Northwest Airlines (© 800/225-2525; www.nwa.com); United Airlines (© 800/ 241-6522; www.ual.com); and US Airways and US Airways Express (© 800/ 428-4322; www.usairways.com). *Note:* At press time, the German carrier Lufthansa (© 800/399-5838; http://lufthansa.com) announced that it would begin daily service between Charlotte and Munich.

The daily Amtrak (© 800/USA-RAIL; www.amtrak.com) service to Washington, D.C., and Atlanta through Charlotte both depart in the early-morning hours.

VISITOR INFORMATION   Contact the Charlotte Convention & Visitors Bureau, Visitor Information Center, 330 S. Tryon St., Charlotte, NC 28202 (© 800/231-4636 or 704/331-2700; www.charlottecvb.org), open Monday to Friday from 8:30am to 5pm, Saturday from 9am to 3pm. Charlotte Transit (© 704/336-3366) can furnish local bus routes and schedule information.

SPECIAL EVENTS   In late April, Springfest is a 3-day festival held in uptown Charlotte. The streets come alive with music and other entertainment, and street vendors dispense a wide variety of foods. In late May, the Coca-Cola 600 packs 'em in at the Charlotte Motor Speedway (call © 704/455-3200 for details). For 6 full days in mid-September, the Festival in the Park in Freedom Park celebrates regional arts and crafts.

## SEEING THE SIGHTS

If you're in Charlotte during April and May, drive north on N.C. 49 to the University of North Carolina at Charlotte campus to see the botanical gardens ★ (© 704/547-2364) in full bloom. The gardens are a wonderland of rhododendrons, azaleas, and native Carolina trees, shrubs, wildflowers, and ferns. A tropical-rainforest conservatory in the gardens' McMillan Greenhouse is open Monday to Saturday 10am to 3pm; admission is free. The outdoor garden is open daily during daylight hours.

Mint Museum of Art   With the recently added Dalton Wing, this stately museum displays a fine survey of European and American art, as well as the internationally recognized Delhom Collection of porcelain and pottery. Also featured are pre-Columbian art, contemporary American prints, African objects, vast collections of costumes and antique maps, and gold coins originally minted at the facility. New galleries exhibit studio glass and pottery from North Carolina studios. An admission ticket also gains you admittance to the Mint Museum of Craft & Design (220 N. Tryon St.).

2730 Randolph Rd. © 704/337-2000. www.mintmuseum.org. Admission $6 adults, $5 students and seniors, $3 children 6–17, free for children 5 and under, free for everyone Tues 5–10pm. Tues 10am–10pm; Wed–Sat 10am–5pm; Sun noon–5pm. Closed Mon and holidays.

Discovery Place & the Nature Museum   Discovery Place is one of the top hands-on science and technology museums in the region. This uptown center features such permanent exhibits as a tropical rain forest and an aquarium. There's also an OMNIMAX theater. The static-electricity demonstration, which literally makes your hair stand on end, is a perennial favorite. Temporary exhibits on loan from other science centers keep the place forever changing.

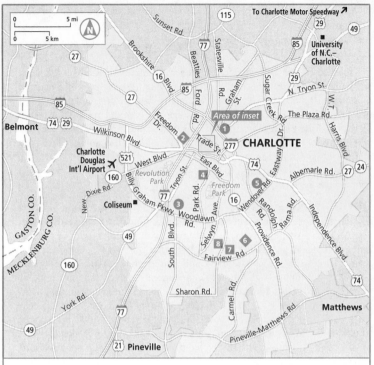

# Charlotte

## Downtown Charlotte

**ACCOMMODATIONS** ◼

Dunhill **9**
Hyatt Charlotte **8**
The Morehead Inn **4**
Park Hotel **7**

**DINING** ◆

The Coffee Cup **2**
La Bibliothéque **6**
La Vecchia's
Seafood Grille **11**

**ATTRACTIONS** ●

Bank of America
Stadium **10**
Discovery Place &
the Nature Museum **1**
Mint Museum of Art **5**
Wing Haven Gardens
& Bird Sanctuary **3**

301 N. Tryon St. ✆ **800/935-0553** or 704/372-6261. www.discoveryplace.org. Admission $14 adults, $11 children 2–14, free for children under 2. Mon–Sat 10am–6pm; Sun 12:30–6pm.

**Wing Haven Gardens & Bird Sanctuary** ✪ *Finds*    Since 1927, one of Charlotte's special attractions, created by Elizabeth and Edwin Clarkson, has been a 3-acre enclosed area in the heart of a residential neighborhood. Mrs. Clarkson was known as the city's "bird lady." Some 142 winged species have been sighted in the walled garden, which was once a bare clay field. Birders and garden lovers will have a field day as they browse through the Upper, Lower, Main, Wild, Herb, and Rose gardens. The gardens are at their most splendid in the spring, when birds are returning from their winter migration. A bulletin board tells you which birds are around at the moment.

248 Ridgewood Ave. ✆ **704/331-0664.** www.winghavengardens.com. Free admission. Tues 3–5pm; Wed 10am–noon; Sun 2–5pm.

## OUTDOOR PURSUITS

Charlotte is ringed by nature preserves and parks, including the nearly 1,000-acre **McDowell Park and Nature Preserve,** about 12 miles south of the city center on N.C. 49 (✆ **704/588-5224**). Its heart is Lake Wylie. The preserve has many hiking trails, and paddleboats can be rented on the lake. Swimming isn't allowed, but fishing is. Call for more information.

Even bigger is **Latta Plantation Park,** the largest in the county, at 6211 Sample Rd. in Huntersville (✆ **704/875-1391**), 12 miles northeast of the city center. It's a favorite resting place for waterfowl, and has some 2,500 acres devoted to nature. It also has stables where you can rent horses and ride along some 7 miles of trail. A nature center and picnic tables are available. Fishing is permitted; swimming is not.

For **bikers,** the best route is between Southpark and uptown Charlotte. If you'd like a route map, write the North Carolina Department of Transportation, P.O. Box 25201, Raleigh, NC 27611.

Because there are so many **fishing** possibilities in the Greater Charlotte area, you may want to obtain a state license from the North Carolina Wildlife Commission; call ✆ **919/733-3391** for more information.

**Tennis** is available at many places in the area, including several city parks. Among the best are Hornet's Nest, Park Road, and Freedom. The **Charlotte Park and Recreation Department** (✆ **704/336-3854;** www.parkandrec.com) will advise you on which ones are closest to your hotel or motel, assuming that there isn't a court where you're staying. The people of Charlotte, like those in all Piedmont cities, are devoted to **golf.** The **Visitor Information Center** (✆ **704/334-2282**) has a complete list of courses that are open to the public.

## WHERE TO STAY

At press time, the massive 700-room **Westin Charlotte** (✆ **704/375-2600;** www.starwood.com/westin) was open for business, in a prime location uptown near the Convention Center and the Bank of America Stadium (home of the Carolina Panthers); look for weekend bargains.

### EXPENSIVE

**Hyatt Charlotte** ✪    In the luxury market, this would be choice no. 2 in Charlotte, outdistanced only by the Park (see below). One of the most stunning choices in western North Carolina, it's 4 miles south of the heart of the city. A seven-story brown brick building accented by greenish glass, it has a four-story atrium and a lobby with a Mexican fountain and an inviting atmosphere. The guest rooms have a decor of inoffensive pastels, and the well-equipped bathrooms have tub/shower combinations and marble vanity tables. Rooms are also equipped with dataports for laptops and fax machines. The slant in the more formal restaurant, **Scalini's,** is northern Italian. You can have a before-dinner drink in the bar.

5501 Carnegie Blvd. (opposite South Park Mall), Charlotte, NC 28209. © **704/554-1234.** Fax 704/554-8319. www.hyatt.com. 262 units. Sun–Thurs $137–$300 double; Fri–Sat $90–$110 double; $375–$715 suite. Children 18 and under stay free in parent's room. AE, DC, DISC, MC, V. Free parking. **Amenities:** Restaurant; bar; indoor pool; fitness center; Jacuzzi; sauna; limited room service; babysitting; laundry service/dry cleaning; nonsmoking rooms; rooms for those w/limited mobility. In room: A/C, TV, hair dryer.

**The Morehead Inn** ★★ (Finds) This southern estate lies in one of Charlotte's oldest neighborhoods, just minutes from uptown. With its tranquil elegance and fine antiques, it is easily one of the finer inns in western North Carolina. Installed in the historic Dilworth home, the inn is a popular center for local weddings. Its public areas are spacious but offer many cozy nooks, often with intimate fireplaces. Eight private suites are in the main house, and a secluded carriage house across the courtyard offers an additional quartet of suites. The furnishings are tasteful and comfortable. One favorite is "The Romany," a corner room with a queen-size four-poster and a separate office den. "The Mount Vernon" has a king-size sleigh bed facing an original fireplace, along with a large sun room. All units have well-kept bathrooms, most with tub/shower combinations.

Breakfast is the only meal served, but the staff will direct you to many good restaurants nearby for lunch and dinner.

1122 E. Morehead St., Charlotte, NC 28204. © **888/MOREHEAD** or 704/376-3357. Fax 704/335-1110. www. moreheadinn.com. 12 units. $120–$190 double. Rates include breakfast. AE, DC, DISC, MC, V. **Amenities:** Breakfast room; nonsmoking rooms. In room: A/C, TV, dataport, hair dryer.

**Park Hotel** ★★ This is Charlotte's government-rated four-star hotel. If money is no object, stay here and enjoy the classic styling, with fluted columns and tasteful, luxurious appointments. In Southpark's commercial center, this six-story hostelry attracts those discriminating travelers who want the ultimate in city

## Finger-Lickin' Down-Home Cooking

Locals are proud of their fancy new restaurants, but sometimes they just want to escape to a roadside dump where—as they say in the South—"all God's children got chicken grease on their fingers." **The Coffee Cup** ★ is where to go. It's in a cinder-block structure across from a garage in an area of truck firms and warehouses. Expect Formica-topped tables, with a bottle of Texas Pete on every one. Vintage soul pours from a jukebox at least 3 decades old. When the place opened in the '40s, only whites could dine inside; black customers had to order takeout through a side window (still here, but covered in plywood). Even the toilets once used by black patrons are still outside. The kitchen cooks pan-fry chicken the old-fashioned way. Locals drive for miles to eat this chicken with their fingers. Daily lunch specials include meatloaf and liver and onions.

The Coffee Cup is at 914 S. Clarkson St. (© **704/375-8855**). It's open Monday to Friday from 6am to 4pm and Saturday from 7am to 1pm. Breakfast costs from $3.95 to $9.95, lunch from $4.95 to $11. The restaurant takes MasterCard and Visa.

comfort. The green marble floors are matched by upholstery in Caribbean sea-green colors—an effect that is tasteful and stylish. The guest rooms, the best in town, often have a set of double beds or sometimes a four-poster king-size bed. Commodious bathrooms with tub/shower combinations and marble vanity tables are featured, along with thoughtful extras such as irons and ironing boards. Some accommodations contain refrigerators. The restaurant is elegant, the serv-ice attentive and unobtrusive. A refined and quite sophisticated cuisine is served. In summer, guests can enjoy piano music Thursday to Saturday.

2200 Rexford Rd., Charlotte, NC 28211. © 800/334-0331 or 704/364-8220. Fax 704/365-4712. www.the parkhotel.com. 192 units. $99–$220 double; $225–$895 suite. Children 17 and under stay free in parent's room. AE, DC, DISC, MC, V. Free parking. **Amenities:** Restaurant; outdoor pool; putting green; fitness center; health spa; sauna; boutiques; 24-hr. room service; massage; laundry service/dry cleaning; nonsmoking rooms; rooms for those w/limited mobility. *In room:* A/C, TV, dataport, hair dryer, safe.

## MODERATE

**Dunhill** ⭐ Constructed in 1929, this is one of Charlotte's oldest and most his-toric hotels. These days, the big names often go elsewhere, but old-timers still prefer the Dunhill's European-style comfort and charm. (The doorman out front often greets returning guests by name.) In the old days, it was called the Mayfair Manor, and some of its most loyal clients still refer to it that way. The artwork in the public areas is by North Carolinian Philip Moose, and a piano player entertains in the stylish lobby. The restored guest rooms have a warm, cozy feeling; they're furnished with handsome reproductions and often with four-poster beds. All units have well-kept bathrooms with tub/shower combina-tions. **Monticello's** is the hotel restaurant, offering excellent cuisine throughout the day. Health-club privileges can be arranged.

237 N. Tryon St., Charlotte, NC 28202. © 800/354-4141 or 704/332-4141. Fax 704/376-4117. www.dunhill hotel.com. 60 units. Sun–Thurs $199 double, Fri–Sat $149 double; $599 suite. Children 15 and under stay free in parent's room. AE, DC, DISC, MC, V. **Amenities:** Restaurant; bar; 24-hr. room service; babysitting; laundry service/dry cleaning; nonsmoking rooms. *In room:* A/C, TV, hair dryer.

## WHERE TO DINE

Getting good buzz at press time was **Bonterra Dining & Wine Room** (1829 Cleveland Ave.; © **704/333-9465;** www.bonterradining.com), which offers some 200 wines by the glass. It's situated in an 1895 church in Charlotte's his-toric Southend District.

**La Bibliothèque** ⭐ FRENCH/INTERNATIONAL Relaxation and ele-gance are virtually guaranteed the moment you step inside this formal dining room, which serves the city's finest French cuisine. The service is formal and effi-cient, yet friendly and not intimidating. Some of Charlotte's rising young pro-fessionals take their favored business clients here for dinner. "We're not New York, but we're getting there," one of them said to me. The cooking is worth traveling across the city to sample, and the chef is especially talented in handling seafood from the Carolina coast, although beef and veal dishes are also prepared with flair. Much of the menu depends on the inspiration of the moment. Sig-nature dishes include Dover sole, chateaubriand, and rack of lamb.

In the Roxborough Office Building, 1901 Roxborough Rd. © 704/365-5000. www.labibliotheque.net. Reservations required. Jackets and ties preferred for men. Main courses $16–$37 at dinner. AE, DC, DISC, MC, V. Mon–Sat 5:30–10pm.

**LaVecchia's Seafood Grille** ⭐⭐ SEAFOOD This family-owned and -oper-ated business is celebrated locally as the best all-around restaurant and the best seafood dining room in greater Charlotte. It's an elegant setting with many works of art and sculpture by the Columbia, South Carolina–born artist Mike Williams. We can't wait to go back to dig into such delights as Maine lobster, aged beef, and both fresh- and saltwater fish, along with the finest assortment of shellfish in the area. In warm weather, tables on the patio fill up quickly, with diners sampling such dishes as she-crab soup (exceptional) and stuffed shrimp with crabmeat. The calamari with rosemary sauce is a delight, as is a platter of rope-cultured mussels steamed with white wine, garlic, and shallots with a touch of Pernod. Our favorite is the cedar-plank Maine salmon wood-roasted over truffled whipped potatoes. For dessert, why not the pumpkin cheesecake?

325-E 6th St. C 704/370-6776. www.lavecchias.com. Reservations required. Main courses $24–$41. AE, DC, MC, V. Mon–Thurs 5:30–10pm; Fri–Sat 5:30–11pm.

## CHARLOTTE AFTER DARK

The **Charlotte Symphony Orchestra** (C 704/972-2003; www.charlotte symphony.org) season runs from September to May; check local newspapers or call for performance dates. **Opera Carolina** (C 704/332-7177; www.opera carolina.org) presents performances from October to April, and the **Charlotte Pops** (C 704/332-0468; www.charlottesymphony.org) gives outdoor concerts (small fee) in Freedom Park on Sunday evenings in the summer. Classic plays are often performed by **Theatre Charlotte,** 501 Queens Rd. (C 704/376-3777; www.theatrecharlotte.org), usually Thursday to Sunday. The **Blumenthal Performing Arts Center,** 130 N. Tryon St. (C 704/372-1000; www.blumenthal center.org), is the newest facility to join the performance venues; it features three theaters for productions ranging from rock concerts to intimate stage events.

If you're in town and want to catch a live professional football game, a limited number of single-game tickets are available. For tickets to see the **Carolina Panthers,** visit the Bank of America Stadium Ticket Office (C 704/358-7800; 800 S. Mint St., southeast side of the stadium; Mon–Fri 8:30am–5:30pm); or order through Ticketmaster (C 704/522-6500; www.cpanthers.com or www. ticketmaster.com). The city also has a pro basketball team, the **Charlotte Bobcats** (C 704/262-2287; www.nba.com/bobcats). The majority holder is Robert Johnson, the Black Entertainment Channel (BET) multimillionaire and the first prominent African-American owner in U.S. sports. The Bobcats were scheduled to play their first season in 2004; the team's new $265-million uptown arena will open in 2005.

**Double Door Inn**    Some of the blues musicians who appeared here went on to become famous: Willie Dixon, Buddy Guy, and Stevie Ray Vaughn. The setting is a renovated 1920s house on the border of downtown Charlotte and the Elizabeth district, with a likable, battered, absolutely unpretentious ambience. You might catch a zydeco band, if you're lucky. Although the place is open Monday to Friday from 11am to 2am and Saturday and Sunday from 8:30pm to 2am, live music is featured only between 10pm and 2am nightly. 218 E. Independence Blvd. C 704/376-1446. Cover $6–$15 when music is offered.

**Scorpio**    This popular lesbian and gay nightclub has been going strong for years. Many gays drive for miles—even from across the border in Tennessee—to have a lively night on the town at this bustling joint. Actually, it's several clubs within a club. There's a large dance bar that attracts "same-sexualists" (to use Gore Vidal's term). There's also a country bar called the Queen City Saloon. On certain Friday and Saturday nights, the crowd is so vast here that you'll think everybody in Charlotte has gone gay—at least for the night. The club is open nightly from 9pm to 2am. 2301 Freedom Dr. C 704/373-9124. Cover $5–$7.

# 7

# Southern Pines & the Pinehurst Sandhills

The Sandhills' porous, sandy soil is a reminder that in prehistoric times, this land was under the rolling waters of the Atlantic. This soil provides the ideal drainage that's crucial to the "Golf Capital of the World," for no matter what the rainfall, no puddles accumulate on its rolling golf courses. And with mean temperatures ranging between 44° and 78°F (7°–26°C), the game is played here year-round.

But golf hasn't always been king. When Boston philanthropist James Walker Tufts bought 5,000 acres of land in 1895 for $1 per acre, his plan was to build the little resort village of Pinehurst as a retreat for wealthy Northerners from harsher climes. Recreation then consisted mainly of croquet on the grassy lawns, outdoor concerts, hayrides, and quiet walks through the pines.

Tufts' attention first turned to golf, which had only recently arrived from Great Britain, when one of his dairy employees complained that guests were "hitting the cows with a little white ball." By 1900, Tufts had enlisted Donald Ross (who had honed his skills at Scotland's St. Andrews) to come to Pinehurst and introduce golf. Ross designed courses here that drew some of the most distinguished golfers in the world: Ben Hogan, Walter Travis, Bobby Jones, Walter Hagen, Patty Berg, Sam Snead, Arnold Palmer, Gary Player, and Jack Nicklaus, to name just a few.

For years, golfing on the superb courses of the Pinehurst Country Club was by invitation only. Even though the golf world's top players still consider Pinehurst their own turf, these days you don't have to wait for an invitation—or be a millionaire—to play. Prices are high, but they're not exorbitant compared with those of other luxury resorts around the country. And there are hotels and motels here in almost any price range for experts or duffers who want to play the Pinehurst courses.

In 1973, the first World Open Championship was played in Pinehurst; the event was replaced in 1977 by the Colgate Hall of Fame Classic. In September 1974, President Gerald Ford presided at the opening of the World Golf Hall of Fame, overlooking Ross's famous No. 2 Course (one of the top 10 in the country).

**Midland Road** (N.C. 2), a highway divided by a stately 6-mile row of pine trees and bordered by sedate homes and lavish gardens, sets the tone for this golf mecca. From the second green of the Pinehurst No. 2 Golf Course (site of the 1999 U.S. Open) at one end to the little village of Southern Pines at the other, Midland offers an array of both golf courses and lodges. About a third of the area's more than 35 courses are accessible via this road. Also on Midland Road, you'll pass a rambling white building called **Midland Crafters,** which houses a virtual survey of American crafts, from beanbags to paintings to furniture to pottery to glassware, or almost any handcraft you can conjure up. Over the years, this region has drawn artists, craftspeople, and potters. Scattered around the vicinity in rustic, pine-sheltered workshops, many of the potters welcome visitors, and most are quite happy to have you watch them at their work.

In addition to golf, competitive **tennis** made its mark when the first major tournament, the United North and South Tennis Tournament, hit the courts of the Pinehurst Tennis Club in 1918. That amateur event ran until 1942 and was the proving ground for many nationally ranked players, including the Davis Cup Team of the 1930s. Today, this area enjoys a reputation for having some of America's best tennis facilities and programs.

The Sandhills region is also known for its **equestrian competitions.** Most of these events are free to spectators. *Horse Days,* a monthly publication about events that features calendar listings, is available locally at information offices. From late October to May, there are horse trials, shows, or even fox hunts. "Is there really a fox?" we asked a dapper man in a traditional "pink" hunt jacket, knee-high riding boots, and a tall hat, who was sitting straight in his saddle. "Sometimes," he responded.

## 1 Pinehurst ⓐ★

71 miles SW of Raleigh

Pinehurst, built by Frederick Law Olmsted (the architect/landscaper who planned New York's Central Park), has retained its New England village air, with a town green and shaded residential streets. Year-round greenery is provided by pines (some with needles 15 in. long), stately magnolias, and hollies. Moderate temperatures mean color through all seasons: camellias, azaleas, wisteria, dogwoods, and summer-blooming flowers. Shops, restaurants, hotels, and other business enterprises make this community self-sufficient. Pinehurst offers plenty of recreational facilities for those who aren't interested in chasing after that little white ball: a tennis club with excellent courts; more than 200 miles of riding trails, as well as stables with good mounts for hire; boating on a 200-acre lake; trap and skeet ranges; archery; 9,000 acres of woods to explore via meandering pathways; and, of course, shopping in the boutiques.

But golf is definitely king. If there's a hotel or motel in the area that doesn't arrange play for its guests, we couldn't find it. For a complete list of golf courses, ask the Visitors Bureau (see "Essentials," below) for its "Accommodations/Golfing" brochure.

## ESSENTIALS

**GETTING THERE**   U.S. 1 runs north and south through Southern Pines; N.C. 211 runs east and west; U.S. 15/501 reaches Pinehurst from the north; and there's direct area access to I-95, I-85, and I-40. You really need a car to get around this entire area.

Raleigh/Durham is the nearest commercial airport (see "Raleigh," in chapter 6). Moore County has a small private airport with a 5,500-foot runway. If you are flying in yourself, call for ramp-space reservations (© **910/692-3212**). A Hertz car-rental desk is at the terminal (© **910/692-5858**). Call ahead for reservations. **Amtrak** (© **800/USA-RAIL;** www.amtrak.com) has one northbound and one southbound train daily through Southern Pines.

**VISITOR INFORMATION**   We strongly recommend that you write or phone ahead for details on golfing and other sports, sightseeing, accommodations, and dining. Contact the **Pinehurst Area Convention and Visitors**

**Bureau,** P.O. Box 2270, Southern Pines, NC 28388 (© **800/346-5362;** fax 910/692-2493; www.homeofgolf.com).

## HITTING THE LINKS

Pinehurst is like a quaint village with the kind of total-golf atmosphere you find in St. Andrews in Scotland. With its more than 35 superb championship golf courses, some of which are among the highest-rated in the world, the town represents golf's grandest era. Legends were born here—names such as Nelson, Zaharias, Jones, Hogan, Snead, and Palmer. Some of the finest golf architects of the 20th century designed courses in the area—Donald Ross, Ellis Maples, and Robert Trent Jones among them.

The courses here are too numerous to list. Following are our favorites.

**The Club at Longleaf,** Pinehurst (© **910/692-6100**), was called by *Golf Digest* "the most playable course in Pinehurst." It was designed by Dan Maples, architect of the nationally acclaimed Pit Golf Links. The front 9 at Longleaf was designed in the Scottish open style, with rolling fairways. Greens fees cost $40 to $100 with cart rental.

**Legacy Golf Links,** U.S. 15/501 South, Aberdeen (© **800/344-8825** or 910/944-8825), is the only links in the area to blend the accessibility of a public course with the amenities of a private club. It's also the only public course to receive *Golf Digest*'s four-star rating. Greens fees are $49 to $69 per person including cart rental.

**Pine Needles Lodge** ★★, Southern Pines (© **910/692-7111**), is a Donald Ross masterpiece built in 1927, a challenging par-71 course for golfers of all skill levels. The course, playing to 6,708 yards from the championship tees, has been immaculately groomed and restored to its original splendor. Its Bermuda fairways and bent-grass greens are available only to guests staying at the Pine Needles and Mid Pines (for resort details, see listing below). Greens fees are $175. Package rates are also available in combination with hotel tariffs.

**The Carolina Hotel Golf Courses** ★★★, 1 Carolina Vista at Pinehurst (© **800/ITS-GOLF** or 910/295-6811), is the only resort with seven signature courses, and you must be a guest of the resort to play. Many guests book in on golf packages. The original architect was Donald Ross. This is golf in the grandest tradition, and shots played by Hogan, Nelson, and Jones still echo down the fairways. For these 126 holes of golf, the classic designs are by Donald Ross and Ellis Maples; the modern concepts are by Tom Fazio and Rees Jones.

## OTHER OUTDOOR PURSUITS

**Tennis** buffs will find nearly 100 public courts in the area; call © **910/692-3330** for locations, hours, and fees. Most of the resorts have their own court facilities. The Pine Needles Lodge and Golf Club has the only local grass courts, and lighted courts are available in both Southern Pines and Aberdeen.

**Bicycling** is another major sport. The Pinehurst area has long been regarded as a top-flight training area and proving ground for the U.S., Canadian, and other international cycling teams. Riders of all skill levels can enjoy a variety of mapped courses along peaceful lanes and through country villages. Annual cycling events include the **Tour de Moore,** a grueling 100-mile road race held the last Saturday in April around the perimeter of Moore County. This race draws cyclists from all over the world, who compete for the coveted Pinehurst Cup.

Because of the lack of bicycle-rental shops in the area, hotels keep their own stocks to rent to guests who'd like to cycle along the relatively easy terrain. Traffic is generally light, and conditions for cycling are good.

## The Links of Pinehurst

Nowhere in America do golf past and golf present walk hand in hand as they do in Pinehurst/Southern Pines. The area is a museum of golf architecture and a living laboratory of golf design. The first 18-hole course was opened in 1899 and was laid out by Dr. D. LeRoy Culver of New York. Since then, the array of architects has included Ellis and Dan Maples, Tom Fazio, Robert Trent Jones, Peter Tufts, and (one of the latest) Arnold Palmer. When the greens of Pinehurst No. 2 were dug up and resurfaced with bent grass in 1987, workers found an old horseshoe buried under the 18th green—a souvenir left by one of the animals that used to drag and shape the putting surface some 80 years ago. When Rees Jones, the famous golf architect, was laying out holes for Pinehurst No. 7 in 1984, he came across several ancient bunkers of a long-abandoned golf course. He ordered the bunkers restored, and they sit today in front of the tee to the 4th hole.

Some holes are nearly a century old, and others have small greens rounded off on the corners—the "upside-down-saucer" effect that Scotsman Donald Ross used so frequently. Some courses have huge greens that require a 7-iron approach if the pin's at the front and a 4-iron if it's in the rear. Still other holes require heroic shots over water or pits of sand, and some have open green entrances that invite the old bump-and-run shot.

North Carolina's Pinehurst/Southern Pines firmly re-established itself as the "Golf Capital of the World" when the United States Golf Association in 1999 made it the site of the U.S. Open Championship, which marked the second time that the U.S. Open has been played in the Southeast (the first time since 1976).

## WHERE TO STAY

Although the **Carolina Hotel** is still *the* place to stay in Pinehurst, several other hotels in the village offer luxury on a smaller scale and graciousness at the same level, at somewhat more moderate prices.

**The Carolina Hotel** ★★★   Established in 1901, this is one of the premier golf and tennis resorts in America. Set on 10,000 acres of landscaped grounds, it's a white, four-story clapboard landmark, with porches lined with comfortable rocking chairs. Here, the art of gracious living is still practiced. The public spaces and guest rooms have undergone extensive renovation. Bright, cheerful colors predominate in the spacious accommodations, which have an air of subdued elegance. In addition, the resort offers recently renovated villas, which are ideal for foursomes or eightsomes; and there's always the cozy Manor Inn for quiet getaways. Some guests prefer a condo by one of the golf courses or facing Lake Pinehurst. Each unit contains well-kept bathrooms with tub/shower combinations. The resort also owns the hotel's divinely comfortable neighbor, the Holly Inn, a charming turn-of-the-20th-century structure that offers deluxe accommodations and an imported Scottish bar.

For the **Carolina Dining Room,** see "Where to Dine," below.

Carolina Vista (P.O. Box 4000), Pinehurst, NC 28374. © **800/ITS-GOLF** or 910/295-8553. Fax 910/235-8507. www.pinehurst.com. 270 units, 170 condos. 3-day, 2-night golf packages $546–$888 per person double. Rates include breakfast and dinner. AE, DC, DISC, MC, V. **Amenities:** 9 restaurants; 3 bars; 3 pools; 8 18-hole golf courses; 24 tennis courts; fitness center; spa; Jacuzzi; sauna; boat rental; kids' club; business center; limited room service; babysitting; nonsmoking rooms; rooms for those w/limited mobility. *In room:* A/C, TV, dataport, minibar, hair dryer, safe.

**Magnolia Inn**  This three-story, white clapboard building, dating from 1895, is set in the midst of well-landscaped gardens. *Casablanca*-style fans rotate overhead on the front porch, and out back is a little pool. The rooms are sunny and flowery, with double, queen-size, or twin beds. Some of the bathrooms, with their claw-foot tubs, are a little too old-fashioned for comfort; the others have tub/shower combinations. The Olmsted and Page rooms, each of which has a fireplace, are our favorites. A tavern offers your basic pub menu. Breakfast and dinner are served in the dining room. The fare's seasonings (or lack of them) won't frighten away this inn's mostly older patrons.

65 Magnolia Rd. (at Chinquapin Rd.; P.O. Box 818), Pinehurst, NC 28370. © **800/526-5562** or 910/295-6900. Fax 910/215-0858. www.themagnoliainn.com. 11 units. $90–$110 per person. Rates include breakfast and dinner. AE, MC, V. **Amenities:** Restaurant; pub; pool. *In room:* A/C, TV, no phone.

**The Pine Crest Inn**  Right in the heart of the village, the Pine Crest Inn has been described by an English visitor as having "all the flavor and courtesies of our countryside inns." It draws people back year after year. Bob Barrett (proprietor since 1961) tells us that approximately 80% of his guests are returnees—and small wonder, for the three-story, white-columned building radiates warmth from the moment you enter the lobby, with its comfortable armchairs, fireplace, and bar. Each room is well maintained and has a bathroom with combination tub/shower. Our favorite place to stay is the Telephone Cottage, named after its former function as a telephone switching station. Roomy and comfortable, it's a separate cottage nestled under the trees. Meals in the three dining rooms (with fireplaces and tasteful wallpaper) are of such quality that they draw people from as far away as Raleigh and Charlotte.

50 Dogwood Rd. (P.O. Box 879), Pinehurst, NC 28370. © **800/371-2545** or 910/295-6121. Fax 910/295-4880. www.pinecrestinnpinehurst.com. 40 units. $136–$212 double. Rates include breakfast and dinner. Golf and sports packages available. AE, DC, DISC, MC, V. **Amenities:** Restaurant; bar; nonsmoking rooms; rooms for those w/limited mobility. *In room:* A/C, TV, dataport.

## WHERE TO DINE

**Carolina Dining Room** ★★ AMERICAN   The food here is the finest in the area. Only fresh, first-rate ingredients are used, and the dining room itself is worthy of the cuisine, with its series of Murano (Venetian) chandeliers. Breakfast, which is more expensive than the luncheon buffet, is the best in the area and recommended even if you're not a guest. Chefs prepare made-to-order omelets and waffles. The dinner menu is extensive, and the service is impeccable. Seafood fresh from Carolina coastal waters is presented in classic style. Beef so tender that you can cut it with your fork, along with baby veal and succulently flavored chicken (depending on the whim of the chef that evening) also appear on the menu. There may be either a buffet or a four- or five-course set menu. In either case, the price is the same, although surcharges appear if you order costly items such as rack of lamb, lobster, or prime rib. In summer, there's top-flight entertainment, as well as dinner dancing.

In the Carolina Hotel, 80 Carolina Vista. © **910/295-6811.** Reservations required. Jacket required for men at dinner. Breakfast buffet $24; lunch buffet $23; lunch main courses $4–$20; fixed-price 4-course dinner $60. AE, DC, DISC, MC, V. Daily 6–10am, noon–2pm, and 6:30–9:30pm (6–9pm in winter).

**Digins Pub** CONTINENTAL/IRISH   Across from the Holly Inn, this is the town's leading independent restaurant. Featuring a nautical decor, with natural woods, it also has a pub. Sandwiches and salads are lunch favorites. At night, a selection of seafood, mainly from Carolina coastal waters, is available. Pasta dishes are often overcooked, but the veal is great. Live music is offered here on Friday and Saturday nights.

2 Market Sq. (©) **910/295-3400.** Main courses $7.95–$18 lunch, $9–$20 dinner. AE, MC, V. Mon–Sat 11:30am–10pm; Sun noon–9pm. Bar Mon–Sat closes at 2am.

## PINEHURST AFTER DARK
Entertainment is mostly available at the golf resorts. Check, though, to see what's going on at **Sandhills Community College,** Airport Road (© **800/338-3944** or 910/692-6185), which often stages jazz and other variety shows, with tickets costing from $5 to $15. There are also free outdoor summer concerts.

## SIDE TRIPS IN THE AREA
**SEAGROVE & THE POTTERIES**   About an hour's drive to the northwest on U.S. 220 is the little town of Seagrove, which has been turning out quality pottery for more than 200 years. This region's red and gray clays were first used by settlers from Staffordshire, England; the first items produced were jugs for transporting whisky. The same art is practiced today just as it was then. Clays are ground and mixed by machines turned by mules, simple designs are fashioned on kick wheels, and glazing is done in wood-burning kilns. Many of the potters work in or behind their homes, with only a small sign outside to identify their trade. If you have difficulty finding them, stop and ask; everybody does, so don't be shy. There are some sales rooms in town, but the real fun is seeing the pottery actually being made.

While you're here, visit **Jugtown Pottery,** a group of rustic, log-hewn buildings in a grove of pines, at 330 Jugtown Rd. (© **910/464-3266;** www.jugtownware.com). The main potters here are owner Vernon Owens and his wife, Pam, both award-winning craftspeople. You'll find traditional jugs and candlesticks in wood-fired salt glaze and frog skin, among many other items. **Friends of the North Carolina Pottery Center** (© **336/873-8430** or 336/873-7887) is located at 250 East Ave., and offers 30-minute demonstrations scheduled between 11:30am and 2:30pm during regular opening days. This center displays examples of most of the potters' wares in the area and also serves as an information source, with guide maps available upon request. It's open Tuesday to Saturday 11:30am to 3:30pm. Admission is $3 adults, $1 children under 12.

Of some 40 potters operating in the Seagrove area, one especially has caught our fancy. At the **Fish House and Blue Moon Gallery,** 1387 Hwy. 705 S., Seagrove (© **336/879-3270;** www.blue-moon-gallery.com), Brian and Georgia Knight's potter's wheel turns out delicate cutout candleholders, as well as a full line of more traditional bowls, vases, teapots, and casseroles. The shop is open Monday to Saturday from 10am to 5pm. The gallery features the work of artists from all over the country.

**ASHEBORO & THE ZOO**   A few miles north of Seagrove on U.S. 220 is the town of Asheboro, and 6 miles southeast of Asheboro off U.S. 64 and U.S. 220 is the **North Carolina Zoological Park** ⊕, 4401 Zoo Pkwy., Asheboro (© **800/488-0444;** www.nczoo.org). The 300-acre Africa region and the 200-acre North America region are the first of seven continental regions planned for the 1,448-acre park, featuring more than 1,000 animals in natural habitats. In this still-developing world-class zoo, gorillas and 200 rare animals such as meerkats inhabit the African Pavilion. Lions, elephants, bears, bison, elk, alligators, chimpanzees, and many other animals dwell in spacious outdoor habitats. A 37-acre African Plains exhibit is the home of a dozen species of antelope, gazelle, and oryx. The R. J. Reynolds Forest Aviary displays 150 exotic birds flying free amid lush tropical trees and plants. There are picnic areas, restaurants, gift shops, and a tram ride. The zoo is open daily 9am to 5pm from April 1 to September 30, and 9am to 4pm October 1 to March 14. The park is closed Christmas Day. Adults pay $10; seniors, students, and children (2–12) pay $6; free for children under 2.

## 2 Southern Pines

5 miles E of Pinehurst

The pleasant village of Southern Pines has its own attractions lying among longleaf and loblolly pines in what is known as "sand country." A resort since the 1880s, it became a golfing mecca in 1920. It's rare for a building here to be more than two stories tall. Locals readily admit that the main reason to come here is to follow that little white ball, but they are quick to point out that the town has some interesting sights as well.

### SEEING THE SIGHTS

The **Campbell House,** a handsome, Georgian former family residence on East Connecticut Avenue, now houses the Arts Council of Moore County, and its galleries display the work of local artists.

**Shaw House,** at Southwest Broad Street and Morganton Road (✆ **910/692-2051** or 910/692-4885), is a stylish antebellum house with unusual carved-cypress mantels. It's the oldest structure in town, dating from the 1770s, and serves as headquarters of the Moore County Historical Association. It's open Wednesday to Sunday from 1 to 4pm, and admission is free. It's closed during the summer, but tours are available. For information on tour times and operators, call the Shaw House.

On the Fort Bragg–Aberdeen road, 1 mile southeast of Southern Pines, you'll come to **Weymouth Woods–Sandhills Nature Preserve** (✆ **910/692-2167**), a nature spot with foot and bridle paths and about 600 acres of pine-covered "sand ridges." The natural history museum is open daily 9am to 6pm; admission is free. It's closed on Christmas Day.

You'll find a lot of fine horse farms in the Sandhills. Steeplechasers trained here show up regularly at tracks around the country, and trotters and pacers are also trained in the area. The late Del Cameron, renowned three-time winner of the Hambletonian, kept a winter training stable here for more than 30 years.

**SPECIAL EVENTS**   Expect a full calendar of equestrian events throughout the year, including the **Southern Pines Horse Trials** at Carolina Horse Park at Five Points, annually in mid-March (✆ **910/246-9808;** www.carolinahorsepark. com). During the first week of April, the **Pinehurst Harness Track Matinee Races** are held at the Pinehurst Harness Mile Track along Route 5 in Pinehurst (✆ **910/295-4446;** www.pinehurstharness.com). **The Carolina Carriage Classic in the Pines** is presented at the end of April and in early May at the Pinehurst Harness Mile Track, Route 5, Pinehurst (✆ **910/295-4446**). This is one of the major driving events in the Southeast, with three rings of competition— dressage, pleasure classes, and obstacles. The **Pinehurst Area Convention and Visitors Bureau** (✆ **800/346-5362;** www.homeofgolf.com), P.O. Box 2270, Southern Pines, NC 28388, can furnish exact dates and full details on all these events, as well as others throughout the year.

Seek out **Downtown Southern Pines,** U.S. 1 in the Broad Street area, for a collection of shops and restaurants in the historic district.

# WHERE TO STAY

**Hampton Inn Southern Pines**    Hampton Inn is one of the two leading motels in the area, though it's not quite as good as its major competitor, the Holiday Inn (recommended below). Although decorated in standard chain format, it is one of the better-run inns, with styling in the Early American mode. Guest rooms are comfortably furnished, making for an inviting family atmosphere. Each unit comes with a well-kept bathroom with a tub/shower combination. Rates rise during special events, such as NASCAR races, the PGA tournament, and the Stoneybrook Steeplechase races. Tennis and golf can be arranged, as can entrance to a nearby health club. There is also a restaurant nearby.

1675 U.S. 1 N., Southern Pines, NC 28387. ℭ **910/692-9266.** Fax 910/692-9298. www.hamptoninn.com. 126 units. $69–$89 double. Children 17 and under stay free in parent's room. Golf packages available. Rates include continental breakfast. AE, DC, DISC, MC, V. **Amenities:** Breakfast room; lounge; outdoor pool; laundry service/dry cleaning. *In room:* A/C, TV, dataport, coffeemaker, iron/ironing board.

**Holiday Inn**    This is the best motel in the area, attracting a lot of golfers. Although lacking personality, it compensates with good-size rooms, a high level of housekeeping, and personal service. All units have well-maintained bathrooms with tub/shower combinations. The staff is helpful, providing such extras as free cribs for families who need them. Room service is also available. The fare in the **Hennings Restaurant** is only ordinary, but the restaurant is conveniently open throughout the day. Charbroiled steaks are a specialty.

P.O. Box 1467 on U.S. 1 at Morganton Rd., Southern Pines, NC 28387. ℭ **800/262-5737** or 910/692-8585. Fax 910/692-5213. www.holiday-inn.com. 160 units. $85 double. Children 17 and under stay free in parent's room. AE, DC, DISC, MC, V. **Amenities:** Restaurant; bar; outdoor pool; fitness center; limited room service; nonsmoking rooms; rooms for those w/limited mobility. *In room:* A/C, TV, dataport, hair dryer, iron/ironing board.

**Hyland Hills Resort**    In an attractive wooded setting, this small resort is nowhere near the match of such better-known places as Mid Pines, but what it has going for it is economy. The efficiencies and rather spacious guest rooms, often with patios, aren't luxurious in any way, but they're comfortable and well maintained, and you can prepare light meals here. All units contain well-kept bathrooms with tub/shower combinations.

U.S. 1 N., Southern Pines, NC 28387. ℭ **800/841-0638** or 910/692-7615. 41 units. $64 double; $68 efficiency. Golf packages available. DISC, MC, V. **Amenities:** Restaurant; bar; pool. *In room:* A/C, TV, coffeemaker.

**Mid Pines Inn and Golf Club** ✪    Five miles east of Pinehurst, this 1921 hotel retains its old-fashioned comfort and a certain flair. It is owned and run by Pine Needles (see below). Every hole on the golf course remains as it was in 1921 when Donald Ross first conceived this challenging course. A devoted clientele returns every year, but newcomers are also given a hearty welcome. It consists of a graceful three-story, Colonial-style main building with wings flanking the entrance. The lobby rotunda is gracious, with twin white staircases. The rooms are decorated with style and taste, although you may prefer one of the golf cottages or villas on the grounds—some have their own fireplaces. The villas are the most spacious choices. Generous meals are prepared in the formal dining room. In summer, lunch is served on an informal terrace overlooking the fairways of the championship golf course.

1010 Midland Rd., Southern Pines, NC 28387. ℭ **800/747-7272** or 910/692-2114. Fax 910/692-4615. www. pineneedles-midpines.com. 113 units, 7 cottages, 10 lakeside villas. $130–$150 per person double; $175 per person cottage or villa. Children 11 and under stay free in parent's room. AE, DC, DISC, MC, V. **Amenities:** Restaurant; bar; pool; 18-hole golf course; tennis court; health club privileges; limited room service; babysitting; laundry service/dry cleaning; nonsmoking rooms. *In room:* A/C, TV, dataport, hair dryer.

**Pine Needles Lodge**   With all the pine trees in the area, someone had to name a hotel "Pine Needles," and someone did. The resort—home to the U.S. Women's Open Championships—is the creation of local legend Peggy Kirk Bell, a champion golfer and golf instructor, who opened it with her late husband. It has won many a devoted fan over the years. The golf course here was designed in 1927 by Donald Ross, the famous golf architect. The handsome rooms are spread across 10 rustic two- or four-story lodges that can hold groups of 10 to 20 people each; returnees often select their favorites. Decidedly informal, the accommodations have rustic styling, often with exposed beams. The Bell family purchased the Mid Pines Inn and Golf Club in 1994 (see above).

1005 Midland Rd., Southern Pines, NC 28387. © **800/747-7272** or 910/692-7111. Fax 910/692-5349. www. pineneedles-midpines.com. 85 units. $130–$365 per person double. Golf packages available. Children 4 and under stay free in parent's room. AE, MC, V. **Amenities:** 2 restaurants; 3 bars; outdoor pool; 2 18-hole golf courses; tennis court; fitness center; health club privileges; bike rentals; business services; gift shop; limited room service; babysitting; laundry service/dry cleaning. *In room:* A/C, TV, dataport, coffeemaker, hair dryer, iron.

## WHERE TO DINE

**La Terrace** ♣ CONTINENTAL/FRENCH   This is the best restaurant at the resort, and dining here is a real pleasure. It offers flavorful cuisine in a charming setting, both intimate and formal. Local seafood, including frogs' legs, is featured, as is the chef's specialty: stuffed Dover sole. Lamb is prepared with just the right seasonings. The service is the finest in town.

270 SW Broad St. © **910/692-5622.** Reservations recommended. Lunch $8.50–$11; main courses $17–$25. MC, V. Mon–Fri 11:30am–2pm and 5:30–9pm; Sat 6–9:30pm.

**The Lob Steer Inn** *Kids* STEAK/SEAFOOD   This family favorite is a sure bet for fine dining at a reasonable cost. Tasty preparations of the kind of fare locals like are served, including broiled seafood and prime rib. Guests help themselves at the freshly prepared salad bar and somehow always find room to go to the dessert bar to finish their meal. This is a rather upscale dining choice, despite the casual dress. As a waiter confided, "We're no redneck joint." It's deservedly one of the best and most popular places in the area. Children's plates are offered in a wider variety than usual.

U.S. 1 N. © **910/692-3503.** Reservations recommended Fri–Sat. Main courses $10–$30. AE, DC, DISC, MC, V. Sun–Thurs 5–10pm; Fri–Sat 5–10:30pm.

## SOUTHERN PINES AFTER DARK

Most area golf resorts offer dancing and occasional evening entertainment. In addition, check the following for current goings-on.

The **Arts Council of Moore County,** P.O. Box 405, Southern Pines, NC 28388 (© **910/692-4356;** www.artscouncil-moore.org), maintains a cultural calendar at the **Sandhills Theater Company** (© **910/944-7853**) and sponsors local concert and entertainment groups and periodic arts-council shows.

## A SIDE TRIP TO CAMERON

The entire little town of **Cameron,** 10 miles north of Southern Pines (off U.S. 1/15/501), has been designated a historic district, with some 19 vintage sites and buildings. More than 60 antiques dealers have shops here, and an annual antiques street fair is held the first Saturday in May and again in October. Most shops are open Wednesday to Saturday from 10am to 5pm. After a morning of sightseeing and shopping, have lunch at the **Dewberry Deli,** 485 Carthage St. (© **910/245-3697**), open Tuesday to Saturday 10am to 5pm. Located in an old hardware store, this eatery is ideal for a salad or a sandwich.

# 8

# Asheville & the High Country

Men and women have made their homes in North Carolina's Blue Ridge Mountains since the first push westward, but nature endures. In late spring, green creeps up the peaks as trees leaf out. In summer, wildflowers make a carpet of colorful blooms. Fall brings vivid reds, yellows, and oranges to give every mountainside a flamelike hue. Wildlife still flourishes; streams are clear; and forests of birch, poplar, beech, hickory, and oak are undisturbed. This is one of those rare places where civilization has been smart enough to protect the natural environment as well as enjoy it.

The largest city in the High Country is handsome Asheville, home of author Thomas Wolfe (*Look Homeward, Angel*) and long a residence of the wealthy and famous. In recent years, neighboring Boone, Banner Elk, and Blowing Rock have become important ski centers in the South, especially since the introduction of snowmaking equipment. The best skiing in the area includes Ski Beech, Appalachian Ski Mountain, Hawksnest Golf & Ski Resort, and Sugar Mountain.

## 1 Enjoying the Great Outdoors in the High Country

Sparkling white winters, fragrant springs, cool summers, and brisk, burnished autumns characterize North Carolina's High Country. Skiing in winter gives way in milder weather to swimming, golfing, fishing, tennis, rafting, horseback riding, backpacking, rock climbing, and rappelling.

The **Blue Ridge Parkway,** a unit of the U.S. National Park System, passes through all five counties of the High Country, offering a vista of natural beauty and rural landscapes (see "The Blue Ridge Parkway," later in this chapter).

Moses Cone Memorial Park, near Blowing Rock on the parkway, has 25 miles of easily graded **hiking** trails. It's also popular for cross-country skiing. The Linville Falls/Linville Gorge area on the parkway has several trails leading to the head of the falls, with views of the cataract and the Linville Gorge Wilderness Area. Moderate trails lead to Grandfather Mountain, and challenging hikes take in part of the fabled Appalachian Trail, stretching from Georgia to Maine. In North Carolina, the trail crosses Roan Mountain, Hump Mountain, and Yellow Mountain, all of which are known for their large expanses of meadows with panoramic views. Trail heads are in Elk Park and at Carver's Gap on Roan.

The High Country is also filled with **state and federal parks,** including Moses Cone Memorial Park, north of Blowing Rock. This 3,600-acre park offers bridle paths, hiking trails, trout streams, and two lakes. The other major park is the Linville Gorge Wilderness Area, a 7,600-acre tract set aside to provide a natural environment. The steep walls of the gorge enclose the Linville River, which descends 2,000 feet in only 12 miles. Access is by foot trails via the Forest Service Road off U.S. 221 at the Linville Falls exit.

# Blue Ridge Parkway

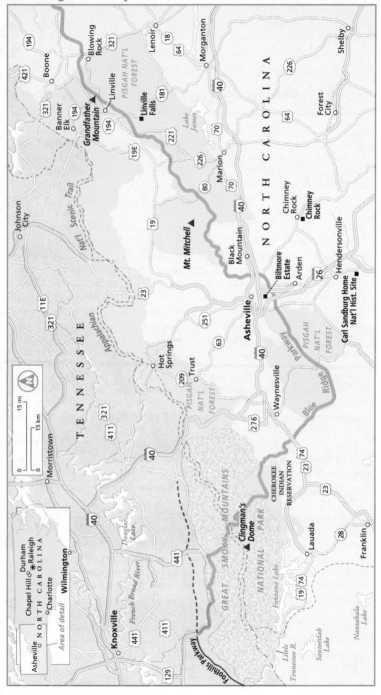

Cross-country **skiing** is the finest in the South. Excellent trails are at Moses Cone Memorial Park, Beech Mountain, and several other locations along the Blue Ridge Parkway.

For **fishing,** area streams and lakes abound in trout, bass, catfish, blue gill, and other varieties. The game fish waters of the Blue Ridge Parkway (Price, Cone, and Doughton parks) are under federal regulation and require a license or permit. The fishing season begins the first Saturday in April and runs through the last day of February.

## 2  Asheville ✦✦✦

241 miles W of Raleigh

Asheville, once just a tiny mountain trading village at the confluence of the French Broad and Swannanoa rivers, has grown up and turned into a year-round resort, complete with architectural gems from several eras and a lively cultural scene.

People who could have lived almost anywhere in the world, including Thomas Edison, settled in Asheville. Those Jazz Age kids, F. Scott and Zelda Fitzgerald, were among the most famous visitors. Fitzgerald arrived in the summer of 1935, recuperating from a mild case of tuberculosis, and his wife, Zelda, who had suffered a series of nervous breakdowns, was incarcerated at Highland Hospital, a private sanitarium charging $240 a month—an exorbitant fee in those days.

The most famous person associated with Asheville is Thomas Wolfe, whose mother ran a boardinghouse here called "The Old Kentucky Home." It was disguised as "Dixieland" in Wolfe's autobiographical novel, *Look Homeward, Angel.* Fitzgerald and Wolfe had some things in common: TB, an eye for the women, and alcohol. They even shared an editor: the famous Maxwell Perkins. Wolfe's novel (still called "that book" by old-timers in Asheville) was blacklisted here as late as 1949. Although he claimed that "you can't go home again," he eventually did, in 1938. Thousands assembled outside his mother's old boardinghouse to bid him farewell upon his premature death.

## ESSENTIALS

**GETTING THERE**    I-40 passes through Asheville from the east and west, I-26 runs southeast (as far as Charleston); U.S. 23/19A runs north and west, and I-240 is a perimeter highway circling the city. For AAA services, contact the **Carolina Motor Club,** 1000 Merrimon Ave., Suite B, Asheville, NC 28804 (© **800/274-2621** or 828/253-5376).

**Asheville Regional Airport** (© **828/684-2226;** www.flyavl.com) is just off I-26. Major airlines serving this airport are **Delta ASA** and **Comair** (© **800/221-1212;** www.delta.com), **Continental Express** (© **800/525-0280;** www.continental.com), and **US Airways** (© **800/428-4322;** www.usairways.com).

**VISITOR INFORMATION**    The **Asheville Convention and Visitors Bureau,** 151 Haywood St. (P.O. Box 1010), Asheville, NC 28802 (© **800/257-1300** or 828/258-6101; www.exploreasheville.com or www.ashevillechamber.com), is open Monday to Friday from 8:30am to 5:30pm and on Saturday and Sunday from 9am to 5pm. You can also request an *Asheville Visitor Guide* from the **Asheville Chamber of Commerce** (© **888/247-9811;** www.ashevillechamber.org).

**SPECIAL EVENTS**   Special happenings at the **Biltmore Estate** (see "Seeing the Sights," below) include a spring Festival of Flowers, September International Exposition, and Christmas at Biltmore—ask ahead for specific dates.

Special events at the **Folk Art Center,** www.southernhighlandguild.org (see "Side Trips from Asheville," later in this chapter), include Fiber Day in May, the World Gee Haw Whimmy Diddle Competition in August, Celebrate Folk Art in September, and Christmas with the Guild in December. In July and October, *Mountain Sweet Talk* is a two-part, two-act play presented by Barbara Freeman and Connie Regan-Blake, who are among this country's best mountain storytellers. Call ahead for dates and times.

If you're here the first weekend of August, you can attend the **Annual Mountain Dance and Folk Festival** (www.folkheritage.org), held at the Civic Center on Haywood Street. The fiddlers, banjo pickers, ballad singers, dulcimer players, and clog dancers don't call it quits until nobody is interested in one more dance. This is the oldest such festival in the country, and you're encouraged to join in even if you don't know a "do-si-do" from a "swing-your-partner." Every Saturday night from early July to August (except for the first Sat in Aug), there's a **Shindig-on-the-Green** (www.folkheritage.org) at the City/County Plaza (College and Spruce sts.), where you'll find many of the same mountain musicians and dancers having an old-fashioned wingding. It's free, and lots of fun. Take along a blanket or chair.

Brevard, 27 miles southwest of Asheville, hosts a music festival from late June through mid-August at the **Brevard Music Center** (www.brevardmusic.org). Nationally and internationally famous artists perform daily in symphony, chamber-music, band, and choral concerts, as well as musical comedy and opera. Write P.O. Box 312, Brevard, NC 28712; or call © **888/384-8682** or 888/862-2105 for schedules and reservations. Some events are free; others cost from $10 to $60.

**The North Carolina International Folk Festival (Folkmoot),** Waynesville, is an annual cultural heritage of folk music and dances. Participants travel from around the world to join in the event. For information, get in touch with Folkmoot USA, 112 Virginia Ave. in Waynesville (© **877/FOLK-USA** or 828/452-2997; www.folkmoot.com; second and third weeks in July).

Billed as "the largest free outdoor street festival in the Southeast," **Bele Chere** is a great summer festival of food and entertainment in Arts Park in Asheville. In 2005 it will be held July 29, 30, and 31. Feast on such delights as hickory smoked pork, peach and blueberry pie, and corn dogs. "A Taste of Asheville" food booths feature local cuisine along with specialties ranging from Mexican to Chinese. In addition, top regional artisans and craftspeople showcase handmade clothing, pottery, and jewelry. Such big-name artists as De La Soul and John Anderson have played the festival. Contact the Department of Parks and Recreation (© **828/259-5800;** www.belechere.com).

## SEEING THE SIGHTS

In recent years, a vigorous local effort has been made to preserve and restore remnants of the city's colorful past. "The Asheville Urban Trail" brochure, available free from the Asheville Chamber of Commerce or at the Asheville Visitor Center, is a self-guided tour through the historic downtown district.

**Biltmore Village** (www.biltmorevillage.com) is a cluster of 24 cottages housing boutiques, crafts shops, and restaurants. The best of these shops is the **New Morning Gallery,** 7 Boston Way (© **828/274-2831**); it started in 1972 and today is a 6,000-square-foot showcase of "Art for Living." The New Morning Gallery is one of the South's largest galleries of arts and crafts. It offers a fresh

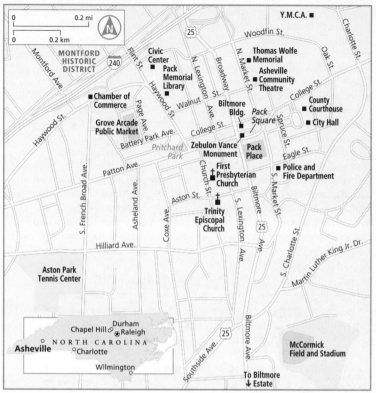

mix of functional and sculptural pottery, fine-art glass, furniture, jewelry, and other handmade objects. It's open Monday to Saturday from 10am to 7pm and on Sunday from noon to 5pm.

Another attraction, the **Montford Historic District,** has more than 200 turn-of-the-20th-century residences. In the downtown area, amid Art Deco buildings, you'll see the **Lexington Park** area, a center for artists and artisans whose workshops are tucked down a little alleyway; and **Pack Place,** a developing center for a wide variety of cultural activities.

**Thomas Wolfe,** a native of Asheville, immortalized the town and its citizens in his first novel, *Look Homeward, Angel.* His mother's **boardinghouse,** at 48 Spruce St., is maintained as a literary shrine. The house was severely damaged by a fire set by an arsonist in 1998, but the building was restored and reopened in 2004. The author lived here from 1906 to 1916. ("I was a child here, here the stairs, and here was darkness; this was I, and this was Time.") Called Old Kentucky Home, the 30-room house with a wooden porch was referred to as "Dixieland" in his novels. Tours of the house are offered Tuesday to Sunday every hour on the half-hour, costing $1 and lasting 45 minutes. Before the fire, the city of Asheville opened the **Thomas Wolfe Memorial;** because many of his personal belongings, such as his typewriter and writing table, were on display in the site's visitor center, they were not destroyed. The exhibit was expanded just after the fire to include a 22-minute video biography and a slide show that depicts the Wolfe house as it was before the devastation. The biography is shown at the

beginning of every half-hour from 9am to 4pm, and the slide show is held from
9:30am to 4:30pm. For information, call, visit, or write the **Visitors Center,** 52
N. Market St., Asheville, NC 28801 (© **828/253-8304;** www.ah.dcr.state.
nc.us/sections/hs/wolfe/wolfe.htm). Hours are Tuesday to Saturday 9am to
5pm, Sunday 1 to 5pm (winter hours Tues–Sat 10am–4pm).

Both Wolfe and short-story writer **O. Henry** (William Sydney Porter) are
buried in **Riverside Cemetery** (entrance on Birch St. off Pearson Dr.).

Asheville's **Grovewood Gallery** (© **877/622-7238** or 828/253-7651; www.
grovewood.com) features the work of some of the Southeast's finest craftspeople,
including the artists of **Grovewood Studios,** whose workshops are in the adjoining buildings. The gallery is located in what was for 70 years the home of the
Biltmore Homespun Shops, adjacent to the Grove Park Inn Resort (see "Where
to Stay," later in this chapter). Grovewood Studios continues the tradition of
craftsmanship begun by Edith Vanderbilt in 1901 as Biltmore Estate Industries.
Established as an industrial school to teach boys and girls the traditional skills of
woodcarving and hand-weaving, the Industries became a thriving business, producing homespun cloth and woodcarvings and furniture. The Industries were sold

## The Greatest Mansion in the Mountains

George Washington Vanderbilt, a young man of 25 in the late 1880s,
came upon the perfect spot in the Blue Ridge for his French Renaissance–style château, which was to be built by his friend, architect
Richard Morris Hunt.

The great château would be called Biltmore. His initial purchase of
125,000 acres outside Asheville has diminished to 8,000. It includes formal and informal gardens designed by the father of landscape architecture in America, Frederick Law Olmsted.

Biltmore remains the largest private residence in the United States,
a National Historic Landmark now owned by Vanderbilt's grandson.
Begun in 1890, the house is constructed of tons of Indiana limestone,
transported by a special railway spur built specifically to bring the massive amounts of material and supplies to the site. It took hundreds of
workers 5 years to complete the house. On Christmas Eve 1895, George
Vanderbilt formally opened the doors for the first time to friends and
family members.

Like William Randolph Hearst, Vanderbilt journeyed through
Europe and Asia buying paintings, porcelains, bronzes, carpets, and
antiques, all of which would become part of the collection of 50,000
objects that are still in Biltmore today. Artwork is by Renoir, Sargent,
Whistler, Pellegrini, and Boldini, and furniture includes designs by
Chippendale and Sheraton.

Fully electric and centrally heated, Biltmore was one of the most
technologically advanced structures ever built at the time of its com-
pletion. It used some of Thomas Edison's first light bulbs and boasted
a fire-alarm system, an electrical call-box system for servants, two elevators, elaborate indoor plumbing for all 34 bedrooms—and a relatively newfangled invention called the telephone.

in 1917 to Fred Seely, manager of the Grove Park Inn, who built the charming cluster of English-style workshops known as the Biltmore Homespun Shops and further developed the woolen cloth into a product known around the world. Cloth production finally ceased in 1980, but the history of the Industries and the Homespun Shops is told here at the **North Carolina Homespun Museum.** Also on the grounds are the **Estes-Winn Memorial Automobile Museum** and the **Grovewood Cafe.** The gallery is open year-round Monday to Saturday 10am to 5pm (closed Sun). The museums are open April to December Monday to Saturday 10am to 5pm and Sunday 1 to 5pm. Admission to the two museums is free. You can reach the gallery and the Grove Park Inn via Charlotte Street and Macon Avenue. When you are on the grounds of the inn, follow the signs.

As interesting as all the preceding attractions may be, they're dwarfed by the premier attraction in Asheville: the magnificent Biltmore Estate.

**Biltmore Estate** ★★★   The French Renaissance château, built by George W. Vanderbilt, has 250 rooms. This is one of the largest and most impressive privately owned historic estates in the world, still under the control of the rich Vanderbilt clan.

Visitors should allow a minimum of 5 hours to see the place—it's huge. Many sightseers make a day of it. If your pass is stamped when you leave the estate at the end of your first day, you can return anytime the following day for a flat fee of $10.

A visit is divided into four different attractions, including the mansion itself, part of a 2- to 2½-hour self-directed tour. Visitors are supplied with a map that covers three floors of the building and the basement. Immediately adjacent to the mansion lie the Greenhouses and Conservatories. Three miles from the main house is the Winery and Biltmore Farm Village, the most visited winery in the U.S., featuring tours and wine tastings. It sells wine that's produced on the grounds. Finally, there's the Explore Biltmore Center, devoted to outdoor sports and family activities, including horseback riding, cycling, trips on the French Broad River, and other events. There isn't an ordinary spot in the place—not even the kitchen. Vanderbilt gathered furnishings and art treasures from all over the world for this palace (Napoleon's chess set and table from St. Helena are here, for example) and then went further, creating one of the most lavish formal gardens you'll ever see.

Two tours are presented. The "Behind the Scenes Tour" provides further access to the house, and the "Rooftop Tour" provides panoramic views. Both are offered for an additional charge of $14.

1 N. Pack Sq. (on U.S. 25, 2 blocks north of I-40). ℂ 800/543-2961 or 828/225-1333. www.biltmore.com. House and gardens $39 adults, $27 seniors, $20 children 6–16; free for children 5 and under when accompanied by paying adult. Daily 9am–6pm.

## OUTDOOR PURSUITS

**BICYCLING**   The Asheville area is terrific for mountain biking. Bicycle shops and outfitters can provide trail maps and bike rentals. Call the chamber of commerce at ℂ **828/258-6101** for a complete list.

**FISHING**   Best for lake fishing is **Lake Julian,** south of Asheville, which is well stocked with bass and bream. Canoes and picnicking are available. **Lake Powhatan,** on N.C. 191 in the Pisgah National Forest, has a sand beach, swimming, camping, and picnicking in addition to fishing. No boats are available, however. **Lake Lure,** on U.S. 74 about 30 minutes southeast of Asheville, has trout, bass, bream, and watersports; motorboats are available. There's also an abundance of well-stocked rivers and highland streams within easy reach of Asheville. For more information about fishing in the area, call the **Hunter Banks Store** (© 828/252-3005).

**GOLF**    The rolling terrain of the mountains around Asheville presents golfers with hundreds of uncrowded fairways. There are more than 50 golf courses in the state's western region. Our favorite is the course at the **Grove Park Inn Resort,** 290 Macon Ave. (© 828/252-2711; www.groveparkinn.com), newly renovated after being closed for a year for a $2.3-million restoration. Open daily throughout the year, the par-71 course is steeped in tradition, having first opened in 1899. It was redesigned in 1924 by master golf architect Donald Ross. The oldest operating course in North Carolina, it evokes memories of Harry Vardon, Bobby Jones, and Ben Hogan. Arnold Palmer and Jack Nicklaus are only two of the great golfers who have played here. Greens fees are $85 for 9 holes and $145 for 18 holes.

**HIKING**    The famous **Appalachian Trail** (www.appalachiantrail.org) passes through a large section of Pisgah National Forest and Great Smoky Mountains National Park. The Greater Asheville area is a hiker's paradise, with trails in almost every direction and in every major park. You can purchase the booklet *100 Favorite Trails* at the Visitors Bureau (© 828/258-6101). You can also contact the North Carolina division of the USDA Forest Service (© 828/257-4200; www.cs.unca.edu/nfsnc) for trail maps and more information.

**HORSEBACK RIDING**    Stables in the area offer trail riding with experienced guides. Some stables also offer pack trips in the surrounding mountains. The Visitors Bureau keeps a complete list; call © 828/258-6101.

**TENNIS**    The **Grove Park Inn Resort,** 190 Macon Ave. (© 828/252-2711; www.groveparkinn.com), leads not only in golf but also in tennis. The resort has been ranked as one of the 50 greatest tennis resorts in the U.S. by *Tennis* magazine. It offers three outdoor courts and three indoor courts. Rates per hour range from $20 outdoors to $25 indoors.

**WHITE-WATER RAFTING**    You can choose a raft, kayak, or canoe to ride the white-water rapids. The rivers of western North Carolina and the Tennessee border offer rapids of Class I–V difficulty. Outfitters offer trips ranging from a half-day to a full weekend. Try the Nolichucky and French Broad rivers to the north or the Nantahala, Ocoee, Chattooga, and Green rivers to the west and south. Call the chamber of commerce for more information (© 828/258-6101).

## SHOPPING

The historic **Grove Arcade Public Market** at 1 Page Ave. (© 828/252-7799; www.grovearcade.com) reopened in 2002, and in the life of this edition it will embrace some 50 shops and restaurants. The arcade is the largest commercial building in the city, and the market itself has been restored to its previous prominence. This 269,000-square-foot structure (ca. 1929), closed since World War II, was in its heyday a bustling part of the city landscape and one of the country's first indoor public markets. It is much in the style of Seattle's Pike Place Market, with food stalls, restaurants, crafts stalls, and more. One of the more popular shops in the Grove Arcade is **Morning Star Galleries** (© 828/350-8585). It stocks heirloom-quality replicas of armoires from the Victorian Age, Art Deco lithographs and prints, stained-glass lamps inspired by Louis Comfort Tiffany, lots of estate jewelry and, perhaps best of all, a staggering number of handmade quilts imported from at least 20 different quilting co-ops in Kentucky and Missouri. A few come from India and Eastern Europe, so if you're passionate about the authenticity of your quilts and quilting patterns, ask before you buy.

Crafts are so important in the hills of western North Carolina that shopping for them is almost like sightseeing. In Asheville, sights and crafts shops are often combined. One of the foremost arts-and-crafts shops is the **Grovewood Gallery** at the **Homespun Shops,** which also enjoys the distinction of being a historical landmark (see "Seeing the Sights," above).

Asheville is the home of more than 50 galleries exhibiting works by local and national artists, including folk art, Native American art, and antiques. A gallery worth noting is the **Appalachian Craft Center,** 10 N. Spruce St. (© **828/253-8499**). Hours are Monday to Saturday from 10am to 5pm.

A popular counterculture bookstore and gathering place is **Malaprop's Bookstore/Cafe,** 55 Haywood St. (© **828/254-6734;** www.malaprops.com). This is the most interesting and most deeply entrenched, independently owned bookstore in western North Carolina, a cultural beacon by anyone's standards and the subject of devoted loyalty from thousands of readers in the surrounding towns and counties. It's divided into more than 300 different subject categories, with specific emphasis on regional studies, Asheville lore, films and movies, women's studies, astrology, New Age philosophy, and more, with a distinctive interest in the liberal, countercultural venues with which Asheville has long been associated. The bookstore is open most nights until 9 or 10pm.

**Biltmore Village**   This shopping village is reminiscent of a time capsule. As you walk the cobblestone sidewalk, you feel that you might catch a glimpse of old George Vanderbilt himself. Shops, restaurants, and galleries abound, so allow yourself plenty of time to see everything. One store, the Biltmore Village Co., is quite charming and affordable; it bills itself as a gift shop containing everything—at half price. Hours are Monday to Saturday 9:30am to 6pm, and Sunday 1 to 5pm. Across from main entrance gate of the Biltmore Estate, Swan St. off Biltmore Ave. © 828/274-8788. www.biltmorevillage.com.

**Blue Spiral 1**   This is one of the hottest galleries in Asheville, representing some 100 Southeastern artists in a three-story space. Hours are Monday to Saturday 10am to 6pm; May through October also Sunday noon to 5pm. 38 Biltmore Ave. © 800/291-2513 or 828/251-0202. www.bluespiral1.com.

**The Chocolate Fetish**   This is the home of the most delicious, elegant, and sophisticated chocolates in the entire region. Bill and Sue Foley have been the owners of this place since the mid-1980s, supervising the manufacture, on-site, of small-scale batches of more than 21 kinds of chocolate that are made according to the highest standards of chocolate-manufacturing in Belgium. Some of the bestsellers include truffles, sold by the piece; Ecstasy Blossom, which is flavored with lemon zest, saffron, and ginger and embellished with a crystallized violet; and a divine "Dragon's Kiss" that's artfully flavored with Japanese wasabi. Open Monday to Thursday 11:30am to 6pm, Friday and Saturday 11am to 9pm, Sunday noon to 5pm. 36 Haywood St. © 828/258-2353.

**The Kress Emporium** ★ *Finds*   This store serves as a showcase for more than 80 artists and craftspeople in the area. Stained-glass mosaics, lace handwork, fine miniature-furnishing collectibles, silk paintings, frames, and prints are just a few of the things that you will find here. The 1928 building that houses the emporium is a reason to visit in its own right; it is an architectural landmark designed in neoclassical style. Hours are Monday to Thursday 11am to 6pm, Friday and Saturday 11am to 7pm. Between summer and Christmas, they are open on Sunday from noon to 5pm. 19 Patton Ave., Asheville. ℂ 828/281-2252.

**The Mast General Store** In terms of down-home Blue Ridge shopping options, the Mast has it all. It's situated on the sprawling premises of a general department store from the 1940s. The merchandise here is more rustic, more rural, and more folksy than you'll find in more modern department stores. You can buy the accessories you'd need (from lingerie to camping supplies) for a season in the "hillbilly hollers" of the region. Don't overlook the furniture stocked in the balcony. Hours are Monday to Thursday 10am to 6pm, Friday to Saturday 10am to 9pm, and Sunday noon to 5pm. 15 Biltmore Ave. ℂ 828/232-1883.

**Old Europe** This shop sells the most elaborate and luscious pastries in Asheville. What you're likely to see behind display cases evokes Habsburgundian Vienna at its most lavish and most intensely high-caloric. At least some of the inspiration for the pastries here (both at tiny tables and as part of take-away food) comes from the Hungarian-born owners, Melanda and Zoltan Vetran. Pastries go for between 45¢ and $4 a slice. Open Monday to Friday 8:30am to midnight, Saturday and Sunday 9:30am to midnight. 18 Battery Park Ave. ℂ 828/252-0001.

**Woolworth Walk** The best crafts emporium in town lies on the main street in the sprawling premises of what was originally built as—you guessed it—a Woolworth's Department Store from the 1930s. Inside, clustered into a series of side-by-side self-contained boutiques, and scattered over two separate floors, are the carefully displayed works of 175 local artists, each of whose work had to be approved by a local jury. Representative art forms include silversmithing, pottery, leatherware, stained glass, metalwork, bookbindery, and cabinetmaking. Adding to the ambience might be live music from a flute player or guitarist. Open Monday to Thursday 11am to 6pm, Friday and Saturday 11am to 8pm, and Sunday 11am to 5pm. 25 Haywood St. ℂ 828/252-9234. www.woolworthwalk.com.

## WHERE TO STAY

**Beaufort House Victorian Inn** ★★ Designed in 1894 by A. L. Melton, a well-known local architect, this landmark Queen Anne confection is among the top two or three B&Bs in Asheville. It lies half a mile from the center of town, in the Grove Park district. The house is operated by Jacqueline and Robert Glasgow, and is listed on the National Register of Historic Places. The individually decorated guest rooms are full of antiques. One accommodation occupies the top floor, and another is in a carriage house with a loft bedroom, kitchenette, private deck, and living room. Three of the four units in the main house have whirlpools. All units have well-kept bathrooms, most of which have tub/shower combinations. The country breakfast with freshly squeezed juice is a serious reason to stay here. No smoking.

61 N. Liberty St., Asheville, NC 28801. ℂ 800/261-2221 or 828/254-8334. Fax 828/251-2082. www.beaufort house.com. 11 units. $125–$275 double. Rates include full breakfast and afternoon tea. MC, V. **Amenities:** Breakfast room; lounge; nonsmoking rooms. *In room:* A/C, TV, dataport, hair dryer.

**Cedar Crest Inn** ★ A stay here is like entering a time capsule and going back to the Victorian era. This Queen Anne mansion is one of the largest and most opulent residences surviving from Asheville's 1890s boom. The mansion has a captain's walk, projecting turrets, and expansive verandas, and the inside is a fantasy of leaded glass, ornately carved fireplaces, and antique furnishings, with a massive oak staircase. Owners Rita and Bruce Wightman have indulged their romantic and whimsical imaginations in furnishing the guest rooms: All have period antiques and individual decor—a canopied ceiling in the Romeo and Juliet room, a carved walnut bed in another room, and brass bedsteads in a third. Each room has a private bathroom with a tub/shower combination (Jacuzzi tubs), and several contain working fireplaces. A cottage with two suites is adjacent to the main house.

674 Biltmore Ave., Asheville, NC 28803. ⓒ 800/252-0310 or 828/252-1389. Fax 828/253-7667. www.cedar crestvictorianinn.com. 11 units. $170–$200 double; $175–$285 suite. Rates include breakfast and afternoon refreshments. AE, DC, DISC, MC, V. Free parking. No children under 12. **Amenities:** Breakfast room; lounge; nonsmoking rooms. *In room:* A/C, TV, dataport, kitchenette (in some), hair dryer, iron/ironing board.

**Great Smokies Holiday Inn SunSpree Resort**    This is Asheville's leading motor hotel, lying directly off I-240, 3 miles from the center of town. Rooms are in a rather bland international style but are clean, comfortable, generous in size, and well maintained, with good tiled bathrooms containing tub/shower combinations and adequate space. Standard double rooms, with either two double beds or a king-size bed, have such extras as refrigerators and coffeemakers. The least expensive suite has a king-size bed with a couch that can be converted to a double bed; mid-range suites contain two bedrooms with two double beds in one and a king-size bed in the other. The most expensive suites offer three bedrooms and a living room, and can easily sleep six. There are tennis courts and an 18-hole golf course nearby. The restaurant, popular with families, serves typically American fare—perfectly acceptable cuisine, nothing more.

1 Holiday Inn Dr., Asheville, NC 28805. ⓒ 800/HOLIDAY or 828/254-3211. Fax 828/285-2688. www.holiday-inn. com. 272 units. $109–$150 double; $300 suite. AE, DC, DISC, MC, V. **Amenities:** Restaurant; bar; outdoor pool; 18-hole golf course; 4 tennis courts; fitness center; sauna; indoor soccer center; sand volleyball court; 24-hr. room service; babysitting; nonsmoking rooms; rooms for those w/limited mobility. *In room:* A/C, TV, dataport, minibar, coffeemaker, hair dryer, iron/ironing board.

**Grove Park Inn Resort & Spa** ★★★    This resort, built in 1913, is one of the oldest and most famous in the South. Listed on the National Register of Historic Places, it's a favorite year-round destination, providing panoramic views of the city's skyline and the Blue Ridge Mountains, old-world charm, and a long tradition of hospitality. Completely renovated in recent years, it's our favorite choice in the entire western section of North Carolina.

The two newer wings reflect the spirit of the original design. Novelist F. Scott Fitzgerald stayed at the hotel while his wife, Zelda, spent her nights in a sanitarium nearby. The hotel offers a romantic-getaway package called the Great Gatsby, although Fitzgerald's stay was hardly romantic. Over the years, the resort has hosted some of the most famous names of the 20th century, including Thomas Edison, Henry Ford, and Harvey Firestone. Presidents Franklin Delano Roosevelt and Woodrow Wilson also slept here.

The inn is built on the side of Sunset Mountain at an elevation of 3,100 feet. Its great-hall lobby is flanked by 14-foot fireplaces; comfortably padded chairs and sofas create a feeling of coziness despite the size of the 120-foot-long room. Twenty-eight of the bedrooms are oversize, containing such extras as whirlpools. All units contain well-kept bathrooms with tub/shower combinations.

**Horizons Restaurant,** featuring an innovative but classic cuisine, is the finest in the area (see "Where to Dine," below). Guests can also dine in the moderately priced **Blue Ridge Dining Room,** which has a legendary outdoor dining veranda. The **Carolina Cafe** also overlooks the mountains.

290 Macon Ave., Asheville, NC 28804. ⓒ 800/438-5800 or 828/252-2711. Fax 828/253-7053. www. groveparkinn.com. 510 units. Summer $209–$429 double, $800–$1,000 suite; off season $150–$300 double, $600–$1,000 suite. AE, DC, DISC, MC, V. **Amenities:** 3 restaurants; 3 bars; 2 pools (1 indoor); 18-hole golf

course; 6 tennis courts; fitness center; health spa; sauna; limited room service; babysitting; laundry service/ dry cleaning; nonsmoking rooms; rooms for those w/limited mobility. *In room:* A/C, TV, dataport, kitchenette, coffeemaker, hair dryer, iron/ironing board, safe.

**Haywood Park Hotel** ⋆   In the heart of downtown Asheville, this rather elegant all-suite place is the leading hotel in the city center. The suites are crisp and airy, a blend of luxury—some have Iberian marble bathrooms, recessed closets, showers with oversize tubs and whirlpools—combined with practical details such as computer hookups. All beds are either queen- or king-size. The hotel's deluxe restaurant has a Continental menu specializing in French, German, and Indian cuisine, as well as an extensive wine list. It also has a beer garden.

1 Battery Park Ave., Asheville, NC 28801. © 800/228-2522 or 828/252-2522. Fax 828/253-0481. www.haywood park.com. 33 units. $175–$335 suite for 2. Rates include continental breakfast. Children 17 and under stay free in parent's room. AE, DC, DISC, MC, V. Free parking. **Amenities:** Restaurant; bar; fitness center; sauna; limited room service; laundry service/dry cleaning; nonsmoking rooms; rooms for those w/limited mobility. *In room:* A/C, TV, dataport, minibar, coffeemaker, hair dryer, iron/ironing board, safe.

## STAYING NEARBY

**The Greystone Inn** ⋆   Henry Ford and John D. Rockefeller once whiled away their summers on the 14 miles of leafy shoreline around Lake Toxaway. Set on a wooded peninsula along the lake, this imposing Swiss Revival mansion, listed on the National Register of Historic Places, was created for Savannah heiress Lucy Armstrong Moltz as a seasonal "cottage." Refurbished in 1985, it welcomes guests with an engaging mix of antique furnishings and modern comforts. Each guest room has its own character, and many have working fireplaces; all have well-maintained bathrooms with showers and whirlpools. The stone fireplace is also a focal point in the oak-paneled living room, the library is a tastefully appointed oasis, and the terrace is the ideal setting for before-dinner drinks. For dedicated do-nothings, there are wicker rocking chairs on the glassed-in sun porch overlooking the lake.

Meals in the **Lakeside** dining room (for guests only) feature such gourmet selections as seared Texas antelope and Georgian pecan chicken. Dinner is a six-course affair.

Greystone Lane, Lake Toxaway, NC 28747. © 800/824-5766 or 828/966-4700. Fax 828/862-5689. www. greystoneinn.com. 33 units. Sept–Mar $315 double, $595 suite; Apr–Aug $360 double, $595 suite. Rates include breakfast, dinner, champagne, afternoon tea, and sports activities except golf. MC, V. **Amenities:** Restaurant; bar; outdoor pool; 4 tennis courts; health spa; sauna; massage; limited room service; babysitting; laundry service/dry cleaning; nonsmoking rooms; rooms for those w/limited mobility. *In room:* A/C, TV, coffeemaker (in some), hair dryer (in some), iron/ironing board, dataport.

**Inn on Biltmore Estate** ⋆⋆⋆   Here's your rare chance to have a glimpse of what it was like to stay on the lavish Vanderbilt estate at the turn of the 20th century. A.V. Cecil, Jr., great-grandson of George W. Vanderbilt, poured $31 million into the creation of this elegant inn, set 2 miles from the French Renaissance country estate originally built by the tycoon himself. The hotel lies deep within the grounds of the Biltmore Estate. No one can drive up to it without proof of a reservation or a general pass to tour the compound. Most rooms are sold as part of packages that include admission to the grounds and mansion.

Each season brings new pleasures here—cozy fireside evenings in the library, tranquil Indian summer afternoons rocking on the big veranda, or spring brunches on the dining terrace as daffodils burst into bloom. The inn faces Mount Pisgah, with 270 degrees of uninterrupted wilderness on view from the windows.

Guest rooms are spacious, comfortable, and elegantly furnished, with state-of-the-art bathrooms with tub/shower combinations. Suites are sometimes named for friends of Vanderbilt, including the suite honoring novelist Edith Wharton. The fine furnishings throughout were inspired by English and French manor houses. The cuisine—one of the reasons to stay here—is among the finest in western North Carolina.

1 Antler Hill Rd., Asheville, NC 28803. ©️ **800/858-4130** or 828/225-1600. Fax 828/225-1629. www.biltmore. com. 249 units. $149–$319 double; $400–$900 suite. AE, DC, MC, V. **Amenities:** 2 restaurants; bar; outdoor pool; fitness center; Jacuzzi; 24-hr. room service; babysitting; laundry service/dry cleaning; nonsmoking rooms; rooms for those w/limited mobility. *In room:* A/C, TV, dataport, coffeemaker, hair dryer, iron/ironing board, safe.

## The Lion and the Rose ⭐    This inn opened in 1987 in a Georgian/Queen Anne–style home in the historic Montford district. The house was built in 1898, during the heyday of Asheville's summer resort boom. Restored to its original grandeur, the inn is run by Jim and Linda Palmer. Oriental rugs and antiques, some of which are precious family pieces, are used throughout the inn. Sherry (served on the porch) and discreetly placed fresh flowers add grace notes that make this a tranquil retreat—one of the best-run B&Bs in Greater Asheville. Guests dine around the fireplace in cold weather or on the porch in summer. For breakfast, try the fresh blueberry blintzes and banana pecan waffles with butter rum sauce. The traditionally styled guest rooms have queen-size beds, and some have a sitting area with a couch. The two-bedroom suite is decorated with white wicker and lace. One bedroom has a queen-size bed, and the other has twin beds; there are also well-kept bathrooms with walk-in shower or tub/shower combinations, and a private balcony. Children 13 and over are welcome on weekends only.

276 Montford Ave., Asheville, NC 28801. ©️ **800/546-6988** or 828/255-7673. Fax 828/285-9810. www.lion-rose.com. 5 units. $155–$195 double; $195 suite. Rates include full breakfast and afternoon tea. AE, DISC, MC, V. Free parking. **Amenities:** Breakfast room; lounge; limited room service; nonsmoking rooms. *In room:* A/C, TV, dataport, hair dryer, iron/ironing board.

## Old Reynolds Mansion ⭐    An antebellum brick house—one of the few left in Asheville—this three-story inn, set on 4 acres, dates from 1855, when Colonel Daniel Reynolds built it just before the Civil War. It was substantially altered over the years before falling into disrepair. Helen Faber rescued it from the bulldozer and earned it a position on the National Register of Historic Places. Today, the inn is furnished with antiques, and some of the beautifully decorated guest rooms have fireplaces or 12-foot ceilings and provide panoramic vistas of the mountains. The mansion also has one cottage located on the grounds, with a queen-size bed, a living room with fireplace, a kitchen, and a sleeper sofa; it's generally rented to a party of three guests. All units have private bathrooms with either a tub/shower combo or a stall shower. Breakfast can be served by the fireplace (on nippy days) or on the veranda. A 1930s swimming pool is nestled among the pines. Children 6 or older are accepted Monday to Friday only. On Saturday and Sunday only children ages 12 and up are accepted.

100 Reynolds Heights, Asheville, NC 28804. ©️ **800/709-0496** or 828/254-0496. www.oldreynoldsmansion. com. 10 units, 1 cottage. $95–$165 double; $150 cottage for 2. Rates include full breakfast and afternoon wine and snacks. AE, DISC, MC, V. Take U.S. 25 for a 10-min. drive north of the center, past Beaver Lake. **Amenities:** Breakfast room; lounge; outdoor pool; breakfast-only room service; nonsmoking rooms. *In room:* A/C, TV, hair dryer.

## Owl's Nest Inn and Engadine Cabins ⭐ *(Finds*    On 12 acres of landscaped grounds with beautiful mountain views, this discovery lies just a 15-minute drive west of downtown Asheville. Built by a Confederate captain in the army after the Civil War, the small inn has been sensitively restored and is a charmer.

Walking paths lead in many directions, and there are also picnic areas. The house retains much Victorian character, and the guest rooms are handsomely furnished and spacious, each with a private bathroom with tub and shower or just shower. In cooler months, guests gather around the fireplace in the living room. On warm days, you can take in the views from the house's wraparound porches or from benches in the meadow. Each room, from the Captain's Room to the Howell Room, is decorated differently. The Engadine Suite is very private and romantic with a queen-size iron canopy bed and a whirlpool built for two. On a hilltop overlooking the inn, three cabins are rented, each with a kitchen, living area, bathroom with whirlpool, and panoramic porches. A hearty breakfast is served (try those cheese grits!).

2630 Smokey Park Hwy., Candler, NC 18715. © **800/665-8868** or 828/665-8325. Fax 828/667-2539. www.engadineinn.com. 9 units. $135–$160 double; $195 suite; $195–$225 cabin. AE, DISC, MC, V. **Amenities:** Breakfast room. *In room:* A/C, hair dryer, ceiling fans.

**Richmond Hill Inn** ⭐⭐   Listed on the National Register of Historic Places, this inn was named one of the "Ten Outstanding New Inns in America" by *Inn Review Newsletter.* Constructed in 1889 of granite, slate, and local woods, the house was designed by James Hill, the supervising architect of the U.S. Treasury buildings. The place is Asheville's premier remaining example of Queen Anne–style architecture. The main building is a spacious two-story mansion, painted yellow, with a wraparound porch. The interior is graced by family-heirloom portraits and the house's original oak paneling. Guest rooms are charming, featuring bathrooms with showers and claw-foot tubs, balconies overlooking a small stream, canopied beds, and fireplaces. The seven rooms on the second floor are preferable to the smaller rooms on the third. Nine cottages containing rooms and suites, all with small porches and rockers, are across the way. Other than the much-larger Grove Park, this is our favorite address in Asheville. The inn also has an excellent restaurant, **Gabrielle** (named for the former mistress of the house), featuring American contemporary cuisine.

87 Richmond Hill Dr., Asheville, NC 28806. © **888/742-4536** or 828/252-7313. Fax 828/252-8726. www. richmondhillinn.com. 36 units. $195–$395 double; $325–$495 suite. Rates include full breakfast. Children 16 and under stay free in parent's room. AE, MC, V. Free parking. **Amenities:** Restaurant; lounge; fitness center; massage; babysitting; dry cleaning; nonsmoking rooms; rooms for those w/limited mobility. *In room:* A/C, TV, dataport, coffeemaker (in some), hair dryer, iron/ironing board.

## WHERE TO DINE

**Blue Ridge Dining Room** AMERICAN   This is the moderately priced choice at Asheville's premier resort. The food is not as good as at the Horizon, but the prices are more affordable, and you get excellent quality and generous helpings. The view of the Blue Ridge Mountains alone is worth the trip here. This longtime family favorite is an Asheville tradition, known for its sumptuous international buffet tables laden with many "plantation extras." Omelets and waffles are on the buffet at breakfast. The Friday-night seafood buffet and Saturday prime-rib buffet are so popular with locals that early reservations are recommended. Sunday brunch is Asheville's best, and it's usually packed.

In the Grove Park Inn Resort, 290 Macon Ave. © **828/252-2711.** Reservations recommended. Jackets and collared shirts for men. Main courses $15–$27; Fri seafood buffet $30; Sat prime-rib buffet $30; Sun brunch $30. AE, DC, DISC, MC, V. Mon–Sat 6:30–11am and 3–9:30pm; Sun 6:30–10am and 2:30–9:30pm.

**Cafe on the Square** ⭐ AMERICAN   This eatery is hip and urban, with a decor and ambience that might have been lifted directly from a stylish restaurant in a posh neighborhood in California. Breezy, airy, and comfortable, it offers seating on the sidewalk in front, or inside a high-ceilinged, artfully simple, long and narrow dining room. Owners Tracy and Mitchell Adler supervise the dining room and kitchen, respectively, of this place, whipping up dishes that are obviously making their diverse clientele happy. Lunches focus on salads, sandwiches, and platters such as rainbow trout with a blueberry-and-lime red butter sauce. Dinners are more elaborate, more leisurely, and more romantic, with dishes that include flash-seared tuna with pickled ginger and wasabi-flavored vinaigrette; mesquite-seared breast of duck with balsamic-roasted shiitake mushrooms and garlic-flavored mayonnaise; and breast of chicken dredged in pecans and finished with a whiskey-and-dijon-mustard glaze.

1 Biltmore Ave. ⓒ 828/251-5565. www.cafeonthesquare.com. Reservations recommended. Lunch sandwiches and platters $7–$9; dinner main courses $16–$32. AE, MC, V. Daily 11am–3pm; Mon–Sat 5–9pm.

**Café Soleil** CONTINENTAL    If Gaudí, the brilliant architect of late-19th-century Barcelona, could have designed a modern-day cafe, it might look a lot like this earth-toned hideaway in downtown Asheville, all curved walls and sinuous lines. Since its establishment by a team of French and Argentine expatriates, it has positioned itself as *the* gathering place for members of Asheville's foreign (mostly European) community, as such evoking some aspects of a busy, arts-conscious cafe in, say, Paris or Madrid. The cafe has a list of interesting wines, many sold by the glass; an impressive roster of both salted and sweet crepes made with buckwheat flour in the French tradition and stuffed with your choice of dozens of different fillings; and quiches and salads. (The version with pine nuts, goat cheese, fresh vegetables, and spring greens is, indeed, named after Gaudí.) Live music is presented most nights after 8pm, and every Friday and Saturday the music is likely to be something that the management refers to as "Gypsy Jazz."

62 N. Lexington Ave. ⓒ 828/350-1140. Reservations recommended at dinner on weekends. Main courses $5–$17. Tues–Wed 11:30am–10pm; Thurs–Sat 11:30am–1:30am; Sun 10am–3pm.

**The Frog Bar Deli/The Flying Frog Café** CONTINENTAL/GERMAN/ "URBAN INDIAN"    This is the most culturally diverse, and in some ways the most intriguing, cafe and restaurant in Asheville, with enough different themes to keep prospective diners moving through its premises until they settle on the venue they like best. The street level (the Frog Bar Deli) offers a disjointed and relatively informal warren of outdoor and indoor tables in at least four different seating areas, each accented with copper trim, beige tiles, and a New Wave sense of "live and let live." Downstairs, in the cellar, is a more formal dining area (the Flying Frog Café), one that celebrates the enigmatic fusion of French, German, and Indian cuisine. Here, at banquettes that romantically engulf their occupants in yard upon yard of milk-colored mosquito netting, you can order from a menu that's 50% devoted to the spicy cuisine of Bombay (the lamb vindaloo is delicious), and 50% devoted to French and German items that include sauerbraten, Wiener schnitzel, and bouillabaisse.

At the corner of Haywood St. and Battery Park. ⓒ 828/254-9411. Reservations recommended for the cellar-level restaurant, not necessary in street-level deli. In deli section, sandwiches and platters $5.75–$8.95; in cellar-level restaurant, main courses $14–$28. AE, DC, MC, V. Deli Sun–Thurs 11:30am–midnight; Fri–Sat 11:30am–2am; Sun 11:30am–3pm. Restaurant Wed–Mon 5:30–11pm.

**Horizons Restaurant** ⓡⓡ CONTINENTAL    If the Great Gatsby were alive today, Horizons would surely be his first choice for dining. It certainly would have been the choice of Gatsby's creator, F. Scott Fitzgerald, who was a frequent visitor to the inn some 60 years ago. The most formal, and also the best, restaurant in greater Asheville occupies a prominent position in the city's grandest resort. It's consistently rated among the finest in the nation and has won the AAA Four Diamond Award for 7 consecutive years.

Patrons are rewarded with exceptional service and gratifying cuisine. In the formal, ground-level setting in the resort's Sammons Wing, innovative yet classic cuisine is served. Specialties depend on what's fresh at the market on any given day. It may be brook trout, bouillabaisse, or medallions of venison. Dinner includes soup or salad, a main course, dessert, and a nonalcoholic beverage. One food critic declared that the dinner was on a scale that recalled "the scope of Thomas Wolfe's 626-page magnum opus." The wine list is very extensive.

In the Grove Park Inn Resort, 290 Macon Ave. © 828/252-2711. Reservations required. Jacket and collared shirts required for men. Fixed-price menu $66. AE, DC, DISC, MC, V. Mon–Sat 5:30–9:30pm.

**The Market Place** CONTINENTAL   An upscale casual restaurant with candlelit tables, this establishment has impeccable service. The chef uses extra-fresh ingredients, and all herbs and vegetables are grown locally. For all its attributes, the restaurant—although popular with savvy locals—seems to be somehow undervalued and underappreciated, and rarely appears in a guidebook. Yet some of its dishes rival those at the Grove Park Inn. Try, for example, the fresh grilled salmon, the fresh tenderloin, or the duo—a platter of lamb and marinated grilled venison. Many dishes are nouvelle in style and preparation, and the professional staff is knowledgeable about the extensive wine list.

20 Wall St. © 828/252-4162. www.marketplace-restaurant.com. Reservations recommended. Main courses $12–$27. AE, DC, MC, V. Mon–Sat 5:30–9:30pm.

**Tupelo Honey Café** SOUTHERN   No other restaurant in Asheville so effectively captures the imagination of both the down-home breakfast crowd and, on weekends only, the very-late-night supper crowd. Set behind a storefront in downtown Asheville, it's a place where Sunday-morning breakfast crowds line up and wait (in some cases for up to an hour) for an available table. Students at the nearby university also drag their parents here for a sense of how much Asheville really does respect old-fashioned Southern virtues and cooking. Breakfast is served throughout the day and as such provides nourishment late into the afternoon with such dishes as grit cakes stuffed with cheddar cheese and served with green tomato salsa; sweet-potato pancakes; many kinds of omelets; and crab cakes topped with poached eggs and hollandaise sauce. Lunches and dinners focus on updated Southern favorites such as shrimp and grits (in this case, the grits are flavored with goat cheese); Cajun-seared catfish; and Tupelo burgers. And in honor of Elvis ("The King"), you can order a grilled peanut butter and banana sandwich, prepared with either honey or (if you're a "hard-core Southerner") mayonnaise.

14 College St. © 828/255-4404. Breakfast platters $5–$13; salads, sandwiches, and platters $6–$14; dinner main courses $13–$17. AE, MC, V. Tues–Sun 9am–3pm; Fri–Sat 5pm–3am.

**Vincenzo's** NORTHERN ITALIAN   The premier Italian restaurant in Asheville is in the central part of the historic district. A bustling trattoria with a piano bar, it has an eclectic decor with Art Deco overtones. True, chances are that you will have had finer Italian dinners than this in your life, but what you get isn't bad. Try veal chop Milanese with pasta; or filet mignon with cream sauce, mussels, and asparagus. Cioppino is filled with goodies, including fresh whitefish, scallops, and shrimp, over linguine flavored with a spicy red sauce. The penne pasta with charbroiled chicken, peppers, pepperoni, and spinach is excellent, as are the veal dishes.

10 N. Market St. © 828/254-4698. www.vincenzos.com. Reservations suggested but not required. Main courses $10–$25. AE, DC, DISC, MC, V. Mon–Thurs 5–10pm; Fri–Sat 5–11pm; Sun 5:30–9:30pm.

## ASHEVILLE AFTER DARK

**Barley's**   This pub has a vast array of imported beer. There's never a cover charge, although the club is a venue for live entertainment, including jazz, blues, rock, and alternative rock. Pizza, nachos, salads, and soups are offered. Hours are Monday to Saturday from 11:30am to 2am and Sunday from noon to midnight. 42 Biltmore Ave. © 828/255-0504.

**Club Hairspray**   Named after the John Waters camp classic starring the late drag queen, Divine, this club attracts mainly a gay and lesbian crowd but welcomes "open-minded straights" as well. There's a funky bar here along with several pool tables, and downstairs is a cabaret and dance club. Call to inquire about their "special events" for the week. Dancing is usually on the weekends. Technically, this is a private club, but you can gain membership at the door for $5. Open daily at 8pm, as late as business warrants. 38N French Broad Ave. © 828/258-2027.

**Fine Arts Theatre**   See first-run, art, and independent films at this elegant Art Deco/Moderne theater. Call for movie titles, times, and ticket prices. No credit cards. 36 Biltmore Ave. © 828/232-1536. www.fineartstheater.com.

**Hannah Flanagan's Irish Pub**   Asheville's most authentically Irish pub draws after-hours workers who congregate either on an outdoor terrace, surrounded with masonry walls draped with ivy, or inside a woodsy-looking interior that evokes the early 20th century. The pub was named after the owner's grandmother Hannah Flanagan, whose sepia-toned portrait hangs above the bar. Menu items derive from Irish traditions (corned beef and cabbage; Irish stew laced with Guinness; chargrilled salmon with mashed potatoes and a "wee" dinner salad). Open Monday to Saturday 11:30am to 2am, Sunday noon to 2am. 27 Biltmore Ave. © 828/252-1922.

**Smokey's**   This is Asheville's favorite gay and lesbian tavern. Established in the 1960s, it's the oldest continuously operating bar of any persuasion in Asheville and contains a collection of barroom kitsch that would gladden the heart of any antiques dealer. An amiable crowd of multi-generational drinkers begins tippling every afternoon a few minutes after the place opens. You'll find a pair of pool tables, plenty of local homeowners to ask for advice, and, as the night progresses, enough good-looking local gays to make any visiting queer feel interested. Open daily 4pm till last call at 2am. 18 Broadway. © 828/253-2155.

**Vincent's Bar**   This two-level beer hall and coffeehouse is Asheville's hip address. You reach it through a small side alley. The live entertainment includes everything from jazz to heavy metal. The coffeehouse offers an alternative atmosphere for those who don't want to join the bar crowd. Cover charge varies. The food includes cold-cut sandwiches and chicken wings. Hours are Sunday to Thursday from noon to midnight, Friday and Saturday from noon to 2am. 68B N. Lexington Ave. © 828/259-9119.

## SIDE TRIPS FROM ASHEVILLE

About 5 miles east of downtown Asheville, at milepost 382 on the Blue Ridge Parkway, the **Folk Art Center** ☆, P.O. Box 9545, Asheville, NC 28815 (© 828/298-7928), is operated by the Southern Highland Handicraft Guild, a not-for-profit organization of craftspeople in the nine-state southern Appalachian region. The contemporary wood-and-stone structure houses the finest of both traditional and contemporary handcrafts of the region. The **Allanstand Craft Shop,** established in 1895, is one of the oldest crafts shops in the country, featuring exhibitions and museum areas. Offered for sale are pottery, ceramics, weavings, jewelry, and handmade quilts, among other merchandise. The center does not charge for admission but does accept donations. It's open daily from 9am to 6pm. The crafts shop maintains the same hours.

**Chimney Rock Park** (www.chimneyrockpark.com) is 25 miles southeast of Asheville on U.S. 64/74A. The granite monolith rises to a height of 360 feet; you can reach its top by a stairway, a trail, or an elevator. An observation lounge is open daily (weather permitting), and the charge is $14 for adults, $6 for children 4 to 12, free for children under 4. Trails lead to Needle's Eye, Moonshiner's Cave, and Devil's Head (on the way to Hickory Nut Falls, which is twice the height of Niagara). *The Last of the Mohicans* was filmed here, and costumes and other artifacts from the movie are on display in the observation lounge. Food service is available for $8 or less, and there are picnic facilities. For full details, a free color brochure, and a trail map, contact Chimney Rock Park, P.O. Box 39, Chimney Rock, NC 28720 (© **800/277-9611** or 828/625-9611; www.chimney rockpark.com).

Stately **Mount Mitchell,** highest point in the eastern U.S., is in Mount Mitchell State Park, 2388 State Hwy. 128, Burnsville (© **828/675-4611**), some 33 miles northeast on the parkway and then 5 miles north on N.C. 128. Mount Mitchell has a museum, a tower, and an observation lodge; camping and picnicking facilities are available in the park.

About 30 miles southeast of Asheville on I-26 is the pastoral little town of Flat Rock, most famous as the former home of Carl Sandburg. The two-time Pulitzer Prize–winning writer/poet/historian known for his biography of Abraham Lincoln lived at **Connemara Farms** ⟨★, 81 Carl Sandburg Lane, just west of I-26 (© **828/693-4178;** www.nps.gov/carl). It's open daily from 9am to 5pm, charging an admission of $5 for adults; children 16 and under are admitted free. Now a National Historic Site, the big white farmhouse is administered by the National Park Service, which offers guided formal tours. Sandburg purchased the 240-acre farm in 1945 for $40,000. He called it Connemara after the mountains of Ireland. Sandburg was quite a reader: The walls of his modest abode are filled with approximately 10,000 volumes of books, bookmarked and dog-eared; in the living room is his collection of walking sticks. The grounds include a goat house occupied by the charming descendants of a prize herd of goats raised by Sandburg's wife. Sandburg died of a stroke in his bedroom here when he was 90.

Flat Rock is also the home of the North Carolina State Theater's **Flat Rock Playhouse** (© **828/693-0731;** www.flatrockplayhouse.org), which opened in 1952. It hosts the popular Vagabond Players, a troupe launched on Broadway in 1937. The group presents *The World of Carl Sandburg* and *The Rootabaga Stories* annually, not at the actual playhouse, but across the street at Sandburg's Connemara Farms.

## 3 Boone ⟨★

95 miles NE of Asheville

In the heart of the Blue Ridge Mountains, Boone has long been a favorite vacation destination. During the 1880s, Southerners came here to escape the summer heat. In recent years, Boone has become a winter ski destination. Daniel Boone traveled through this area on his way to Kentucky in the late 1700s—hence, the town's name.

Boone has been called "the coolest spot in the South," with an average temperature of 68°F (20°C) in summer. Golf, tennis, swimming, fishing, skiing, and sightseeing are part of the local attractions. The region's rugged terrain lends itself to a variety of high-adventure outdoor sports, from mountain biking and canoeing to white-water rafting and rock climbing. For summer visitors, there's also the outdoor drama, Kermit Hunter's *Horn in the West,* as well as an Appalachian Summer Festival of concerts, drama, and art exhibits.

## ESSENTIALS

**GETTING THERE**   Boone lies 1 hour from I-77, I-81, and I-40 and is accessible from a trio of major highways, including U.S. 321, U.S. 421, and U.S. 221. N.C. 105 provides access from U.S. 221.

The nearest **airport** is at Asheville (℃ **828/687-9446**).

**VISITOR INFORMATION**   The **Boone Convention and Visitors Bureau,** 208 Howard St., Boone, NC 28607 (℃ **800/852-9506** or 828/262-3516; http://visitboonenc.com), is open Monday to Friday from 9am to 5pm. Information is also available at the **High Country Host,** 1700 Blowing Rock Rd. (℃ **828/264-1299;** www.mountainsofnc.com), which is open Monday to Saturday from 9am to 5pm, and Sunday 9am to 3pm.

## SEEING THE SIGHTS

**Daniel Boone Native Gardens,** Horn in the West Drive, 1 mile east of U.S. 421 (℃ **828/264-6390**), next door to the Daniel Boone Theatre, offers a collection of native North Carolina plants in an informal landscaped design set amid 6 acres. Weather permitting, the gardens are open daily from May 1 to October 15, and on weekends in October from 9am to 6pm. June 15 to August 15, they remain open until 8pm. Admission is $2 for visitors 16 and older.

Also adjacent to the theater is the **Hickory Ridge Homestead Museum** (℃ **828/264-2120;** www.horninthewest.com/museum.htm), an 18th-century living-history museum in a re-created log cabin. Traditional craftspeople demonstrate their skills, and there's a homestead store. An apple festival is held on the grounds in late October, and Christmas events are on tap in mid-December. Hours are as follows: May to October, Tuesday to Sunday 1 to 5pm; October to April, Saturday 10am to 4pm and Sunday 1 to 4:30pm. Admission is $2.

**Tweetsie Railroad Theme Park,** Blowing Rock Road, halfway between Boone and Banner Elk (℃ **800/526-5740** or 828/264-9061; www.tweetsie.com), is not just for the kids; the whole family can enjoy it. An old narrow-gauge train winds along a 3-mile route, enduring mock attacks by "Indians" and "outlaws." There's mountain music and other entertainment, along with restaurants, Western shops, country-fair rides, a petting zoo, and a crafts area. The park is open April 30 to May 28, Friday to Sunday from 9am to 6pm; May 29 to August 19, daily from 9am to 6pm; and August 20 to October 31, Friday to Sunday from 9am to 6pm. The park is also open on Labor Day. Admission is $25 for adults and $18 for children 3 to 12. Children 2 and under ride free. Get your tickets early for the popular "Ghost Train" night rides, part of Tweetsie's Halloween Festival, held on October weekends. An assortment of entertainment and games is available for very young children, for whom the Ghost Train ride is not recommended. Admission is $20 per person, and gates open at 7:30pm.

## OUTDOOR PURSUITS

**GOLF**   The **Boone Golf Club,** U.S. 321/221, Blowing Rock Road (℃ **828/264-8760;** www.boonegolfclub.com), an 18-hole, par-70 course designed by

Ellis Maples, is 6,400 yards long from its longest tees. It's the standard against which all High Country public courses are measured. Opened in 1958, with its natural routing and electrifying greens, it remains a perennial favorite. Greens fees from June to October are $49 Monday to Thursday, rising to $54 Friday to Sunday. Off-season fees range from $44 to $49. Depending on the weather, the course is open April to November, daily from 8am to 7pm. Professional instruction costs $40 to $50 per hour, and clubs are available for rent at $20 for 18 holes. A pro shop is on-site, and there's a restaurant at the clubhouse.

**RAFTING & OTHER SPORTS**    **Wahoos,** on U.S. 321 between Boone and the Tweetsie Railroad Theme Park (© **800/444-RAFT** or 828/262-5774; www.wahooadventures.com), is the best all-around center to connect you with outdoor adventures, ranging from white-water rafting to tubing. Tours are available for all ages. The office is open daily 8am to 8pm in summer.

Nolichucky River rafting is for those 6 years or older, costs $65 to $85 per person, and lasts 4 to 5 hours, including transportation and lunch. Watauga River rafting, for those 3 and older, lasts 2 hours and costs $40 to $55 per person, including lunch and transportation. Canoeing is possible in the New River, with three 1- to 3½-hour excursions costing $20 per person. Wahoos can also make reservations at local campsites.

## SHOPPING

In the tiny town of Valle Crucis, 10 miles west of Boone, **Mast General Store** ⚐, 3565 Hwy. 194 S. (© **828/963-6511;** www.mastgeneralstore.com), is arguably the most famous store in Appalachia. Dating from 1883, it is listed on the National Register of Historic Places. Its plank floors are worn to a smooth sheen, and on cold mountain mornings, a potbellied stove is still fired up. From overalls to brogans, red ribbons to calico patterns, the store has a wide assortment of sturdy clothing, shoes, and boots—all the outdoor gear you'll need to become a mountain man or mountain mama. You'll also find old-time salves, wind-up toys, regional music, rock candy, and peanut brittle on sale. Hours are Monday to Saturday 7:30am to 6:30pm. If you don't want to drive out to the hamlet of Valle Crucis, you'll find similar merchandise at the outlet in Boone, **Old Boone Mercantile,** 630 E. King St. (© **828/262-0000**), in business since 1883. Hours are Monday to Saturday 10am to 6pm, Sunday 1 to 6pm.

## WHERE TO STAY

**Holiday Inn Express**    Within 20 minutes of the downhill ski runs, this is one of the best motels in the Boone area. The rooms are well maintained and exactly what you'd expect from this dependable chain. Each unit has a well-kept bathroom with a tub/shower combination. There's no on-site restaurant, although several restaurants and diners are within walking distance.

1943 Blowing Rock Rd., Boone, NC 28607. © **888/733-6867** or 828/264-2451. Fax 828/265-3861. www.holiday-inn.com. 129 units. $90–$130 double; $209–$250 suite. Rates include continental breakfast. AE, DC, DISC, MC, V. **Amenities:** Breakfast room; outdoor pool; fitness center; dry cleaning and coin-operated laundry; nonsmoking rooms; rooms for those w/limited mobility. *In room:* A/C, TV, dataport, kitchenette (in some), coffeemaker, hair dryer, iron/ironing board.

**Lovill House Inn** ⚐    Dating from 1875, this inn was originally a private home. The house stands on 11 wooded acres. Scott and Anne Peecook welcome you to one of the finest places to stay in the area. Floors and walls are double-insulated, and the guest rooms are tastefully furnished. Quality linens and comforters are just two of the thoughtful touches. Each unit has a well-maintained bathroom with a tub/shower combination. Three of the original brick fireplaces remain. Breakfast is served in a dining room with picture-view windows. In summer, guests gather on a spacious veranda before dinner to meet one another.

404 Old Bristol Rd., Boone, NC 28607. ℂ **800/849-9466** or 828/264-4204. www.lovillhouseinn.com. 6 units. $135–$195 double. Rates include full breakfast. MC, V. No children under 12. **Amenities:** Breakfast room; lounge; Jacuzzi; nonsmoking rooms. *In room:* TV, dataport, hair dryer, ceiling fans.

## WHERE TO DINE

**Dan'l Boone Inn** ⭐ SOUTHERN    So legendary is this place in this part of North Carolina that many motorists will drive the 5 miles from the parkway to dine here. The inn is one of the oldest buildings in town, with a rustic atmosphere that attracts a huge family trade. But what really brings 'em in is the down-home Southern cooking, served family-style and based on fresh ingredients. That means Southern fried chicken, country-fried steak, and a choice of five vegetables. Lunch or dinner comes with soup or salad, vegetables, a choice of three meats, homemade biscuits, a homemade dessert (usually rich and creamy), and a beverage. Breakfast includes such Southern savories as country ham, grits, and stewed apples. If you come here on New Year's Day, you can participate in the Southern tradition of eating black-eyed peas and collard greens, for good luck in the coming year. The cuisine is in the style of fill 'em up, with heaping platters and bowls of everything. What you get isn't bad, and it's so reasonable that you'll wonder if the waiter left several items off your bill when it comes time to settle up.

130 Hardin St. ℂ **828/264-8657.** www.danlbooneinn.com. Reservations accepted only for parties of 15 or more. Breakfast $7.95; lunch/dinner $13; children's plates (4–11 years old) $2.95–$5.95; children 3 years and younger eat free. No credit cards. Breakfast Sat–Sun 8–11am year-round. Dinner June–Oct Mon–Fri 11:30am–9pm, Sat–Sun 11am–9pm; off season Mon–Fri 5–8pm, Sat–Sun 11am–9pm.

## BOONE AFTER DARK

Kermit Hunter's ***Horn in the West*** ⭐ is presented in the Daniel Boone Theatre, 591 Horn in the West Dr., Boone, NC 28607 (ℂ **828/264-2120;** www.horn inthewest.com), every night except Monday from late June through mid-August. The play tells a vivid story of the pioneers' efforts to win freedom during the American Revolution. Performances begin at 8pm, and admission is $15 (half price for children 12 and under). Tickets can be ordered in advance by mail and will be held at the box office for pickup.

## 4  Banner Elk ⭐

136 miles NW of Charlotte

The village of Banner Elk used to be about the sleepiest place in the High Country until it was discovered by scenery hounds in summer and skiers in winter. Banner Elk is on N.C. 194, enclosed by mountains. In winter, skiers can head for Sugar Mountain or Ski Beech. The town also makes a good center for exploring Grandfather Mountain, just north of Linville, a wealthy enclave where many owners have summer homes.

## ESSENTIALS

**GETTING THERE**    To reach Banner Elk from Asheville, take I-40 East to U.S. 221 North, passing through Marion to Linville. Exit onto N.C. 105 North at Linville until you reach the intersection of N.C. 194 East. Turn left onto N.C. 194 East and proceed for roughly 4 miles into Banner Elk.

**VISITOR INFORMATION** The **Avery/Banner Elk Chamber of Commerce,** N.C. 184, no. 2 Shoppes at Tynecastle (P.O. Box 335), Banner Elk, NC 28604 (© **800/972-2183** or 828/898-5605; www.banner-elk.com), will mail you information on activities in the area. It's open Monday to Friday from 9am to 4pm, Saturday 10am to 4pm, and Sunday noon to 4pm.

**SPECIAL EVENTS** Kilt-clad Scots from Scotland (as well as all parts of North America) gather here early in July for the annual **Grandfather Mountain Highland Games and Gathering o' Scottish Clans** (www.gmhg.org). Bagpipe music, dancing, wrestling, and tossing the caber (a shaft that resembles a telephone pole), as well as the colorful mix of people bent on 4 days of fun, make this a spectacle not to be missed.

## GRANDFATHER MOUNTAIN

**Grandfather Mountain** ★★, on U.S. 221 near Linville (© **828/733-4337;** www.grandfather.com), a mile off the Blue Ridge Parkway, is the highest peak in the Blue Ridge. You can see as far as 100 miles from the **Mile High Swinging Bridge;** the **Environmental Habitat** is the home of Mildred the Bear and her black-bear friends. In a spacious separate section, you can view native deer, cougars, and bald and golden eagles (which have been injured and cannot live in the wild on their own). Grandfather Mountain is open daily except Thanksgiving and Christmas from 8am to 5pm in winter, to 6pm in spring and fall, and to 7pm in summer. Admission is $12 for adults, $6 for children 4 to 12.

## OUTDOOR PURSUITS

**GOLF** The **Hawksnest Golf & Ski Resort,** 2058 Skyland Dr., off N.C. 105 in Seven Devils (© **800/822-4295** or 828/963-6561; www.hawksnest-resort. com), is a scenic 18-hole, par-72, 6,200-yard championship course at the cool elevation of 4,200 feet. It's a true mountain course with good putting surfaces. From mid-March to November, the course is open daily from 7am to 7pm. Including the use of a cart, greens fees are $39 Monday to Friday before 2pm, or $29 after 2pm. On Saturday and Sunday, greens fees are $44 before 2pm, $34 after 2pm. Clubs can be rented for $15 for 18 holes. Reserved tee times are recommended.

**Village of Sugar Mountain Golf Course,** N.C. 184 (© **800/SUGAR-MT** or 828/898-6464), outside Banner Elk, is an 18-hole, par-64 course at the foot of the Sugar Mountain Ski Resort. This executive course offers variety and a par-5 hole designed by Arnold Palmer. It charges $38 for greens fees, which includes cart.

**SKIING** The **Hawksnest Golf & Ski Resort,** 1800 Skyland Dr., Seven Devils, NC 28604 (© **800/822-HAWK** or 828/963-6561; www.hawksnest-resort.com), is northeast of Banner Elk and 10 miles south off N.C. 105. It offers 12 slopes— one expert, three advanced, five intermediate, and three beginner—with a peak elevation of 4,819 feet and a 669-foot vertical drop. Lift tickets cost $25 to $45, depending on the time of season and the length of time for which you plan to ski. Ski rentals range from $20. The resort also offers a children's camp, costing $45 for a half-day or $75 for a full day. During the December-to-March season, the resort is open Sunday to Thursday from 9am to 10pm, on Friday from 9am to 2am, and on Saturday from 9am to midnight. Professional ski instruction is available for $35 for a 1-hour session.

**Sugar Mountain Resort,** N.C. 194, a mile from N.C. 105 (P.O. Box 369), Banner Elk, NC 28604 (© **800/SUGAR-MT** or 828/898-4521; www.skisugar. com), has 20 slopes—20% expert, 40% intermediate, and 40% beginner—with an elevation of 5,300 feet and a vertical drop of 1,200 feet. The resort is open from mid-November to mid-March. Lifts operate daily from 9am to 4:30pm and 6 to 10pm, with tickets ranging from $20 to $53. Ski rentals range from $10 to $20, depending on the time of day and the type of skis, and professional lessons are also available, at $20 per member of a group or $42 per person hourly. Children 5 to 10 can participate in a Sugarbear Ski School from 10am to 3pm daily, including lunch, for $70 per student. The resort also offers snowboarding, with lift tickets costing from $19 to $29.

## WHERE TO STAY

**Archers Mountain Inn**   Located on Beech Mountain between the towns of Banner Elk and Beech Mountain, this resort is a good choice if you want to sample all the skiing in the area. The inn features 15 rooms in two buildings plus five separate log cabins. Laurel Lodge and the Hawks View both have views of Sugar Mountain and the Grandfather Mountains just outside your window. The rooms in Laurel Lodge are essentially designed for couples; all have fireplaces. Some of the more expensive rooms and suites feature whirlpools. Hawk's View offers more spacious rooms, with efficiency kitchens and fireplaces. These rooms are better equipped for serving large parties. All units contain well-kept bathrooms with tub/shower combinations. The building has large porches with rockers where the guests can take in views of the mountain range. The inn's restaurant, Jackalope's View, serves international fare prepared by the restaurant's two chefs.

2489 Beech Mountain Pkwy., Banner Elk, NC 28604. (© **888/827-6155** or 828/898-9004. www. archersinn.com. 15 units. $77–$185 double; $125–$200 suite. Top rates include full breakfast. Each additional person $10. DISC, MC, V. **Amenities:** Restaurant; bar; babysitting; nonsmoking rooms. *In room:* TV, hair dryer, no phone.

## WHERE TO DINE

**Jackalope's View Restaurant** AMERICAN   In the cozy Archers Mountain Inn (see above), Jackalope's is nestled on the side of Beech Mountain. Even if you're not a guest at the inn, you'll want to dine here—the cuisine is among the finest in the area. After dinner in winter, guests relax in front of fireplaces; in summer they sit on rockers on the porch. The personal service in the dining room makes you feel pampered. The menu changes from time to time, but you might begin with a sweet Vidalia onion stuffed with sautéed mushrooms, roasted garlic, and Gorgonzola cheese; or else a venison pâté with red bell-pepper purée. Jackalope's has more imaginative salads than we've encountered elsewhere in the region—caramelized fennel and orange salad; or else ripe summer strawberries dusted with black pepper (you heard right) with mixed greens and red onions. The main courses are always tantalizing, especially the delectable sautéed North Carolina trout atop shrimp and crab stuffing, or the tiger shrimp flavored with bacon and tomatoes and tossed in an Alfredo sauce with ziti. Homemade desserts are featured nightly.

2489 Beech Mountain Pkwy. (© **828/898-9004**. Reservations recommended. Main courses $16–$30. DISC, MC, V. Daily 5–9pm.

**Morels** ✯ NEW AMERICAN   Many local foodies consider this to be the resort's finest dining room, and we concur. Every edible item in the kitchen is homemade, and you can count on cooking with imaginative touches. It's served in a somewhat cramped dark-green dining room. Standout dishes include roast monkfish with lobster sauce and seasonal vegetables; grilled veal chop with mushrooms and onions; honey and tamari-seared salmon with a sauce made of leeks, cream, and vinegar; and sautéed sweetbreads with a mustard-cream sauce. The restaurant is very popular with skiers in winter.

1 Banner St. (off N.C. 194). ✆ **828/898-6866.** Reservations required. Main courses $19–$32. MC, V. Tues–Sun 6–10pm.

## 5 Beech Mountain

141 miles NW of Charlotte; 5 miles NW of Banner Elk

This resort boasts the highest elevated ski area in the east, with a peak of 5,506 feet. It was voted the number-one ski area by readers of *Blue Ridge Country,* competing with the slopes in Tennessee, West Virginia, Virginia, and other areas of North Carolina. The Ski Beech mountain area lies on N.C. 184 along the Beech Mountain Parkway.

Beech Mountain is a resort of all seasons. You can enjoy golf, tennis, hiking, and biking in summer; or else skiing, tubing, and snowboarding—among the best in the Southeast—in winter.

A former hunting ground for the Cherokees, Beech Mountain was once called *Klonteska,* or "pheasant." The Great Trading Path that ran from Virginia to Georgia is said to have passed through Beech Mountain, and the 1864 Battle of Beech Mountain was fought here during the Civil War.

### ESSENTIALS
**GETTING THERE**    After you reach Banner Elk (see above), you'll see Beech Mountain signposted. It's a 5-mile drive along the Beech Mountain Parkway to the top of the mountain.

**VISITOR INFORMATION**    Dispensing information is the very helpful staff at the **Beech Mountain Chamber of Commerce,** 403–A Beech Mountain Pkwy. (✆ **800/468-5506** or 828/387-9283; www.beechmtn.com). It's open Monday to Saturday 9am to 5pm.

### FUN IN THE OUTDOORS
**SUMMER**    The private **Beech Mountain Club** has a magnificent Willard Byrd–designed 18-hole championship golf course. Access to the course is available to guests renting a qualified lodging; ask your rental office for more details.

This same private club has both hard-surface and clay tennis courts. Access to tennis is available to guests renting a qualified lodging; ask your rental office for details. The **Pinnacle Inn** (✆ **800/405-7888**) offers two asphalt courts for registered guests.

The swimming pool at the Beech Mountain Club is available to guests renting a qualified lodging. There are indoor pools at the Pinnacle Inn and at **Cedar Village Condos** (✆ **800/258-6198**) for registered guests.

**Beech Mountain Sports** offers rentals of mountain bikes for the eight marked trails on Beech Mountain. For more information, call ✆ **828/387-2795** or 828/387-2373.

Fishermen will find the 7-acre Buckeye Lake stocked throughout the year with trout. Facilities here include a boat ramp, picnic pavilion, and toilet facilities. The fishing season runs from the first Saturday in April until the end of February. Lake Coffey, another lake on Beech Mountain, is also stocked with trout. Persons over the age of 16 need a license; you can get one at **Fred's General Mercantile** (✆ **828/387-4838**).

If you like hiking, the best trail is **Pond Creek Trail,** stretching for 2 miles beginning at Tarnarack Road, following the creek past Lake Coffey, and continuing to Locust Ridge Road. The lower end of the trail has a few small waterfalls.

**WINTER**    The **Ski Beech Express,** a high-speed quad chairlift, is one of 10 lifts that service 15 slopes in the area: three beginner, eight intermediate, and four advanced. There is an 830-foot vertical drop from the summit to the base.

The ski season lasts from mid-November until mid-March. Daily lift rates are $28 Monday to Friday and $45 on Saturday and Sunday. Lifts operate daily from 8:30am to 4:30pm and from 6 to 10pm. Ski rental is $16 Monday to Friday and $20 on weekends. Professional lessons are available at $15 per hour for group lessons or $40 for private lessons. Snow tubing and ice-skating are also available for $10 each for a 2-hour period.

The town has created a free sledding hill next to the town hall. This is eastern America's highest sled run, and it's open daily from 8am to 10pm.

## WHERE TO STAY

**The Banner Elk Inn** ★★    This is one of our favorite getaways in the Appalachian Mountains. Built in 1912 and recently renovated, it retains its old-fashioned mountain aura. The location is only 2 miles from Sugar Mountain ski resort and a few more miles up to Ski Beech ski resort. The inn lies in the village across the street from the Banner Elk Town Park, with its walking path and meandering stream. You can sit out on the side porch enjoying the mountain breezes or else admire the prize-winning gardens. Innkeeper and owner Beverly Lait is one of the more gracious hosts in western Carolina.

The cozy and comfortable guest rooms have a certain charm, and bathrooms come with tub and shower. In addition to the two Briarwood cottages, a new room/cottage is available, with a wood-burning stove, a sleigh bed, and a kitchenette. Hearty and memorable breakfasts are served on fine china. There are many nooks and crannies in which to escape. The collection of carvings and crafts is interspersed with antique furnishings.

407 Main St. E., Banner Elk, NC 28604. © **828/898-6223.** Fax 828/898-6224. www.bannerelkinn.com. 9 units. $85–$165 double; $140–$180 4-person suite; $140–$200 cottage. MC, V. **Amenities:** Breakfast room; nonsmoking rooms; rooms for those w/limited mobility. *In room:* TV, kitchenette (in some).

**The Pinnacle Inn** ★ (Kids)    Among the vast array of accommodations at this modern resort are the one- or two-bedroom Ski Suites. The one-bedroom units can sleep two to four guests comfortably, and the two-bedroom accommodations can hold up to six. Each unit is well maintained and comfortably furnished, and comes with a fully equipped kitchen, a fireplace, and a private balcony for taking in those mountain views. All the rooms have been painted and decorated with bright colors and furnished in a cozy style. Each unit contains a well-kept bathroom equipped with a tub/shower combination. Rates are extremely complicated and depend on the time of year and a host of other factors. It's always best to talk directly to the hotel, state your requirements, and try to negotiate the best deal for yourself. There is no restaurant on-site, but nine different dining choices lie within a 3-mile driving radius, and twice as many are only minutes away in Banner Elk.

301 Pinnacle Inn Rd., Banner Elk, NC 28604. © **800/405-7888** or 828/387-2231. Fax 828/387-3745. www. pinnacleinn.com. 242 units. Winter $85–$140 double, $195 2-bedroom; summer $65–$100 double. AE, MC, V. **Amenities:** Heated indoor pool; tennis courts; exercise room; Jacuzzi; sauna; steam room; children's playground; free supervised children's activities mid-June to mid-Sept; coin-operated laundry; nonsmoking rooms; picnic tables; grills. *In room:* TV, hair dryer, kitchen, coffeemaker, iron/ironing board.

## 6 Blowing Rock

90 miles NE of Asheville

One of the oldest resorts in North Carolina, Blowing Rock dates back to the 1800s. Sitting on the Continental Divide at an elevation of 4,000 feet, Blowing Rock is filled with little B&Bs, inns, and galleries. It makes a good base for exploring and offers some of the state's best snow-skiing (at Appalachian Mountain).

### ESSENTIALS

**GETTING THERE  By Car**  To reach Blowing Rock from Asheville, head north on the Blue Ridge Parkway or take I-40 East out of Asheville to U.S. 321 North and follow the signs into Blowing Rock. From Boone, take U.S. 321 South directly into Blowing Rock.

**VISITOR INFORMATION**  The **Blowing Rock Chamber of Commerce,** 132 Park Ave., Blowing Rock, NC 28605 (© **800/295-7851** or 828/295-7851; www.blowingrock.com), is open Monday to Saturday 9am to 5pm, dispensing information about the area.

### EXPLORING THE AREA

The area's biggest attraction, from which the town takes its name, is the **Blowing Rock** ✦ (© **828/295-7111;** www.theblowingrock.com), on U.S. 321, 2 miles south of town. Rising 4,000 feet above John's River Gorge, the mountain has a strong updraft that returns any light object (such as a handkerchief) that's thrown into the void. The observation tower, gazebos, and gardens offer panoramic views of John's River Gorge and nearby Blue Ridge peaks. You can visit the mountain Friday to Monday December to March from 9am to 5pm; April to Memorial Day daily 9am to 6pm; Memorial Day to Labor Day daily 8:30am to 7pm; September and October Sunday to Thursday 9am to 6pm, Friday and Saturday 9am to 7pm; November weekends 9am to 5pm. Admission is $6 for adults, $1 for children 4 to 11.

Another natural phenomenon at Blowing Rock is **Mystery Hill,** where balls and water run uphill. The pioneer museum is interesting, and you'll get a kick out of the mock grave marked simply HE WAS A REVENOOR—a pile of dirt with boots sticking out one end.

### OUTDOOR PURSUITS

**HORSEBACK RIDING**  Some 30 horses are available for guided trail rides that take in 26 miles. Bookings are possible at the **Blowing Rock Stables,** 1500 Laurel Lane (© **828/295-4700**). Minimum age for riders is 9 years, and reservations must be made 1 day in advance. Both English and Western saddles are used. The cost is $35 for 1 hour or $50 for 2 hours.

**SKIING**  The **Appalachian Ski Mountain,** P.O. Box 106, Blowing Rock, NC 28605 (© **800/322-2373** or 828/295-7828; www.appskimtn.com), lies 2 miles off U.S. 221/321 between Boone and Blowing Rock near the Blue Ridge Parkway intersection. It offers nine slopes: two beginner, four intermediate, and three advanced. It stands at an elevation of 4,000 feet, with a 365-foot vertical drop. The season runs from the weekend before Thanksgiving to the third weekend in March, when it's open daily from 9am to 4pm and 6 to 10pm. Lift tickets cost $30 for adults Monday to Friday and $40 on weekends and holidays. Children 12 and under are charged $20 and $30, respectively. Ski lessons are available for $35 per hour for private instruction, but cost only $15 per person in a group. Skis can be rented for $12 to $16.

## SHOPPING

The **Main Street Gallery,** Main Street (© **828/295-7839**), is a cooperative gallery featuring handmade contemporary art and crafts from the North Carolina mountains. The location is in the center of Blowing Rock across from the post office. Hours are daily 10am to 6pm.

Orchard at Altapass, milepost 328.4 on the Blue Ridge Parkway, at Spruce Pine on Orchard Road (© **828/765-9531**), sells apples from July to November; you pick, or they pick. The orchard has an array of fresh baked goods, free tours, and even music and tall tales. The proprietors will arrange hayrides for you on Saturday and Sunday. From May to October, hours Monday to Saturday are 10am to 6pm; on Sunday they're 11am to 6pm. The rest of the year, the store is open only on Saturday 10am to 6pm, Sunday noon to 6pm. Finally, **Parkway Craft Center** (© **828/295-7938**) is at milepost 294 on the Blue Ridge Parkway in the Moses Cone Manor just off Route 321. Here, you'll find the finest-quality Appalachian Mountain crafts, handmade by members of the Southern Highland Craft Guild. Craft demonstrations are presented on the porch. Open daily 9am to 5pm.

## WHERE TO STAY

**Crippen's Country Inn and Restaurant** (see "Where to Dine," below) also rents guest rooms.

**Chetola Resort at Blowing Rock** ★★ *Kids*   *Chetola,* Cherokee for "rest haven," is the right name for this idyllic spot. This is the grandest resort in the area, set on 87 acres within walking distance of the center of the village, with the 3,600-acre Moses H. Cone National Park and the Blue Ridge Mountains enveloping it. Guests can select first-class accommodations in the lodge or choose one of the luxury condos.

Since antebellum days, the property has known many owners, including J. Luther Snyder, the Coca-Cola king of the Carolinas in the 1920s. Much of it is new, but remnants of yesterday remain, including the fireplace (from the mid-1800s) in the manor house. Many private homes are also part of the complex. In 1988, the Chetola Lodge & Conference Center opened on-site. We prefer staying in the lodge, where the spacious rooms and suites are comfortably and attractively furnished. (The condos' decor depends on the taste of the individual owners.) The on-site restaurant, **Manor House,** offers a superb cuisine, showcasing local produce whenever possible, including trout from nearby mountain streams.

N. Main St., Blowing Rock 28605. © **800/243-8652** or 828/295-5500. Fax 828/295-5529. www.chetola.com. 104 units. May–Dec $131–$246 double, $275–$295 condos. Off-season reductions. AE, DISC, MC, V. **Amenities:** Restaurant; soda shop; bar; entertainment; indoor heated pool; golf privileges; 4 tennis courts; boat rentals; fishing; fitness center; gym; sauna; children's playground and activities; limited room service; massage; babysitting; laundry service and coin-operated laundry; nonsmoking rooms; rooms for those w/limited mobility. *In room:* A/C, TV, minibar, kitchenette (in some), coffeemaker, hair dryer, iron/ironing board.

**The Green Park Inn** ★   Once upon a time, this 1882 hotel, listed on the National Register of Historic Places, received such guests as John D. Rockefeller, Franklin D. Roosevelt, and Calvin Coolidge. That illustrious list of names might make you think that the place needs refurbishing today, but the old-fashioned and timeworn charm is part of its appeal. The hotel's fans are mostly an older crowd that likes to while away the time in the wicker rocking chairs on the veranda. The sprawling, three-story Victorian inn straddles the Eastern Continental Divide at an elevation of 4,300 feet near John's River Gorge. The inn has air-conditioning, as well as ceiling fans in the guest rooms. Rooms have one or two queen-size beds and quilted spreads, as well as neatly kept bathrooms with tub/shower combinations. Golf is available at a nearby country club.

P.O. Box 7, Blowing Rock, NC 28605. © 800/852-2462 or 828/295-3141. Fax 828/295-3141. www.green parkinn.com. 87 units. $129–$169 double; $149–$209 suite. AE, DISC, MC, V. Take U.S. 321 2 miles southeast of town. **Amenities:** 3 restaurants; bar; exercise room; spa; limited room service; babysitting; nonsmoking rooms. *In room:* A/C, TV, dataport, coffeemaker, hair dryer, iron/ironing board.

**Hound Ears Lodge** ⋆⋆ If you want high style, this exclusive resort should be your mountain retreat. Its unusual name derives from a nearby rock formation. The setting is panoramic, on 700 acres with an 18-hole golf course. Guest rooms, except for seven in the main clubhouse, are in chalets complete with "Oh, that view!" balconies and pitched roofs. Guest rooms are spacious and have well-kept bathrooms containing tub/shower combinations. The hotel doesn't serve liquor, but guests are welcome to "brown-bag" it: Bring your own. Fishing and skiing are the major pastimes.

Off N.C. 105 S. near Boone, P.O. Box 188, Blowing Rock, NC 28605. © 828/963-4321. Fax 828/963-8030. www.houndears.com. 28 units. $175–$195 double; $245–$275 for 4. Rates include breakfast and dinner. AE, MC, V. **Amenities:** Restaurant; bar; outdoor pool; 18-hole golf course; 6 tennis courts; sauna; limited room service; nonsmoking rooms. *In room:* A/C, TV, dataport.

## WHERE TO DINE

**Best Cellar Incorporated** ⋆ CONTINENTAL This restaurant is housed inside an authentic log cabin dating from 1938. Set on a hillside off the bypass in Blowing Rock, it's run by Rob Dyer and Lisa Stripling, who welcome visitors from all over the world. They've turned their kitchen over to chef Richard Jones (everybody calls him "Dickie"), a master at his craft. He admits that he didn't learn to cook from his mama, whose specialty was TV dinners. Dickie is a heavy-cream-and-butter type of chef—South Beach dieters might prefer to book a table elsewhere. Fresh seafood and aged beef are the chef's delightful specialties, and he also does wonders with rack of lamb and duck. We've enjoyed the sesame-seed tuna over sautéed fresh spinach and shiitake mushrooms, and pan-seared scallops over pasta primavera. The homemade desserts are worth making room for; the chef's favorite is a rich brownie with vanilla ice cream and hot fudge.

267 Little Springs Rd. (off 321 Bypass). © 828/295-3466. Reservations required. Main courses $19–$26. AE, MC, V. Daily 5:30–10pm (closes 9:30pm Dec–Apr, and Tues–Wed and Sun May–Nov).

**Crippen's Country Inn and Restaurant** ⋆ AMERICAN The restaurant's sophisticated cuisine is one of the reasons people stay at Crippen's Country Inn. The spacious dining area with circular tables offers a surprising amount of intimacy despite the crowds. The menu changes daily, offering many creative delights. Ever had Coca-Cola–marinated kangaroo or chocolate steak with Bailey's sauce? You may begin with a shrimp brûlée, pan-roasted with blue-spot prawns, or a crispy duck confit with spring rolls and peanut-ginger dressing. The chef's specialties round out the main courses: grilled loin of venison wrapped with applewood-smoked bacon, and pan-seared tuna with fried oysters and ham-and-scallions sauce. Reservations are extremely important; the restaurant's closing hours often reflect the number of reservations it receives for the evening. The inn also rents nine guest rooms, each of which is comfortable and well furnished; prices range from $129 to $159 (double occupancy).

239 Sunset Dr., Blowing Rock, NC 28607. © 828/295-3487. Fax 828/295-0388. www.crippens.com. Reservations required. Main courses $18–$40. AE, DISC, MC, V. Daily 6–9pm.

## 7 The Blue Ridge Parkway ★★★

The **Blue Ridge Parkway** takes up where Virginia's Skyline Drive leaves off at Rockfish Gap, between Charlottesville and Waynesboro. It then continues winding and twisting along the mountain crests for 469 miles, passing through most of western North Carolina before it reaches Great Smoky Mountains National Park near the Tennessee border.

The parkway links the southern end of Shenandoah National Park in Virginia with the eastern entrance of Great Smoky Mountains National Park in North Carolina. When it was begun 60 years ago, the parkway was a great engineering challenge. During the Roosevelt era, it was designed as a federal public-works project to relieve massive unemployment in the region. Its final segment, the Linn Cove Viaduct, was constructed in the 1980s.

The northern section of the parkway skims the crest of the towering Blue Ridge Mountains, with panoramic views of grand valleys on both sides of the road. But when the parkway twists and curls in the more rugged Pisgah and Black mountains to the south, the panoramas become even more dramatic.

Because the mountains are higher in the south—and the temperatures are lower—fall foliage is at its most brilliant here earlier in October than in the northern part. October, in fact, is the peak visiting month, as thousands of people come to see the incredible scarlet of sourwoods, orange sassafras, and golden poplars, to name only a few. Traffic moves at a snail's pace in October, and Saturday and Sunday are especially crowded on the parkway. Reservations for lodging and certain attractions in summer and especially in October are essential.

You can detour to Waynesville around the third week of October for the best apple festival in the region. On sale are crafts, cider, apple butter, and fresh and dried apples. Square dancers perform, and bluegrass bands entertain the crowds. Waynesville lies 7 miles from the parkway at milepost 443.1. For more information, write **Haywood County Apple Harvest Festival,** P.O. Box 600, Waynesville, NC 28786 (© **828/456-3021**).

Elevations range from 649 to 6,053 feet above sea level. The parkway has frequent exits to nearby towns but no tolls. There are 11 visitor contact stations, nine campgrounds (May–Oct only; some need reservations) with drinking water and comfort stations but no shower or utility hookups; restaurants and gas stations; and three lodges, plus one location featuring rustic cabins for overnight stays (reservations recommended). Opening and closing dates for campgrounds and cabins are flexible, so be sure to check in advance. Before you set out, write ahead for maps and detailed information. Contact Superintendent, **Blue Ridge Parkway,** 199 Hemphill Knob Rd., 1 Pack Sq., Asheville, NC 28803 (© **828/ 298-0358;** www.nps.gov/blueridge).

At many overlooks, you'll see a man with a hiking stick symbol and the word *Trail,* which means that there are marked walking trails through the woods. Some trails take only 10 or 20 minutes and provide a leg-stretching break from the confines of the car; others are longer and steeper and may take an hour or more if you go the entire way.

A few simple rules have been laid down by the National Park Service, which administers the parkway: no commercial vehicles; no swimming in lakes and ponds; no hunting; no pets without a leash; and above all, no fires except in campground or picnic-area fireplaces. Another good rule is to keep your gas tank half-filled at all times; this is no place to be stranded. The speed limit is 45 miles an hour, and they're quite serious about that.

Don't plan to hurry down the Blue Ridge: Take time to amble and drink in the beauty. If you want to drive the entire length of the parkway, allow at least 2 or 3 days. On the first day, drive the Virginia half; then stop for the night at Boone, North Carolina, not far from the state border. The final two legs of the trip—from Boone to Asheville and from there to Fontana Village—can easily be accomplished in another day's drive.

**SIGHTS NEAR THE PARKWAY**   You can veer off the parkway to see several attractions, including **Linville Falls Visitor Center** (© 828/765-1045), between Linville and Marion. Parking is available at milepost 316 on the parkway. This is a series of two falls, with an upper level of 12 feet and a lower level of 90 feet. The falls plunge into the 2,000-foot-deep Linville Gorge. A 1-mile round-trip hike takes you to the upper falls; other trails lead to more views. Some of the trails are quite challenging. Open year-round, the falls are free.

The 7,600-acre **Linville Gorge Wilderness Area** is a primitive natural environment, accessed by foot trails off N.C. 183. You need a permit to enter the area and can obtain one at the district ranger's office (signposted) in Marion.

Another major attraction, **Linville Caverns,** lies about 65 miles north of the Folk Art Center (milepost 382 on the Blue Ridge Pkwy.), just off U.S. 221 between Linville and Marion (© 828/756-4171; www.linvillecaverns.com). The only caverns in North Carolina, these tunnels go 2,000 feet underground. The year-round temperature is 51°F (11°C). Admission is $5 for adults, $4 for seniors, and $3 for children 5 to 12. The caverns are open June 1 to Labor Day, daily 9am to 6pm; April, May, September, and October daily 9am to 5pm; November to March daily 9am to 4:30pm; and December to February weekends 9am to 4:30pm.

**SHOPPING**   The best shopping for handmade mountain crafts is at **Allanstand Craft Shop,** Folk Art Center Building, Blue Ridge Parkway, milepost 382 (© 828/298-7928). Here you'll find beautifully made quilts, Granny style, along with pottery, wooden bowls, and even musical instruments. Works displayed were made by members of the Southern Highland Craft Guild.

# 9

# Great Smoky Mountains National Park

Cloaked in mystery, the **Great Smoky Mountains** ✏★★★ were once known by the Cherokee as *sha-cona-ge,* "land of the blue mist" (or smoke). According to Cherokee legend, people and animals originally lived in the sky above the ocean. When the sky became overcrowded, a water beetle was sent to find land but could not, so it dived to the bottom of the ocean and brought up mud to form the Earth. The Smokies were then formed by a great buzzard whose wings touched the mud, hardening it into a mountain range. Geologists have a counter theory that says this range was actually formed by many upheavals and erosions of the land. Choose the one that appeals to you.

The Great Smoky Mountains, formed hundreds of millions of years ago, are the oldest mountains in the world. They're comprised of peaks that range in elevation from 840 to 6,642 feet. The mountainsides are covered with a wide variety of flora and fauna that have few equals throughout the Temperate Zone.

To preserve the pristine beauty of this environment, Great Smoky Mountains National Park was officially established in June 1934. The area was threatened with destruction by the logging industry. A librarian from St. Louis, Horace Kephart, spearheaded the effort to save the area. He was joined by several prominent citizens from Knoxville. The National Park Service, John D. Rockefeller, and eventually the federal government backed their efforts. The people gave the government the land, making it the first national park to be created in this fashion. In September 1940, Great Smoky Mountains National Park was dedicated by President Franklin D. Roosevelt at the Rockefeller monument at Newfound Gap. The park has become one of the most-frequented national parks in the United States, hosting more than nine million visitors annually.

The oval park, bisected by the North Carolina–Tennessee border, encompasses more than 520,000 acres of forests, streams, rivers, waterfalls, and hiking trails. These trails pass through valleys, peaks, forests, and overlooks that provide scenic views. The park also contains balds—patches of clear land in the midst of the wooded slopes. It's still a mystery why these spots do not support tree growth.

The United Nations has designated the park an International Biosphere Reserve because of its multitude of plants, trees, mammals, birds, and fish. More than 100 species of trees thrive in the park. Growing on some of the relatively drier slopes in the lower to middle elevations (up to 4,500 ft.) are pines, oaks, hickories, yellow poplars, and dogwood trees. Hike the trails at Cades Cove and Laurel Falls to see the species that are typical of this elevation. In several areas, you can find gigantic ancient hemlocks that escaped the loggers' destruction; these hemlocks are located along trails leading from the Roaring Fork Motor Nature Trail to

# Great Smoky Mountains National Park

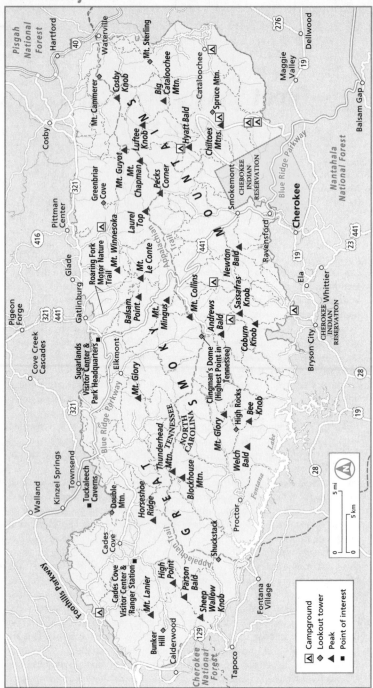

Grotto Falls or from the Newfound Gap Road to Alum Cave Bluffs. At slightly higher elevations are hardwoods typical of those that grow in northern states: beeches and yellow birches. Look for these species at Newfound Gap and along Clingmans Dome Road. The higher elevations (above 4,500 ft.) support the kinds of evergreens that are typical of areas such as Maine and Quebec at sea level. Varieties include the Fraser fir and red spruce, which you can find along the Appalachian Trail through most of the eastern half of the park, as well as along Clingmans Dome Road.

Abundant wildflowers offer a kaleidoscope of colors in spring and early summer and a blanket of lush greenery in later summer. Often, non-native flowers—trilliums, violets, lady's slippers, and jack-in-the-pulpits —have taken over entire areas. Blooming shrubs, numbering more than 1,500 species, are scattered throughout the park. The height of the blooming season is in mid-June, when you'll find rhododendrons, mountain laurels, and azaleas displaying all their beauty. The best places to look for these blooms are among the various balds (such as Gregory, Andrews, and Silers) and along the Cove Hardwoods Nature, the Chimney Tops, and the Noah Bud Ogle Farm trails.

As you ascend the peaks, you'll travel through the blue mists that once were wholly the work of Mother Nature. Unfortunately, they are now composed of almost 70% pollution from factories and cities, and are causing damage to the delicate balance of this area's ecosystem. Pollution has also reduced visibility by 30% over the past several decades. Yet, as you traverse the park, the mists still surround you with a centuries-old aura of mystery.

The park is the home of more than 200 species of birds. The junco, a small gray bird with white outer tail feathers, patrols the parking lots of Newfound Gap and Clingmans Dome. Although wild turkeys appear throughout the park, you'll most likely view them in the early morning and evening hours around Cades Cove. More than 70 types of fish and 30 varieties of amphibians can be found in the streams, including the red-cheeked salamander, which lives only in the park.

Nearly everyone is interested in the park's wildlife. More than 70 species of mammals live here. The park is known especially for its black bears, which weigh an average 200 to 300 pounds. Other mammals are white-tailed deer, groundhogs, raccoons, skunks, and bobcats. Park rangers stress that no visitor should try to approach or feed these creatures—for the safety of both humans and animals.

## 1 Cherokee: Gateway to the Smokies ⭒

48 miles SW of Asheville

The Cherokee Nation once claimed around 135,000 square miles of land encompassing sections of South Carolina, North Carolina, Tennessee, Virginia, West Virginia, and Kentucky. When Hernando de Soto, the Spanish explorer, moved into the southern mountains of the Appalachian range in 1540, the Cherokee numbered only about 25,000—a very small number compared with the millions who now occupy former Cherokee land.

When de Soto arrived, he forever changed the way the Cherokee lived. With him on his quest for gold in the name of Spain came misery, disease, and death. Some of de Soto's men killed or enslaved many of the Native Americans, believing that they were holding back information about the location of treasure. It's estimated that during the first 200 years of European occupation, 95% of the

Cherokee died of diseases that the foreigners brought with them. The treatment of the Cherokee did not improve in later centuries. When the Cherokee adapted well to the white man's ways and set up a flourishing society, greed and envy eventually culminated, in 1838, in the Trail of Tears. Most of the Cherokee were driven out of the area by military force, and their ancestral lands were taken away.

Today, the Smoky Mountain home of the Cherokee has dwindled to 56,000 acres that make up the Qualla Boundary, also known as the Cherokee Indian Reservation. This land was purchased by a white man, Will Thomas, who gave it to the Cherokee people in the late 1800s. When you visit the reservation, you're entering a sovereign land held in trust specifically for the tribe by the United States government. Known as the Eastern Band of the Cherokee Nation, the Cherokee who still reside here are descendants of the approximately 1,000 Cherokee who hid in these mountains to avoid forced removal to Oklahoma. These people can rightfully claim to be the original inhabitants of the vast Smoky Mountains.

Only a generation ago, the Cherokee language—both the spoken form and the written form—was in danger of becoming extinct. But since the late 1940s, annual increases in tourist-related business and the resultant growth of tribal resources have helped keep it alive. Today, visitors can hear the language spoken at attractions such as the Oconaluftee Indian Village and during the outdoor drama *Unto These Hills.* In Cherokee schools, it's a required subject, and it has also become part of the curriculum of universities such as Western Carolina University in Cullowhee, North Carolina. Tourism is the mainstay of the economy; about 75% of the tribe's revenue is derived from this industry. All business locations within the Qualla Boundary are Native American–owned, but by the authority of the Tribal Council, Native Americans can lease their buildings or businesses to other people. Nearly 30 businesses hold trader's licenses and collect a 6% tribal levy on sales. No other sales tax applies within the boundary, including North Carolina sales tax.

On your visit here, you'll notice several "chiefs" dressed in Western attire. You can have your picture taken with them for a small fee or tip. Many of these "chiefs" have been around for quite a while, priding themselves on having their pictures taken with two or three generations of the same family.

## ESSENTIALS

**GETTING THERE**    From the southern end of the Blue Ridge Parkway and points south, U.S. 441 leads to Cherokee; U.S. 19 runs east and west through the town.

The nearest airport is at Asheville (see "Essentials," in the "Asheville" section of chapter 8).

**VISITOR INFORMATION**    For more information, contact the **Cherokee Visitor Center,** 498 Psali Blvd., off 441 North, Cherokee, NC 28719 (**©** **800/438-1601** or 828/497-9195), open in summer Monday to Saturday 8am to 8pm, Sunday 8am to 7pm; in winter Monday to Saturday 8am to 5pm, Sunday 8am to 5pm. Or go to the website www.cherokee-nc.com.

## DISCOVERING CHEROKEE CULTURE

**The Museum of the Cherokee Indian** ⭐    The objective of this museum is to "authentically present and preserve thousands of years of Cherokee history and culture." This it does, displaying one of the finest exhibits of Native American artifacts in the United States. One exhibit includes a digital movie of the creation of the Cherokee Nation. When you enter the building, you begin walking along a timeline, beginning with the Paleolithic era some 10,000 years ago and continuing chronologically to modern times. Also included are lighting special effects, the most impressive of which is a holographic exhibit of the Cherokee. A gift shop is also open in the museum. On the entrance grounds is a 20-foot-tall, hand-carved statue of Sequoyah, the inventor of the Cherokee alphabet. Artifacts that you'll find inside include farming utensils, weapons for hunting and war, clothing, copies of the first photographs taken of the Cherokee people, pottery, baskets, and an art gallery displaying native art and photography.

U.S. 441 at Drama Rd. ℂ **828/497-3481.** www.cherokeemuseum.org. Admission $8 adults, $5 children, free for children 5 and under. Closed major holidays.

**Oconaluftee Indian Village**    Operated by the Cherokee Historical Association, this living museum offers a step back in time to the mid-1750s Cherokee way of life. On your tour of the village, you'll see women shaping clay into pottery, arrowheads being chipped, naturally dyed river cane being woven into baskets, and blowguns being demonstrated. Lectures are held at the Ceremonial Grounds, where you'll hear about dances, masks, rattles, feathers, and other facets of Cherokee life, and at the Council House, where presentations are given about Cherokee government, Council House designs, territories, language, and other nonceremonial topics. There's also a mile-long nature trail adjacent to the village. The seven-sided Council House conjures up images of the leaders of seven tribes gathered to thrash out problems or to worship their gods together.

U.S. 441. ℂ **828/497-2315.** www.oconalufteevillage.com. Admission $13 adults, $6 children 6–13. Mid-May to Oct daily 9am–5:30pm.

## SHOPPING

You'll find many opportunities to take some Cherokee culture home with you. A wide selection of handmade Cherokee products is available, as well as authentic Native American items from other areas. About 16 stores on the Cherokee reservation specialize in crafts, clothing, paintings, or jewelry made by local craftspeople or craftspeople from other tribes. The largest is **Qualla Arts and Crafts Mutual** (ℂ **828/497-3103**), on U.S. 441 at Drama Road, at the entrance to the *Unto These Hills* arena. Formed in the mid-1940s as a cooperative, Qualla has a current membership of 300 Cherokee, whose items are sold exclusively at the store. It ships products worldwide and is frequently visited by other tribal representatives who are interested in establishing a similar facility on their lands. Whether the craftsperson is a woodcarver, pottery maker, finger-weaver, artist, or basket maker, the products show individual artistry and convey a personal link to the makers' ancestors. Hours are Monday to Saturday 8am to 7pm, Sunday 9am to 5pm.

## TROUT FISHING

The major outdoor pursuit on the reservation is **fishing.** Thirty miles of streams are stocked with 400,000 trout annually. Supplemental fish stocks include rainbow, brook, and brown trout, ranging up to trophy size.

Anyone 12 or older needs a tribal permit to fish the Cherokee streams and ponds. No other type of fishing license is accepted on the reservation. The annual season begins the last Saturday of March and ends the last day of February in the following year. Fishing is allowed beginning a half-hour before sunrise and ending a half-hour after sunset. The creel limit is 10 trout per day per permit holder. Certain enterprise waters are open only to tribal members.

## Unto These Hills

*Unto These Hills* ★★★, the most popular outdoor drama in America, is presented each summer at Cherokee. The drama began in 1950 and has been seen by some five million summer visitors since then. It relates the story of the Cherokee from 1540 until the Trail of Tears exodus to Oklahoma in 1838, during which thousands died.

As you watch the first encounter with Hernando de Soto, you'll hear voices echoing off the mountainside—the very mountainside that became a hiding place for Cherokee who were determined to remain in their homeland instead of joining the long march to exile in Oklahoma.

The powerful drama re-creates the inspiration of the great Sequoyah, who created the alphabet that enabled Cherokee to become a written language; the wise leadership of Junaluska; and the sacrifices of Tsali, who gave his life so that a few of his people could remain on their ancestral lands. The emotional impact of this tragic story is supported by a strong musical score.

The 2½-hour show, written by Kermit Hunter, involves 130 performers and technicians. All performances are at the 2,800-seat **Mountainside Theater**, off U.S. 441 (© **888/554-4557** or 828/497-2111; www.untothese hills.com). Traditionally, the drama has a 9-week run. Opening night is around June 10, and the curtain goes down for the last time at August's end. Tickets cost $18 for reserved seating or $16 for general admission; children 6 to 13 years old are charged $8. Children under 6 are free in the general-admission seating area. No shows are presented on Sunday.

For complete fishing information, contact **Cherokee Fish and Game Management,** P.O. Box 302, Cherokee, NC 28719, or the visitor center (see "Essentials," above).

## WHERE TO STAY

Cherokee has an abundance of motel and hotel rooms offering basic accommodations. In addition to the following listings is the **Holiday Inn-Cherokee,** U.S. 19 South (© **800/HOLIDAY** or 828/497-9181). You'll also find some nifty retro choices that seem to be straight out of a family road trip from the 1940s and 1950s.

**Baymont Inn**   Built in 1995, this economy choice offers comfortable but decidedly straightforward accommodations. Guest rooms are basic, with neatly kept bathrooms with tub/shower combinations. Suites offer such amenities as small refrigerators, microwaves, and sleeper sofas. The rates include in-room coffee and continental breakfast delivered to your door. Stay here only for the value.

1465g Acquoni Rd. (P.O. Box 1865), Cherokee, NC 28719. © **828/497-2102.** Fax 828/497-5242. www.baymont inns.com. 67 units. $50–$95 double; $90–$115 suite. Rates include continental breakfast. AE, DC, DISC, MC, V. **Amenities:** Breakfast room; lounge; outdoor pool; coin-operated laundry; nonsmoking rooms; rooms for those w/limited mobility. *In room:* A/C, TV, dataport, coffeemaker, hair dryer, iron/ironing board.

**Harrah's Cherokee Casino & Hotel** ★   Directly connected to the casino, this first-class hotel rises 15 floors, each level decorated with local Indian crafts and art work. An elevated mountain walkway over a fast-flowing stream takes patrons from the casino into the hotel precincts, where the spacious lobby is adorned with Native American artifacts. Guest rooms are big and attractively furnished.

777 Casino Dr. (✆ 800/HARRAHS or 828/497-7777. Fax 828/497-5076. www.harrahs.com/our_casino/che/index/html. 252 units. $80–$175 double. AE, DC, DISC, MC, V. **Amenities:** 4 restaurants; indoor pool; exercise room; sauna; limited room service; babysitting; laundry service/dry cleaning; nonsmoking rooms; rooms for those w/limited mobility. *In room:* A/C, TV, dataport, minibar (nonalcoholic), beverage maker, fridge, hair dryer, iron/ironing board, safe.

**Newfound Lodge**    Located on the Oconaluftee River, this motel is divided into two sections. One section is set on the mountainside; the other is located across the street and contains balconied rooms overlooking the river. The rooms are spacious; some are decorated in the standard floral motif, whereas others display a more modern geometric design. The bathrooms are rather small but are equipped with tub/shower combinations. The grounds include picnic areas with grills and a deck that leads down to the rocks below. The motel is centrally located for Cherokee attractions, shopping, and Great Smoky Mountains National Park.

1192 Tsa lagi Blvd., N. Cherokee, NC 28719. (✆ **828/497-2746.** Fax 828/497-7136. 72 units. Late Mar to mid-June $58 double; mid-June to Oct $88 double. AE, DISC, MC, V. Closed Nov to late Mar. **Amenities:** Outdoor pool; nonsmoking rooms; rooms for those w/limited mobility. *In room:* A/C, TV, fridge, coffeemaker.

**Riverside Motel and Campground**    Set off the road, this motel offers comfortable, standard rooms overlooking the river. Each well-kept unit has a bathroom containing a tub/shower combination. The stone structure fits in well with the environment, not distracting from the beauty of the mountains. The grounds hold a sheltered picnic area plus a campground with 30 rental sites. Overnighters bring their own camper, RV, or tent.

U.S. 441 S. at Old Rte. 441 (P.O. Box 58), Cherokee, NC 28719. (✆ **828/497-9311.** www.riversidemotelnc.com. 34 units. $74–$78 double. DISC, MC, V. Closed Nov–Mar. **Amenities:** Outdoor pool; coin-operated laundry; nonsmoking rooms. *In room:* A/C, TV.

## WHERE TO DINE

Most restaurants here serve your basic chicken, steak, seafood, and (of course) freshwater fish from local waters. Also, the familiar national chains have long since arrived.

**Happy New Restaurant** CHINESE    Adorned with traditional Chinese artwork, this red-and-gold restaurant offers hearty helpings. The staff makes you feel welcome and is quite attentive throughout the meal. The specialties include battered shrimp lightly fried with a five-spice/salt blend, green peppers, and green onions; and Seven Star around the Moon, which is scallops, chicken, and barbecued pork with broccoli, carrots, snow peas, bamboo shoots, and rice in a brown sauce, with seven fried shrimp surrounding the entire concoction. Although it's not the most original Chinese restaurant, it is consistent and a welcome relief from all the Big Macs.

Acquoni Rd., Saunooke Village. (✆ **828/497-4310.** Buffet $5.95–$7.25 lunch, $8.95 dinner. AE, MC, V. Tues–Sun 11am–8pm.

**Peter's Pancakes & Waffles** AMERICAN    This pancake house offers hearty breakfasts and light lunches featuring sandwiches, soups, and salads. The birdhouse-adorned dining room has tables as well as counter service. Lunch options include Reubens, hot ham and cheese, chili dogs, and even PB&J, but the meal to eat here is breakfast. As you walk in the door, the aroma of fresh-cooked waffles and pancakes greets you. Waffles come topped with fresh fruit, and pancakes can be made with pecans. Hearty breakfast platters include the Ranch Hand: country ham, two eggs, two pancakes or biscuits, and grits.

34 Hwy. 441. (©) **828/497-5116.** Breakfast items $2.95–$6.95; lunch $3.75–$5. DISC, MC, V. Apr–Oct daily 7am–2pm.

## CHEROKEE AFTER DARK

Drawing people from across the state is **Harrah's Cherokee Casino,** 777 Casino Dr. ((©) **828/497-7777**), open 24 hours daily. All your favorite games of chance are here, plus a 1,500-seat Cherokee Pavilion Theater and five major restaurants. You must be 21 years of age or older to enter. This complex is part of a vast project that has transformed the Cherokee tribe's chronically depressed reservation into the only place in North Carolina where people can legally gamble. Rows of slots, video poker, and blackjack machines, along with other games, provide the tribe with an annual payout from Harrah's of $155 million—each member gets a $6,000 check every year. Once that news was announced, "Cherokees" began to emerge from behind every bush. About once a month, the theater presents a headliner, such as Jay Leno, Loretta Lynn, Bill Cosby, or B. B. King. Depending on the entertainment booked, tickets range from $15 to $55.

## 2 The Smokies: Just the Facts

**GETTING THERE**  Take I-40 from Asheville to U.S. 19; then take U.S. 441 to the park's southern entrance near Cherokee, a distance of 50 miles west.

**ACCESS POINTS & ORIENTATION**  Although there are several side roads into the park, the best routes are through one of the three main entrances, two of which are located on Newfound Gap Road, U.S. 441, a 33-mile road that stretches north–south through the park. The southern entrance is near Cherokee, North Carolina, whereas the northern entrance is located 33 miles away near Gatlinburg, Tennessee. The third main entrance is on the western side of the park at Townsend, Tennessee. Other access points are from the campgrounds at the edge of the park. The park is open year-round, and admission is free.

**VISITOR CENTERS**  At each of the three main entrances are visitor centers for the park. Each center offers information on roads, weather, camping, and backcountry conditions. You'll also find books, maps, and first-aid information.

The **Sugarlands Visitor Center and Park Headquarters** ((©) **865/436-1291;** www.nps.gov/grsm; for park headquarters and all three visitor centers) is at the northern entrance, near Gatlinburg, Tennessee. This center is the largest and offers a 20-minute movie. A natural-history exhibit features stuffed animals such as a wild boar and other wildlife of the region.

The smaller **Oconaluftee Visitor Center** is at the southern entrance and offers a few exhibits on what to see and do in the park.

**Cades Cove Visitor Center,** at the western end of the park on Parson Branch Road about 12 miles southwest of Townsend, Tennessee, is set among a cluster of historic 19th-century farms and buildings.

The visitor centers are open daily from April to October: in April, May, and August 31 to October from 8am to 6pm (9am at the Cades Cove center); June to August 30, from 8am to 7pm (9am at the Cades Cove center).

**FEES, REGULATIONS & PERMITS**  Entrance to the park, backcountry permits, and parking permits for people with disabilities (which can be obtained from the visitor centers and ranger stations) are all free.

Park visitors must adhere to quite a few regulations, which help preserve the surroundings and safety of visitors as well as that of the wildlife:

- Alcohol is allowed only in designated picnic and campsite areas and at LeConte Lodge. Open containers in automobiles are illegal.
- No hunting, weapons, or fireworks are allowed, including bows, arrows, and slingshots.
- Fires are allowed only in designated areas, such as established fire rings and fireplaces. No trees can be cut down for firewood, although dead and downed wood may be used. Firewood is sold by concessionaires at the Cades Cove, Elkmont, and Smokemont campgrounds.
- You may camp in designated areas only. To camp overnight in the back-country, you must obtain a permit from a ranger station, one of the camp-grounds, or one of the visitor centers (but not at Cades Cove).
- Motorcycles, bicycles, and mountain bikes are allowed on paved roads and campgrounds. They are not permitted on trails and administrative roads. Hel-mets are required for motorcyclists. Skateboarding is prohibited in the park.
- Pets are allowed in parking lots, campgrounds that are accessible by motor vehicle, and along paved roads. They are not allowed on the trails, in public buildings, or in the backcountry—with the exception of Seeing Eye and hearing guide dogs, which are permitted to travel throughout the park.
- It is illegal to pick, damage, destroy, and/or disturb any natural feature of the park. Federal law protects the forests and wildflowers of the Great Smokies.
- Food should never be left out for bears to find. You'll find specially designed trash cans and dumpsters throughout the park for deposit of any food, wrap-pings, and containers.

**SEASONS**    With each season come new scenery and several changes in the weather. From late March to June, spring brings great bursts of color from the wildflowers. Flowering shrubs spread across the countryside. This time is known as the wildflower season, although to a lesser degree, summer and fall also pro-duce a panoramic variety. At the higher elevations, mild daytime temperatures around the mid-70s (mid-20s Celsius) are recorded, although evenings are much cooler, dipping into the mid-40s (single digits Celsius).

As the season changes over to summer, which lasts from June to August, the lush greenery comes into its full splendor, and the weather gets warm and humid. Although the higher elevations offer milder temperatures, ranging from the low 50s to the mid-60s (teens Celsius), the lower ones can bring on days that

---

**Tips** **Avoiding the Crowds**

The height of the tourist season lasts from late May until late August. As autumn approaches, the greatest number of visitors come to the park on weekends, with the crowds much more manageable during weekdays. From March to November, the best crowd-avoiding times are the early morning hours. Although the National Park Service tries to keep all roads and trails open and clear in the winter, sometimes that's impossible (espe-cially at the higher elevations), making travel across the park an iffy propo-sition. Only those who are very well-equipped and skilled in the winter outdoor scene should brave the elements in the park's backcountry during the winter months.

are in the 90s (30s Celsius). Autumn colors first appear at higher elevations when the leaves on the fire cherry tree change to brilliant shades of crimson. Around the beginning of October, elevations above a mile have seen the end of fall, but lower elevations are just coming into their own with brilliant reds, yellows, oranges, purples, and browns. The best time to experience this change is from mid- to late October. Winter in the park can be very scenic, with snowfalls blanketing the countryside. At higher elevations, the temperature can drop below zero (−18°C). Throughout the year, one factor remains constant: Weather can change often and rapidly. During the course of a day, you may witness several thunderstorms and breaks of clear, sunshiny skies, while temperatures switch from cool and comfortable to hot and humid. The wettest months are generally March and July.

**RANGER PROGRAMS**    Park rangers provide assistance to visitors at the ranger stations scattered throughout the park, as well as at the visitor centers. Rangers also offer films, short talks, guided nature and history walks, and evening campfire programs, along with slide presentations covering geology, bears, plant life, and early settler life. These programs are posted daily at the visitor centers.

## 3 Seeing the Park's Highlights

If you have only a couple of days to tour the park, you must start early in the morning to avoid the crowds that increase during the day. When crossing the park on the Newfound Gap Road (U.S. 441), you should allow, at the very least, 1 hour. The speed limit does not rise above 45 mph anywhere in the park. When ascending the mountain slopes, you can rarely go over 25 to 30 mph because of the winding roads. Pack a lunch; the park has no restaurants, but picnic sites abound.

Following are suggestions for seeing some of the park's most popular sights:

**DAY 1**    Your best strategy is to visit the sights along the Newfound Gap Road. Begin at the **Oconaluftee Visitor Center,** where you can pick up park information and get details about the weather. Oconaluftee (which means "by the river") was owned by the Cherokee until settlers acquired the land through treaties. Today, the **Oconaluftee Mountain Farm Museum,** a replica of a pioneer farmstead, operates here in a collection of original log buildings. It features such artifacts as a sorghum molasses mill; a blacksmith shop; a mountain house; a corncrib; and a barn with cows, horses, pigs, geese, and roosters. Park staff members, dressed in period costumes, make this a living-history farm from April to October.

Travel about half a mile north on the Newfound Gap Road to the **Mingus Mill,** constructed in 1886 by Dr. John Jacob Mingus, son of this area's first permanent settler. It closed in 1940 and was reopened in 1968 by the park service. This water-powered mill is still in operation, grinding wheat and corn for flour and cornmeal from mid-April to October.

As you travel north, you'll come to a turnoff for **Clingmans Dome,** the highest peak in the park, soaring 6,642 feet and named for Thomas Lanier Clingman, a 19th-century North Carolina senator. After you turn onto this road, you travel 7 miles southwest to a parking lot, where you can walk a steep half-mile to a viewing platform that features one of the park's best views. The platform is generally closed from December to April.

Next comes **Newfound Gap,** which at 5,048 feet is the center of the park. A path that the Cherokee traveled was located 2 miles west of the present-day gap. Later, the path was widened and renamed Indian Gap Road. If the sky is clear, you can see for miles around; on other days, you find yourself literally in the clouds. It's best to call 📞 **865/436-1291** or -1200, the park's main number, for weather conditions before you set out.

The next point of interest is the **Chimney Tops,** twin peaks that rise close to 2,000 feet. The Cherokee named these peaks *Duniskwalguni* (which means "forked antlers"), whereas the settlers called them Chimney Tops because of the 30-foot-deep, fluelike cavity located in one of them. If you'd like a closer look, you can hike a 4-mile trail round-trip.

The drive across the park leads you to the **Sugarlands Visitor Center,** where you can stroll through the nature exhibit, view a slide show, or browse through the gift shop. At this point, you can either head into Gatlinburg for the night or go west about 5 miles on Little River Road to **Elkmont Campground.** It's best to make reservations (accepted only from mid-May to Oct).

**DAY 2** Continue your journey west on Little River Road to **Cades Cove,** where you'll find more pioneer structures than at any other location in the park. The best time to go is early in the morning, when you have a better chance of spotting deer grazing in the fields. Plan to spend half a day exploring the many attractions along the 11-mile Cades Cove Loop. Stop at the visitor center for a pamphlet that contains a key to the numbered sights.

Originally called Kate's Cove, after the wife of John Oliver, the cove's first settler, the name evolved over the years into Cades Cove. Founded in 1818, the cove was a thriving, self-supporting community for more than 100 years. Original homesites, such as the log homes of John Oliver, Elijah Oliver, Becky Cable, and Carter Shields, still stand today, giving visitors a glimpse into the lives of the original settlers. The other buildings include smokehouses, cantilevered barns, a blacksmith shop, and corncribs. You'll also find cemeteries with such epitaphs as one from the Civil War that reads BAS SHAW—KILLED BY REBELS. There are three historic churches: **Methodist Church; Missionary Baptist Church;** and the oldest, **Primitive Baptist Church,** built in 1827. Included on the loop is the John P. Cable farm, where you'll find the **1868 Cable Mill** still in operation. Cades Cove offers several nature trails; the shortest in the Cable Mill area consists of a half-mile round-trip.

After you complete the Cades Cove loop, head toward the **Sugarlands Visitor Center** to the Newfound Gap Road to recross the park, this time taking advantage of the numerous pulloff areas dotting the roadside. At most of them, you'll find Quiet Walkways—short paths created for moments of solitude in which visitors can experience nature. Remember to take your camera, because these stops offer a multitude of photo opportunities. Don't be discouraged if a pulloff is full, because another one will appear within a mile.

## 4 Sports & Outdoor Pursuits

**BACKPACKING** Backpacking enthusiasts are required to obtain permits from one of the ranger stations, the Oconaluftee and Sugarlands visitor centers, or the Cades Cove Campground Kiosk, before setting out. These permits are used to keep track of visitors for safety reasons, as well as to prevent popular campsites from becoming overcrowded. Campers are allowed to use only designated campsites and shelters. You will be fined if you're caught camping outside one of these sites. A rationing program limits the number of campers at 13 of the 80 campsites and at all 18 of the shelters. It's best to plan your route before visiting the park to determine whether you'll need any of these designated areas. The maximum number of people allowed in a hiking group is eight.

You must obtain shelter and ration (those with electrical and water hookups) campsite permits in person before departing on any given trail, calling for permits between 8am and 6pm only. Stays are limited to 1 night at shelters and 3 nights at campsites. Tents are not allowed in the shelter areas or along the Appalachian Trail. Shelters are located on the Appalachian Trail and at Laurel Gap, Kephart Prong, Mount LeConte, Rich Mountain, and Scott Gap. Permits for nonration sites can be obtained upon arrival. For more information, call © **865/436-1297** from 8am to 6pm daily; or write **Great Smoky Mountains National Park,** Attn.: Backcountry Office, Gatlinburg, TN 37738.

**BIKING**    Bicycles are not allowed on the trails, so areas for cyclists are limited. You can ride on roads, but traffic can be very heavy and the inclines quite steep. Try the 11-mile **Cades Cove Loop** from May to mid-October on Saturday mornings before 10am, when it's closed to all automobile traffic. Another possibility is the **Cataloochee Valley.** From April to October, you can rent a bicycle from the **Cades Cove Campground Store** (© **865/448-9034**) for $4 an hour or $20 for a full day. Hours are daily 9am to 7pm.

**BIRDING**    With more than 200 species of birds in the park, you should be able to spot a few on your ramblings. The higher elevations support bird life that's typical of parts of northern New England. Also to be seen in the high country along mountain crags are falcons, hawks, and ravens. Throughout the park, you may spot grouse and wild turkey, although the latter are quite shy of people.

**FISHING**    The park contains more than 700 miles of streams suitable for fishing. Fishers must have a valid North Carolina or Tennessee state fishing license, which can be purchased in the gateway towns at sporting-goods stores. In North Carolina, anyone 16 or older must have a license. Trout stamps are not required. Fishing is permitted from sunrise to sunset year-round, although the optimum seasons are spring and fall. Popular fishing areas include **Abrams Creek, Big Creek, Fontana Lake,** and **Little River.** The limit is five fish, with the exception of brook trout, which are illegal to possess.

**GOLF**    One of the best courses in the area is the **Maggie Valley Golf Course,** on U.S. 19 35 miles east of Asheville (© **828/926-6013**). A par-72, 6,500-yard course, it offers 18 holes. Greens fees range from $30 to $65 but are always $30 for 18 holes after 3pm. Carts are included.

**HIKING**    With more than 800 miles of trails, the park offers visitors of all fitness levels a chance to experience the great outdoors firsthand (see "Nature Trails," below). Before setting out, make sure to check the weather forecast for the duration of your trip, be it a few hours or a few days. If you find yourself caught in a thunderstorm, make sure to avoid all open areas, thereby lessening your chance of being struck by lightning. Carry rain gear, because sudden storms are normal for this area, and leave a copy of your itinerary at one of the ranger stations or visitor centers in case you become lost or injured.

Following are a few of the most popular trails that the park offers:

The **Indian Creek Falls Trail** has an elevation gain of 100 feet and begins at Deep Creek Road near the Deep Creek Campground. The 1-mile flat trail leads to the 60-foot-high Indian Creek Falls. Physical level: easy.

The **Laurel Falls Trail** ☆ is the most popular waterfall trail in the park, with an elevation gain of 200 feet. You travel 1.25 miles to the falls from the Laurel Falls parking area, a few miles from the Sugarlands Visitor Center. It's paved and relatively flat. Physical level: easy.

**Abrams Falls Trail** has an elevation gain of 340 feet. You travel 2.5 miles from the Abrams Falls parking lot at the west end of Cades Cove Loop Road to a 20-foot-high waterfall. The trail follows a clear stream and is relatively flat. Physical level: easy to moderate.

**Alum Cave Bluffs Trail** is deceiving because it starts off easy and grows more difficult. The elevation gain is 2,800 feet, and the distance is 11 miles round-trip. The first 1.5 miles takes you to Arch Rock, which contains a tunnel created by erosion. Then the trail becomes steeper and takes you to the 100-foot-high Alum Cave Bluffs. The last leg of the trail is quite steep, and many hikers find it necessary to use trailside cables to maneuver the cliffs. The journey is worth the trouble, because it ends at Mount LeConte, which offers one of the park's best views. Begin at Newfound Gap Road at the Alum Cave Bluffs parking lot, 9 miles south of the Sugarlands Visitor Center. Physical level: moderate.

**Charlies Bunion Trail** is a 4-mile trek to a 1,000-foot-high cliff where the forest was destroyed by fire in 1925. Part of the Appalachian Trail, it offers an elevation gain of 980 feet and begins at the Newfound Gap Overlook parking lot. Physical level: moderate.

Although the **Boulevard Trail** is the easiest and most popular trail to Mount LeConte, the 16-mile round-trip categorizes it as strenuous for a lot of people. The elevation gain is 1,545 feet. You must travel the Appalachian Trail from Newfound Gap to reach this trail. Physical level: moderate to strenuous.

**Ramsay Cascades Trail** has a total elevation gain of 2,375 feet and is 8 miles long round-trip. This trail also leads to Ramsay Cascades, a 100-foot-high waterfall, the park's highest. From Greenbrier Cove, follow the signs to the trail head. Physical level: strenuous.

The **Appalachian Trail** ❀❀❀ is the most famous trail, stretching from Maine to Georgia, and has 68 of its 2,100 miles situated in the park, following the Smokies ridgeline from east to west almost the entire length of the park. Access points are Newfound Gap, Clingmans Dome, the end of Tenn. 32 just north of the Big Creek Campground, and the Fontana Dam. The most popular section is from Newfound Gap to Charlies Bunion (see above). Elevation gain is 980 feet. Physical level: strenuous.

**HORSEBACK RIDING**    The park offers some of the state's most panoramic scenery for equestrians. All off-trail and cross-country riding, as well as use of trails designated as foot trails, is prohibited in the park. Horses are restricted from developed campgrounds and picnic areas and on maintained portions of park roadways. Any overnight riders must obtain backcountry permits (see "Backpacking," above). The following five drive-in horse camps offer easy access to designated horse trails: Anthony Creek, Big Creek, Cataloochee, Round Bottom, and Towstring. You can make reservations 30 days in advance with the **Backcountry Reservations Office** by calling ✆ **865/436-1231.**

If you have your own horse, write for an information packet that describes the park's trails, campsites, and regulations. Contact the Superintendent at Great Smoky Mountains National Park, 107 Park Headquarters Rd., Gatlinburg, TN 37738 (✆ **865/436-1200**).

Horses can be rented for $20 an hour April to October. Ask for details at the individual concessions within the park at **Cades Cove** (✆ **865/448-6286**); **Smokemont Riding Stable** (✆ **828/497-2373**); and **Smoky Mountains Riding Stables,** U.S. 321 (✆ **865/436-5634**). The park service requires that a guide accompany all rental treks.

**NATURE TRAILS**   Self-guided nature trails offer even couch potatoes an opportunity to commune with nature. These trails are staked and keyed to pamphlets with descriptions of points of interest along the way. You can obtain a keyed pamphlet from one of the visitor centers or stands at the trail heads. There are about a dozen such trails, ranging in length from a third of a mile to 6 miles. All offer easy walks through peaceful surroundings.

**WHITE-WATER RAFTING** ★★   Starting at the Waterville Power Plant, a 5-mile stretch of the Pigeon River has 10 rapids and offers some of the most challenging white-water rafting in the South. Water for rafting is released by the Carolina Power & Light Company. **Rafting in the Smokies** rafts both the Pigeon and the Nantahala rivers. A trip on the Pigeon costs $39 per person, but only $30 on the Nantahala. For reservations and details, call the company's central office in Gatlinburg, Tennessee (✆ **865/436-5008**).

**WILDLIFE-WATCHING**   Your chances are best in the spring, summer, and fall. Mammals are the main interest for many park visitors. As in all national parks, native wildlife is protected by federal law. Printed material, available at the visitor center, can provide additional information. For your safety as well as the protection of the wildlife, do *not* tease, harass, feed, or approach any wild animal, and be especially cautious when encountering mothers with their young.

The best-known park mammal is the black bear, which has been known to stop traffic—a situation that park officials try to keep from happening, because bears can become too used to humans. If this happens, bears are relocated to other, less-traveled areas of the park. When bears lose their innate fear of humans, they become more susceptible to poachers. Visitors should heed the rules about bears and the warnings given out by the park authorities.

Frequently sighted smaller mammals include cottontail rabbits, squirrels, and woodchucks (groundhogs). Mammals that are seldom seen are raccoons, skunks, opossums, weasels, bobcats, red and gray foxes, mink, and beavers.

The park is the home of at least 23 varieties of snakes. The poisonous ones are timber rattlesnakes and copperheads. If you stay on the trails and away from warm rocky slopes, abandoned buildings, and stone fences, you should have no close encounters. These snakes are not aggressive and generally stay away from areas used by people. Among the nonpoisonous snakes, the most common are the Eastern garter and Northern water snakes. Other varieties include the Northern ringneck, the Eastern king snake, and the Northern black racer.

## 5 Camping

The park contains 10 campgrounds with picnic tables, fire grills, cold running water, and flush toilets, but they don't have showers or water and electrical hookups (see "Backpacking," above). There are three major campgrounds. **Cades Cove** (151 sites) features a camp store, bike rentals, a disposal station, wood for sale, and naturalist programs held in the small amphitheater. **Elkmont** (220 sites) offers a disposal station, firewood for sale, vending machines, and a telephone. **Smokemont** (142 sites) has a disposal station and firewood for sale.

**Reservations** (✆ **800/365-CAMP**; www.reservations.nps.gov) can't be made more than 5 months in advance. It is possible to make reservations online at reservations.nps.gov daily from 10am to 10pm. The campgrounds are full on weekends beginning in April and daily from July to October. The busiest months are July and October, and you should make reservations at least 4 weeks in advance. Mid-May to October, there's a 7-day maximum stay, and the charge is $17 per day. November to mid-May, with limited sites available, the maximum stay is 14 days, and the charge is also $17 per day. The seven smaller campgrounds, open mid-May to October, are along the boundaries of the park and are slightly cheaper, costing $14 per day.

## 6 Where to Stay

### IN THE PARK

The park's only accommodations, **LeConte Lodge** ★ (② 865/429-5704 for reservations; www.lecontelodge.com), is located on the top of Mount LeConte. The lodge is very back-to-basics: It has no electricity, TV, phone, or indoor plumbing, although there are four flush toilets in outhouses. The only means of access to the lodge is by hiking. The shortest and steepest route is the Alum Cave Bluffs Trail (see "Hiking," above), a 5.5-mile one-way trip. Lodgings include private bedrooms in cabins with shared living rooms, as well as private cabins. The rates include breakfast, dinner (served family style), and lunch for those staying more than 1 night. There are eight rooms to rent, costing $85 per adult. A two-bedroom lodge costs $444 for up to eight people, plus $28 extra per person for meals. Two three-bedroom lodges cost $666 for up to 12 people, plus $28 per person for meals. An additional person can stay in any of the lodges at a cost of $55 per person, plus meals. Reservations are difficult to come by if you don't make them in October for the following year. The lodge is open from the last week in March to late November. No credit cards are accepted.

### BRYSON CITY

**Carriage Inn**    This is a survivor of the roadside motels that dotted the countryside during the 1940s and 1950s, offering basic but clean and comfortable accommodations. (Think Clark Gable and Claudette Colbert in the classic film, *It Happened One Night*.) It's a fine choice if you're planning to spend most of your time in the park anyway. All the rooms are ground-level, offering double or king-size beds, and well-maintained bathrooms with tub/shower combinations. The rates include free morning coffee. It has a small playground and a picnic area; restaurants are nearby.

U.S. 19N (5 miles east of Bryson City; P.O. Box 1506), Cherokee, NC 28719. ② 800/480-2398 or 828/488-2398. Fax 828/488-2398. www.carriageinn.bizland.com. 25 units. Apr–May and Nov $38 double; June–Oct $54–$78 double. AE, DISC, MC, V. Closed Dec–Mar 31. **Amenities:** Outdoor pool; nonsmoking rooms. *In room:* A/C, TV, dataport, coffeemaker.

**The Chalet Inn**    On 22 acres of forested mountainsides and ridges with trails, this inn offers the blend of rusticity and traditional comforts of an alpine *Gasthaus*. George and Hanneke Ware own this inn, which offers uniquely decorated rooms with private bathrooms containing tub/shower combinations and balconies or porches. Although the rooms have no phones, you have access to cordless phones that you're welcome to use in your room. You can view Doubletop Mountain from the Chalet's Great Room, and if the window is open, you can hear the sounds of the babbling brook that winds its way around the inn. On wintry evenings, you can enjoy one of the books from the inn's library while sitting in front of the fire in the stone fireplace. The grounds include lawn games and a picnic area, as well as hiking trails. Children are welcome, but from Labor Day until January 1, only children 8 and older are accepted. In winter, only children 12 and older are accepted. A whirlpool is available in the Romantic suite. All rooms are nonsmoking.

U.S. 74/441 between Bryson City and Dillsboro (285 Lone Oak Dr., Whittier, NC 28789). (C) **800/789-8024** or 828/586-0251. www.thechaletinn.com. 6 units. $89–$145 double; $140–$180 suite. Rates include full breakfast. AE, DISC, MC, V. Closed Jan 2–Mar. **Amenities:** Breakfast room; lounge; privileges at a nearby country club. *In room:* A/C, dataport, no phone.

**The Folkestone Inn** 🐾 Originally a 1920s farmhouse, the Folkestone Inn, which bills itself as a place to escape and explore, has the benefit of location. The structure is framed by a grove of Norway spruce trees, with a mountain stream serving as a boundary with the wilderness. Guests can explore the park and play golf at a nearby course. Asheville and other towns are just an hour's drive away. "Rustic" is the most apt term to describe the rooms, which are furnished with antiques, including the beds (some have queen-size beds). Each unit features its own bathroom with a shower and an old-fashioned claw-foot tub. The upstairs rooms have balconies with mountain views; the downstairs rooms have flagstone floors and pressed-tin ceilings. Breakfast is the only meal served, and what you get is a little less common than your standard eggs and bacon; you might see eggs Benedict when you sit down at the table. Smoking is not allowed in the building.

101 Folkestone Rd., Bryson City, NC 27813. (C) **888/812-3385** or 828/488-2730. Fax 828/488-0722. www. folkestone.com. 10 units. $88–$148 double. Additional person $20 per night. Rates include full breakfast. AE, DISC, MC, V. Children 10 and under not allowed. **Amenities:** Breakfast room; lounge. *In room:* A/C, hair dryer, fireplace (in some), no phone.

**Fryemont Inn** 🐾🐾 Listed on the National Register of Historic Places, this inn has been in operation since 1923. Amos Frye, head of a timber empire in the late 1800s, built it of the best chestnut, oak, and maple in the region. The exterior is covered with the bark of huge poplar trees, as sturdy today as when the strips were first cut. Sue and George Brown are the owners of the inn, which the *Atlanta Journal-Constitution* cited as being "a rustic, bark-covered architectural masterpiece." Each of the chestnut-paneled rooms is individually decorated, and some bathrooms contain old-fashioned pedestal tubs; all have showers. The large rooms have country touches such as homespun curtains. Units are not air-conditioned, but for the most part, air-conditioning is not needed. The cottage suites, open all year, are housed in a stone structure. Each suite has a loft bedroom overlooking a living area with a fireplace, TV, and wet bar. There is also a secluded and well-furnished cabin near the pool. Meals are served in the dining room in the main lodge, open April 14 through October 29. The lobby has a TV, two game tables, and a fireplace that can burn 8-foot logs, and the porch has rocking chairs. Closely supervised children are allowed in the main lodge, but the cottage suites are for adults only.

Fryemont St. (P.O. Box 459), Bryson City, NC 28713. (C) **800/845-4879** or 828/488-2159. www.fryemont inn.com. 41 units. $135–$150 double; $200–$250 suite; $155–$215 cottage; $225–$275 cabin. Additional person $20–$30. Rates include breakfast and dinner. DISC, MC, V. Main lodge closed Dec to mid-Mar. **Amenities:** Restaurant; bar; outdoor pool; nonsmoking rooms; basketball court. *In room:* A/C, no phone.

**Lloyd's on the River** This inn offers clean, decent rooms in a relaxed atmosphere, with comfortable furnishings and wood paneling or tasteful wallpaper. All units contain neatly kept bathrooms with tub/shower combinations. No meals are served, although the grounds contain picnic tables along the river and outdoor grills. With its columned porches accented by hanging plants and rocking chairs, the look is that of an oversize country home—or, as one guest stated, "It's like staying at a B&B without the breakfast." The owner, Bob Starks, offers warm hospitality and can create a personalized trail guide for you.

## The Great Smoky Mountains Railroad

Among the most popular attractions in the mountains are year-round scenic excursions departing Dillsboro and Bryson City. For schedules and reservations, call © **800/872-4681** or 828/586-8811 (www.gsmr.com). This scenic train journey, an exercise in nostalgia, takes you across valleys and river gorges and through tunnels. In all, there are 53 miles of track, two tunnels, and 25 bridges. A variety of round-trip excursions are offered, departing from depots in both Dillsboro and Bryson City. The trip takes from 4 to 4½ hours. You have a choice of diesels or steam trains. Prices for adults are $35 for diesel or $41 for steam; for kids 3 to 12, $16 diesel, $20 steam. Ages 2 and under ride for free.

U.S. 19 (P.O. Box 429), Bryson City, NC 28713. © **828/488-3767.** Fax 828/488-9020. www.lloydsonthe river.com. 21 units. Mid-Apr to mid-June and mid-Aug to mid-Sept $35–$88 double; mid-June to mid-Aug and mid-Sept to Oct 31 $80–$145 double. DISC, MC, V. Closed Nov to mid-Apr. **Amenities:** Lounge; outdoor pool; nonsmoking rooms; rooms for those w/limited mobility. *In room:* A/C, TV, dataport, coffeemaker.

# DILLSBORO & BALSAM

**Applegate Inn Bed & Breakfast** *Value* Owned by John and Andree Faulk, this inn is situated on a half-acre of land across Scott's Bridge. Although it's just "a footbridge away from the train station," it feels more remote. The inn welcomes children 12 and older. Decorating themes include mountain rustic, Victorian, French provincial, and country charm. Two units include a full kitchen, two bedrooms, and a living area. All units have well-kept bathrooms with tub/shower combinations. Breakfast is hearty, so come with an appetite.

163 Hemlock St. (P.O. Box 1051), Dillsboro, NC 28725. © **800/353-0377** or 828/586-2397. Fax 828/ 631-9010. www.applegatebed-breakfast.com. 11 units. $75–$125 double. Rates include full country breakfast. DC, DISC, MC, V. Free parking. **Amenities:** Breakfast room; lounge; nonsmoking rooms; rooms for those w/limited mobility. *In room:* A/C, TV, dataport (in some), coffeemaker, iron/ironing board.

**Balsam Mountain Inn** ★★ Only a 5- to 7-minute drive from Dillsboro, this long-established inn is on the National Register of Historic Places, as is Jarrett House, below. It's set a drop-dead-gorgeous part of the mountains, overlooking the little town of Balsam. For those who want to escape the curse of cheapskate roadside motels, this is the place. Lying just a quarter of a mile from the Blue Ridge Parkway, the inn was constructed in a neoclassical style, with a mansard roof and wraparound porches; it welcomed its first guests in 1908. Completely restored, it offers comfortably furnished and well-maintained units, either with a claw-foot tub or a shower. The more expensive and much better "bedsitting" rooms—minisuites—are more spacious, each opening onto mountain views. Suites range from cozy, romantic havens for couples to units suitable for families. Grace notes include a piano in the dining room, a library, a lobby with fireplaces, and 24 acres of trails.

68 Seven Springs Dr., Balsam, NC 28707. © **800/456-9298** or 828/456-9498. www.balsaminn.com. 50 units. $95–$125 double; $130–$160 suite. Rates include breakfast. DISC, MC, V. **Amenities:** Restaurant; nonsmoking rooms. *In room:* No phone.

**Jarrett House** ★★ *Value* One of the oldest inns in western North Carolina, this 1884 hostelry goes back to the days of the horse and buggy. It is on the National Register of Historic Places. Expect home-style food such as hot biscuits served with honey, affordable prices, and an old-time ambience (rockers on the front porch) where guests can practice the lost art of loafing. Units are handsomely furnished and come with neat, well-maintained bathrooms. The on-site restaurant is open to the public daily April to December.

100 Haywood St., Dillsboro, NC 28725. ✆ **800/972-5623** or 828/586-0265. www.jarretthouse.com. 22 units. $80 double. No credit cards. Closed Dec–Easter. **Amenities:** Restaurant; nonsmoking rooms; rooms for those w/limited mobility. *In room:* A/C, no phone.

**Olde Towne Inn** This inn is a restored 1878 home in the heart of Dillsboro. The rooms have a country flair and are tastefully appointed with antiques and ceiling fans. Each unit comes equipped with a well-kept bathroom with a tub/shower combination. The inn has been referred to as "a comfortable old home place"—ideally located near shops, restaurants, and the train station. You'll find many guests enjoying the breezes that roll off the mountainside as they rock on the front porch. In the morning, you're greeted by the aroma of a freshly prepared breakfast that's sure to fill you up. Children 10 and older are welcome.

300 Haywood Rd (P.O. Box 485), Dillsboro, NC 28725. ✆ **888/528-8840** or 828/586-3461. www.dillsboro-olde towne.com. 4 units. $100–$135 double; $135 suite. Rates include full breakfast. AE, DC, MC, V. **Amenities:** Breakfast room; lounge; nonsmoking rooms. *In room:* A/C, TV, hair dryer.

**Squire Watkins Inn** A casual lodging set in peaceful surroundings on 3 acres of gardens, this 1880s inn touts itself as "a place to enjoy the sunrise and fireflies, peaches from the garden and eggs from the farm." That's right. Tom and Emma Wertenberger, who bought and restored this old home in 1983, make their guests feel right at home, providing helpful advice on places to go and activities not to miss. Each morning, you're greeted with freshly baked breads, homemade casseroles, eggs from a farm just down the road, and fresh fruits and juices, all served on sparkling china and silver. Units are furnished with period antiques and have well-maintained bathrooms.

U.S. 441 and Haywood Rd. (P.O. Box 430), Dillsboro, NC 28725. ✆ **800/586-2429** or 828/586-5244. www. bbonline.com/nc/squirewatkins. 5 units. $85–$95 double; $125 suite. Rates include full breakfast. No credit cards. No children under 12. **Amenities:** Breakfast room; lounge; nonsmoking rooms. *In room:* A/C, no phone.

## FONTANA DAM

**Fontana Village Resort** On January 1, 1942, 24 days after the attack on Pearl Harbor, the Tennessee Valley Authority (TVA) got permission to build a dam 480 feet high to produce critically needed hydroelectric energy. This led to the birth of a village to support the workers and their families, including a school, a 50-bed hospital, churches, and space to play. This village has become the largest and most complete resort in the Great Smoky Mountains. Choose a room at the inn, a cottage with a kitchenette, or a campsite. All rooms and cottages have well-kept bathrooms with tub/shower combinations. (There are 20 campsites, 10 with hookups; the cost is $15 a night without hookup and $20 with hookup.)

Activities abound for every taste: biking (30 trails), horseback riding, cook-outs, square dancing, crafts classes, mountain-bike races, and boating.

N.C. 28 (P.O. Box 68), Fontana Dam, NC 28733. ✆ **800/849-2258** or 828/498-2211. Fax 828/498-2345. www.fontanavillage.com. 64 units, 135 cottages. $79–$149 double; $89–$229 cottage with kitchenette. AE, DISC, MC, V. **Amenities:** Restaurant; 3 pools; minigolf course; 4 tennis courts; fitness center; sauna; horseback riding; crafts shop; coin-operated laundry; nonsmoking rooms; rooms for those w/limited mobility. *In room:* A/C, TV, kitchenette (in some), hair dryer.

## MAGGIE VALLEY

**The Abbey Inn** On the northern slope of Setzer Mountain, this hostelry has a 1950s feel and offers views up to 5 miles away. Owners Mike and Natalie Nelson deliver friendly hospitality and advice on what to see in the area. The rooms are small yet reasonably comfortable and contain refinished furniture specifically made for the inn. Some rooms have kitchenettes with small refrigerators, stoves, and microwaves. All units have ceiling fans, bathrooms with oversize showers, and front porches with great views where you can while away the hours. The 2-acre grounds boast patio swings, a picnic area, and grills.

6375 Soco Rd. (U.S. 19), Maggie Valley, NC 28751. ☎ **800/545-5853** or 828/926-1188. Fax 828/926-2389. www.abbeyinn.com. 20 units. Apr 1–Oct 31 $45–$84 double. DISC, MC, V. Closed Nov–Mar. **Amenities:** Lounge; nonsmoking rooms. *In room:* TV, kitchenette (in some).

**Cataloochee Ranch** ★★    On the border of Great Smoky Mountains National Park, this 1,000-acre ranch offers a wide range of activities. The property includes a main lodge with six double rooms; the Silver Belle, containing the remaining rooms; and six cabins, each of which is rustic and individual. All units contain well-kept bathrooms with tub/shower combinations. One small house is suitable for four. Meals are served family style, and very few people ever leave hungry. The property includes a trout pond for fishing, and trails for hiking.

119 Ranch Dr., Maggie Valley, NC 28751. ☎ **800/868-1401** or 828/926-1401. Fax: 828/926-9249. www.cataloochee-ranch.com. 25 units. Apr–Nov $150–$200 double, $200–$400 cabin. Rates include breakfast and dinner. AE, MC, V. Closed Dec–Mar. **Amenities:** Dining room; lounge; outdoor pool; tennis court; horseback riding; nonsmoking rooms; rooms for those w/limited mobility. *In room:* TV (in some), kitchenette (in some), coffeemaker, no phone.

**The Ketner Inn & Farm** *Value*    Set on the mountainside on 27 acres, this B&B is housed in an 1898 farmhouse that has been completely restored by Randall McCrory. Decor highlights include hardwood floors, Victorian and country antiques such as a 7-foot rice-planter bed, and washstands. The rooms were decorated with different themes in mind, including doll, swan, and cat motifs. All units come with well-maintained bathrooms with tub/shower combinations. A hearty turn-of-the-20th-century-style breakfast is served in the dining room. You're welcome to sit on the porches overlooking Jonathan Valley and the rolling hills of the farm or to explore the grounds, where you'll find antique farm equipment, an old barn, a natural spring, and wooded trails. Children under 6 not welcome.

1154 Jonathan Creek Rd., Waynesville, NC 28786. ☎ **800/714-1397** or 828/926-7791. www.bbonline.com/nc/ketner. 5 units. $70–$80 double. Rates include full breakfast. MC, V. **Amenities:** Breakfast room; lounge; nonsmoking rooms. *In room:* A/C, TV, no phone.

**Maggie Valley Resort and Country Club**    Opening onto panoramic vistas, this resort offers a wide variety of activities to accommodate the whole family. The spacious rooms come with a rather standard decor. The premium ones overlook the front 9 holes of the golf course; the villas open onto the back 9. All units have well-kept bathrooms with tub/shower combinations. Greens fees for the golf course range from $53 to $58. A dining room serves steak, seafood, and an array of international dishes. Live entertainment is featured Wednesday to Saturday evenings.

1819 Country Club Rd. (near the intersection of U.S. 19 and U.S. 276), Maggie Valley, NC 28751. ☎ **800/438-3861** or 828/926-1616. Fax 828/926-2906. www.maggievalleyresort.com. 75 units. Apr–Oct $109–$129 double, $129–$209 villa; Dec–Feb $69–$89 double, $99–$119 villa; Mar and Nov $79–$89 double, $109–$139 villa. Golf packages available. AE, DISC, MC, V. **Amenities:** Restaurant; bar; outdoor pool; 18-hole golf course; exercise room; nonsmoking rooms. *In room:* A/C, TV, dataport, kitchenette (in some), coffeemaker, hair dryer, iron/ironing board.

## 7 Where to Dine

Forget the tourist brochures. Some of the worst restaurants in the South are in the towns that cater to the millions of visitors to the Smokies. Fast-food joints are everywhere, and many a cook's idea of a good dinner is a frozen hamburger slapped on a grill. Some good places with country cooking do exist, but they can be hard to find. Here's a representative sampling to get you going.

### BRYSON CITY

**Nantahala Village Restaurant** SOUTHERN    The food at this family-style haven ranges from down-home favorites like mountain trout, fried chicken, and country ham to more eclectic and lighter varieties that reflect an up-to-date approach to dining. Of the latter, dig into wild forest pasta, sautéed shrimp, and nightly vegetarian specialties. Many guests arrive early to enjoy the sunsets over the Smoky Mountains through the large windows. In cool weather, a fireplace burns brightly. Homemade soups (such as corn chowder or lentil) and homemade pies and cakes round out the wide variety of meats, poultry, and fish offered as main courses. As one local habitué informed us, "This place serves portions big enough to satisfy the biggest, hungriest bear."

9400 Hwy. 19. © 828/488-2826. www.nvnc.com. Breakfast $4–$9; main courses $5–$12 lunch, $9–$22 dinner. DC, MC, V. Daily 7:30–9:30am, 11am–2pm (May 24–Sept 1 only), and 5:30–8:30pm (to 9pm May 24–Sept 1). Weekend breakfasts 7:30–11am Apr 7–Oct 27. Closed Dec 1–Mar 8.

**Relia's Garden** 𝐾𝑖𝑑𝑠 AMERICAN/SOUTHERN    Part of the Nantahala Outdoor Center, this lodgelike place is worth the trip out of town. Hearty food and a helpful staff make it a family favorite, with a kids' menu and a policy of doggie-bagging. The menu is a bit overfamiliar, but time-tested favorites include rainbow trout and beef kebabs. Everybody likes the baked Cajun catfish. Vegetarian meals are also available. In fair weather, try for a table on the porch. You can "brown bag" your own alcohol if you choose to do so.

U.S. 19 S. (13 miles southwest of the Nantahala Outdoor Center). © 828/488-2175. Main courses $6–$12. MC, V. Sun–Thurs 5–9pm; Fri–Sat 5–10pm.

### DILLSBORO

**Dillsboro Smokehouse** BARBECUE    One of your best bets in town is hickory-flavored mountain barbecue at this smokehouse, 2 blocks down the street from the post office. It's known mainly for the fall-off-the-bones baby back ribs in a peach-flavored sauce. The pork barbecue, served chopped or sliced, has the best flavor, and the smoked brisket of beef is excellent. The chicken, either dark or white meat, can dry out fast when barbecued. Dinners are served with coleslaw, barbecue beans, yams, french fries, and hush puppies (what else?). The restaurant also sells barbecue by the pound to go, in case you've rented a cabin nearby.

403 Haywood St. © 828/586-9556. Main courses $5.65–$6.75 lunch; $9.25–$14 dinner. AE, DISC, MC, V. Mon–Thurs 11am–9pm; Fri–Sat 11am–10pm; Sun 11am–8pm (closed at 4pm in winter). Closes an hour earlier Nov–Feb.

### MAGGIE VALLEY

**J. Arthur's Restaurant** AMERICAN/BEEF    In a classic mountain building, J. Arthur's (which is affiliated with Manero's Restaurant in Palm City, Florida) is an odd name for a Smoky Mountain restaurant. It's a winning choice, however; in fact, it's the best in town. Offering a loft dining area, the restaurant is a family favorite and tailors its menus to diners 12 and under. The kitchen is known for its Gorgonzola cheese salad, which is backed by a choice of prime rib,

New York sirloin, broiled filet mignon, and grilled rib-eye. The meat is succulent and very tender (in other words, not the kind that you can purchase in a supermarket). Southerners really know how to cook pork chops, and this joint doesn't diminish that culinary reputation. The menu is limited but quite choice. You can also order fresh North Carolina rainbow trout, which is delicious.

2843 Soco Rd. (U.S. 19). © 828/926-1817. www.jarthurs.com. Main courses $12–$27. MC, V. May–Oct daily 5–9:30pm; Nov–Apr Wed–Sat 5–9:30pm.

**Joey's Pancake House** *Kids* PANCAKES/SOUTHERN   A popular family dining room for Ma and Pa Kettle and all the kids, this eatery was featured in the book *100 Secrets of the Smokies*. It has been pleasing hungry diners for some 40 years. Pancakes are made according to the chefs' secret formula, featuring such delights as Smoky Mountain blueberry, peanut butter, chocolate chip, pecan, and whole wheat smothered in cinnamon apples. A wide variety of specialty items are offered, including a hash brown casserole, French toast, and savory eggs Benedict. Biscuits are made from scratch and served along with country-sausage gravy, Southern grits, and creamed chipped beef.

4309 Soco Rd. © 828/926-0212. www.joeyspancake.com. Main courses $5–$7. Children's menu $2.60. Reservations not required. MC, V. Mon–Wed and Fri–Sat 7am–noon; Sun 7am–1pm..

# 10

# Planning Your Trip to South Carolina

This chapter tackles the nuts and bolts of your trip to South Carolina. Refer also to chapter 3, "Planning Your Trip to North Carolina," and chapter 2, "For International Visitors." Some of the information you need may be discussed in those chapters.

## 1 The Regions in Brief

**THE HEARTLAND**   The attraction of these backwater stops is the interaction with the people who live here. A Southern drawl as long as Rhett Butler's coattails prevails here, as do "Yes, ma'am," "No, ma'am," and afternoon naps. You're likely to come upon an old gas station complete with working Pure pumps and ice-cold Coca-Cola in bottles, and you're even more likely to pass a flock of camouflage-clad deer hunters lining a country road with trucks and guns.

A rail and highway hub, **Florence** is simply a convenience off the interstate, with fast-food joints, clean inexpensive motels, and a midsize mall with a cafeteria and restrooms.

A more charming town for a half-day visit is **Darlington,** home of the famed raceway. The small, old-time downtown area features attractive Victorian-style homes and several good restaurants serving home-cooked meals. The Mountain Dew Southern 500, held each Labor Day, and the Stock Car Hall of Fame are ideal for a taste of NASCAR-style racing.

With that small-town feel, South Carolina is a film producer's dream location and a delight for Northerners seeking a taste of the traditional South. There are courthouses that rival the national Capitol building (on a smaller scale) sitting smack in the middle of Main Street. There are white-picket-fenced homes sporting Victorian woodwork lining two-lane, moss-hung streets. There's a General Hardware store that doubles as a Greyhound bus station. There are a couple of churches where the membership has stayed pretty much the same (with the annual number of births equaling the number of deaths) for who knows how long. There are places such as **Camden** (the home of William F. Buckley, Jr.), which hosts two nationally known horse races: the Camden Classic and the Carolina Classic. **Kingstree** is the home of Nobel Peace Prize–winner Dr. Joseph Goldstein.

**COLUMBIA**   The state capital, located in the heart of South Carolina, is the home of "The Worst Boiled Peanuts in the World," at Cromer's, a state institution for munchies.

Columbia also happens to be the state's largest city, hosting more than 300 factories. In addition, the city is the marketing and distribution center for a large farming area, and it's crawling with college students who attend the University of South Carolina.

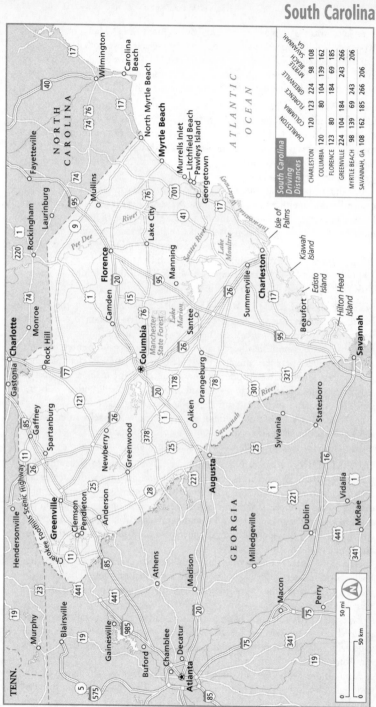

| South Carolina Driving Distances | CHARLESTON | COLUMBIA | FLORENCE | GREENVILLE | MYRTLE BEACH | SAVANNAH, GA |
|---|---|---|---|---|---|---|
| CHARLESTON | | 120 | 123 | 224 | 98 | 108 |
| COLUMBIA | 120 | | 80 | 104 | 139 | 162 |
| FLORENCE | 123 | 80 | | 184 | 69 | 185 |
| GREENVILLE | 224 | 104 | 184 | | 243 | 266 |
| MYRTLE BEACH | 98 | 139 | 69 | 243 | | 206 |
| SAVANNAH, GA | 108 | 162 | 185 | 266 | 206 | |

A day's worth of exploring will take you to Ainsley Hall Mansion, President Woodrow Wilson's boyhood home; the State House and Governor's Mansion; the Columbia Museum of Art; and the Town Theatre (1919), one of the oldest theaters in the country. The Riverbanks Park Zoo is an outstanding modern zoo that celebrates Christmas by draping thousands of twinkling lights throughout the park.

**THE UPSTATE** The northwestern region of South Carolina lies in the foothills of the Blue Ridge Mountains. Originally it was the place where residents of Charleston fled to escape the summer heat and the mosquitoes. What they discovered was a land of scenic wonders, with mountain peaks, unspoiled forests, waterfalls, and country hamlets. The chief city is **Greenville,** and the "second city," is **Spartanburg.**

But these cities are not the major reason to visit the Upstate. Escape instead to **Pendleton,** an entire town listed on the National Register of Historic Places. Here, you can visit Ashtabula Plantation, dating from the 1820s and once the most beautiful farm in the Upstate. Parks and battlefields abound, including Cowpens National Battlefield at Chesnee, famous for Daniel Morgan's 1781 defeat of the British. Finally, the Cherokee Foothills Scenic Highway curves for 130 miles through the heart of South Carolina's Blue Ridge foothills.

*Note:* The Upstate is not covered in this guide.

**MYRTLE BEACH & THE GRAND STRAND** Like Las Vegas in the desert, Myrtle Beach rises above the Southern coastline in a blaze of neon so bright that you might want to keep your shades handy, even after sunset. This city, a far cry from the historic South, has been transformed into a megawatt entertainment mecca. A golfer's paradise, the area now boasts more than 120 championship golf courses. There are water slides, arcades, giant shopping malls, and a host of kids' attractions. Numerous country-music shows are available and, as in Branson, Missouri, renowned musicians appear here year-round.

If you're hungry for seafood, dining is best at nearby **Murrells Inlet,** a strip along the marsh that's packed with seafood places. You might catch a glimpse of mystery novelist Mickey Spillane, who makes his home here.

**CHARLESTON** What can we possibly say about a city so charming that nearly every celebrity who visits ends up driving around town with a real-estate agent? Located on the peninsula between the Cooper and Ashley rivers in southeastern South Carolina, Charleston is the oldest and second-largest city in the state, full of antebellum homes and carefully preserved buildings. Each spring, Charleston hosts the Spoleto Festival, one of the most prestigious performing-arts events in the South.

One of the finest examples of Colonial architecture in the country is Drayton Hall, a mansion set amid huge oaks draped with Spanish moss. This National Historic Landmark is the only Ashley River plantation house to survive the Civil War intact.

Every day of the week, Charleston's City Market bustles with craftspeople jammed under the covered breezeways. Sweet-grass basket-weavers hum old spirituals; horse-drawn carriages clop down the street; and thousands of tourists eat, drink, and shop their way along.

A minimum 3-day stay is required if you are to discover Charleston by day and night. Try to include a trip over the Cooper River Bridge to the string of islands that have rebounded from the massive destruction of Hurricane Hugo. Take time to stop in **Beaufort,** the inspiration for Pat Conroy's novel *The Prince* *of Tides* (among other bestsellers). The town is full of old-fashioned inns, rustic pubs, and tiny stores along a tailored waterfront park.

**HILTON HEAD**   Much more commercial than Charleston is Hilton Head Island, home of wealthy Northerners (mostly retired) and vacationers from all parts of the country. With myriad contemporary beachfront restaurants and rows of hotels, timeshare villas, and cottages, the island has recently sprouted boutiques and upscale shopping areas. Although the traffic is horrendous (there is only one main thoroughfare both on and off the island), development hasn't obliterated nature on Hilton Head, and you can find solitude at the north end of the beach.

On the positive side, the island has become socially and culturally oriented, playing host to presidents and world leaders and also supporting its own symphony orchestra and ballet company. Sea Pines on Hilton Head is one of the country's premier golf resorts, located on a 605-acre Wildlife Foundation Preserve that's home to birds, squirrels, dolphins, and alligators. Hilton Head has 15 miles of bike paths and 5 miles of pristine beaches.

## 2 Visitor Information

Before leaving home, write or call ahead for specific information on sports and sightseeing. Contact **South Carolina Division of Tourism,** 1205 Pendleton St. (P.O. Box 71), Columbia, SC 29202 (© **803/734-0122;** fax 803/734-0138; www.discoversouthcarolina.com). It can also furnish *South Carolina: Smiling Faces, Beautiful Places,* a detailed booklet with photos that covers each region of the state.

When you enter South Carolina, look for one of the 10 **travel information centers** located on virtually every major highway near the border with neighboring states. Information sources for specific destinations in the state are listed in the South Carolina chapters that follow.

## 3 When to Go

## CLIMATE

Although parts of South Carolina can be very hot and steamy in summer (to say the least), temperatures are never extreme the rest of the year, as shown in the average highs and lows in the accompanying charts.

### Charleston Average Temperatures & Rainfall

|            | Jan | Feb | Mar | Apr | May | June | July | Aug | Sept | Oct | Nov | Dec |
|------------|-----|-----|-----|-----|-----|------|------|-----|------|-----|-----|-----|
| High (°F)  | 59  | 61  | 68  | 76  | 83  | 87   | 89   | 89  | 85   | 77  | 69  | 61  |
| High (°C)  | 15  | 16  | 20  | 24  | 28  | 31   | 32   | 32  | 29   | 25  | 21  | 16  |
| Low (°F)   | 40  | 41  | 48  | 56  | 64  | 70   | 74   | 74  | 69   | 49  | 49  | 42  |
| Low (°C)   | 4   | 5   | 9   | 13  | 18  | 21   | 23   | 23  | 21   | 9   | 9   | 6   |
| Rain (in.) | 3.5 | 3.3 | 4.3 | 2.7 | 4.0 | 6.4  | 6.8  | 7.2 | 4.7  | 2.9 | 2.5 | 3.2 |

### Columbia Average Temperatures & Rainfall

|            | Jan | Feb | Mar | Apr | May | June | July | Aug | Sept | Oct | Nov | Dec |
|------------|-----|-----|-----|-----|-----|------|------|-----|------|-----|-----|-----|
| High (°F)  | 56  | 59  | 67  | 77  | 84  | 89   | 91   | 85  | 76   | 68  | 67  | 59  |
| High (°C)  | 13  | 15  | 19  | 25  | 29  | 32   | 33   | 29  | 24   | 20  | 19  | 15  |
| Low (°F)   | 33  | 35  | 42  | 50  | 59  | 66   | 70   | 69  | 64   | 50  | 41  | 35  |
| Low (°C)   | 1   | 2   | 6   | 10  | 15  | 19   | 21   | 21  | 18   | 10  | 5   | 2   |
| Rain (in.) | 4.4 | 4.1 | 4.8 | 3.3 | 3.7 | 4.8  | 5.5  | 6.1 | 3.7  | 3.0 | 2.9 | 3.6 |

## SOUTH CAROLINA CALENDAR OF EVENTS

### January

**Low-Country Oyster Festival,** Charleston. Steamed buckets of oysters greet visitors at Boone Hall Plantation. Enjoy live music, oyster-shucking contests, kids' events, and other activities. Contact the Greater Charleston Restaurant Association at © **843/577-4030.** End of January.

### February

**Southeastern Wildlife Exposition,** Charleston. More than 150 of the finest artists and more than 500 exhibitors participate at 13 locations in the downtown area. Enjoy carvings, sculpture, paintings, live-animal exhibits, food, and much more. Call © **843/723-1748** (www.sewe.com) for details. Mid-February.

**Africa Alive,** Rock Hill. Learn about the African heritage by way of storytelling, craft activities, exhibits, music, and dance from the Museum of York County. Call © **803/329-2121** for information (www.yorkcounty.org). Late February.

### March

**Festival of Houses and Gardens,** Charleston. For nearly 50 years, people have been enjoying some of Charleston's most historic neighborhoods and private gardens on this tour. Contact the Historic Charleston Foundation, P.O. Box 1120, Charleston, SC 29402 (© **843/723-1623;** www.historic charleston.org) for details. Mid-March to mid-April.

### April

**Cooper River Bridge Run,** Charleston. Sponsored by the Medical University of South Carolina, this run and walk starts in Mount Pleasant, goes over the Cooper River Bridge, and ends in the center of Charleston. *Note:* The April 2, 2005, race is the last one on the old Cooper River Bridge; the 28th annual race in 2006 will go over the new bridge. For information, call © **843/792-0345** (www.bridgerun.com). Early April.

**Carolina Cup,** Camden. The elaborate picnics with silver candelabras and crystal champagne flutes make this annual steeplechase race an event to remember. Contact the Springdale Race Course at © **803/432-6513** (www.carolina-cup.org). Early April.

**Flowertown Festival,** Summerville. More than 180 booths of arts and crafts, a road race, a "Youth Fest," and lots of entertainment are set in this historic city surrounded by brilliant azalea and dogwood blossoms. Contact the YMCA at © **843/871-9622** or online at www.flowertown festival.com/flowertown to learn more. First weekend in April.

**Family Circle Cup,** Charleston. Moved from Hilton Head to a tennis center in Charleston, the Family Circle Cup WTA tournament is one of the oldest on the women's pro tour. For information, call © **843/856-7900,** or go to www.family circlecup.com. April 9 to April 17.

**MCI Heritage,** Hilton Head. This $1.3-million tournament brings an outstanding field of PGA tour professionals to this event each year. The weeklong tournament is held at Harbour Town Golf Links in Sea Pines Plantation. Contact Classic Sports, Inc., 71 Lighthouse Rd., Suite 414, Hilton Head, SC 29928 (© **843/671-2448**). Mid-April.

**World Grits Festival,** St. George. This unique festival is a celebration of that famous Southern staple, grits! For years, contestants have competed in grits-grinding, corn-shelling, grits-eating, and best recipes, as well as traditional festivities. Call ✆ **843/563-7943** to find out more. April 15 to 17.

## May

**Spring Fling,** Spartanburg. Live entertainment mixed with arts, crafts, and games make this a popular annual event. Contact Spartanburg Community Events at ✆ **864/594-5080** for details. First weekend in May.

**Iris Festival,** Sumter. The world-famous Swan Lake Iris Gardens is the setting for this elaborate festival of arts and crafts, food, concerts, garden tours, and a parade. Call ✆ **800/688-4748** (www.irisfestival.org). Late May.

**Carolina Dodge Dealers 500** and **Diamond Hill Plywood 200,** Darlington. Stock car racing's original superspeedway will inaugurate an entirely new race weekend in May 2005. The NASCAR NEXTEL Cup Series' 104th visit to Darlington Raceway will be Darlington's first-ever full weekend of night racing. For tickets, contact ✆ **843/395-8499** (www.darlingtonraceway.com). Mother's Day weekend.

**Pontiac GMC Freedom Weekend Aloft,** Anderson. This 4-day extravaganza features big-name entertainment, amusement rides, 100 hot-air balloons, fireworks, and more at the city's Sports & Entertainment Center. Contact Freedom Weekend Aloft at ✆ **864/232-3700** or go to www.freedomwkend.org. Memorial Day weekend.

**Spoleto Festival U.S.A.,** Charleston. This is the premier cultural event in the tri-state area. This famous international festival—the American counterpart of the equally celebrated one in Spoleto, Italy—showcases world-renowned performers in drama, dance, music, and art in various venues throughout the city. For details and this year's schedule, contact Spoleto Festival U.S.A., P.O. Box 157, Charleston, SC 29402 (✆ **843/722-2764;** www.spoletousa.org). Late May through early June.

## June

**Edisto Riverfest,** Walterboro. The main attractions at this festival are guided trips down the "blackwater" (water darkened from tree tannins) Edisto River. Call ✆ **843/549-5591** (www.edistoriver.org) for details. Mid-June.

## July

**Lake Murray's July 4th Celebration,** Columbia. Lake Murray plays host to some 100 boats decorated in red, white, and blue. A fireworks display is held at night. Contact the Lake Murray Tourism and Recreation Association at ✆ **866/SC-JEWEL** (www.lakemurraycountry.com). First Saturday in July.

**Two Days, Round the Fourth,** Conway. You can gather along the banks of the Waccamaw River for 2 days full of arts and crafts, live entertainment, food, Jell-O jumps, raft races, boat rides, and fireworks. Contact the Conway Area Chamber of Commerce at ✆ **843/248-2273;** www.roundthefourth.com. Early July.

## August

**Shawfest,** Shaw Air Force Base, near Sumter and Cherryvale. This annual event takes the form of a community-appreciation festival. Onlookers are treated to an air show featuring some of the Air Force's top pilots and jets. Call ✆ **800/511-SHAW** for additional information. Early August.

**Summerfest,** York. Loads of live entertainment is presented here with four stages, crafts, country food, and a classic car show. Contact the York County Convention and Visitors Bureau at ✆ **803/684-2590.** Fourth Saturday in August.

## September

**South Carolina's Largest Garage Sale,** Myrtle Beach. One person's trash is another person's treasure, and you're likely to find yours here. Vendors set up shop in a large parking garage to sell clothing, furniture, household goods, and hundreds of other bargains. Contact the Myrtle Beach Parks and Recreation Department at ✆ **843/918-1242.** Early September.

**Scottish Games and Highland Gathering,** Charleston. This gathering of Scottish clans features medieval games, bagpipe performances, Scottish dancing, and other traditional activities. Call the Scottish Society of Charleston at ✆ **843/224-7867** (www.charlestonscots.com). Third Saturday in September.

**Candlelight Tour of Homes & Gardens,** Charleston. Sponsored by the Preservation Society of Charleston, this annual event provides an intimate look at many of the area's historic homes, gardens, and churches. For more information, call ✆ **800/968-8175** or 843/722-4630 (www.preservationsociety.org). Mid-September to late October.

## October

**Fall for Greenville,** Greenville. This annual 2-day event features more than 40 restaurants and food vendors from around the city presenting a wide variety of their tasty wares. Events include a chili "cook-off," a cooking school, an ice carving, a bartender's mix-off, a waiter's race, and a bike race, along with free entertainment. For more information, call **864/467-5780.** Early October.

**Jubilee: Harvest of the Arts,** Rock Hill. Concerts featuring national recording artists, and events showcasing regional and local talents, are held at this arts festival. Call ✆ **803/328-ARTS** (www.rockhillarts.org). Early October.

**MOJA Festival,** Charleston. Celebrating the rich African-American heritage in the Charleston area, this festival features lectures, art exhibits, stage performances, historical tours, concerts, and much more. Contact the Charleston Office of Cultural Affairs at ✆ **843/724-7305** (www.mojafestival.com). Late September to early October.

**A Taste of Charleston,** Charleston. Held in 2004 at Boone Hall Plantation, this annual event offers an afternoon of food, fun, entertainment, and more. A selection of Charleston-area restaurants offers their specialties in bite-size portions, so you can sample them all. For more information, call ✆ **843/577-4030** (www.charlestoncvb.com). Early October.

**Fall Festival of Houses,** Beaufort. Frank Lloyd Wright's Aldbrass Plantation is only one of the beautiful homes on this tour. The public is invited to get a rare view of this coastal city's most stately residences during a 3-day tour. Call ✆ **843/379-3331** or go to www.historicbeaufort.org. Late October.

**Governor's Cup,** Columbia. This event, more than half a century old, is comprised of a half marathon, an 8km run, a 4-mile EdVenture Walk, and a Kids Fun Run beginning at 8:30am on the State Capitol grounds. Conducted by the Carolina Marathon Association. Call ✆ **803/929-1996** (www.carolina marathon.org). Mid-October.

## November

**Mountain Dew Southern 500,** Darlington. The NASCAR NEXTEL Cup Series returns to the track for the Mountain Dew Southern 500, where the checkered flag will wave under the lights for the very first time. It's a new date as well, as top racers battle not only for the win but, in the next-to-last race of

| What Things Cost in Charleston | US$ |
| --- | --- |
| Taxi from Charleston airport to city center | 20.00–25.00 |
| Bus fare (exact change) | 1.25 |
| Local telephone call | 0.50 |
| Double room at the Planters Inn (expensive) | 195.00 |
| Double room at 1837 Bed & Breakfast (moderate) | 129.00 |
| Double room at Best Western King Charles Inn (inexpensive) | 105.00 |
| Lunch for one at Magnolias (moderate) | 16.00–25.00 |
| Lunch for one at A.W. Shucks (inexpensive) | 12.00 |
| Dinner for one, without wine, at Charleston Grill (expensive) | 45.00 |
| Dinner for one, without wine, at Magnolias (moderate) | 30.00 |
| Dinner for one, without wine, at Hyman's Seafood Co. Restaurant (inexpensive) | 18.00 |
| Bottle of beer | 2.50–3.00 |
| Coca-Cola | 1.00 |
| Cup of coffee | 1.25–1.50 |
| Roll of 35mm Kodak film, 36 exposures | 8.50 |
| Admission to the Charleston Museum | 9.00 |
| Movie ticket | 7.50 |
| Ticket to a Charleston Symphony concert | 22.00 |

the season, for the 2004 NASCAR NEXTEL Cup Series Championship. Call ✆ **843/395-8499** (www.darlingtonraceway.com) for tickets and information. Mid-November.

**St. Francis Festival of Trees,** Greenville. Professionally decorated trees are displayed in the Hyatt Regency. A Teddy Bear tea, Gingerbread Land, and family brunch are special attractions. Call ✆ **864/255-1199.** Late November to late December.

**Merrily Myrtle—A Holiday Celebration,** Myrtle Beach. The Grand Strand is decorated in a profusion of lights. This months-long celebration has a lineup that includes concerts, parades, and festivals. Contact the Myrtle Beach Area Chamber of Commerce at ✆ **800/356-3016** (www.mbchamber.com). November to January 15.

**Colonial Cup, Camden.** Every year, this prestigious steeplechase race determines the champion and winner of the NSA's Eclipse award. Tailgating in style is a trademark of this event, with tables covered in linen and patrons dressed in hats and sport coats. Contact the Springdale Race Course at ✆ **803/432-6513** or go to www.carolina-cup.org. November 21.

**December**

**Lights Before Christmas,** Columbia. The Riverbanks Zoo becomes a holiday wonderland when thousands of lights are strung around the park. Contact the Riverbanks Zoo at ✆ **803/779-8717.** December 1 to 30.

**Christmas in Charleston,** Charleston. This month-long celebration features home and church tours, Christmas-tree lightings, craft shows, artistry, and a peek at how

Old Charleston celebrated the holiday season. For more information on how to participate or to visit, call ℂ **843/853-8000.** December 1 to 31.

## 4 The Active Vacation Planner

**BEACHES**   The South Carolina coast is the true gem of the state. Along more than 280 miles of seashore are white-sand beaches shaded by palms, stretching from the Grand Strand to the mouth of the Savannah River. Myrtle Beach offers a carnival atmosphere and emphasizes family entertainment. Edisto Beach is a secluded spot. Fripp Island and Hilton Head are luxury resorts.

**BIKING**   South Carolina's basically flat terrain offers some of the country's best biking. The hard-packed sand of the beaches is particularly good for bike riding. Resorts such as Hilton Head have extensive paved bike trails, and many rental outfits operate just off the beaches.

**CAMPING**   Many of South Carolina's lakes have lakefront campsites. Reservations are not necessary, but you are strongly advised to make reservations for big weekends such as Memorial Day or Labor Day. Campsites are also available in South Carolina's 34 state parks. For more information, contact **South Carolina Department of Parks, Recreation, and Tourism,** 1205 Pendleton St., Columbia, SC 29202 (ℂ **888/887-2757** or 803/734-0159; www.southcarolina parks.com).

**CANOEING**   The Broad and Saluda rivers, which flow near Columbia in the center of the state, provide excellent canoeing.

**FISHING & HUNTING**   On the coast, fish for amberjack, barracuda, shark, king mackerel, and other species. In South Carolina's many lakes and streams, fish for trout, bass, and blue and channel catfish. No license is required for saltwater fishing, but a freshwater license is required. The Upstate is a mecca for waterfowl and wild turkey. The season stretches over fall and winter and sometimes into spring. Hunting on public lands is illegal, but many hunting clubs will allow you to join temporarily if you provide references. For information, write the **South Carolina Department of Natural Resources,** P.O. Box 167, Columbia, SC 29202 (ℂ **803/734-3447;** www.dnr.state.sc.us).

**GOLF**   Some of the best golf in the country is available in South Carolina, at courses such as the one at the fabled Harbor Town at Hilton Head. For information, contact the **South Carolina Department of Parks, Recreation, and Tourism,** 1205 Pendleton St., Columbia, SC 29202 (ℂ **888/867-2757** or 803/ 734-0159; www.southcarolinaparks.com). Ask for the *South Carolina Golf Guide.*

**HORSEBACK RIDING**   Without question, Aiken County is king of the equine industry in the area. The Carolina Cup and the Colonial Cup steeplechase races are held in Camden each year. For information, contact **Thoroughbred Country** at ℂ **803/649-7981;** or write the **Aiken Chamber of Commerce,** 121 Richland Ave. E., Aiken, SC 29801 (ℂ **803/641-1111**).

**THE LAKES**   South Carolina's rivers feed lakes all over the state, offering boating, fishing, and camping. With 450 miles of shoreline, the lakes are a magnet for commercial development. While lakeside resort communities are booming, 70% of the lakeshore is slated to remain in a natural state. Many operators and marinas rent boats and watercraft. For information about staying lakeside, contact the **South Carolina Department of Parks, Recreation, and Tourism,** 1205 Pendleton St., Columbia, SC 29202; or call ℂ **888/887-2757.**

**STATE PARKS**   Camping, fishing, boating, and extensive hiking are available in South Carolina's many state parks. Cabin accommodations are rented all year in 14 of the parks. All cabins are heated, air-conditioned, and fully equipped with cooking utensils, tableware, and linens. Rates range from $60 to $144 per night or $288 to $959 per week. Cabins can accommodate any number from 4 to 12 people. Advance reservations are necessary for summer. For full details, write the **South Carolina State Parks,** 1205 Pendleton St., Columbia, SC 29201 (② **803/734-0156**).

**WHITE-WATER RAFTING**   The Chattooga River forms part of the lower northeast border with Georgia and offers some of the best white-water rafting and canoeing in the country. **Wildwater Ltd.,** P.O. Box 309, Long Creek, SC 29658 (② **800/451-9972**; www.wildwaterrafting.com), offers white-water trips on the Chattooga. Packages including instruction, meals, and lodging are available.

## 5 Specialized Travel Resources

The Columbia telephone directory contains a special section of "Community Service Numbers." It's quite comprehensive and includes services for most of these groups.

**TRAVELERS WITH DISABILITIES**   South Carolina has numerous agencies that assist people with disabilities. For specific information, call the **South Carolina Handicapped Services Information System** (② **888/978-2273**; www.scsis.org). Two other agencies that may prove to be helpful are the **South Carolina Protection & Advocacy System for the Handicapped** (② **803/782-0639**) and the **Commission for the Blind** (② **803/898-8700**; www.sccb.state.sc.us). For more information, see "Specialized Travel Resources," in chapter 3.

**GAY & LESBIAN TRAVELERS**   The most important information center in the state is the **South Carolina Pride Center,** 1108 Woodrow St., Columbia 29205 (② **803/771-7713**; www.scglpm.org). It's open on Wednesday and Sunday from 1 to 6pm, on Friday from 7 to 11pm, and on Saturday from 1 to 8pm. On the premises are a library, an archives, a "gay pride" shop, an inventory of films, and a meeting space. It also functions as a conduit for such other organizations as the **Low Country Gay and Lesbian Alliance** (② **843/720-8088**).

For information before you go, refer to "Specialized Travel Resources," in chapter 3.

**SENIOR TRAVEL**   Seniors may want to contact the **Retired Senior Volunteer Program** (② **803/252-7734**). When you're sightseeing or attending entertainment events, always inquire about senior discounts; they're plentiful. Also see "Specialized Travel Resources," in chapter 3.

**FOR FAMILIES**   A great vacation idea is to rent a cabin in one of South Carolina's 14 state parks. Rates range from $60 to $144 per night, $339 to $946 per week. Cabins accommodate anywhere from 4 to 12 people. For details on advance reservations and on accommodations at the 34 other state parks, contact **South Carolina State Parks,** 1205 Pendleton St., Columbia, SC 29201 (② **803/734-1056**).

## 6 Getting There

**BY PLANE**   **American Airlines** and **American Eagle** (② **800/433-7300**; www.aa.com), **Continental Airlines** (② **800/525-0280**), **Delta** and **Delta Connection** (② **800/221-1212**; www.delta.com), **United Airlines** and **United Express**

(© **800/241-6522;** www.united.com), and **US Airways** (© **800/428-4322;** www.usairways.com) are the major airlines serving South Carolina. **Independence Air** (© **800/FLY-FLY;** www.flyi.com) has entered the competition, flying six to seven daily nonstop flights from Washington's Dulles International Airport to Charleston. The airline has immediately been hailed by its visitors and locals alike for its low-cost airfares. If money is an object, check its fares and compare them with those of the better-known carriers. **Myrtle Beach** has scheduled air service via Continental, Delta, and US Airways. You can fly into **Charleston** on Continental, Delta, United and United Express, and US Airways. **Columbia** is served by American and American Eagle, Delta and Delta Connection, and US Airways. **Greenville/Spartanburg** is served by Continental, Delta, and US Airways. If you're traveling to **Hilton Head,** you have the option of flying US Airways directly to the island or flying into the Savannah (Georgia) International Airport via Continental or Delta and then driving or taking a limousine to Hilton Head, which is 1 hour away.

**BY CAR** Interstate 95 enters South Carolina from the north near Dillon and runs straight through the state to Hardeeville on the Georgia border. The major east–west artery is I-26, running from Charleston northwest through Columbia and on up to Hendersonville, North Carolina. U.S. 17 runs along the coast, and I-85 crosses the northwestern region.

South Carolina furnishes excellent travel information to motorists, and has well-equipped, efficiently staffed visitor centers at the state border on most major highways. If you have a cellphone and need help, dial ***HP** for Highway Patrol Assistance.

**BY TRAIN** South Carolina is on the **Amtrak** (© **800/USA-RAIL;** www.amtrak.com) New York–Miami and New York–Tampa runs, serving Camden, Charleston, Clemson, Columbia, Denmark, Dillon, Florence, Greenville, Kingstree, Spartanburg, and Yemassee. Amtrak also has tour packages that include hotel, breakfast, and historic-site tours in Charleston at bargain rates. Be sure to ask about the money-saving "All Aboard America" regional fares or any other current fare specials. Amtrak also offers attractively priced rail/drive packages in the Carolinas and Georgia.

**BY BUS** Greyhound/Trailways (© **800/231-2222;** www.greyhound.com) has good direct service to major cities in South Carolina from out of state, with connections to almost any destination. With a 21-day advance purchase, you can get a discounted "Go Anywhere" fare (some restrictions apply).

**PACKAGE TOURS** Conducting 8-day tours of the South, specifically South Carolina and Georgia, **Mayflower Tours** (© **800/365-5359**) sweeps across the antebellum South from Atlanta, cultural capital of the South, to historic Charleston, which is often called a "living museum." The tour also encompasses the 300-year-old Boone Hall Plantation, the best example of antebellum plantation life.

The tour launches its excursions in Charleston, with its cobblestone streets and antebellum houses, and proceeds to some of the most appealing tourist destinations in Georgia or South Carolina, including Jekyll Island, Savannah, and Hilton Head. Land prices for the weeklong tours start at $1,249.

## 7 Getting Around

**BY PLANE** Delta and US Airways (see "Getting There," above) both have flights within South Carolina, although connections are sometimes awkward.

**BY CAR**    South Carolina has a network of exceptionally good roads. Even when you leave the major highways for the state-maintained roadways, driving is easy on well-maintained roads. AAA services are available through the **Carolina Motor Club** in Charleston (© **843/766-2394**), Columbia (© **803/798-9205**), and Greenville (© **864/583-2766**).

In South Carolina, vehicles must use headlights when windshield wipers are in use as a result of inclement weather. Remember that drivers and front-seat passengers must wear seat belts.

Also see "Getting Around," in chapter 3.

For driving times and distances in South Carolina, see the "South Carolina" map on p. 191.

---

### FAST FACTS: South Carolina

*American Express* Services in South Carolina are provided through **B&A Travel Service,** 2001 Greene St., Columbia (© **803/732-5847**).

*Area Code* It's 803 for Columbia and environs; 843 for Charleston and the South Carolina coast; and 864 for Greenville, Anderson, Spartanburg and the Upstate area.

*Emergencies* Dial © **911** for police, ambulance, paramedics, and the fire department. You can also dial 0 (zero, *not* the letter O) and ask the operator to connect you to emergency services.

*Fishing* A **fishing hot line** (© **800/ASK-FISH**) gives you an up-to-date fishing report on South Carolina's major lakes, as well as information on fishing regulations. For more information, contact **South Carolina Department of Natural Resources,** P.O. Box 167, Columbia, SC 29202 (© **803/734-3886;** http://water.dnr.state.sc.us).

*Liquor Laws* The minimum drinking age is 21. Some restaurants are licensed to serve only beer and wine, but many offer those plus liquor in minibottles, which can be added to cocktail mixers. Beer and wine are sold in grocery stores 7 days a week, but all package liquor is offered through local government-controlled stores, commonly called "ABC" (Alcoholic Beverage Control Commission) stores, which are closed on Sundays.

*Newspapers & Magazines* The major papers are the *State* (Columbia), the *Greenville News,* and the *Charleston Post and Courier.*

*Taxes* South Carolina has a 6% sales tax. Cities often tack an accommodations tax (room or occupancy tax) on to your hotel bill. Counties also have the option of adding an extra .5% to 3% use tax.

*Time Zone* South Carolina is in the Eastern Standard Time zone and goes on daylight saving time in summer.

*Weather* Phone © **803/822-8135** for an update.

# 11

# Charleston

In the closing pages of *Gone With the Wind*, Rhett tells Scarlett that he's going back home to Charleston, where he can find "the calm dignity life can have when it's lived by gentle folks, the genial grace of days that are gone. When I lived those days, I didn't realize the slow charm of them." In spite of all the changes and upheavals over the years, Rhett's endorsement of Charleston still holds true.

If the Old South lives on in South Carolina's Low Country, it positively thrives in Charleston. All our romantic notions of antebellum days—stately homes, courtly manners, gracious hospitality and, above all, gentle dignity—are facts of everyday life in this old city, in spite of a few scoundrels here and there, from pirates to politicians.

Notwithstanding a history dotted with earthquakes, hurricanes, fires, and Yankee bombardments, Charleston remains one of the best-preserved cities in America's Old South. It boasts 73 pre–Revolutionary War buildings, 136 from the late 18th century, and more than 600 built before the 1840s. With its cobblestone streets and horse-drawn carriages, Charleston is a place of visual images and sensory pleasures. Jasmine and wisteria fragrances fill the air; the aroma of she-crab soup (a local favorite) wafts from sidewalk cafes; and antebellum architecture graces the historic cityscape. "No wonder they are so full of themselves," said an envious visitor from Columbia, which may be the state capital but has little of Charleston's style and grace.

In its annual reader survey, *Condé Nast Traveler* magazine named Charleston the number-three city to visit in America, which places it ahead of such perennial favorites as Boston, Washington, D.C., and Santa Fe. Visitors are drawn here from all over the world, and it is now quite common to hear German and French spoken on local streets.

Does this city have a modern side? Yes, but it's well hidden. Chic shops abound, as do a few supermodern hotels, but Charleston has no skyscrapers. You don't come to Charleston for anything cutting-edge, though. You come to glimpse an earlier, almost-forgotten era.

Many local families still own and live in the homes that their planter ancestors built. Charlestonians manage to maintain a way of life that in many respects has little to do with wealth. The simplest encounter with Charleston natives seems to be invested with a social air, as though the visitor were a valued guest. Yet there are those who detect a certain snobbishness in Charleston—and truth be told, you'd have to stay a few hundred years to be considered an insider here.

## 1 Orientation

### ARRIVING

**BY PLANE** See "Getting There," in chapter 10. **Charleston International Airport** is in North Charleston on I-26, about 12 miles west of the city. Taxi fare into the city runs about $25, and the airport **shuttle service** (© 843/767-1100) has a $10 fare. All major car-rental facilities, including Hertz and Avis, are available at the airport. If you're driving, follow the airport-access road to I-26 into the heart of Charleston.

**BY CAR**   The main north–south coastal route, U.S. 17, passes through Charleston; I-26 runs northwest to southeast, ending in Charleston. Charleston is 120 miles southeast of Columbia via I-26 and 98 miles south of Myrtle Beach via U.S. 17.

**BY TRAIN**   **Amtrak** (© **800/USA-RAIL;** www.amtrak.com) trains arrive at 4565 Gaynor Ave., North Charleston.

## VISITOR INFORMATION

**Charleston Area Convention and Visitors Bureau (CACVB),** 375 Meeting St., Charleston, SC 29402 (© **843/853-8000;** www.charlestoncvb.com), just across from the Charleston Museum, provides maps, brochures, and access to South Carolina Automated Ticketing. The helpful staff can also assist you in finding accommodations. Numerous tours depart hourly from the Visitors Bureau, and restroom facilities, as well as parking, are available. Be sure to allow time to view the 24-minute multi-image presentation *Forever Charleston* and pick up a copy of the visitor's guide. The center is open daily from 8:30am to 5:30pm (closing at 5pm Nov–Feb; closed Christmas Day, New Year's Day, and Thanksgiving Day).

## CITY LAYOUT

Charleston's streets are laid out in an easy-to-follow grid pattern. The main north–south thoroughfares are King, Meeting, and East Bay streets. Tradd, Broad, Queen, and Calhoun streets cross the city from east to west. South of Broad Street, East Bay becomes East Battery.

Unlike most cities, Charleston offers a most helpful map, and it's distributed free. Called **"The Map Guide—Charleston,"** it includes the streets of the historic district as well as surrounding areas, and offers tips on shopping, tours, and what to see and do. Maps are available at the **Visitor Reception & Transportation Center,** 375 Meeting St., at John Street (© **843/853-8000**).

## NEIGHBORHOODS IN BRIEF

**The Historic District** In 1860, according to one Charlestonian, "South Carolina seceded from the Union, Charleston seceded from South Carolina, and south of Broad Street seceded from Charleston." The city preserves its early years at its southernmost point: the conjunction of the Cooper and Ashley rivers. The White Point Gardens, right in the elbow of the two rivers, provide a sort of gateway into this area, where virtually every home is of historic or architectural interest. Between Broad Street and Murray Boulevard (which runs along the south waterfront),

you'll find such sightseeing highlights as St. Michael's Episcopal Church, the Edmondston-Alston House, the Heyward-Washington House, Catfish Row, and the Nathaniel Russell House.

**Downtown** Extending north from Broad Street to Marion Square at the intersection of Calhoun and Meeting streets, this area encloses noteworthy points of interest, good shopping, and a gaggle of historic churches. Just a few of its highlights are the Old City Market, the Dock Street Theatre, Market Hall, the Old Powder Magazine, the Thomas

Elfe Workshop, Congregation Beth Elohim, the French Huguenot Church, and St. John's Church.

**Above Marion Square** The visitor center is located on Meeting Street north of Calhoun. The Charleston Museum is just across the street, and the Aiken-Rhett Mansion, Joseph Manigault Mansion, and Old Citadel are within easy walking distance in the area bounded by Calhoun Street to the south and Mary Street to the north.

**North Charleston** Charleston International Airport is at the point at which I-26 and I-526 intersect. This makes North Charleston a Low Country transportation hub. Primarily a residential and industrial community, it lacks the charm of the historic district. It's the home of the North Charleston Coliseum, the largest indoor entertainment venue in the state.

**Mount Pleasant** East of the Cooper River, just minutes from the historic district, this community is worth a detour. Filled with lodgings, restaurants, and some attractions, it encloses a historic district along the riverfront known as the Old Village, which is on the National Register's list of historic buildings. Its major attraction is Patriots Point, the world's largest naval and maritime museum; it's also the home of the aircraft carrier *Yorktown.*

**Outlying Areas** Within easy reach of the city are Boone Hall Plantation and the public beaches at Sullivan's Island and Isle of Palms. Head west across the Ashley River Bridge to pay tribute to Charleston's birth at Charles Towne Landing, and visit such highlights as Drayton Hall, Magnolia Gardens, and Middleton Place.

## 2 Getting Around

**BY BUS** City bus fares are $1.25, and service is available from 5:35am to 10pm (until 1am to North Charleston). Between 9am and 3:30pm and after 6pm, seniors pay 60¢. The fare for persons with disabilities (all day) is 30¢. Exact change is required. For route and schedule information, call © **843-724-7420.**

**BY TROLLEY** The **Downtown Area Shuttle (DASH)** is the quickest way to get around the main downtown area daily. The fare is $1.25, and you'll need exact change. A day pass costs $4. For hours and routes, call © **843/724-7420.**

**BY TAXI** Leading taxi companies are **Yellow Cab** (© **843/577-6565**) and **Safety Cab** (© **843/722-4066**). Each company has its own fare structure. Within the city, however, fares seldom exceed $3 or $4. You must call for a taxi; there are no pickups on the street.

**BY CAR** If you're staying in the city proper, park your car and save it for day trips to outlying areas. You'll find **parking facilities** scattered about the city, with some of the most convenient at Hutson Street and Calhoun Street, both of which are near Marion Square; on King Street between Queen and Broad; and on George Street between King and Meeting. If you can't find space on the street to park, the two most centrally located **garages** are on Wentworth Street (© **843/724-7383**) and at Concord and Cumberland (© **843/724-7387**). Charges are $8 all day.

Leading car-rental companies are **Avis Rent-a-Car** (© **800/331-1212** or 843/767-7030), **Budget Car and Truck Rentals** (© **800/527-0700,** 843/767-7051 at the airport, 843/760-1410 in North Charleston, or 843/577-5195 downtown), and **Hertz** (© **800/654-3131** or 843/767-4554).

## FAST FACTS: Charleston

*American Express* The local American Express office is at 10 Carriage Lane (© **843/556-9051**), open Monday to Friday from 9am to 5pm.

*Camera Repair* The best option is **Focal Point**, 4 Apollo Rd. (© **843/571-3886**), open Monday to Thursday from 9am to 1pm and 2 to 5pm, and on Friday from 9am to noon.

*Car Rentals* See "Getting Around," above.

*Climate* See "When to Go," in chapter 10.

*Dentist* Consult **Palmetto Dental Clinics**, 34 Morris St. (© **843/577-9444**).

*Doctor* For a physician referral or 24-hour emergency-room treatment, contact **Charleston Memorial Hospital**, 326 Calhoun St. (© **843/792-2300**); or **Roper Hospital**, 316 Calhoun St. (© **843/724-2970**). Contact **Doctor's Care** (© **843/556-5585**) for the names of walk-in clinics.

*Emergencies* In an emergency, dial © **911**. If the situation isn't life threatening, call © **843/577-7070** for the fire department, © **843/577-7077** for the police.

*Eyeglass Repair* Try **Jackson Davenport Vision**, 379 King St. (© **843/722-4416**), open Monday to Friday 9am to 3pm and Saturday 9am to 5pm.

*Hospitals* Local hospitals operating 24-hour emergency rooms include **AMI East Cooper Community Hospital**, 1200 Johnnie Dodds Blvd., Mount Pleasant (© **843/881-0100**); **Charleston Memorial Hospital**, 326 Calhoun St. (© **843/792-2300**); and **Medical University of South Carolina**, 171 Ashley Ave. (© **843/792-1414**). For medical emergencies, call © **911**.

*Hot Lines* Crisis counseling is available at © **843/744-HELP**.

*Newspapers & Magazines* The *Post and Courier* is the local daily.

*Pharmacies* Try **CVS Drugs**, 1603 Hwy. 17 N. (© **843/971-0764**), open Monday to Saturday from 8am to 10pm and on Sunday from 10am to 8pm.

*Post Office* The main post office is at 83 Broad St. (© **843/577-0688**), open Monday to Friday from 9am to 5pm.

*Restrooms* These are available throughout the downtown area, including at Broad and Meeting streets, at Queen and Church streets, on Market Street between Meeting and Church streets, and at other clearly marked strategic points in the historic and downtown districts.

*Safety* Downtown Charleston is well lighted and patrolled throughout the night to ensure public safety. People can generally walk about downtown at night without fear of violence.

*Taxes* South Carolina has a 6% sales tax. Charleston tacks a 6% accommodations tax (room or occupancy) onto your hotel bill and 7% on food.

*Transit Information* Contact the **Charleston Area Convention Visitor Reception & Transportation Center**, 375 Meeting St. (© **843/853-8000**).

*Weather* Call © **843/744-3207** for an update.

## 3 Where to Stay

Charleston has many of the best historic inns in America, surpassing even those of Savannah. Hotels and motels are priced in direct ratio to their proximity to the 789-acre historic district; if prices in the center are too high for your budget, find a place west of the Ashley River, and drive into town for sightseeing. In the last decade, the restoration of inns and hotels in Charleston has been phenomenal, although it's slowing somewhat. Charleston ranks among the top cities of America for hotels of charm and character.

Bed-and-breakfast accommodations range from historic homes to carriage houses to simple cottages, and they're located in virtually every section of the city. For details and reservations, contact **Historic Charleston Bed and Breakfast,** 57 Broad St., Charleston, SC 29401 (© **800/743-3583** or 843/722-6606; www.historiccharlestonbedandbreakfast.com; Mon–Fri 9am–5pm).

During the Spring Festival of Houses and the Spoleto Festival, rates go up, and owners charge pretty much what the market will bear. Advance reservations are essential at those times.

In a city that has rooms of so many shapes and sizes in the same historic building, classifying hotels by price is difficult. Price often depends on the room itself. Some expensive hotels may in fact have many moderately priced rooms. Moderately priced hotels, on the other hand, may have special rooms that are quite expensive. When booking a hotel, ask about package plans—deals are most often granted to those who are staying 3 days or more.

The downside regarding all these inns of charm and grace is that they are among the most expensive in this tri-state guide. Staying at an inn or B&B in the historic district is one of the reasons to go to Charleston and can do more to evoke the elegance of the city than almost anything else. Innkeepers and B&B owners know this all too well and charge accordingly, especially in the summer season.

If you simply can't afford a stay at one of these historic inns, you can confine your consumption of Charleston to dining in the old city and sightseeing and, at night, retire to one of the many clean, comfortable—and yes, utterly dull—chain motels on the outskirts. See the most representative samples under our "Inexpensive" category, below.

By and large, the double rooms in the recommended hotels and inns below have private bathrooms with tub/shower combinations, unless otherwise noted.

### VERY EXPENSIVE

**Charleston Place Hotel** ★★★    Charleston's premier hostelry, an Orient Express Property, is an eight-story landmark in the historic district that looks like a postmodern French château. It's big-time, uptown, glossy, and urban—at least, a former visitor, Prince Charles, thought so. Governors and prime ministers from around the world, as well as members of Fortune 500 companies, even visiting celebs such as Mel Gibson, prefer to stay here instead at one of the more intimate B&Bs. Guest rooms are among the most spacious and handsomely furnished in town—stately, modern, and maintained in state-of-the-art condition. This hotel represents the New South at its most confident, a stylish giant in a district of B&Bs and small converted inns. Acres of Italian marble grace the place, leading to plush guest rooms with decor inspired by colonial Carolina. The deluxe restaurant, **Charleston Grill,** is recommended in the "Where to Dine" section, later in the chapter. A cafe provides a more casual option.

205 Meeting St., Charleston, SC 29401. © **800/611-5545** or 843/722-4900. Fax 843/724-7215. www. charlestonplacehotel.com. 440 units. $229–$450 double; $579–$1,575 suite. Seasonal packages available.

# Charleston Accommodations

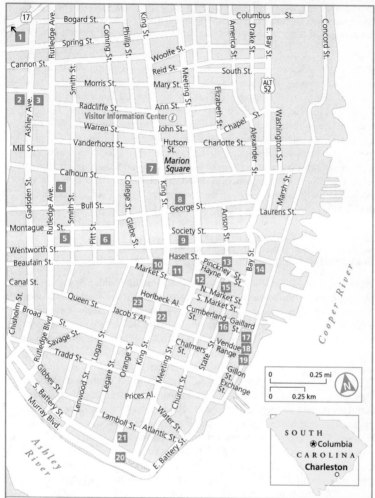

Anchorage Inn **17**

Ansonborough Inn **14**

Ashley Inn **2**

Best Western King Charles Inn **9**

The Cannonboro Inn **3**

Charleston Place Hotel **11**

Doubletree Guest Suites **15**

1843 Battery Carriage House Inn **20**

1837 Bed & Breakfast **6**

The Elliott House Inn **22**

Francis Marion Hotel **7**

HarbourView Inn **18**

Indigo Inn/Jasmine House **13**

The Inn at Middleton Place **1**

Kings Courtyard Inn **10**

King George IV Inn **8**

La Quinta Charleston **1**

The Lodge Alley Inn **16**

Philip Porcher House **23**

Planters Inn **12**

The Rutledge Victorian
Guest House **4**

Two Meeting Street Inn **21**

Vendue Inn **19**

Wentworth Mansion **5**

AE, DC, DISC, MC, V. Parking $10–$15. **Amenities:** 2 restaurants; bar; indoor/outdoor pool; 2 tennis courts; fitness center; health spa; sauna; 24-hr. room service; nonsmoking rooms; rooms for those w/limited mobility. *In room:* A/C, TV, dataport, minibar, kitchenette (in some), hair dryer, iron/ironing board, safe.

**Planters Inn** ★★★    For many years, this distinguished brick-sided inn next to the City Market was left to languish. In the 1990s, a multimillion-dollar renovation transformed the place into a cozy but tasteful and opulent enclave of Colonial charm, turning it into one of the finest small luxury hotels of the South. The inn has a lobby filled with reproductions of 18th-century furniture and engravings, a staff clad in silk vests, and a parking area with exactly the right amount of spaces for the number of rooms in the hotel. The spacious guest rooms have hardwood floors, marble bathrooms, and 18th-century decor (the work of award-winning decorators). The suites are appealing, outfitted very much like rooms in an upscale private home. Afternoon tea is served in the lobby, and a well-recommended restaurant, the **Peninsula Grill,** is described in the "Where to Dine" section, later in the chapter.

112 N. Market St., Charleston, SC 29401. ℭ **800/845-7082** or 843/722-2345. Fax 843/577-2125. www.planters inn.com. 62 units. $195–$325 double; $450–$700 suite. AE, DC, DISC, MC, V. Parking $16. **Amenities:** Restaurant; lounge; limited room service; laundry service/dry cleaning; nonsmoking rooms; rooms for those w/limited mobility. *In room:* A/C, TV, dataport, hair dryer, iron/ironing board, safe.

**Wentworth Mansion** ★★★    An example of America's Gilded Age, this 1886 Second Empire Inn touts such amenities as hand-carved marble fireplaces, Tiffany stained-glass windows, and detailed wood and plasterwork. If it is grand accommodations that you seek, you've found them. When a cotton merchant built the property in the 1800s, it cost $200,000, an astronomical sum back then. In the mid-1990s a team of local entrepreneurs spent millions renovating it into the smooth and seamless inn you see today. Prior to its reopening in 1998, it had been a run-down office building. The guest rooms and suites are large enough to have sitting areas. All units have a king-size bed and a well-kept bathroom with a shower and whirlpool tub, and most have working gas fireplaces. The mansion rooms and suites also come with a sleeper sofa for extra guests, who are charged an additional $50 per night.

A full European breakfast is served in the inn's sun room each morning, and guests are invited to relax each evening in the lounge for cordials or spend some quiet time reading in the library. The inn's **Circa 1886 Restaurant,** one of the grandest in Charleston, is recommended even if you're not a guest of the Wentworth (see "Where to Dine," later in this chapter).

149 Wentworth St., Charleston, SC 29401. ℭ **888/466-1886** or 843/853-1886. Fax 843/720-5290. www. wentworthmansion.com. 21 units. $315–$415 double; $495–$695 suite. Rates include breakfast buffet and afternoon tea and cordials. AE, DC, DISC, MC, V. Free parking. **Amenities:** Restaurant; bar; limited room service; babysitting; laundry service/dry cleaning; nonsmoking rooms; rooms for those w/limited mobility. *In room:* A/C, TV, dataport, minibar (soft drinks only), hair dryer, iron/ironing board, safe.

## EXPENSIVE

**Ansonborough Inn** ★ *Kids*    This is one of the oddest hotels in the historic district. Most visitors really like the unusual configuration of rooms, many of which are spacious enough to house families. Set close to the waterfront, the massive building, once a 1900 warehouse, has a lobby that features exposed timbers and a soaring atrium filled with plants. Despite the building's height, it only has three floors, which allows guest rooms to have ceilings of 14 to 16 feet and, in many cases, sleeping lofts. Guest rooms are outfitted with copies of 18th-century furniture and accessories, and the bathrooms contain tubs and shower stalls.

Breakfast is the only meal served, but many fine dining rooms are located nearby.

21 Hasell St., Charleston, SC 29401. (C) **800/522-2073** or 843/723-1655. Fax 843/577-6888. www.ansonboroughinn.com. 37 units. Mar–Nov $149–$259 suite; off season $99–$229 suite. Rates include continental breakfast. Children 11 and under stay free in parent's room. AE, DISC, MC, V. Parking $10. **Amenities:** Breakfast room; lounge; babysitting; nonsmoking rooms; rooms for those w/limited mobility. *In room:* A/C, TV, dataport, fridge, hair dryer, iron/ironing board, safe.

**1843 Battery Carriage House Inn** 🏠   In one of the largest antebellum neighborhoods of Charleston, this inn offers guest rooms in a carriage house behind the main building. In other words, the owners save the top living accommodations for themselves but have restored the bedrooms out back to a high standard. Recent renovations added four-poster beds and a Colonial frill to the not-overly-large bedrooms. All units contain well-managed bathrooms with mostly tub/shower combinations. Don't stay here if you want an inn with lots of public space; that, you don't get. But you can enjoy the location, which is a short walk off the Battery—a seafront peninsula where you can easily imagine a flotilla of Yankee ships enforcing the Civil War blockades.

Unfortunately, if you call, you're likely to get only a recorded message until the owners are able to call you back. Despite the inaccessibility of the main house and the difficulty of reaching a staff member, this place provides comfortable and convenient lodging in a desirable neighborhood.

Breakfast, during nice weather, is served in a carefully landscaped brick courtyard. Evening wine is also served to guests.

20 S. Battery, Charleston, SC 29401. (C) **800/775-5575** or 843/727-3100. Fax 843/727-3130. www.batterycarriagehouse.com. 11 units. $99–$299 double. Rates include continental breakfast served in courtyard or room. AE, DISC, MC, V. Free parking. No children under 12. **Amenities:** Lounge; nonsmoking rooms. *In room:* A/C, TV, dataport.

**Francis Marion Hotel** 🏠   A $14-million award-winning restoration has returned this historic hotel to its original elegance. Although the 12-story structure breaks from the standard Charleston decorative motif and has rooms furnished in traditional European style, it is not devoid of Charleston charm. Guest rooms feature a king-size, queen-size, or double bed, and the renovated bathrooms contain tub/shower combinations with brass fixtures. The hotel's restaurant, **Swamp Fox Restaurant & Bar,** serves breakfast, lunch, and dinner, and features classic Southern cuisine.

387 King St., Charleston, SC 29403. (C) **877/756-2121** or 843/722-0600. Fax 843/723-4633. www.francismarioncharleston.com. 226 units. $88–$230 double; $251–$293 suite. Children 11 and under stay free in parent's room. AE, DC, DISC, MC, V. Parking $10–$15. **Amenities:** Restaurant; bar; fitness center; limited room service; babysitting; laundry service/dry cleaning; nonsmoking rooms; rooms for those w/limited mobility. *In room:* A/C, TV, dataport, minibar, coffeemaker, hair dryer, iron/ironing board.

**HarbourView Inn** 🏠   Spruced up and looking better than ever, this four-story inn lies in the heart of Charleston, across from the landmark Waterfront Park. From its windows you can see some of the best seascapes in the city. Known for its Old South hospitality and attentive service, this is one of the best and most comfortable inns in the historic zone. Guest rooms have an understated elegance, with plush four-poster beds, wicker chests, sea-grass rugs, and rattan chairs—decor very much in the style of an old-time Charleston sea captain's town house. Expect pampering here, from morning (when a continental breakfast is delivered to your door) to night (when turndown service comes with "sweet dream good night candy" on your pillow). The beautifully maintained private bathrooms come with both tub and shower. The most elegant unit is the penthouse with its whirlpool bathroom, working fireplace, and private balcony.

2 Venue Range, Charleston, SC 29401. © **888/853-8439** or 843/853-8439. Fax 843/853-4034. www.harbour viewcharleston.com. 52 units. Sun–Thurs $159–$219 double, Fri–Sat $189–$269 double; Sun–Thurs $209–$249 penthouse, Fri–Sat $249–$299 penthouse. Rates include continental breakfast. AE, DC, DISC, MC, V. Parking $6. **Amenities:** Business services; limited room service; babysitting; laundry service/dry cleaning; nonsmoking rooms; rooms for those w/limited mobility. *In room:* A/C, TV, dataport, hair dryer, iron/ironing board.

**Indigo Inn/Jasmine House** ⭐   These two hotels are set across the street from each other, with the same owners and the same reception area in the Indigo Inn. Built as an indigo warehouse in the mid–19th century, and gutted and radically reconstructed, the Indigo Inn (the larger of the two) offers rooms with 18th-century decor and comfortable furnishings. Rooms in the Jasmine House, an 1843 Greek Revival mansion whose exterior is painted buttercup yellow, are much more individualized. Each unit in the Jasmine House has a ceiling of about 14 feet, its own color scheme and theme, crown moldings, bathrooms with shower and whirlpool tubs, and floral-patterned upholsteries. Parking is available for $6 a day in the lot at the Indigo Inn. Both inns serve breakfast on-site for their respective guests. Children are welcome at the Indigo Inn, but not at the Jasmine House.

1 Maiden Lane, Charleston, SC 29401. © **800/845-7639** or 843/577-5900. Fax 843/577-0378. www. indigoinn.com. 40 units (Indigo Inn), 10 units (Jasmine House). $99–$235 double in the Indigo Inn; $125–$295 double in the Jasmine House. Rates include continental breakfast. 10% discounts available in midwinter. AE, DC, DISC, MC, V. Parking $6. **Amenities:** Breakfast room; lounge; Jacuzzi; babysitting; nonsmoking rooms; rooms for those w/limited mobility. *In room:* A/C, TV, hair dryer, gas fireplace (in some).

**Kings Courtyard Inn** ⭐   The tiny entry to this three-story 1854 inn in the historic district is deceiving, because it opens into a brick courtyard with a fountain. A fireplace warms the small lobby, which has a brass chandelier. Besides the main courtyard, two courts offer fine views from the breakfast room. The owners bought the building next door and incorporated 10 more rooms into the existing inn. Your room might be outfitted with a canopy bed, an Oriental rug over a hardwood floor, an armoire, or even a gas fireplace. A whirlpool is on-site. A continental breakfast is included in the rate; a full breakfast is available at an additional charge.

198 King St., Charleston, SC 19401. © **800/845-6119** or 843/723-7000. Fax 843/720-2608. www.charming inns.com. 41 units. $150–$210 double. Rates include continental breakfast. Children 11 and under stay free in parent's room. Off-season 3-day packages available. AE, DC, DISC, MC, V. Parking $10. **Amenities:** Breakfast room; lounge; Jacuzzi; limited room service; babysitting; laundry service/dry cleaning; nonsmoking rooms. *In room:* A/C, TV, dataport, hair dryer.

**The Inn at Middleton Place** ⭐⭐ *Finds*   It's a long way from Tara and Rhett Butler, but if your lodging preferences south of the Mason-Dixon line run toward strikingly modern luxury hotels, this is the place for you. The inn is a direct counterpoint to the adjoining Middleton Place (p. 226), an 18th-century plantation that's a sightseeing attraction. Charles Duell, a descendant of Middleton's original owners, wanted a departure from ersatz Colonial and deliberately commissioned architects to create an inn devoid of "Scarlett and her antebellum charm." That said, the inn, with its live oaks and setting on the bluffs of the Ashley River, still has Southern grace and a warm and inviting interior. The guest rooms are filled with handcrafted furniture, wood-burning fireplaces, and cypress paneling; bathrooms have oversize tubs and private showers. You can patronize the inn's restaurant if you're not a guest, enjoying classic plantation fare ranging from pan-fried quail to crawfish cakes. Ever had pecan-encrusted duck breast?

4290 Ashley River Rd., Charleston, SC 29414. © 800/543-4774 or 843/556-0500. Fax 843/556-5673. www.middletonplace.org/inn. 52 units. $170–$240 double; $400 suite. Rates include full breakfast. AE, DISC, MC, V. Free parking. **Amenities:** Restaurant; lounge; outdoor pool; kayaking; free bikes; babysitting; laundry service/dry cleaning; admission to Plantation. *In room:* A/C, TV, dataport, coffeemaker, hair dryer, iron/ironing board.

**The Lodge Alley Inn** ★   This sprawling historic property extends from its entrance on the busiest commercial street of the Old Town to a quiet brick-floored courtyard in back. It was once a trio of 19th-century warehouses. Today, it evokes a miniature village in Louisiana, with a central square, a fountain, and landscaped shrubs basking in the sunlight. Units include rather standard hotel rooms, suites, and duplex arrangements with sleeping lofts. Throughout, the decor is American country, with pine floors and lots of Colonial accents. Some rooms have fireplaces, and most retain the massive timbers and brick walls of the original warehouses. The staff is usually polite and helpful, but because the hotel hosts many small conventions, they may be preoccupied with the demands of whatever group happens to be checking in or out. A full or continental breakfast is available each morning.

195 E. Bay St., Charleston, SC 29401. © 843/722-1611. Fax 843/577-7497. www.bluegreenrentals.com. 87 units. $169 double; $189–$225 suite. Children 12 and under stay free in parent's room. AE, DISC, MC, V. Parking $10. **Amenities:** Limited room service; laundry service/dry cleaning; nonsmoking rooms; rooms for those w/limited mobility. *In room:* A/C, TV, dataport, minibar, kitchenette, coffeemaker, hair dryer, iron/ironing board.

**Philip Porcher House** ★★   Hailed by *Travel & Leisure* as one of the top B&Bs in the South, this beautifully restored 1770 Georgian home stands in the heart of the historic district. Built by a French Huguenot planter, Philip Porcher, the house was renovated in 1997. Handsome Georgian Revival oak paneling was installed from the demolished executive offices of the Pennsylvania Railroad in Pittsburgh. The one rental unit in the house, an apartment on the ground floor, consists of five rooms, and is rented to only one party (with two bedrooms, the apartment can accommodate up to four guests, ideal for families). It's attractively furnished with period antiques and 18th-century engravings; good books and music create a cozy environment. A comfortable sitting room has a working fireplace. One twin-bedded bedroom has a fireplace. One bathroom has an elegant glass shower and double sinks. A screened gallery opens onto a wonderful secret walled garden.

19 Archdale St., Charleston, SC 29401. © 843/722-1801. www.bbonline.com/sc/porcher. 1 unit. 2-bedroom apt $250 for 2, $350 for 4. Rates include continental breakfast. No credit cards. Free parking. No children under 12. **Amenities:** Nonsmoking rooms. *In room:* A/C, kitchenette, hair dryer.

**Two Meeting Street Inn** ★   Set in an enviable position near the Battery, this house was built in 1892 as a wedding gift from a prosperous father to his daughter. Inside, the proportions are as lavish and gracious as the Gilded Age could provide. Stained-glass windows, mementos, and paintings were either part of the original decorations or collected by the present owners, the Spell family. Most guest rooms contain bathrooms with tub/shower combinations, four-poster beds, ceiling fans, and (in some cases) access to a network of balconies. A continental breakfast with home-baked breads and pastries is available.

2 Meeting St., Charleston, SC 29401. © 843/723-7322. www.twomeetingstreet.com. 9 units. $190–$350 double. Rates include continental breakfast and afternoon tea. No credit cards. No children under 12. **Amenities:** Breakfast room; lounge; nonsmoking rooms. *In room:* A/C, TV, hair dryer, iron/ironing board, safe.

**Vendue Inn** ★   This three-story inn manages to convey some of the personalized touches of a B&B. Its public areas—a series of narrow, labyrinthine spaces—are full of antiques and Colonial accessories that evoke a cluttered, and slightly cramped, inn in Europe. Guest rooms do not necessarily follow the lobby's European model, however, and appear to be the result of decorative experiments by the owners. Room themes may be based on aspects of Florida, rococo Italy, or 18th-century Charleston. Marble floors and tabletops, wooden sleigh beds, and (in some rooms) wrought-iron canopy beds, while eclectically charming, might be inconsistent with your vision of colonial Charleston. Overflow guests are housed in a historic, brick-fronted annex across the cobblestone-covered street. The inn's restaurant is called the **Kitchen House** (for dinner only). The chef here offers a menu of local favorites with unusual twists. The other restaurant, the **Roof Top Terrace,** offers a more informal atmosphere with a panoramic view of the harbor and of the historic district. A complete luncheon and dinner menu of local and American favorites is offered here.

19 Vendue Range, Charleston, SC 29401. (© **800/845-7900** or 843/577-7970. Fax 843/577-2913. www.vendue inn.com. 65 units. $169–$189 double; $239–$339 suite. Rates include full Southern breakfast. AE, DC, DISC, MC, V. Parking $14. **Amenities:** 2 restaurants; bar; limited room service; babysitting; laundry service/dry cleaning; nonsmoking rooms; rooms for those w/limited mobility. *In room:* A/C, TV, dataport, kitchenette (in some), hair dryer, iron/ironing board, safe.

## MODERATE

Reliable motel accommodations are also available at the **Hampton Inn Historic District,** 345 Meeting St. (© **800/HAMPTON** or 843/723-4000), across from the visitor center.

**Anchorage Inn** ★★  Other than a heraldic shield out front, few ornaments mark this bulky structure, which was built in the 1840s as a cotton warehouse. The inn boasts the only decorative theme of its type in Charleston: a mock-Tudor interior with lots of dark paneling; references to Olde England; canopied beds with matching tapestries; pastoral or nautical engravings; leaded casement windows; and, in some places, half-timbering. Because bulky buildings are adjacent to the hotel on both sides, the architects designed all but a few rooms with views overlooking the lobby. (Light is indirectly filtered inside through the lobby's overhead skylights—a plus during Charleston's hot summers.) Each room's shape is different from that of its neighbors, and the expensive ones have bona-fide windows overlooking the street outside. The inn serves a continental breakfast and an afternoon tea (complete with sherry, wine and cheese, and fruit and crackers).

26 Vendue Range, Charleston, SC 29401. (© **800/421-2952** or 843/723-8300. Fax 843/723-9543. www. anchoragencharleston.com. 19 units. $89–$189 double; $179–$279 suite. Rates include continental breakfast and afternoon tea. AE, MC, V. Parking $10. **Amenities:** Breakfast room; babysitting; laundry service/dry cleaning; nonsmoking rooms. *In room:* A/C, TV, dataport, hair dryer, iron/ironing board.

**Ashley Inn** ★  Partly because of its pink clapboards and the steep staircases that visitors must climb to reach the public areas, this imposing bed-and-breakfast inn might remind you of an antique house in Bermuda. Built in 1832 on a plot of land that sold at the time for a mere $419, it has a more appealing decor than the Cannonboro Inn (below), which belongs to the same owners. Breakfast and afternoon tea are served on a wide veranda overlooking a brick-paved driveway whose centerpiece is a formal fountain/goldfish pond evocative of Old Charleston. The public rooms, with their high ceilings and deep colors, are appealing. If you have lots of luggage, know in advance that negotiating this inn's steep and frequent stairs might pose something of a problem.

201 Ashley Ave., Charleston, SC 29403. (© **800/581-6658** or 843/723-1848. Fax 843/723-8007. www. charleston-sc-inns.com. 8 units. $110–$185 double; $150–$230 suite; $185–$265 carriage house. Rates

include full breakfast and afternoon tea. AE, DISC, MC, V. Free off-street parking. No children under 10. **Amenities:** Breakfast room; nonsmoking rooms. *In room:* A/C, TV, kitchenette (in carriage house), no phone.

### The Cannonboro Inn

This buff-and-beige 1853 house was once the private home of a rice planter. The decor isn't as carefully coordinated or as relentlessly upscale as those of many of its competitors; throughout, it has a sense of folksy informality. Although there's virtually no land around this building, a wide veranda on the side creates a "sit-and-talk-a-while" mood. Each unit contains a canopy bed; formal, old-fashioned furniture; and a cramped, somewhat dated bathroom with shower.

184 Ashley Ave., Charleston, SC 29403. $\textcircled{C}$ **800/235-8039** or 843/723-8572. Fax 843/723-8007. www. charleston-sc-inns.com. 6 units. $130–$250 double. Rates include full breakfast and afternoon tea and sherry. AE, DISC, MC, V. Free parking. No children under 10. **Amenities:** Breakfast room; lounge; bicycles; nonsmoking rooms. *In room:* A/C, TV, kitchenette.

### Doubletree Guest Suites *Kids*

A somber five-story 1991 building adjacent to the historic City Market, the Doubletree offers family-friendly suites instead of rooms, each outfitted with a wet bar, refrigerator, and microwave oven. The accommodations tend to receive heavy use, thanks to their appeal to families, tour groups, and business travelers. Breakfast is the only meal served.

181 Church St., Charleston, SC 29401. $\textcircled{C}$ **843/222-TREE.** Fax 843/577-2697. www.doubletree.com. 212 units. $109–$279 1-bedroom suite; $169–$568 2-bedroom suite. AE, DC, DISC, MC, V. Parking $16. **Amenities:** Breakfast room; fitness center; babysitting; laundry service/dry cleaning; nonsmoking rooms; rooms for those w/limited mobility. *In room:* A/C, TV, dataport, coffeemaker, hair dryer, iron/ironing board, free cribs.

### 1837 Bed & Breakfast

Built in 1837 by Nicholas Cobia, a cotton planter, this place was restored and decorated by two artists. It's called a "single house" because it's only a single room wide, which makes for some interesting room arrangements. Our favorite room is no. 2 in the Carriage House, which has authentic designs, exposed-brick walls, warm decor, a beamed ceiling, and three windows. All the rooms have refrigerators and separate entrances because of the layout, and all contain well-kept bathrooms and canopied poster rice beds. On one of the verandas, you can sit under whirling ceiling fans and enjoy your breakfast (sausage pie or eggs Benedict, and homemade breads) or afternoon tea. The parlor room has cypress wainscoting and a black-marble fireplace; the breakfast room is really part of the kitchen.

126 Wentworth St., Charleston, SC 29401. $\textcircled{C}$ **877/723-1837** or 843/723-7166. Fax 843/722-7179. www. 1837bb.com. 9 units. $79–$165 double. Rates include full breakfast and afternoon tea. AE, DISC, MC, V. Free off-street parking. No children under 7. **Amenities:** Breakfast room; lounge. *In room:* A/C, TV, fridge, coffeemaker, hair dryer, iron/ironing board.

### The Elliott House Inn

Historians have researched anecdotes about this place going back to the 1600s, but the core of the charming inn that you see today was built as a private home—probably for slaves—in 1861. You get a warm welcome from a very hip staff, and there's lots of Colonial inspiration in the decor of the comfortable and carefully maintained rooms. But despite all the grace notes and the landscaping (the flower beds are touched up every 2 weeks), the place seems like a raffish, indoor/outdoor motel, which some guests find appealing. The rooms are arranged in a style that you might expect in Key West—off tiers of balconies surrounding a verdant open courtyard. Each room contains a four-poster bed (the one in no. 36 is especially nice) and provides a feeling of living in an upscale cottage. Avoid those rooms with ground-level private outdoor terraces, however; they're cramped and claustrophobic, don't have attractive views, and tend to be plagued by mildew problems. Conversation often becomes free and easy beneath the city's largest wisteria arbor, near a bubbling whirlpool designed for as many as 12 people at a time.

78 Queen St. (between King and Meeting sts.), Charleston, SC 29401. ℂ 800/729-1855 or 843/723-1855. Fax 843/722-1567. www.elliotthouseinn.com. 24 units. $95–$180 double. Rates include continental breakfast. AE, DISC, MC, V. Parking $6. **Amenities:** Breakfast room; lounge; Jacuzzi; free bikes; nonsmoking rooms. *In room:* A/C, TV, dataport, hair dryer.

## INEXPENSIVE

To avoid the high costs of the elegant B&Bs and deluxe inns of historic Charleston, try one of the chain motels such as **Days Inn,** 2998 W. Montague Ave., Charleston, SC 29418 (ℂ 843/747-4101; fax 843/566-0378), near the international airport. Doubles range from $60 to $80. Children under 12 stay free in their parent's room, and cribs are also free. **Lands Inn,** 2545 Savannah Hwy., Charleston, SC 29414 (ℂ 843-763-8885; fax 843/556-9536), is another bargain, with doubles costing from $69 to $89, and $10 extra charged for each additional person. Children under 16 stay free. A final bargain is **Red Roof Inn,** 7480 Northwoods Blvd., Charleston, SC 29406 (ℂ 843/572-9100; fax 843/572-0061), where doubles cost $50 to $60, and $6 is charged for each additional person. Those 18 and under are housed free.

**Best Western King Charles Inn** *Kids* One block from the historic district's market area, this three-story hotel has rooms that are better than you might expect from a motel and are likely to be discounted off season. Some rooms have balconies, but the views are limited. Although short on style, the hotel is a good value and convenient to most everything. An all-you-can-eat buffet breakfast is served in a Colonial-inspired restaurant, and the hotel has a small pool and a helpful staff.

237 Meeting St. (between Wentworth and Hazel sts.), Charleston, SC 29401. ℂ 800/528-1234 or 843/723-7451. Fax 843/723-2041. www.kingcharlesinn.com. 93 units. $105–$130 double. Children 18 and under stay free in parent's room. AE, DC, DISC, MC, V. Free parking. **Amenities:** Restaurant; lounge; outdoor pool; limited room service; laundry service/dry cleaning; nonsmoking rooms; rooms for those w/limited mobility. *In room:* A/C, TV, dataport, coffeemaker, hair dryer, iron/ironing board.

**King George IV Inn** This four-story 1790 Federal-style home in the heart of the historic district serves as an example of the way Charleston used to live. Named the Peter Freneau House, it was formerly the residence of a reporter and co-owner of the *Charleston City Gazette*. All rooms have wide-planked hardwood floors, plaster moldings, fireplaces, and 12-foot ceilings, and are furnished with

---

*Kids* **Family-Friendly Hotels**

**Ansonborough Inn** (p. 208) This is a good value for families who want to stay in one of the historic inns. Many of the high-ceilinged rooms in this converted warehouse have sleeping lofts.

**Best Western King Charles Inn** (see above) This is one of the best family values in Charleston. Children 18 and under stay free in their parent's room. The location is only a block from the historic district's market area.

**Doubletree Guest Suites** (p. 213) This is a good choice for families who want extra space and a place to prepare meals. Some suites are bi-level, giving families more privacy.

antiques. Beds are either Victorian or four-poster double or queen-size. Each unit has a well-kept bathroom, most with tub/shower combinations. All guests are allowed access to the three levels of porches on the house. The location is convenient to many downtown Charleston restaurants; tennis is a 5-minute drive, the beach is 15 minutes away, and some 35 golf courses are nearby. The continental breakfast consists of cereals, breads, muffins, pastries, and fruit.

32 George St., Charleston, SC 29401. (C) **888/723-1667** or 843/723-9339. Fax 843/723-7749. www.king georgeiv.com. 10 units, 2 with shared bathrooms. $89–$179 double. Rates include continental breakfast. AE, MC, V. Free parking. **Amenities:** Breakfast room; nonsmoking rooms. *In room:* A/C, TV, dataport.

**The Rutledge Victorian Guest House**    This 19th-century structure is a sibling property of the King George IV Inn (described above). The Italianate building is kept immaculate; rooms, as well as the inn, are furnished with Victorian antiques and have four-poster, rice, mahogany, or Italian rope beds in double, queen-size, and twin sizes. The location is just a short trek from many of Charleston's notable restaurants, and activities such as golf and tennis are just minutes away. Some rooms have working fireplaces, and most have private bathrooms with shower units. In addition, the Rutledge Victorian Guest House has accommodations at another nearby property, **Number Six Ambrose Alley.** Specify your room requests and accommodations when you make your reservation; doing so as far in advance as possible is highly recommended.

114 Rutledge Ave., Charleston, SC 29401. (C) **888/722-7553** or 843/722-7551. Fax 843/722-0065. www. charlestonvictorian.com. 10 units, 8 with private bathroom. No children under 12. $90–$150 double without private bathroom; $110–$170 double with private bathroom. Rates include continental breakfast. MC, V. Free parking. **Amenities:** Breakfast room; nonsmoking rooms. *In room:* A/C, TV, dataport (in most), hair dryer, iron/ironing board.

## NORTH CHARLESTON
### INEXPENSIVE

**La Quinta Charleston**    This sturdy, well-designed, and childproof member of a nationwide hotel chain has an exterior that's attractively designed like a Spanish hacienda, replete with terra-cotta roof tiles, thick stucco walls, a bell tower, and references to the mission churches of California. It lies in the rather nondescript jumble of North Charleston, near the busy interstate and close to row upon row of shopping malls, chain restaurants, and fast-food joints. Historic Charleston is a clearly signposted 25-minute drive away. Each guest room is midsize and comfortably laid out with upholstered chairs, a writing (or dining) table, and a sense of Tex-Mex whimsy.

2499 La Quinta Lane, Charleston, SC 29420. (C) **800/531-5900** or 843/797-8181. Fax 843/569-1608. www. laquinta.com. 122 units. $62–$85 double; $92–$98 suite. Rates include continental breakfast. AE, DC, DISC, MC, V. Free parking. Children under 18 stay free in parent's room. **Amenities:** Outdoor pool; nonsmoking rooms; rooms for those w/limited mobility. *In room:* A/C, TV, kitchenette, coffeemaker, hair dryer, iron/ironing board.

## 4 Where to Dine

Foodies from all over flock to Charleston for some of the finest dining in the tri-state area. You get not only the refined cookery of the Low Country, but also an array of French and international specialties. Space does not permit us to preview all the outstanding restaurants of Charleston—much less the merely good ones.

### VERY EXPENSIVE

**Circa 1886 Restaurant**  ★★ AMERICAN/FRENCH   Situated in the carriage house of the Wentworth Mansion (see earlier in this chapter), this deluxe restaurant offers grand food and formal service. Begin by taking the invitation of the concierge for a view of Charleston from the cupola, where you can see all the bodies of water surrounding the city. Seating 50, two main rooms are beautifully set in the most idyllic place for a romantic dinner in Charleston. The chef prepares an updated version of Low Country cookery, giving it a light, contemporary touch but retaining the flavors of the Old South. Menus are rotated seasonally to take advantage of the best and freshest produce. For a first course, try the candied carrot custard with roasted garlic and a stuffed morel, or the summer sausage of wild boar and sun-dried peaches. Here the traditional gazpacho comes with cucumber instead of tomato and is studded with pickled crawfish. Featured main courses are prepared with consummate skill, especially the French sea bass with lobster mousse, or the lemon-tea-infused halibut with a butter-poached leek-and-potato mousseline. We're still smacking our lips over the raspberry soufflé hazelnut tart with a vanilla bean ice milk.

Special attention is paid to the salad courses, as exemplified by a concoction of baby spinach, strawberries, wild mushrooms, and red onion, all flavored with a champagne-and-poppyseed vinaigrette.

Desserts, ordered at the beginning of the meal, include a unique "baked Carolina" with orange and raspberry sorbets, or pan-fried angel food cake with fresh berries and peach ice cream.

In the Wentworth Mansion, 149 Wentworth St. (C) **843/853-1886.** www.circa1886.com. Reservations recommended. Main courses $23–$35. AE, DC, DISC, MC, V. Mon–Sat 5:30–10pm.

**Robert's of Charleston** ✸✸✸ AMERICAN/FRENCH   One of the most unusual restaurants in Charleston, and one of the best and most exclusive, this formal choice is a winner in cuisine, service, and ambience. Chef/owner Robert Dickson brings a whole new dimension to dining in Charleston. His set menu, served in a long, narrow room that evokes an intimate dinner party, is the town's finest.

Guests peruse the menu while listening to music from a pianist. The waiter will explain each course on a menu that is seasonally adjusted. He'll also give you a preview of each wine that you'll be served. Don't be surprised if the chef himself suddenly bursts through the door from the kitchen in the back, singing *Oliver*'s "Food, Glorious Food." Each dish we've ever sampled here has been a delight in flavor and texture, ranging from sea scallops mousse in a Maine lobster sauce as an appetizer, to very tender, rosy duck breast in a yellow-pepper cream sauce. The garnishes served with the dishes—often ignored in most restaurants—are especially tasty here, including roasted red pepper or hot fried eggplant. Tossed in a homemade vinaigrette, salads are zesty with wild mixed greens and such vegetables as mushrooms and artichokes. For a main course, dig into a chateaubriand with a demi-glace flavored with mushrooms from the woods, or perhaps steamed salmon. Desserts often include the best and richest chocolate cake in Charleston. It comes with vanilla sauce, strawberries, and almond praline, but perhaps that's gilding the lily.

182 E. Bay St. (C) **843/577-7565.** www.robertsofcharleston.com. Reservations essential. 5-course fixed-price menu including wine and coffee $80 per person. AE, DC, DISC, MC, V. 1 seating Thurs–Sat 7:30pm.

## EXPENSIVE

**Anson** ✸✸✸ LOW COUNTRY/MODERN AMERICAN   We think it's simply the best. Charlestonians know that they can spot the local society types here; newcomers recognize it as a hip, stylish venue with all the grace notes of a top-notch restaurant in New York or Chicago, but with reminders of Low

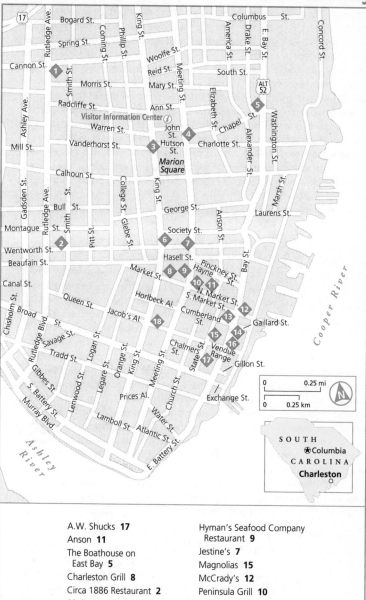

A.W. Shucks **17**

Anson **11**

The Boathouse on
East Bay **5**

Charleston Grill **8**

Circa 1886 Restaurant **2**

82 Queen **18**

Fish **3**

High Cotton Maverick
Bar & Grill **13**

Hominy Grill **1**

Hyman's Seafood Company
Restaurant **9**

Jestine's **7**

Magnolias **15**

McCrady's **12**

Peninsula Grill **10**

Robert's of Charleston **16**

Sermet's Corner **6**

S.N.O.B. (Slightly North
of Broad) **14**

39 Rue de Jean **4**

Country charm. The setting is a century-old, brick-sided ice warehouse. The present owners have added New Orleans–style iron balconies, Corinthian pilasters salvaged from demolished colonial houses, and enough Victorian rococo for anyone's taste. A well-trained staff in long white aprons describes dishes that are inspired by traditions of the coastal Southeast. But this isn't exactly down-home cookery, as you'll see after sampling such appetizers as fried calamari with an apricot and shallot sauce, or cornmeal-dusted okra with chile oil and goat cheese. France meets the Deep South in one seafood selection: cashew-crusted grouper with hoppin' John, green beans, and a champagne cream sauce. Our favorite is the crispy flounder, which rival chefs have tried to duplicate but haven't equaled. Some of the best meat selections include slow-roasted duck with dried cranberries, pecans, wild rice, and orange sauce, or else a New York strip with Maytag blue cheese and an onion marmalade. A children's menu is available.

12 Anson St. (C) 843/577-0551. www.ansonrestaurant.com. Reservations recommended. Main courses $16–$29. AE, DC, DISC, MC, V. Sun–Thurs 5–10pm; Fri–Sat 5–11pm.

**Charleston Grill** ★★★ LOW COUNTRY/FRENCH Chef Bob Waggoner, from the Wild Boar in Nashville, has a devoted local following. This is the most ostentatiously formal and pleasing restaurant in Charleston, with superb service, grand food, an impeccably trained staff, and one of the city's best selections of wine. His French cuisine draws rave reviews, earning the restaurant the Mobil Four-Star rating—the only restaurant in South Carolina to have such a distinction. The decor makes absolutely no concessions to Southern folksiness, and the marble-floored, mahogany-sheathed dining room is one of the city's most luxurious. Menu items change with the seasons, and you will be pleasantly surprised by how well Low Country and French cuisine meld. Absolutely delightful appetizers include chilled beet and watermelon soup garnished with ruby-red grapefruit and fresh mint, or else bay scallops and mussels stuffed in lobster and encased in pastry over a saffron-laced Vidalia onion mousseline in an orange-scented emulsion. The chef's creativity is reflected in such main dish offerings as roasted tenderloin of venison over a caramelized pearl onion and sun-dried cranberry compote, or a duo of milk-fed veal slowly grilled and served with roasted sweetbreads with tapenade over baked eggplant. For dessert, nothing quite matches the "pistachio mousse martini" layered with bittersweet chocolate.

In the Charleston Place Hotel, 224 King St. (C) 843/577-4522. Reservations recommended. Main courses $18–$29. AE, DISC, DC, MC, V. Sun–Thurs 6–10pm; Fri–Sat 6–11pm.

**McCrady's** ★★ AMERICAN/FRENCH Charleston's oldest eating establishment, where none other than George Washington dined, is back in business under chef/partner Michael Kramer, who has turned it into one of the finest kitchens in the Low Country. Praising both its wine list and well-chosen menu, *Esquire* named it one of the best new restaurants in America. Entered down a mysterious-looking "Jack the Ripper" alley, it looks like an elegant wine cellar, with rough brick walls, exposed beams, and wide-plank floors. Cooking times are unerringly accurate, and a certain charm and fragrance is given to every dish. We still remember the creamy potato soup with chive oil, truffles, and leek foam—it doesn't get much better. Ditto for the tartare of "big eye" tuna with a wake-up-the-taste-buds fresh wasabi and a cucumber coulis. A perfectly done sautéed halibut appears on your plate with sides of salsify, yellow squash, and white beans. Slow-roasted Moulard duck breast comes with celery root purée, or else you might happily settle for the herb-marinated rack of lamb. Desserts are expensive but worth it, especially the pumpkin pie with a cranberry-apple compote and cinnamon-flecked whipped cream.

2 Unity Alley. ✆ **843/577-0025.** www.mccradysrestaurant.com. Reservations required. Main courses $25–$34. AE, MC, V. Sun–Thurs 5–10pm; Fri–Sat 5–11pm.

**Peninsula Grill** ✪✪ CONTINENTAL/INTERNATIONAL  There's an old Southern saying about "country come to city." This is one case where "city has come to country." The Peninsula Grill, in the historic Planters Inn, has caused quite a stir in the gastronomic world—not just in Charleston, but also around the country. Quaint and quiet, the setting has a 19th-century charm unlike any other restaurant in Charleston. The kitchen does a marvelous job of bringing new cuisine to an old city without compromising the delicacies that have made dining in Charleston famous. The menu changes frequently. You might start with a delicious lobster and corn chowder, or chilled cucumber buttermilk soup. Worthy of your palate are such dishes as a cracklin' pork *osso buco* with a sweet potato risotto, or the bourbon-grilled jumbo shrimp with Low Country hoppin' John and (a first for many) lobster-and-basil-infused hush puppies. Even the *New York Times* and *Bon Appetit* have praised "the ultimate coconut cake," based on a recipe from the chef's grandmother.

In the Planters Inn, 112 N. Market St. ✆ **843/723-0700.** www.peninsulagrill.com. Reservations required. Main courses $20–$34. AE, DC, DISC, MC, V. Mon–Thurs 5:30–10pm; Fri–Sat 5:30–11pm.

## MODERATE

**The Boathouse on East Bay** SEAFOOD  Briny delights await you at this bustling restaurant at the corner of Chapel and East Bay. It is a curious blend of family friendliness and two-fisted machismo, appealing to a wide range of denizens from Charleston plus visitors who are just discovering the place. The setting is in a turn-of-the-20th-century warehouse where boats were once repaired. Massive antique timbers on the heavily trussed ceiling remain. On the northern perimeter of the historic core, the restaurant has a raw bar open daily from 4pm to midnight. Shellfish platters are the chef's specialty, including the "J Boat," which can be shared. On it are some of the city's best oysters, littleneck clams, smoked mussels, king crab legs, and fresh shrimp. Every night four different types of fish, ranging from mahimahi to black grouper, are grilled and served with a range of sauces, from mustard glaze to hoisin ginger.

Familiar Charleston specialties include spicy shrimp and grits, and crab cakes with green Tabasco sauce, the latter one of our favorites. For those who don't want fish, a selection of pasta, beef, and chicken dishes is also served. For dessert, opt for the strawberry cobbler or Key lime pie.

549 E. Bay St. ✆ **843/577-7171.** Reservations recommended. Main courses $9.95–$28. AE, DISC, MC, V. Sun–Thurs 5–10pm; Fri–Sat 5–11pm; Sun 10am–2pm.

**82 Queen** ✪ LOW COUNTRY  In its way, this is probably the most unusual compendium of real estate in Charleston: three 18th- and 19th-century houses clustered around an ancient magnolia tree, with outdoor tables arranged in its shade. Menu items filled with flavor and flair include an award-winning version of she-crab soup laced with sherry. Some of the best Low Country meals in Charleston are served here, especially the Charleston bouillabaisse made with market-fresh seafood or the seasoned shrimp and crawfish jambalaya with tasso ham and red rice. Grilled dinners are also a specialty of the chef, especially the black-pepper rib-eye with mashed red-skin potatoes and caramelized onions.

82 Queen St. ✆ **843/723-7591.** Reservations recommended for dinner. Main courses $17–$24. AE, DC, DISC, MC, V. Daily 11:30am–4pm and 5:30–10:30pm.

**Fish** ⭐ SEAFOOD   With a name like fish, you know what to expect. Restaurant owners Charles and Celeste Patrick spearheaded the revitalization of North King Street when they restored and opened a restaurant in this 1830s former private home. Now visitors are flocking to an area once viewed as unsafe to enjoy some of the freshest and best seafood in the Low Country. The menu is seasonally adjusted. We recently dined on fire-roasted Prince Edward Island mussels in a shallot-laced white-wine sauce, whereas other members of our party opted for the seared foie gras with a roasted corn soufflé or the fish spring rolls in a ginger mango sauce. For a main course, perhaps "naked fish" is best. It's the fresh catch of the day and is prepared simply to bring out its natural flavor. Seared North Carolina trout with grilled asparagus and an herbed risotto is always a winning combination—as is the seared halibut in a cucumber yogurt sauce. An array of "sides," or fresh vegetables, is among the city's best and freshest.

442 King St. ⓒ 843/722-3474. Reservations recommended. Main courses $6–$13 lunch, $16–$20 dinner. AE, MC, V. Mon–Fri 11:30am–2pm; Sat 11:30am–2pm and 5:30–10pm.

**High Cotton Maverick Bar & Grill** SOUTHERN/STEAK   Established in 1999, this blockbuster of a restaurant caters to an increasingly devoted clientele of locals who prefer its two-fisted drinks in an upscale macho decor, and a tasty cuisine that defines the restaurant as a Southern-style steakhouse. It's also a good choice for nightlife because of its busy and cozy bar. If you decide to stick around for dinner, expect more than steaks. Dig into the buttermilk-fried oysters with arugula in a green goddess dressing, or the house-made sausage and grits with a mushroom sauce and roasted tomatoes. Gourmets gravitate to the "Something Wild" section of the menu, featuring brace of Carolina quail with a tomato chive mousse, or the venison medallions with grilled shiitakes. Most diners go for one of the juicy, tender steaks, which are served with sauces ranging from bourbon to béarnaise. The chef's dessert specialties are soufflés; the signature treat is a Charleston praline soufflé in chocolate sauce.

199 E. Bay St. ⓒ 843/724-3815. Reservations recommended. Main courses $18–$27. AE, DC, DISC, MC, V. Daily 5:30–10pm; Sat 11:30am–2:30pm; Sun brunch 10am–3pm.

**Magnolias** (Kids) SOUTHERN   Magnolias manages to elevate the regional, vernacular cuisine of the Deep South to a hip, postmodern art form that's suitable for big-city trendies, but is more likely to draw visiting families instead. The city's former Customs House has been revised into a sprawling network of interconnected spaces with heart-pine floors, faux-marble columns, and massive beams. Blackened catfish—how Southern can you get? And the side dishes—including fried green tomatoes, cheese grits, and yellow corn salsa—make the platters whistle Dixie. Many diners fill up on soups and salads at lunch, ranging from a creamy tomato with lump crabmeat to a seafood Cobb salad. The "Down South" main dishes are the favorites and are good tasting, especially the Low Country bouillabaisse made with fresh fish and shellfish; or the buttermilk fried chicken breast with cracked pepper biscuits, collard greens, and cream-style corn. A recently sampled dessert wins a prize: warm peach potpie with orange blossom syrup and white-chocolate ice cream.

185 E. Bay St. ⓒ 843/577-7771. Reservations recommended. Main courses $8–$20 lunch, $15–$25 dinner. AE, DC, MC, V. Mon–Thurs 11:30am–3:45pm and 5–10pm; Fri–Sat 11:30am–3:45pm and 4–11pm.

**S.N.O.B. (Slightly North of Broad)** ⭐ (Finds) SOUTHERN   You'll find an exposed kitchen, a high ceiling crisscrossed with ventilation ducts, and vague references to the South of long ago—including a scattering of wrought iron—in this snazzily rehabbed warehouse. The place promotes itself as being

Charleston's culinary maverick, priding itself on updated versions of the vittles that kept the South alive for 300 years but, frankly, the menu seems to be tame compared with the innovations being offered at many of its upscale, Southern-ethnic competitors. After you get past the hype, however, you might actually enjoy the place. Former diners include Timothy ("007") Dalton, Lee Majors, Sly Stallone, and superlawyer Alan Dershowitz. Main courses can be ordered in medium and large sizes—a fact appreciated by dieters. An array of freshly made salads, soups, sandwiches, and daily specials greet you at lunch. Dinners are more elaborate, including a classic red-bean soup, complete with tomato and jalapeño salsa, or an arugula salad with julienned apples and blue cheese. Tuesday night is devoted to roast prime rib suppers. You can enjoy such main courses as jumbo lump crab cakes over a sauté of corn, okra, and roasted yellow squash, or else sautéed duck breast with a plum glaze. Together with sibling restaurants **Slightly Up the Creek** and **Swamp Fox Restaurant & Bar,** the restaurant has launched a private-label wine, dubbed MSK (for "Maverick Southern Kitchen").

192 E. Bay St. ℂ **843/723-3424.** Reservations accepted only for parties of 5 or more at lunch, recommended for all at dinner. Main courses $8–$13 lunch, $9–$26 dinner. AE, DC, DISC, MC, V. Mon–Fri 11:30am–3pm and 5:30–11pm; Sat–Sun 5:30–11pm.

**39 Rue de Jean** ⭑ *Value* FRENCH/SUSHI You'll think you've been transported back to the Left Bank at this new bistro, which pays homage (exceedingly well) to the classic brasserie cuisine of Paris. Justifiably popular for its inexpensive French cuisine, the restaurant comes complete with a traditional zinc bar, steak *frites,* and a great bottle of wine. Patio dining is an added attraction. The only incongruous note is the sudden culinary departure into Japanese sushi. All our favorite French appetizers are on the menu, including onion soup, truffle potato soup, frisée lettuce with bacon lardoons, and even an Alsatian onion tart. Each day a special *plat du jour* is featured, and we always go for that, especially the Sunday rendition of a delectable bouillabaisse. It wouldn't be a Parisian bistro without escargots gratinée, steak *frites,* and foie gras, and the chefs do these time-honored dishes well. Special features are six preparations of mussels, and a whole fish *du jour* from the marketplace that morning.

39 John St. ℂ **843/722-8881.** Reservations required. Main courses $5.95–$12 lunch, $9–$24 dinner. AE, DC, DISC, MC, V. Mon–Fri 11:30am–1am; Sat 5:30pm–1am; Sun 5:30–11pm.

## INEXPENSIVE

**A. W. Shucks** ⭑ *Value* SEAFOOD This hearty oyster bar is a sprawling, salty tribute to the pleasures of shellfish and the fishermen who gather them. A short walk from the Public Market, set in a solid, restored warehouse with rough timbers, the restaurant has a long bar where thousands of crustaceans have been cracked open and consumed, as well as a dining room. The menu highlights oysters and clams on the half-shell, tasty seafood chowders, deviled crab, shrimp Creole, and succulent oysters prepared in at least half a dozen ways. Chicken and beef dishes are also listed on the menu, but they're nothing special. A wide selection of international beers is sold. Absolutely no one cares how you dress; just dig in.

70 State St. ℂ **843/723-1151.** Lunch $5–$11; main courses $12–$18. AE, DC, DISC, MC, V. Sun–Thurs 11am–10pm; Fri–Sat 11am–11pm.

**Hominy Grill** ⭑ *Kids* LOW COUNTRY Owned and operated by chef Robert Stehling, Hominy Grill features simply and beautifully prepared dishes inspired by the kitchens of the Low Country. Since its opening, it has gained a devoted family following, who come here to feast on such specialties as barbecue chicken

**Kids  Family-Friendly Restaurants**

**Magnolias** (p. 220)   Southern hospitality and charm keep this place buzzing day and night. Lunch is the best time for families and children. An array of soups, appetizers, salads, sandwiches, and pastas is available. But in-the-know local kids go easy on these items, saving room for homemade fare such as the warm cream-cheese brownie with white-chocolate ice cream and chocolate sauce.

**Hominy Grill** (p. 221)   Locally loved, this grill has been a friendly, home-like family favorite since 1996. Fair prices, good food, and an inviting atmosphere lure visitors to sample an array of Southern specialties at breakfast, lunch, or dinner.

sandwich, avocado and wehani rice salad and grilled vegetables, okra and shrimp beignets, and—a brunch favorite—smothered or poached eggs on homemade biscuits with mushroom gravy. At night, opt for one of the down-home specials such as grilled soft-shell crab with baked cheese grits and almond slaw, or else country-style pork ribs with red rice and pinto beans. For extra flavor, you can slather your chops with some blackstrap-molasses barbecue sauce. Stehling claims that he likes to introduce people to new grains in the place of pasta or potatoes; many of his dishes, including salads, are prepared with grains such as barley and cracked wheat. The menu is well balanced between old- and new-cookery styles. Dropping in for breakfast? Go for the buttermilk biscuits, the meaty bacon, and the home-style fried apples. There's even liver pudding on the menu. A lunch of catfish stew with cornbread is a temptation on a cold, rainy day, and the banana bread is worth writing home about.

207 Rutledge Ave. ✆ 843/937-0930. Brunch from $10; main courses $5.25–$11 lunch, $8.50–$22 dinner. MC, V. Mon–Fri 7:30–11am and 11:30am–2:30pm; Mon–Thurs 5:30–9:30pm; Fri–Sat 5:30–10pm; Sun 9am–2:30pm.

**Hyman's Seafood Company Restaurant** ⚐ SEAFOOD   Hyman's was established a century ago and honors old-fashioned traditions. The building sprawls over most of a city block in the heart of Charleston's business district. Inside are at least six dining rooms and a take-away deli loaded with salmon, lox, and smoked herring, all displayed in the style of the great kosher delis of New York City. One sit-down section is devoted to deli-style sandwiches, chicken soup, and salads; another to a delectably messy choice of fish, shellfish, lobsters, and oysters. We can ignore the endorsement of now-deceased Senator Strom Thurmond, but we take more seriously the praise of such big-time foodies as Barbra, Oprah, and Baryshnikov.

215 Meeting St. ✆ 843/723-6000. Lunch $5–$10; seafood dinners and platters $9–$23. AE, DC, DISC, MC, V. Daily 11am–11pm.

**Jestine's** SOUTHERN/SOUL FOOD   When the tourist board is asked "for a native place to eat," they most often send visitors here for some real Low Country flavors. This restaurant was named after the cook and housekeeper who reared the founder of the restaurant, Shera Lee Berlin. All of Jestine's recipes have been preserved to delight a new generation of diners who like to feast on such local favorites as country-fried steak, okra gumbo, fried chicken, shrimp

Creole, fried oyster po' boys, country cream corn, black-eyed peas, and blueberry cobbler. There is a daily blue-plate special, and even a green-plate special for vegetarians. If you ever wondered what "red rice" is, ask for it here. The "table wine" is actually sugary tea in tumblers.

251 Meeting St. ℂ **843/722-7224.** No reservations accepted. Main courses $7.95–$13. AE, DC, DISC, MC, V. Tues–Thurs 11am–9:30pm; Fri–Sat 11am–10pm; Sun 11am–9pm. Closed Dec 25 and Jewish holidays.

**Sermet's Corner** ⋆ *Finds* MEDITERRANEAN/ITALIAN   With its large windows overlooking a bustling intersection, its good and modestly priced food, and its fun atmosphere, this discovery attracts a young crowd. Fresh, informal, and healthy, the cuisine contains any number of delightful dishes, including imaginative soups, appetizers, and salads. Try the cold cucumber with yogurt soup; or a crabmeat-stuffed portobello mushroom topped with a roasted pepper, scallion, and lavender sauce. Or go for the savory shrimp, crawfish, and scallops with sun-dried tomatoes; or the grilled seafood cakes in a Sambuca sauce. A special treat is walnut-encrusted salmon with a ginger-flavored butternut squash. Most dishes are at the lower end of the price scale. Live jazz is heard on the mezzanine Tuesday to Saturday from 5pm to 2am.

276 King St. ℂ **843/853-7775.** Main courses $11–$17. AE, MC, V. Daily 11am–10pm.

## 5 Exploring Charleston

We always head for the **Battery** (officially, the White Point Gardens) to get into the feel of this city. It's right on the end of the peninsula, facing the Cooper River and the harbor. It has a landscaped park, shaded by palmettos and live oaks, with walkways lined with old monuments and other war relics. The view toward the harbor goes out to Fort Sumter. We like to walk along the seawall on East Battery and Murray Boulevard and slowly absorb the Charleston ambience.

Before you go, contact the **Charleston Area Convention and Visitors Bureau** (**CACVB;** ℂ **800/774-0006** or 843/853-8000; www.charlestoncvb.com) for information on tours, attractions, and special events.

*Note:* You can visit six of the attractions listed in this section by buying a **Heritage Passport ticket** for $40 ($23 children). The ticket provides admission to Middleton Place, Drayton Hall, the Nathaniel Russell House, the Gibbes Museum, the Aiken-Rhett House, and the Edmondston-Alston House. You can purchase a ticket at the main CACVB branch, 375 Meeting St. (Mon–Fri 8:30am–5pm), or at the attractions themselves.

## THE TOP ATTRACTIONS
### A CONFEDERATE FORT & A SUBMARINE

**Fort Sumter National Monument** ⋆⋆⋆   It was here that the first shot of the Civil War was fired on April 12, 1861. Confederate forces launched a 34-hour bombardment of the fort. Union forces eventually surrendered, and the Rebels occupied federal ground that became a symbol of Southern resistance. This action, however, led to a declaration of war in Washington. Amazingly, Confederate troops held onto Sumter for nearly 4 years, although it was almost continually bombarded by the Yankees. When evacuation finally came, the fort was nothing but a heap of rubble.

Park rangers today are on hand to answer your questions, and you can explore gun emplacements and visit a small museum filled with artifacts related to the siege. A complete tour of the fort, conducted daily from 9am to 5pm, takes about 2 hours.

Though you can travel to the fort via your own boat, most people take the tour of the fort and harbor offered by **Fort Sumter Tours,** 360 Concord St., Suite 201 (© **843/722-1691**). You can board at either of two locations: Liberty Square in downtown Charleston; or Mount Pleasant's Patriots Point, the site of the world's largest naval and maritime museum. Sailing times change every month or so, but from March to Labor Day, there generally are three sailings per day from each location, beginning at 9:30 or 10:45am. Winter sailings are more curtailed. Call for details. Each departure point offers ample parking, and the boats that carry you to Fort Sumter are sightseeing yachts built for the purpose; they're clean, safe, and equipped with modern conveniences.

In Charleston Harbor. © **843/883-3123.** www.spiritcruises.com. Admission to fort free; boat trip $12 adults, $11 seniors, $6 children 6–11, free for children 5 and under.

*H.L. Hunley* **Confederate Submarine** ✦✦✦ One of the greatest and most sought-after artifacts in the history of naval warfare can now be viewed by the public. The Confederate submarine *H.L. Hunley,* a hand-cranked vessel fashioned of locomotive boilers, sank the Union blockade vessel USS *Housatonic* in February of 1864. The sinking of the Union ship launched the age of submarine warfare. The submarine and its nine-member crew mysteriously vanished off Sullivan's Island shortly after completing its historic mission. The vessel was finally located in 1995, sparking headlines across the world. The submarine was eventually raised and brought to the old Charleston Navy Base for preservation. The bones of its crew members were buried in a historic ceremony on April 17, 2004, at the Magnolia Cemetery. The sub, which rests in a tank of 50°F water, can only be visited weekends on 20-minute tours.

Warren Lasch Conservation Center, 1250 Supply St., Building 255, North Charleston. © **866/866-9938** or **888/202-3849.** www.hunley.org. Admission $12, free for children 5 and under. Sat 9am–5pm; Sun noon–5pm.

## HISTORIC HOMES

**Aiken-Rhett House** ✦✦✦ There is no better insight into antebellum life than that provided by the Aiken-Rhett House, built by merchant John Robinson in 1818 and greatly expanded by Governor and Mrs. William Aiken in the 1830s and 1850s. The property still looks as it did in 1858, 2 years before the outbreak of the Civil War. From Europe the governor and his lady brought back crystal and bronze chandeliers, classical sculpture and paintings, and antiques with which to furnish the elegant abode. Original outbuildings include the kitchens, slave quarters, stables, privies, and cattle sheds.

48 Elizabeth St. © **843/723-1159.** Admission $8. Mon–Sat 10am–5pm; Sun 2–5pm.

**Edmondston-Alston House** ✦✦✦ On High Battery, an elegant section of Charleston, this house (built in 1825 by Charles Edmondston, a Charleston merchant and wharf owner) was one of the earliest constructed in the city in the late Federal style. Edmondston sold it to Charles Alston, a Low Country rice planter, who modified it in Greek Revival style. The house has remained in the Alston family, which opens the first two floors to visitors. Inside are heirloom furnishings, silver, and paintings. It was here in 1861 that General Beauregard joined the Alston family to watch the bombardment of Fort Sumter. Gen. Robert E. Lee once found refuge here when his hotel uptown caught on fire.

21 E. Battery. © **843/722-7171.** Admission $10. Guided tours Tues–Sat 10am–4:30pm; Sun 1:30–4:30pm; Mon noon–4:30pm.

**Nathaniel Russell House** ✦✦✦ One of America's finest examples of Federal architecture, this 1808 house was completed by Nathaniel Russell, one of

# Charleston Sights

Aiken-Rhett House **2**

Charleston Ballet Theatre **3**

The Charleston Museum **4**

Charleston Symphony Orchestra **5**

The Citadel **1**

Dock Street Theatre **8**

Edmondston-Alston House **15**

Fort Sumter National Monument **14**

French Huguenot Church **9**

The Gibbes Museum of Art **7**

The Heyward-Washington House **12**

*H.L. Hunley* Confederate Submarine **18**

Joseph Manigault House **4**

Nathaniel Russell House **13**

Old City Market **6**

Old Exchange & Provost Dungeon **10**

South Carolina Aquarium **17**

St. Michael's Episcopal Church **11**

White Point Gardens **16**

Charleston's richest merchants. It is celebrated architecturally for its "free-flying" staircase, spiraling unsupported for three floors. The staircase's elliptical shape is repeated throughout the house. The interiors are ornate with period furnishings, especially the elegant music room with its golden harp and neoclassical-style sofa.

51 Meeting St. (✆ 843/724-8481. www.historiccharleston.org. Admission $8, free for children under 6. Guided tours Mon–Sat 10am–5pm; Sun and holidays 2–5pm.

**The Heyward-Washington House** ★★★    In a district of Charleston called Cabbage Row, this 1772 house was built by Daniel Heyward, called "the rice king," and was the setting for Dubose Heyward's *Porgy.* It was also the home of Thomas Heyward, Jr., a signer of the Declaration of Independence. President George Washington bedded down here in 1791. Many of the fine period pieces in the house are the work of Thomas Elfe, one of America's most famous cabinetmakers. The restored 18th-century kitchen is the only historic kitchen in the city that is open to the public. It stands behind the main house, along with the servants' quarters and the garden.

87 Church St. (between Tradd and Broad sts.). (✆ 843/722-0354. Admission $8 adults, $4 children 3–12; combination ticket to the Charleston Museum and Joseph Manigault House $18 adults. Mon–Sat 10am–5pm; Sun 1–5pm. Tours leave every half-hour until 4:30pm.

**Joseph Manigault House** ★    This 1803 Adams-style residence, a National Historic Landmark, was a wealthy rice planter's home. The house features a curving central staircase and an outstanding collection of Charlestonian, American, English, and French period furnishings. It's located diagonally across from the visitor center.

350 Meeting St. (at John St.). (✆ 843/723-2926. Admission $8 adults, $4 children 3–12; combination ticket to the Heyward-Washington House and Charleston Museum $18 adults. Mon–Sat 10am–5pm; Sun 1–5pm. Last tour is at 4:30pm.

## NEARBY PLANTATIONS

**Middleton Place** ★★★    This was the home of Henry Middleton, president of the First Continental Congress, whose son, Arthur, was a signer of the Declaration of Independence. Today, this National Historic Landmark includes America's oldest landscaped gardens, the Middleton Place House, and the Plantation Stableyards.

The gardens, begun in 1741, reflect the elegant symmetry of European gardens of that period. Ornamental lakes, terraces, and plantings of camellias, azaleas, magnolias, and crape myrtle accent the grand design.

The Middleton Place House itself was built in 1755, but in 1865, all but the south flank was ransacked and burned by Union troops. The house was restored in the 1870s as a family residence and today houses collections of fine silver, furniture, rare first editions by Catesby and Audubon, and portraits by Benjamin West and Thomas Sully. In the stable yards, craftspeople demonstrate life on a plantation of yesteryear. There are also horses, mules, hogs, cows, sheep, and goats.

A plantation lunch is served at the **Middleton Place Restaurant,** which is a replica of an original rice mill. *American Way* magazine cited this restaurant as one of the top 10 representing American cuisine at its best. Specialties include she-crab soup, hoppin' John and ham biscuits, okra gumbo, Sea Island shrimp, and corn pudding. Service is daily from 11am to 3pm. Dinner is served daily 5 to 9pm, and is likely to include panned (pan-seared) quail with ham (a recipe from famed chef Edna Lewis, who was a consultant-in-residence here for years), sea scallops, or broiled oysters. For dinner reservations, call (✆ **843/556-6020.**

Ashley River Rd. (©) 843/556-6020. www.middletonplace.org. Admission to gardens $20 adults, free for children 15 and under. Tour of house additional $10 adults, $6 children 6–12. Gardens and stable yards daily 9am–5pm; house Mon noon–4:30pm, Tues–Sun 10am–4:30pm. Take U.S. 17 W. to S.C. 61 (Ashley River Rd.) 14 miles northwest of Charleston.

## Magnolia Plantation ★★★

Ten generations of the Drayton family have lived here continuously since the 1670s. They haven't had much luck keeping a roof over their heads; the first mansion burned just after the Revolution, and the second was set afire by General Sherman. But you can't call the replacement modern. A simple, pre-Revolutionary house was barged down from Summerville and set on the basement foundations of its unfortunate predecessors.

The house has been filled with museum-quality Early American furniture, appraised to exceed $500,000 in value. An art gallery has been added to the house as well.

The flowery gardens of camellias and azaleas—among the most beautiful in America—reach their peak bloom in March and April but are colorful year-round. You can tour the house, the gardens (including an herb garden, horticultural maze, topiary garden, and biblical garden), a petting zoo, and a waterfowl refuge, or walk or bike through wildlife trails.

Other sights include an antebellum cabin that was restored and furnished, a plantation rice barge on display beside the Ashley River, and a Nature Train that carries guests on a 45-minute ride around the plantation's perimeter.

Low Country wildlife is visible in marsh, woodland, and swamp settings. The **Audubon Swamp Garden,** also on the grounds, is an independently operated 60-acre cypress swamp that offers a close look at other wildlife, such as egrets, alligators, wood ducks, otters, turtles, and herons.

S.C. 61. (©) 800/367-3517 or 843/571-1266. www.magnoliaplantation.com. Admission to garden and grounds $13 adults, $12 seniors, $7 children 13–19, free for children under 6. Tour of plantation house is an additional $7 for ages 6 and up; children under 6 not allowed to tour the house. Admission to Audubon Swamp Garden $5 adults and seniors, $5 children 13–19, $3 children 6–12. Magnolia Plantation and Audubon Swamp Gardens summer daily 8am–5:30pm; winter daily 10am–5pm.

## Drayton Hall ★★

This is one of the oldest surviving plantations, built in 1738 and owned by the Drayton family until 1974. Framed by majestic live oaks, the Georgian-Palladian house is a property of the National Trust for Historic Preservation. Its hand-carved woodwork and plasterwork represent New World craftsmanship at its finest. Because such modern elements as electricity, plumbing, and central heating have never put in an appearance, the house is much as it was in its early years; in fact, it is displayed unfurnished.

Old Ashley River Rd. (S.C. 61). (©) 843/766-0188. www.draytonhall.org. Admission $12 adults, $8 children 12–18, $6 children 6–11; included in Passport Ticket (see "Exploring Charleston," above). Mar–Oct daily 10am–4pm, with tours on the hour; Nov–Feb daily 9:30am–3pm. Closed Thanksgiving Day and Dec 25. Take U.S. 17 S. to S.C. 61; it's 9 miles northwest of Charleston.

## Boone Hall Plantation & Gardens

This unique plantation is approached by a famous **Avenue of Oaks ★★★**, huge old moss-draped trees planted in 1743 by Captain Thomas Boone. The first floor of the plantation house is elegantly furnished and open to the public. Outbuildings include the circular smokehouse and slave cabins constructed of bricks made on the plantation. A large grove of pecan trees lies behind the house. Note that Boone Hall is not an original structure, but a replica; die-hard history purists may be disappointed in the plantation house, but the grounds are stunning and very much worth visiting.

1235 Long Point Rd. (U.S. 17/701), Mt. Pleasant. (©) 843/884-4371. www.boonehallplantation.com. Admission $15 adults, $13 seniors 55 and over, $7 children 6–12. Apr to Labor Day Mon–Sat 8:30am–6pm, Sun

1–5pm; day after Labor Day to Mar Mon–Sat 9am–5pm, Sun 1–4pm. Take U.S. 17/701 9 miles north of Charleston.

## SPECTACULAR GARDENS

See also the listing for Magnolia Plantation in "Nearby Plantations," above.

**Cypress Gardens** ★★   This 163-acre swamp garden was used as a freshwater reserve for Dean Hall, a huge Cooper River rice plantation, and was given to the city in 1963. Today, the giant cypress trees draped with Spanish moss provide an unforgettable setting for flat-bottom boats that glide among their knobby roots. Footpaths in the garden wind through a profusion of azaleas, camellias, daffodils, and other colorful blooms. Visitors share the swamp with alligators, pileated woodpeckers, wood ducks, otters, barred owls, and other abundant species. The gardens are worth a visit at any time of year, but they're at their most colorful in March and April. Also on-site are a reptile center, aquarium, and aviary, plus a butterfly house.

U.S. 52, Moncks Corner. ✆ 843/553-0515. www.cypressgardens.org. $9 adults, $8 seniors, $3 children 6–12, free for children 5 and under. Daily 9am–5pm. Closed major holidays. Take U.S. 52 some 24 miles north of Charleston.

## MUSEUMS

**The Charleston Museum** ★★   The Charleston Museum, founded in 1773, is the first and oldest museum in America. The collections preserve and interpret the social and natural history of Charleston and the South Carolina coastal region. The full-scale replica of the famed Confederate submarine *Hunley* standing outside the museum is one of the most-photographed subjects in the city. The museum also exhibits the largest silver collection in Charleston; early crafts; historic relics; and the "Discover Me" room, which has hands-on exhibits for children.

360 Meeting St. ✆ 843/722-2996. www.charlestonmuseum.org. Admission $9 adults, $4 children 3–12. Combination ticket to the Joseph Manigault House and Heyward-Washington House $18 adults, $4 children. Mon–Sat 9am–5pm; Sun 1–5pm.

**The Gibbes Museum of Art** ★   Established in 1905 by the Carolina Art Association, the Gibbes Museum contains an intriguing collection of prints and drawings from the 18th century to the present. On display are landscapes, genre scenes, panoramic views of Charleston harbor, and portraits of South Carolinians (see *Thomas Middleton* by Benjamin West, *Charles Izard Manigault* by Thomas Sully, or *John C. Calhoun* by Rembrandt Peale). The museum's collection of some 400 miniature portraits ranks as one of the most comprehensive in the country.

The Wallace Exhibit has 10 rooms, eight replicated from historic American buildings and two from classic French styles. Styles range from the plain dining room of a sea captain's house on Martha's Vineyard to the elegant drawing room of Charleston's historic Nathaniel Russell House (see "Historic Homes," above).

135 Meeting St. ✆ 843/722-2706. www.gibbesmuseum.org. Admission $7 adults; $6 seniors, students, and military; $4 children 6–18; free for children under 6; included in Passport Ticket (see "Exploring Charleston," earlier in this chapter). Tues–Sat 10am–5pm; Sun 1–5pm. Closed Mon and holidays.

## MORE ATTRACTIONS

**Charles Towne Landing** ★★★   This 663-acre park is located on the site of the first 1670 settlement. Underground exhibits show the colony's history, and the park features a re-creation of a small village. You can rent a bike for $3 an hour. Because trade was such an important part of colonial life, a full-scale reproduction of the 17th-century trading vessel *Adventure* is an excellent addition to the site. After touring the ship, you can step into the Settler's Life Area

## Frommer's Favorite Charleston Experiences

**Playing Scarlett & Rhett at Boone Hall.** Over in Mount Pleasant, you can pretend that you're one of the romantic figures in Margaret Mitchell's *Gone With the Wind* by paying a visit to this 738-acre estate, a cotton plantation settled by Major John Boone in 1681. It was used for background shots in the films *Gone With the Wind* and *North and South*.

**Going Back to Colonial Days.** At Charles Towne Landing, you get insight into how colonists lived 300 years ago, when they established the first English settlement in South Carolina. A visit here features hands-on activities. Even the animals that the settlers encountered, from bears to bison, roam about. You can also enjoy 80 acres of gardens by walking or bicycling along the marsh and lagoons.

**A Walk into the Past.** With its architecturally gracious and historic buildings and its magnificent gardens, Charleston has more of the charm and flavor of the Old South than any other American city. There's nothing finer than wandering at random and discovering the historic core of this remarkable city block by intriguing block.

and view a 17th-century crop garden where rice, indigo, and cotton were grown. There's no flashy theme-park atmosphere here: What you see as you walk under huge old oaks, past freshwater lagoons, and through the Animal Forest (with the same species that lived here in 1670) is what those early settlers saw.

1500 Old Towne Rd. (S.C. 171, between U.S. 17 and I-126). (©) 843/852-4200. www.discoversouthcarolina. com. Admission $5 adults, $3.75 seniors, $3 children 6–15, free for those with disabilities. Daily 8:30am–5pm. Closed Dec 24–25.

**The Citadel** ⋆    The all-male (at that time) Citadel was established in 1842 as an arsenal and a refuge for whites in the event of a slave uprising. In 1922, it moved to its present location. Pat Conroy's novel *The Lords of Discipline* is based on his 4 years at the school. Since 1995, when the first woman notoriously joined the ranks of cadets, women now join the ranks with young men. The campus of this military college features buildings of Moorish design, with crenellated battlements and sentry towers. It is especially interesting to visit on Friday, when the college is in session and the public is invited to a precision-drill parade on the quadrangle at 3:45pm. For a history of the Citadel, stop at the **Citadel Memorial Archives Museum** ((©) 843/953-6846).

Moultrie St. and Elmwood Ave. (©) 843/953-3294. www.citadel.edu. Free admission. Daily 24 hr. for drive-through visits; museum Sun–Fri 2–5pm, Sat noon–5pm. Closed religious, national, and school holidays.

**Old Exchange and Provost Dungeon** ⋆    This is a stop that many visitors overlook, but it's one of the three most important Colonial buildings in the United States because of its role as a prison during the American Revolution. In 1873, the building became City Hall. You'll find a large collection of antique chairs, supplied by the local Daughters of the American Revolution, each of whom brought a chair here from home in 1921.

122 E. Bay St. (©) 843/727-2165. www.oldexchange.com. Admission $7 adults, $3.50 children 7–12. Daily 9am–5pm. Closed Thanksgiving Day and Dec 23–25.

**Fort Moultrie**    Only a palmetto-log fortification at the time of the American Revolution, the half-completed fort was attacked by a British fleet in 1776. Colonel William Moultrie's troops repelled the invasion in one of the first decisive American victories of the Revolution. The fort was subsequently enlarged into a five-sided structure with earth-and-timber walls 17 feet high. The British didn't do it in, but an 1804 hurricane ripped it apart. By the War of 1812, it was back and ready for action. Osceola, the fabled leader of the Seminoles in Florida, was incarcerated at the fort and eventually died here. During the 1830s, Edgar Allen Poe served as a soldier at the fort. He set his famous short story "The Gold Bug" on Sullivan's Island. The fort also played roles in the Civil War, the Mexican War, the Spanish-American War, and even in the two World Wars, but by 1947, it had retired from action.

1214 Middle St., on Sullivan's Island. © 843/883-3123. Admission $3 adults, $1 seniors over 62, $5 family, free for children under 15. Federal Recreation Passports honored. Daily 9am–5pm. Closed Christmas Day and New Year's Day. Take S.C. 703 from Mt. Pleasant to Sullivan's Island.

**South Carolina Aquarium**  ☆   Visitors can explore Southern aquatic life in an attraction filled with thousands of enchanting creatures and plants in amazing habitats, from five major regions of the Appalachian Watershed. Jutting into the Charleston Harbor for 2,000 feet, the focal point at this attraction, which opened in 2000, is a 93,000-square-foot aquarium featuring a two-story Great Ocean Tank Exhibition. Contained within are more than 800 animals, including deadly sharks but also sea turtles and stingrays. Every afternoon at 4pm the aquarium offers a dolphin program, where bottle-nosed dolphins can be viewed from an open-air terrace. One of the most offbeat exhibits replicates a blackwater swamp, with atmospheric fog, a spongy floor, and twinkling lights. The newest attraction here is called **Secrets of the Amazon,** which features the diversity of this endangered region in sights, sounds, and adventure. You'll meet such creatures as a giant green anaconda, poison dart frogs, four-eyed fish, and flesh-devouring piranhas.

100 Aquarium Wharf. © 843/720-1990. www.scaquarium.org. Admission $15 adults, $13 students 13–17 and seniors 60 and over, $8 children 3–12, free for children under 2. Apr 1–Aug 15 Mon–Sat 9am–6pm, Sun noon–6pm; Aug 16–Mar 31 Mon–Sat 9am–5pm, Sun noon–5pm.

## ESPECIALLY FOR KIDS

For more than 300 years, Charleston has been the home of pirates, patriots, and presidents. Your child can see firsthand the **Great Hall at the Old Exchange,** where President Washington danced; view the **Provost Dungeons,** where South Carolina patriots spent their last days; and touch the last remaining structural evidence of the **Charleston Seawall.** Children will take special delight in **Charles Towne Landing** and **Middleton Place.** At **Fort Sumter,** they can see where the Civil War began. Children will also enjoy **Magnolia Plantation,** with its Audubon Swamp Garden.

Kids and Navy vets will also love the aircraft carrier **USS *Yorktown,*** at Patriots Point, 2 miles east of the Cooper River Bridge. Its World War II, Korean, and Vietnam exploits are documented in exhibits, and general naval history is illustrated through models of ships, planes, and weapons. You can wander through the bridge wheelhouse, flight and hangar decks, chapel, and sick bay, and view the film *The Fighting Lady,* which depicts life aboard the carrier. Also at Patriots Point are the World War II destroyer *Laffey;* the World War II submarine *Clamagore;* and the cutter *Ingham.* Patriots Point is open daily from 9am to 6pm April to October, until 5pm November to March. Admission is $14 for adults, $12 for seniors over 62 and military personnel in uniform, $7 for kids 6 to 11. Adjacent is the fine 18-hole public Patriots Point Golf Course. For further information, call © 843/884-2727 or visit www.patriotspoint.org.

## 6 Organized Tours

**BY HORSE & CARRIAGE**   The **Old South Carriage,** 14 Anson St. (© 843/577-0042;** www.oldsouthcarriagetours.com), offers narrated horse-drawn-carriage tours through the historic district daily from 9am to dusk. A 1-hour carriage tour goes for 2½ miles, covering 30 blocks of the historic district. The cost is $19 for adults, $8 for children 3 to 11.

**BY MULE TEAM**   **Palmetto Carriage Tours,** 40 N. Market St., at Guignard Street (© 843/723-8145), uses mule teams instead of the usual horse and carriage for its guided tours of Old Charleston. Tours originate at the Big Red Barn behind the Rainbow Market. The cost is $17 for adults and seniors, and $8 for children 4 to 11. Daily 9am to 5pm.

**BY BOAT**   **Fort Sumter Tours/Spiritline Cruises,** 360 Concord St., Suite 201 (© 800/789-3678), offers a **Harbor and Fort Sumter Tour** by boat, departing daily from the City Marina and from the Patriots Point Maritime Museum. This is the only tour to stop at Fort Sumter, target of the opening shots of the Civil War. Rates are adults $12, seniors $11, children 6 to 11 $6, children under 6 free. The operator also has an interesting **Charleston Harbor Tour,** with daily departures from Patriots Point. The 2-hour cruise passes the Battery, Charleston Port, Castle Pinckney, Drum Island, Fort Sumter, and the aircraft carrier *Yorktown,* and sails under the Cooper River Bridge and on to other sights. Prices are the same as those for Fort Sumter Tours.

**WALKING TOURS**   One of the best offbeat walking tours of Charleston is the **Charleston Tea Party Walking Tour** (© 843/577-5896). It lasts 2 hours and costs $15 for adults or $7 for children up to age 12. Departing year-round Monday to Saturday at 9:30am and 2pm, tours originate at the Kings Courtyard Inn, 198 Kings St. The tour goes into a lot of nooks and crannies of Charleston, including secret courtyards and gardens. Finally, you get that promised tea. Reservations are required.

The embattled city of Charleston during one of the worst phases in its history comes alive again on the **Civil War Walking Tour,** conducted daily at 9am by a guide well versed in the lore of "The War of Northern Aggression." You can stroll down cobblestone streets and listen to firsthand accounts and anecdotes of Charleston during its years of siege by Union troops. Tours depart March to December, daily at 9am from the Mills House Hotel lobby at 115 Meeting St. Adults pay $17, and children 12 and under go free. Call Jack Thomson at © 843/722-7033 for more information; reservations are appreciated.

Tours of Charleston's 18th-century **architecture** in the original walled city begin at 10am and 2pm, and tours of 19th-century architecture along Meeting Street and the Battery begin at 2pm. Departures are from in front of the Meeting Street Inn, 173 Meeting St. Tours last 2 hours and are given every day but Tuesday and Sunday. The 9am tour covers 18th-century architecture; the 2pm tour encompasses the 19th century. The cost is $15 (free for children 12 and under). For reservations, call © 843/893-2327.

## 7 Beaches & Outdoor Pursuits

**BEACHES**    Three great beaches are within a 25-minute drive of the center of Charleston.

In the West Islands, **Folly Beach,** which had degenerated into a tawdry Coney Island–type amusement park, is making a comeback following a multi-million-dollar cleanup, but it remains the least-pristine beach in the area. The best bathroom amenities are located here, however. At the western end of the island is the **Folly Beach County Park,** with bathrooms, parking, and shelter from the rain. To get here, take U.S. 17 East to S.C. 171 South to Folly Beach.

In the East Cooper area, both the **Isle of Palms** and **Sullivan's Island** offer miles of public beaches, mostly bordered by beachfront homes. Windsurfing and jet-skiing are popular here. Take U.S. 17 East to S.C. 703 (Ben Sawyer Blvd.). S.C. 703 continues through Sullivan's Island to the Isle of Palms.

**Kiawah Island** has the area's most pristine beach—far preferable to Folly Beach, to our tastes—and draws a more upmarket crowd. The best beachfront is at **Beachwalker County Park,** on the southern end of the island. Get there before noon on weekends; the limited parking is usually gone by then. Canoe rentals are available for use on the Kiawah River, and the park offers not only a boardwalk but also bathrooms, showers, and a changing area. Take U.S. 17 East to S.C. 171 South (Folly Beach Rd.), turn right onto S.C. 700 Southwest (Maybank Hwy.) to Bohicket Road, which turns into Betsy Kerrigan Parkway. Where Betsy Kerrigan Parkway dead-ends, turn left on Kiawah Parkway, which takes you to the island.

For details on the major resorts on Kiawah Island and the Isle of Palms, see "Kiawah Island & the Isle of Palms," later in this chapter.

**BIKING**    Charleston is basically flat and relatively free of traffic, except on its main arteries at rush hour. Therefore, biking is a popular local pastime and relatively safe. Many of the city parks have biking trails. Your best bet for rentals is **The Bicycle Shoppe,** 280 Meeting St. (© 843/722-8168), which rents bikes for $5 per hour or $20 for a full day. A credit-card imprint is required as a deposit.

**BOATING**    A true Charlestonian is as much at home on the sea as on land. Sailing local waters is a popular family pastime. One of the best places for rentals is **Wild Dunes Yacht Harbor,** Isle of Palms (© 843/886-0209), where 16-foot boats, big enough for four people, rent for around $185 for 4 hours, plus fuel. A larger pontoon boat, big enough for 10, goes for about $360 for 4 hours, plus fuel.

**DIVING**    Several outfitters provide rentals and ocean charters, as well as instruction for neophytes. At **Atlantic Coast Diving,** 426 W. Coleman Blvd., Mt. Pleasant (© 843/884-1500), you can rent both diving and snorkeling equipment. Diving equipment costs $40 per day. It's open Monday to Saturday from 10am to 6pm.

**FISHING**    Freshwater fishing charters are available year-round along the Low Country's numerous creeks and inlets. The waterways are filled with flounder, trout, spot-tail, and channel bass. Some of the best striped-bass fishing available in America can be found at nearby Lake Moultrie.

Offshore-fishing charters for reef fishing (where you'll find fish such as cobia, black sea bass, and king mackerel) and for the Gulf Stream (where you fish for sailfish, marlin, wahoo, dolphin, and tuna) are also available. Both types of charters can be arranged at the previously recommended **Wild Dunes Yacht Harbor,** Isle of Palms (© **843/886-5100**). A fishing craft holding up to six people rents for $600 to $750 for 6 hours, including everything but food and drink. Reservations must be made 24 hours in advance.

**Folly Beach Fishing Pier** at Folly Beach is a wood pier, 25 feet wide, that extends 1,045 feet into the Atlantic Ocean. Facilities include restrooms, a tackle shop, and a restaurant. It's accessible to people with disabilities.

**GOLF**    Charleston is said to be the home of golf in America. Charlestonians have been playing the game since the 1700s, when the first golf clubs arrived from Scotland. With 17 public and private courses in the city, there's a golf game waiting for every buff.

**Wild Dunes Resort,** Isle of Palms (© **888/798-1876** or 843/886-6000; www.wilddunes.com), offers two championship golf courses designed by Tom Fazio. **The Links** ★★★ is a 6,722-yard, par-72 layout that takes the player through marshlands, over or into huge sand dunes, through a wooded alley, and into a pair of oceanfront finishing holes once called "the greatest east of Pebble Beach, California." The course opened in 1980 and has been ranked among the 100 greatest courses in the United States by *Golf Digest* and among the top 100 in the world by *Golf Magazine. Golf Digest* has also ranked the Links as the 13th-greatest resort course in America. **The Harbor Course** offers 6,402 yards of Low Country marsh and Intracoastal Waterway views. This par-70 layout is considered to be target golf, challenging players with 2 holes that play from one island to another across Morgan Creek. Greens fees at these courses can range from $60 to $165, depending on the season. Clubs can be rented at either course for $25 for 18 holes, and professional instruction costs $85 for a 1-hour session. Both courses are open daily from 7am to 6pm year-round.

Your best bet, if you'd like to play at any of the other Charleston-area golf courses, is to contact **Charleston Golf, Inc.** (© **800/774-4444;** www.charlestongolfguide.com; Mon–Fri 8:30am–5pm). The company represents 20 golf courses, offering packages that range from $100 to $150 per person March to August. Off-season packages range from $75 to $110 per person. Prices include greens fees on one course, a hotel room based on double occupancy, and taxes. Travel pros here will customize your vacation with golf-course selections and tee times; they can also arrange rental cars and airfares. Reservations must be made 1 week in advance.

**HIKING**    The most interesting hiking trails begin around Buck Hall in **Francis Marion National Forest** (© **843/887-3257**), located some 40 miles north of the center of Charleston via U.S. 52. The site consists of 250,000 acres of swamps, with towering oaks and pines. Also in the national forest, **Buck Hall Recreation,** reached by U.S. 17/701 North from Charleston, has 15 camping sites ($15–$20 per night), plus a boat ramp and fishing. Other hiking trails are at **Edisto Beach State Park,** State Cabin Road, on Edisto Island (© **843/869-2156**).

**HORSEBACK RIDING**    One of the best riding stables in South Carolina is found at **M&M Farms,** 1859 Hoover Rd., Huger (© **843/336-5700**). These outfitters offer daily trail rides in the Francis Marion National Forest for $25; rides last 1 hour and depart daily at 10am, noon, 2pm, and 4pm. The stables lie only a 20-minute drive from Charleston. Call for directions.

**TENNIS**    Charlestonians have been playing tennis since the early 1800s. The **Charleston Tennis Center,** 19 Farmfield Ave. (2 miles west of Charleston on U.S. 17; © **843/724-7402**), is your best bet, with 15 well-maintained outdoor courts lighted for night play. The cost is only $3.50 per person per hour of court time. The center is open Monday to Thursday from 8:30am to 9pm, on Friday from 8:30am to 7pm, on Saturday from 9am to 3pm, and on Sunday from 10am to 6pm.

## 8 Shopping

**King Street** is lined with many special shops and boutiques. The **Shops at Charleston Place,** 130 Market St., is an upscale complex of top designer-clothing shops (Gucci, Jaeger, Ralph Lauren, and so on). The historic **Old City Market,** which sprawls across four buildings from Meeting Street to East Bay Street, offers local crafts (including traditional sweetgrass baskets, an art form brought over from Africa by slaves in the 19th century), antiques, jewelry, tapestries, and even local foodstuffs. The lively **State Street Market,** just down from the City Market, is another cluster of shops and restaurants.

### ART

**Gallery Chuma**   With some 2,900 square feet of exhibition space, this is the largest African-American art gallery in the South. The original pieces change every 2 months. On permanent display are the works of prominent artists, including Dr. Leo Twiggs and historical artist Joe Pinckney (prints only). Hours are Monday to Saturday 10am to 6pm. 43 John St. ℃ **843/722-8224.**

**Lowcountry Artists**   In a former book bindery, this gallery is operated by eight local artists, who work in oil, watercolor, drawings, collage, woodcuts, and other media. Hours are Monday to Saturday 10am to 5pm, Sunday noon to 5pm. 148 E. Bay St. ℃ **843/577-9295.**

**Waterfront Gallery**   Facing Waterfront Park, this gallery is the premier choice for the work of South Carolina artists. The works of 21 local artists are presented. For sale are pieces ranging from sculpture to oils. Hours are Monday to Thursday 11am to 6pm, Friday to Saturday 11am to 10pm, Sunday noon to 5pm. 215 E. Bay St. (across from Custom House). ℃ **843/722-1155.**

**Wells Gallery**   Works by artists from the Low Country and all over the Southeast are on display at this Charleston gallery. Specializing in Low Country landscapes, the gallery also offers works by artists from all over the U.S. Prices range from $600 to $12,000. Hours are Monday to Saturday 10am to 5pm. 103 Broad St. ℃ **843/853-3233.**

### ANTIQUES

**George C. Birlant and Co.**   If you're in the market for 18th- and 19th-century English antique furnishings, this is the right place. This Charleston staple prides itself on its Charleston Battery Bench, which is seen (and sat upon) throughout the Battery. The heavy iron sides are cast from the original 1880 mold, and the slats are authentic South Carolina cypress. It's as close to the original as you can get. Hours are Monday to Saturday 9am to 5:30pm. 191 King St. ℃ **843/722-3842.**

**Livingston Antiques**   For nearly a quarter of a century, discriminating antiques hunters have patronized the showroom of this dealer. Both authentic antiques and fool-the-eye reproductions are sold. If you're interested, the staff will direct you to the shop's 30,000-square-foot warehouse on West Ashley. Hours are Monday to Saturday 10am to 5pm. 163 King St. ℃ **843/723-9697.**

## BOOKS

**Preservation Society of Charleston Bookstore**   Near Queen Street in the historic district, this shop features a collection of books about Charleston and the Low Country. The outlet also sells art books, Southern literature, and even early recordings of Low Country lore told in the Gullah dialect. Local handcrafts, art prints, and the acclaimed architectural drawings of Jim Polzois are featured among the merchandise. Hours are Monday to Saturday 10am to 5pm. 147 King St. © **843/722-4630.**

## CANDIES

**Lucas Belgian Chocolate**   This is one of the truly fine chocolatier shops in South Carolina, in business for more than 2 decades. In the historic district near Market Street, it sells imported Belgian chocolates, chocolate truffles, "turtles," and "clusters," among other mouthwatering confections. The store, in fact, features just about anything made of chocolate you might be seeking. Your purchases, incidentally, are beautifully wrapped. Hours are Tuesday to Saturday 10am to 6pm, Sunday 12:30 to 5:30pm. 73 State St. © **843/722-0461.**

## CIVIL WAR ARTIFACTS

**Sumter Military Antiques & Museum**   Relics from that "War of Northern Aggression" are sold here. You'll find a collection of authentic artifacts that range from firearms and bullets to Confederate uniforms and artillery shells and bullets. There are some interesting prints, along with a collection of books on the Civil War. By appointment only. 341 King St. © **843/577-7766.**

## CRAFTS & GIFTS

**Charleston Crafts**   This is a permanent showcase for Low Country crafts artists who work in a variety of media, including metal, glass, paper, clay, wood, and fiber. Handmade jewelry is also sold, along with basketry, leather, traditional crafts, and even homemade soaps. Hours are Monday to Saturday 10am to 5:30pm. 87 Hasell St. © **843/723-2938.**

**Clown's Bazaar**   Deanna Wagoner's heart is as big as her smile. Her store is indeed one of a kind—the city's only tax-exempt, self-help crafts organization. Originally, it was in Katmandu, Nepal, founded to help Third World families help themselves. Economic and political circumstances forced the store's relocation to Charleston, but the objective of helping Third World families hasn't changed. The store features handmade carvings, silks, brasses, and pewter from exotic locales such as Africa, Nepal, India, Bangladesh, and the Philippines, as well as wooden toys and books, including some in Gullah, a lost language that is still spoken in some areas of the city. Oh, and if you're looking for clown dolls, Deanna has those, too. Hours are Monday to Saturday 11am to 6pm, Sunday 10am to 5pm. 56 Broad St. © **843/723-9769.**

## DISHES & CRYSTAL

**Mikasa Factory Outlet Store**   You'll have to drive out of town to partake of these bargains, but at this factory outlet northwest of Charlestown in the town of Wondo, you can pick up amazing bargains in dishes and crystal. These wares are sold alongside table accessories such as napkins and place mats. Many Mikasa items represent top quality and aren't rejects or "seconds." Sometimes only a damaged carton will cause an entire shipment to be rejected, which means the other crystal and dishes are top rate with no imperfections. The little town of Wondo is the only Mikasa distribution center in America. Hours are Monday to Saturday 10am to 6pm, Sunday noon to 5pm. It's a 30-minute drive to Wondo from the center of Charleston. Take Highway 17 North to Highway 526 West, exiting at the Clements Ferry Road. Follow the signs from here. 1980 Clements Ferry Rd. © 843/856-5064.

## FASHION

**Ben Silver**    One of the finer men's clothiers in Charleston, this is the best place to get yourself dressed like a member of the city's finest society. The store specializes in blazers and buttons; it has a collection of more than 600 blazer-button designs that are unique in the city. The store features house names and designs only, so don't go looking for Ralph Lauren here. Hours are Monday to Saturday 9am to 6pm. 149 King St. © 843/577-4556.

**Nancy's**    On the main street, Nancy's specializes in clothing for the woman who wants to be both active and stylish. Complete outfits in linen, silk, and cotton are sold, along with such accessories as belts and jewelry. Hours are Monday to Saturday 10am to 5:30pm. 342 King St. © 843/722-1272.

## FURNISHINGS

**Historic Charleston Reproductions**    It's rare that a store with so much to offer could be not-for-profit, but that's the case here. All items are approved by the Historic Charleston Foundation, and all proceeds benefit the restoration of Charleston's historic projects. Licensed-replica products range from furniture to jewelry. The pride of the store is its home-furnishings collection by Baker Furniture, an esteemed company based in Michigan. What makes this collection unusual is the fact that the pieces are adaptations of real Charleston antiques, made of mahogany, a rich dark wood with an authentic feel that can only be found here.

If one of Charleston's iron designs around town has caught your eye, there's a chance that you'll find a replica of it in the form of jewelry. A collection of china from Mottahedeh is also featured. Hours are Monday to Saturday 10am to 5pm.

The store operates shops in several historic houses, and for slightly more than basic souvenirs, see its Francis Edmunds Center Museum Shop at 108 Meeting St. (© 843/724-8484). Hours are Monday to Saturday 10am to 5pm, Sunday 1 to 5pm. 105 Broad St. © 843/723-8292.

## JEWELRY

**Croghan's Jewel Box**    You'll find gift ideas for any situation, from baby showers to weddings. Estate jewelry and some contemporary pieces are featured. This store also sets diamonds for rings and pendants, and can even secure the diamond for you, with the price depending on the type of stone and grade that you choose. Hours are Monday to Friday 9:30am to 5:30pm, Saturday 10am to 5pm. 308 King St. © 843/723-3594.

**Dazzles**    One-of-a-kind jewelry is sold here, along with the finest collection of handmade 14-karat-gold slide bracelets in town. Some of the jewelry is of heirloom quality. The staff will also help you create jewelry of your own design, including a choice of stones. Hours are Monday to Wednesday 10am to 6pm, Thursday to Saturday 10am to 7pm, Sunday noon to 5pm. Charleston Place, 226 King St. © 843/722-5951.

**Geiss & Sons Jewelers**    Jewelry here is custom-designed by old-world-trained craftspeople. This is a direct offshoot of a store opened by the Geiss family in Brazil in 1919. It's an official watch dealer for names such as Rolex,

Bertolucci, and Raymond Weil. Hours are Monday to Friday 10am to 5pm. 116 E. Bay St. ℭ **843/577-4497**.

## JOGGLING BOARDS

**Old Charleston Joggling Board Co.**   Since the early 1830s, joggling boards have been a Charleston tradition. These boards are the creation of Mrs. Benjamin Kinloch Huger, a native who sought a mild form of exercise for her rheumatism. Mrs. Huger's Scottish cousins sent her a model of a joggling board, suggesting that she sit and gently bounce on the board. The fame of the device soon spread, and the board soon turned up in gardens, patios, and porches throughout the Charleston area. After World War II, joggling boards became rare because of the scarcity of timber and the high cost of labor, but the tradition was revived in 1970. The company also produces a joggle bench, a duplicate of the joggling board but only 10 feet long (as opposed to the original 16 ft.) and 20 inches from the ground. Hours are Monday to Friday 8am to 5pm. 652 King St. ℭ **843/723-4331**.

## PERFUME

**Scents of Charleston**   Favorite fragrances are found here, and prices (for the most part) are relatively reasonable. The shop evokes a perfumery in Europe. Scents creates its own exclusive brands, and also features classic and popular fragrances. Hours are Monday to Thursday 10am to 9pm, Friday and Saturday 10am to 10pm, Sunday 10am to 6pm. 92 N. Market St. ℭ **843/853-8837**.

## SMOKESHOP

**The Smoking Lamp**   This is Charleston's oldest smokeshop, with the most complete array of tobacco products in the city. You'll find an assortment of pipes, tobacco, cigars, even walking canes and other paraphernalia. Hours are Monday to Wednesday 10am to 10pm, Thursday to Saturday 10am to 11pm, Sunday 11am to 8pm. 189 E. Bay St. ℭ **843/577-7339**.

## 9 Charleston After Dark

### THE PERFORMING ARTS

Charleston's major cultural venue is the **Dock Street Theatre,** 133 Church St. (ℭ **843/965-4032;** www.charlestonstage.com), a 463-seat theater. The original was built in 1736 but burned down in the early 19th century, and the Planters Hotel (not related to the Planters Inn) was constructed around its ruins. In 1936, the theater was rebuilt in a new location. It's the home of the **Charleston Stage Company,** a local not-for-profit theater group whose season runs from mid-September to May. Dock Street hosts performances ranging from Shakespeare to *My Fair Lady.* It's most active during the Spoleto Festival USA in May and June. The box office (ℭ **843/577-7183**) is open Monday to Friday 10am to 5pm, Saturday 10am to 5pm and a half-hour before curtain, and Sunday from 10am to 3pm.

The **Robert Ivey Ballet,** 1910 Savannah Hwy. (ℭ **843/556-1343**), offers both classical and contemporary dance, as well as children's ballet programs. The group performs at various venues throughout the Charleston area, with general-admission prices of $20 for adults and $15 for children.

**Charleston Ballet Theatre,** 477 King St. (ℭ **843/723-7334;** www. charlestonballet.com), is one of the South's best professional ballet companies. The season begins in late October and continues into April. Admission is $15.

**Charleston Symphony Orchestra,** 14 George St. (© **843/723-7528;** www. charlestonsymphony.com), performs throughout the state, but its main venues are the Gaillard Auditorium and Charleston Southern University. The season runs from September to May.

## THE CLUB & MUSIC SCENE

**Blind Tiger Pub**    Near Bay Street, this pub occupies a historic location, a bar having operated here since 1803. The name comes from the days when Charlestonians opened up illegal "parlors of consumption" before the days of speakeasies—these parlors were known as "blind tigers." The legend was that admission fees were paid to see the mythical beast known as a Blind Tiger, with "complimentary" cocktails served. The tiger never showed up, of course, and the drinks weren't really free. Lawyers and businessmen in suits frequent the on-site Four Corners Café at lunch, but at night more casual attire is worn by the crowd, usually in the 30-to-40 age range. Live jazz or other kinds of music is played in the evening. Out back is a walled deck with subdued lighting and fountains. Café hours are Monday to Saturday from noon to 3pm and 5 to 10pm. The bar is open Monday to Friday from 4pm to 2am, Saturday 1:30pm to 2am, and Sunday 2pm to 2am. 38 Broad St. © **843/577-0088.**

**Cumberland's**    If your musical tastes run from Delta blues to rock to reggae, this is the place for you. The dominant age group at this bar depends on the act playing. You will find that the generation gap isn't strong here, with college students toasting glasses with midlifers. Greasy chicken wings and lots of suds make this place ever popular. Music is the common bond. Daily 11am to 2am. 301 King St. © **843/577-9469.** Cover varies.

**Henry's**    One of the best places for jazz in Charleston, this club features a live band on Friday and Saturday. Otherwise, you get taped top-40 music for listening and dancing. If you're a single man or woman with a roving eye, this is one of the hottest pickup bars in town. It attracts a mainly over-30 crowd. Happy hour, with drink discounts and free appetizers, is Monday to Friday from 4 to 7pm. Hours are Monday to Saturday 4pm to 2am and Sunday noon to 2am. 54 N. Market St. © **843/723-4363.**

**Music Farm**    This club is self-described as being "Charleston's premier music venue." It covers nearly every taste in music, from country to rock. You're as likely to hear funkster George Clinton as you are country legend George Jones. The club hosts local and regional bands, as well as national acts. Music is present anywhere from 2 to 6 nights a week from 8am to 2am. Call **843/853-FARM** for schedules and information. 32 Ann St. © **843/722-8904.** Cover $10–$25.

## THE BAR SCENE

**The Brick**    Set in what was built in the 19th century as a warehouse, this neighborhood bar is lined with hand-made bricks and capped with heavy timbers. It receives a wide medley of drinkers, everyone from college students to local dockyard workers, as well as a scattering of travelers from out of town. Appetizers and burgers are the only food served, but at least a dozen beers are on tap. Live music begins at 9:30pm Wednesday to Saturday. The tavern is open daily 5pm to 2am. 213 E. Bay St. © **843/720-7788.**

**Club Habana**    With the ambience of a private club, this second-floor house from 1870 is where the Ernest Hemingway of today would head if he were in

Charleston. Relax in one of three Gilded Age salons, each evocative of the Reconstruction era of the Old South. The house specializes in exotic cigars and martinis, and serves appetizers, desserts, fruit and cheese plates, and even some miniature beef Wellingtons. When filming *The Patriot,* Mel Gibson made Habana his second home in the city. You pass through a well-stocked tobacco store downstairs to reach the club. Hours are Monday to Thursday 4:30pm to midnight, Friday and Saturday 4:30pm to 2am, Sunday 4:30pm to midnight. 177 Meeting St. ② 843/853-5900.

**First Shot Bar** Our preferred watering hole is this old standby, where we've seen such visiting celebs as Gerald Ford and Elizabeth Taylor (not together, of course) over the years. The bar is one of the most elegant in Charleston, a comfortable and smooth venue for a drink. If you get hungry, the kitchen will whip up some shrimp and grits for you. Hours are from 4 to 10:30pm. In the Mills House Hotel, 115 Meeting St. ② 843/577-2400.

**Roof Top at the Vendue Inn** If you like your drinks with a view, there is none more panoramic than the rooftop of the Vendue Inn (see "Where to Stay," earlier in this chapter). As you down your cocktails, you can take in a sweeping vista of Charleston that includes Waterfront Park, the Cooper River Bridges, and embattled Fort Sumter. Patronize this upmarket bar for your sundowner. From Sunday to Friday you can listen to live music, including jazz, reggae, and bluegrass. There's never a cover charge. Hours are daily 11:30am to 11pm. 19 Vendue Range. ② 800/845-7900.

**Vickery's Bar & Grill** This is one of the most popular gathering places in Charleston for the younger crowd, especially students. It's also a good dining choice, with an international menu that includes jerk chicken and gazpacho. But the real secrets of the place's success are its 16-ounce frosted mug of beer for $2.50 and the convivial atmosphere. It's open from 11:30am to 1am. 15 Beaufain. ② 843/577-5300.

## GAY & LESBIAN BARS

**Déjà Vu II** Some people say this is the coziest and warmest "ladies' bar" in the Southeast. The owners have transformed what used to be a supper club into a cozy enclave with two bars, weekend live entertainment (usually by "all-girl bands"), and a clientele that's almost exclusively gay and 75% lesbian. The ambience is unpretentious and charming, and definitely does not exclude sympathetic patrons of any ilk. This is a late-night spot, but hours vary; call ahead. 4634 Prulley Ave, N. Charleston. ② 843/554-5959; www.dejavuii.com. Cover varies.

**Patrick's Pub & Grill** If you like your men in leather, chances are you'll find Mr. Right here. A gay pub and grill, right outside Charleston, this is a late-night venue for some of the hottest men in Charleston. Levi's take second place to leather. Hours are 5pm to 2am daily. 1377 Ashley River Rd. (Hwy. 61). ② 843/571-3435.

## LATE-NIGHT BITES

**Kaminsky's Most Excellent Café** Following a night of jazz or blues, this is a good spot to rest your feet and order just the power boost you need to make it through the rest of the evening. The handsome bar offers a wide selection of wines and is ideal for people-watching. Visitors who like New York's SoHo will feel at home here. The desserts are sinful, especially the Italian cream cake and mountain chocolate cake. Daily noon to 2am. 78 N. Market St. ② 843/853-8270.

## 10 A Side Trip to Edisto Island ⟨★

Isolated, and offering a kind of melancholy beauty, Edisto lies some 45 miles south of Charleston (take U.S. 17 W. for 21 miles; then head south along Hwy. 174 the rest of the way). By the late 18th century, Sea Island cotton made the islanders wealthy, and some plantations from that era still stand. Today, the island attracts families from Charleston and the Low Country to its white sandy beaches. Watersports include shrimping, surf-casting, deep-sea fishing, and sailing.

**Edisto Beach State Park,** State Cabin Road, sprawls across 1,255 acres, opening onto 2 miles of beach. There's also a signposted nature trail. Enjoy a picnic lunch under one of the shelters. The park has 75 campsites with full hookups and 28 with no hookups. Campsites cost $25 per night (the price is the same for RV hookups). Five cabins are also available for rent, ranging from $62 to $67 daily. Two restaurants are within walking distance of the campsite. Call ⓒ 843/869-2156 for reservations.

You can stay in a hotel in Charleston and commute here during the day.

### WHERE TO DINE

Barbecue fanciers—and what Southerner isn't one?—flock to **Po-Pigs BBQ Restaurant,** 2410 Hwy. 174 (ⓒ **843/869-9003**), for the finest barbecue on island, with all the Southern fixin's. An all-you-care-to-eat barbecue buffet is a daily feature for only $7.50 for adults or $3.50 for children. In addition to the barbecue, you get grilled or fried chicken, liver hash, red rice, and an assortment of vegetables served the long-cooked Southern way, including turnip greens, field peas, and squash casserole. Hours are Thursday to Saturday 11am to 9pm; no credit cards.

**The Old Post Office** SOUTHERN   This is the most prominent building that you're likely to see as you drive through the forests and fields across Edisto Island. About 5 miles from the beach, the restaurant was once a combination post office and general store, as its weathered clapboards and old-time architecture imply. Partners David Gressette and Philip Bardin, who transformed the premises in 1988, prepare a worthy compendium of Low Country cuisine and serve it in copious portions. Try island corn and crabmeat chowder, Orangeburg onion sausage with black bean sauce, scallops and grits with mousseline sauce, fried quail with duck-stock gravy, and "fussed-over" pork chops with hickory-smoked tomato sauce and mousseline.

Hwy. 174 at Store Creek. ⓒ 843/869-2339. Reservations recommended. Main courses $17–$23. MC, V. Mon–Sat 5:30–10pm.

**Sunset Grille** SEAFOOD   This is the sibling restaurant to the Old Post Office just recommended, and it is a family favorite. It opens onto Big Bay Creek overlooking the Intracoastal Waterway. The fresh fish and locally caught shellfish are delivered to the restaurant dock daily, and you can request them broiled, grilled, or fried. The lunch and dinner menus have variety and the freshest of ingredients. The brunch on Sunday is the island's best. At lunch an array of fresh salads (including one made with local oysters) is served along with burgers, chicken grills, and a selection of the best-stuffed sandwiches on Edisto. You can also order a big bowl of South Carolina she-crab soup. The menu at night is more elaborate, with a selection of appetizers ranging from a fish stew in a robust tomato and fish stock to fried alligator served with honey mustard. New York strip appears as a main course, as do delicious Edisto crab cakes. "Bell Boil" is a local favorite, fresh shrimp boiled in seasoned stock and served hot. There is a children's menu.

3702 Docksite Rd. at the Edisto Marina. © **843/869-1010.** Main courses $6–$21. MC, V. Daily 11am–2:30pm and 5–11pm; Sun brunch 11am–2:30pm.

## 11 Kiawah Island ⭐ & the Isle of Palms ⭐

# KIAWAH ISLAND

This eco-sensitive private residential and resort community sprawls across 10,000 acres located 21 miles south of Charleston. Named for the Kiawah Indians who inhabited the islands in the 17th century, it today consists of two resort villages: East Beach and West Beach. The community fronts a lovely 10-mile stretch of Atlantic beach; magnolias, live oaks, pine forests, and acres of marsh characterize the island.

Kiawah boasts many challenging golf courses, including one designed by Jack Nicklaus at Turtle Point that *Golf Digest* has rated among the top 10 courses in South Carolina. Golf architect Pete Dye designed a 2½-mile oceanfront course to host the 1991 PGA Ryder Cup March. *Tennis* magazine rates Kiawah as one of the nation's top tennis resorts, with its 28 hard-surface or Har-Tru clay courts. Anglers are also attracted to the island, especially in spring and fall.

For more information on golf and the beaches, see "Beaches & Outdoor Pursuits," earlier in this chapter.

**The Sanctuary at Kiawah Island** ⭐⭐⭐    One of the greatest resorts in the Southeast opened in the summer of 2004. With its sweeping views of the Atlantic, this $125-million ultra-luxury resort and spa lies just south of Charleston. It is nestled among majestic live oak stands along the island's 10-mile beachfront. It was constructed in the grand tradition of a seaside mansion, offering guests preferred tee times at the island's five championship golf courses. The sprawling resort features some of the largest and most luxurious guest rooms in America, with 90% of the units opening onto the water. In addition, the resort offers two oceanfront restaurants, plus other dining choices. The entrance to the resort is lined with some 150 transplanted live oak trees.

12 Kiawah Beach Dr., Kiawah Island, SC 29455. © **800/576-1570** or 843/768-2121. Fax 843/768-6099. www.kiawahresort.com. 255 units. $275–$575 double; from $900 suite. AE, DC, DISC, MC, V. **Amenities:** 5 restaurants; 4 bars; 3 pools (1 indoor); 5 18-hole golf courses; 28 tennis courts; fitness center; sauna; spa; 24-hr. room service; babysitting; laundry service/dry cleaning; nonsmoking rooms; rooms for those w/limited mobility. *In room:* A/C, TV, dataport, minibar, hair dryer, safe.

# THE ISLE OF PALMS

A residential community bordered by the Atlantic Ocean and lying 10 miles north of Charleston, this island, with its salt marshes and wildlife, has been turned into a vacation retreat, but one that is more downscale than Kiawah Island. The attractions of Charleston are close at hand, but the Isle of Palms is also self-contained, with shops, dining, an array of accommodations, and two championship golf courses. Charlestonians have been flocking to the island for holidays since 1898. I-26 intersects with I-526 heading directly to the island via the Isle of Palms Connector (S.C. 517). Seven miles of wide, white, sandy beach are the island's main attraction, and sailing and windsurfing are popular. The more adventurous will go crabbing and shrimping in the creeks.

**Wild Dunes Resort** ⭐⭐    A bit livelier than Kiawah Island, its major competitor, this complex is set on landscaped ground on the north shore. The 1,600-acre resort has not only two widely acclaimed golf courses, but an array of other outdoor attractions. Many families settle in here for a long stay, almost never venturing into Charleston. Guests are housed in condos and a series of cottages and villas. Many accommodations have only one bedroom, but others have as many as six. Villas and cottages are built along the shore, close to golf and tennis. Furnishings are tasteful and resortlike, with kitchens, washers and dryers, and spacious bathrooms with dressing areas. Some of the best units have screened-in balconies.

**Edgar's Restaurant** serves standard American cuisine and regional specialties. The hotel also maintains a lounge, which stays open until 2am.

Isle of Palms (P.O. Box 20575), Charleston, SC 29413. (C) **800/845-8880** or 843/886-6000. Fax 843/886-2916. www.wilddunes.com. 500 units. $120–$299 double/suite; $234–$1,280 villa or cottage. Golf packages available. AE, DC, DISC, MC, V. Free parking. **Amenities:** 2 restaurants; bar; 4 outdoor pools; 2 18-hole golf courses; 18 tennis courts; fitness center; Jacuzzi; sauna; limited room service; massage; babysitting; laundry service/dry cleaning; nonsmoking rooms; rooms for those w/limited mobility. *In room:* A/C, TV, dataport, minibar, coffeemaker, hair dryer, iron/ironing board, safe.

# 12

# Hilton Head & the Low Country

The largest sea island between New Jersey and Florida and one of America's great resort meccas, Hilton Head is surrounded by the Low Country, where much of the romance, beauty, and graciousness of the Old South survives. Broad white-sand beaches are warmed by the Gulf Stream and fringed with palm trees and rolling dunes. Palms mingle with live oaks, dogwood, and pines, and everything is draped in Spanish moss. Graceful sea oats, anchoring the beaches, wave in the wind. The subtropical climate makes all this beauty the ideal setting for golf and for some of the Southeast's finest saltwater fishing. Far more sophisticated and upscale than Myrtle Beach and the Grand Strand, Hilton Head's "plantations" (as most resort areas here call themselves) offer visitors something of the traditional leisurely lifestyle that's always held sway here.

Although it covers only 42 square miles (it's 12 miles long and 5 miles wide at its widest point), Hilton Head feels spacious, thanks to judicious planning from the beginning of its development in 1952. And that's a blessing, because about 2.3 million resort guests visit annually (the permanent population is about 35,000). The broad beaches on its ocean side, sea marshes on the sound, and natural wooded areas of live and water oak, pine, bay, and palmetto trees in between have all been carefully preserved amid commercial explosion. This lovely setting attracts artists, writers, musicians, theater groups, and craftspeople. The only city (of sorts) is Harbour Town, at Sea Pines Plantation, a Mediterranean-style cluster of shops and restaurants.

## 1 Essentials

**GETTING THERE**   It's easy to fly into Savannah, rent a car, and drive to Hilton Head (about 65 miles north of Savannah). See chapter 20 for complete details on all the airlines flying into Savannah. If you're driving from other points south or north, exit I-95 to reach the island (exit 28 off I-95 South, exit 5 off I-95 North). U.S. 278 leads over the bridge to the island. It's 52 miles northeast of Savannah and located directly on the Intracoastal Waterway.

**VISITOR INFORMATION**   The **Island Visitors Information Center** is on U.S. 278 at S.C. 46 (© **843/785-4472;** www.islandvisitorcenter.com), just before you cross over from the mainland. It offers a free *Where to Go* booklet, including a visitor map and guide. It's open Monday to Saturday from 9:30am to 5:30pm.

The **Hilton Head Visitors and Convention Bureau (chamber of commerce),** 1 Chamber Dr. (© **843/785-3673;** www.hiltonheadisland.org), offers free maps of the area and will assist you in finding places of interest and outdoor activities. It will even make hotel reservations. It's open Monday to Friday 8:30am to 5:30pm.

# Hilton Head Island

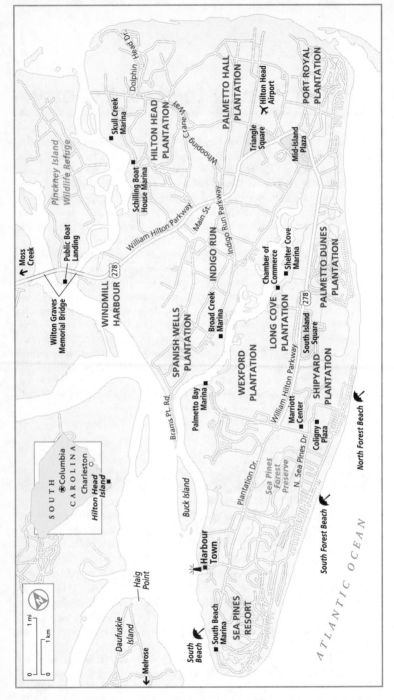

**GETTING AROUND**    U.S. 278 is the divided highway that runs the length of the island.

The **Downtown Area Shuttle (DASH;** © **843/724-7420)** is the quickest way to get around the main downtown area daily. The fare is $1.25, and you'll need exact change. A pass good for the whole day costs $4 and can be purchased on the bus.

**Yellow Cab** (© **843/686-6666**) has two-passenger flat fares determined by zone, with an extra $2 charge for each additional person.

**SPECIAL EVENTS**    The earliest annual event is **Springfest,** a March festival featuring seafood, live music, stage shows, and tennis and golf tournaments. Outstanding PGA golfers also descend on the island in mid-April for the **MCI Heritage Tournament** at the Harbour Town Golf Links. To herald fall, the **Hilton Head Celebrity Golf Tournament** is held on Labor Day weekend at Palmetto Dunes and Sea Pines Plantation.

## 2  Beaches, Golf, Tennis & Other Outdoor Pursuits

You can have an active vacation here any time of year; Hilton Head's subtropical climate ranges in temperature from the 50s (10°–15°C) in winter to the mid-80s (around 30°C) in summer. And if you've had your fill of historic sights in Savannah or Charleston, don't worry—the attractions on Hilton Head mainly consist of nature preserves, beaches, and other places to play.

**Coastal Discovery Museum,** 100 William Hilton Pkwy. (© **843/689-6767;** www.coastaldiscovery.org), hosts 12 separate guided tours and cruises. Tours go along island beaches and salt marshes or stop at Native American sites and the ruins of old forts or long-gone plantations. Children can search for sharks' teeth with an identification chart. The nature, beach, and history tours generally cost $10 for adults and $5 for children. The dolphin and nature cruise costs $15 per adult, $10 per child; and a kayak trip costs $35 per person. Hours are Monday to Saturday 9am to 5pm, Sunday 10am to 3pm.

**BEACHES**    *Travel & Leisure* ranked Hilton Head's **beaches** ✦✦✦ among the most beautiful in the world. We concur. The sands are extremely firm, providing a sound surface for biking, hiking, jogging, and beach games. In summer, watch for the endangered loggerhead turtles that lumber ashore at night to bury their eggs.

All beaches on Hilton Head are public. Land bordering the beaches, however, is private property. Most beaches are safe, although there's sometimes an undertow at the northern end of the island. Lifeguards are posted only at major beaches, and concessions are available to rent beach chairs, umbrellas, and watersports equipment.

There are a number of public-access sites to popular beach areas. Our favorites are **Coligny Beach** at Coligny Circle at Pope Avenue and South Forest Beach Drive. This is the island's busiest strip of sand with toilets, sand showers, a playground, and changing rooms. **Alder Lane,** entered along South Forest Beach Road at Alder Lane, offers parking and is less crowded. Toilets are also found here. Off the William Hilton Parkway, **Dreissen Beach Park** at Bradley Beach Road has toilets, sand showers, and plenty of parking as well as a playground and picnic tables. Of the beaches on the island's north side, we prefer **Folly Field Beach,** on Starfish Road, which has more limited parking but offers toilets and sand showers. The island also has a number of other less accessible and less desirable beaches. Technically, all beaches are public.

**BIKING**   Enjoy Hilton Head's 25 miles of bicycle paths. There are even bike paths running parallel to U.S. 278. Beaches are firm enough to support wheels, and every year, cyclists seem to delight in dodging the waves or racing the fast-swimming dolphins in the nearby water.

Most hotels and resorts rent bikes to guests. If yours doesn't, try **Hilton Head Bicycle Company,** off Sea Pines Circle at 112 Arrow Rd. (© **843/686-6888**). The cost is $12 per day, but only $18 for 3 days and $25 per week. Baskets, child carriers, locks, and headgear are supplied, and the inventory includes cruisers, BMXs, mountain bikes, and tandems. Hours are daily 9am to 5pm.

Another rental place is **South Beach Cycles,** South Beach Marina Village in Sea Pines (© **843/671-2453**), offering beach cruisers, tandems, child carriers, and bikes for kids. There's free delivery to Sea Pines. Cost is $10 per half-day, $15 for a full day, or $23 for 3 days. Hours are 9am to 6pm daily.

**CRUISES & TOURS**   To explore Hilton Head's waters, contact **Adventure Cruises, Inc.,** Shelter Cove Harbour, Suite G, Harbourside III (© **843/785-4558**). Outings include a 1½-hour dolphin-watch cruise, which costs adults $19 and children $9. A 3-hour sunset cruise aboard the vessel *Adventure* costs adults $20 and children $10.

Another outfitter, **Drifter & Gypsy Excursions,** South Sea Pines Dr., South Beach Marina (© **843/363-2900**), takes its 65-foot *Gypsy,* holding 89 passengers, on dolphin watches, sightseeing cruises, and nature cruises. Call for more information to see what's happening at the time of your visit.

**FISHING**   No license is needed for saltwater fishing, although freshwater licenses are required for the island's lakes and ponds. The season for fishing offshore is April through October. Inland fishing is good between September and December. Crabbing is also popular; crabs are easy to catch in low water from docks, boats, or right off banks.

Off **Hilton Head** ⊛, you can go deep-sea fishing for amberjack, barracuda, shark, and king mackerel. Many rentals are available; we've recommended only those with the best track records. The previously recommended **Drifter & Gypsy Excursions,** South Sea Pines Drive, South Beach Marina (© **843/363-2900**), features a 50-passenger, 50-foot drifter vessel that offers 5-hour offshore and inshore fishing excursions. The 32-foot *Boomerang* fishing boat is available for private offshore and inshore custom fishing charters lasting up to 8 hours.

**Harbour Town Yacht Basin,** Harbour Town Marina (© **843/671-2704**), has four boats of various sizes and prices. *The Manatee,* a 40-foot vessel, can carry a group of six. The rates, set for six passengers, are $400 for 4 hours, $600 for 6 hours, and $800 for 8 hours. A charge of $13 per hour is added for each additional passenger.

*The Hero* and *The Echo* are 32-foot ships. Their rates for a group of six are $375 for 4 hours, $570 for 6 hours, and $750 for 8 hours. A smaller three-passenger inshore boat is priced at $295 for 4 hours, $445 for 6 hours, and $590 for 8 hours.

A cheaper way to go deep-sea fishing—only $47 per person—is aboard *The Drifter* (© **843/363-2900**), a party boat that departs from the South Beach Marina Village. Ocean-bottom fishing is possible at an artificial reef 12 miles offshore.

**GOLF**   With 24 challenging **golf courses** ⊛⊛⊛ on the island and an additional 16 within a 30-minute drive, this is heaven for both professional and novice golfers. Some of golf's most celebrated architects—including George and

Tom Fazio, Robert Trent Jones, Pete Dye, and Jack Nicklaus—have designed championship courses on the island. Wide, scenic fairways and rolling greens have earned Hilton Head the reputation of being the resort with the most courses on any number of the "World's Best" lists.

Many of Hilton Head's championship courses are open to the public, including the **George Fazio Course** ⭐ at Palmetto Dunes Resort (© **843/785-1130**), an 18-hole, 6,534-yard, par-70 course that *Golf Digest* ranked in the top 50 of its "75 Best American Resort Courses." The course has been cited for its combined length and keen accuracy. The cost is $90 for 18 holes, and hours are daily from 6:30am to 6pm.

**Old South Golf Links** ⭐⭐⭐, 50 Buckingham Plantation Dr., Bluffton (© **800/257-8997** or 843/785-5353), is an 18-hole, 6,772-yard, par-72 course, open daily from 7:30am to 7pm. It's recognized as one of the "Top 10 New Public Courses" by *Golf Digest,* which cites its panoramic views and setting ranging from an oak forest to tidal salt marshes. Greens fees range from $65 to $92. The course lies on Highway 278, 1 mile before the bridge leading to Hilton Head.

**Hilton Head National,** Highway 278 (© **843/842-5900**), is a Gary Player Signature Golf Course, including a full-service pro shop and a grill and driving range. It's a 27-hole, 6,779-yard, par-72 course with gorgeous scenery that evokes Scotland. Greens fees range from $50 to $95, and hours are daily 7am to 6pm.

**Island West Golf Club,** Highway 278 (© **843/689-6660**), was nominated in 1992 by *Golf Digest* as the best new course of the year. With its backdrop of oaks, elevated tees, and rolling fairways, it's a challenging but playable 18-hole, 6,803-yard, par-72 course. Greens fees range from $29 to $59, and hours are from 7am to 6pm daily.

**Robert Trent Jones Course** at the Palmetto Dunes Resort (© **843/785-1138**) is an 18-hole, 6,710-yard, par-72 oceanfront course. The greens fees are $90 to $130 for 18 holes, and hours are daily from 7am to 6pm.

**HORSEBACK RIDING**    Riding through beautiful maritime forests and nature preserves is reason enough to visit Hilton Head. We like **Lawton Stables,** 190 Greenwood Dr., Sea Pines (© **843/671-2586**), offering rides for both adults and kids (kids 7 and under ride ponies) through the Sea Pines Forest Preserve. The cost is $50 per person for a ride that lasts somewhat longer than an hour. Riders must weigh under 240 pounds. The stables are open Monday to Saturday 8:30am to 5:30pm. Reservations are necessary.

**JOGGING**    Our favorite place for jogging is Harbour Town at Sea Pines. Go for a run through the town just as the sun is going down. Later, you can explore the marina and have a refreshing drink at one of the many outdoor cafes. In addition, the island offers lots of paved paths and trails that cut through scenic areas. Jogging along U.S. 278, the main artery, can be dangerous because of heavy traffic, however.

**KAYAK TOURS    Eco-Kayak Tours,** Palmetto Bay Marina (© **843/785-7131**), operates guided tours in Broad Creek. About four to five trips are offered each day; the cost is $30 to $50 per person, and anyone age 7 to 82 is welcome to participate.

**South Beach Marina Village** (© **843/671-2643**) allows you to tour Low Country waterways by kayak. A 2-hour Dolphin Nature Tour costs $46 (half-price for children under 12). The tour takes you through the salt-marsh creeks of the Calibogue Sound or Pinckney Island Wildlife Refuge. The trip begins with instructions on how to control your boat.

## Moments   Hilton Head's Wonderful Wildlife

Hilton Head has preserved more of its wildlife than almost any other resort destination on the East Coast.

Hilton Head Island's **alligators** are a prosperous lot and, in fact, the South Carolina Department of Wildlife and Marine Resources uses the island as a resource for repopulating state parks and preserves in which alligators' numbers have greatly diminished. The creatures represent no danger if you stay at a respectful distance. (Strange as it may seem, some unsuspecting tourists, thinking that the dead-still alligators are props left over from Disney, often approach the reptiles and hit them or kick at them—obviously, not a very good idea.)

Many of the large **water birds** that regularly grace the pages of nature magazines are natives of the island. The island's Audubon Society reports around 200 species of birds every year in its annual bird count, and more than 350 species have been sighted on the island during the past decade. The snowy egret, the large blue heron, and the osprey are among the most noticeable. Here, too, you may see the white ibis, with its strange beak that curves down, plus the smaller cattle egret, which first arrived on Hilton Head Island in 1954 from a South American habitat. They follow the island's cows, horses, and tractors to snatch grasshoppers and other insects.

A big part of the native story includes **deer, bobcat, otter, mink,** and a few **wild boars.** The bobcats are difficult to see, lurking in the deepest recesses of the forest preserves and in the undeveloped parts of the island. The deer, however, are easier to encounter. One of the best places to watch these timid creatures is Sea Pines Plantation, on the southern end of the island. With foresight, the planners of this plantation set aside

**NATURE PRESERVES**   The **Audubon-Newhall Preserve,** Palmetto Bay Road (© **843/689-2989**), is a 50-acre preserve on the south end of the island. Here, you can walk along marked trails to observe wildlife in its native habitat. Guided tours are available when plants are blooming. Except for public toilets, there are no amenities. The preserve is open from sunrise to sunset; admission is free.

The second-leading preserve is also on the south end of the island. **Sea Pines Forest Preserve** ★★, Sea Pines Plantation (© **843/363-4530**), is a 605-acre public wilderness with marked walking trails. Nearly all the birds and animals known to live on Hilton Head can be seen here. (Yes, there are alligators, but there are also less fearsome creatures, such as egrets, herons, osprey, and white-tailed deer.) All trails lead to public picnic areas in the center of the forest. The preserve is open from sunrise to sunset year-round. Maps and toilets are available.

**SAILING**   *Pau Hana* and *Flying Circus,* Palmetto Bay Marina (© **843/686-2582**), are two charter sailboats on Hilton Head piloted by Capt. Jeanne Zailckas. You can pack a picnic lunch and bring your cooler aboard for a 2-hour trip—in the morning or afternoon, or at sunset. The cost is $25 for adults and $15 for children 11 and under. Flying Circus offers private 2-hour trips for up to six people costing $150, and a sunset cruise for $180.

areas for a deer habitat back in the 1950s, when the island master plan was conceived.

The **loggerhead turtle,** an endangered species, nests extensively along Hilton Head's 12 miles of wide, sandy beaches. Because the turtles choose the darkest hours of the night to crawl ashore and bury eggs in the soft sand, few visitors meet these 200-pound giants.

Ever-present is the **bottle-nosed dolphin,** usually called a porpoise by those unfamiliar with the island's sea life. Hilton Head Plantation and Port Royal Plantation adjacent to Port Royal Sound are good places to meet up with the playful dolphins, as are Palmetto Dunes, Forest Beach, and all other oceanfront locations. In the summer, dolphins feed on small fish and sea creatures very close to shore. Island beaches are popular with bikers, and this often offers a real point of interest for curious dolphins, who sometimes seem to swim along with the riders. Several excursion boats offer tours that provide an opportunity for fellowship with dolphins. Shrimp boats are a guaranteed point of congregation for the hungry guys.

The Sea Pines Forest Preserve, the Audubon-Newhall Preserve, and the Pinckney Island Wildlife Preserve, just off the island between the bridges, are of interest to nature lovers. The **Coastal Discovery Museum** hosts several guided nature tours and cruises; call © **843/689-6767.** Tours, conducted weekdays, generally cost $10 for adults and $5 for children. Check the museum's online Events Calendar at www.coastal discovery.org for specific dates and times; you can even reserve your tour online in advance.

**H2 Sports,** Harbour Town Marina (© **843/671-4386**), offers a 27-foot catamaran with captain for scenic sails costing $29 for a 1½-hour trip or $39 for a 2-hour jaunt. In addition, the outfitter offers jet-skiing, parasailing, eco-tours, and water-skiing. We especially recommend their eco-tours (or "enviro" as they are called). Passengers head out on Zodiac inflatable boats for close encounters with wildlife, including dolphin sightings and bird-watching. Rates are $24, $20 for kids 12 and under.

**TENNIS**   *Tennis* magazine ranked Hilton Head among its "50 Greatest U.S. Tennis Resorts." No other domestic destination can boast such a concentration of **tennis facilities** ★★★: more than 300 courts that are ideal for beginning, intermediate, and advanced players. The island has 19 tennis clubs, seven of which are open to the public. A wide variety of tennis clinics and daily lessons are available.

**Sea Pines Racquet Club** ★★★, Sea Pines Plantation (© **843/363-4495**), has been ranked by *Tennis* magazine as a top-50 resort and was selected by the *Robb Report* as the best tennis resort in the United States. The club has been the site of more nationally televised tennis events than any other location. Two hours of tennis are complimentary for guests of the hotel; otherwise, there's a $22-per-hour charge. The club has 23 clay courts (two are lighted for night play).

**Port Royal Racquet Club,** Port Royal Plantation (© **843/686-8803**), offers 10 clay and four hard courts, plus two natural-grass courts. Night games are possible on all courts. Charges range from $20 to $32 per hour, and reservations should be made a day in advance. Clinics are $20 per hour for adults and $12 to $14 for children.

**Hilton Head Island Beach and Tennis Resort,** 40 Folly Field Rd. (© **843/842-4402**), features a 10 lighted hard courts, costing only $15 per hour (free to guests).

**Palmetto Dunes Tennis Center,** Palmetto Dunes Resort (© **843/785-1152**), has 23 clay and two hard courts (some lighted for night play). Hotel guests pay $20 per hour; otherwise, the charge is $25 per hour.

**WINDSURFING**   Hilton Head is not recommended as a windsurfing destination. Finding a place to windsurf is quite difficult, and one windsurfer warns that catching a tailwind at the public beaches at the airport and the Holiday Inn could land you at the bombing range on Parris Island, the Marine Corps' basic-training facility. Your resort may have equipment for rent, although what's usually available has been described as antiquated.

## SHOPPING

Hilton Head is browsing heaven, with more than 30 shopping centers spread around the island. Chief shopping sites include **Pinelawn Station** (Matthews Dr. and U.S. 278), with more than 30 shops and half a dozen restaurants; and **Coligny Plaza** (Coligny Circle), with more than 60 shops, food stands, and several good restaurants. We've found some of the best bargains in the South at **Factory Outlet Stores I and II** (© **843/837-4339**), on Highway 278 at the gateway to Hilton Head. The outlet has more than 45 factory stores, including Ralph Lauren, Brooks Brothers, and J. Crew. The hours of most shops are Monday to Saturday 10am to 9pm and Sunday 11am to 6pm.

## 3 Where to Stay

Hilton Head has some of the finest hotel properties in the South, and prices are high—unless you book into one of the motels run by national chains. Most facilities offer discount rates from November to March, and golf and tennis packages are available.

The most comprehensive central reservations service on the island, **The Vacation Company,** P.O. Box 5312, Hilton Head Island, SC 29938 (© **800/845-7018** in the United States and Canada; www.hiltonheadcentral.com), can book you into private homes or villas on the island at no charge. It's open Monday to Saturday 9am to 5pm.

Another option is renting a private home, villa, or condo. Families might consider a villa rental if it fits into their budget. For up-to-date availability, rates, and bookings, contact **Island Rentals and Real Estate,** P.O. Box 5915, Hilton Head Island, SC 29938 (© **800/845-6134** or 843/785-3813). The toll-free number is in operation 24 hours, but office hours are Monday to Saturday 8:30am to 5:30pm.

By and large, the double rooms in the recommended hotels and inns below have private bathrooms with tub/shower combinations, unless otherwise noted.

## VERY EXPENSIVE

**Hilton Head Marriott Beach & Golf Resort** ★★   After a much-needed $23-million renovation, this aging property has emerged in its latest reincarnation as a

---

*Finds* **Halfway between Manhattan & Miami**

At last there's a great place to stay that's close to I-95 between the borders of the Carolinas. Spend the night in a seven-room country inn, **Abingdon Manor,** in Latta, South Carolina (© **888/752-5090;** www.abingdonmanor. com). It lies 5 miles east of I-95 at exit 181, at the halfway point between New York City and Miami. In this turn-of-the-20th-century town, the manor is an opulent Greek Revival house listed on the National Register of Historic Places. The grand entry hall leads to elegant public rooms and luxurious bedrooms. The inn offers complete dining and liquor service. Rates range from $150 to $190, with gourmet dinners costing $40 per person.

---

Marriott. Set on 2 acres of landscaped grounds and bordering the oceanfront, the hotel is surrounded by the much more massive acreage of Palmetto Dunes Plantation and is just 10 minutes from the Hilton Head airport. But the hotel's 10-story tower of rooms dominates everything around it.

Rooms open onto either ocean or island views. Some are smaller and less opulent than you might expect of such a well-rated hotel, but all are comfortably furnished, each coming with a tiled, midsize bathroom. Most rooms open onto small balconies overlooking the garden or the ocean. The hotel's program of sports and recreation is among the best on the island.

In Palmetto Dunes Plantation, Hilton Head Island, SC 29938. © **800/228-9290** or 843/686-8400. Fax 843/686-8450. www.marriott.com. 512 units. $205–$249 double; $500–$700 suite. AE, DC, DISC, MC, V. Valet parking $15. **Amenities:** Restaurant; 2 bars; coffee shop; 1 indoor and 2 outdoor pools; 3 18-hole golf courses; 25 tennis courts nearby; health club; full spa; sauna; gift shop; hair salon; limited room service; babysitting; laundry service/dry cleaning; nonsmoking rooms; rooms for those w/limited mobility. *In room:* A/C, TV, dataport, minibar, coffeemaker, hair dryer, iron/ironing board, safe, bathrobe.

**Main Street Inn** ★★★ *Finds*    Don't expect cozy Americana from this small, luxurious inn, as it's grander and more European in its motifs than its name would imply. Designed like a small-scale villa that you might expect to see in the south of France, it was built in 1996 in a format that combines design elements from both New Orleans and Charleston, including cast-iron balustrades and a formal semi-tropical garden where guests are encouraged to indulge in afternoon tea. Inside, you'll find artfully clipped topiary, French provincial furnishings, and accommodations that are more luxurious and more richly appointed than those of any other hotel in Hilton Head. Color schemes throughout make ample use of golds, mauves, and taupes; floors are crafted from slabs of either stone or heart pine; fabrics are richly textured; and plumbing and bathroom fixtures are aggressively upscale. Overall, despite a location that requires a drive to the nearest beach, the hotel provides a luxe alternative to the less personalized megahotels that lie nearby. AAA, incidentally, awarded it a much-coveted four-star rating. Breakfast and afternoon tea are served here. A fixed-price dinner is available for $35.

2200 Main St., Hilton Head Island, SC 29926. © **800/471-3001** or 843/681-3001. Fax 843/681-5541. www.mainstreetinn.com. 33 units. $185–$250 double. $35 surcharge for 3rd occupant of double room. Rates include breakfast. AE, DISC, MC, V. Free parking. **Amenities:** Breakfast room; outdoor pool; spa; massage; laundry service/dry cleaning; nonsmoking rooms; rooms for those w/limited mobility. *In room:* A/C, TV, dataport, minibar, coffeemaker, hair dryer, iron/ironing board.

**The Westin Resort** ★★    Set near the isolated northern end of Hilton Head Island on 24 landscaped acres, this is the most opulent European-style hotel in town. Its Disneyesque design, including cupolas and postmodern ornamentation that looks vaguely Moorish, evokes fanciful Palm Beach hotels. If there's a drawback, it's the stiff formality. Adults accompanied by a gaggle of children and bathers in swimsuits will not necessarily feel comfortable in the reverently hushed corridors. The rooms, most of which have ocean views, are outfitted in Low Country plantation style, with touches of Asian art thrown in for additional glamour. The **Carolina Café** or the **Barony Grill** are the best places for food. Poolside dining is available, and there's also a seafood buffet restaurant.

Two Grasslawn Ave., Hilton Head Island, SC 29928. ② **800/WWESTIN-1** or 843/681-4000. Fax 843/681-1087. www.westin.com. 412 units. $209–$459 double; $450–$1,900 suite. Children 17 and under stay free in parent's room; children 4 and under eat free. Special promotions offered. AE, DC, DISC, MC, V. **Amenities:** 3 restaurants; bar; 3 pools; 3 18-hole golf courses; 16 tennis courts; health spa; Jacuzzi; room service; laundry service/dry cleaning; nonsmoking rooms; rooms for those w/limited mobility. *In room:* A/C, TV, dataport, minibar, coffeemaker, hair dryer, iron/ironing board, safe.

## EXPENSIVE

**Disney's Hilton Head Island Resort** 🏠🏠   This family-conscious resort is on a 15-acre island that rises above Hilton Head's widest estuary, Broad Creek. When it opened in 1996, it was the only U.S.-based Disney resort outside Florida and California. About 20 woodsy-looking buildings are arranged into a compound. Expect lots of pine trees and fallen pine needles, garlands of Spanish moss, plenty of families with children, and an ambience that's several notches less intense than that of hotels in Disney theme parks. Part of the fun, if you like this sort of thing in concentrated doses, are the many summer-camp-style activities. Public areas have outdoorsy colors (forest green and cranberry), stuffed game fish, and varnished pine. References are made to Shadow the Dog (a fictitious golden retriever that is the resort's mascot) and Mathilda (a maternal figure who conducts cooking lessons for children as part of the resort's planned activities). All accommodations contain minikitchens, suitable for feeding sandwiches and macaroni to the kids but hardly the kind of thing that a gourmet chef would enjoy, as well as wooden furniture consistent with the resort's vacation-home-in-the-forest theme. For elaborate restaurants and bars, look elsewhere. **Tide Me Over** is a walk-up window serving Carolina cookery for breakfast and lunch. Those who don't cook their meals in-house can trek a short distance to the dozen or so eateries and bars in the nearby marina complex at Shelter Cove Harbour.

22 Harbourside Lane, Hilton Head Island, SC 29928. ② **407/DISNEY** or 843/341-4100. Fax 843/341-4130. www.dvcresorts.com. 123 units. $105–$275 studio; $150–$710 villa. AE, DC, DISC, MC, V. **Amenities:** 3 restaurants; bar; 3 outdoor pools; fitness center; health spa; babysitting; laundry service. *In room:* A/C, TV, dataport, coffeemaker, kitchenette, hair dryer, iron/ironing board, safe.

**Hilton Head Crowne Plaza Resort** 🏠   Tucked away within the Shipyard Plantation, and designed as the centerpiece of that plantation's 800 acres, this five-story inn gives its major competitor, Westin Resort, stiff competition. It underwent a $10-million renovation in 1993 and today has the island's most dignified lobby: a mahogany-sheathed postmodern interpretation of Chippendale decor. The golf course associated with the place has been praised by the National Audubon Society for its respect for local wildlife. Guest rooms are nothing out of the ordinary, with simple furnishings, yet the sheer beauty of the landscaping, the attentive service, the omnipresent nautical theme, and the well-trained staff (dressed in nautically inspired uniforms) can go a long way toward making your stay memorable. On the premises are three restaurants. The most glamorous is **Portz,** off the establishment's main lobby. A good middle-bracket choice is **Brella's,** serving both lunch and dinner. Certain nights in the premier bar, **Signals,** feature line dancing and shag dancing.

130 Shipyard Dr., Shipyard Plantation, Hilton Head Island, SC 29928. ✆ **800/465-4329** or 843/842-2400. Fax 843/785-8463. www.cphilton.com. 340 units. $199–$325 double; $375–$615 suite. AE, DC, DISC, MC, V. Free parking. **Amenities:** 2 restaurants; bar; 2 pools (1 indoor); fitness center; Jacuzzi; bikes; room service; laundry service/dry cleaning; nonsmoking rooms; rooms for those w/limited mobility. *In room:* A/C, TV, dataport, minibar, coffeemaker, hair dryer, iron/ironing board, safe.

**Hilton Oceanfront Resort** ✦ This award-winning property isn't the most imposing on the island. Many visitors, however, prefer the Hilton because of its hideaway position: tucked at the end of the main road through Palmetto Dunes. The low-rise design features hallways that open to sea breezes at either end. The guest rooms are some of the largest on the island, and balconies angling out toward the beach allow sea views from all accommodations. **Mostly Seafood** is the resort's premier restaurant, although cafes and bars—and even a Pizza Hut on the grounds—serve less expensive fare.

23 Ocean Lane (P.O. Box 6165), Hilton Head Island, SC 29938. ✆ **800/845-8001** or 843/842-8000. Fax 843/341-8037. www.hilton.com. 324 units (with kitchenette). $99–$159 double; $299–$499 suite. AE, DC, DISC, MC, V. Parking $6. **Amenities:** 3 restaurants; bar; 2 outdoor pools; fitness center; limited room service; laundry service/dry cleaning; coin-operated laundry; nonsmoking rooms; rooms for those w/limited mobility. *In room:* A/C, TV, dataport, coffeemaker, hair dryer, iron/ironing board, safe.

## MODERATE

**Holiday Inn** ✦ The island's leading motor hotel, across from Coligny Plaza, this five-story high-rise opens onto a quiet stretch of beach on the southern side of the island, near Shipyard Plantation. The rooms are spacious and well furnished, decorated in tropical pastels, but the balconies are generally too small for use. The upper floors have the views, so you should try for accommodations there. In summer, planned children's activities are offered.

1 S. Forest Beach Dr. (P.O. Box 5728), Hilton Head Island, SC 29938. ✆ **800/HOLIDAY** or 843/785-5126. Fax 843/785-6678. www.holiday-inn.com. 201 units. $169–$239 double. AE, DC, DISC, MC, V. Free parking. **Amenities:** Restaurant; bar; outdoor pool; exercise room; limited room service; laundry service; nonsmoking rooms; rooms for those w/limited mobility. *In room:* A/C, TV, dataport, coffeemaker, hair dryer, iron/ironing board, safe.

**Residence Inn by Marriott** Set on the eastern edge of Hilton Head's main traffic artery, midway between the Palmetto Dunes and Shipyard plantations, this is a three-story complex of functionally furnished but comfortable one-bedroom suites. The setting is wooded and parklike, and both cost-conscious families and business travelers on extended stays appreciate the simple cooking facilities in all accommodations. Each unit has an icemaker, microwave, and coffeemaker.

12 Park Lane (in Central Park), Hilton Head Island, SC 29938. ✆ **800/331-3131** or 843/686-5700. Fax 843/686-3952. www.marriott.com. 156 units. Apr–Sept $109–$149 suite; Oct–Mar $109–$119 suite. Rates include continental breakfast. AE, DC, DISC, MC, V. **Amenities:** Breakfast room; outdoor pool; 2 tennis courts; basketball court; fitness center; Jacuzzi; laundry service/dry cleaning, coin-operated laundry; nonsmoking rooms; rooms for those w/limited mobility. *In room:* A/C, TV, dataport, kitchenette, coffeemaker, hair dryer, iron/ironing board.

**The South Beach Marina Inn** ✦ *Finds* Of the dozens of available accommodations in Sea Pines Plantation, this 1986 clapboard-sided complex of marina-front buildings is the only place offering traditional hotel-style rooms by the night. With lots of charm, despite its aggressive theme, the inn meanders over a labyrinth of catwalks and stairways above a complex of shops, souvenir kiosks, and restaurants. Each unit is cozily outfitted with country-style braided rugs, pinewood floors, and homespun-charm decor celebrating rural 19th-century America. All units include a kitchenette.

232 S. Sea Pines Dr. (in Sea Pines Plantation), Hilton Head Island, SC 29920. © **800/367-3909** or 843/671-6498. www.southbeachvillage.com. 17 units. $69–$200 suite. AE, DISC, MC, V. Free parking. **Amenities:** Outdoor pool; nonsmoking rooms; courtyard. *In room:* A/C, TV, kitchenette, coffeemaker, hair dryer, iron/ironing board.

## INEXPENSIVE

**Fairfield Inn and Suites by Marriott**    This three-story motel in Shelter Cove has all the features of Marriott's budget chain, including complimentary coffee in the lobby, nonsmoking rooms, and same-day dry cleaning. The inn provides easy access to the beach, golf, tennis, marinas, and shopping. The rooms are wheelchair-accessible and, although they're unremarkable, they are a good value for expensive Hilton Head. Families save money by using one of the grills outside for a home-style barbecue, to be enjoyed at one of the picnic tables. In addition, a heated pool is provided.

9 Marina Side Dr., Hilton Head Island, SC 29938. © **800/228-2800** or 843/842-4800. Fax 843/842-5388. www.marriott.com. 119 units. $59–$129 double; $159 suite. Rates include continental breakfast. Senior discounts available. AE, DISC, MC, V. Free parking. **Amenities:** Breakfast room; lounge; outdoor pool; coin-operated laundry; nonsmoking rooms; rooms for those w/limited mobility. *In room:* A/C, TV, dataport, hair dryer, iron/ironing board, safe.

**Hampton Inn**    Although slightly edged out by its major competitor, the Fairfield Inn by Marriott, this is the second-most sought-after motel on Hilton Head, especially by families and business travelers. It's 5 miles from the bridge and the closest motel to the airport. Rooms in pastel pinks and greens are quite comfortable and well maintained. Some units have refrigerators. Local calls are free.

1 Dillon Rd., Hilton Head Island, SC 29926. © **800/HAMPTON** or 843/681-7900. Fax 843/681-4330. www.hamptoninn.hilton.com. 125 units, 11 with kitchen units. $79–$119 double. Children under 18 stay free in parent's room. Rates include continental breakfast. AE, DC, DISC, MC, V. **Amenities:** Breakfast room; outdoor pool; putting green; fitness center; coin-operated laundry; nonsmoking rooms; rooms for those w/limited mobility. *In room:* A/C, TV, dataport, coffeemaker, hair dryer, iron/ironing board, safe.

## VILLA RENTALS

**Palmetto Dunes Resort** 🌟 *Kids*    This relaxed and informal enclave of privately owned villas is set within the sprawling 1,800-acre complex of Palmetto Dunes Plantation, 7 miles south of the bridge. Accommodations range all the way from one-bedroom condos, booked mostly by groups, to four-bedroom villas, each of the latter furnished in the owner's personal taste. This is the place for longer stays, ideal for families who want a home away from home when they're traveling. In fact, in 2003 it was ranked as the number-one family resort in the continental U.S. and Canada by *Travel & Leisure Family.* Villas are fully equipped and receive housekeeping service; they're located on the ocean, fairways, or lagoons. Each villa comes with a full kitchen, washer and dryer, living room and dining area, and balcony or patio.

Palmetto Dunes (P.O. Box 5606), Hilton Head Island, SC 29938. © **800/845-6130** or 843/785-1161. Fax 843/686-2877. www.palmettodunesresort.com. 500 units. $700–$3,500 per week condo or villa. Golf and honeymoon packages available. 2-night minimum stay. 50% deposit for reservations. AE, DC, DISC, MC, V. Free parking. **Amenities:** 20 restaurants; 12 bars; 28 pools; 3 18-hole golf courses; 25 tennis courts; 200-slip marina; nonsmoking rooms; rooms for those w/limited mobility. *In room:* A/C, TV, dataport, safe (in some).

**The Sea Pines Resort** 🌟🌟🌟    Since 1955, this has been one of the leading condo developments in America, sprawling across 5,500 acres at the southernmost tip of the island. Don't come to Sea Pines looking for quick overnight accommodations. The entire place encourages stays of at least a week. Lodgings vary—everything from one- to four-bedroom villas to opulent private homes that are available when the owners are away. There is a minimum 1-week stay. The clientele here includes hordes of golfers, because Sea Pines is the home of the WorldCom Classic, a major stop on the PGA tour. If you're not a Sea Pines guest, you can eat, shop, or enjoy aspects of its nightlife. For full details on this varied resort/residential complex, write for a free "Sea Pines Vacation" brochure.

Sea Pines (P.O. Box 7000), Hilton Head Island, SC 29938. ℂ **888/807-6873** or 843/785-3333. Fax 843/842-1475. www.seapines.com. 400–500 units (with kitchenette or kitchen). $150–$230 1-bedroom villa; $225–$320 2-bedroom villa; $250–$375 3-bedroom villa. Rates are daily, based on 3-night stay. AE, DC, DISC, MC, V. **Amenities:** 12 restaurants; 12 bars; 2 outdoor pools; 3 18-hole golf courses; 28 tennis courts; fitness center; health spa; watersports; horseback riding; massage; babysitting; nonsmoking rooms; rooms for those w/limited mobility. *In room:* A/C, TV, kitchen, washer/dryer.

## 4 Where to Dine

Hilton Head has the dubious distinction of having the most expensive restaurants in South Carolina. What on island might be ranked as moderate would be considered very expensive in other parts of the state.

### EXPENSIVE

**The Barony Grill** ✦✦✦ INTERNATIONAL    The Barony, quick to promote itself as one of only two AAA four-star restaurants on Hilton Head Island, didn't shy away from installing decor that's a hybrid between a stage set in Old Vienna and a brick-lined, two-fisted steakhouse. The lighting is suitably dim; the drinks are appropriately stiff; and as you dine in your plushly upholstered alcove, you can stare at what might be the largest wrought-iron chandelier in the state. The place caters to a resort-going crowd of casual diners. Everything is well prepared and in copious portions, although the chef doesn't experiment or stray far from a limited selection of tried-and-true steak-and-lobster fare. Your meal might include New York strip steak, tenderloin of pork with purée of mangos, lobster thermidor, or fresh Atlantic swordfish with pistachios.

In the Westin Resort, 2 Grass Lawn Ave. ℂ 843/681-4000. Reservations recommended. Main courses $26–$35. AE, DC, DISC, MC, V. Wed–Sun 6–10pm.

### MODERATE

All of these so-called moderately priced restaurants have expensive shellfish dishes. However, if you order from the lower end of the price scale, enjoying mainly meat and poultry dishes, you'll find platters that cost $20 or less. Helpings for the most part are generous, so you'll rarely need to order appetizers, which will keep your overall cost in the more affordable price range.

**Alexander's** ✦ SEAFOOD/INTERNATIONAL    One of the most visible independent restaurants (in other words, not associated with a hotel) on Hilton Head lies in a gray-stained, wood-sided building just inside the main entrance into Palmetto Dunes. The decor includes Oriental carpets, big-windowed views over the salt marshes, wicker furniture, and an incongruous—some say startling—collection of vintage Harley Davidson motorcycles, none with more than 1,000 miles on them, dating from 1946, 1948, 1966, and 1993, respectively. Each is artfully displayed as a work of sculpture and as a catalyst to dialogues. Powerful flavors and a forthright approach to food are the rules of the kitchen. The chefs don't allow a lot of innovation on their menu—you've had all these dishes before—but fine ingredients are used, and each dish is prepared with discretion and restraint. Try the oysters Savannah or the bacon-wrapped shrimp, and most definitely have a bowl of Low Country seafood chowder. Guaranteed to set you salivating are the seafood pasta and the grilled Chilean sea bass in an herb vinaigrette. Steak, duck, rack of lamb, and pork—all in familiar versions—round out the menu.

76 Queen's Folly, Palmetto Dunes. ℂ **843/785-4999.** Reservations recommended. Main courses $19–$29. AE, DC, DISC, MC, V. Daily 5–10pm.

**Charlie's L'Etoile Verte** ★★ INTERNATIONAL   Outfitted like a tongue-in-cheek version of a Parisian bistro, our favorite restaurant on Hilton Head Island was also a favorite with former President Clinton during one of his island conferences. The atmosphere is unpretentious but elegant. The service is attentive, polite, and infused with an appealingly hip mixture of old- and new-world courtesy. Begin with shrimp-stuffed ravioli, and move on to grilled tuna with a jalapeño beurre blanc (white butter) sauce, grilled quail with shiitake mushrooms and a merlot sauce, or veal chops in peppercorn sauce. End this rare dining experience with biscotti or a "sailor's trifle." The wine list is impressive.

8 New Orleans Rd. ℂ **843/785-9277.** Reservations required. Lunch $10–$15; main courses $23–$30. AE, DISC, MC, V. Tues–Sat 11:30am–2pm; Mon–Sat 6–9pm.

**Café Europa** ★ CONTINENTAL/SEAFOOD   This fine European restaurant is at the base of the much-photographed Harbour Town Lighthouse, opening onto a panoramic view of Calibogue Sound and Daufuskie Island. In an informal, cheerful atmosphere, you can order fish that's poached, grilled, baked, or even fried. Baked Shrimp Daufuskie was inspired by local catches; it's stuffed with crab, green peppers, and onions. Grilled grouper is offered with a sauté of tomato, cucumber, dill, and white wine. Specialty dishes include a country-style chicken recipe from Charleston, with honey, fresh cream, and pecans. Tournedos au poivre is flambéed with brandy and simmered in a robust green-peppercorn sauce. The omelets, 14 in all, are perfectly prepared at breakfast (beginning at 10am) and are the island's finest. The bartender's Bloody Mary won an award as the island's best in a *Hilton Head News* contest.

Harbour Town, Sea Pines Plantation. ℂ **843/671-3399.** Reservations recommended for dinner. Lunch $8–$13; main courses $18–$28. AE, DC, MC, V. Daily 9am–2:30pm and 5:30–10pm.

**The Crazy Crab North** Kids SEAFOOD   This is a branch of the chain that's most likely to be patronized by locals. In a modern, low-slung building near the bridge that connects the island with the South Carolina mainland, it serves baked, broiled, or fried versions of stuffed flounder; seafood kabobs; oysters; the catch of the day; and any combination thereof. She-crab soup and New England–style clam chowder are prepared fresh daily; children's menus are available; and desserts are a high point for chocoholics.

U.S. 278 at Jarvis Creek. ℂ **843/681-5021** or 843/363-2722. Reservations not accepted. Lunch $6–$15; main courses $17–$35. AE, DC, DISC, MC, V. Daily 11:30am–10pm.

**Harbour Town Grill** ★ Finds AMERICAN   For years, this woodsy-looking refuge of golfers and their guests was open only to members of the nearby golf club. Several years ago, however, it opened to the public at large, a fact that's still not widely publicized in Hilton Head, and which sometimes seems to catch some local residents by surprise. Looking something like a postmodern version of a French château, this small-scale affair has views over the 9th hole and room for only about 50 diners at a time. Inside, it's sporty-looking and relatively informal during the day, when most of the menu is devoted to thickly stuffed deli-style sandwiches and salads named in honor of golf stars. Dinners are more formal and more elaborate, with good-tasting dishes such as local shrimp sautéed with ginger, Vidalia onions, and collard greens; roasted rack of American lamb with white beans, spinach, and rosemary; and an array of thick-cut slabs of meat that include beef, lamb, veal, and chicken.

In the Harbour Town Golf Links Clubhouse, Sea Pines. © **843/363-4080**. Reservations recommended for dinner only. Lunch sandwiches and platters $9–$13; dinner main courses $20–$35. AE, DC, DISC, MC, V. Daily 7–11am and 11am–3pm; Wed–Sun 6–10pm.

### Hudson's Seafood House on the Docks SEAFOOD

Built as a seafood-processing factory in 1912, this restaurant still processes fish, clams, and oysters for local distribution, so you know that everything is fresh. If you're seated in the north dining room, you'll be eating in the original oyster factory. We strongly recommend the crab cakes, the steamed shrimp, and the especially appealing blackened catch of the day. Local oysters (seasonal) are also a specialty, breaded and deep-fried. Before and after dinner, stroll on the docks past shrimp boats, and enjoy the view of the mainland and nearby Parris Island. Sunsets here are panoramic. Lunch is served in the Oyster Bar.

1 Hudson Rd. (go to Skull Creek just off Square Pope Rd. signposted from U.S. 278). © **843/681-2772**. Reservations not accepted. Main courses $8–$15 lunch, $15–$35 dinner. AE, DC, MC, V. Daily 11am–2:30pm and 5–10pm.

### Mostly Seafood ★★ SEAFOOD/AMERICAN

The most elegant and innovative restaurant in the Hilton resort, Mostly Seafood is noted for the way its chefs make imaginative dishes out of fresh seafood. Something about the decor—backlighting and glass-backed murals in designs of sea-green and blue—creates the illusion that you're floating in a boat. Menu items include fresh grouper, snapper, swordfish, flounder, salmon, trout, halibut, and pompano, prepared in any of seven ways. Dishes that consistently draw applause are corn-crusted filet of salmon with essence of hickory-smoked veal bacon and peach relish; and "fish in the bag," prepared with fresh grouper, scallops, and shrimp, laced with a dill-flavored cream sauce and baked in a brown paper bag.

In the Hilton Oceanfront Resort, Palmetto Dunes Plantation. © **843/842-8000**. Reservations recommended. Main courses $18–$35. AE, DC, DISC, MC, V. Daily 5:30–10pm.

### The Old Oyster Factory ★ SEAFOOD/STEAK

Built on the site of one of Hilton Head's original oyster canneries, this landmark offers waterfront dining overlooking Broad Creek. The restaurant's post-and-beam decor has garnered several architectural awards. At sunset, every table enjoys a panoramic view as diners sip their "sundowners."

All the dishes here can be found on seafood menus from Maine to Hawaii. But that doesn't mean they're not good. The cuisine is truly palate friendly, beginning with such appetizers as a tangy kettle of clams steamed in a lemon-butter sauce, or else a delectable crab cake sautéed and served in a chile-garlic tartar sauce. Will it be oysters Rockefeller (baked with spinach and a béarnaise sauce) or oysters Savannah (shrimp, crabmeat, and smoked bacon)? Almond-crusted mahimahi is among the more tantalizing main courses, as are seafood pasta and broiled sea scallops. Non-seafood eaters can go for a chargrilled chicken breast.

101 Marsh Rd. © **843/681-6040**. Reservations not accepted. Main courses $18–$23. AE, DC, DISC, MC, V. Daily 5–10pm (closing times can vary).

### Rendez-Vous Café ★ *Finds* FRENCH/PROVENÇAL

Some of the best French dining in eastern South Carolina is served here in this bistro, which offers a piano player on Wednesday and Thursday nights. Its decor transports you to the south of France. Inventive cookery with fresh flavors characterizes this popular dining spot. The list of hors d'oeuvres is the island's finest, ranging from many of the classics such as French onion soup gratinée or escargots bourguignon, but also taking in such delights as a French country pâté with duck mousse combo. The main courses are prepared with finesse, including crab cakes Mediterranean with ratatouille and polenta, or frogs' legs Provençal on a bed of couscous. Grouper is prepared Riviera style—that is, sautéed in olive oil with sweet red bell peppers. The chefs are diligent about maintaining high standards, and rely on market-fresh products. The good news: The dishes are nowhere as heavy or as laden with sauces as you might expect from a classic French restaurant serving food in the Escoffier tradition.

14 Greenwood Dr., Seapines Circle. © **843/785-5070.** Reservations recommended. Main courses $8.95–$15 lunch, $15–$27 dinner. MC, V. Mon–Fri 11:30am–2pm; Mon–Sat 5:30–9pm.

**Santa Fe Cafe** ⭐ MEXICAN    The best, most stylish Mexican restaurant on Hilton Head, the Santa Fe Cafe has rustic, Southwestern-inspired decor and cuisine that infuses traditional recipes with nouvelle flair. Menu items are often presented in colors as bright as the Painted Desert. Dishes might include tequila shrimp; herb-roasted chicken with jalapeño cornbread stuffing and mashed potatoes laced with red chiles; grilled tenderloin of pork with smoked habañero sauce and sweet-potato fries; and worthy burritos and chimichangas. The chiles rellenos are exceptional, stuffed with California goat cheese and sun-dried tomatoes. The quesadilla is one of the most beautifully presented dishes of any restaurant in town.

700 Plantation Center. © **843/785-3838.** Reservations recommended. Main courses $6–$8 lunch, $20–$30 dinner. AE, DISC, MC, V. Mon–Fri noon–2pm; daily 6–10pm.

## INEXPENSIVE

**Hofbrauhaus** _Kids_ GERMAN    A sanitized German beer hall, this family favorite serves locals and visitors such classics as grilled bratwurst and smoked Westphalian ham, along with Wiener schnitzel and sauerbraten. One specialty we like is roast duckling with spaetzle, red cabbage, and orange sauce. Helpings are so big here that one main course is more than adequate for most appetites—there really is no need for appetizers. For example, a recent serving of a house specialty, prime strip of sirloin, turned out to be 14 ounces of aged beef, charbroiled and served with buttered whipped potatoes, fresh crisp garden vegetables, and a red-wine mushroom sauce. Note the stein and mug collection as you're deciding which of the large variety of German beers to order. A children's menu is available. Live music is offered on Tuesday, Wednesday, Thursday, and Friday nights.

In the Pope Ave. Mall. © **843/785-3663.** Reservations recommended. Early-bird dinner (5–6:30pm only) $14; main courses $16–$24. AE, MC, V. Daily 5–10pm.

**Taste of Thailand** ⭐ _Finds_ THAI    Offering exotic flavors, this eatery does a bustling business among cost-conscious diners who appreciate the emphasis on exotic curries, lemon grass, and coconuts. Among scattered examples of Thai woodcarvings and handicrafts, you can enjoy a limited but choice menu offering beef, pork, chicken, shrimp, mussels, or tofu in a choice of different flavors. One of our favorite dishes is chicken with stir-fried vegetables, Thai basil, and oyster sauce. The hottest dish is the green curry, but equally delectable is the curry with roasted peanuts and red chiles flavored with cumin seeds. Thai spring rolls appear as an appetizer. A hot and sour soup is always on the menu, as is a spicy squid salad. Most dishes are at the low end of the price scale.

Plantation Center, 807 William Hilton Pkwy., Suite 1200. ✆ **843/341-6500.** Reservations recommended. Main courses $12–$25. AE, DC, MC, V. Mon–Sat 5–11pm.

## 5 Hilton Head After Dark

Hilton Head doesn't have Myrtle Beach's nightlife, but enough is here, centered mainly in hotels and resorts. Casual dress (but not swimming attire) is acceptable in most clubs.

Cultural interest focuses on the **Arts Center of Coastal Carolina,** in the Self Family Arts Center, 14 Shelter Cove Lane (✆ **843/842-ARTS;** www.artscenter-hhi.org), which enjoys one of the best theatrical reputations in the Southeast. The Elizabeth Wallace Theater, a 350-seat, state-of-the-art theater, was added to the multiplex in 1996. The older Dunnagan's Alley Theater is located in a renovated warehouse. A wide range of musicals, contemporary comedies, and classic dramas is presented. Show times are 8pm Tuesday to Saturday, with a Sunday matinee at 2pm. Adult ticket prices range from $45 for a musical to $35 for a play. Children 16 and under are charged $18 to $23. The box office is open 10am to 5pm Monday to Friday.

The island abounds in sports bars, far too many to document here. We recommend **Callahan Sports Bar & Grill,** 38 New Orleans Rd. (✆ **843-686-7665**); and **Casey's Sports Bar & Grill,** 37 New Orleans Rd. (✆ **843/785-2255**).

**Quarterdeck**   Our favorite waterfront lounge is the best place on the island to watch sunsets, but you can visit at any time during the afternoon and in the evening until 2am. Try to go early and grab one of the outdoor rocking chairs to prepare yourself for nature's light show. There's dancing every night to beach music and top-40 hits. Daily 11am to 2am. Harbour Town, Sea Pines Plantation. ✆ **843/671-2222.**

**Remy's**   Got the munchies? At Remy's, you can devour buckets of oysters or shrimp, served with the inevitable fries. The setting is rustic and raffish, and live music is provided. Daily 11am to 4am. 28 Arrow Rd. ✆ **843/842-3800.**

**The Salty Dog Cafe**   Locals used to keep this laid-back place near the beach to themselves, but now more and more visitors are showing up. Soft guitar music or Jimmy Buffett is often played. Dress is casual. Sit under one of the sycamores, enjoying your choice of food from an outdoor grill or buffet. Daily until 2am. South Beach Marina. ✆ **843/671-2233.**

## 6 Side Trip to Beaufort ★★

Some 30 miles north of Hilton Head Island, Beaufort (Low Country pronunciation *bew*-fort) is an old seaport with narrow streets shaded by huge live oaks and lined with 18th-century homes. The oldest house (at Port Republic and New sts.) was built in 1717. This was the second area in North America to be discovered by the Spanish (1520), the site of the first fort on the continent (1525), and the first attempted settlement (1562). Several forts have been excavated, dating from 1566 and 1577.

Beaufort has been used as a setting for several films, including *The Big Chill.* Scenes from the Paramount blockbuster *Forrest Gump,* starring Tom Hanks, and *The Prince of Tides* were also shot here.

If you're traveling from the north, take I-95 to exit 33; then follow the signs to the center of Beaufort. From the south, take I-95 to exit 8 and follow the signs. From Hilton Head, go on U.S. 278 West, and after S.C. 170 North joins U.S. 278, follow S.C. 170 into Beaufort.

**Beaufort Chamber of Commerce,** 1106 Carteret St. (P.O. Box 910), Beaufort, SC 29901 (© **843/524-3163;** www.beaufortsc.org), has information and self-guided tours of this historic town. It's open daily 9am to 5:30pm. If your plans are for early to mid-October, contact the **Historic Beaufort Foundation,** P.O. Box 11, Beaufort, SC 29901 (© **843/379-3331;** www.historic-beaufort.org), for dates and details regarding its 3 days of antebellum house and garden tours.

A tour called **The Spirit of Old Beaufort,** 103 West St. extension (© **843/ 525-0459;** www.spiritofoldbeaufort.com), takes you on a journey through the old town, exploring local history, architecture, horticulture, and Low Country life. You'll see houses that are not accessible on other tours. Your host, clad in period costume, will guide you for 2 hours from Monday to Saturday at 10:30am and 2:30pm. The cost is $13 for adults, $7.50 for children 6 to 12. Tours depart from just behind the John Market Verdier House Museum.

**John Mark Verdier House Museum,** 801 Bay St. (© **843/379-6335**), is a restored 1802 house partially furnished to depict the life of a merchant planter during the period 1800 to 1825. It's one of the best examples of the Federal period and was once known as the Lafayette Building, because the Marquis de Lafayette is said to have spoken here in 1825. It's open Monday to Saturday from 11:30am to 3:30pm, charging $6 for adults, $3 for children; children under 6 are admitted free.

**St. Helena's Episcopal Church,** 507 New Castle St. (© **843/522-1712**), traces its origin back to 1712. Visitors, admitted free Monday to Saturday from 10am to 4pm, can see its classic interior and visit the graveyard, where tombstones served as operating tables during the Civil War.

## WHERE TO STAY

**The Beaufort Inn** ★★ Built in 1897, this is the most appealing hotel in Beaufort and the place where whatever movie star happens to be shooting a film in town is likely to stay. The woodwork and moldings inside are among the finest in Beaufort, and the circular, four-story staircase has been the subject of numerous photographs and architectural awards. The guest rooms, each decorated in brightly colored individual style, are conversation pieces. The inn also has a wine bar, a grill room, and a rose garden. Children under 8 are not welcome.

809 Port Republic St., Beaufort, SC 29902. © **843/521-9000.** Fax 843/521-9500. www.beaufortinn.com. 21 units. $145–$350 double; $215–$350 suite. Rates include full gourmet breakfast. AE, DISC, MC, V. **Amenities:** Restaurant; bar; limited room service; nonsmoking rooms. *In room:* A/C, TV, dataport, coffeemaker, hair dryer, iron/ironing board.

**The Cuthbert House Inn** ★★ One of the grand old B&Bs of South Carolina, this showcase Southern home was built in 1790 in classic style. The inn was remodeled shortly after the Civil War to take on a more Victorian aura, but its present owner, Sharon Groves, has worked to modernize it without sacrificing its grace or antiquity. Graffiti carved by Union soldiers can still be seen on the fireplace mantel in the Eastlake Room. Guest rooms are elegantly furnished in Southern plantation style, and some have four-poster beds. All units come equipped with bathrooms containing tub/shower combinations; some bathrooms have old cast-iron soaking tubs. The inn is filled with large parlors and sitting rooms, and has spacious hallways and 12-foot ceilings characteristic of Greek Revival homes. At breakfast in the conservatory, you can order such delights as Georgia ice cream (cheese grits) and freshly made breads.

1203 Bay St., Beaufort, SC 29901. © **800/327-9275** or 843/521-1315. Fax 843/521-1314. www.cuthberthouse inn.com. 7 units. $145–$215 double; $195–$265 suite. Rates include full breakfast and afternoon tea or refreshments. AE, DISC, MC, V. Free parking. **Amenities:** Breakfast room; lounge; bikes; nonsmoking rooms. *In room:* A/C, TV, dataport, fridge, hair dryer, iron/ironing board.

**The Rhett House Inn** ★★★    This inn is certainly very popular, at least with Hollywood film crews. Because it was a site for *Forrest Gump, The Prince of Tides,* and *The Big Chill,* chances are that you've seen it before. It's a Mobil and AAA four-star inn in a restored 1820 Greek Revival plantation-type home. Rooms are furnished with English and American antiques, and ornamented with Oriental rugs; eight contain whirlpools. The veranda makes an ideal place to sit and view the gardens. The inn is open year-round. Children under 5 are not accepted.

1009 Craven St., Beaufort, SC 29902. ✆ 888/480-9530 or 843/524-9030. Fax 843/524-1310. www.rhett houseinn.com. 17 units. $195–$325 double. Rates include full breakfast, afternoon tea, and evening hors d'oeuvres. AE, DISC, MC, V. Free parking. **Amenities:** Breakfast room; lounge; nonsmoking rooms. *In room:* A/C, TV, dataport, minibar (in some), hair dryer, iron/ironing board.

**Two Suns Inn**    When this place was built in 1917, it was one of the grandest homes in its prosperous neighborhood, offering views of the coastal road and the tidal flatlands beyond. Every imaginable modern (at the time) convenience was added, including a baseboard vacuum-cleaning system, an electric call box, and steam heat. Later, when it became housing for unmarried teachers in the public schools, the place ran down. Now it's a cozy B&B. Part of the inn's appeal stems from its lack of pretension, as a glance at the homey bedrooms with simple furnishings and neatly kept bathrooms will show. Children under 12 are not welcome.

1705 Bay St., Beaufort, SC 29902. ✆ 800/532-4244 or 843/522-1122. Fax 843/522-1122. www.twosuns inn.com. 5 units. $135–$200 double. Rates include full breakfast and afternoon cordials. AE, DISC, MC, V. Free parking. **Amenities:** Breakfast room; lounge; nonsmoking rooms; rooms for those w/limited mobility. *In room:* A/C, TV, dataport, hair dryer.

## WHERE TO DINE

Fans of the former Ollie's by the Bay in downtown Beaufort should know that it has moved to Lady's Island and changed its name to **Ollie's Seafood Restaurant,** 71 Sea Island Pkwy. (✆ **843/525-6333**). It still serves some of the best steak in the area, and shrimp burgers are a house specialty. The catch of the day can be broiled, blackened, or sautéed.

**The Beaufort Inn Restaurant & Wine Bar** ★ INTERNATIONAL    Stylish and urbane, and awash with colonial lowland references, this is the local choice for celebratory or business dinners, amid candlelit surroundings. Meat courses include chicken piccata with artichokes and sun-dried tomatoes, and an excellent grilled filet mignon with herbal Gorgonzola butter and shiitake mushrooms; vegetarian main courses include roasted-pepper-and-eggplant torte. On the menu is a variation on a dish whose invention has been claimed by a string of other restaurants in the South Carolina Low Country: crispy whole flounder with strawberry-watermelon chutney.

In the Beaufort Inn, 809 Port Republic St. ✆ **843/521-9000.** Reservations recommended. Main courses $17–$30. AE, DISC, MC, V. Mon–Sat 6–10pm; Sun 11:30am–2pm and 6–10pm.

**Emily's** INTERNATIONAL    This is our favorite restaurant in Beaufort, a spot whose ambience and attitude put us in mind of Scandinavia. That's hardly surprising, because the bearded owner is an émigré from Sweden who feels comfortable in the South Carolina lowlands after years of life at sea. Some folks just go to the bar to sample tapas: miniature portions of tempura shrimp, fried scallops, stuffed peppers, and at least 50 other items. Menu items might include rich cream of mussel and shrimp soup; filet "black and white" (filets of beef and pork served with béarnaise sauce); duck with orange sauce; and a meltingly tender Wiener schnitzel. Everything is served in stomach-stretching portions.

906 Port Republic St. (**€**) **843/522-1866.** Reservations recommended. Tapas $8; main courses $20–$27. AE, DISC, MC, V. Drinks and tapas Mon–Sat 4–10pm; main courses Mon–Sat 6–10pm.

**Kathleen's Grille** *(Finds)* SEAFOOD/SOUTHERN   This local eatery has plenty of Low Country atmosphere and is known for its fresh fish dinners. We'd go here for its Southern starters alone, including fried green tomatoes topped with a shrimp salsa, or the "classy" crab chowder. For lunch, try an offering from the "sandwich showcase," including soft-shell crab or fresh grouper. Salads, including a seafood pasta version, are made fresh daily. At night the restaurant serves some of the best fish platters in the area, including grilled shrimp and boiled oysters. For the meat lover, there is the inevitable rib-eye or pork chop, the latter coming with a sweet and spicy berry glaze. One section of the menu is reserved for "Kathleen's kids," but the offerings are so meager (fresh boxed cereals, a hot dog), your little ones may end up nutritionally deprived.

822 Bay St. (**€**) **843/524-2500.** Reservations not required. Lunch $7–$9; main courses $15–$18. AE, DISC, MC, V. Mon–Fri 11am–10pm; Sat–Sun 7am–9pm.

# 13

# Myrtle Beach & the Grand Strand

One of the top vacation destinations along the East Coast, the Myrtle Beach/Grand Strand area stretches south from the South Carolina state line at Little River to Georgetown. It's 98 miles north of Charleston but a world away in ambience.

On a summer day, the population here exceeds half a million people. The Grand Strand hosts more than twice as many visitors each year as Hawaii. The beach is not the only reason people come—shopping, golfing, sightseeing, and live theater are also draws. In the past few years, Myrtle Beach has grown into a year-round destination, and as a result, South Carolina now ranks second only to Florida as a vacation destination, ahead of California, New Jersey, and North Carolina. The Travel Channel has voted it the "Best Family Beach."

Myrtle Beach is at the center of the Grand Strand, a 60-mile string of beaches. Named for the abundance of myrtle trees in this area, Myrtle Beach is an ideal base for a Grand Strand vacation. As the largest beach resort along the Grand Strand, it has the most facilities, entertainment, and restaurants, and as a result, it attracts the most visitors. But if you're looking for a wild, swinging kind of beach resort, this isn't it. The tone is that of a family resort, with almost as much attention paid to children's needs as to those of adults. Many hotels and motels provide activity programs and playgrounds

with supervision, and nearly all have babysitter lists for parents who like a little nightlife.

The big attraction in the area is the beach, of course. Sunbathing, swimming, boating, and all the other watersports rank first among things to do. Fishing is first-rate, whether you cast your line from the surf, a public pier, or a charter boat. Surf fishing is permitted all along the beach. Charter boats ("head boats," as the locals say) are available at marinas up and down the Strand, and even at the height of the season, you'll be able to book a trip without much difficulty.

You can swing a golf club at any of 120 courses. Most motels and hotels hold guest-membership privileges, entitling you to reduced greens fees. The season extends from February to November. There are also more than 200 public and private tennis courts in the Grand Strand area.

But although the area's tourist growth may be almost unparalleled in America, there are some clouds on the horizon. Environmentalists are concerned that the rampaging development puts the region's natural beauty at risk. Longtime promoters fear that Myrtle Beach's family-friendly atmosphere may be threatened. (Families make up an important part of the trade, and efforts to keep it that way have meant banning thong bathing suits and relegating topless clubs to an industrial park.) Others bemoan the

# Myrtle Beach & the Grand Strand

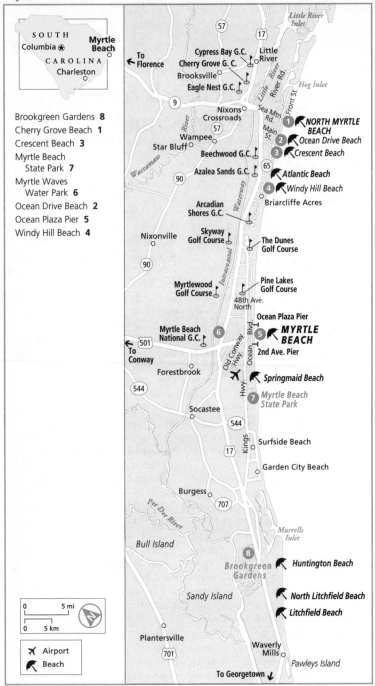

SOUTH
Columbia ✦
CAROLINA
Charleston

Myrtle
Beach

Brookgreen Gardens **8**
Cherry Grove Beach **1**
Crescent Beach **3**
Myrtle Beach
State Park **7**
Myrtle Waves
Water Park **6**
Ocean Drive Beach **2**
Ocean Plaza Pier **5**
Windy Hill Beach **4**

To Florence

Cypress Bay G.C.
Cherry Grove G. C.
Brooksville
Eagle Nest G.C.

Little
River

Little River Rd.

Front St.

Hog Inlet

Nixons
Crossroads
Wampee
Star Bluff
Beechwood G.C.
Azalea Sands G.C.

River

Waccamaw

Sea Mtn. Rd.
Main St.

**1** ↖ **NORTH MYRTLE BEACH**
**2** ↖ *Ocean Drive Beach*
**3** ↖ *Crescent Beach*
↖ *Atlantic Beach*
**4** ↖ *Windy Hill Beach*
Briarcliffe Acres

Arcadian
Shores G.C.

Waterway

Intracoastal

Skyway
Golf Course
The Dunes
Golf Course

Nixonville

Myrtlewood
Golf Course
Pine Lakes
Golf Course
48th Ave.
North

Ocean Plaza Pier
Myrtle Beach
National G.C.
**6**
**5** ↖ **MYRTLE BEACH**
2nd Ave. Pier

To
Conway
Forestbrook

Old Conway Hwy.

Ocean Blvd.

✈ Springmaid Beach
**7** Myrtle Beach State Park

Hwy.

Socastee

Kings

Surfside Beach

Garden City Beach

Burgess

Pee Dee River

Murrells
Inlet

Bull Island

**8**
Brookgreen
Gardens

↖ *Huntington Beach*

Sandy Island

↖ *North Litchfield Beach*
↖ *Litchfield Beach*

0      5 mi
0      5 km

Plantersville

Waverly
Mills
*Pawleys Island*

✈ Airport
↖ Beach

To Georgetown ↓

theme-park atmosphere, likening the Grand Strand to a combination of Disneyland and Las Vegas (without the casinos).

Change is slowly coming to Myrtle Beach. North European tour groups are coming to the Grand Strand in increasing numbers, drawn by advertisements that tout the area as a seaside resort that evokes heartland America at its most authentic, least apologetic, and most unselfconscious. Food and booze are super-cheap. And corporate entrepreneurs are pouring money into less expensive versions of Disney World, where a family can amuse itself at rates much, much lower than those offered in Orlando.

## 1 Essentials

**GETTING THERE**    **Myrtle Beach International Airport** (© 843/448-1589) has scheduled air service via **Air Tran** (© 800/247-8726; www.airtran.com), **Delta/ASA/ComAir** (© 800/221-1212; www.delta.com); **Spirit Airlines** (© 800/ 772-7117; www.spiritair.com), and **US Airways** (© 800/428-4322; www.us air.com). If you're driving, U.S. 17 runs north and south along the Grand Strand, and U.S. 17 Business runs through Myrtle Beach; U.S. 501 runs east from I-95.

**VISITOR INFORMATION**    The **Myrtle Beach Area Chamber of Commerce** is at 1200 N. Oak St. (P.O. Box 2115), Myrtle Beach, SC 29578 (© **800/ 356-3016** or 843/626-7444 to order literature only; www.myrtlebeachinfo.com), open Monday to Friday from 8am to 5pm. One publication jam-packed with specific area information is *Stay & Play* (available from the chamber of commerce).

## 2 The Beaches, the Links & Beyond

**Myrtle Beach Pavilion Amusement Park** *(Kids)*    Named the number-one family attraction in the area by the Travel Channel, this horseshoe-shaped entertainment complex offers all the summer fun you may remember from the 1960s and 1970s, with rock 'n' roll blasting away, carnival rides, and a carousel. Along with the kiddie rides, the park has the largest flume in the Carolinas, not to mention sidewalk cafes, video games, and even a teenage nightclub where no alcohol is served. The pavilion covers nearly a dozen acres and features more than 40 rides. One of the biggest attractions is the Hurricane roller coaster.

9th Ave. N. and Ocean Blvd. © 843/448-6456. www.mbpavilion.com. All-day pass $24 ages 7–53, $15 seniors 54 and up and children 3–6. Individual tickets $5 (allows 7 rides). Open Mar–Sept. Summer hours daily 1pm–midnight. Call ahead in other months—times vary according to seasons.

**Myrtle Beach Waves Water Park** *(Kids)*    Myrtle Beach is hot as hell in summer, so it's little wonder that June through August this place is jam-packed with families escaping the heat. The state's largest water park has some 20 acres of curves, waves, and swerves, and employs 1 million gallons of water. Attracting

---

*Tips* **Cutting Your Driving Time**

If you're heading from Myrtle Beach to North Myrtle Beach, the opening of the 29-mile Conway Bypass has cut driving time by half an hour. The road brings to life the "Bridge to Nowhere," which for 3 years stood astride the Intracoastal Waterway without a road. The bypass, also State Road 22, runs between U.S. 501, the major route to the coast, northwest of Conway, and U.S. 17 in North Myrtle Beach.

some 200,000 visitors a year, the park offers 32 rides and various attractions, including an Ocean in Motion Wave pool; the LayZee River, a slow, 3 mph ride around the park; and Bubble Bay, a 7,000-foot leisure pool with a trio of cascading water umbrellas. Other amusements include a Saturation Station with splashes, slides, and waterfalls, including a Caribbean-themed "volcano"—the world's tallest tubular slides (10 stories high).

U.S. 17 Bypass at 10th Ave. N. ✆ 843/448-1026. Admission $24 ages 7–54, $15 ages 3–6, $15 ages 55 plus, free for ages 3 and under. Mid-May to mid-Sept daily 10am–5pm (until 6pm June–Aug).

**NASCAR Speed Park** *Kids*   The entrepreneurs of the park claim that "if you got any closer to the real thing, you'd have to hire a pit crew!" Opened in 1998, it's practically a Disneyland devoted to racing, complete with seven thrilling racetracks and such attractions as speed bumper boats, an indoor climbing wall, and kiddie rides. The most exciting track is a half-mile course featuring ⅝-scale Nextel Cup–style cars. (*Note:* Drivers must be 16 years old with a valid license.) All sorts of games, some 50 in all, are a feature of the Speed Dome Arcade, including side-by-side linked racing machines.

Hwy. 17 at Bypass at 21st Ave. N. (across from Broadway at the Beach). ✆ 843/918-8725. Single ticket $75, family ticket $175. Tax extra. Year-round daily 10am–10pm (closes at 8pm in winter).

**Ripley's Aquarium** ★★ *Kids*   This is the most visited attraction in South Carolina, and deservedly so. Located in Broadway at the Beach, this aquarium—one of the greatest in America—was built at a cost of $40 million and is maintained in state-of-the-art condition. Visitors are surrounded on all sides by menacing 10-foot sharks as they travel through Dangerous Reef, a 750,000-gallon tank. The question always asked is why these don't monsters gobble up the other fish in the tank. The answer: They're so well fed they don't bother. Most of the habitats in the various holding tanks are saltwater. The only freshwater exhibit is of the Rio Amazon, displaying fearsome piranhas, Aruana and Pacu. You can spend at least 4 hours here, enjoying such pleasures as Rainbow Rock, with its view of thousands of brilliantly colored fish from the Pacific. Children are drawn to the Sea-for-Yourself Discovery Center, an interactive, multimedia playground. Dive shows and marine education sessions are presented hourly.

1110 Celebrity Circle. ✆ 843/916-0888. www.ripleysaquarium.com. Admission $17 ages 12 and up, $10 ages 5–11, $3.95 ages 2–4, free for children under 2. Daily 9am–11pm.

## BEACHES

The Myrtle Beach sand is mostly hard-packed and the color of brown sugar, to which it's often compared. The main action is around the Myrtle Beach Pavilion Amusement Park (see above) at Ocean Boulevard and Ninth Avenue North. If you'd like more seclusion, head north of 79th Avenue for several miles.

The beach has lifeguards and plenty of fast-food joints. Amazingly, there are no public toilets. South Carolina law, however, obligates hotels to allow beach buffs to use their facilities. (Many male beachgoers don't bother to go inside the hotels but use walls instead—a habit that has provoked endless local-newspaper comment.)

At the southern tier of the beach, **Myrtle Beach State Park** (✆ 843/238-5325) offers 312 acres of pinewoods and a sandy beach. Admission to the park is $3 adults, $2.50 seniors, free for ages 15 and younger. It has toilets, along with pavilions, picnic tables, and a swimming pool. It's possible to fish from the pier for $4.50. The park is full of nature trails and offers 302 campsites. You can either reserve a campsite in advance (winter $18, summer $24) or take your chances on a first-come, first-served site (winter $17, summer $23). The park is open daily from 6am to 10pm.

## GOLF

Golf enthusiasts can tee off at 120 **championship golf courses** ★★★, making it possible to play a different course every day for almost 3 months straight. Many local courses host major professional and amateur tournaments, such as the DuPont World Amateur Tournament. One of the sport's most prestigious events, the Energizer Senior Tour, is held November 6 to November 12.

Variety is a contributing factor to the success and popularity of Grand Strand golf courses, which come in many shapes, sizes, and degrees of difficulty. Courses have been designed by some of the best-known names in golf: Jack Nicklaus, Arnold Palmer, Rees Jones, Tom Fazio, Gary Player, Don Ross, Dan Maple, Tom Jackson, and Pete and P. B. Dye.

Golf-course architects have taken care to protect the habitats of indigenous wildlife. Players find themselves in the midst of towering Carolina pines or giant live oaks draped in Spanish moss. Some courses overlook huge bluffs with the Atlantic Ocean or Intracoastal Waterway in the background. Some unusual attractions are featured: a private airstrip adjoining a clubhouse, a cable car that crosses the Intracoastal Waterway, and alligators lurking in water hazards. Some courses are built on the grounds of historic rice plantations, which offer Old South atmosphere.

Although golf is played all year, spring and autumn are the busiest seasons. Many golf packages include room, board, and greens fees. For information, call **Golf Holiday** (© **800/845-4653;** www.golfholiday.com).

**Aberdeen Country Club,** S.C. 9, North Myrtle Beach (© **800/882-3902** or 843/235-6079), is a 27-hole course designed by Tom Jackson, charging greens fees of $29 to $60. Along the banks of the Waccamaw River, this course has Bermuda greens, along with a pro shop and a practice area with a driving range.

**Arcadian Shores,** 701 Hilton Rd. (© **866/326-5275** or 843/449-5217), an 18-hole, par-72 course, opened in 1974, when it was created by noted golf architect Rees Jones. Just 5 miles north of Myrtle Beach off U.S. 17, the course has bent-grass greens winding through a stately live-oak grove. Electric carts are required, and greens fees are $33 to $56.

**Azalea Sands,** 2100 U.S. 17, North Myrtle Beach (© **800/253-2312** or 843/272-6191), opened in 1972. The 18-hole course features white-sand traps and blue lakes. Designed by architect Gene Hamm, it's a popular course for golfers of all handicaps. Greens fees range from $34 to $48.

**Beachwood,** 1520 U.S. 17, Crescent Section, North Myrtle Beach (© **800/ 526-4889** or 843/272-6168), is another course designed by Gene Hamm. Opened in 1968, it has 18 holes, charging greens fees ranging from $33 to $51. It's a par-72 course with blue tees of 6,825 yards. The course annually hosts the Carolinas' PGA Senior's Championship and DuPont World Amateur.

**Caledonia Golf Course and Fishing Club,** Pawleys Island (© **800/483- 6800** or 843/237-3675), is set atop what used to be a series of marshy rice paddies, and some of its links are graced with century-old oak trees. This golf course has an intelligent layout favored by pros, and a clubhouse whose architecture was inspired by an antique Low Country plantation house. Its only drawback is a location that's about a 30-minute drive south of Myrtle Beach. A flotilla of charter boats and deep-sea fishing pros are associated with this place as well. Greens fees range from $82 to $132.

**Grand Dunes Golf Club** ★★, 8700 Golf Village Lane (© **843/449-7070**), is one of the newer and better courses, set on a bluff overlooking the Intracoastal Waterway with panoramic views. Rated by *Golf Magazine* as one of the best courses in the nation, it is a par-72 course with numerous elevation changes and wide Bermuda grass fairways, including 34 acres of lakes. Greens fees range from $94 to $186.

**Legends** ★★★, U.S. 501, Myrtle Beach (© **800/530-1873** or 843/236-9318), designed by Pete Dye and Tom Doak, opened in 1990. The 54-hole, par-72 course charges greens fees of $70 to $120. Its Mooreland Course was ranked by *Golf Digest* as one of the top five new public courses in America in 1991. Dye's flair for deep bunkers, undulating fairways and greens, and signature bulkheads have transformed this course into one of the strongest challenges along the East Coast. The 42,000-square-foot Scottish-style clubhouse is an impressive entry to the course. Heathland, designed by Doak, has been called "the next best thing to visiting Scotland."

**Myrtlewood,** 48th Avenue (U.S. 17 Business), North Myrtle Beach (© **800/283-3633** or 843/449-5134), a 36-hole, par-72 Pinehills course, was designed by architect Arthur Hills. Greens fees range from $44 to $63. Bordering the Intracoastal Waterway, the Pines Course is the fourth oldest at Myrtle Beach, measuring 6,640 yards. The Palmetto Course is one of the best in the area, with bent-grass putting greens. It stretches for 6,953 yards.

**Pine Lakes Country Club,** 5603 Woodside Ave., Myrtle Beach (© **800/446-6817** or 843/449-6459), is semi-private, but under some conditions (such as whenever the fairways aren't too crowded), out-of-towners are allowed to play. Established in 1920, it's the oldest golf course in the region, despite a name change that occurred in 1944. Linked to the early days of *Sports Illustrated* magazine, the course is permeated with a more distinctive Scottish flavor than any other golf course in town. It can even get very posh, as when mimosas and/or Low Country stews and chowders are served on the links. Greens fees range from $44 to $76.

## OTHER OUTDOOR PURSUITS

**FISHING** Because of the warming temperature of the Gulf Stream, fishing is good from early spring until around Christmas. You can pursue king mackerel, spadefish, amberjack, barracuda, sea bass, and Spanish mackerel, along with grouper and red snapper. Great fishing is available aboard any boat of **Captain Dick's,** Business Highway 17, at Myrtle Beach South Strand and Murrells Inlet (© **866/557-FISH** or 843/651-3676; www.captdicks.com). Captain Dick offers three charters that go as far as 60 miles offshore. The Sea Bass Fishing Adventure is a half-day trip priced at $39 for adults and $23 per child (12 and under). The rates include rod and reel, bait, tackle, license. Sightseers can also take this trip for $18 per person.

The Sundown Special Fishing trip is a 9-hour trip that goes slightly farther out than the Sea Bass Adventure, in search of bigger fish. Rates are $55 for adults and $29 for children (12 and under), including rod and reel, bait, tackle, and license. Electric reels are available for $9. The All Day Gulf Stream trip is an 11-hour jaunt that departs at 7am in search of red snapper, grouper, triggerfish, and amberjack. The rate of $75 for adults and $49 for children (12 and under) includes rod and reel, bait, tackle, and license. Electric reels are also available for this trip for an additional $12.

Once a month, between March and November, Captain Dick's hosts the Overnight Gulf Stream fishing expedition for the true fishing enthusiast. The

## Building a Better Bear

One of the most Disneyesque shopping and entertainment malls anywhere is **Broadway at the Beach.** Identified by the neo-Pharaonic pyramid of the Hard Rock Cafe, the complex sprawls between 22nd and 29th boulevards. It's here where you'll find the most unusual shop in Myrtle Beach. **Build a Bear Workshop,** Celebrity Circle, Broadway at the Beach (© 843/445-7675), functions more as a family-entertainment attraction than a conventional store. It's part of a national chain established by St. Louis-based Maxine Clark in the late 1980s. Ever since, it has proven amazingly popular with the arts-and-crafts crowd who, with or without their children, come to this place in droves. You'll be confronted with all the raw materials you'll need to make the teddy bear of your dreams, selecting its eyes, clothing, smiles (or lack thereof), and gender. You can choose your bear's "voice" from a prerecorded selection, the houses or caves it inhabits, and any accessories that will communicate very clearly to everyone your bear's unique eccentricities, quirks, and lifestyle. Come here to see how you behave when confronted with the opportunity to play genetic engineer, and also for an insight into the passion with which this creative expression is favored both by conventional-looking families with children and single adults of all ilk—including motorcycle fetishists dressed in highly unconventional ways. By the time the stuffing and compilation of your bear is complete, it will cost anywhere from $10 to $50, depending on the raw materials that went into it. In the latest development, you can build your own Elmo from Sesame Street. Be prepared to spend at least 90 minutes on-site. An advisory dialogue with an on-site "bear counselor" can be enormously helpful in figuring out the nuances of this place, but the shop is well-equipped with a perky staff ready to indulge you, your kids, or your grandparents in equally cheerful good measure. In the summer, expect long lines even to get into the store. Open daily 10am to 9pm.

cost of the 21-hour trip, which departs at 10am on Saturday morning and returns at 11am on Sunday, is $145 plus a $4 fuel surcharge. Rates include rod and reel, bait, tackle, and license; an electric reel is an additional $12. On this trip, the price of the electric reel may well be worth it.

**SAILING & WINDSURFING  Captain Dick's,** Business Highway 17, at Myrtle Beach South Strand and Murrells Inlet (© 866/557-FISH or 843/651-3676), has cruises that offer stunning views of the Grand Strand. The Saltwater Marsh Explorer Adventure is a 2½-hour ecology trip that allows you to see marine life in its true element. Rates are $19 for adults and $11 for children 12 and under. The "Cruising the Beach" Ocean Sightseeing Cruise along the coast of Myrtle Beach wraps up the trip with a sunset at sea. Rates are $16 for adults and $6 for children ages 6 to 12 (free for children under 6).

You can rent windsurfers at **Sail and Ski,** 515 Hwy. 501, Myrtle Beach (© 843/626-7245), from April to September.

**SCUBA DIVING**  Several wrecks off the coast and a wide variety of tropical fish make scuba diving a popular pastime. One of the best outfitters is **Coastal Scuba,** at 1626 Hwy. 17 S., North Myrtle Beach (© **800/249-9388** or 843/361-3323; www.coastalscuba.com), which has full PADI certification. Charters range from $63 to $110 per person, and boats go anywhere from 6 to 55 miles offshore.

**TENNIS**  The **Myrtle Beach Public Courts,** 3200 Oak St., on Myrtle Beach (no phone), offer a trio of outdoor and asphalt courts next to the Myrtle Beach Recreation Center. A more elegant place to play is the **Kingston Plantation Sport & Health Club,** 9760 Kings Rd., Myrtle Beach (© **843/497-2444**), home of the annual GTE Tennis Festival. Such greats as Pete Sampras and Jimmy Connors have played these five Har-Tru courts. There are also four outdoor clay courts. Courts cost $20 per hour.

**Grand Dunes Tennis Club,** U.S. 17 Business, across from Dixie Stampede, at Myrtle Beach (© **843/449-4486**), has 10 composition courts, 5 of which are lighted for night play. Courts cost $30 for two people for 2 hours and $50 for four people for 2 hours. There's also an on-site pro shop and fitness room.

**WATERSPORTS**  A family-oriented business, **Adventure Water Sports** will hook you up with jet ski rentals, sports boats, kayaks, and other equipment. Boat rentals range from $250 to $350 for a half-day or $400 to $600 for a full day. Kayak rentals begin at $35 for a single. A $100 credit card deposit is required for jet ski rentals, a $400 credit card deposit for sports boats. The outfitter is open daily 9am to 7pm at its main office at 3947 B Hwy. 544 in Myrtle Beach (© **843/444-2969**).

**SHOPPING**  **Coastal Grand** (© **843/839-9100;** www.coastalgrand.com), one of South Carolina's greatest shopping centers, opened in the spring of 2004 at the intersection of Highway 17 Bypass and Highway 501. With three competing department stores, including Sears, it also features dozens of specialty retail outlets along with restaurants and specialty food vendors. You can shop until you drop here at outlets that range from Radio Shack to Victoria's Secret.

## 3 Where to Stay

The Grand Strand is lined with hotels, motels, condominiums, and cottages. The highest rates are charged June 15 to Labor Day. Myrtle Beach is becoming more of a year-round destination, however, and you can find great off-season discounts in the winter. Golfers in particular take advantage of these low-cost rooms in the off season.

By and large, the double rooms in the recommended hotels and inns below have private bathrooms with tub/shower combinations, unless otherwise noted.

### VERY EXPENSIVE

**Kingston Plantation** ★★  This is the most desirable, and one of the best-landscaped, hotel and condominium complexes in Myrtle Beach. Set on 145 rolling acres of intensely manicured gardens, it combines a conventional hotel—the 20-story Embassy Suites—with a labyrinthine collection of individually owned one-, two-, and three-bedroom villas and condos. Be sure to specify your tastes in condo living, either when you reserve or at the time of check-in—some units are in soaring high-rises, others are low-slung town house–style accommodations. A few are free-standing, woodsy-looking buildings in their own right. Registration is in the lobby of the above-mentioned Embassy Suites Hotel. Each of the conventional hotel accommodations contains a kitchen, dining area, living room, and at least one bedroom, and is outfitted with a private balcony and a tasteful blend of light-grained woods and pale sand-and-sea colors. Residents of the suites benefit from slightly more intensive service rituals than those in the outlying condos and villas. All units are extremely comfortable and contain beautifully kept bathrooms.

For such an enormous resort development, it's surprising to find only one restaurant, **Azaleas Cafe,** on the premises. Set on the ground floor of the high-rise Embassy Suites, it segues from breakfast to lunch to dinner without breaking stride, serving a well-prepared but not particularly ambitious menu of American and international specialties.

9800 Queensway Blvd., Myrtle Beach, SC 29572. (C) **800/876-0010** or 843/449-0006. Fax 843/497-1110. www.kingstonplantation.com. 255 units, 600 condos and villas. $199–$219 Embassy Suites; $199–$299 condo or villa. Children 18 and under stay free in parent's room. Rates include breakfast in Embassy Suites. AE, DC, DISC, MC, V. Take Hwy. 17 to a location near the border of Myrtle Beach and N. Myrtle Beach. **Amenities:** 3 restaurants; bar; 11 outdoor pools; 9 tennis courts; fitness center; Jacuzzi; sauna; limited room service; nonsmoking rooms; rooms for those w/limited mobility. *In room:* A/C, TV, dataport, kitchenette, hair dryer, iron/ironing board.

**Myrtle Beach Marriott Resort at Grande Dunes** ★★★    Constructed at a cost of $50 million, the 2,200-acre chain hotel is one of the most luxurious on the South Carolina coastline. Opening onto the beach, it lies 1 mile from the Carolina Opry and 10 miles from the international airport. The smartly modern guest rooms are midsize to spacious, each with a luxurious bathroom. Most units open onto ocean views, and nearly all have panoramic vistas of some sort. Because it is part of the greater Grande Dunes community, a plantation-style residential and leisure development, the resort offers more amenities than any other in the Carolinas, including a championship golf course and a European spa with an indoor pool. The 15-floor structure offers everything from an excellent on-site restaurant with an international menu to an array of in-room extras, ranging from voice mail to free coffee.

8400 Costa Verde Dr., Myrtle Beach, SC 29572. (C) **800/228-9290** or 843/449-8880. Fax 843/449-8669. www.marriott.com. 405 units. $199–$289 double; from $629 suite. AE, DC, DISC, MC, V. Parking $12. **Amenities:** Restaurant; bar; cafe; indoor and outdoor pools; tennis (can be arranged by hotel); full spa; business center; hair salon; 24-hr. room service; babysitting; laundry (valet and self-service); dry cleaning; nonsmoking rooms; rooms for those w/limited mobility. *In room:* A/C, TV, dataport, hair dryer.

## EXPENSIVE

**Hilton Myrtle Beach Resort** ★★ *(Kids*    This imposing high-rise is shaped like a Y, with accommodations radiating from the central core, where a huge tapestry hangs down 10 floors. Because the hotel lies in the center of the 145-acre Kingston Plantation resort community, it's a more tranquil choice than other hotels right in the bustling heart of Myrtle Beach. The guest rooms open onto the ocean and are furnished in a light, contemporary style, often with rattan pieces. There is an outdoor pool with a children's section and a separate toddlers' pool. A formal restaurant offers a Continental menu, although you can also patronize the informal coffee shop. Entertainment is featured at the mezzanine-level bar, and light snacks are offered at the poolside cafe in good weather.

10000 Beach Club Dr., Myrtle Beach, SC 25972. (C) **877/887-9549** or 843/449-5000. Fax 843/497-0168. www.hilton.com. 385 units. $179–$209 double; from $259 suite. AE, DC, DISC, MC, V. Free parking. Take U.S. 17 for 9 miles north of Myrtle Beach to Arcadian Shores. **Amenities:** 2 restaurants; 2 bars; 2 pools (1 indoor); 13 tennis courts; fitness center; Jacuzzi; children's activities; limited room service; babysitting; laundry service/dry cleaning; nonsmoking rooms; rooms for those w/limited mobility. *In room:* A/C, TV, dataport, kitchenette, coffeemaker, hair dryer, iron/ironing board.

## MODERATE

In addition to the following listings, a good choice is the **Holiday Inn Ocean-front,** 415 S. Ocean Blvd. at 6th Ave. S. (© **800/845-0313** or 843/448-4481) in Myrtle Beach.

**Beachcomber Inn & Suites**   These well-furnished oceanfront units, located 2 miles south of the town center, have private balconies. They attract families in summer. Connecting units are available, as are deluxe rooms (with refrigerators) and fully equipped one- and two-bedroom efficiencies. There are two pools (one for children) and a laundry room on the premises. Golf, tennis, shopping, amusement centers, and restaurants are nearby.

1705 S. Ocean Blvd., Myrtle Beach, SC 29577. © **800/262-2113** or 843/448-4345. Fax 843/626-8155. www.beachcombermyrtlebeach.com. 45 units. $56–$114 double; $69–$119 efficiency. Weekly, monthly, and golf packages available. Complimentary doughnuts and coffee for breakfast. AE, DISC, MC, V. Free parking. **Amenities:** 2 outdoor pools; laundry service/dry cleaning and coin-operated laundry. *In room:* A/C, TV, kitchenette (in some), safe.

**The Breakers Resort** ⭐ (Kids)   This longtime family favorite is better than ever. With one of the best north beachfront locations, it occupies both a multi-story complex and a 19-floor North Tower 7 blocks away. You can book here on any number of plans, so study them carefully. The newer North Tower has its own registration desk and some 140 condos. The accommodations are wide-ranging, from tastefully furnished guest rooms to efficiencies with kitchenettes, and even one- to three-bedroom suites. Extra beds in the form of foldout sofas, Murphy beds, and twin sets of doubles make for flexible family units. Many rooms have balconies and refrigerators.

   The **Sidewalk Vendor Cafe** serves breakfast and dinner, and the Top of the Green rooftop lounge opens onto a panoramic view of the sea, providing enter-tainment 6 nights weekly under a mirrored ceiling.

2006 N. Ocean Blvd. (P.O. Box 485), Myrtle Beach, SC 29578. © **800/952-4503** or 843/444-4444. Fax 843/626-5001. www.breakers.com. 538 units. $119–$149 double; $164–$205 suite. Ask about off-season rates. Children 16 and under stay free in parent's room. AE, DC, DISC, MC, V. Free parking. **Amenities:** 2 restaurants; bar; 3 pools (1 indoor); fitness center; Jacuzzi; sauna; limited room service; laundry service/dry cleaning; nonsmoking rooms; 1 room for those w/limited mobility. *In room:* A/C, TV, kitchenette (in some), hair dryer, washer/dryer (in some).

**Four Points Sheraton** ⭐ (Kids)   On oceanfront beach property, this 16-floor tower, lined with balconies, is the most southerly at the resort. It's a family favorite and also the darling of the convention crowd. A moderately priced but first-class operation, it has a lobby that suggests the Caribbean, with ceiling fans and nautical colors. Some rooms are efficiencies, and units come with a double bed (or two) or a king-size bed. All rooms include refrigerators and well-kept bathrooms. Some of the units open onto spacious balconies overlooking the ocean. American cuisine is offered at the slightly formal restaurant, and enter-tainment is presented in the lounge.

2701 S. Ocean Blvd., Myrtle Beach, SC 29577. © **800/992-1055** or 843/448-2518. Fax 843/448-1506. www.sheratonresort.com. 223 units. $136–$148 double; $217 suite. Children under 18 stay free in parent's room. AE, DC, DISC, MC, V. Free parking. **Amenities:** Restaurant; bar; 2 pools (1 indoor); fitness center; Jacuzzi; children's program; free airport transfers; limited room service; laundry service/dry cleaning; nonsmoking rooms; rooms for those w/limited mobility. *In room:* A/C, TV, dataport, fridge, coffeemaker, hair dryer, iron/ironing board, safe.

**Landmark Resort** ⭐   Standing 14 stories tall amid the beach action, the Landmark is one of the Grand Strand's better examples of midpriced accommo-dations, with the South's largest resort indoor-pool complex. Its pink-and-green lobby makes a favorable impression, as do the gardenlike restaurant and bar. For more action, try the nightclub or the grill by the outdoor pool. In winter, the same pool is enclosed for year-round use. Almost half a dozen floors have small balconies. Units are equipped with one king-size or two double beds, well-kept bathrooms, tropical colors, refrigerators, and some ocean vistas. The lowest rates are available in December and January.

1501 S. Ocean Blvd., Myrtle Beach, SC 29577. © **800/845-0658** or 843/448-9441. Fax 843/448-6701. www.landmarkresort.com. 570 units. $95–$142 double; $129–$165 suite. $15 each additional person. Children 18 and younger stay free in parent's room. Off-season discounts granted. AE, DC, DISC, MC, V. **Amenities:** Restaurant; bar; 14 pools (1 indoor); exercise room; 5 Jacuzzis; sauna; limited room service; laundry service/dry cleaning; nonsmoking rooms. *In room:* A/C, TV, dataport, fridge, hair dryer.

**Ocean Creek Resort** *(Kids)*    One of the finest resorts along the beach, this first-class choice features studios and condos in half a dozen complexes on almost 60 acres. The Beach Club on the ocean operates in summer. Condominiums may be categorized as studios, one-bedrooms, two-bedrooms, three-bedrooms, lodge units, beachside towers, or tennis villas.

10600 N. Kings Hwy., Myrtle Beach, SC 29572. © **877/844-3800** or 843/272-7724. Fax 843/272-9627. www.oceancreek.com. 750 units. $54–$295 studio or condo. AE, DISC, MC, V. Take U.S. 17 N. almost to N. Myrtle Beach. **Amenities:** Restaurant; bar; 7 pools (1 indoor); 7 tennis courts; fitness center; Jacuzzi; summer children's program; coin-operated laundry. *In room:* A/C, TV, dataport, kitchen (in most), hair dryer, iron/ironing board.

**Ocean Reef Resort** *(Kids)*    Lying north of the bustling beach center, this 16-floor oceanfront resort is better than most other moderately priced choices. The bar is Caribbean-style, complete with bamboo, and the restaurant has tall windows opening onto ocean views. (The views, we have to say, are often better than the food.) All the rooms and efficiency units are oceanfront and tropically inspired; most have two double beds, good-size bathrooms, and balconies. Some units contain refrigerators and microwave ovens. The best accommodations are the suites (with whirlpool baths) at the top.

7100 N. Ocean Blvd. (at 71st Ave. N.), Myrtle Beach, SC 29572. © **888/322-6411** or 843/449-4441. Fax 843/497-3041. www.oceanreefmyrtlebeach.com. 284 units. $114–$131 double; $146 suite. Children 17 and under stay free in parent's room. Off-season discounts granted. AE, DC, DISC, MC, V. Free parking. **Amenities:** Restaurant; bar; 3 pools (1 indoor); fitness center; Jacuzzi; sauna; children's activities; kids' water playground; limited room service; dry cleaning; coin-operated laundry; nonsmoking rooms; rooms for those w/limited mobility. *In room:* A/C, TV, kitchenette (in some), coffeemaker, hair dryer, iron/ironing board, safe.

**Yachtsman Resort Hotel**    Some 8 blocks from the Convention Center, this 20-floor glass tower stands between two more-dated 11-story towers. Rooms in the older towers are timeshare units, available for nightly rentals when the owners aren't in residence. The main tower alone houses 144 well-furnished, albeit somewhat run-of-the-mill, units. Timeshares range from small studios to larger two-bedroom units. Tour groups, golfers, and sometimes honeymooners book accommodations at the hotel.

1400 N. Ocean Blvd., Myrtle Beach, SC 29577. © **800/868-8886** or 843/448-1441. Fax 843/626-6261. www.yachtsman.com. 142 units. $95–$260 unit for 4. AE, DC, DISC, MC, V. Free parking. **Amenities:** 2 outdoor pools; minigolf; 2 Jacuzzis; sauna; laundry service/dry cleaning; nonsmoking rooms. *In room:* A/C, TV, dataport, kitchen, hair dryer.

## INEXPENSIVE

**Coral Beach Hotel** *(Kids)*    As its name implies, the Coral Beach Hotel is decked out in fresh coral paint, with more trendy colors inside. This is an ideal place to take the kids, and in 2003 the Travel Channel voted it "best family accommodations." In case the sun doesn't shine, you can use the indoor pool or game room. For food choices, you have a snack bar, a full-service restaurant, and a grill and food bar. The units are comfortably furnished but basic, with sofa beds or Murphy beds, kitchens with microwave ovens, one or two TVs, and balconies. Rooms that don't have full kitchens have refrigerators.

1105 S. Ocean Blvd., Myrtle Beach, SC 29577. © **800/556-1754** or 843/448-8421. Fax 843/626-0156. www.holidayinnresort.com/cb. 300 units. $145–$155 double; $165 efficiency; $199–$209 suite. AE, DC, DISC, MC, V. Free parking. **Amenities:** Restaurant; bar; 10 pools (1 indoor); exercise room; spa; 4 Jacuzzis (3 indoor); children's activity center; game room; arcade; limited room service; massage; laundry service/dry cleaning; coin-operated laundry; bowling alley. *In room:* A/C, TV, dataport, fridge, coffeemaker, hair dryer, iron/ironing board, safe, microwave.

**Hampton Inn** *Value*   This is the most appealing of the quartet of Hampton Inns in Myrtle Beach. It's clean, affordable, and stylish, with an Iberian-inspired design that emulates a blockbuster version of Spanish-Colonial/American Mission. Best of all, it's the only hotel in Myrtle Beach that's within walking distance (across a mammoth parking lot) of the vast nightlife and entertainment complex, Broadway at the Beach. Rising eight floors, it contains a seashell-colored, vaguely tropical decor, and an attentive, youthful staff that's well-versed in the facilities at the nearby Broadway complex. Each of the standard-size guest rooms has a neatly kept bathroom. Breakfast is the only meal served. The restaurants of Broadway at the Beach are close at hand.

Broadway at the Beach, 1140 Celebrity Circle, Myrtle Beach, SC 29577. © **888/916-2001** or 843/916-0600. Fax 843/946-6308. www.hamptoninn.com. 141 units. $139–$229 double. Children under 18 stay free in parent's room. Rates include deluxe continental breakfast. AE, DC, DISC, MC, V. Free parking. **Amenities:** Breakfast room; bar; 2 pools (1 indoor); fitness center; Jacuzzi; sauna; business center; laundry service/dry cleaning; coin-operated laundry; nonsmoking rooms; rooms for those w/limited mobility. *In room:* A/C, TV, dataport, fridge, coffeemaker, hair dryer, iron/ironing board, microwave.

**St. John's Inn** ✸   This three-story motel, north of the town center and across from the beach, is more than just a motel. The fine landscaped grounds and Mediterranean-style building lend themselves to a pleasant stay. The former Caribbean motif has been replaced by more contemporary decor, investing heavily in colors such as hunter green with mauve and gold trim to evoke a rich look. Breakfast is the only meal served (you must walk across the street to the Caravelle Hotel), aside from an occasional Friday or Saturday dinner, depending on arbitrary factors such as the number of guests staying at the hotel. About one unit in three is an efficiency, and the rooms have one king-size bed or two double beds.

6803 N. Ocean Blvd., Myrtle Beach, SC 29572. © **877/326-8669** or 843/449-5251. Fax 843/449-3306. www.stjohnsinn.com. 88 units. $73–$99 double; $109 efficiency. Golf and entertainment packages available. AE, DISC, MC, V. Pets accepted for $10 per night and $50 refundable deposit. **Amenities:** Restaurant across the street; lounge; outdoor pool; fitness center; Jacuzzi; nonsmoking rooms. *In room:* A/C, TV, fridge, hair dryer, microwave.

**Serendipity Inn** ✸   This is a Spanish-style inn located on a quiet side street, a block and a half from the beach. All the rooms are decorated and furnished individually, and the suites are ideal for honeymooners or for anyone who wants a little pampering. All units have well-kept bathrooms, most of which contain tub/shower combinations. A breakfast buffet includes fresh fruit, hard-boiled eggs, and hot breads. You can cook your own steaks and chicken on the grill, which is provided for and shared by all guests. All rooms are nonsmoking.

407 71st Ave. N., N. Myrtle Beach, SC 29572. © **800/762-3229** or 843/449-5268. www.serendipityinn.com. 15 units. $89–$99 double; $109–$139 suite. Rates include continental breakfast. Off-season discounts available. AE, DISC, MC, V. Take Kings Hwy. (U.S. 17 N.) to 71st Ave. N., then turn east toward the ocean. **Amenities:** Breakfast room; lounge; outdoor pool; Jacuzzi; babysitting 1 room for those w/limited mobility. *In room:* A/C, TV, kitchenette in minisuite, hair dryer, no phone.

## CAMPING

You'll find plenty of campsites along the Grand Strand, many on the oceanfront, and rates drop considerably after Labor Day. Most accept families only—no singles. On the ocean, about halfway between Myrtle Beach and North Myrtle Beach, 430 sites are available at **Apache Family Campground,** 9700 Kings Rd., Myrtle Beach (© **843/449-7323**). Amenities include a swimming pool and recreation pavilion, water, electricity, shade shelters, modern bathhouses with hot water, sewer hookups, laundry, trading post, playground, public telephones, and ice. Reserve here year-round, except for the week of July 4. Rates are $44 to $48.

## 4 Where to Dine

Prices are no measure of quality here; dining costs are unexpectedly moderate at even the better restaurants.

## EXPENSIVE

**Collectors Cafe, Gallery & Coffee House** ★ *Finds* MEDITERRANEAN
This unique fine-dining restaurant, art gallery, and coffeehouse is a culinary delight, as well as a feast for the eyes. It was named by *Southern Living* as a "Reader's Choice Favorite" and by *Golf Magazine* as "A Gourmet Experience." Diners are seated in one of six rooms, which feature more than 100 original paintings, sculptures, and craftwork by 40 artists. In the afternoon you can relax and listen to cool jazz music while you sip special blends of coffee or tea. Everything, including the tables, is for sale, so feel free to shop while you eat. If you stay for dinner, we recommend starting with smoked chicken ravioli in a brown-butter sauce with shiitake mushrooms, tomatoes, shallots, and garlic. For main courses, specialties include pan-sautéed scallop cakes in a tomato, scallion, and butter sauce served with grilled vegetables, and herb-roasted New Zealand baby lamb rack with Middle Eastern vegetable pine-nut couscous and mint cucumber yogurt sauce. A children's menu is available.

7726 N. Kings Hwy., Myrtle Beach. © **843/449-9370**. Reservations recommended. Main courses $23–$28. AE, DC, DISC, MC, V. Collectors Cafe: Mon–Sat 6–10pm. Art Gallery and Coffeehouse: Mon–Sat noon–midnight.

**Greg Norman's Australian Grille** ★ INTERNATIONAL/AUSTRALIAN
This is the most internationally hip, best-designed, and most prestigious restaurant in Myrtle Beach, with enough big-city inspiration to keep out-of-staters comfortable, and enough redneck references to keep locals from getting defensive. It was established in 1999 by one of the most visible pro golfers in the world, Australia-born Greg Norman, across a saltwater estuary from a Greg Norman–endorsed golf course. It occupies what looks like a mock-medieval watchtower on the Rhine, with a soaring, flatteringly lighted, woodsy-looking interior designed by Norman's wife. There's a cigar bar on the premises, a somewhat cumbersome emphasis on the establishment's self-image as a citadel of fine dining, an impressive wine list, and a two-fisted, somewhat macho emphasis on nouvelle Australian cuisine. Its menu promotes itself as "the Upper Crust of Down-Under Dining," although some of the more aggressively promoted items, including an imported Australian crawfish known as "Yabbies," are over-rated. Better choices include any of the succulent cuts of steak or game fish. Wood-grilled and rotisserie classics are favored, including Australian rib-eye steak or rack of lamb from Down Under. A good-tasting dish is the Aussie potpie, a classic beef pie baked under puff pastry. You can also opt for Australian lobster tails, tempura fried and served with seared vegetables on sticky rice. The appetizers are

some of the best in Myrtle Beach, including fried calamari tossed in a sweet-and-sour chile glaze, cilantro, and lemon juice and served with a light-red curry aioli.

4930 Hwy. 17 S., N. Myrtle Beach. (?) **843/361-0000.** www.shark.com/australliangrille. Reservations recommended. Main courses $16–$30. AE, DISC, MC, V. Daily 5–11pm. Pub opens at 4pm (happy hour 4–7pm).

**The Library** ⚜ CONTINENTAL/FRENCH   In downtown Myrtle Beach, this is the most formal and classic restaurant along the Grand Strand, an area that is not known for its classy food joints. Evoking a library, the walls are lined with old and new volumes. The tables are covered in crisp white linens, and the food service is the best. Serving dinner only, The Library is not innovative in its array of seafood, duck, beef, chicken, and veal dishes, but only first-class ingredients are used. Start perhaps with such appetizers as soft-shell crabs or artichoke hearts, going on to a delightful chicken Chardonnay or else duckling in orange sauce. Reserve this place for that special occasion.

1212 N. Kings Hwy. (U.S. 17 Business). (?) **843/448-4527.** www.thelibraryrestaurantsc.com. Reservations recommended. Main courses $18–$36. AE, DC, DISC, MC, V. Mon–Sat 5–10pm. Open on major holidays.

## MODERATE

**Dick's Last Resort** AMERICAN   This is the most consistently irreverent restaurant in town, a fact that the owners proudly advertise in a large sign above the entrance. It might remind you of Dante's description of the lettering above the gateway to hell in *Divine Comedy:* ABANDON HOPE ALL YE WHO ENTER HERE. Most of the loyal fans of this place seem to revel in the ongoing banter provided by the waitstaff, members of whom compete for the role of sassiest, and/or most abrasive, on-site.

You'll enter the equivalent of a wood-trussed airplane hangar with a scattering of motorcycles displayed as cultural icons, and a randomly arranged inventory of bras and panties hanging from rafters above the rough-hewn bar. Table linens are nonexistent—if you don't count the big tear-off sheets of craft paper that soak up the grease from the burgers and ribs that everyone seems to favor. If all of this appeals to you, and if you utterly abandon any ideas about political correctness, you won't be alone, as the cavernous interior of the ample wraparound porches are usually mobbed with everyone from singles who swing to families with young children. How did this place develop into something with a personality so distinct? It was born out of the collapse of a relatively restrained "fine dining" restaurant in Dallas. After its bankruptcy, its owners decided to "go sloppy." They did, literally dipping into aspects of "grunge dining," where spectacularly greasy food is served in huge portions—and sometimes in buckets. Expect pork that's grilled in half-slabs, full slabs, and a genuinely humongous size known as "a full porker." There's also chicken, shrimp, steaks, burgers, and grilled combinations that are evocatively designated as "cluck and moo" (chicken and steak) and "oink and cluck" (pork and chicken). Live music is on offer between 7 and 11pm between June and October.

4700 Hwy. 17 S., in N. Myrtle Beach. (?) **843/272-7794.** www.dickslastresort.com. Reservations not accepted. Lunch platters and sandwiches $5–$13; dinner main courses $11–$30. AE, DC, DISC, MC, V. Daily 11:30am–11pm.

**Hard Rock Cafe** AMERICAN   Even if you're a die-hard fan of the Hard Rock Cafe chain, you won't be prepared for this nonstandard Hard Rock Cafe. Set a short distance north of Myrtle Beach's center, in the Broadway at the Beach shopping center, it's designed like an ancient Egyptian pyramid, entirely without windows and covered with hieroglyphs. True, there's a vintage motorcycle displayed in front, but no trademark Cadillac is suspended from the ceiling—which appeals to New Agers, who believe that cosmic and psychic forces are amplified beneath any pyramid. After a few beers or party-colored cocktails, you might believe that the psychics are right. This is one of the most successful and popular Hard Rock Cafes in the worldwide chain. Proudly displayed is all the rock memorabilia you'd expect; the most prized possession is a guitar used in concert by the late Jerry Garcia (of the Grateful Dead). Menu items include the usual Americana: french fries, tacos, burgers, barbecued chicken, milkshakes, and banana splits. In midsummer be prepared for waits up to 2 hours.

1322 Celebrity Circle. ⓒ 843/946-0007. Reservations not accepted. Main courses $8–$21. AE, DC, DISC, MC, V. Daily 11am–11pm (Fri–Sat until midnight).

**Joe's Bar & Grill** ⭐ *Finds* AMERICAN   It's worth the drive north to sample the fare at this plainly named restaurant with a rustic atmosphere. Joe's is known for its fresh fish and its homemade soups and sauces. With both downstairs and upstairs dining, it has a panoramic view of the saltwater marsh. Beef, veal, and seafood dominate the menu. The roast prime rib of beef is the best in the area, or you may prefer Low Country shrimp sautéed in a peppery butter sauce. Fish specials (look for the board) are from the Carolina coast. Service is excellent.

810 Conway Ave., N. Myrtle Beach. ⓒ 843/272-4666. www.dinejoes.com. Reservations recommended. Main courses $17–$27. AE, DISC, MC, V. Daily 5–10pm. Drive 15 miles north on U.S. 17; it's across from Barefoot Landing in N. Myrtle Beach.

**Sea Captain's House** ⭐ AMERICAN   Consistently crowded, and evocative of the kind of American Colonial seafood restaurant you might have expected on Cape Cod, this place originated in 1930 as a privately owned beachfront cottage. Today, it retains a few of its original nostalgic touches, including a masonry fireplace that's lighted on cold evenings. More prevalent, however, is a sense of decent, well-managed modernity, with glassed-in views overlooking the sea. The menu is absolutely typical of coastal Carolina—and that's no putdown. When regional cuisine is done well, as it is here, it's excellent, especially the fresh coastal crab dishes, either served as an appetizer or in she-crab soup, or perhaps in a salad or else as sautéed crab cakes. Locals order the Low Country crab casserole topped with sherry. Any dish you order is likely to be decorated with hush puppies. A few poultry and meat dishes such as grilled pork chops are offered, but there's nothing special in that department.

3000 N. Ocean Blvd. ⓒ 843/448-8082. www.seacaptains.com. Reservations not accepted. Breakfast $5.25–$7.40; lunch platters, salads, and sandwiches $5.95–$13; lunch and dinner main courses $5.75–$27. AE, DISC, MC, V. Daily 7–10:30am, 11:30am–2:30pm, and 4:45–10pm.

**Thoroughbreds** ⭐ SEAFOOD/CONTINENTAL   Rivaled only by the Library, Thoroughbreds is one of the few places along the Grand Strand that truly specializes in fine dining. It has been a hit ever since it opened in 1990. Guests select one of four handsomely appointed rooms; it also has a garden terrace and a piano bar. The latest addition is a dining room that seats 30 and features a fireplace. The staff is among the best-trained at the resort, but the food is what keeps people coming back for more. The Caesar salad is prepared tableside by your server; or you might begin with a Caribbean seafood chowder. The steaks are among the juiciest and most tender along the Strand. You can order blackened prime rib or grilled rib-eye, among other selections. Several excellently prepared veal, duck, and chicken dishes are offered. Call for the entertainment schedule.

9706 N. Kings Hwy. ⓒ 843/497-2636. Reservations recommended. Main courses $18–$29. AE, DC, DISC, MC, V. Daily 5–11pm.

## INEXPENSIVE

**House of Blues** *Kids* AMERICAN/SOUTHERN    Many visitors come to this restaurant looking for a burger and a stiff drink, and leave with a newfound appreciation for American folk art. With virtually every inch of its interior plastered over with vernacular art by largely untrained Southern artists, this Grand Strand version of the House of Blues franchise is by far the most aesthetically interesting bar, restaurant, and musical venue in Myrtle Beach. You'll recognize it by a design that emulates a rusted hulk you might have found deep in the Mississippi Delta, the kind of battered venue that might be appropriate for a religious revival and the laying-on of hands. Redolent of bourbon and live jazz, however, it's more urbanized and hip than the folk-art setting would imply. The labyrinthine interior features indoor/outdoor bars and several dining areas. There's even a rear veranda where a collection of antique hubcaps is elevated to a kitschy, and very charming, art form. Culinary fare includes fish, burgers, salads, steaks, ribs, and all the Southern staples you can handle. There's a "Gospel Brunch" ("Have mercy and say yeah") every Sunday from 9am to 2pm, with a buffet that's priced at $17 per person, $8.50 children 6 to 12. No one will mind if you come here just to drink, mingle, gossip, and flirt. And, if you're interested in music, concerts are scheduled almost every night in the summer, with tickets priced from $15 to $85 each. Box office hours are from 11am to 6pm daily.

Barefoot Landing, 4640 Hwy. 17 S., N. Myrtle Beach. ℰ **843/272-3000.** Reservations not accepted. Breakfast buffet $6; main courses $7.95–$16 lunch, $11–$27 dinner. AE, DC, DISC, MC, V. Mon–Sat 8–10:30am, 11:30am–3pm, and 4–10pm; Sun Gospel brunch 9am–2pm and 4–9pm.

**NASCAR Cafe** AMERICAN    This is the most intriguing of the many theme restaurants of Myrtle Beach. It's devoted to the history and memorabilia of the National Association of Stock Car Auto Racing (NASCAR), which, if you didn't already know, includes fans, worldwide, who are almost fanatically devoted to the lore and minutiae of the subculture. Set within a building that vaguely evokes a temple to some exotic high-tech god, the dining room is prefaced with one of the most complete collections of NASCAR memorabilia in the world. Look for Americana that will sometimes make nostalgia buffs weep, including bar stools made from oil barrels, balustrades crafted from the springs of old cars, and the out-of-date logos of spare-parts companies that no longer exist. Food is relentlessly geared to the kind of fare you might expect at Indy on a super-heated race day. Your waiter (who will identify him- or herself as a member of your "pit crew") will bring you heaping portions of food that includes six kinds of burgers, "supercharged chili," chargrilled shrimp, barbecued ribs, and chicken potpie.

1808 21st Ave. N. ℰ **843/946-7223.** Reservations not accepted. Sandwiches and platters $7–$18. AE, DC, DISC, MC, V. Daily 11am–10pm (until 11pm Fri–Sat).

---

### For Bikers Only

A major biker weekend takes place in early May. Unless you plan to roar into town on your Harley-Davidson, you may want to skip it. This event draws a slightly older crowd. Things get more out of hand later in the year during the Memorial Day weekend, when some 100,000 hell-raising bikers, most of them young, show up. Numerous complaints of traffic being brought to a virtual standstill occur at this time. *Bottom line:* Both are best to avoid unless you're part of the rowdy fun.

---

## 5 . The Grand Strand After Dark

# VARIETY SHOWS & THEATERS

**The Alabama Theatre**   The country-music supergroup Alabama unveiled this $7-million, 2,200-seat theater, located in an expanding waterside shopping complex, on the Fourth of July 1993. The theater features three kinds of shows. Alabama performs at least 10 shows a year; celebrities such as George Jones, The Lettermen, and Loretta Lynn fill in at about 20 others. Typical shows combine Opryland-style singing, dancing, and music on the other nights. Alabama began by singing for tips around Myrtle Beach before going on to sell millions of records.

Shows are given daily at 7:30pm. The "One for the Holidays Christmas Show" is presented November 1 to January, daily at 8pm, with matinees at 2pm on Saturday. Celebrity concerts are booked for some Friday or Saturday nights, as announced.

Barefoot Landing, N. Myrtle Beach. ✆ **800/342-2262** or 843/272-1111. www.alabama-theatre.com. Shows $33–$37 adults, $17 children 3–16, free for children 2 and under. "Christmas in Dixie" holiday shows $36–$39 adults, $17–$18 children.

**The Carolina Opry** ⭐   Missouri-born musician/entrepreneur Calvin Gilmore has been called a better businessman than a guitarist. He's credited with starting the incredible entertainment explosion in Myrtle Beach by launching this theater back in 1986 and attracting a host of imitators. In 1992, the original Carolina Opry moved into this new 2,200-seat facility, complete with its own recording studio. Shows offer a variety of music, including country, bluegrass, western swing, big band, patriotic, and show tunes, as well as comedy. The Christmas show is so popular that it's often sold out by June. Performances are daily at 8pm.

N. Kings Hwy. at U.S. 17, Myrtle Beach. ✆ **800/843-6779** or 843/238-8888. www.carolinaopry.com. Tickets $32–$39 adults, $20 students, $15 children 3–16, free for children 2 and under. Christmas show tickets $36–$39 adults, $21 students and children 3–16.

**Dixie Stampede Dinner and Show**   Owned by Dolly Parton's Dollywood Productions, this show house features a rodeo with a Civil War theme. While you eat a four-course meal with your fingers, you're entertained by some 30 horses, riders, and singing Southern belles. Locals and visitors flock here to feast on chicken, ribs, and corn on the cob while cheering whichever side they're on—usually, the side of Dixie. Drinks (definitely nonalcoholic) are served in the Dixie Belle Saloon before the show. Shows are given mid-February to May and in September and October, daily at 6pm; June to August, daily at 6 and 8:30pm; and in November and December on Wednesday, Friday, and Saturday at 6pm.

N. Kings Hwy. at U.S. 17, Myrtle Beach. ✆ **800/433-4401** or 843/497-9700. www.dixiestampede.com. Tickets $36 adults, $19 children 4–11.

**Legends in Concert**   Calvin Gilmore also brought another venture to the town, a show that features impersonations of the biggest stars in the business, including Cher, Dolly, Reba, the Blues Brothers, and (inevitably) Elvis and Marilyn Monroe—the latter two being perhaps the easiest to imitate. Michael Jackson, the Beatles, Nat King Cole, Elton John, Judy Garland, John Lennon, and even Liberace get into the act. Singers, dancers, and a live band are featured.

301 U.S. 17, Surfside Beach. ✆ **800/843-6779** or 843/238-8888. www.legendsinconcertsc.com. Tickets $31 adults, $15 children 3–16, free for children 2 and under.

**Medieval Times & Dinner Show**    This family-entertainment spectacle provides a sanitized look at the Middle Ages in a 1,300-seat arena. Before going into the arena, guests inspect the Hall of Banners & Flags and a Museum of Torture. Falconry, sorcery, and swordplay, along with some horsemen who are "gallant knights," add to guests' amusement. Guests consume a four-course banquet (without utensils) while watching the show. The highlight of the evening is a joust.

2904 Fantasy Way. ℂ **888/935-6878** or 843/236-4655. www.medievaltimes.com. $41 adults, $24 children 12 and under.

**The Palace Theater**    This 2,700-seat theater features three different shows throughout the year. The award-winning *Spirit of the Dance* is a foot-stomping international production that features dances from all over the world. *Lullabies of Broadway* is a star-spangled salute to Broadway and features a cast of 30 dancers and singers. *The Rat Pack* is a tribute to Frank Sinatra, Dean Martin, and Sammy Davis, Jr. Touring Broadway productions like *Cats, Smokey Joe's Café*, and *Thoroughly Modern Millie* also appear at the Palace. Featured performers like Neil Sedaka and Debbie Reynolds and popular musical groups perform here as well. During the holiday season, the theater presents a holiday show and *The Nutcracker.*

1420 Celebrity Circle. ℂ **800/905-4228** or 843/448-0588. www.palacetheatremyrtlebeach.com. In-residence shows are $33–$40 adults, $5 children. Call for prices for special holiday shows, featured theater shows, or performing groups.

## THE CLUB & MUSIC SCENE

**Barefoot Landing,** Highway 17 South, straddling the civic boundary between Myrtle Beach and North Myrtle Beach, has 13 restaurants; a variety-music venue known as the Alabama Theatre (see above), an endlessly popular nightclub—the House of Blues—and a reptilian theme park known as Alligator Adventure. Everything about this place, frankly, is well-orchestrated except for parking which, during peak seasons or weekends, is very, very hard to come by.

**Broadway at the Beach,** lying between 22nd and 29th boulevards, is the most appealing nightlife, shopping, dining, and entertainment venue in South Carolina. It's a less glossy, and much less expensive, version of Disney World, but with very few of the rides, and less emphasis on myths and legends. It sprawls across a vast acreage bisected with saltwater estuaries and lakes in the heart of town. Some of its most visible features include the most famous chain restaurant in town, the pyramid-shaped Hard Rock Cafe, as well as Margaritaville, Murray Brothers Caddy Shack, and the Aquarium (Ripley's) where fish swim in translucent turquoise waters behind a thick layer of Plexiglas. There are shops, a free-standing IMAX theater, a 16-screen conventional movie theater, a gaggle of theme-oriented bars (many with big-screen TVs for sports-watching), and a collection of late-night bars and dance clubs—each within a cluster known as Celebrity Circle—that includes everything from country-western line dancing to Latino salsa. For more information, go to **www.broadwayatthebeach.com**.

**2001**    With three clubs (and three different styles), this is a major stop on the Grand Strand's nightlife circuit. The newest club is **Echelon,** billing itself as a "seductive dance environment." A lighting centerpiece with digital video and laser graphics above a three-tier dance floor is an unusual and more urban offering for the Redneck Riviera. The **Indigo Lounge** is for drinking, "chilling," and dancing, also offering billiards and plush seating areas. Adjoining is **Razzies Beach Club,** where patrons dance the Shag and listen to golden oldies played by the in-house band. 920 Lake Arrowhead Rd., Myrtle Beach. ℂ **843/449-9434.** Cover $6–$10. Open year-round.

## 6 Murrells Inlet ⍟: The Seafood Capital of South Carolina

11 miles S of Myrtle Beach; 11 miles N of Pawleys Island

Murrells Inlet is often invaded by Myrtle Beach hordes in quest of a seafood dinner. Just take U.S. 17 (Business) south from Myrtle Beach, and prepare to dig in. This centuries-old fishing village has witnessed a parade of humanity, from Confederate blockade runners to Federal gunboats, from bootleggers to today's pleasure craft. The island was also visited by Edward Teach, better known as Blackbeard. Drunken Jack Island lies off Murrells Inlet. During the 1600s, Blackbeard's ship allegedly left a sailor on the island by accident; when the ship returned 2 years later, the crew discovered the abandoned sailor's bones bleaching in the sun, along with 32 empty casks of rum.

In addition to its seafood restaurants (a few are recommended in this chapter), Murrells Inlet is the setting of Brookgreen Gardens, one of the most-visited attractions along the Grand Strand (see below).

### BROOKGREEN GARDENS ⍟

Halfway between Myrtle Beach and Georgetown on U.S. 17 (near Litchfield Beach), Brookgreen Gardens, 1931 Brookgreen Dr. (✆ **843/237-4218;** www.brookgreen.org), is a unique sculpture garden and wildlife park on the grounds of a Colonial rice plantation. It was laid out in 1931 as a setting for a collection of American garden sculptures from the mid–19th century to the present. Archer Milton and Anna Hyatt Huntington planned the garden walks in the shape of a butterfly with outspread wings. All walks lead back to the central space, which was the site of the plantation house. On opposite sides of this space are the Small Sculpture Gallery and the original plantation kitchen. In the wildlife park, an outstanding feature is the Cypress Bird Sanctuary, a 90-foot-tall aviary housing species of wading birds within half an acre of cypress swamp.

Admission is $12 for adults, $10 for seniors and students, free admission for ages 12 and under. Hours are daily 9:30am to 5pm. June 15 through August 31, it stays open until 9pm. It's closed on Christmas Day.

### WHERE TO DINE

**Bovine's** ⍟ SOUTHWESTERN   On the waterfront at Wahoo's Marina, with large windows opening onto marshland, the restaurant evokes the Southwest with its use of cowhide and mounted bulls' heads. In the heart of Seafood Row, the restaurant has made a name for itself with its wood-fired specialties. You can order honey-crust pizza from the brick oven, along with grilled or blackened ribeye steak. Barbecued baby back ribs are roasted with bourbon, honey, and aged balsamic vinegar. Appetizers include crab gazpacho (a refreshing change) and Cajun oyster stew.

3979 Hwy. 17 Business. ✆ 843/651-2888. Reservations recommended. Main courses $16–$24. AE, DC, DISC, MC, V. Daily 5–10pm.

**Capt. Dave's Dockside** ⍟ *Kids* SEAFOOD/SOUTHERN   Family owned and run since 1974, this is one of the best seafood restaurants in the area, offering dining indoors or on the patio outside overlooking the waterfront. Chef Richard takes special care to ensure that the seafood is fresh, and his dinner specials every evening feature what's best in the catch of the day. Arrive early if you want to enjoy a sundowner at the waterfront **Gazebo Bar.** We like to start our meal here with a bowl of the Low Country steamed mussels or she-crab soup, either one a delight to the palate. Among the dinner specials are such sublime dishes as a *zuppa di pesce,* a kettle of fish with everything from lobster meat to clams; or flounder filets stuffed with lump crabmeat. Beef-eaters can order a tender rib-eye steak or prime rib of beef au jus. Each day a selection of homemade desserts is featured—count yourself lucky if it's New Orleans bread pudding with a Jack Daniel's sauce. A children's menu is also offered.

On the Waterfront (4037 Hwy. Business 17). © 843/651-5850. Reservations recommended. Main courses $16–$24. AE, DISC, MC, V. Tues–Sun 11:30am–2:30pm; daily 5–10pm.

## 7 Pawleys Island ⚓ & Litchfield

25 miles S of Myrtle Beach; 12 miles N of Georgetown

One of the oldest resorts in the South, Pawleys Island has been a popular hideaway for vacationers for more than 3 centuries. Over the years, everyone from George Washington to Franklin Roosevelt to Winston Churchill has arrived. During the 18th century, rice planters made the island their summer home so that they could escape the heat and humidity of the Low Country and enjoy ocean breezes. Storms have battered the island, but many of the weather-beaten old properties remain, earning for the island the appellation of "arrogantly shabby."

This area of South Carolina is sometimes called Waccamaw Neck, a reference to a strip of land 30 miles long and 3 miles wide that extends from the Waccamaw River to the Atlantic Ocean. Both North Litchfield and Litchfield Beach lie between Murrells Inlet and Pawleys Island. (To get here from Myrtle Beach, take Hwy. 17 S.)

The beaches here are among the best-maintained, least-polluted, and widest along coastal South Carolina. Because so much of the land is private, however, access to public beach areas is severely limited.

Many visitors from Myrtle Beach come to Pawleys Island to shop for handcrafts, such as the famous Pawleys Island rope hammock. The best place to purchase one is the **Original Pawleys Island Rope Hammock** (© **800/332-3490** or 843/237-9122), on Highway 17 at Pawleys Island. It's open year-round Monday to Saturday from 9:30am to 6pm and on Sunday from noon to 5pm. At various plantation stores (known as the hammock shops), you'll find pewter, miniature doll furniture, clothing, candles, Christmas items, brass, and china.

The **Pawleys Island Visitors Center,** Highway 17 at the Planter's Exchange (© **843/237-1921**), provides complete information about the area. Hours are Monday through Saturday from 9am to 5pm, and Sunday 10am to 2pm.

## ENJOYING THE OUTDOORS

**Huntington Beach State Park** ⚓, along Highway 17, 3 miles south of Murrells Inlet, across from Brookgreen Gardens (© **843/237-4440**), offers one of the best beaches along the Grand Strand. Entrance is $5 for adults, $4.25 for seniors and children 6 to 15, free for children 5 and under. The 2,500-acre park has a wide, firm beach, which is slightly orange. Anna Hyatt Huntington and her husband, Archer, the creators of Brookgreen Gardens, once owned this coastal wilderness. The park is the site of their Iberian-style castle, Atalaya. In the park are 137 campsites, along with picnic shelters and a boardwalk. There's terrific birding, as well as bike rentals and toilets. Swimming in specially marked sections is excellent, as is fishing from the jetty at the north side of the beach. Crabbing along the boardwalk is another popular pastime. Campsites are rented on a first-come, first-served basis, at a cost of $14 to $23 per day (price depends on sites with electricity and water). The park is open April through September daily from 6am to 10pm; off season Saturday to Thursday from 6am to 6pm, Friday 6am to 8pm.

**Caledonia Golf & Fish Club,** King River Road, Pawleys Island (© **800/ 483-6800** or 843/237-3675), opened in 1993. Each tee is marked by replicas of native waterfowl that inhabit the old rice fields. The centerpiece of the course is a clubhouse, a replica of a 1700s Colonial plantation house. Architect Mike Strantz, a former assistant to Tom Fazio, took care to highlight the natural beauty of the area: huge, centuries-old live oaks; pristine natural lakes; scenic views of the old rice fields; and glimpses of native wildlife. Greens fees are $82 to $132.

## WHERE TO STAY

**Litchfield Beach and Golf Resort** ★   One of the largest developments along coastal South Carolina, this complex sprawls across 4,500 acres, with 7 miles of private beach and some of the best tennis courts in the South. Often catering to groups, it offers a wide range of accommodations, including suites, condos, and cottages. Furnishings are hit-or-miss, described by one returning guest as being "residential beach stuff." The property is well maintained and forms its own private enclave away from the crowds of the Grand Strand. Many of the units have lake, ocean, and marshland views, complete with waterfowl. A restaurant on-site serves standard American food, and there's a grill at the golf club.

14276 Ocean Hwy., Pawleys Island, SC 29585. © **888/766-4633** or 843/237-3000. Fax 843/237-4282. www.litchfieldbeach.com. 300 units. $119–$449 suite/condo; $194–$650 2–4 bedroom cottage. AE, DC, DISC, MC, V. Free parking. **Amenities:** Restaurant; bar; 4 pools (2 indoor); 3 18-hole golf courses; 17 tennis courts; fitness center; salon; health spa; Jacuzzi; sauna; business center; massage; babysitting; laundry service/dry cleaning; nonsmoking rooms; rooms for those w/limited mobility. *In room:* A/C, TV, dataport, coffeemaker, hair dryer, iron/ironing board, safe.

**Litchfield Plantation**   Along the banks of the Waccamaw River, Litchfield Plantation is at the end of a quarter-mile avenue of live oaks. Here, a stately manor house (ca. 1750) overlooks former rice fields. A fine country inn, fully restored, it offers four suites. The Ballroom Suite, for example, occupies the north wing of the second floor. This suite includes a bedroom and fireplace, a bathroom with whirlpool, and a large living room (formerly the ballroom) with a Pullman-type kitchen area and a veranda overlooking the grounds. Rates include the use of a cabana, and a private beach club at Pawleys Island. There are numerous championship golf courses in the area. There's also a 31-acre equestrian center nearby. Children under 12 are not permitted.

Kings River Rd. (P.O. Box 290), Pawleys Island, SC 29585. © **800/869-1410** or 843/237-9121. Fax 843/237-1041. www.litchfieldplantation.com. 38 units. Summer $220–$240 junior suite, $374–$416 2-bedroom villa; off season $154 junior suite, $266 2-bedroom villa. Rates include full plantation breakfast. AE, DC, DISC, MC, V. **Amenities:** Restaurant; bar; outdoor pool; 2 tennis courts; marina; business center; coin-operated laundry; nonsmoking rooms. *In room:* A/C, TV, dataport, hair dryer.

**Pawleys Plantation Golf & Country Club** ★★★   A group of elegant, regional-style structures border a nature preserve, offering a luxurious country-club aura for those discriminating clients who don't want to pile into a hotel or resort on overcrowded Myrtle Beach. Guests are housed in one-, two-, or three-bedroom luxury villas, each elegantly furnished with a living and dining room, outdoor patio, and full kitchen, plus a tiled bathroom. Many of the villas feature whirlpools, wet bars, and fireplaces. The villas, with screened-in porches and patios, open onto views of the Jack Nicklaus signature course. The location is 25 miles south of Myrtle Beach on Highway 17 and about an hour's drive north of Charleston. Some of the Low Country's best recreational facilities, such as outdoor pools and tennis courts, along with beautiful beaches, are found here.

The elegantly appointed clubhouse has four different dining venues, each serving a first-rate cuisine.

70 Tanglewood Dr., Pawleys Island, SC 29585. ℂ 800/367-9959 or 843/237-6009. Fax 843/237-0418. www.pawleysplantation.com. 179 units. $65–$95 double; $105–$155 1-bedroom suite; $135–$290 2-bedroom villa; $215–$330 3-bedroom villa. AE, DISC, MC, V. **Amenities:** 3 restaurants; bar; 2 outdoor pools; golf course; tennis; limited room service; laundry service/dry cleaning; nonsmoking rooms. *In room:* A/C, TV, dataport, kitchen (in some), washer/dryer (in some).

## WHERE TO DINE

**Frank's Restaurant & Bar** ⊛ LOW COUNTRY/INTERNATIONAL Frank's has been a Grand Strand tradition since 1988. Its fans think that it's the best restaurant along the beach strip. Chef Pierce Culliton borrows inspiration wherever he finds it, from Arizona to Provence, from China to Thailand. Your grilled yellowfin tuna might arrive with a Moroccan-inspired barbecue sauce. The rack of lamb with garlic-laced mashed potatoes is better than many versions of this dish we've sampled in France. With its painted tin ceilings and wood floors, Frank's is an intimate, cozy place. The menu changes every day, based on the chef's inspiration.

In back of the restaurant is **Frank's Out Back,** the home of Frank Marlow's mother before its conversion. Frank has turned it into another candlelit restaurant, although it's slightly less formal than the restaurant up front. In fair weather, tables are set outside in a garden under a canopy of trees. Menu items range from wood-fired pizza to sautéed crab cakes.

10434 Ocean Hwy., Pawleys Island. ℂ 843/237-3030 or 843/237-1581. Reservations recommended. Main courses $21–$25 at Frank's Restaurant. Main courses $20–$25 at Out Back, pizza $11–$15. AE, DC, DISC, MC, V. Frank's Mon–Sat 6–10pm; Frank's Out Back Tues–Sat 6–10pm.

## 8 Georgetown ⊛⊛

28 miles S of Myrtle Beach

The lifestyle of pre–Revolutionary War days comes alive here. Named after George II, this enclave of only 11,000 people boasts more than 50 historic homes and buildings dating back as far as 1737. Masted ships sailed from this riverfront, bound for England with their cargoes of indigo, rice, timber, and "king cotton." You can take a leisurely stroll along the Harbor Walk, tour the antebellum homes, or dine at some of our favorite spots. Georgetown is rarely crowded with visitors. Located 12 miles from the Atlantic, this community is South Carolina's third-oldest city, and it was recently rated among the 100 best small towns in America. When Elisha Screven laid out the town in 1729, he couldn't know that it was to become a lively shopping enclave.

## ESSENTIALS

**GETTING THERE** From Myrtle Beach, take U.S. 17 South. From I-95, take U.S. 521 into Georgetown. From Charleston, take U.S. 17/701.

**VISITOR INFORMATION** Providing information about sights, accommodations, and tours, the **Georgetown Chamber of Commerce,** 1001 Front St. (P.O. Box 1776), Georgetown, SC 29442 (ℂ 800/777-7705 or 843/546-8436; www.georgetownchamber.com), is most helpful. The staff will also provide you with maps and brochures. It's open Monday to Saturday from 9am to 5pm.

## SEEING THE SIGHTS

**Harold Kaminski House Museum** A pre–Revolutionary War home (ca. 1760), this house is visited mainly for its collection of antiques, including a 15th-century

Spanish wedding chest, a Chippendale dining table, and some excellent pieces from Charleston in the 1700s. Many of the interior architectural details, including moldings and the original floors, have been left intact. At one time, the house was occupied by Thomas Daggett, a Confederate sea captain. There's also a museum shop selling items related to the decorative arts and the history of Georgetown.

1003 Front St. ℂ 843/546-7706. Admission $5 adults, $2 children 6–12, free for children 5 and under. Mon–Sat 9am–5pm; Sun 1–5pm. Closed holidays.

**Prince George Winyah Episcopal Church**   Built around 1750 with brick from English ships' ballast, this church was occupied by British troops during the Revolutionary War and by Union troops during the Civil War. The latter occupation resulted in a great deal of damage. The stained glass behind the rebuilt altar was once part of a slaves' chapel on a nearby plantation. In the churchyard is one of the state's oldest cemeteries, the most ancient marker dating back to 1767.

Broad and Highmarket sts. ℂ 843/546-4358. Free admission but donations welcome. Sanctuary tours Mar–Oct Mon–Fri 11:30am–4:30pm.

**Rice Museum**   This museum is easy to locate. It's in the Old Market Building, which local residents call "The Town Clock"—Georgetown's answer to Big Ben. The first building in town to be listed on the National Register of Historic Places, it houses a museum devoted to the once-flourishing rice trade. The museum is a repository of maps, artifacts, dioramas, and other exhibits, tracing the development of rice cultivation (which was long Georgetown's primary economic base) from 1700 to 1900. There's also a scale model of a rice mill.

1842 Old Market Building, Front and Screven sts. ℂ 843/546-7423. Admission $5 adults, $4 seniors, $2 ages 12–21, free for children under 12 with an adult. Mon–Sat 10am–4:30pm.

## ORGANIZED TOURS

Nell Morris Cribb, a Georgetown native who conducts tours wearing period dress, complete with a bonnet, provides personalized walking tours of the downtown historic district. **Miss Nell's Tours** takes in about 12 history-rich blocks, lasts about 1¼ hours, and costs $9 for adults (free for children 12 and under). Tours begin at HarborWalk Books, 723 Front St. (ℂ **843/546-3975**). The tour is given Tuesday to Thursday at 10:30am and 2:30pm, and on Saturday and Sunday by appointment.

## OUTDOOR PURSUITS

**CANOEING & KAYAKING**   **Black River Expeditions** can be arranged at Kensington Gardens, U.S. 701, 3 miles north of Georgetown (ℂ **843/546-4840**). Half-day kayak, tandem kayak, and canoe excursions cost $45 for adults and $25 for children under 13.

**GOLF**   One of the popular Georgetown championship courses, **Wedgefield Plantation** ✦, just north of Georgetown (ℂ **843/546-8587** or 843/448-2124), is on the site of a former Black River plantation and has wildlife in abundance. It was designed by Porter Gibson, and *Golf Week*'s "America's Best" honored it as one of the top 50 golf courses in South Carolina in 1994. Greens fees are $50 to $79, including cart. The signature hole is the par-4 14th, with both tee and approach shots over water.

**RIVER CRUISES**   The *Carolina Rover* and the *Jolly Rover* (ℂ **843/546-8822**) set sail from Georgetown Harbor. The *Carolina Rover* offers a 3-hour trip aboard a 40-foot pontoon boat, including a docked stop on North Island. The

45-minute excursion to this rather remote island includes a nature walk and beach shelling. Trips leave at 9am, 1pm, and 5pm Monday to Saturday. It costs $25 for adults and $15 for children under 12. The *Jolly Rover* is a 2-hour tour of Winyah Bay aboard an 80-foot topsail schooner. On board is a storyteller in a pirate's costume, who relates tales about pirates and ghosts who have prowled the Carolina coast. Trips depart Monday to Saturday at 10am, 1pm, and 6pm. The 10am and 1pm tours are pirate adventures. The cost is $20 for adults and $10 for children under 12. The 6pm trip is a sunset cruise for adults only and costs $25 per person. Reservations are strongly recommended.

## WHERE TO STAY

**DuPre House** ★ *Finds*    Sam Murphy and Karen Komar transformed this 1740 New England–style house into a highly appealing bed-and-breakfast hotel where the owners take personal interest in the well-being of their guests. Only a 2-minute walk from Georgetown's center and 1 block from the waterfront, it features a working fireplace near the entrance, glowing oaken floors, durable but tasteful furnishings, and five bedrooms that are interconnected via steeply sloping Colonial-style staircases. An outdoor swimming pool and a hot tub are on the premises. The good-size bedrooms are conservatively but tastefully decorated with contemporary furnishings. The daily social and gastronomic highlight is breakfast, when the host prepares his personalized version of French toast. *Note:* Children are not welcome at the DuPre House. All rooms are nonsmoking.

921 Prince St., Georgetown, SC 29440. ℂ 877/519-9499 or 843/546-0298. Fax 843/546-0298. www.dupre house.com. 5 units. $110–$150 double. Rates include full breakfast and evening reception. AE, MC, V. Free parking. **Amenities:** Breakfast room; lounge; outdoor pool; Jacuzzi. *In room:* A/C, TV, hair dryer.

**Live Oak Inn** ★ *Finds*    Innkeepers Fred and Jackie Hoelscher welcome you to one of Georgetown's most historic homes, a 1905 Victorian landmark that is the site of a 7-centuries-old live oak tree. They have decorated their midsize-to-spacious guest rooms most tastefully with antiques or reproductions, each with a fireplace and a private bathroom (three with whirlpool tubs). One of the town's best breakfasts, featuring such delights as freshly made breads, is served in the elegantly formal dining room. Homelike touches abound—for example, the dresses of Fred's grandmother appear decoratively in Dawn's Room.

515 Prince St., Georgetown, SC 29440. ℂ 888/730-6004 or 843/545-8658. www.liveoakinn.com. 5 units. $115–$150 double. Rates include breakfast. AE, DISC, MC, V. **Amenities:** Breakfast room. *In room:* A/C, TV.

**The Shaw House Bed and Breakfast** ★★    Nestled among pine trees overlooking miles of marshland, this recently upgraded Colonial B&B has spacious rooms with impressive antiques that evoke the grandeur and culture of the Old South. Each unit has a neatly maintained bathroom with a shower. Mary and Joe Shaw are the gracious innkeepers, and their knowledge of the area is encyclopedic. Your day begins with a full Southern breakfast that's probably more than you can eat. Historic walking tours and boat tours can be arranged. All rooms are nonsmoking.

613 Cypress Court, Georgetown, SC 29440. ℂ/fax **843/546-9663**. www.bbonline.com/sc/shawhouse. 3 units. $65–$90 double. Each additional person $15. Rates include full breakfast. AE, MC, V. **Amenities:** Breakfast room; lounge. *In room:* A/C, TV.

## WHERE TO DINE

**The Rice Paddy** SEAFOOD/AMERICAN    The Rice Paddy continues the Georgetown tradition of everything historic. This early-20th-century structure has a minimalist decor that relies on the effectiveness of its exposed-brick walls.

The river side of the restaurant offers views of the Sampit River, and if you want to sit even closer to the river, an outdoor dining patio with awnings and ceiling fans seats up to 40 patrons comfortably. Cookery has flair and flavor, with a finesse and consistency that keep the most discriminating palates of Georgetown returning again and again. Main-course choices range from lump crab cakes to rack of lamb. The menu changes seasonally to take advantage of the freshest ingredients.

732 Front St. ℂ **843/546-2021.** Reservations recommended. Main courses $17–$25. AE, MC, V. Mon–Sat 11:30am–2:30pm and 6–10pm.

**River Room** SEAFOOD    This is about the best Georgetown gets in terms of seafood dining. Some dishes are a bit overcooked, but locals seem to prefer them that way. Guests are rewarded by waterfront views from cozy precincts; an equally inviting bar is decked out in wood and exposed brick. Diners are smartly dressed in a casual way. Daily specials might include seafood fettuccine or a soft-shell-crab sandwich. Of the main dishes, we fared well with the grilled tuna. Grouper, crab cakes, and other seafood are regularly featured, and you can order such Low Country dishes as yellow grits sautéed with shrimp and sausage.

801 Front St. ℂ **843/527-4110.** Reservations not accepted. Main courses $9.95–$25. AE, MC, V. Mon–Sat 11am–2:30pm and 5–10pm.

**Thomas Cafe** LOW COUNTRY    This is the kind of cafe where Charles Kuralt might have come to talk with the locals. With only five tables, a few booths, and a handful of counter stools, it's real Americana. Your waitress might be a spry 80-year-old. Breakfast is a very filling event: grits or hash browns served with eggs, a Cajun omelet, or blueberry pancakes. At lunch, you can have selections like jambalaya, fried chicken, mashed potatoes, and fried green tomatoes. This is the Old South—plenty of hospitality but no nonsense.

703 Front St. ℂ **843/546-7776.** Reservations not accepted. Breakfast $4–$7; plate lunches $6–$8; sandwiches $5.75–$7.50. MC, V. Mon–Sat 7am–2pm; Sun 11am–3pm.

# 14

# Columbia & the Heartland

Moving inland, today's visitor comes face to face with vivid reminders of South Carolina's past, as well as with the New South. Industries such as textiles, chemicals, precision-tool making, and metalworks thrive alongside large farms producing dairy products, tobacco, soybeans, peaches, wheat, and cotton, plus large pine forests for an ever-growing paper industry.

Since the days of George Washington, who once visited Columbia, this area of South Carolina has been known for its equestrian tradition. Horses are ranked number three on the state's commodities list. Camden and Aiken are centers for training racehorses that compete on racetracks around the country. Camden's Springdale Race Course plays host to two major steeplechases each year:

the Carolina Cup and the Colonial Cup. The latter event is run in November, with a purse of $100,000. Aiken stages its yearly Aiken Triple Crown on three consecutive Saturdays in the spring.

Most outdoor recreation is in Santee Cooper Country, which offers fishing, golf, camping, hunting, and boating, among other diversions. Lake Marion and Lake Moultrie draw anglers in search of catfish, striped bream, crappie and, above all, bass—white, large-mouth, and striped. There's no closed season for fishing.

The center is Columbia, the state capital, 3 miles from the geographic center of the state. It not only has its own attractions, but it's a good base for exploring several historic Piedmont towns, including Camden and York.

## 1 Columbia ⊱

120 miles NW of Charleston; 131 miles W of Myrtle Beach

Columbia, unlike many of America's older cities, has the orderly look of a planned community, with streets laid out like an almost-unbroken checkerboard and wide boulevards giving it a graceful beauty. The city was created in 1786 as a compromise capital, located just 3 miles from the exact geographical center of the state, to satisfy both Low Country and Upstate factions. George Washington paid a visit to Columbia in 1791, just a year after the first General Assembly convened in the brand-new city.

It was here that a convention, held in the First Baptist Church, passed the first Ordinance of Secession in the Southern states on December 17, 1860. (Because of a local smallpox epidemic, however, it was actually signed in Charleston.) Columbia itself was little touched by battle until General Sherman arrived with his Union troops on February 17, 1865, and virtually wiped out the town by fire: An 84-block area and some 1,386 buildings were left in ashes. Although recovery during Reconstruction was slow, the city that emerged from almost-complete devastation is one of stately homes and public buildings, with government and education (seven colleges are located here) playing leading roles in its economy. Fort Jackson, a U.S. Army basic-training post on the southeastern edge of town, adds another element to the economic mix.

Long a well-patronized shopping village, **Five Points** contains restaurants, bars, galleries, specialty shops, and other establishments lying next to the University of South Carolina. The increasingly hip part of town is **Congaree Vista,** which is giving the Five Points area competition as the place to hang out and patronize restaurants, bars, and galleries. The old warehouses around the Adluh Flour Mill have been turned into clubs and restaurants; and offices, condos, and private homes are springing up here.

## ESSENTIALS

**GETTING THERE**    I-20 reaches Columbia from the northeast (connecting with I-95 running north and south) and southwest, I-26 from the southeast from Charleston (crossing I-95) and northwest, and I-77 from the north.

If you're flying, the **Columbia Metropolitan Airport** (© 803/822-5000) is served by **Continental Airlines** (© 800/525-0280; www.continental.com), **Delta** (© 800/221-1212; www.delta.com), **US Airways** (© 800/428-4322; www.usair.com), **Northwest Airlines** (© 800/225-2525; www.nwa.com), and **Independence Air** (© 800/359-3594; www.flyi.com).

For **Amtrak** service, contact © 800/USA-RAIL (www.amtrak.com).

**VISITOR INFORMATION**    The **Columbia Metropolitan Convention and Visitors Bureau** is at 1101 Lincoln St., Columbia, SC 29201 (© 800/264-4884 or 803/545-0000; www.columbiacvb.com). Its visitor center is open Monday to Friday from 9am to 5pm and Saturday from 10am to 4pm.

An excellent Web resource for information about South Carolina cities, including Columbia and surrounding points of interest, is **www.sciway.net**. It is the largest and most comprehensive site documenting South Carolina information on the Web. The site includes thousands of links to other South Carolina websites, as well as maps and other resources.

**SPECIAL EVENTS**    One of the country's best state fairs, the **South Carolina State Fair,** is held annually in early October on the Fairgrounds at 1200 Rosewood Dr. (© 803/799-3387; www.scstatefair.org), with shows, a carnival, food stalls, and entertainment, along with crafts, agricultural, and livestock exhibits.

## EXPLORING THE AREA
### THE STATE CAPITOL

**The State House,** at Main and Gervais streets (© 803/734-2430), begun in 1855, was only half-finished when General Sherman bombarded Columbia in 1865. Today, the west and south walls are marked with bronze stars where the shells struck. In the fire that wiped out so much of the city, the State House escaped destruction, but the architect's plans were burned. As a result, the dome is not the one that was originally envisioned. Despite that fact, the building, with its Corinthian granite columns, is one of the most beautiful state capitols in the U.S. The landscaped grounds hold memorial tablets and monuments; inside are portraits and statues of South Carolina's greats. A more recently dedicated African-American monument also stands on the grounds. The Confederate flag has come down from the dome, where its flying generated nationwide protest. (It's still displayed on the grounds, however, and its presence remains a temper-raising issue in South Carolina.) The State House is open Monday to Friday 9am to 5pm, Saturday 10am to 5pm, and the first Sunday in each month 1 to 5pm.

> ⌒ *Fun Fact* **Why George Has a Broken Walking Stick**
> When visiting the State House, note the statue of George Washington on
> the front steps with its broken walking stick. It was broken by Union sol-
> diers when they invaded Columbia during the Civil War. The people of
> South Carolina, who have nothing if not long memories, decided to leave
> it the way the soldiers left it. The statue has been touched so many times
> since then that the stump of the cane is worn smooth.

## FOUR HISTORIC HOMES

At the **Historic Columbia Foundation,** 1616 Blanding St. (℃ **803/252-
1770**), you can purchase tickets and get a tour map of the capital's most historic
homes. Tickets for each property cost $5 for adults and $2.50 for children. A
combination ticket to all four properties is $18 for adults; $14 for ages 65 and
older, military, and college students; $10 for children 6 to 17 years old; and free
for children 5 and under. Hourly tours are conducted Tuesday to Saturday from
10am to 4pm and on Sunday from 1 to 5pm, with tours starting every hour on
the hour. On Tuesday to Saturday, the last tour is at 3pm; on Sunday, the last
tour is at 4pm.

**Woodrow Wilson's Boyhood Home** ⍟, 1705 Hampton St., was built by the
president's father in 1872. Much Wilson memorabilia remains, including the
family's heirloom furnishings. The red-velvet music room and the plush parlor
evoke the Victorian age. The 28th president lived here until 1875, leaving at age
14 when his family decided to move out of state.

**Hampton-Preston Mansion,** 1615 Blanding St., was purchased by Wade
Hampton and occupied by his family until 1865, when Union Gen. J. A. Logan
took over it. Much memorabilia of the antebellum period remains, including
furnishings and decorative arts. The house dates from 1818. The Hamptons
were once called "the Kennedys of the Old South," having grown rich from cotton instead of liquor.

**Manns-Simons Cottage,** 1403 Richmond St., is a small house from the early
1850s. It was the former abode of Celia Mann, an African-American slave who
bought her freedom and walked from Charleston to Columbia. She'd earned
money by working on the side as a midwife and started a church for blacks in
her basement at the end of the Civil War. Today, her former home houses a
museum of African-American culture and an art gallery.

**Robert Mills Historic House & Park** is at 1616 Blanding St. Mills served
seven presidents as the first federal architect, designing such landmarks as the
Washington Monument, the U.S. Treasury Building, and the Old Patent Office
in Washington, D.C. This is one of the few residences that he actually designed.
It's rich in art and furnishings of the Regency and neoclassical periods.

## MORE ATTRACTIONS

**Columbia Museum of Art** ⍟   The museum's plaza has four quadrants: one
containing an amphitheater; another, a dining terrace; and two others designed
to feature plants and sculptures. The dining section's fountains and pools create
an ambience matched nowhere in Columbia. The museum entry is at the rear
of the plaza. The museum houses a permanent collection of more than 5,000
items, including paintings; furniture; baroque and Renaissance sculptures; and
work by native South Carolinians, including turn-of-the-20th-century photos.

Of special interest are *The Seine at Giverny*, painted by Claude Monet; and *Nativity*, a painting by the great Sandro Botticelli. The Tiffany art glass is also of exceptional interest. Call the museum for a schedule of events.

Corner of Main and Hampton sts. ⓒ 803/799-2810. www.columbiamuseum.org. Admission $5 adults, $4 seniors, $2 students, free for children 5 and under. Wed–Thurs and Sat 10am–5pm; Fri 10am–9pm (10am–5pm in Dec); Sun 1–5pm.

**Governor's Mansion** This house was built in 1855 as an officers' quarters for Arsenal Academy. When General Sherman swept through town, this was the only building on the academy grounds left standing. South Carolina governors have lived here since 1868. Visitors get to see the state dining room, the private drawing rooms, and the library, each furnished with antiques, mostly 19th century. Many of these furnishings, including a railroad baron's bed, were made in the state. Portraits of the state's more famous governors hang in the Hall of Governors. The gardens can also be visited.

800 Richland St. (at Lincoln St.). ⓒ 803/737-1710. www.scgovernorsmansion.org. Free admission. 20-min. guided tours by appointment only. Tues–Thurs 10–11am, by appointment only.

**South Carolina State Museum** The State Museum is housed in what was once the world's first all-electric textile mill. Each of the four floors is dedicated to one of four important areas: art, history, natural history, and science and technology. Hands-on exhibits, realistic dioramas, and laser displays make for exciting browsing through South Carolina's past, from prehistory to the present. Some of the decorative pottery on display was made by slaves. Look for the 1904 Oldsmobile "horseless carriage." Other exhibits focus on "king cotton" and slavery. One exhibit honors African-American astronauts, including Dr. Ronald McNair, a South Carolina native who was killed on the *Challenger*.

301 Gervais St. ⓒ 803/898-4921. www.museum.state.sc.us. Admission $5 adults, $4 seniors and children 13–18; $3 children 3–12. Tues–Sat 10am–5pm; Sun 1–5pm.

**University of South Carolina** The scenic 218-acre campus is covered with buildings dating from the early 1800s. The campus is filled with ancient oaks and magnolias. Note especially the historic Horseshoe, at the corner of Pendleton and Bull streets. It's worth half an hour or so to go by the **McKissick Museum** (ⓒ 803/777-7251; www.cla.sc.edu/mcks), located in a fine old building at the head of the Horseshoe. The museum features changing exhibitions on regional folk art, history, natural science, and fine art, and contains the university's collection of historic 20th-Century Fox Movietone newsreels.

Gregg, Pendleton, and Main sts. ⓒ 803/777-7000. Free admission. Museum Mon–Fri 8:30am–5pm; Sat 11am–3pm.

**Riverbanks Zoo and Garden** ★★★ *Kids* Named one of the 10 great zoos in America, Riverbanks Zoo is known for its worldwide conservation work. The zoo is a refuge for many endangered species, including the American bald eagle, and shelters more than 2,000 animals. Animals live in natural habitats, and botanically significant trees and plants are labeled throughout the park. All kinds of domestic animals live at the **Farm,** including cows, goats, pigs, and chickens. The **Aquarium Reptile Complex** introduces the aquatic and reptilian creatures of South Carolina. The zoo continues to improve its physical geography and its animals, with the addition of **Gorilla Island** and the arrival of koalas. A 15-minute 3-D **Action Theater** is an interactive film experience for kids. Your admission ticket includes entrance to the **Botanical Garden** ★★, located across the river from the zoo, connected by a bridge that offers a panoramic view of the river. Named by HGTV as one of the "20 Great Botanical Gardens and Arboretums Across America," the Botanical Gardens feature more than 70 acres of gardens, ruins, scenic views, and natural plants and woodlands. The easiest way to get to the Botanical Garden is to hop aboard one of the free trams. Another one of the zoo's real treats is actually not inside, but behind it—a place where you can picnic, swim, and revel in the mild rapids along the Saluda River. Wear your swimming trunks, and look for the rope that swings from a tree out over the river a la Tarzan.

500 Wildlife Pkwy. (🕐 803/779-8717. www.riverbanks.org. Admission $8.75 adults, $6.25 seniors, $6.25 children 3–12, free for children under 3. Daily 9am–5pm; summer weekends 9am–6pm.

## NEARBY ATTRACTIONS
### EDISTO MEMORIAL GARDEN ★★
To reach the gardens, drive 45 miles southeast of Columbia on I-26 and take U.S. 601 South to Orangeburg. The 165-acre park, on U.S. 301, is located along the banks of the Edisto River, the world's longest blackwater river. The garden is one of three test gardens in the United States and is known especially for its experimentation in roses. Some 5,000 varieties bloom from mid-April until October. Other vegetation and trees include camellias, dogwood, cherry trees, and thousands of azaleas that bloom from mid-March to mid-April. South Carolina's Festival of Roses, one of the 20 top festivals in the Southeast, is held here annually during the last weekend in April. The gardens are open daily from dawn to dusk, charging no admission.

### THE SANTEE COOPER LAKE ★★
From Orangeburg, it's a short drive on U.S. 301 to I-95 North to Lake Marion and Lake Moultrie, known collectively as the Santee Cooper Lakes, which cover more than 171,000 acres. Anglers, note: Three world-record and eight state-record catches have been recorded here. These waters have been stocked with striped, largemouth, hybrid, and white bass; catfish; and other panfish. The lakes are ringed with fish camps, marinas, campgrounds, and modern motels.

You don't have to be an angler to enjoy this scenic region, however; you'll find numerous golf courses, tennis courts, and wildlife sanctuaries. The best place for camping is Santee State Park, which offers 150 sites at two lakefront campgrounds on Lake Marion. Amenities include swimming, tennis, a boat ramp, fishing boats, a tackle shop, and nature programs (including a nature trail).

The **Santee-Cooper Counties Promotion Commission,** P.O. Drawer 40, Santee, SC 29142 (🕐 **800/227-8510** or 803/854-2131 within South Carolina; www.santeecoopercountry.org), can furnish full details on recreational facilities

---

### State Farmers' Market
Serving Columbia since 1952, the 50-acre **State Farmers' Market** ★, 1001 Bluff Rd. (🕐 **803/734-2506**), is ranked in the top 10 in the nation for sales volume. Selling fruits and vegetables, as well as flowers and plants, the market has more than 500 open stalls, as well as wholesale and retail units. It also has four restaurants and a U.S. Post Office. Don't worry about rain or inclement weather—a 100,000-square-foot drive-through building provides shelter to both sellers and buyers. The market is open Monday to Saturday 6am to 9pm and Sunday 1 to 6pm. It's across the street from the University of South Carolina's football stadium.

and accommodations. For more on lakefront vacation cabins on Lake Marion, contact the Superintendent, **Santee State Park,** 251 State Park Rd., Box 79, Santee, SC 29142 (© **803/854-2408;** www.southcarolinaparks.com). In all cases, be sure to inquire about fishing and golf package deals. To reach the state park from Columbia, take I-26 East to U.S. 301 North to I-95 North; take exit 98 to Santee and head 3 miles northwest.

Columbia residents also go to **Santee Cooper Country** for 270 holes of golf. For a complete golf kit, contact Santee Cooper Country, P.O. Box 40, Santee, SC 29142 (© **800/227-8510** or 803/854-2131 within South Carolina).

## WHERE TO STAY

By and large, the double rooms in the recommended hotels and inns below have private bathrooms with tub/shower combinations, unless otherwise noted.

### EXPENSIVE

**Adam's Mark** ✿   Near state offices and the University of South Carolina, this upscale, 14-story downtown landmark is the capital's best, lying near the State Capitol. With its atrium design, Adam's Mark is clearly far superior to its major competitor, the Embassy Suites at 200 Stoneridge Dr. But it lacks the traditional charm of Claussen's Inn at Five Points (recommended below). The rooms have subtle color schemes and a king-size bed or two double beds. The hotel dining room serves up American cuisine in a family-style atmosphere—*Columbia Metro,* a local magazine, consistently cites it for serving the best Sunday brunch.

1200 Hampton St., Columbia, SC 29201. © 800/444-2326 or 803/771-7000. Fax 803/254-8307. www.adams mark.com. 301 units. $120 double; $159 suite. Children 17 and under stay free in parent's room. AE, DC, DISC, MC, V. Parking $10. **Amenities:** Restaurant; bar; indoor pool; fitness center; Jacuzzi; free airport shuttle; limited room service; laundry service/dry cleaning; coin-operated laundry; nonsmoking rooms; rooms for those w/limited mobility. *In room:* A/C, TV, hair dryer, iron/ironing board.

**The Whitney Hotel** ✿   Southeast of the center, this all-suite hotel is the premier motor hotel in the capital. It's about a 20-minute walk from the University of South Carolina and a mile from Five Points. It's an eight-floor stucco building, traditional in style from its classic marble lobby to its wood-trimmed lounge. All suites are tastefully furnished, with full kitchens with stoves, microwaves, and refrigerators. The suites also have washers and dryers, butler's tables, and balconies. The small staff is congenial, but the hotel is not quite as luxurious as it appears to be in its promotional material.

700 Woodrow St. (at Devine St.), Columbia, SC 29205. © 800/637-4008 or 803/252-0845. Fax 803/771-0495. www.whitneyhotel.com. 74 units. $129 1-bedroom suite; $139 2-bedroom suite. Rates include full buffet breakfast. AE, DC, DISC, MC, V. Free parking. **Amenities:** Breakfast room; lounge; outdoor pool; free airport transfers; dry cleaning; nonsmoking rooms; rooms for those w/limited mobility. *In room:* A/C, TV, full kitchen, coffeemaker, hair dryer, iron/ironing board, safe, washer/dryer.

### MODERATE

**Clarion Town House Hotel** ✿   In a tranquil area about 3 blocks from the State Capitol, this is a two-in-one complex, with a main six-floor building that forms the hotel proper, plus an adjoining, motel-like annex. The hotel was constructed on the site of the 1800s Minnaugh Mansion, General Sherman's headquarters when he marched on Columbia. The hotel is well maintained and charges moderate prices for top-grade (though not spectacular) accommodations. Each well-furnished and midsize-to-spacious unit contains a well-scrubbed bathroom. The especially considerate staff is reflected in the basket of fresh cookies at reception. The hotel is noteworthy for its amenities, both public and in each room (see below).

1615 Gervais St., Columbia, SC 19102. © **803/771-8711.** Fax 803/252-9347. www.clariontownhouse.com. 163 units. $71–$100 double; $100–$139 Jacuzzi suite. AE, DC, DISC, MC, V. Free parking. **Amenities:** Restaurant; bar/lounge; outdoor pool; room service; valet services; coin-operated laundry; nonsmoking rooms; rooms for those w/limited mobility. *In room:* A/C, TV, dataport, coffeemaker, iron/ironing board, safe.

**Claussen's Inn** ⭐ *Finds*   Just 2 miles southeast of downtown, this is the premier inn of Columbia. It's in the fashionable Five Points district, near the University of South Carolina, and it offers far more charm than any other in the local landscape. The tastefully decorated rooms may have watermelon-color walls, pine armoires, Windsor chairs, and small patios; some have four-poster beds. Sherry and wine are offered in the lobby.

2003 Greene St., Columbia, SC 29205. © **800/622-3382** or 803/765-0440. Fax 803/799-7924. www. claussensinn.com. 29 units. $125–$140 double; $155 suite. Rates include deluxe continental breakfast. AE, DC, DISC, MC, V. Free parking. **Amenities:** Breakfast room; lounge; Jacuzzi; laundry service/dry cleaning; nonsmoking rooms; rooms for those w/limited mobility. *In room:* A/C, TV, dataport, coffeemaker, hair dryer, safe.

## WHERE TO DINE

Columbia has a host of restaurants, many with chain affiliations. The area around Five Points, close to the USC campus, is ideal for snacks, coffee, or something more substantial, as is the newly emerging Congaree Vista section.

### EXPENSIVE

**Hennessy's** ⭐ CONTINENTAL   This converted hardware store provided us with our finest meal on our latest rounds in Columbia. It's the most intriguing in town, and we like it even better than Garibaldi's. The kitchen may not be particularly daring, but it's in capable hands, and the service staff is ready for the big time; it's that good. The food is nicely prepared and fresh tasting. Begin perhaps with such South Carolina favorites as Low Country seafood cocktail or the very enticing she-crab soup. Carnivores seeking "butcheries from the block" might opt for our favorite—an 8-ounce filet of beef tenderloin topped with blue cheese and served with a wild mushroom demi-glace. You can also order filet mignon marinated in teriyaki and flavored with ginger. Seafood fanciers are advised to sample the grouper encrusted with almonds and herbs and served with a lemon beurre blanc, or the jumbo shrimp Creole in a zesty tomato sauce.

1649 Main St. © 803/799-8280. www.hennessyssc.com. Reservations recommended. Main courses $16–$25. AE, DISC, MC, V. Mon–Fri 11:30am–2:30pm; Mon–Thurs 6–9:30pm; Fri–Sat 6–10pm.

### MODERATE

**California Dreaming** AMERICAN   This large, popular restaurant in a restored 1902 depot is usually filled with both students and the uptown crowd. You just show up and wait for a seat, because you won't have much luck trying to reserve a table. The freshly made salads are quite good, and the typical fare is prime rib or seafood. Barbecued ribs, homemade pasta, and Tex-Mex dishes are also featured. This place is renowned for its large portions. Don't miss the hot apple walnut cinnamon pie—a special recipe—topped with French vanilla ice cream for dessert.

401 S. Main St. (2 blocks south of Blossom St.). © 803/254-6767. www.californiadreaming.com. Main courses $9–$20. AE, DISC, DC, MC, V. Sun–Thurs 11am–10pm; Fri–Sat 11am–11pm.

**Garibaldi's of Columbia** ⭐ ITALIAN/SEAFOOD   Near the university campus, with an inviting ambience, Garibaldi's is the first name that comes to mind when a local wants to eat Italian. Art Deco furnishings add a traditional note, and the helpful staff provides service with a smile. The menu is familiar— the usual array of seafood, beef, and chicken—but ingredients are fresh and deftly handled by the kitchen, even if Granddad would recognize the recipes. Try the shrimp marinara over angel-hair pasta. Every dish is so generously appor-tioned that you may not have room for dessert, but that would be no great loss here. Jazz pours forth from the speakers.

2013 Greene St. ⓒ **803/771-8888.** Reservations recommended. Main courses $10–$20. AE, MC, V. Daily 5:30–11pm.

**Motor Supply Company Bistro** INTERNATIONAL    Despite its unappe-tizing name, this restaurant serves decent food. It's in an 1890s building, now listed on the National Register of Historic Places, that was once a motor-supply-parts warehouse and has been completely restored. You'd never suspect the building's former role as you sit at the oak German bar or a marble-topped Eng-lish table. Outside is a sculpture garden, and diners can browse through the gift shop or art gallery inside. At night, the kitchen works harder than at lunch, turning out such well-prepared appetizers as grilled quail with balsamic barbe-cue and chicken satay with peanut sauce (definitely Thai-influenced). Main dishes might include peppercorn-encrusted pink salmon with champagne beurre blanc (white butter), or filet of beef with crabmeat and hollandaise.

920 Gervais St. ⓒ **803/256-6687.** Reservations recommended. Main courses $15–$20. AE, DC, MC, V. Tues–Sat 11:30am–2:30pm and 6–10pm; Sun 11am–3pm and 6–11pm.

**Mr. Friendly's New Southern Cafe** ★★ NEW SOUTHERN    In the down-town business district, this award-winning bistro is hailed by many food critics as one of the finest and most innovative restaurants in South Carolina—and we concur. The chefs call their food "good old-fashioned, New Southern cuisine." That may seem a contradiction, but no matter. What matters is the taste and the freshness of the food platters offered, and in that regard this casual place suc-ceeds most admirably. Look for specialties on the ever-changing menu that focus on seafood delights and innovative wild game dishes. Some favorite dishes recently sampled include pecan crab cakes with a sherry-laced cayenne mayon-naise, or a delectable grilled chicken breast with a sun-dried peach sauce (instead of sun-dried tomatoes, for a change). Their *carte* has been placed by *Wine Spec-tator,* and there is also a wide variety of microbrew beers.

2001-A Greene St. ⓒ **803/254-7828.** www.mrfriendlys.com. Reservations recommended. Main courses $13–$23. AE, DISC, MC, V. Mon–Fri 11:30am–2:30pm; Mon–Thurs 5:30–10pm; Fri–Sat 5:30–10:30pm.

## INEXPENSIVE

**Adriana's Café & Gelateria** COFFEES/DESSERT    This most quintessen-tially appealing coffeehouse in the area is frequented by university students who drop in either to chill out or warm up. Black-and-white art decorates the walls, and you sit at marble-topped tables on ice-cream-parlor chairs. The homemade desserts are delectable. Try the cheesecake, the velvety homemade gelato and sor-bet, the yogurt, or one of the flavorful coffees.

721 Saluda Ave. ⓒ **803/799-7595.** Reservations not accepted. Coffee $1.25–$3.75; desserts $2.35–$4.50; food $4–$10. MC, V. Mon–Thurs 8am–noon; Fri 8am–12:30pm; Sat 9:30am–12:30am; Sun 11am–11pm.

**Lizard's Thicket** ★ *Kids* SOUTHERN/AMERICAN    If you aren't from the South and want to experience true home-style, stick-to-your-ribs, lip-smacking country food, then head here. With 11 locations scattered throughout the Columbia area, this restaurant is an annual winner of the *Metropolitan Colum-bia Magazine*'s "Best in State Country Cooking and Family Restaurant." Three meals a day are served by friendly waitresses wearing country-style dresses with frilly white aprons. The restaurant has printed menus, but it's more fun to pick

## Right Wing Barbecue

**Maurice Bessenger's Piggie Park,** 1600 Charleston Hwy. (© 803/796-0200; www.mauricesbbq.com), may be the South's most controversial eatery. All because of the Confederate flag–waving Maurice himself. Even though his politics are to the right of Attila the Hun, he has his fans, who claim his barbecue is the best in the South. Critics, on the other hand, dismiss his sauce as a "gloppy mess." Go or not—it's up to you. As our astute editor put it, to ignore Maurice is "like ignoring a 800-pound gorilla in the room." The sauce of this self-proclaimed "Undisputed Barbecue King" is mustard based, his meats hickory smoked. So, to be called "yellow-bellied" means you've eaten his sauce. Good ol' Bubbas and "Bubba-ettes" file into this dive at the rate of 20,000 customers a week. So what's the rub? Maurice's politically incorrect views turn off many diners. Maurice isn't big on flying the U.S. flag—not when he has the South Carolina state flag and the Confederate flag to fly over his joint. He doesn't have much good to say about "left-wing one worlders," and don't even ask him what he thinks of same-sex marriage! Even Lincoln comes under attack for issuing "illegal" executive orders. And if there's anyone left in the world who is a budding Aunt Jemima, Maurice will be happy to sell them a Confederate bandanna. The most damning charge made against Maurice is that he has a "racist past and approves of things that most Americans would find offensive—such as slavery," to quote a column by newspaper reporter John Monk. In truth, many chains, sensitive to public reaction, no longer carry Maurice's food products—and lots of folks simply bypass the loopy diatribes to get to the pig. For a full blast of Bessinger's message, you can purchase his book, *Defending My Heritage,* in the so-called "Truth Store" on-site. If you simply want to try his food, a "Big Pig" chopped barbecue and ribs begin at $9.99. Open daily 10am to 10pm.

your "meat and three's" from the huge menu boards located throughout the restaurant. For breakfast, your choices may include hearty combinations of eggs with grits or hash browns, toast, or thick homemade biscuits (highly recommended), along with bacon, sausage, or country ham (particularly good and salty here). Pancakes, waffles, and other specialties, like "the slightly Northern" corned beef and hash, or "the Southern staple" fried bologna breakfast, are offered as well. The "meat and three vegetable" lunch and dinner options include sweet Southern cornbread or rolls. We highly recommend the fried chicken, fried flounder, and country-fried steak. Vegetable options change seasonally, but staples include macaroni and cheese, Alabam' Slaw, green beans, fried okra, and squash. If you have any room for dessert, try any of the cobblers or our favorite, banana pudding. Don't miss the sweet tea, some of the best we've ever tasted in the South. You won't leave Lizard's Thicket hungry, and you won't break the bank either—the meat-and-three combination is less than $6.

818 Elmwood Ave. © 803/779-6407. www.lizardsthicket.com. Main courses $2.75–$8.95 breakfast, $5.50–$8.95 lunch and dinner. AE, DC, DISC, MC, V. Daily 6am–10pm.

**Yesterday's** ★ (Kids) SOUTHERN/AMERICAN The neon cowboy in a bathtub over the entrance sets the tone for what you'll find inside this Old West–style tavern known for its good food and robust drinks. It's also the unofficial headquarters of the St. Patrick's celebration in Five Points. Everyone from students to politicians makes this their hangout. Run by locals, it attracts patrons with its casual tavern atmosphere and affordable prices. Tex-Mex, pastas, vegetarian selections, Cajun cookery—you get a little bit of everything here, even Confederate fried steak and stuffed yucca. It's also a great choice for families, with a special menu for the kiddies.

2030 Devine St. © **803/799-0196.** Lunch specials $6–$11; dinner main courses $7–$11. AE, DISC, MC, V. Sun–Thurs 11:30am–midnight; Fri–Sat 11:30am–1am.

## COLUMBIA AFTER DARK
### PERFORMING ARTS

The **South Carolina Philharmonic** and the **Chamber Orchestra Association,** 1237 Gadsden St. (© **803/771-7937** or box office 803/254-7445; www.sc philharmonic.com), perform concerts at various venues throughout Columbia and the surrounding area. The music runs from classical music to pop to jazz. The season lasts from September to May. Call for information about performances and tickets.

One of the best little regional theaters in South Carolina is **Trustus Theater** ⭐, 520 Lady St. (© **803/254-9732;** www.trustus.org), in the Congaree Vista neighborhood. Launched in the 1980s, the theater presents many regional premieres and develops new works in a regular season and its "late night series." It's also one of the most comfortable theaters in the state: All reserved seats are large armchairs, with a bowl of popcorn between every other seat and a place to put your drink (which the staff lets you bring in from the bar). Low-cost bleacher seats are available at every performance.

The **Workshop Theater of South Carolina,** 1136 Bull St. (© **803/799-4876;** www.workshoptheatre.com), which has a season lasting from October to March, produces musicals, comedies, and dramas. You can obtain ticket information from the box office from noon to 6pm on performance days only. For announcements of presentations, look in the local newspapers or call the theater.

The **Columbia Marionette Theatre,** 401 Laurel St. (© **803/252-7366**), offers shows for all ages every Saturday at 11am and 3pm. Tickets are $4 per person, free for children 2 and under. Productions include adaptations of classics, as well as original and innovative new shows.

Less than an hour's drive from Columbia is the historic **Newberry Opera House,** 1201 McKibben St. (© **803/276-5179** or box office 803/276-6264; fax 803/276-9993; www.newberryoperahouse.com), in Newberry, S.C. The Opera House served the community for more than 100 years, primarily as a theatrical venue and movie theater. Celebrated performers ranging from Tallulah Bankhead to Tex Ritter graced the stage in its heyday. After the performance hall turned into administrative offices in the 1950s, the historic building was in danger of being torn down until the Newberry Historical Society stepped in and saved this community treasure. It was placed on the National Register of Historic Places in 1970. After a $5.5-million renovation, the 426-seat theater is now equipped with state-of-the-art acoustics and lighting systems. Performances range from beach music to big band to Broadway and, of course, opera.

### THE CLUB & BAR SCENE

It used to get very sleepy in Columbia after dark, but in the past few years the town has been coming to life, thanks to the preponderance of young people. The best wine tavern and tapas bar is **Gervais & Vine,** 620A Gervais St. (© **803/799-8463**). Drop in to partake of the expanding list of tapas—Spanish for "small bites." If you order enough of them, these tapas can turn into a full meal.

---

### Shop 'til You Drop

**Columbiana Centre,** 100 Columbiana Circle (© 803/732-6255), one of the largest malls in the Columbia area, features more than 100 stores, including Dillards, Belks, Ann Taylor, Sears, Banana Republic, and Build-A-Bear workshop. The mall has an antique carousel for the kids to ride and a 420-seat food court with a variety of dining options. Hours are Monday to Saturday 10am to 9pm, Sunday 1:30 to 6pm.

---

Bartenders also serve you more than five different wines by the glass. Other bars and nightspots include **Bailey's Sports Grille,** 115 Alton Court, across the street from the Columbiana Centre (© 803/407-3004). Columbia's best sports bar, with big-screen TVs, attracts a macho crowd of good ol' boys. Food is served—and in such a spot, you expect ribs to be a specialty. **Damon's Clubhouse,** 900 Senate St. (© 803/758-5880), is another sports bar with big TVs. Barbecue ribs are a specialty here as well. This lively place is popular with the college and Congaree Vista crowds.

An amusing late-night bar is **Group Therapy,** 2107 Green St. (© 803/256-1203), which draws a diverse crowd. Even though it has a happy hour, it's best to go late at night. It's popular with the college crowd, many of whom drop in after their studies are done for the night. A neighborhood bar, **Hemingway's,** 7467 St. Andrews Rd. (© 803/749-6020), has a real macho atmosphere, as befits its namesake. Its happy hour is the longest in town, extending from 4 to 8pm. Burgers and sandwiches emerge from the back, and live music and entertainment are presented every Friday and Saturday.

The gay hangout is **PT's 1109,** 1109 Assembly St. (© 803/253-8900), which is a private club—but call for arrangements if you're visiting. Across from the State House, this is mainly a gentlemen's club, promising "gorgeous men, tasty beverages, upbeat music, and diverse customers." It's the home bar for a camp for kids dedicated to families of children affected by HIV, and it's also the home bar for the Carolina Bear Lodge. Cabaret is often presented, featuring such "Party Time Gals" as the "Lesbian Drag Queen of Columbia."

## 2 Side Trips from Columbia

North-central South Carolina was the scene of several significant battles of the American Revolution. Camden was actually an important garrison for British general Lord Cornwallis, and the battle of Kings Mountain, many people believe, was the turning point of the Revolutionary War. Battles of another sort are regularly waged these days on Darlington's raceway here, as stock cars engage in fierce competition.

### LAKE MURRAY & IRMO

Located 10 miles from Columbia, this bustling suburb offers one of the crown jewels of South Carolina—**Lake Murray** ★★, a premiere recreational area covering more than 500 miles of shoreline. When the 1½-mile-long earthen dam was constructed to create a lake in 1927 (completed in 1930), it was the largest earthen dam in the world. Owned by South Carolina Electric and Gas, the power-generating plant below the dam provides electricity for the entire Midlands region.

Offering boating, swimming, fishing, and a variety of watersports, Lake Murray is also recognized for hosting major fishing tournaments such as Bassmasters and the FLW tour. The swimming area on the Lexington side of the dam is open from the first week in April to the last weekend in September, daily 10am to 8pm. The cost is $3 per vehicle. A boat ramp area that also provides picnic tables is located on the Irmo side of the dam and is open 24 hours a day. A fishing pier is also available. Entrance fees are $3 per car. You must have a fishing license to fish on Lake Murray (age 16 and older), even from the pier. You may purchase a 7-day license for $11 on the Lexington side of the dam at **Lake World,** 1757 N. Lake Dr. (© **803/957-6548**). For more information about boat rentals, watersports equipment providers, or fishing guides, contact **Capital City/Lake Murray Country,** 2184 N. Lake Dr. (© **866/SC JEWEL [866/725-3935]** or 803/781-5940.

Named by *Travel & Leisure* magazine as one of the top 10 food festivals in the U.S., the **Okra Strut** ★★ (© **803/781-6122;** www.irmookrastrut.com) draws 80,000 to 100,000 visitors to Irmo each fall. Held in late September or early October, the 2-day festival features food (yes, plenty of okra and an okra-eating contest, too), arts and crafts, a parade, street dance, rides, a petting zoo, a golf tournament, a cycling ride and a 10km "Dam Run to Irmo" across Lake Murray Dam. Proceeds of the festival benefit the community and provide scholarships and civic improvements.

## CAMDEN ★

The 24-mile drive northeast to Camden, via I-20 and U.S. 521, takes you straight back to this nation's beginnings. Founded by Irish Quakers in 1751, it's the state's oldest inland town. During the Revolutionary War, 14 battles raged within a 30-mile radius here. Cornwallis held Camden until the British retreated in 1781, burning the town behind them. During the Civil War, another invader, General Sherman, brought his Union troops to burn the town once more, because it had served the Confederates as a storehouse and as a hospital. Historic relics are everywhere you look.

Camden is equally well known for the training of fine thoroughbred horses; the internationally known **Colonial Cup** steeplechase, held at the nearby Springdale Course, draws huge crowds.

Make your first stop the **Kershaw County Chamber of Commerce,** 607 S. Broad (P.O. Box 605), Camden, SC 29020 (© **800/968-4037** or 803/432-2525; www.camden-sc.org). Pick up a guidebook and a self-guided driving tour to point you to 63 historic sites in the area. The chamber is open Monday to Friday from 9am to 5pm.

**Historic Camden,** 222 Broad St. (© **803/432-9841**), is a Revolutionary War park affiliated with the National Park Service. There are restored log houses with museum exhibits, fortifications, the Cornwallis House, a powder magazine, an 80-building model of the original town, and miniature dioramas depicting military actions between 1780 and 1781. The guided tour includes a narrated slide presentation and access to all museums. The park is open Tuesday to Saturday from 10am to 5pm and on Sunday from 1 to 5pm. Adults pay $5, seniors pay $4, students are charged $2, and children 5 and under enter free. Self-guided tours are free.

Nearby **Goodale State Park** (© **803/432-2772**), 2 miles north of Camden on Old Wire Road (off U.S. 1), offers lake swimming and fishing, with pedal and fishing boats for rent. Bring along a picnic, and wander the nature trail.

### WHERE TO STAY

**The Greenleaf Inn at Camden** ★    This inn, located in Camden's historic district, consists of two separate houses and includes the Reynolds House, which dates from 1805. There are seven rooms in the Reynolds House, the main house of a plantation that once stood here. There are also four rooms to rent on the second floor. The entire inn is decorated with Victorian furnishings appropriate to its era. Two of the rooms are virtual minisuites, each with a small sitting area. It also has a two-bedroom cottage with two bathrooms and a kitchenette, suitable for up to five guests. The bathroom in each unit is well maintained and equipped with a tub/shower combination.

1308 Broad St., Camden SC 29020 ✆ 800/437-5874 or 803/425-1806. Fax 803/425-5853. www.greenleaf inncamden.com. 10 units. $89–$129 double. Rates include full breakfast. AE, DISC, MC, V. Free parking. **Amenities:** Restaurant; bar; limited room service. *In room:* A/C, TV, dataport, hair dryer, iron/ironing board.

## WHERE TO DINE

**The Mill Pond Restaurant** ✰ INTERNATIONAL   One of the finest restaurants in the heartland, this establishment attracts diners from miles away. Constructed in the 1890s, it's listed on the National Register of Historic Places. It has Early American decor and offers a view overlooking the millpond. The chef chooses prime, rigorously fresh ingredients and, with the help of a skillful staff, fashions dishes that are often sublime. The menu typically includes such traditional favorites as fried green tomatoes and other Southern delicacies.

84 Boykin Mill Rd., Boykin. ✆ 803/425-8825. Reservations required. Main courses $19–$35. MC, V. Tues–Thurs 5–10pm; Fri–Sat 5–11pm. Take U.S. 521 S. to S.C. 261 to Boykin, 10 miles south of Camden.

# DARLINGTON

Stock-car fans in the thousands invade Darlington (70 miles northeast of Columbia via I-20 and U.S. 52/401) in March for NASCAR's **Dodge Dealers 400** race and again on Labor Day weekend for the **Mountain Dew Southern 500.** The **Darlington County Chamber of Commerce,** 38 Public Sq., Darlington, SC 29540 (✆ **843/393-2641;** www.visitdarlingtoncounty.org), can furnish detailed information on racing as well as on sightseeing in this area. Hours are Monday to Friday 9am to noon and 2 to 5pm.

If you arrive between the year's two main races, hike over to the **NMPA Stock Car Hall of Fame/Joe Weatherly Museum** (✆ **843/395-8821;** www.darlington raceway.com) at the Darlington Raceway, 1 mile west of town on S.C. 34. It holds the world's largest collection of stock cars, including those of such racing greats as Richard Petty and Fireball Roberts. Hours are 9am to 5pm daily, and admission is $5 (free for kids 12 and under).

## LOCAL FISH CAMPS

This is fish-camp country. Very often, you'll find down-home fish dinners (all you can eat for practically nothing) in rustic cafes on unpaved side roads. Stop at a gas station, grocery store, or some other local shop, and just ask; everybody has a favorite, and it's often worth a detour. A good place to begin your search is Route 6 (Porter Rd.). The best time to show up is on a Friday or Saturday night. The operators of these dives are likely to have gone fishin' the rest of the week.

# YORK ✰

York is at the heart of South Carolina's northern Piedmont. To get here from Columbia, take I-77 North to Rock Hill, then S.C. 5 about 15 miles northwest to York. The Department of the Interior has granted York one of the largest historic districts in the United States. The restored downtown area is filled with specialty shops—in all, 180 historical structures and landmarks. Get a detailed map from the **Greater York Chamber of Commerce,** 23 E. Liberty St. (P.O. Box 97), York, SC 29745 (✆ **803/684-2590**), open Monday to Friday from 9am to 5pm.

Nearby **Historic Brattonsville,** 1444 Brattonsville Rd., McConnells (© **803/ 684-2327;** www.yorkcounty.org/brattonsville), is a restored Southern village of 18th- and 19th-century buildings. To reach it, take U.S. 321 South from York or S.C. 322 from Rock Hill. Restorations include a dirt-floor backwoodsman's cabin, a 1750s frontier home, an authentic antebellum plantation home, hand-hewn log storage buildings, and a brick slave cabin. It's open Monday to Saturday 10am to 5pm and Sunday 1 to 5pm. Admission is $6 adults, $5 seniors, $3 children 5 to 17, free for children under 5.

## KINGS MOUNTAIN
Just across the border from North Carolina, **Kings Mountain Military Park** (© **864/936-7921;** www.rps.gov/kimo) marks the site of the Revolutionary War battle that was crucial to the eventual colonial victory. The park is on I-85, 20 miles northeast of Gaffney; from York, take S.C. 5 northwest for about 20 miles.

The southern Appalachians were virtually undisturbed by the war until 1780, when British Major Patrick Ferguson, who had threatened to "lay the country waste with fire and sword," set up camp here with a large loyalist force. The local backwoodsmen recruited Whigs from Virginia and North Carolina to form a largely untrained, but very determined, army to throw the invaders out. In spite of wave after wave of British bayonet charges, the ill-trained and outnumbered colonists converged on Kings Mountain and kept advancing on Ferguson's men until they took the summit. Ferguson was killed in the battle, and the Appalachians were once more under colonial control. You can see relics and a diorama of the battle at the visitor center. It's open every day of the year (except Thanksgiving Day, Christmas Day, and New Year's Day) from 9am to 5pm (weekends 9am to 6pm Memorial Day to Labor Day); admission is free.

## 3 Aiken: Thoroughbred Country
60 miles SW of Columbia; 17 miles E of Augusta

The international horse set hangs out in the country around Aiken at the Georgia–South Carolina border, where horse training and racing are major preoccupations. When you're driving, you might find yourself sharing the road with a horse and its mount. There's even a stoplight just for horses on Whiskey Road. Nearly a thousand horses winter and train in this area, and Aiken has two racetracks, as well as polo grounds.

The fame of Aiken began in the 1890s, when rich Northerners flocked here in winter, often erecting lavish mansions. It was a rival of Thomasville, Georgia, which also attracted the wintering wealthy. The horsey set amused themselves with horse shows, fox hunts, and lavish parties.

## ESSENTIALS
**GETTING THERE**    From Columbia, take I-20 West for 55 miles to either exit 22 (Hwy. 1) or exit 18 (Hwy. 19). Both routes lead into downtown Aiken. From Augusta (Georgia), take I-20 East, getting off at either exit 18 or 22.

**VISITOR INFORMATION**    The **Aiken Chamber of Commerce,** 121 Richland Ave. E. (© **803/641-1111;** www.aikenchamber.net), is open Monday to Friday from 8am to 5pm. The City of Aiken (© **803/642-7631**) offers a 90-minute tour of the historic district every Saturday at 10am, at a cost of $6 per person. A 27-passenger bus takes visitors throughout the historic core to view the old Southern homes. Reservations and payment must be made in advance, and only cash or checks are accepted.

## SEEING THE SIGHTS

The three weekends of horse racing in March that make up the **Aiken Triple Crown** are the highlight of the year. Call **Thoroughbred Country** (✆ 888/834-1654 or 803/649-7981; www.tbredcountry.org) to find out about the many sporting activities.

Even nonhorsey folks, however, will delight in the lovely old homes in the town's historic district. The **Aiken County Historical Museum,** 433 Newberry St. SW (✆ 803/642-2015), occupies part of a former millionaire's estate. Of special interest are Native American artifacts, a 1930s drugstore from a little South Carolina town that no longer exists, a 19th-century schoolhouse, and a full miniature circus. Admission is by donation. Hours are Tuesday to Friday 9:30am to 4:30pm, Saturday and Sunday 2 to 5pm.

**Hopeland Gardens,** 100 Dupree Place (at the corner of Whiskey Rd.; ✆ 803/642-7631), are the pride of Aiken, graced with weeping willows, fountains, and shimmering ponds. The grounds hold the **Thoroughbred Racing Hall of Fame** in a restored carriage house. A touch-and-scent trail has plaques in both standard type and in Braille to identify plants and to lead visitors, blind or sighted, to a performing-arts stage. Open-air concerts are given here Monday evenings in summer, and theatrical productions are offered periodically. Admission is free. The gardens are open daily from 10am to dusk; the Hall of Fame is open June to August, Saturday and Sunday from 2 to 5pm.

The 2,200-acre **Hitchcock Woods,** 404 South Boundary Ave., close to the center of town, is one of the best places to go riding in South Carolina. You'll even see some locals taking carriage drives. If you want to go riding, call one of the local centers and discuss your needs and requirements. The best outfitter is the **Black Forest Equestrian Center,** 4343 Bank Mill Rd. (✆ 803/642-0438; www.blackforestfarm.com).

## WHERE TO STAY

Aiken is an easy day trip from Columbia, but this part of the state is so beguiling that you may want to settle in here for a day or so. Note that when special events are on (horse races, the Masters Golf Tournament in neighboring Augusta, Georgia, and so on), rates in the Aiken area often go up.

**The Briar Patch Bed & Breakfast** ★ *Value*   Listed on the National Register of Historic Places, this is Aiken's finest B&B. It's very small, however, so reservations are important. Lying a couple of blocks from the polo grounds and 2 miles from the racetracks, it attracts the horse set. The two guest units were created from a horse stable, and the bedrooms were once a tack room. The guest units are separated from the main house and furnished with Early American antiques. Both units have fireplaces and private bathrooms equipped with tub/shower combinations. Golfers enjoy privileges nearby.

544 Magnolia Lane SE, Aiken, SC 29801. ✆ 803/649-2010. 2 units. $75 double. Rates include continental breakfast. No credit cards. **Amenities:** Breakfast room; lounge. *In room:* A/C, TV, no phone.

**Hotel Aiken**   The main part of the inn dates from 1929 and offers spacious, tastefully decorated rooms with high ceilings typical of the era. More modern but less interesting standard-size rooms are in the motel, offering modest comfort. Maintenance is excellent. All units have well-kept bathrooms with tub/shower combinations.

235 Richland Ave., Aiken, SC 29801. ℂ **877/817-6690** or 803/648-4265. Fax 803/649-6910. www.hotel aiken.com. 70 units. Hotel $70–$80 double; motel $56–$69 double. Rates include continental breakfast. AE, DISC, MC, V. **Amenities:** Restaurant; bar; outdoor pool; fitness center (nearby); salon; laundry service/dry cleaning. *In room:* A/C, TV, hair dryer.

**Willcox Inn** ★★   This 1897 inn, with its English country–house decor and antique furnishings, is one of the premier inns of South Carolina. Washington didn't sleep here, but Winston Churchill and Franklin D. Roosevelt did. So did the Astors, the Duke of Windsor, and an array of other glittering names. Six two-story columns line the front porch in the style of the antebellum South.

The lobby is graced with rosewood and pine woodwork, oak floors, stone fireplaces, and Oriental carpets. Guest rooms are individually decorated, often with four-poster beds and ornamental fireplaces and a liberal use of Second Empire furnishings. Each unit has a marble bathroom, the size of a compact car, with a tub/shower combination. The Vanderbilt Suite contains a 6-foot-long tub.

The inn's **Pheasant Room** is also the top restaurant in Aiken. The dining room is lovely, with fresh flowers and sparkling goblets. Well-prepared dishes are drawn from a changing repertoire of creative Continental fare based on seasonally fresh produce. The Pheasant Room is open for breakfast, lunch, and dinner. Have a drink in the **Polo Pub,** which displays artifacts such as fly rods, cricket bats, and polo mallets. All rooms are nonsmoking.

100 Colleton Ave. (at the corner of Whiskey Rd.), Aiken, SC 29801. ℂ **877/648-1898** or 803/648-1898. Fax 803/643-0971. www.willcoxinn.com. 22 units. $175–$225 double; $400–$500 suite. AE, DC, DISC, MC, V. Free parking. **Amenities:** Restaurant; bar; exercise room; health spa; limited room service; massage; babysitting; laundry service/dry cleaning. *In room:* A/C, TV, minibar, hair dryer, safe, fireplace (in some).

## WHERE TO DINE

**Linda's Bistro** ★ *Finds* STEAKS/SEAFOOD   Come here for the best steaks and seafood in town. In the heart of historic downtown Aiken, this casual bistro lies close to the newly completed Aiken Playhouse. Wine-tasting dinners are a special feature here (call and see if one is scheduled at the time of your visit). The menu is seasonally adjusted to showcase the best produce. The service is peerless, and most of the ingredients are fresh from the country. Delightful appetizers include roasted leek and lobster tart; and fresh jumbo lump crabmeat with horseradish sauce. The main courses never get overly elaborate but deliciously combine flavors, as in the seared Chilean sea bass with minced sun-dried tomatoes, or the creamy risotto with roasted mushrooms and Italian fontina. For dessert, how can you resist the sweet chocolate truffle cake with macerated peaches and Chantilly cream? *Note:* The street may be a little hard to find—it's only 1 block long, stretching from Laurens Street to Newberry Street.

210 The Alley. ℂ **803/648-4853.** Reservations required. Main courses $16–$30. AE, MC, V. Tues–Sat 5:30–10pm.

---

*Finds*   **Breakfast of Jockeys**

Near the racetrack, the breakfast-only **Race Track Kitchen,** 20 Mead Ave. (ℂ **803/641-9628**), is where the jockeys go to eat between sets. If you want racing tips, this is the place to hear them. It's just a hole in the wall, but we love its down-home atmosphere. The food is basic breakfast fare— ham and eggs, grits—costing $4 to $6. Hours are daily from 6am to 1pm.

## AIKEN AFTER DARK

The **Aiken Community Playhouse,** Washington Center for the Performing Arts, 124 Newberry St. (© **803/648-1438**), is firmly ensconced in its new home. Its repertoire mainly sticks to the standard road show fare, from *Butterflies Are Free* to *Gypsy.* On Friday and Saturday, performances are at 8pm, with a Sunday matinee at 3pm. Adults pay $15, seniors (60 and up) $13, students $10, and children under 12 $6.

# 15

# Planning Your Trip to Georgia

This chapter tackles the practical details of organizing your trip to Georgia. Also look at chapter 2, "For International Visitors"—some of the information you need may have already been discussed there.

## 1 The Regions in Brief

**THE ATLANTA AREA**   Gateway to the Deep South, Atlanta is one of the most progressive cities in America. The hometown of Martin Luther King, Jr., bears no relationship to the city from which Scarlett O'Hara and Aunt Pittypat fled during Sherman's March. It's a fast-paced capital city that, while still sporting a few magnolia blossoms and mint juleps, is marching forward in commerce and culture. *Fortune* magazine has called Atlanta "America's Best City for Business," and the title still holds into the 21st century.

**NORTHERN GEORGIA**   This area, within 70 to 120 miles of Atlanta, may be the best-kept travel secret in the South. Northern Georgia is a virtual national or state park, a rugged outback that stands in sharp contrast to the Blue Ridge Mountains in the northeastern part of the state. The northwest has many Native American sites, as well as the Chickamauga and Chattanooga National Military Park, where critical Civil War battles were staged. Lookout Mountain rises like a 100-mile linear barrier from the valleys below.

The southern Appalachians contain a mountain culture that hasn't been completely wiped out, and many of the old ways prevail. **Dahlonega** makes a great base for exploring Georgia's Blue Ridge Mountains, much of which lies within 727,000-acre **Chattahoochee National Forest.**

**SAVANNAH**   The very name evokes a romantic antebellum aura. Savannah is the city that General Sherman gave President Lincoln as a Christmas present.

Founded in 1733 by James Oglethorpe as Georgia's first settlement, the city is located 18 miles inland on the Savannah River at the South Carolina border. A deep channel connects Savannah to the ocean, attracting massive freighters to the terminals at the Georgia Ports Authority. Visitors can almost touch the ships as they slowly make their way up the river. Lined with classy nightspots and upscale restaurants, as well as a few rough pubs and artsy boutiques, cobblestone River Street has become a hub for tourists.

**MACON & THE SOUTHWEST**   Macon is best seen in March during the Cherry Blossom Festival, but this historic town has year-round attractions, too. It once grew fat on the cotton trade and still boasts some antebellum homes that Sherman's armies didn't completely destroy. Today, it's one of the most rewarding destinations in Georgia. The two other major attractions in the state's southwest are **Callaway Gardens** and **Warm Springs** (where Franklin Delano Roosevelt died). You can visit both towns on a day trip from Atlanta, or you can find plenty of old inns in the area if you want to spend the night.

# Georgia

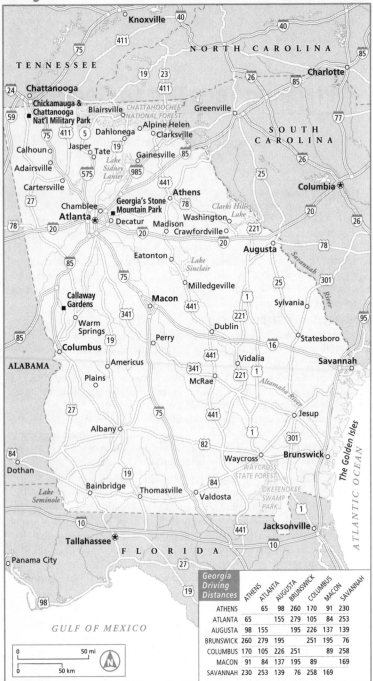

| Georgia Driving Distances | ATHENS | ATLANTA | AUGUSTA | BRUNSWICK | COLUMBUS | MACON | SAVANNAH |
|---|---|---|---|---|---|---|---|
| ATHENS | | 65 | 98 | 260 | 170 | 91 | 230 |
| ATLANTA | 65 | | 155 | 279 | 105 | 84 | 253 |
| AUGUSTA | 98 | 155 | | 195 | 226 | 137 | 139 |
| BRUNSWICK | 260 | 279 | 195 | | 251 | 195 | 76 |
| COLUMBUS | 170 | 105 | 226 | 251 | | 89 | 258 |
| MACON | 91 | 84 | 137 | 195 | 89 | | 169 |
| SAVANNAH | 230 | 253 | 139 | 76 | 258 | 169 | |

**THE GOLDEN ISLES**   Don't leave Georgia without exploring the Golden Isles. Start at U.S. 17 about 17 miles south of Darien (or exit off I-95 South at the Golden Isles Pkwy.), head toward Brunswick, and then travel to St. Simons and Sea Islands. The drive culminates in **Jekyll Island,** once the private enclave of wintering wealthy like the Rockefellers and the Vanderbilts, but now open to all.

If you can afford it, plan to spend at least one night at the **Cloister** on Sea Island, the grandest resort in the tri-state area. For escapists, there are also Little St. Simons Island and Cumberland Island, the idyllic wilderness where John Kennedy, Jr., married Caroline Bessette 3 years before their tragic plane crash.

Based at a hotel on the Golden Isles, you can make a day trip to one of the greatest attractions in Georgia: the **Okefenokee Swamp,** the largest freshwater swamp still preserved in the United States.

## 2  Visitor Information

For advance reading and planning, contact the **Division of Tourism,** Georgia Department of Industry, Trade & Tourism, P.O. Box 1776, Atlanta, GA 30301-1776 (© **800/VISIT-GA** or 404/962-4000; www.georgiaonmymind.org). Ask for information on your specific interests, as well as a calendar of events (Jan–June or July–Dec).

**State Information Centers** are located near Atlanta, Augusta, Columbus, Kingsland, Lavonia, Plains, Ringgold, Savannah, Sylvania, Tallapoosa, Valdosta, and West Point. They're open Monday to Saturday from 9am to 6pm and on Sunday from noon to 6pm. Information sources for specific destinations in the state are listed in the Georgia chapters that follow.

| What Things Cost in Atlanta | US$ |
|---|---|
| Taxi from Atlanta airport to downtown (for one passenger) | 25.00 |
| Fare between any two MARTA stops | 1.75 |
| Local telephone call | 0.50 |
| Four Seasons Hotel Atlanta (very expensive) | 275.00 |
| The Westin Peachtree Plaza (expensive) | 199.00 |
| Ansley Inn (moderate) | 120.00 |
| Hampton Inn (inexpensive) | 109.00 |
| Lunch for one at the Atlanta Fish Market (moderate) | 28.00 |
| Lunch for one at Mary Mac's Tea Room (inexpensive) | 10.00 |
| Dinner for one, without wine, in the Dining Room of the Ritz-Carlton Buckhead (expensive) | 77.00 |
| Dinner for one, without wine, at the Buckhead Diner (moderate) | 30.00 |
| Dinner for one, without wine, at Mick's (inexpensive) | 16.00 |
| Bottle of beer | 5.50 |
| Coca-Cola | 1.75 |
| Cup of coffee in a cafe | 2.00 |
| Roll of 35mm Kodak film, 36 exposures | 8.25 |
| Admission to Fernbank Museum of Natural History | 12.00 |
| Movie ticket | 8.50 |
| Theater ticket to the Alliance | 20.00–55.00 |

## 3 When to Go

## CLIMATE

The average high and low temperatures at coastal Savannah and central Atlanta show Low Country coastal areas to be warmer year-round than those farther inland. Winter temperatures seldom drop below freezing anywhere in the state. Spring and fall are the longest seasons, and the wettest months are December to April.

Spring is a spectacular time to visit. Many areas become a riot of color, as the azaleas, dogwoods, and camellias are bursting into bloom.

**Savannah Average Temperatures & Rainfall**

|            | Jan | Feb | Mar | Apr | May | June | July | Aug | Sept | Oct | Nov | Dec |
|------------|-----|-----|-----|-----|-----|------|------|-----|------|-----|-----|-----|
| High (°F)  | 60  | 62  | 70  | 78  | 84  | 89   | 91   | 90  | 85   | 78  | 70  | 62  |
| High (°C)  | 16  | 17  | 21  | 26  | 29  | 32   | 33   | 32  | 29   | 26  | 21  | 17  |
| Low (°F)   | 38  | 41  | 48  | 55  | 63  | 69   | 72   | 72  | 68   | 57  | 57  | 41  |
| Low (°C)   | 3   | 5   | 9   | 13  | 17  | 21   | 22   | 22  | 20   | 14  | 14  | 5   |
| Rain (in.) | 3.6 | 3.2 | 3.8 | 3.0 | 4.1 | 5.7  | 6.4  | 7.5 | 4.5  | 2.4 | 2.2 | 3.0 |

**Atlanta Average Temperatures & Rainfall**

|            | Jan | Feb | Mar | Apr | May | June | July | Aug | Sept | Oct | Nov | Dec |
|------------|-----|-----|-----|-----|-----|------|------|-----|------|-----|-----|-----|
| High (°F)  | 51  | 55  | 61  | 71  | 79  | 85   | 87   | 86  | 81   | 73  | 62  | 53  |
| High (°C)  | 11  | 13  | 16  | 22  | 26  | 29   | 31   | 30  | 27   | 23  | 17  | 12  |
| Low (°F)   | 33  | 36  | 41  | 51  | 59  | 67   | 69   | 69  | 63   | 52  | 41  | 34  |
| Low (°C)   | 1   | 2   | 5   | 11  | 15  | 19   | 21   | 21  | 17   | 11  | 5   | 1   |
| Rain (in.) | 4.8 | 4.8 | 5.8 | 4.3 | 4.3 | 3.6  | 5.0  | 3.7 | 3.4  | 3.1 | 3.9 | 4.3 |

## GEORGIA CALENDAR OF EVENTS

### January

**Martin Luther King Celebration,** Atlanta. This event, occurring over the King holiday weekend, honors one of Atlanta's native sons in a celebration of the life and accomplishments of the civil rights leader. The program includes a "Salute to Greatness" dinner on Saturday, and a commemorative at Ebenezer Baptist Church on the Monday holiday, with speeches by notables from the Reverend King's former pulpit. Contact the King Center at ℂ **404/ 526-8923** (www.thekingcenter.org). Second week in January.

**Rattlesnake Roundup,** Whigham. This event, held at 84 E. Whigham Rattlesnake Grounds, features arts, crafts, food, entertainment, and snake handling that includes a milking demonstration. Call ℂ **229/762- 3774.** Last Saturday in January.

**Augusta Cutting Horse Futurity,** Augusta. This prestigious annual event attracts cowboys and cowgirls from all over the country and the world. Held in the Augusta-Richmond County Civic Center, this event marks the first big date on any equestrian lover's calendar. Call ℂ **706/823-3417.** Late January.

### February

**Wormsloe's Colonial Faire and Muster,** Savannah. Wormsloe was the colonial fortified home of Noble Jones, one of Georgia's first colonists. Costumed demonstrators portray skills used by those early settlers. Tickets cost $2 for adults, and $1 for children. Call ℂ **912/ 353-3023** or go to www.wormsloe. org. First Saturday and Sunday in February.

**Savannah Irish Festival,** Savannah. This Irish heritage celebration promises fun for the entire family, with music, dancing, and food. There's both a children's stage and a main stage. Contact the Irish Committee of Savannah at ℂ **912/232-3448** (www.savannahirish.org).Mid-February.

## March

**St. Patrick's Day Celebration on the River,** Savannah. The river flows green and so does the beer in one of the largest celebrations held on River Street each year. Enjoy live entertainment, lots of food, and tons of fun. Contact the Savannah Waterfront Association at ℂ **912/234-0295** (www.savriverstreet.com). St. Patrick's Day weekend.

**Golden Corral 500,** Hampton. This suburb outside Atlanta is the site of the Atlanta International Raceway and home to this first of two annual NASCAR NEXTEL Cup events. Tickets to the races range from $25 to $100. For information and tickets, call ℂ **770/946-4211** (www.atlanta motorspeedway.com). Mid-March.

**Cherry Blossom Festival,** Macon. You'll find everything from hot-air ballooning to a giant parade with 100 bands. The entire city is ablaze with thousands of blooming cherry trees. For more information, contact the Macon Cherry Blossom Festival at ℂ **478/751-7429** (www.cherry blossom.com). Mid- to late March.

**Aiken-Augusta Spring Regatta,** Augusta. The Augusta Rowing Club is perched over the waters of the Savannah River. From this point the water continues for 11 miles downstream from the boathouse, ideal

rowing territory, as it is one of the longest stretches of rowable water in the world. This is a well-tended event attracting enthusiasts from all over America. For more information, call ℂ **706/821-2875** or go to www.augustarowingclub.org. Mid-March.

**The Savannah Tour of Homes & Gardens,** Savannah. Each spring Savannahians open the doors to many of their historic homes and gardens during 4-day self-guided walking tours where you are allowed to visit six to eight private homes and gardens every day. Afternoon teas and special luncheons are also staged. Contact 18 Abercorn St. (ℂ **912/234-8054;** www.savannah tourofhomes.org). March 31 to April 3, 2005; March 23 to March 26, 2006.

## April

**Masters Golf Tournament,** Augusta. The first of professional golf's four "major" tournaments, this event was conceived by golf legend Bobby Jones, an Atlantan, who mastered the links as an amateur in the 1920s. Tickets ("badges," as the Augusta National "patrons" call them) are sold out years in advance. However, those who plan well in advance are able to enter a lottery to obtain tickets to practice rounds, which allows you to walk the grounds. "Ike's Tree," along the 18th fairway, was named for former President Dwight D. Eisenhower. Call ℂ **706/667-6700** or go to www.masters.org for additional information. The deadline for lottery registration is usually the middle of July for the following year's event. First weekend in April.

**Georgia Renaissance Festival,** Fairburn. Of the more than 100 shows every day, see the King's Joust and the Birds of Prey Show. There are also games, rides, and crafts items, not to mention giant stilt-walkers, minstrels, jousters, and magicians in the re-creation of a 16th-century English county fair. Buy tickets at the gate. Adults $15, children $7. Contact the Georgia Renaissance Festival at © 770/964-8575 (www.garenfest.com). Weekends April to June.

**Atlanta Dogwood Festival.** Georgia celebrates the coming of spring with garden and house tours, bicycle tours of exclusive Buckhead, concerts, and tons of azaleas and dogwoods in full bloom. On the final weekend, food booths, kids' activities, and concerts are among the events. Piedmont Park events are free, but there are admission fees to many other activities. Call © 404/329-0501 (www.dogwood. org). Three days in mid-April.

**Riverfest Weekend,** Columbus. This family-oriented festival offers an art show and sale, a custom and classic automobile show, a 5km (3.1-mile) road race, an orchid show and sale, parades, river events, and lots of food and music. Contact Riverfest at © 706/323-7979 (www. columbusriverfest.com). Late April.

**May**

**The Cotton Pickin' Fair,** Gay. Active for more than half a century, this award-winning festival is a family affair, filled with antiques, arts and crafts, food, and entertainment. You can make a day of it. Admission is $5 for adults or $2 for children. For more information, call © 706/538-6814 (www.cpfair.com). Held semi-annually, first weekend in May and October.

**Savannah Symphony Duck Race,** Savannah. Each year the Savannah Symphony Women's Guild plays host as a flock of rubber ducks hits

the water to go with the flow of the tides along historic River Street. There's a $5,000 grand prize for the winning ducky. All proceeds benefit the Savannah Symphony. Call © 912/236-9536. Early May.

**Memorial Day at Old Fort Jackson,** Savannah. The ceremonies have a flag-raising ceremony and a memorial service featuring "Taps." Contact the Coastal Heritage Society at © 912/651-6840 (www.chsgeorgia. org). Late May.

**June**

**Arts Festival of Atlanta,** Atlanta. One of the nation's oldest and largest outdoor art events, this contemporary visual and performing-arts festival features regional, national, and international artists. Call © 404/521-6600. Second week in June.

**Juneteenth,** Savannah. This event highlights the contributions of more than 200,000 African Americans who fought for their freedom and that of future generations. This event is a celebration of the Emancipation Proclamation. Although this promise of freedom was announced in January, it was not until the middle of June (actual date unknown) that the news reached Savannah, thus prompting the remembrance of "Juneteenth." For more information, contact **Savannah Trade & Tourism** at © 912/944-0456. Mid-June.

**The Atlanta Film Festival,** Atlanta. This 7- to 10-day festival celebrates the rising independent movie scene in Atlanta. More than 80 films, videos, shorts, and documentaries are screened to the public throughout the city. Steven Spielberg credits this festival with giving his work its first big boost. Call © 404/352-4225 or go to www.image fv.org/aff2004. Late June to early July.

## July

**Fourth of July Fireworks and Laser Show,** Stone Mountain. Stone Mountain makes a picturesque canvas for the artistry of the popular laser show. You need not enter the park to enjoy the show—you can join the thousands who simply pull off to the shoulder of the road to witness the spectacle. Call ✆ 770/498-5600 for more information. July 4.

**Augusta Southern National Dragboat Races,** Augusta. The stretch of the Savannah River that runs along the Augusta Riverwalk makes for an ideal setting for this annual thunderous event. High speeds and danger fuel these races as boats "fly" by with engines larger than what is found in most cars. Tickets range from $15 to $50. For information, call ✆ 706/724-2452. Mid- to late July.

## August

**Georgia Mountain Fair,** Hiawassee. Enjoy fun-filled days and nights of activities on the shores of Lake Chatuge. There will be country, bluegrass, or gospel music along with clogging, a parade, a midway, and arts and crafts shows. Call ✆ 706/896-4191 (www.georgia-mountain-fair.com). Early to mid-August.

## September

**Savannah Jazz Festival,** Savannah. This festival features national and local jazz and blues legends. A jazz brunch and music at different venues throughout the city are among the highlights. Contact Ike Carter at ✆ 912/356-2399; www.coastal jazz.com. Mid-September.

**Yellow Daisy Festival,** Stone Mountain. Every year Georgians gather at Stone Mountain Park to celebrate the blooming of the yellow daisy. Enjoy the arts and crafts, but please don't eat the daisies—they're rare. Call ✆ 770/498-5600. Mid-September.

**Helen's Oktoberfest,** Helen. Alpine Helen celebrates the South's longest Oktoberfest (starting in Sept) with live Bavarian music, German food and beverages, and dancing. Tickets cost $7 to $9. Contact the Helen Welcome Center at ✆ 800/858-8027; www.helenga.org. September to early November.

**Georgia State Fair,** Macon. The state's most joyous occasion takes place at this fair, which has everything from rides to competitions, regional specialties to live music. It's strictly family fun. Usually you pay one price ($15) and get unlimited rides. Late September or early October (dates vary).

## October

**Andersonville October Fair,** Andersonville. History comes alive in Andersonville, near the site of the Andersonville Prison, of Civil War infamy. Reenactments and demonstrations take you back to the time of the War Between the States. Contact ✆ 229/924-2558 or go to www.andersonvillegeorgia. com. Two days in October (dates vary).

**The Cotton Pickin' Fair,** Gay. Active for more than half a century, this award-winning festival is a family affair, filled with antiques, arts and crafts, food, and entertainment. Admission is $5 for adults or $2 for children. For more information, call ✆ 706/538-6814 or go to www.cpfair.com. Held semi-annually, first weekend in October and May.

**Big Pig Jig,** Vienna. Hailed by *Travel Agent* magazine as one of the "Top 20 Events in the Southeast," the state's barbecue-cooking championship was born in 1982 when a group of people competed to see who could cook the most succulent pig. The festival has expanded today to include a parade, sidewalk art contest, "Hog Jog" race, and carnival rides. Go to www.bigpigjig.com. Mid-October.

**Yank/Reb Blues Festival,** Fitzgerald. This celebration of blues music and folk art is expressed in a hundred different media and displayed on brick streets among blooming plaza parks in this historic downtown. Call ✆ **800/FUN-IN-GA** or go to www.fitzgeraldga.org/yank-reb.html. Third weekend in October.

**November**

**Crafts Festival and Cane Grinding,** Savannah. More than 75 craft artists from four states sell and demonstrate their art. Music is provided by the Savannah Folk Music Society. Contact Oatland Island at ✆ **912/897-3773.** Mid-November.

**Candlelight Tours,** Atlanta. These evening tours of historic homes and gardens offer music and storytelling in the spirit of the holidays. Contact the Atlanta History Center at ✆ **404/814-4000** (www.atlanta historycenter.com). Late November.

**December**

**Candles and Carols of Christmases Past,** Mount Berry. This is a Victorian Christmas in the best tradition of the Old South, with candlelight tours and seasonal music and drama. Contact Oak Hill and the Martha Berry Museum at ✆ **800/220-5504.** First Friday and Saturday in December.

**Christmas 1864,** Savannah. Fort Jackson hosts the dramatic re-creation of its evacuation on December 20, 1864. More than 60 Civil War re-enactors play the part of Fort Jackson's Confederate defenders, who were preparing to evacuate ahead of Union Gen. William Tecumseh Sherman. Contact Old Fort Jackson at ✆ **912/232-3945.** Early December.

**Holiday Tour of Homes,** Savannah. The doors of Savannah's historic homes are opened to the public during the holiday season. Each home is decorated, and a different group of homes is shown every day. Contact the Downtown Neighborhood Association at ✆ **912/236-8362** (www. dnaholidaytour.net). Mid-December.

## 4 The Active Vacation Planner

The 2000 Super Bowl and the 1996 Olympics brought attention to Atlanta and helped show the rest of the world that Georgia offers a variety of outdoor experiences. From the Golden Isles to the North Georgia uplands, the Peach State offers fishing, golf, sailing, and everything in between.

**BEACHES**    Georgia's beaches don't enjoy the fame of those in the Carolinas. But at one time, the Georgia coast was frequented by the likes of Rockefellers and Vanderbilts, and even though this grand life has faded, the coast remains a quiet retreat for those seeking a true getaway. The Georgia coast is dotted with what are known as the Golden Isles: Historic Jekyll Island, luxurious Sea Island, and secluded Cumberland Island are the Eastern Seaboard's best-kept secrets. For information, call ✆ **800/VISIT-GA** or write the **Division of Tourism,** Georgia Department of Industry, Trade & Tourism, P.O. Box 1776, Atlanta, GA 30301.

**CAMPING**    For information on Georgia's state parks and their camping facilities, contact the **Georgia Department of Natural Resources,** Office of Information, 205 Butler St. SE, Suite 1352, Atlanta, GA 30334. Forty of the state parks in Georgia welcome campers to sites that rent for $10 to $20 per night.

Some 25 parks have vacation cottages that rent for $50 to $135 per night. These rates are for the summer and are reduced during other months. Reservations may be made by calling © **800/864-PARK,** or visit www.gastateparks.org. Be aware that some of the Georgia state parks have become privatized. Site and cabin rentals could be higher at these parks. **Georgia State Parks & Historic Sites** (© **404/656-3530**) can provide additional information, including details on hiking.

**GOLF**    Golf is big in Georgia. Augusta is home to the venerable Augusta National Golf Club, where the Masters Golf Tournament is played (the club's course is not open to the public). Lake Oconee is the golf capital of Georgia, boasting more than seven championship courses by designers like Jack Nicklaus and Ben Crenshaw. Mickey Mantle loved it so much that he spent most of his last days at the Harbor Club golf resort. Its neighbor, Reynolds Plantation, is host to the American qualifications for the World Championship. For information on private and public golf courses across the state of Georgia, call the Georgia State Golf Association at © **800/949-4742** (www.gsga.org) to receive your free guide, *Georgia Golf on My Mind.*

**FISHING & HUNTING**    No license is needed for saltwater fishing, but fishing in Georgia's lakes, streams, and ponds does require a license. Hunting is a sport used to curtail the annual exponential growth of the white-tailed deer population. Wild turkey and quail also abound. For information on hunting and fishing regulations, contact the **Georgia Department of Natural Resources,** 205 Butler St., Atlanta, GA 30334 (© **800/241-4113;** www.georgiawildlife.com). Many hunting clubs will allow you to join provided that you have references or can be sponsored by a local friend or family member.

**HIKING**    The Appalachian Trail begins in North Georgia. For those who want easier hikes, some 40 state parks in Georgia offer trails of varying difficulty. Call © **800/864-PARKS** for more information.

**LAKES**    Georgia is a virtual land of lakes, providing water, electricity, and recreation. East Georgia's Clarks Hill Lake (the Georgia side of South Carolina's Thurmond Lake), northeast Georgia's Lake Hartwell, and middle Georgia's lakes Oconee, Sinclair, and Lanier are the premier spots for boating and fishing. Contact the **Georgia Department of Natural Resources,** Office of Information, 205 Butler St. SE, Atlanta, GA 30334; or call © **800/241-4113.**

**PANNING FOR GOLD**    Believe it or not, the San Francisco gold rush fever actually started in Dahlonega, Georgia. For a trip back in time, contact the **Dahlonega Georgia Visitor Center** at © **800/231-5543** (www.dahlonega.org) for information on vacations and day trips to the gold mines, 250 feet below the surface. You get to keep the gold you find, but don't expect a king's ransom.

**WHITE-WATER CANOEING & RAFTING**    The Amicalola River (pronounced am-e-co-*lo*-la) is one of the state's more stunning sites, with the towering Amicalola Falls. **Appalachian Outfitters** (© **800/426-7117;** www.canoe georgia.com) is the leading outfitter, offering trips for beginners through experienced rafters.

## 5 Specialized Travel Resources

**TRAVELERS WITH DISABILITIES**    Many hotels and restaurants in Georgia provide easy access for persons with disabilities. However, it's always a good idea to call ahead to make sure.

The **Georgia Governor's Developmental Disabilities Council** (© 404/657-2126; www.gcdd.org) may also be of help. The Georgia Department of Industry, Trade & Tourism publishes a guide, *Georgia on My Mind*, that lists attractions and accommodations with access for persons with disabilities. To receive a copy, contact **Tour Georgia**, P.O. Box 1776, Atlanta, GA 30301 (© **800/VISIT-GA**, ext. 1903).

For information on associations for persons with disabilities, see "Specialized Travel Resources," in chapter 3.

For transportation within Atlanta, individuals with disabilities can contact **Handicapped Driver Services** (© 770/422-9025; www.hdsvans.com) or **Wheelchair Getaways, Inc.** (© 770/457-9851; www.wheelchairgetaways.com).

**GAY & LESBIAN TRAVELERS**  Atlanta is famous for its thriving gay community. You can access its gay offerings through the listings and articles in the *Southern Voice*. Call © 404/876-1819 for information about distribution points throughout the South and gay resources and activities in Atlanta.

For more information before you go, refer to "Specialized Travel Resources," in chapter 3.

**FAMILY TRAVEL**  All Georgia visitor centers offer discount coupons for families as well as the *Atlanta Street Map & Visitors Guide*. Families might also pick up the book *A Guide for Family Activities*, by Denise Black, with a host of ideas and activities for children in the Metro Atlanta area. Another local guide is called *Fun Family Vacations—Southeast.*

## 6 Getting There

**BY PLANE**  Virtually every major national airline flies through Atlanta's **Hartsfield International Airport**, 13 miles south of downtown off I-85 and I-285. From Atlanta, there are connecting flights to points around the state, including Augusta, Columbus, and Savannah. **Delta** (© **800/221-1212**; www.delta.com), based at Hartsfield, is the major carrier to Atlanta, connecting it to pretty much the entire country as well as 32 countries internationally. Other major carriers are **America West** (© 800/235-9292; www.americawest.com), **American** (© 800/433-7300; www.aa.com), **British Airways** (© 800/AIRWAYS; www.britishairways.com), **Continental** (© 800/525-0280; www.continental.com), **KLM** (© 800/374-7747; www.klm.nl), **Lufthansa** (© 800/645-3880; www.lufthansa-usa.com), **Northwest** (© 800/225-2525; www.nwa.com), **United** (© 800/241-6522; www.ual.com), and **US Airways** (© 800/428-4322; www.usairways.com).

American, Delta, United, and US Airways all serve Savannah's airport.

**BY CAR**  Georgia is crisscrossed by major interstate highways: I-75 bisects the state from Dalton in the north to Valdosta in the south; I-95 runs north–south along the Eastern Seaboard. The major east–west routes are I-16, running between Macon and Savannah; and I-20, running from Augusta through Atlanta and into Alabama. I-85 runs northeast–southwest in the northern half of the state. The state-run welcome centers at all major points of entry are staffed with knowledgeable, helpful Georgians. The highway speed limit of 65 mph and the seat-belt law are strictly enforced.

**BY TRAIN**  Amtrak (© **800/USA-RAIL**; www.amtrak.com) has stops in Atlanta, Savannah, Jesup, Gainesville, and Toccoa. Bargain fares are in effect for limited periods. Ask about Amtrak's money-saving "All Aboard America" regional fares.

**BY BUS**    Greyhound/Trailways (© **800/231-2222;** www.greyhound.com) has good direct service to major cities in Georgia from out of state, with connections to almost any destination you want.

## 7 Getting Around

**BY CAR**    In addition to the interstates, U.S. 84 cuts across the southern part of the state from the Alabama state line through Valdosta and Waycross, and eventually connects to I-95 south of Savannah. U.S. 441 runs from the North Carolina border south to Athens, Dublin, and the Florida state line. For 24-hour road conditions, call © **404/656-5267. AAA** services are available in Atlanta, Augusta, Columbus, Macon, Savannah, Smyrna, and Tucker.

**BY PLANE**    From Atlanta, there are connecting flights into Albany, Augusta, Brunswick (for the Golden Isles), Savannah, and (by commuter line) several smaller cities. Check with your travel agent. See also "Getting There," above.

**BY TRAIN    Amtrak** (see "Getting There," above) runs from Toccoa to Gainesville and Atlanta, as well as from Savannah to Jesup. The **Georgia Railroad** operates between Atlanta and Augusta.

---

### FAST FACTS: **Georgia**

*American Express* American Express services are available in Albany, Atlanta (five locations; see "Fast Facts: Atlanta," in chapter 16), Augusta (two locations), Columbus, Dalton, Duluth, Macon, and Valdosta.

*Emergencies* Dial © **911** for police, an ambulance, paramedics, or the fire department.

*Liquor Laws* If you're 21 or over, you can buy alcoholic beverages in package stores between 8am and midnight (except on Sun, election days, Thanksgiving, and Christmas).

*Newspapers & Magazines* The *Atlanta Journal-Constitution* is the state's leading daily newspaper.

*Taxes* Georgia has a 7% sales tax, and an accommodations tax (room or occupancy tax) is often tacked onto your hotel bill. Counties also have the option of adding an extra .5% to 3% use tax.

*Time Zone* Georgia is in the Eastern Time zone, and goes on daylight saving time in summer.

# 16

# Atlanta

Atlanta is the gateway to the New South. Bustling and ever-growing—not always attractively—Georgia's capital is the 13th-largest metropolitan area in the United States. If only Rhett and Scarlett could see it now—or, better yet, if only General Sherman could rise from the grave to witness the phenomenal growth of a city that he was able to burn to the ground but whose spirit he couldn't destroy.

Atlanta has enlarged its rail system, brought in six interstate highways, and acquired an airport to rival Chicago's O'Hare. Some 450 of the Fortune 500 corporations have offices or home offices here.

Perversely (though predictably), it seems that the more progress Atlanta makes, the more serious its problems become. Yet, in spite of overcrowding, unemployment, traffic-clogged streets, and a high crime rate, Atlanta remains the showcase of the New South. It's filled with the homes of the rich and famous (everybody from Ted Turner to Elton John) and is also the Promised Land to immigrants from as far away as Vietnam and as close as the Caribbean and (especially) Mexico.

Ever since Atlanta was selected as the site of the 2000 Super Bowl and the 1996 Summer Olympic Games, the city's face has changed. Massive construction began in the early 1990s with the $215-million, 70,500-seat Georgia Dome, and continued in 1994 and 1995 with the creation of a $50-million, 60-acre Centennial Park, the heart of the public area for the Games. The hard work and construction were not wasted when the Olympics left town. Centennial Park is used for leisure by Atlantans today; the $169-million Olympic Village became housing for Georgia Tech and Georgia State University; the $170-million Olympic Stadium, scaled down to become Turner Field, is the home of the Atlanta Braves; and the Olympic Cauldron still stands in remembrance of the Games. The city's major sports and entertainment facility, the Philips Arena, opened in late 1999 and hosts the Atlanta Hawks NBA team and the Atlanta Thrashers NHL expansion team. The Thrashers join the Atlanta Braves and the Atlanta Hawks as the crown jewels in mogul Ted Turner's sports empire.

All this commerce with the outside world has energized the city's cultural life. More than ever before, there are concerts and cabarets, art galleries and avant-garde "happenings," and the many late-night diversions of "Hotlanta." The influx of restaurants featuring international cuisine has put Atlanta on the gastronomic map, but has made it harder and harder to find fried chicken, country ham, hot biscuits, and grits. Locals like to boast that Atlanta has arrived—and they'll be happy to take you by the hand and prove it. You won't have to convince Elton John. The rock star, who owns homes of varying degrees of pomp and elegance all over the world, is said to favor living Southern-style in his Atlanta apartment best of all.

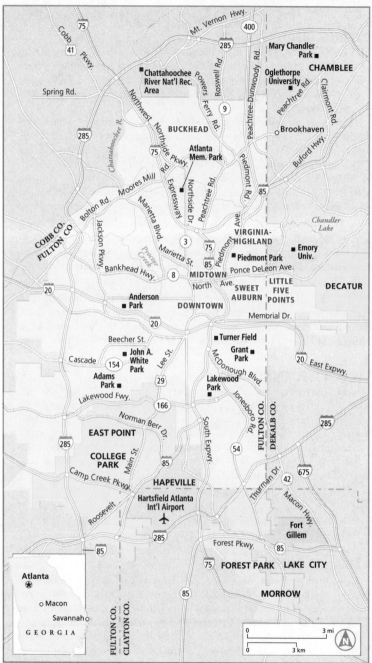

## 1 Orientation

## GETTING THERE

**BY PLANE**    Atlanta's **Hartsfield International Airport** is the home of **Delta** (*C* 800/221-1212; www.delta.com) and served by dozens of other international and domestic carriers, including **American** (*C* 800/433-7300; www. aa.com), **United** (*C* 800/241-6522; www.united.com), and **US Airways** (*C* 800/ 428-4322; www.usairways.com).

The Atlanta **airport shuttle** (*C* **404/524-3400**) connects the airport with downtown and major hotels between 6am and midnight, for a $16 fare downtown, $18 midtown, and $20 Buckhead. **MARTA**'s (Metropolitan Atlanta Rapid Transit Authority; *C* **404/848-4711**) rapid-rail trains run from 4:45am to 1am, with a downtown fare of $1.75. Taxi fare to downtown is $20 for one passenger, $22 for two passengers, and $30 for three. *Warning:* Be sure the taxi driver knows how to get to where you want to go before you leave the airport.

**BY CAR**    Atlanta is accessible by car via three interstate highways: I-75, which runs north–south between Tennessee and Florida; I-85, which runs northeast–southwest between South Carolina and Alabama; and I-20, which runs east–west between South Carolina and Alabama. I-285, more commonly known as the Perimeter Highway, circles the Atlanta metropolitan area.

**BY TRAIN**    Amtrak trains arrive at the **Brookwood Railway Station,** 1688 Peachtree St. (*C* **800/USA-RAIL**), providing daily service to and from Washington, New York, Boston, and intermediate points to the northeast, and to New Orleans and intermediate points to the southwest. This is a very central location, within easy reach of most downtown or midtown hotels.

## VISITOR INFORMATION

**Atlanta Convention and Visitors Bureau (ACVB),** 233 Peachtree St. NE, Suite 100, Atlanta, GA 30303 (*C* **404/521-6600;** www.atlanta.net), can supply a wealth of information on sightseeing, accommodations, dining, cultural happenings, and special interests. The ACVB also offers the "Atlanta Passport," a vacation packet filled with coupons, discounts, and an events calendar.

After your arrival, stop by one of the helpful **ACVB visitor information centers,** at Hartsfield International Airport, in the Lenox Square Shopping Center (Buckhead), at 3393 Peachtree Rd., and in Underground Atlanta at 65 Upper Alabama St.

For a more in-depth exploration of the city, look for *Frommer's Atlanta,* available at many bookstores.

## NEIGHBORHOODS IN BRIEF

**Downtown** Atlanta's commercial center is home to numerous gleaming skyscrapers, the most outstanding of which is Peachtree Center. Underground Atlanta, the Georgia World Congress Center, department stores (Macy's, and so on), the downtown branch of the High Museum of Art (in the Georgia-Pacific Center), Grant Park (with its zoo and Cyclorama), and the state capitol are all here. Adjacent to central downtown is the Martin Luther King, Jr. Historic District, a predominantly black neighborhood that bred and nurtured the revered civil rights leader. The safest downtown streets (particularly after dark) are in the well-traveled "hotel corridor"—bordered by Ellis, Courtland,

Baker, and Peachtree streets. Private security officers and the Atlanta Police carefully patrol this area.

**Midtown**  North of downtown, the midtown area extends roughly from Ponce de Leon Avenue to 26th Street. Major attractions include the Woodruff Arts Center (housing the High Museum of Art), the Alliance Theatre, the Atlanta Symphony Orchestra, and the Fox Theatre.

**Ansley Park**  Adjacent to midtown and designed by Frederick Law Olmsted around the turn of the 20th century, this is chiefly a residential area of landscaped greenery. It also houses Colony Square, a complex of shops, restaurants, and offices.

**Buckhead**  About 6 miles north of downtown is Atlanta's affluent district, the setting of gorgeous mansions surrounded by landscaped gardens, posh shops and boutiques, some of the city's top hotels and restaurants, and two top-of-the-line shopping centers—Lenox Square and Phipps Plaza. It's also well known for its bar and restaurant scene. Even the "border" of Buckhead is easily marked by the first of a long stretch of bars you'll see as you drive through.

**Virginia-Highland**  Northeast of downtown, this is to Atlanta what Greenwich Village is to New York—an area of quirky little shops, bookstores, sidewalk cafes,

art galleries, bistros, and some of the liveliest bars in the city.

**Little Five Points**  Just beyond Virginia-Highland, Little Five Points is centered around the junction of Euclid and Moreland avenues. The Victorian homes here became the renovation craze of city residents and now shine in their original glory. This is also where you'll find the Jimmy Carter Presidential Center and Library.

**Decatur**  This charming village dating from 1823 is clustered around the courthouse square, a 15-minute drive east of downtown. Decatur has the huge, bustling Dekalb Farmer's Market, and is also the setting for a variety of cultural events and festivals. In recent years, it has been a popular destination for immigrants, prompting national publications such as *USA Today* to recognize that Atlanta's immigrant population growth is outpacing that of the rest of the country, especially in the number of Asian immigrants. The neighboring community of Chamblee has been referred to as "Little Hanoi."

**Vining**  Set to the northwest of Buckhead, inside the Beltway, this leafy, pleasant neighborhood's buildings and homes mostly date from the 1950s. Recently, it's been the site of a residential and commercial building boom, and the focus of lots of attention.

## 2 Getting Around

### BY PUBLIC TRANSPORTATION

**BY SUBWAY**  The **Metropolitan Atlanta Rapid Transit Authority** (**MARTA; ℭ 404/848-4711**) is Atlanta's rapid-rail system, with 36 stations. It extends north to the airport, and east–west and north–south lines intersect at the Five Points Station in downtown. **BATMA** (Buckhead Area Transportation Management Association) operates free electric shuttle buses between Lenox and Buckhead, the two MARTA train stations in the district. MARTA operates Monday to Friday 4:45am to 1am, Saturday 5:15am to 12:45am, and Sunday 6am to 12:45am; the regular fare is $1.75. There are token vending machines at all stations, and transfers are free. For schedule and route information, call

# MARTA Rapid Rail

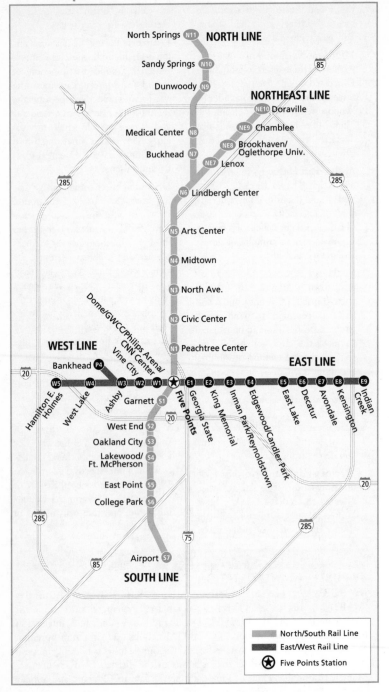

© **404/848-4711** Monday to Friday from 6am to 11pm, and on Saturday, Sunday, and holidays from 8am to 10pm.

**BY BUS   MARTA** also operates some 150 bus routes, which connect with all rapid-rail stations. You must have exact change—no pennies—for the $1.75 fare, and transfers are free. For route and schedule information, call the MARTA number listed above. They can also tell you when special shuttle buses run from downtown to major sports events. MARTA also provides transportation services for persons with disabilities; call © **404/848-5389** for details.

## BY CAR

It's possible to reach most major Atlanta sites by transit system (MARTA), but a car is preferable, with a few caveats.

Parking isn't usually a problem (though it can be expensive downtown during conventions and sporting events), but traffic often is. (There's even a column in the local newspaper devoted to traffic information and difficulties.) Rush hour—roughly 7 to 9am and 4:30 to 6:30pm—can be vicious, especially when you're traveling into town in the morning or out of town in the afternoon on any of the interstates. Besides the commuter traffic, there are travelers passing through Atlanta on their way to points north, south, east, and west. Atlanta drivers are generally courteous, but they tend to travel at breakneck speeds well above the posted limit, so it's wise to avoid the interstates—especially I-285, which supports a lot of truck traffic—during peak hours.

All of the major car-rental companies are, of course, represented here and are reachable via toll-free numbers. These include the following: **Avis** (© 800/331-1212), **Budget** (© 800/527-0700), **Dollar** (© 800/800-4000), **Hertz** (© 800/654-3131), and **Thrifty** (© 800/367-2277). There's also **Atlanta Rent-A-Car** (© 404/763-1160), a local, independently owned company, which also has good rates.

AAA services are available through **AAA Auto Club South,** 4540B Roswell Rd., Atlanta, GA 30342 (© **404/843-4500**).

## BY TAXI

Atlanta's taxis can be a major problem. Many are dirty, mechanically suspect, and manned by drivers unfamiliar with the city. Be sure the fare is settled before you set off. Fares operate on a set schedule downtown and in Buckhead: a flat rate of $6 to $7 for one passenger, $2 to $3 each for additional passengers. For all other destinations, a single passenger pays $3 for the first mile, and $1.50 for each additional mile. You pay $15 per hour for waiting time, and $5 for use of additional space for luggage. Vans or station wagons cost an additional $5. Taxis usually cannot be flagged down on the streets, but must be called or be met at major hotels or the airport. One of the most reliable companies is **Yellow Cab Company** (© **404/521-0200**). If you have a complaint about taxi service, call © **404/658-7600.**

*FAST FACTS:* **Atlanta**

*American Express* There is an American Express Travel Service at 3384 Peachtree Rd., Lenox Plaza (© **404/262-7561**). Offices are open Monday to Friday 9am to 5:30pm and Saturday 10am to 4pm.

*Babysitters* **Friend of the Family** (℅ **770/643-3000**) is a reliable firm with carefully screened, age-21-and-over sitters, some of whom speak foreign languages. Twenty-four-hour advance notice is recommended, and you may interview a sitter before making a commitment.

*Camera Repair* Try **Wolf Camera**, 150 14th St. NW (℅ **404/875-0071**), open Monday to Friday 8:30am to 6:30pm, Saturday 10am to 5pm, and Sunday 12:30 to 5pm. Take the 14th Street exit off I-85.

*Currency Exchange* There's a currency exchange service at the airport. In the city, downtown major banks provide the service. Try **Bank of America**, 35 Broad St. NW (℅ **404/893-8282**).

*Dentists* A free referral service is operated by the Georgia Dental Association of Atlanta (℅ **404/636-7553**).

*Doctors* For physician referrals, contact the **Georgia State Medical Board** (℅ **404/656-3913**). See also "Hospitals," below.

*Drugstores* They're plentiful around the city. **Eckerd Drugs**, 1512 Piedmont Ave. (℅ **404/876-2263**), is open Monday to Saturday 9am to 9pm, Sunday 11am to 6pm.

*Emergencies* Call ℅ **911.**

*Eyeglasses* **LensCrafters**, in the Lenox Square Mall, 3400 Woodlake Dr. in Buckhead (℅ **404/239-0784**), is open Monday to Saturday from 10am to 9pm and on Sunday from noon to 6pm.

*Hospitals* There are 24-hour emergency rooms at the **Atlanta Medical Center**, 303 Parkway Dr. NE (℅ **404/265-4000**); and at Grady Memorial Hospital, 80 Jesse Hill Jr. Dr. (℅ **404/616-4307**).

*Newspapers & Magazines* The *Atlanta Journal-Constitution* is the major daily newspaper. Others include the *Atlanta Business Chronicle* and the *Atlanta Daily World. Atlanta* magazine is an excellent reference for information on current cultural, entertainment, and sightseeing activities. Other periodicals include *Atlanta Now* and *Where* magazine. The *Southern Voice* serves the gay, lesbian, bisexual, and transsexual community; and *Creative Loafing* is to Atlanta what the *Village Voice* is to New York, with concert, movie, and theater listings—an insider's guide to what is going on in the city.

*Post Office* The main post office is Atlanta Post Office, 3900 Crown Rd., Atlanta, GA 30321 (℅ **404/765-7476** or 800/275-8777 for general information).

*Restrooms* In addition to bus, rail, and air terminals, there are public toilets at Underground Atlanta and at Peachtree Center.

*Safety* More than 80% of the city's crimes are property crimes, including thefts from parked cars. Purse-snatchings and muggings are commonplace, especially after dark. After the business clients leave the downtown and midtown areas, it becomes a venue for drug dealers and hookers. But there is improvement. Since the end of the Olympics, crime in Atlanta has dropped off thanks to a program that features a battalion of Atlanta Ambassadors. These are unarmed corps of security guards—clad in pith helmets and white uniforms—that act as the eyes and ears of the Atlanta police force. Concentrated in the downtown area, and paid for by a cooperative association of local business owners, they've gone a long way to discourage crime in downtown Atlanta.

*Taxes*  In addition to the 7% state sales tax, there is a 7% hotel and motel tax. Combined, they make a significant difference in your final hotel bill.

*Transit Information*  Dial ☏ **404/848-5000.**

*Weather*  Call ☏ **770/603-3333.**

## 3 Where to Stay

B&Bs are available in Atlanta in grand style or in modest houses, and are located all over the city. Contact **Bed & Breakfast Atlanta,** 790 North Ave., Suite 202, Atlanta, GA 30306 (☏ **800/96-PEACH** or 404/875-0525; fax 404/876-6544). Rates run $90 to $110 including a continental breakfast, with some exceptional lodgings in the $110-to-$250 range. There's no booking fee, and major credit cards are accepted.

By and large, the double rooms in the recommended hotels and inns below have private bathrooms with tub/shower combinations, unless otherwise noted.

## DOWNTOWN ATLANTA
### VERY EXPENSIVE

**Hyatt Regency Atlanta** ★★   The first of Atlanta's super-hotels, the Hyatt—flanked by two 23-story towers and standing near the Atlanta Mart—launched the chain's atrium look in 1967 when it was first designed by noted architect John Portman. That was a long time ago. To keep up to date, the Hyatt has recently completed a $22-million renovation campaign. The lobby is somewhat subdued, although striking, with a sculpture extending from the 2nd level to the 12th, much greenery, and bubble-glass elevators. The most desirable rooms are the executive rooms on the 21st and 22nd floors of the main building—they are definitely posh. Expense-account junkies like the rooms in the 24-floor International Tower overlooking the atrium and opening onto panoramic views of Atlanta. Guests are also accommodated in the 22-floor Ivy Tower. The lobby coffee shop is nothing special, but the blue-domed Polaris rooftop revolving restaurant and cocktail lounge is almost reason enough to check in. At lobby level is an Italian restaurant with a 1,800-gallon saltwater aquarium, and an additional lounge.

265 Peachtree St. NE (between Baker and Harris sts.), Atlanta, GA 30303. ☏ **800/233-1234** or 404/577-1234. Fax 404/588-4812. www.hyatt.com. 1,260 units. $150–$350 double; from $280 suite. Children 18 and under stay free in parent's room. AE, DC, DISC, MC, V. Parking $20. MARTA: Peachtree Center. **Amenities:** 2 restaurants; bar; outdoor pool; racquetball courts; fitness center; health club privileges; sauna; business center; limited room service; laundry service/dry cleaning; babysitting; nonsmoking rooms; rooms for those w/limited mobility. *In room:* A/C, TV, dataport, coffeemaker (in some), hair dryer, iron/ironing board.

**The Ritz-Carlton Atlanta** ★★★   A premier state-of-the-art hotel in the heart of the business district, this is downtown Atlanta's finest, dating from 1984. It has more personal style and glamour than the Atlanta Hilton or Hyatt Regency. Less ostentatious than its Buckhead counterpart, this hotel is more intimately geared to the day-to-day bustle of business-oriented Atlanta. It's richly decorated with silks, tapestries, Persian carpeting, and 18th- and 19th-century paintings. Even

# Downtown Atlanta Accommodations & Dining

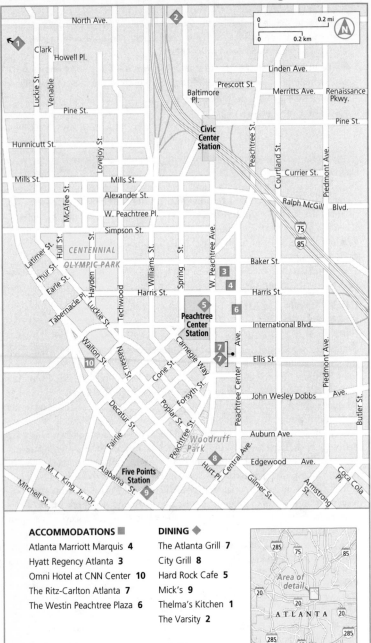

ACCOMMODATIONS ■

Atlanta Marriott Marquis **4**

Hyatt Regency Atlanta **3**

Omni Hotel at CNN Center **10**

The Ritz-Carlton Atlanta **7**

The Westin Peachtree Plaza **6**

DINING ◆

The Atlanta Grill **7**

City Grill **8**

Hard Rock Cafe **5**

Mick's **9**

Thelma's Kitchen **1**

The Varsity **2**

the elevator exudes elegance. The guest rooms are restful refuges in traditional style, with bay windows, fresh flowers, and luxurious marble bathrooms. Both the 24th and 25th floors have been set apart as "The Club," where guests enjoy a private lounge with complimentary refreshments and the services of a concierge.

Beyond the clublike, intimate lounge is an elegant dining room, the **Atlantic Grill,** where gourmet lunches and dinners, with a special fitness cuisine menu, are accompanied by piano music. The lobby lounge serves lighter fare.

181 Peachtree St. NE (at Ellis St.), Atlanta, GA 30303. ☎ **800/241-3333** or 404/659-0400. Fax 404/688-0400. www.ritzcarlton.com. 444 units. $279–$400 double; from $379 suite. AE, DC, DISC, MC, V. Valet parking $16–$25. MARTA: Peachtree Center. **Amenities:** 2 restaurants; bar; fitness center; spa; sauna; children's activities; business center; 24-hr. room service; massage; babysitting; laundry service/dry cleaning; nonsmoking rooms; rooms for those w/limited mobility. *In room:* A/C, TV, dataport, minibar, coffeemaker, hair dryer, iron/ironing board, safe.

## EXPENSIVE

**Atlanta Marriott Marquis** ★★   The futuristic design of this Marriott is evident the moment you walk into the seemingly infinite atrium, softened with greenery and sculpture. Fifty stories tall, this hotel rises dramatically toward the sky, more luxurious than the Hyatt. Reached by bullet elevators, the guest rooms are in soothing shades, each with a king-size bed or two doubles. Two of the six club levels feature upgraded rooms, although all of them have club-level privileges.

At the garden level is a bevy of restaurants, including a sidewalk cafe. The Marquis Steakhouse is casual, with steak and seafood; and the Atrium Express offers gourmet sandwiches, salads, and soups. There's also a piano bar on this floor, plus a noisy sports-theme bar.

265 Peachtree Center Ave. (between Baker and Harris sts.), Atlanta, GA 30303. ☎ **800/228-9290** or 404/ 521-0000. Fax 404/586-6299. www.marriott.com. 1,675 units. $169–$195 double; from $400 suite. Children 11 and under stay free in parent's room. AE, DC, DISC, MC, V. Parking $20. MARTA: Peachtree Center. **Amenities:** 2 restaurants; bar; lounge; 2 pools (1 indoor); health club privileges; Jacuzzi; sauna; business center; 24-hr. room service; massage; babysitting; laundry service/dry cleaning; nonsmoking rooms; rooms for those w/limited mobility. *In room:* A/C, TV, dataport, minibar, hair dryer, iron/ironing board, safe.

**Omni Hotel at CNN Center** ★   Next to the World Congress Center and the Philips Arena (since 1999 the sports home of the NBA Atlanta Hawks and the NHL Atlanta Thrashers), this 15-story modernistic megastructure houses CNN headquarters. In its way, it's the most anonymous hotel in Atlanta, designed as part of a huge commercial complex that disguises the fact it is a hotel at all. Its soaring, marble-covered, split-level lobby and tastefully luxurious guest rooms send a contemporary message. Glass elevators climb to the top floors, where some rooms have balconies overlooking the lobby. The well-furnished guest rooms have well-maintained bathrooms. A VIP floor for the ultimate in luxury and service attracts CNN newshounds.

A coffee shop and two restaurants include one with Northern Italian cuisine. The **Prime Meridian** restaurant and bar overlooks Centennial Olympic Park.

100 CNN Center (at Techwood Dr. and Marietta St.), Atlanta, GA 30335. ☎ **800/843-6664** or 404/659-0000. Fax 404/525-5050. www.omnihotels.com. 1,067 units. $149–$355 double; from $650 suite. AE, DC, DISC, MC, V. Parking $20. MARTA: Omni. **Amenities:** 2 restaurants; bar; lounge; outdoor pool; fitness center; sauna; children's program; 24-hr. room service; massage; laundry service/dry cleaning; nonsmoking rooms; rooms for those w/limited mobility. *In room:* A/C, TV, minibar, coffeemaker, hair dryer, iron/ironing board, safe (in some).

**The Westin Peachtree Plaza** ★★   Atlanta's most famous contemporary hotel is also the tallest, with 73 soaring floors. A bank of 18 elevators will carry you to the roof with its revolving restaurant, a grand spectacle for a special evening on the town. If you're not afraid of heights, you'll reach your room in a glass elevator that goes up the side of the building. Try to get a room high up, as the view becomes panoramic. Executive Club rooms are the most desirable; color-coordinated fabrics, light-wood furniture, and well-designed contemporary bathrooms add to the lavish ambience. The hotel is undergoing a $25-million guest-room refurbishment project.

A refined American cuisine is served at the **Sun Dial Restaurant,** where a 360-degree cityscape comes into view. Three ground-level bars dispense potent libations.

210 Peachtree St. NE (at International Blvd.), Atlanta, GA 30303. © **800/228-3000** or 404/659-1400. Fax 404/589-7424. www.westin.com. 1,067 units. $199–$239 double; from $350 suite. Children 17 and under stay free in parent's room. AE, DC, DISC, MC, V. Valet parking $18, self-parking $16. MARTA: Peachtree Center. **Amenities:** 2 restaurants; 2 bars; lounge; 2 pools (1 indoor and 1 outdoor); fitness center; Jacuzzi; sauna; business center; 24-hr. room service; babysitting; laundry service/dry cleaning; nonsmoking rooms; rooms for those w/limited mobility. *In room:* A/C, TV, dataport, minibar (in some), coffeemaker, hair dryer, iron/ironing board, safe.

## MIDTOWN ATLANTA
### VERY EXPENSIVE

**Four Seasons Hotel Atlanta** ★★★ *Kids*    It's as opulent and plush as its nearest rival, the Buckhead branch of the Ritz-Carlton, but to its growing legion of fans, the Four Seasons is even better, with a midtown location that's increasingly favored as a venue for hip Atlantans. It occupies the bottom 19 floors of a granite-sheathed tower that soars 53 floors above midtown Atlanta—the upper floors contain private, and very upscale, condominiums. Developed by a Spain-based investment group in the late 1980s, and now managed by the world-class Four Seasons chain, it has the most attentive and sophisticated staff, and the most impressive and dramatic lobby, of any hotel in Georgia. You'll register in a stately-looking three-story atrium that vaguely evokes the imperial days of ancient Rome. It's sheathed in thousands of slabs of russet-colored marble, studded with masses of fresh flowers, and ringed with the kind of modern art you want to take time to savor. Accommodations are as plush as you'd expect from this top-notch chain, each room with marble trim, ultra-comfortable chaise longues, beautifully kept bathrooms, and all the electronic extras you'll need to conduct business or enjoy a holiday away from home.

At the **Park 75** (see "Where to Dine," later in this chapter), some of the finest cuisine in the Southeast is dished up with verve by a staff that fully understands its culinary nuances. Nearby, in a setting that evokes a mahogany-sheathed private club in London, you'll find the most urbane and appealing hotel bar in Atlanta.

Trips can be arranged to such family favorites as the Children's Garden at the Atlanta Botanical Gardens. This is one of the most welcoming hotels for families with children in Atlanta, with a special program that includes a kiddie box of toiletries complete with a rubber Donald Duck and baby shampoo, cookies and milk upon check-in, and children's movies and video games.

75 14th St. (between Peachtree and W. Peachtree sts.), Atlanta, GA 30309. © **800/332-3443** or 404/881-9898. Fax 404/873-4692. www.fourseasons.com. 244 units. $275–$375 double; from $600 suite. Reductions granted, depending on occupancy, especially on weekends. Children under 16 stay free in parent's room. AE, DC, DISC, MC, V. Parking $24. MARTA: Arts Center. **Amenities:** Restaurant; bar; indoor pool; fitness center; spa services; Jacuzzi; sauna; business center; 24-hr. room service; massage; babysitting; laundry service/dry cleaning; nonsmoking rooms; rooms for those w/limited mobility. *In room:* A/C, TV, dataport, minibar, hair dryer, iron/ironing board, safe.

### EXPENSIVE

**The Georgian Terrace Hotel** ★★ *Kids*    An Atlanta landmark since 1911, this fabled hotel dodged the wrecking ball and was beautifully restored in 2001. It now receives guests as it did in 1939 when Clark Gable and Vivien Leigh stayed here to attend the premiere of *Gone With the Wind* at the Fox Theater across the street. Listed on the National Register of Historic Places, the hotel is graced with soaring pillars, French windows, and marble floors. The guest rooms have been modernized in grand comfort, with elegant furnishings and marble bathrooms.

Antique furnishings are used, and queen-size "Dream Beds" installed with crisp white European-style duvet covers. The luxury suites are among the best in town; otherwise, the finest rooms are on the two club floors. The staff caters to children, with such extras as video games. Options are studios (the smallest) or else two- or three-bedroom suites, the latter with kitchens and washer-dryers. Staying in these larger units is like having your own private apartment in Atlanta.

659 Peachtree St. (north of Ponce de Leon Ave.), Atlanta, GA 30308. ✆ 800/651-2316 or 404/897-1991. Fax 404/724-9116. www.thegeorgianterrace.com. 326 units. $159 double studio; $189 1-bedroom suite; $299 2-bedroom suite; $409 3-bedroom suite. AE, DC, DISC, MC, V. Valet parking $25. MARTA: North Ave. **Amenities:** Restaurant; bar; outdoor rooftop pool; fitness center; children's amenities; limo service; airport shuttle; business center; limited room service; laundry service/dry cleaning; nonsmoking rooms; rooms for those w/limited mobility. *In room:* A/C, TV, dataport, kitchen, hair dryer, safe, laundry facilities.

## MODERATE

**Ansley Inn** ★ *Finds*    Unique in Atlanta, this former stately home in a prestigious neighborhood (Ansley Park) mimics many of the trappings of an exclusive, small-scale European inn. It occupies a yellow-brick Tudor mansion built in 1907. In 1995, nine additional rooms were added to the back of the house in a less distinguished style. Those in the front of the house retain a semi-antique flair. All but two of the rooms have Jacuzzis. Breakfast is served in a formal dining room outfitted with English Chippendale, carpets, and Italian crystal chandeliers. Classical music or quiet jazz reverberates softly through the carefully furnished public rooms throughout most of the day.

253 15th St. NE (at Lafayette), Atlanta, GA 30309. ✆ 800/446-5416 or 404/872-9000. Fax 404/892-2318. www.ansleyinn.com. 22 units. $120–$250 double. Rates include full breakfast. AE, DC, DISC, MC, V. Free parking. MARTA: Arts Center. **Amenities:** Breakfast room; lounge; nearby health club privileges. *In room:* A/C, TV, dataport, coffeemaker, hair dryer, iron/ironing board.

**Shellmont Inn** ★    Named after the carved seashell adorning the front of this elaborate Victorian from 1891, the Shellmont is a stylish and historically authentic period home for overnight guests, with wicker-laden verandas. Elaborate restoration has filled it with discreetly concealed modern luxuries as well as a historically appropriate collection of Oriental carpets; stained, leaded, and beveled glass; hand-painted stenciling; wall coverings and draperies; furnishings; fresh flowers; and 1890s accessories. Only breakfast is served, featuring seasonal specialties. From the front, you'll be fully aware of your urban location. From the back garden, however, where there are verandas and a fishpond, you'll swear you're in a small town in the Georgia countryside. The largest accommodation is the suite, originally conceived as the servants' quarters.

821 Piedmont Ave. NE (at 6th St.), Atlanta, GA 30308. ✆ 404/872-9290. Fax 404/872-5379. www.shellmont. com. 5 units. $115–$175 double; $150–$250 suite. Rates include full breakfast. AE, DC, DISC, MC, V. Free parking. MARTA: North Ave. or Midtown. **Amenities:** Breakfast room; lounge; laundry service/dry cleaning; nonsmoking rooms. *In room:* A/C, TV, dataport, hair dryer, ceiling fans.

## BUCKHEAD
### VERY EXPENSIVE

**Grand Hyatt Atlanta** ★★    This is one of the most distinctive hotels in Atlanta, an award-winning combination of bold postmodern and Chippendale,

# Midtown Atlanta Accommodations & Dining

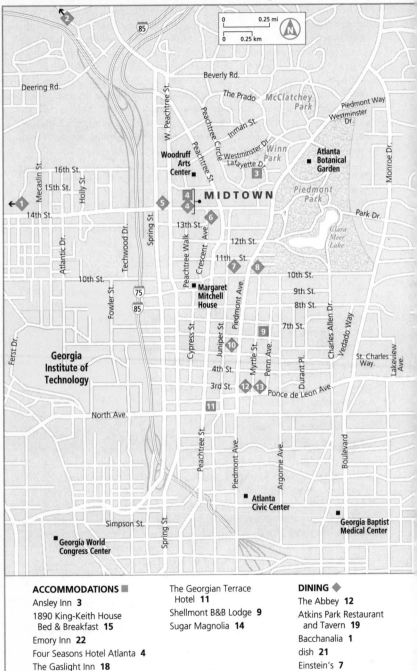

**ACCOMMODATIONS** ■

Ansley Inn **3**

1890 King-Keith House
Bed & Breakfast **15**

Emory Inn **22**

Four Seasons Hotel Atlanta **4**

The Gaslight Inn **18**

The Georgian Terrace
Hotel **11**

Shellmont B&B Lodge **9**

Sugar Magnolia **14**

**DINING** ◆

The Abbey **12**

Atkins Park Restaurant
and Tavern **19**

Bacchanalia **1**

dish **21**

Einstein's **7**

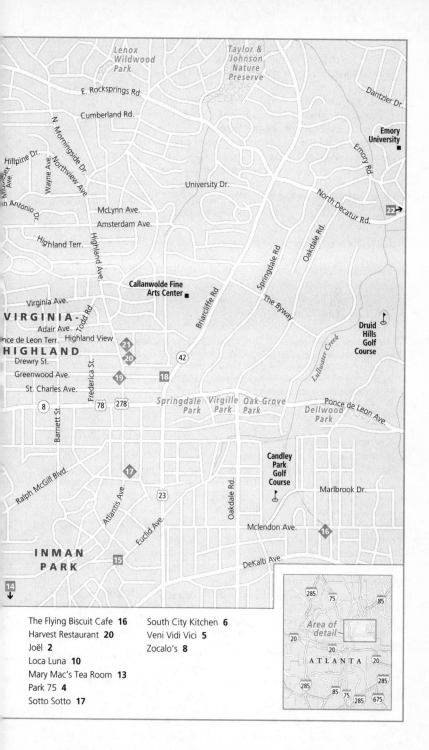

The Flying Biscuit Cafe **16**
Harvest Restaurant **20**
Joël **2**
Loca Luna **10**
Mary Mac's Tea Room **13**
Park 75 **4**
Sotto Sotto **17**

South City Kitchen **6**
Veni Vidi Vici **5**
Zocalo's **8**

Area of detail

ATLANTA

with attention paid to aesthetic detailing. Grand Hyatt, which recently underwent a $5.6-million renovation, is a striking 24-story monolith with a massive motor entrance that some visitors compare to a set design for *The Wizard of Oz.* Register in the striking rotunda faced with marble and accented with massive chandeliers. The accommodations are in earth-color schemes.

The **Cassis** restaurant is international in scope, specializing in a range of food that covers all shores of the Mediterranean. English-style afternoon teas are served in the lobby, and a jazz trio sometimes entertains in the bar.

3300 Peachtree Rd., Atlanta, GA 30305. (C) **800/233-1234** or 404/365-8100. Fax 404/233-5686. www.grand atlantahyatt.com. 437 units. $215–$250 double; from $485 suite. AE, DC, DISC, MC, V. Parking $19. MARTA: Buckhead. **Amenities:** Restaurant; bar; outdoor pool; health club; sauna; business center; 24-hr. room service; massage; babysitting; laundry service/dry cleaning. *In room:* A/C, TV, dataport, minibar, coffeemaker, hair dryer, iron/ironing board.

**Ritz-Carlton Buckhead** ★★★   The Ritz-Carlton is the most sumptuous and elegant hotel in Atlanta. A 22-story tower soaring above Buckhead, it's awash in oiled paneling, tapestries, marble and hardwood, theatrical bouquets of spotlighted flowers, antiques, and a museum's worth of valuable paintings. It's been likened to Claridge's in London. The staff is artful, polite, soft-spoken, and efficient.

The **Dining Room** is one of the most sought-after restaurants in Atlanta (see "Where to Dine," below). There's also a deli with an attendant espresso bar, and both a cafe and a bar-lounge with a frequently blazing fireplace.

3434 Peachtree Rd. NE, Atlanta, GA 30326. (C) **800/241-3333** or 404/237-2700. Fax 404/239-0078. www.ritzcarlton.com. 553 units. $219–$290 double; from $459 suite. AE, DC, DISC, MC, V. Parking $25, self-parking $15. MARTA: Buckhead. **Amenities:** Restaurant; bar; indoor pool; fitness center; Jacuzzi; sauna; beauty treatments; 24-hr. room service; massage; laundry service/dry cleaning; nonsmoking rooms. *In room:* A/C, TV, dataport, minibar, hair dryer, safe.

## EXPENSIVE

**Westin Buckhead Hotel** ★★   Here's a hotel that would ordinarily stand head and shoulders above the others. But in Buckhead, the Westin is hard-pressed to keep up with the Joneses—in this case, the Ritz-Carlton. Still, it's first-class all the way and has a European flavor to it. The guest rooms and suites are the largest in Buckhead, with Biedermeier-style furnishings. The guest rooms have three dual-line phones with call waiting and voice mail. The marble bathrooms feature oversize tubs and makeup and shaving mirrors. The suites are especially luxurious, with VCRs and glass-block bathing areas; the presidential suite houses a fireplace and a terrace with a Jacuzzi.

The **Palm** restaurant (see "Where to Dine," below) is patterned after the famous Palm Restaurant launched in New York in 1926. The menu is that of an all-American steakhouse.

3391 Peachtree Rd. NE (between Lenox and Piedmont roads), Atlanta, GA 30326. (C) **888/737-9477** or 404/ 365-0065. Fax 404/365-8787. www.westin.com. 365 units. $169–$389 double; $470–$1,200 suite. Children 17 and under stay free in parent's room. AE, DC, DISC, MC, V. Valet parking $20. MARTA: Lenox. **Amenities:** Restaurant; bar; indoor pool; fitness center; sauna; salon; 24-hr. room service; laundry service/dry cleaning. *In room:* A/C, TV, minibar, hair dryer.

## INEXPENSIVE

**Hampton Inn**   This hotel is no better than most standard Hampton Inns—it's strictly chain format. But what makes it special are its price and location in upscale Buckhead. Staying in this neighborhood and living well for a reasonable tab brightens the glow of this place. Guest rooms are medium in size and come with all the usual Hampton Inn equipment such as dataports, free newspapers, free local calls, and a private safe. Some of the rooms are suitable for persons with disabilities. The hotel has a pool and can arrange temporary visits to a nearby health club. An adjacent restaurant is open daily from 11am to 11pm.

3398 Piedmont Rd. NE, Atlanta, GA 30305. ℂ **800/426-7866** or 404/233-5656. Fax 404/237-4688. www. hamptoninn.com. 154 units. $109–$119 double. Children under 18 free in parent's room. Rates include full breakfast. AE, DC, DISC, MC, V. MARTA: Lindbergh. **Amenities:** Breakfast room; outdoor pool; laundry/dry cleaning. *In room:* A/C, TV, dataport, hair dryer.

## VIRGINIA-HIGHLAND

**The Gaslight Inn** ★★ *Finds* The most appealing B&B in Virginia-Highland is this 1913 Craftsman-style house that's set above a steeply sloping front garden, behind a commodious front porch. In the 1990s, it was enlarged and renovated, and a well-proportioned annex was added, separated from the main house by a garden illuminated by flickering gas-fired lanterns. Accommodations, especially the suites, are outfitted like private apartments. Four of the six contain working kitchens; the remaining two have access to a kitchen right outside their doors. Breakfast is a high point of the day here: An informal and affable affair, it's served in an early-20th-century dining room accented with a Craftsman-style fireplace and fine paintings. Morning coffee and afternoon wine are offered by the staff, as well as information about attractions and diversions.

1001 St. Charles Ave., Atlanta, GA 30306. ℂ **404/875-1001.** Fax 404/876-1001. www.gaslightinn.com. 8 units. $115–$125 double; $149–$215 suite. Rates include continental breakfast. AE, DC, DISC, MC, V. Free parking. Bus: 2 (Ponce) or 16 (Noble). **Amenities:** Breakfast room; lounge. *In room:* A/C, TV, dataport, hair dryer.

## INMAN PARK

**1890 King-Keith House Bed & Breakfast** ★★ *Finds* One of Atlanta's most photographed houses—on the National Register of Historic Places—might become your temporary home. This Queen Anne–style home dates from 1890 when it was constructed by a hardware magnate, George King. The guest rooms are beautifully furnished, generally with antiques, and the 12-foot ceilings and carved fireplaces evoke oak-shaded Inman Park of another time. Units are spacious, each with a private bathroom, although two are in the hallway but not shared with other guests. The best accommodations here are the downstairs suite with a Jacuzzi, private sitting room, and stained-glass and Empire furnishings; and the Cottage out back with its vaulted ceilings. It, too, has a Jacuzzi for two, and is ideal for a honeymoon or a getaway. Guests also enjoy the inn's private gardens.

889 Edgewood Ave. NE, Atlanta, GA 30307. ℂ **800/728-3879** or 404/688-7330. Fax 404/584-8408. www. kingkeith.com. 6 units, including separate cottage. $90–$180 double. Rates include breakfast. AE, DISC, MC, V. Free parking. MARTA: Inman Park. **Amenities:** Breakfast room. *In room:* A/C, TV, dataport, hair dryer.

**Sugar Magnolia** ★ *Finds* Located in a historic district of Atlanta, this 1892 Victorian house was originally constructed by a Southern colonel but was turned into a B&B of charm and beauty by its owners, Jim Emshoff and Debi Starnes. They have created an oasis that lives up to its name, with a three-story turret, six fireplaces, oval beveled windows, hand-painted plasterwork, and a grand staircase fit for an entrance by Scarlett O'Hara. A nonsmoking house, the inn rents individually styled and commodious guest rooms, including one called the Royal Suite, with a king-size brass bed in a curtained alcove, and a rooftop deck with a waterfall garden. The cottage suite has a fully equipped galley kitchen and a vaulted ceiling with skylight, along with a Jacuzzi and open-loft bedroom with a double bed. The delightful Aviary is furnished with antiques and a fireplace, but best of all, this seven-sided room has a painted ceiling of clouds and birds.

# Buckhead Accommodations & Dining

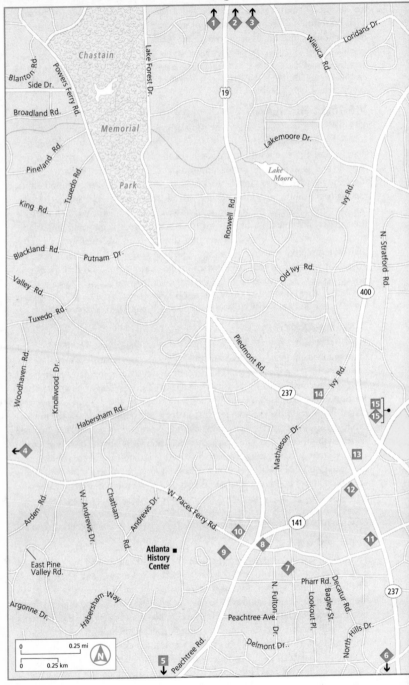

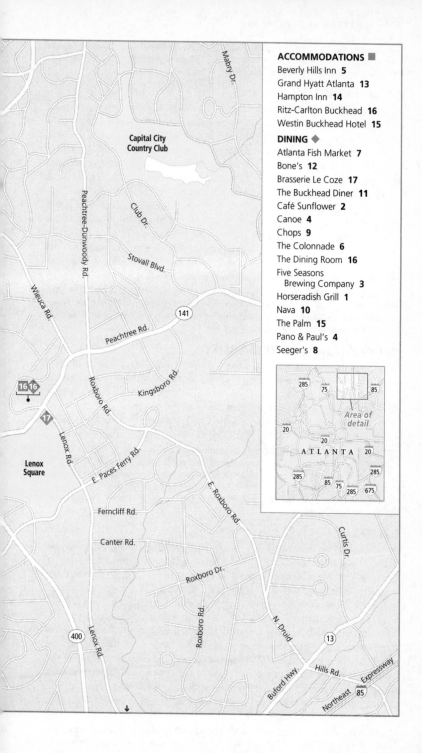

**ACCOMMODATIONS** ■

Beverly Hills Inn **5**
Grand Hyatt Atlanta **13**
Hampton Inn **14**
Ritz-Carlton Buckhead **16**
Westin Buckhead Hotel **15**

**DINING** ◆

Atlanta Fish Market **7**
Bone's **12**
Brasserie Le Coze **17**
The Buckhead Diner **11**
Café Sunflower **2**
Canoe **4**
Chops **9**
The Colonnade **6**
The Dining Room **16**
Five Seasons
   Brewing Company **3**
Horseradish Grill **1**
Nava **10**
The Palm **15**
Pano & Paul's **4**
Seeger's **8**

804 Edgewood Ave. NE, Atlanta, GA 30307. ✆ **404/222-0226.** Fax 404/681-1067. www.sugarmagnolia
bb.com. 4 units. $95–$115 double; $120–$150 suite. Rates include continental breakfast. MARTA: Inman
Park. **Amenities:** Breakfast room; lounge. *In room:* A/C, TV, hair dryer.

## STONE MOUNTAIN

**Marriott Stone Mountain Park Inn** ⭐ *Kids*    This low-rise, neocolonial hotel
was originally built in 1965 for visitors interested in staying as close as possible to
the massive bas-reliefs of Stone Mountain's northern face. Set inside the park
boundaries, about 16 miles east of the city, it offers guest rooms outfitted in reproductions of 18th-century country furniture. Don't expect a mountain view: Many
guest rooms overlook the forest or the hotel's inner courtyard, and you must stand
on the plantation-style front porch to catch a glimpse of the laser-light show illu-
minating the mountain. Views are even better from the hotel's lawns, and better
still across the highway. The in-house restaurant, the **Mountain View,** features a
revolving series of all-you-can-eat buffets. This is an especially good choice for
families, who can enjoy the many recreational opportunities of the park. In addition to enjoying life around a big pool, families can go on hiking, fishing, and
boating trips, and there are plenty of places nearby for a family picnic.

1058 Robert E. Lee Dr., Stone Mountain Park, Stone Mountain, GA 30083. ✆ 770/469-3311. Fax 770/876-5009.
www.marriott.com. 92 units. $125–$145 double. AE, DC, DISC, MC, V. $7 fee into park; otherwise, free parking.
**Amenities:** Restaurant; bar; lounge; outdoor pool; 18-hole golf course; laundry service/dry cleaning. *In room:* A/C,
TV, dataport, fridge, coffeemaker, hair dryer, iron/ironing board.

## DRUID HILLS/EMORY UNIVERSITY

**Emory Inn** ⭐ *Finds*    Owned by Emory University, this hotel lies east of midtown and Buckhead, a 10-minute drive from the center of activity. It's also close
to the famous Centers for Disease Control and Prevention. You'll think you're in
the country: The inn lies in a secluded corner of the university grounds tucked
away among trees. Rooms are handsomely and comfortably furnished. Guests
can explore walking trails at the nearby Hahn Woods Nature Preserve.

1641 Clifton Rd. NE (between Briarcliff and N. Decatur roads), Atlanta, GA 30329. ✆ 800/933-6679 or
404/712-6700. Fax 404/712-6701. www.emoryconferencecenter.com. 107 units. $110 double. AE, DC, DISC,
MC, V. Free parking. Bus no. 6. **Amenities:** Restaurant; outdoor pool; free use of health club on campus (with
heated indoor pool); 12 tennis courts; indoor track; Jacuzzi; complimentary shuttle to Emory University campus; airport shuttle on request; limited room service; coin-operated laundry. *In room:* A/C, TV, coffeemaker,
hair dryer, iron/ironing board.

## PALMETTO

**Serenbe Bed & Breakfast** ⭐⭐ *Finds*    Imagine experiencing rural Georgia
only 32 miles south of Atlanta! This inn lies on a 350-acre farmstead, where you
can hand-feed the cows and chickens, fish from a lake, or top off a perfect day
with a moonlit canoe ride. This is the best example in the Greater Atlanta area
of what is a vanishing trait these days: real Southern hospitality. For families
with children, it is a total delight, complete with marshmallow roasts at a bonfire. The house itself is nearly a century old. Each handsomely furnished guest
room comes with a private bathroom, one with a Jacuzzi tub. Rag rugs, knotty
pine floors, beds piled high with decorative pillows, and even lace curtains at the
windows mark a return to Grandma's house. You can also rent a two-bedroom
cottage with its own kitchen and living room. Steven and Marie Nygren are your
gracious hosts. Guests enjoy a full country breakfast complete with such delights
as fried green tomatoes, cheese grits, and homemade biscuits.

10950 Hutcheson Ferry Rd., Palmetto, GA 30268. ✆ 770/463-2610. Fax 770/463-4472. www.serenbe.com.
7 units, 1 cottage. $140 double; $175 cottage. Rates include farm breakfast. No credit cards. Free parking.

Call for directions. **Amenities:** Outdoor pool with water slide; Jacuzzi; bike rental; massage; babysitting; communal kitchen; barbecue grill; free washers/dryers; dataport available. *In room:* A/C, coffeemaker, hair dryer.

## 4 Where to Dine

**Underground Atlanta,** bounded by Peachtree, Wall, Alabama, Pryor, and Central streets and by Martin Luther King, Jr., Drive (✆ **404/523-2311;** see "Attractions," later in this chapter), is home to a dozen "food courts" and nightclubs centered around Kenny's Alley; most are open nightly until around midnight.

# DOWNTOWN
## EXPENSIVE

**The Atlanta Grill** ✰✰ STEAK  Stylish, well organized, and urbane, this downtown Atlanta steakhouse evokes some of the Southern charm of New Orleans, thanks to an elaborate iron balcony that juts over the sidewalk of one of the busiest sections of Peachtree Street. Inside, flickering gas lanterns and photos of Old Atlanta's political and debutante parties usually evoke dialogues from the most taciturn of local residents. Although meals here are impeccable, this is not a fine-dining enclave. Instead, the hotel that contains it refers to it as a steakhouse with extremely refined service rituals, leaving the culinary finesse to the restaurant within the Ritz-Carlton in Buckhead instead. Also, it's the kind of place where the rich-grained bar top doubles as a dining table for the many single, usually business-related travelers who come here. Menu items include many cuts of juicy steak, prime beef, lobster macaroni with cheese, and buttermilk-marinated fried green tomatoes. For lunch you might begin with a mint julep soup made with chilled Georgia peaches or else a seared crab cake. Sandwiches, such as "pulled pork," are available. At night, the menu expands with such Southern-influenced dishes as molasses-grilled pork tenderloin, or tomato stone-ground grits cake with baby summer squash. Most guests finish with a piece of pecan pie and caramel ice cream covered with a vanilla bourbon syrup.

In the Ritz-Carlton, 181 Peachtree St., Atlanta. ✆ 404/221-6550. Reservations recommended. Main courses $26–$42. AE, DC, MC, V. Daily 11:30am–2:30am; only light fare 2:30–5pm and 11pm–1am. MARTA: Peachtree Center.

**City Grill** ✰✰ CONTEMPORARY AMERICAN  One of Atlanta's most elegant restaurants is still going strong; it remains a venue for movers and shakers at lunch and for Atlanta's social elite at dinner. The setting for this opulent showcase for creative cookery is the 1912 Hurt Building, long known as the Deep South's most spectacular office building, with its rotunda lined in marble with a gold-leaf dome. You'll be impressed by the boneless quail with creamy gravy, the crab cakes with pasta, or the pancake with fennel. We recommend the barbecued shrimp and a wonderful sautéed trout. The duck is succulent and moist, having been slowly smoked over wood chips. The selection of French and California wines is about as good as Atlanta gets.

50 Hurt Plaza (at Edgewood Ave.). ✆ 404/524-2489. Reservations recommended. Main courses $14–$32. AE, DC, DISC, MC, V. Mon–Fri 11:30am–2pm and 5–10pm; Sat 5–10pm. MARTA: Peachtree Center.

## MODERATE

**Hard Rock Cafe** AMERICAN  This enduring favorite can still pack 'em in on a good night. The music is loud and raucous, the hamburgers aren't bad, and the banana splits evoke those halcyon days of James Dean and Marilyn Monroe.

215 Peachtree St. NE (at International Blvd.). ✆ 404/688-7625. Reservations not accepted. Main courses $9–$19. AE, DC, MC, V. Sun–Thurs 11am–midnight; Fri–Sat 11am–1am. MARTA: Peachtree Center.

## INEXPENSIVE

**Mick's** AMERICAN   The tile floors, leather booths, and counter stools here are straight out of a 1950s movie set or an Edward Hopper painting. In a renovated building with high tin ceilings, this is one of the most popular members of an Atlanta chain. The menu still gives you those nostalgic soggy pastas with their watery sauces—better stick to chicken potpie or meatloaf, the famous blue-plate specials of those long-gone years. Or, better yet, go for the sandwiches, salads, and such down-home dishes as hickory-smoked pork chops that can be quite a taste treat. Remember banana splits? They're still served here, along with cherry Cokes.

557 Peachtree St. *C* 404/875-6425. Main courses $8–$15; children's menu $3. AE, DC, MC, V. Sun–Thurs 11am–10pm; Fri–Sat 11am–11pm. MARTA: North Ave.

**Thelma's Kitchen** ⭐ SOUL FOOD/SOUTHERN   On the northern edge of downtown Atlanta, amid Marietta Street's "soot and gravel," this is the legendary soul-food kitchen of Atlanta founded by Thelma Grundy. If you attended grade school in Appalachia in the 1940s and ate in the cafeteria, you'll know what to expect in ambience, complete with plastic tablecloths. Smothered collards, rousing rutabagas, great catfish, greasy fried chicken, rice and gravy, creamy limas, sweet potato pie, country-fried steak, barbecued ribs, corn bread, pineapple upside-down cake—you get the culinary picture. Local attorneys nearby flock here for lunch, as do what one habitué called "slide-rule types from Tech and grimy transmission surgeons." He added, "Just tell your readers everything is finger-lickin' good." Rib-eye steak is the most expensive item on the menu, but everything is cheap, including the specials of the day.

768 Marietta St. NW (just off Means St.). *C* 404/688-5855. Reservations not needed—"just show up." Meals average $15 and under. No credit cards. Mon–Fri 7:30am–4:30pm; Sat 7am–5pm. Bus: Howell Mill from Downtown.

**The Varsity** *Kids* AMERICAN   This local legend offers enough "Grease" for the Broadway show and 80 roadside versions. The world's largest drive-in restaurant, opened in 1928 by Frank Gordy, is run nowadays by his daughter, Nancy Simms, and her children. Some 16,000 people a day dine at this Atlanta institution—on hot dogs, hamburgers, french fries, and 300 gallons of chili. Service is fast both carside and inside, with seats and stand-up eating counters; and prices are definitely low. Yes, the orange freezes are just like the ones you had after the senior prom. Ordering can be an adventure. For example, you may be greeted with "Whadda ya have? Whadda ya have?" Hot dogs are called "dawgs," and hamburgers are "steaks." If you order them plain, just add "naked" to the front of the name—"nekkid dawg" or "nekkid steak," and so on. *Insider's tip:* If you want a cheeseburger, be sure to ask for pimento cheese. True, it's a mess, but you've never had anything like it.

61 North Ave. (at Spring St.). *C* 404/881-1706. Reservations not accepted. Main courses $4–$6.50. No credit cards. Sun–Thurs 10am–11:30pm; Fri–Sat 10am–12:30am. MARTA: North Ave.

## MIDTOWN
### EXPENSIVE

**The Abbey** ⭐ CONTINENTAL   The most lavish and charming ecclesiastical setting in Atlanta doesn't function as a church, but as an always-popular restaurant. It was originally built in 1915 as a Methodist-Episcopal sanctuary by a well-funded Atlanta congregation that gradually disbanded and moved to the suburbs. In 1968, the building was deconsecrated and transformed into a theme restaurant that's devoted to earthly pleasures—including an unapologetic emphasis on drinking and fine dining. The waitstaff wears monks' robes in a soaring, high-church setting of English Gothic design, complete with elaborate stained-glass depictions of the saints in all their humility and majesty. Be warned in advance that every few months or so, a religious fundamentalist manages to become deeply offended by the tongue-in-cheek piety of this place, and storms out in a huff. Most diners, however, interpret the adaptation as charming, a bit bizarre, and a catalyst for some interesting dialogue. Of special interest is the former vestry, once used for the storage of uniforms and communion vessels, which now functions as the Abbot's Cup Bar and Lounge. Because of its location near many of downtown Atlanta's biggest hotels, the place does a roaring business on the corporate convention circuit. A live pianist performs every evening, near a stained-glass depiction of Christ in Majesty, from 7 to 10pm. The cooking is good without being great. Especially satisfying first courses include a foie gras and lobster terrine in a champagne vinaigrette, or mussels delectably steamed in a spicy Thai curry broth. Proceed from there to the main dishes, especially pan-seared red snapper with a potato mousseline and white truffle oil, or the grilled veal strip in a white balsamic vinegar and rosemary sauce. The chargrilled New York strip steak is especially good, served in a Gorgonzola and port-wine sauce with caramelized onions.

163 Ponce de Leon. ✆ 404/876-8532. Reservations recommended. Main courses $18–$36. AE, DC, DISC, MC, V. Daily 6–10pm. MARTA: North Abbey.

**Bacchanalia** ✰✰ CONTEMPORARY AMERICAN    Posh, upscale, and artfully contrived to appeal to the entertainment needs of Atlanta's thousands of upscale consumers, this establishment combines a stylish and sought-after restaurant with a series of boutique-style food shops. The setting is in what was built in the 1920s as a meatpacking plant, in an unlikely-looking drab stretch of commercial real estate at the edge of midtown. Inside is a dining room that's considerably improved from its old days, but still sheathed in the pale yellow tiles of its original construction.

The team of Anne S. Quatrano and Clifford R. Harrison has brought fine dining all the way from the California Culinary Academy. Portions are small in size but big on flavor. Some recipes have been criticized as "pretentiously experimental," but try the Kumamoto oysters on the half shell from Washington State, or the sautéed veal sweetbreads with braised baby artichokes. Full-flavored main courses, inspired by what looks good at the market and by the whims of the chef, include sautéed turbot with baby red kale, pan-seared breast of duck with caramelized apples and turnips, and braised short ribs of Kobe beef with a potato purée. Save room for dessert, especially the blood orange and rosemary soup with a sheep's milk yogurt sorbet, or the ginger soufflé given added zest by a lemon sauce.

1198 Howell Mill Rd. ✆ 404/365-0410. Reservations recommended. Set-price 3-course lunch $48; set-price 4-course dinner $65. AE, DC, MC, V. Wed–Sat 11:30am–1:30pm; Mon–Sat 6–10pm. MARTA: 10th St.

**Park 75** ✰✰✰ NEW AMERICAN    It's chic, it's sexy, and the food that's dished up by the international staff is among the very best in the Southeast. Come here for an insight into the New American cuisine that the Four Seasons chain is promoting with verve, and for a meal you're likely to remember long after it's finished. The setting evokes a dignified-looking pavilion where subtle depictions of lattices and garden ornaments don't interfere with the visual appeal of absolutely superb cuisine. Fish and meats are combined into artful and unexpected combinations that, while sophisticated, never dip into the purely experimental. Menus and wines change frequently and seasonally. Depending on when you arrive, offerings might include a carpaccio of Kobe beef with juniper-flavored foie gras and braised arugula, a succulent version of loin of lamb with cèpe mushrooms and golden tomatoes, and roasted free-range chicken baked with Oregon truffles. Undecided about what to order? Consider one of the set-price menus, which come in both vegetarian and meat-based versions. This restaurant is at its best and most confident at dinner, when your dining experience should probably begin or end within the plush confines of the opulent-looking hotel bar.

In the Four Seasons Hotel Atlanta, 75 14th St. (between Peachtree and W. Peachtree sts.). ℂ **404/881-9898.** Reservations recommended. Main courses $14–$22 lunch; $28–$45 dinner; 4-course set-price dinner $65–$85. AE, DC, DISC, MC, V. Mon–Sat 11am–2pm and 5:30–10:30pm; Sun brunch 11am–2pm. MARTA: Arts Center.

## MODERATE

**Veni Vidi Vici** ⭐⭐ ITALIAN   Hailed by everyone from *Wine Spectator* to *Gourmet* magazine, this is a creative citadel of a finely honed Italian cuisine. You'll want to adopt the executive chef, Jamie Adams, and take him home with you to your own kitchen. Adams has an extraordinary palate, and he knows how to bring authentic Italian flavors to American plates. One of his secrets is using absolutely market-fresh ingredients.

The sophisticated decor of cherrywood and stenciled oak flooring is centered around an exhibition rotisserie kitchen. Among the selection of appetizers, our favorite is the crispy Maine calamari with lemon and capers in a tangy tomato aioli. Adams also serves a baked stuffed Vidalia onion with Scamorza cheese. The handmade pasta dishes are truly succulent: The Italian-style linguine, served with a traditional white clam sauce, is the best we've ever had in Atlanta. The secret? Plump littleneck clams. We gravitate to the rotisserie-meat main dishes, including the Maialino suckling pig with braised Savoy cabbage and scallion-laced mashed potatoes; or the Anatra half-duck served with beans and sautéed spinach.

41 14th St. (between E. Peachtree and Spring sts.). ℂ **404/875-8424.** Reservations recommended. Main courses $11–$15 lunch; $17–$27 dinner. AE, DC, DISC, MC, V. Mon–Fri 11:30am–4pm; Mon–Thurs 4–11pm; Fri 4pm–midnight; Sat 5pm–midnight; Sun 5–10pm. MARTA: Arts Center.

## INEXPENSIVE

**Einstein's** AMERICAN   The setting of this place is a clapboard-sided bungalow (ca. 1904) on a quiet street of midtown, close to some of the neighborhood's tallest towers. Partly because the owner is the godson of the late physicist and partly because scientists appreciate their nuances, you're likely to see several of Einstein's equations decorating blackboards near the bar, sometimes misstated in ways that, during our visit, provoked lots of arguments among this restaurant's clients. You can dine inside, in a woodsy-looking bar, or outside, on an open-air front terrace, elbow-to-elbow with many other residents of this rather liberal neighborhood. The food is well prepared and tasty without being spectacular. Try the grilled pork chop with a pepper and cream sauce, or freshly prepared filet of salmon with a savory barbecue pepper sauce. A signature dish is Einstein's shrimp with a mustard sauce enhanced by mango and orange.

1077 Juniper St. ℂ **404/876-7925.** Reservations recommended. Sandwiches and burgers $6.95–$7.95; main courses $15–$25. AE, DC, DISC, MC, V. Mon–Thurs 11am–11pm; Fri–Sat 11am–midnight; Sat 10am–midnight; Sun 10am–11pm. MARTA: Midtown.

**Loca Luna** ⭐ *Finds* CENTRAL/SOUTH AMERICAN   Nothing about its facade would make you want to enter this tapas restaurant, lying unattractively in a midtown parking lot. But once you get past the door, you'll find a bustling, bright place inside, with walls painted with parrot scenes under a "starry" purple ceiling. Tables are squeezed together, and couples dance to a live salsa band on many evenings. Something's always happening here, perhaps a bachelorette party where a male stripper is hired. The place is so festive you almost forget about the food, but you shouldn't. Against a backdrop of live flamenco guitarists or jazz trios, diners feast on an array of excellent tapas such as meaty ribs or savory chunks of lamb sizzling from the grill. Vegetarians will delight in the grilled portobello mushrooms with garlicky goat cheese. Chicken is marinated and cooked on a skewer with pineapple. We're especially fond of the *patatas bravas,* or spicy hot potatoes.

836 Juniper St., Suite B. ℂ **404/875-4494.** Reservations recommended. Main courses $5–$19. AE, MC, V. Tues–Sat 11:30am–2:30pm; Tues–Thurs 5–11pm; Fri–Sat 5pm–12:30am. MARTA: Midtown.

**Mary Mac's Tea Room** ★ *Kids* SOUTHERN   This landmark follows the tradition of "Southern hospitality with damn Yankee efficiency," a slogan launched in 1945. In a midtown storefront, some 2,000 hungry diners, including lots of families and local politicos, are served daily. Since Jimmy Carter used to drop in for lunch, it's always been a tradition that governors visit for meals. The food is fine if you like the slightly overcooked down-home Southern style. The fried chicken and country ham are really good here, as are the fresh but long-cooked vegetables and the straight-from-the-oven breads. Your best bet might be a sautéed rainbow trout from the North Georgia mountains. For dessert, who would dare order anything but the fresh peach cobbler? Those are Georgia peaches, of course.

224 Ponce de Leon Ave. NE (at Myrtle St.). ℂ **404/876-1800.** www.marymacs.com. Reservations required only for groups of 10 or more. Dinner $8.75–$17. AE, MC, V. Daily 11am–9pm. MARTA: North Ave.

**South City Kitchen** NEW SOUTHERN   Although many critics have found its new-style Southern cookery inconsistent, most Atlantans salute this choice. It's in a renovated two-story building with dining both up and down the stairs. Fireplaces on both floors burn on nippy nights to make the place cozy and inviting. If the weather's fair, patio dining is possible. Try the buttermilk-fried chicken or the sautéed scallops and shrimp over creamy, stone-ground grits. The secret of South City's pork chops is that they're apple-smoked, making them a real winner. Also good are the shredded barbecued pork on jalapeño bread or corn bread with creamy lump crab. The grilled swordfish on a bed of homemade grits with Monterey Jack cheese left us cold, but a taste of pork porterhouse with grilled apples, parsnips, and pepper jelly warmed our souls again.

1144 Crescent Ave. NE (between 13th and 14th sts.). ℂ **404/873-7358.** Reservations recommended. Main courses $14–$22; Sun brunch $8–$15. AE, DC, MC, V. Mon–Sat 11am–3:30pm; Mon–Thurs 5–11pm; Fri–Sat 5pm–midnight; Sun 11am–3:30pm (brunch) and 5–10pm. MARTA: Arts Center or Midtown.

**Zocalo's** MEXICAN   This is one of the most charming and authentic Mexican restaurants in Atlanta, with a growing reputation as a meeting place for the young and the restless of this very hip midtown neighborhood. The venue evokes an open-aired *cantina* on the Gulf of Mexico, in a dining room that's little more than a folklorically decorated veranda protected from winter cold by fold-down plastic flaps. No one will mind if you come only for a fiesta-colored cocktail instead of a full-fledged meal. The bar stocks at least 120 kinds of tequila, priced from $6 to $75 a glass, and their margaritas are, in the words of a local fan, *magnífico.* Menu items do not include any of the Tex-Mex hybrids (burritos, chips with salsa) that you might find in most Mexican-American restaurants. Instead, you'll be treated to authentic, and often creative, Mexican dishes that include *crema de chile poblano* (a creamy soup of stuffed chiles); *molcajete carmelita,* served on a grinding stone and composed of steak, braised cactus leaves, Serrano peppers, and asadero cheese; and *chile en nogada* (chile peppers stuffed with minced veal, pork, and beef).

187 10th St. at corner of Piedmont. ✆ **404/249-7576.** Reservations not accepted. Main courses $15–$25. AE, DC, DISC, MC, V. Sun 10:30am–10pm; Mon–Thurs 11:30am–11pm; Fri–Sat 11:30am–midnight. MARTA: Midtown.

## BUCKHEAD
### VERY EXPENSIVE

**Bone's** ★★ STEAK/SEAFOOD   Yes, that's Ted Turner at the next table, and where else would former president George Bush eat when he's in Atlanta? In an atmosphere one food critic called "boardroom frat house," this is just the type of place to get that juicy rib-eye steak weighing in at 16 ounces. Fresh Maine lobster is flown in daily, and the corn-fed beef is butchered and cut into steaks on the premises. Grits fritters are favored by locals, who invariably end their meal with Georgia pecan pie and vanilla-bean ice cream. A cigar humidor can be brought to your table at your request after dinner, but one female CEO from New York found the service by the waiters "sexist."

3130 Piedmont Rd. NE (half a block below Peachtree Rd.). ✆ **404/237-2663.** Reservations required. Main courses $25–$45 dinner, $12–$35 lunch. AE, DC, DISC, MC, V. Mon–Fri 11:30am–2:30pm and 5:30–10:30pm; Sat–Sun 5:30–11pm. Closed major holidays. MARTA: Buckhead.

**The Dining Room** ★★★ CONTEMPORARY FRENCH/JAPANESE Atlanta's most fashionable hotel boasts one of its stateliest dining rooms, where the food, decor, and service are unequaled in the city. The cuisine of Bruno Ménard is inventive and relentlessly perfect, and you dine luxuriously here while enjoying peerless service. Against a backdrop of fresh flowers, English hunt pictures, and an overall romantic ambience, you're served small portions on exquisitely arranged platters, backed up by an exceptional wine list. The restaurant has been a consistent winner of the AAA five-diamond award and Mobil's five-star rating. Although the menu changes daily, Atlanta's most venerated restaurant is nothing if not dependable. The young French chef led the kitchen at the Ritz-Carlton in Osaka, Japan, so he brings his Ginzu-sharpened techniques to Atlanta. Many of his dishes are rightly called "three-dimensional compositions." Every night a set of new dishes on the tasting menus is created by Ménard to titillate your palate, which he does by starting you off with such dishes as a smoked trout mousse quenelle churned in an ice-cream maker. The marinated loin of rabbit in a celeriac confit is so sensitively handled we want to give it an award. Sweetbreads in any form are a delectable item on the menu, as are the medallions of New Zealand loin of lamb—the most flavorful we've ever ordered in Atlanta. Although some local critics have praised Ménard's meat dishes but faulted his fish, our party found the Japanese-style seafood generally excellent in every way, including lobster with a medley of vegetables ranging from black trumpet mushrooms to baby artichokes. Desserts, as our companion raved, "are too good for ordinary mortals." Try them anyway, including the highly recommended Cuban chocolate tart with a chocolate sorbet.

In the Ritz-Carlton Buckhead, 3434 Peachtree Rd. NE. ✆ **404/237-2700.** Reservations required. Jacket required for men. Fixed-price menu $77 for 3 courses; $85–$135 tasting menu. AE, DC, MC, V. Tues–Sat 6–10pm. MARTA: Lenox.

**The Palm** ⭐ STEAK   The emphasis in this two-fisted, upscale tavern is macho friendliness, macho portions, and a kind of bustling unpretentiousness. Its namesake in Manhattan was established in 1926 by two Italian immigrants who wanted to name a restaurant after their hometown (Parma), and the result was a trattoria whose mistranslated name was "The Palm," which was transformed into an all-American steakhouse. Despite a sense that the place is a bit less glamorous than it was a few years ago, the Palm survives and thrives. There's a long and busy bar where you might be asked to wait for a table; comfortable banquettes within two separate dining rooms (one for smokers); and hundreds of cartoonlike caricatures of former diners, a la Sardi's in New York. (Both Coretta Scott King and Ted Turner have sampled the steaks here.) The Palm's menu is deceptively simple—six different preparations of veal, massive steaks, and chops; pastas and salads that would appeal to a vegetarian; and shellfish (including succulent 3-lb. lobsters and four preparations of clams). Lunchtime choices include less expensive, less filling items like sirloin burgers, grilled chicken sandwiches, crab cakes, and Caesar salads with chicken strips.

In the Buckhead Westin, 3391 Peachtree Rd. (between Lenox and Piedmont roads, just south of Lenox Sq.). ℂ 404/814-1955. Reservations recommended. Main courses $8–$20 lunch, $17–$35 dinner; lobster $60–$200, depending on weight. AE, DC, MC, V. Mon–Sat 11:30am–11pm; Sun noon–10pm. MARTA: Buckhead.

**Seeger's** ⭐⭐⭐ CONTINENTAL   Our trendy foodie friends on whom we rely on for insider dining tips rave about this place, saying it serves "the best food in Atlanta." Indeed, you are treated regally, and your palates will be uplifted in praise many times. Opened in 1997, it's chef Guenter Seeger's own restaurant following the media blitz he created at the swank Ritz-Carlton in Buckhead. Before his move to Atlanta, Seeger received a Michelin star for his restaurant in Germany's Black Forest. This restaurant is in a redecorated 19th-century house, an evocative setting for serving Continental fare in the European tradition. Dining options are limited to daily fixed-price menus, but there is a lot of variety and temptation here. Any chef who serves such amusing whimsies as crab salad on quince gelée must be doing something right. You can opt for the more limited three-course menu or else the virtual feast featured in a six-course repast.

Seeger possesses one of the most fertile and creative culinary minds in Atlanta. An artful touch is the grilled lamb chops on a turnip gratin with eggplant "caviar." The mesclun salad with fresh goat cheese, glazed apples, and pecan oil is the perfect way to glide into a meal that might continue with roasted squab with sweetbreads; or filet of halibut with a cèpe crust, served on a spaghetti squash salad. Desserts are among the most imaginative in the city. After the cherry soup with goat yogurt sorbet, you may want to kidnap the chef and take him home.

111 W. Paces Ferry Rd. ℂ 404/846-9779. Reservations required. Fixed-price 5-course menu $74; fixed-price 8-course tasting menu $95. AE, DC, MC, V. Mon–Thurs 6–10pm; Fri–Sat 5:30–10pm. MARTA: Lenox.

## EXPENSIVE

**Brasserie Le Coze** ⭐⭐ FRENCH   Authentic French food, mainly seafood, is served in what has been called "the most sophisticated of French restaurants," in spite of its location in a shopping mall. Between Neiman Marcus and Cartier, this Paris bistro was founded by the owners of Le Bernardin in New York: Maguy Le Coze and her late brother, Gilbert. The restaurant's signature dish is fish, whisked from the fire and served at the precise point between being overcooked and undercooked, a startling development when it was first introduced in Atlanta, land of the fried-to-death catfish. The service staff in long white aprons appears with mussels marinière in an aromatic bowl of broth flavored with white wine and flecks of shallots. Sautéed grouper follows, served over a mélange of vegetables flavored with curry oil. Believe it or not, some foodies come here for the roast chicken with its crisp skin, a perfectly done dish served with herbed gravy and the best mashed potatoes in Atlanta—creamy and laced with butter and chives. Other dishes include a beautifully seasoned and prepared rack of lamb and even such longtime bistro favorites as *coq au vin* (chicken in wine).

Lenox Sq., 3393 Peachtree Rd. NE. Ⓒ 404/266-1440. Reservations recommended. Main courses $17–$32. AE, DC, MC, V. Mon–Thurs 11:30am–2:30pm and 5:30–10pm; Fri 11:30am–3pm and 5:30–11pm; Sat 11:30am–3:30pm and 5:30–11pm. MARTA: Lenox.

**Chops** ✸ STEAK/SEAFOOD   Leave your vegetarian palate at home while dining at this 1930s-era macho enclave of good steaks, another jewel in the crown of restaurateur Pano Karatassos. Chops is the most informal restaurant in his chain, which includes the Atlanta Fish Market and Veni Vidi Vici. Business types, media stars, and locals flock to this handsome, clubby place, with its low lighting, roomy banquettes, and tri-level seating.

The Chops Lobster Bar, on the lower level, is the best in Atlanta, and large live Maine lobsters are flown in daily. The seared yellowfin tuna with a pepper crust, a shiitake mushroom and scallion potato mash, and a port-wine glaze are worth the trip across town. But the fame of the kitchen rests on its chops and steaks, specially aged and selected from corn-fed beef. The Chops Porterhouse for two (weighing in at 3 lb.) is enough to satisfy two gargantuan appetites. Mega-steaks aside, save room for some of Chops' homemade ice cream: The banana white-chocolate fudge is to die for, as is the chocolate black-bottom pie. Most of the wines are reasonable in price unless you're tempted by the odd $3,000 bottle.

70 W. Paces Ferry Rd. (at Peachtree Rd.). Ⓒ 404/262-2675. Reservations strongly recommended for dinner. Main courses $11–$35 lunch, $25–$85 dinner. AE, DC, MC, V. Mon–Fri 11:30am–2:30pm; Mon–Thurs 5:30–11pm; Fri–Sat 5:30pm–midnight; Sun 5:30–11pm. MARTA: Buckhead.

**Joël** ✸✸✸ FRENCH/MEDITERRANEAN/ASIAN   This is the hot new dining reservation in town. Joël Antunes has escaped from his nest at the Ritz-Carlton Buckhead and established his own chic French brasserie. Against a setting of contemporary design, Antunes sets the standard for casual fine dining in Atlanta. Amazingly, the 40 or so dishes listed don't appear on any other menus in the city. Antunes selected a location on Northside Parkway for his new restaurant and, not surprisingly, Atlanta foodies tracked him down there. (For the location, see the "Midtown Atlanta Accommodations & Dining" map on p. 328.)

The chef is clearly a master, as a sampling of his seared scallops and leek confit with a truffle sauce reveals. Everything looks tempting, including the gazpacho with tomato sorbet. A heavenly breast of duck with baby cabbage, fried polenta, and a fig sauce is served, and the perfectly roasted lamb comes with a butternut squash confit and ricotta and Parmesan tortellini. Potato gnocchi is supreme, with chanterelles and truffles in a frothy cream.

Desserts are not mere desserts; try the crêpes suzette with Grand Marnier sorbet, or a pineapple and coconut sorbet with a lemon-grass sauce.

3290 Northside Pkwy. NE. Ⓒ 404/233-3500. www.joelrestaurant.com. Reservations essential. Main courses $18–$29. AE, MC, V. Tues–Sat 11:30am–2pm; Tues–Thurs 5:30–10:30pm; Fri–Sat 5:30–11pm. MARTA: Lindberg.

**Nava** ✸ CONTEMPORARY/SOUTHWESTERN   It's Atlanta's most sophisticated Southwestern restaurant, with a colorful theme directly inspired by the pueblos, cactus branches, and adobe houses of the Painted Desert. The decor includes beams carved into zigzag patterns, massive lintels resembling those of a Franciscan mission, sculptures apparently used by once-powerful medicine men, and bold, native paintings you may actually be tempted to buy after your meal. Appetizers include a fire-roasted adobe quail with citrus honey, a green chile lobster-sauce taco, and tortilla-crusted shrimp rellenos. Main courses have flair and are spicy, especially the wood-roasted pork tenderloin with a tamarind-bean glaze that seems in perfect harmony, as does the giant shrimp with a mango glaze and white-bean enchiladas. Save room for the raspberry crème brûlée. The service here is first-rate.

3060 Peachtree Rd. © 404/240-1984. Reservations required. Main courses $8.95–$18 lunch, $15–$28 dinner. AE, DC, DISC, MC, V. Mon–Fri 11:30am–2:30pm and 5:30–11pm; Sat 5pm–midnight; Sun 5:30–10pm. MARTA: Buckhead.

**Pano & Paul's** ★★ CONTINENTAL/AMERICAN When this place opened in 1979, it created a dining sensation. The setting is one of Victorian opulence. Impeccable service, refined cuisine, and an extensive wine list drown out complaints that the place is snobby and overpriced. The broiled dry-aged sirloin steak or the roast double beef filet are about the best you'll get in Atlanta. Try white asparagus with smoked salmon and foie gras with an artichoke heart. Some of the Pacific Rim dishes, such as limpid wontons, are to be avoided, but not any of the potato dishes, including souffléd potatoes. Yes, potatoes are a signature dish. Another temptation is the fried baby-lobster tail with waffle fries and a Chinese mustard sauce.

1232 W. Paces Ferry Rd. © 404/261-3662. Reservations recommended. Main courses $20–$39. AE, DC, DISC, MC, V. Mon–Fri 6–10:30pm; Sat 5:30–11pm. MARTA: Buckhead.

## MODERATE

**Atlanta Fish Market** ★★ SEAFOOD/SUSHI This is the best seafood place in Atlanta, and we don't want to have an argument about that. Even Madonna and Senator Zell Miller agree (probably the only thing they do agree on) that the pecan-crusted catfish and the Carolina mountain trout are the best. The jazzy, 475-seat dining room has been compared to an old Southern train station. It's the creation of Pano Karatassos, sometimes known as "Kingfish." Some locals may be taken aback by the grilled halibut over creamy grits, garnished with shards of apple-smoked bacon, but they're quickly won over. Also try the New Orleans seafood gumbo to start—it contains crabmeat, spicy sausage, shrimp, and a peppery oceanic stock. For dessert, a wise choice is the pineapple-macadamia upside-down cake. The extensive menu is changed daily.

265 Pharr Rd. (between Peachtree Rd. and N. Fulton Dr.). © 404/262-3165. Main courses $13–$33 lunch, $13–$40 dinner. AE, DC, DISC, MC, V. Mon–Thurs 11am–3pm and 5:30–11pm; Fri 11:30am–3pm and 5:30pm–midnight; Sat 11:30am–4pm and 5pm–midnight; Sun 4–10pm. MARTA: Buckhead.

**The Buckhead Diner** ★ AMERICAN Since reservations aren't accepted, you may find yourself waiting in line with Elton John. Even though the place sounds like a hash house for truckers, it's one of the hottest spots in Atlanta. A highly theatrical venture, it has a gleaming stainless-steel exterior adorned with neon. Inside, try the crisp, spicy barbecued oysters served over creamy succotash with a Cajun rémoulade on the side, or butternut squash soup—the city's best. The veal and wild-mushroom meatloaf is a bit overrated, but not the seared calamari with a hot red sauce. For dessert, the coconut sorbet or the chocolate-chip crème brûlée will convince you that you've visited no meat-and-taters roadside diner.

*Finds*   **Family-Friendly Restaurants**

**The Varsity** (p. 336)   It's straight from that old movie *American Graf-fiti*. Singing carhops never died but live on here, serving the great American hot dog or the great American hamburger, plus 300 gallons of chili daily.

**Mary Mac's Tea Room** (p. 339)   At this Atlanta institution, you can introduce your kid to the delights of classic Southern cuisine—and per-haps introduce him or her to a former president, Jimmy Carter, who might be at a nearby table. Corn bread and pot liquor, fried catfish and turnip greens—it's the kind of fare Granny on the *Beverly Hillbillies* knows how to cook.

3073 Piedmont Rd. (at E. Paces Ferry Rd.). ☎ 404/262-3336. Reservations not accepted. Main courses $9.95–$20 lunch, $15–$25 dinner. AE, DC, DISC, MC, V. Mon–Sat 11am–midnight; Sun 10am–10pm. MARTA: Lenox.

**Horseradish Grill** ☆ SOUTHERN CUISINE   Overhyped but satisfying seems to be the consensus about this brash restaurant named for its equestrian art, not the root vegetable. Try the maple-smoked Georgia quail. Those inevitable pork chops are moist and made even more delectable with a cheddar-cheese macaroni side dish and cucumber salad. Grilled lamb chops also appear on the menu, as does the catch of the day. Naturally, turnip greens are served, as is cornmeal-battered catfish with home fries.

4320 Powers Ferry Rd. ☎ 404/255-7277. Reservations recommended. Main courses $7.50–$15 lunch, $17–$26 dinner. Mon–Fri 11:30am–2:30pm; Mon–Thurs 5:30–9pm; Fri–Sat 5–11pm; Sun 5–9pm. MARTA: Buckhead.

## INEXPENSIVE

**Café Sunflower** CONTINENTAL/VEGETARIAN   This upscale vegetarian restaurant lies on the Sandy Springs strip. The kitchen takes its inspiration from Mexican, Asian, and Mediterranean cuisine. Against a decor described as Williams-Sonoma, the service is more polite than efficient. The spring rolls are stuffed with shredded vegetables, rice noodles, and tofu; and a red-pepper hum-mus is served with pita triangles and a medley of crunchy raw vegetables. The quesadilla arrives stuffed with black beans, brown rice, tomato, cheese, and corn, a taste sensation in spite of the too-watery salsa. Eggplant and wood-ear mush-rooms are delectable in a garlic-ginger sauce, but forget the house salad. Another good choice is curried vegetables on a bed of couscous spiked with raisins and cashews. Instead of wine or beer, you can order freshly squeezed carrot juice.

5975 Roswell Rd. (at Hammond Dr.). ☎ 404/256-1675. Reservations recommended. Main courses $7.50–$9.95 lunch, $11–$16 dinner. AE, DISC, MC, V. Mon–Fri 11:30am–2:30pm; Mon–Thurs 5–9pm; Sat noon–2:30pm; Fri–Sat 5–9pm. MARTA: Sandy Springs.

**The Colonnade** SOUTHERN   An Atlanta favorite since 1927, and just as drab as ever, this friendly joint lies between Wellborne Drive and Manchester Street. Like a cheerful American restaurant of the 1950s, it offers great value and attracts the family trade with its down-home cookery and gargantuan portions. Inexpen-sively priced steaks, chops, seafood, and the inevitable Southern fried chicken round out the menu, along with vegetables boiled all day long. One regular comes here every day to order sugar-cured ham with red-eye gravy. Some of the menu items might lead to arterial overload, but fans of the Colonnade love this one.

1879 Cheshire Bridge Rd. NE (near Piedmont Rd.). ℂ 404/874-5642. Reservations not accepted. Main courses $6.95–$17. No credit cards. Mon–Tues 5–9pm; Wed–Sat 11:30am–4pm and 5–9pm; Sun 11am–9pm. MARTA: Lindbergh; then bus 27.

## VIRGINIA-HIGHLAND
### EXPENSIVE

**dish** ⭑ CONTEMPORARY GLOBAL & AMERICAN   More self-consciously trendy, and more deliberately cutting edge than its nearby competitor, the also-recommended Harvest Restaurant, this is an enduringly popular spot with a postmodern design that includes lots of copper—both polished and oxidized—in a mostly green decor. Between April and November, its relatively small (55 seats) interior is doubled, thanks to a sought-after outdoor terrace. Don't overlook the merits of this place as a bar, as local hipsters tend to gravitate here to "dish" whatever local or national icon deserves, in their eyes, deflating. Menu items change, sometimes radically, about four times a year, but at the time of our visit, they included such delights as steamed Penn Cove mussels roasted with garlic and saffron in a tomato broth, and shrimp and seaweed roll with a peanut chile dipping sauce. The main courses have robust flavors and reflect the chef's imagination, as evoked by seared scallops and shrimp with a basil fettuccine; sautéed five-spice duck breast with shiitake mushrooms and Chinese cabbage (served with a rhubarb and ginger coulis); and sautéed halibut with grilled salsify and asparagus served with a lemon and shallot vinaigrette.

870 N. Highland Ave. ℂ 404/897-3463. Reservations recommended. Main courses $16–$26. AE, DC, MC, V. Sun–Thurs 5:30–10pm; Fri–Sat 5:30–11pm. Bus: 2 or 16.

**Harvest Restaurant** ⭑ *Finds* AMERICAN   One of the neighborhood's most enduringly popular restaurants is set in one of the few Arts and Crafts–style bungalows that remain within the increasingly commercialized main drag of Virginia-Highland. Built in 1905, and painted an appropriate tone of harvest gold, it offers a two-story interior that might have been inspired by a disciple of Frank Lloyd Wright, with lots of turn-of-the-20th-century stained glass and varnished hardwoods, Stickley-style furnishings, a sextet of gas-fired fireplaces, and unusual sculptures and mobiles hanging from the high, sloping ceilings. (*Tip:* Most romantics and architecture buffs gravitate to a table upstairs.)

Raw ingredients come from several small purveyors, both farmers and fishermen, who haul in very fresh components, many of them organic, from Georgia, the Carolinas, and Florida. You might start with banana-and-coconut-crusted jumbo Gulf shrimp or an Argentine filet carpaccio with shaved fennel. The eggless Caesar salad, as a change of pace, is made with sun-dried tomatoes served with griddled shallot croutons and shaved Parmesan cheese. Main dishes have full flavor and imagination, especially the pumpkin seed–crusted halibut with ancho-chile mashed potatoes, or the jerk pork tenderloin with a mango salsa and raspberry mayonnaise.

853 N. Highland Ave. ℂ 404/876-8244. Reservations recommended. Dinner main courses $15–$25. AE, DC, MC, V. Sun–Thurs 5:30–10pm; Fri–Sat 5:30–11pm; Sun brunch 11am–2pm. Bus: 2 or 16.

### MODERATE

**Atkins Park Restaurant and Tavern** ⭑ *Finds* TRADITIONAL AMERICAN/ CAJUN   With a long and colorful history, this is the city's oldest continuously licensed tavern, with good and affordable family dining. It attracts the chicken wings crowd: Many drinkers come here for the late-night munchies and the beer. Weekend brunch is another popular time, attracting a faithful coterie of Virginia-Highland residents. In fair weather, opt for a table on the patio. Popular food items for the breakfast crowd include buttermilk biscuits and gravy, even Southern fried chicken. The sandwiches can be appropriately described as bulging. The locals dig into the earthy gumbo and jambalaya dishes, though we prefer the crusted Georgia mountain trout. For dinner, things get a little more elaborate, with dishes like drunken pork tenderloin (marinated in bourbon), or a thick-cut pork chop stuffed with goat cheese and served with toasted pecans. A special kids' menu is featured.

794 N. Highland Ave. NE. ⓒ 404/876-7249. www.atkinspark.com. Reservations not needed. Main courses $7.95–$9.95 lunch, $13–$17 dinner. AE, DC, DISC, MC, V. Mon–Fri 11am–4am; Sat 11am–3am; Sun 11am–midnight. Bus: 16.

## INEXPENSIVE

**The Flying Biscuit Cafe** ⓖ SOUTHERN   This cozy Candler Park favorite enjoys renown all over the Atlanta area for its all-day breakfasts and weekend brunches. It made its reputation by serving what are arguably the best biscuits in Georgia—where the competition is stiff. We recommend you pair the biscuits with a jar of cranberry apple butter.

The restaurant decor features oddly matched vinyl tablecloths and funky accessories. The fare is strictly down-home, including "love cakes"—three black-bean and cornmeal cakes sautéed and topped with a tomatillo salsa, sour cream, feta cheese, and spears of red onion. Their most popular dish—enough to get Mike Wallace arrested for—is turkey meatloaf and "pudge." Pudge is based on an old family recipe for mashed potatoes, sun-dried tomatoes, basil, and olive oil. For breakfast, we prefer the orange-scented French toast with raspberry compote and crème Anglaise, but the long-enduring favorite of most diners is the Flying Biscuit breakfast: two large farm-fresh eggs served with the cafe's signature free-range chicken breast sausage. A three-course dinner special with wine costs just $25 on Friday. Kids under 12 eat free from the children's menu Monday to Wednesday after 5pm.

The Biscuit recently opened up a more convenient midtown location at 1001 Piedmont Ave. (ⓒ **404/874-8887**), which charges the same prices and keeps the same hours.

1655 McLendon Ave. at Clifton Rd. ⓒ 404/687-8888. www.flyingbiscuit.com. Breakfast $5.95–$8.95; dinner specials after 5pm $9.95–$15. AE, MC, V. Fri–Sat 7am–10:30pm; Sun–Thurs 7am–10pm. MARTA: Midtown.

## INMAN PARK

**Sotto Sotto** ⓖ TUSCAN/PIEMONTESE/EMILIA-ROMAGNOLA   The best and most appealing restaurant in Inman Park occupies the unpretentious premises of what was built around 1900 as a low-slung row of brick-fronted stores. In 1999, Stefano Volpi and a team of culinary entrepreneurs from Turin and Milan inserted a stylish minimalist decor of glowing hardwoods and immaculate napery, and added a high-tech, open-to-view kitchen where a team of chefs supervises batteries of bubbling pastas and sauces. Today, the Northern Italian ambience is as authentic and accurate to the European motif as anything you're likely to find in Atlanta, a fact that's appreciated by the residents of increasingly upscale Inman Park. Superbly prepared menu specialties include wood-roasted whole fish (either pompano, trout, or snapper) flown in ultra fresh from Florida; risotto with seafood; and a succulent version of scallops braised with arugula, white beans, and truffle oil. A favorite pasta is tortelli di Michelangelo, stuffed with a mixture of minced veal, pork, and chicken, served with brown butter and sage sauce. Most wines here are Italian, including goodly numbers of Barolos, Brunellos di Montalcino, and Barbarescos.

313 N. Highland Ave. ℭ 404/523-6678. Reservations recommended. Main courses $31–$40. AE, DC, MC, V. Mon–Thurs 5:30–11pm; Fri–Sat 5:30pm–midnight.

## NEARBY DINING

For locations of the following two restaurants, see the "Buckhead Accommodations & Dining" map on p. 332.

**Canoe** ★★ CONTEMPORARY AMERICAN    Canoe is located right at the city's outskirts in Cobb County—of Newt Gingrich fame. Remember him? Tables at this hip and fashionable restaurant open onto the Chattahoochee River. After World War II the locale was famous as a dance hall for "big dresses, big hair, senior proms, and *East of Eden* scenes." Today the much-gentrified pair of connected Quonset huts housing the restaurant have been upgraded with burnished wood, exposed brick, and a service staff fetchingly clad in patterned vests.

Canoe's appetizers are among the most sophisticated in the city. Sure, they serve catfish, but it comes with a toasted-pistachio green-curry sauce. The chef is known for his light pastas and risottos, one an outstanding pumpkin tortellini with roasted pine nuts and a spicy lamb ragout. The standing menu includes crispy duck with spicy greens and caramel-ginger sauce; slow-roasted pork with Gorgonzola polenta and a spicy escarole; and bacon-wrapped sturgeon with whipped potatoes and sage butter. The waiters warn you to save room for dessert.

4199 Paces Ferry Rd. NW. ℭ 770/43-CANOE. Reservations strongly recommended. Main courses $7.95–$16 lunch, $17–$24 dinner. AE, DC, DISC, MC, V. Mon–Thurs 11:30am–2:30pm and 5:30–10pm; Fri 11:30am–2:30pm and 5:30–11pm; Sat 5:30–11pm; Sun 10:30am–2:30pm and 5:30–9pm.

**Five Seasons Brewing Company** ★ *Finds* AMERICAN/JAPANESE    When you tire of grits and collards, head for Sandy Springs, just north of Buckhead, for some unique dishes as well as the highest-quality handcrafted beers in Georgia. The signature beer is Seven Sisters, named after the original seven breweries in Munich that hosted Oktoberfest. It's deep amber, soft and rich, with a malty finish. The menu's blend of Japanese dishes with stateside grill fare comes as a surprise and a refreshing change to the palate. We always get stuck on the appetizers, wanting a taste of practically everything before moving on to the main courses. Our favorites here are the fried blue-crab fingers with a honey-mustard aioli, and the calamari with orange-chile dipping sauce. Grilled pizza is a regular feature. The meats are well handled, to judge by the chargrilled Black Angus New York strip with asparagus, or the lamb tenderloin. The chef uses textural contrasts to good effect in dishes like miso-marinated sea bass with sesame spinach. Some sides appear here and nowhere else, such as a sweet-onion spaetzle. Desserts are worth walking a mile for, especially the brioche bread pudding with chocolate, raisins, and pecans.

5600 Roswell Rd., Suite 21, The Prado. ℭ 404/255-5911. Reservations recommended. Main courses $7.95–$8.95 lunch, $11–$22 dinner. AE, DC, DISC, MC, V. Mon–Wed 11am–10pm; Thurs 11am–10:30pm; Fri–Sat 11am–11pm; Sun noon–10pm. MARTA: Medical Center Station.

## 5 Attractions

Sit in the tourist office in Atlanta and, within an hour at least, three visitors will come by and ask for directions to "Tara" or "Twelve Oaks." Regrettably, these places never existed in real life, only in Margaret Mitchell's imagination. Even the movie theater where *Gone With the Wind* premiered in 1939 was gutted by

# Downtown Atlanta Sights

Alonzo F. Herndon Home **1**

APEX Museum **5**

Birth Home of
  Martin Luther King, Jr. **10**

The Carter Center **16**

CNN Center **2**

Cyclorama **14**

Ebenezer Baptist Church **8**

Georgia State Capitol **7**

Grant Park **13**

High Museum of Art Folk Art
  and Photography Galleries **4**

The King Center **9**

Oakland Cemetery **11**

SciTrek **3**

Turner Field **12**

Underground Atlanta **6**

The World of
  Coca-Cola **6**

Zoo Atlanta **15**

fire in the early 1980s. A marble skyscraper sits on the site where Clark Gable and Vivien Leigh launched the film. But even with no Tara, Atlanta has a great deal to offer.

**The Carter Center** ✦  This center, opened in 1986, is the 30-acre site from which former U.S. president Jimmy Carter works to advance peace and human rights, efforts for which he won a Nobel prize in October 2002. Its work in democratization and development, global health, and urban revitalization has touched the lives of people in some 65 countries. The center is 2 miles east of the center of downtown Atlanta, with the skyline as a dramatic backdrop. On the same grounds is the Jimmy Carter Library and Museum, housing millions of documents, photos, gifts, and memorabilia of Carter's career and his years in the White House. You can even view a full-scale reproduction of the Oval Office and use interactive video geared to both children and adults. Displays of gifts received by then-President and Mrs. Carter range from silver, ivory, and crystal from heads of state, to paintings and peanut carvings from around the world. *Presidents,* a 30-minute film, looks at the crises and triumphs that marked his administration.

1 Copenhill, 441 Freedom Pkwy. Ⓒ **404/865-7100.** www.jimmycarterlibrary.org. Admission $7 adults, $5 seniors, free for children 16 and under. Mon–Sat 9am–4:45pm; Sun noon–4:45pm.

**CNN Center** ✦  Located in the heart of Atlanta, the CNN Center anchors the city's dynamic entertainment, news, sports, and business core and is adjacent to the Georgia Dome and the Georgia World Congress Center. It houses CNN, Headline News, and CNN International studios, and offers guided **studio tours** of these facilities daily. Group tours can also be arranged. See the listing information below for tour information and reservations.

The center also features more than 40 one-of-a-kind retail stores. The **Turner Store,** on the ground level in the Atrium, has merchandise from all of broadcasting's networks and properties. Visitors can create their own CNN news tape by reading the day's top stories in the **Turner Studio** from a TelePrompTer while sitting behind an actual CNN anchor desk. Through the magic of chroma-key, you can have your photo taken on the pitcher's mound with your favorite Braves players, relax with Scarlett O'Hara and Rhett Butler in a scene from *Gone With the Wind,* or choose from more than 40 other backgrounds.

Visitors can continue their Turner adventure at the **Braves Clubhouse Store** on the ground level in the Atrium, which holds the largest collection of official Braves merchandise in Atlanta. The store is open 7 days a week 9:30am to 7pm, with extended hours on Braves' and Hawks' game days, and for Georgia Dome special events.

The **Atrium** has a variety of eateries in its international food court, where visitors can sit down for a quick meal.

1 CNN Center (at Marietta St. and Techwood Dr.). Ⓒ **404/827-2300.** www.cnn.com/StudioTour. CNN Studio Tours admission $10 adults, $8 seniors 65 and over, $7 children 4–12 (no children under 12 allowed on tours); $22 VIP tour. Tours given every 10 min. daily 9am–5pm; reservations highly recommended at least 1 day in advance. Turner Store and Studio, daily 9:30am–7pm. Closed major holidays. MARTA: Omni, Dome, or GWCC.

**Fox Theatre**  This Moorish-Egyptian extravaganza, with its minarets and onion domes, began life as a Shriners' temple. It became a movie theater when movie mogul William Fox, after 2 years of extensive work on the block-long structure, threw open its doors to the public. Its exotic lobby was decorated with lush carpeting; in the auditorium itself, a skyscape was transformed to sunrise, sunset, or starry night skies as the occasion demanded, and a striped Bedouin canopy overhung the balcony. The Great Depression came hot on the heels of

# Central Atlanta Sights

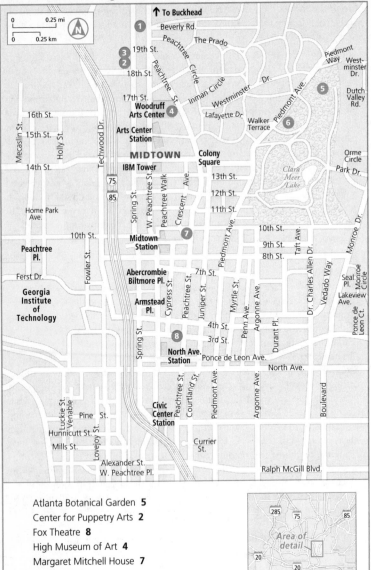

Atlanta Botanical Garden **5**

Center for Puppetry Arts **2**

Fox Theatre **8**

High Museum of Art **4**

Margaret Mitchell House **7**

Piedmont Park **6**

Rhodes Memorial Hall **1**

William Breman Jewish Heritage Museum **3**

the Fox's opening, however, and in 1932 bankruptcy forced its closing. In the 1940s it was brought to life again with installation of a huge panoramic movie screen, but decline closed its doors once more in the 1970s. The Fox was slated for demolition, but Atlantans raised $1.8 million to save their treasured old movie palace. Restored to its former glory, it now thrives as a venue for live entertainment.

660 Peachtree St. NE. ℂ **404/881-2100**. Tours $10 adults, $5 children. Tours given Feb–Nov, Mon and Wed–Thurs 10am; Sat 10am and 11am. Dec–Jan, Mon and Thurs 10am. MARTA: North Ave.

**Georgia State Capitol**    Writer Colin Campbell saw the 1884 capitol building as "weird, colorful, relentlessly Southern; a super attic of flags, paintings, two-headed snakes, scale models, stuffed animals, and weapons." Its gold-topped dome rises 237 feet above the city. Besides a Hall of Fame (with busts of famous Georgians), and a Hall of Flags (U.S., state, and Confederate), it houses the **Georgia State Museum of Science and Industry,** with collections of Georgia minerals and Indian artifacts, dioramas of famous places, and fish and wildlife exhibits. Visit in late January and February to hear Georgia legislators at work. Georgia is a great state, but sometimes these members aren't very up on things—for example, we were treated to a legislator who condemned the 1996 Olympic games out of fear "that it will give all of us AIDS."

Capitol Sq. ℂ **404/656-2844**. Free admission. Mon–Fri 8am–5pm. Apr–Dec tours at 10am, 11am, 1pm, and 2pm; Jan–Mar 9:30am, 10:30am, 1pm, and 2pm. Closed major holidays. MARTA: Georgia State.

**Underground Atlanta**    Right in town, 4 blocks of Atlanta's history lie beneath newer city streets. Underground Atlanta is the city's birthplace, where the Zero Milepost of the Western & Atlantic Railroad was planted in 1837. In post–Civil War days, railroad viaducts were built over its rococo buildings, and they lay deserted for the better part of a century. Restoration of the crumbling area has resulted in an authentic picture of Atlanta in the 1800s. During the mid-1980s the historic city beneath a city was closed for massive redevelopment, and in 1989 it reopened with more than 100 establishments, including shops, restaurants, and nightspots. Regrettably, it is looking a bit seedy these days, as souvenir shops and fast-food joints take over.

Bounded by Peachtree, Wall, Alabama, Pryor, and Central sts. and by Martin Luther King, Jr., Dr. ℂ **404/523-2311**. Free admission. Mon–Sat 10am–9pm; Sun 11am–6pm (clubs and restaurants stay open until midnight or beyond). MARTA: Five Points, with a pedestrian tunnel linking it directly to the Underground.

**The World of Coca-Cola**  ⚐    It has been called "the world's most popular product." It's been called a lot of other things too, including "the Devil's Drink." But Coca-Cola—its recipe still a secret—has been consumed by people all over the world and has endured, even surviving Shirley Temple singing "Sweet Coca-Cola Bush." A three-floor pavilion exhibits memorabilia of the world's most famous drink, from endorsements by fabled stars of yesterday (including those *It Happened One Night* actors, Clark Gable and Claudette Colbert) to campy commercials by the Supremes. The pavilion boasts the most innovative outdoor neon sign ever created for a company—an 11-ton extravaganza hanging 18 feet above the entrance. In all, there are more than 1,000 exhibits, including a 1930s vintage soda fountain, complete with a soda jerk.

55 Martin Luther King, Jr., Dr. SW (at Central Ave., adjacent to Underground Atlanta). ℂ **404/676-5151**. Admission $7 adults, $5 seniors, $4 children 6–11, free for children 5 and under. Mon–Sat 9am–6pm; Sun 11am–6pm; last admission at 5pm. Closed major holidays. MARTA: Five Points.

**Georgia's Stone Mountain Park** ★   A monolithic gray granite outcropping (the world's largest), carved with a massive Confederate memorial, Stone Mountain is a distinctive landmark on Atlanta's horizon and the focal point of its major outdoor recreation area—3,200 acres of lakes and beautiful wooded parkland.

Over half a century in the making, Stone Mountain's neoclassic carving—90 feet high and 190 feet wide—is the world's largest piece of sculpture. Originally conceived by Gutzon Borglum, it depicts Confederate leaders Jefferson Davis, Robert E. Lee, and Stonewall Jackson galloping on horseback throughout eternity. Borglum started work on the mountain sculpture in 1923; after 10 years he abandoned it, because of insurmountable technical problems and rifts with its sponsors. (He went on to South Dakota, where he gained fame carving Mount Rushmore.) It wasn't until 1963, when the state purchased the mountain and its surroundings for a park, that work resumed under Walter Kirtland Hancock and Roy Faulkner. The memorial was completed in 1970.

The best view of the mountain is from below, but you can ascend a walking trail up its moss-covered slopes, especially lovely in spring when they're blanketed in wildflowers, or take the narrated tram ride to the top. Trams run about every 20 minutes in both directions.

A highlight at Stone Mountain is **Lasershow,** a spectacular display of laser lights and fireworks with animation and music. It begins in April, weekends only (Fri–Sun at 9:30pm); from early May to Labor Day it can be seen nightly at 9:30pm. Don't miss it.

Other major park attractions include the **Stone Mountain Scenic Railroad,** which chugs around the 5-mile base of Stone Mountain. The ride takes 25 minutes. Trains depart from Railroad Depot, an old-fashioned train station with an attractive restaurant on-site. The *Scarlett O'Hara,* a paddlewheel riverboat, cruises 363-acre Stone Mountain Lake. The **Antique Auto & Music Museum** is a jumble of old radios, jukeboxes, working nickelodeons, Lionel trains, and carousel horses, along with classic cars.

The 19-building **Antebellum Plantation** is a major sightseeing attraction in itself. Self-guided tours are assisted by hosts in period dress. Highlights include an authentic 1830s country store; the 1845 Kingston House; clapboard slave cabins; the 1790s Thornton House, elegant home of a large landowner; the smokehouse and well; a doctor's office; and the 1850 neoclassical Tara-like Dickey House, formal gardens, and kitchen garden. It takes at least an hour to tour the entire complex (a map is provided at the entrance). Often there are crafts and cooking demonstrations, medicine shows, storytellers, or balladeers on the premises.

**Confederate Hall,** an information center, houses a large narrated exhibit called "The War in Georgia," a chronological picture story of the Civil War.

Additional activities are golf (on a top-rated 36-hole course designed by Robert Trent Jones and John LaFoy), miniature golf, 15 hard-surface tennis courts (the site of the tennis competition for the 1996 Summer Olympic Games), a sizable lakefront beach with wonderful water slides, 20 acres of wildlife trails with natural animal habitats and a petting zoo, boating, bicycle rentals, fishing, and more. Also located in the park is the **Evergreen Conference Resort,** a 249-room state-of-the-art conference facility.

Hwy. 78 E., Stone Mountain (16 miles east of downtown on U.S. 78). © **800/317-2006.** www.stonemountain park.com. Major attractions each $7.50 adults. A ticket for all major attractions is $19 adults, $16 children. Year-round gates open 6am–midnight. Major attractions open fall and winter 10am–5pm; spring and summer Sun–Thurs 10am–6pm, Fri–Sat 10am–8pm. Parking charge $7 a day, $30 annually (1-time-only charge if you stay on the grounds). Only the attractions are closed for Christmas; the park is open. MARTA: Avondale; then transfer to a bus to Stone Mountain Village.

## Martin Luther King, Jr., National Historic Site

Under the auspices of the National Park Service is the Martin Luther King, Jr., National Historic Site, an area of about 10 blocks around Auburn Avenue, established in 1980 to "preserve the birthplace and boyhood surroundings of the nation's foremost civil rights leader." It includes **King's boyhood home** and the **Ebenezer Baptist Church,** of which King, his father, and his grandfather were ministers. Other Auburn Avenue attractions, not under NPS auspices, include the **King Center** (where King is buried) and the **APEX Museum.** A **visitor center** at 449 Auburn Ave., across from the King Center, provides a complete orientation to area attractions and includes a theater for audiovisual and interpretive programs, exhibits, and a bookstore. Guided tours of the area (including those of the Birth Home) originate here. The visitor center is fronted by a beautifully landscaped plaza with a reflecting pool and outdoor amphitheater for park service programs.

**The King Center** ☆    Martin Luther King, Jr.'s commitment to nonviolent social change lives on at this memorial and educational center under the direction of his son, Dexter Scott King. On the premises is an information counter where you can find out about all Auburn Avenue attractions.

The center works with government agencies and the private sector to reduce violence within the community and among nations. It provides day care for low-income families, assists students in developing leadership skills in nonviolence, and holds workshops on topics such as hunger and illiteracy. Its library and archives house the world's largest collection of books and other materials documenting the civil rights movement, including Dr. King's personal papers and a rare 87-volume edition of *The Collected Works of Mahatma Gandhi,* a gift from the government of India. Equally important, it is Martin Luther King's final resting place, a living memorial to an inspiring leader, which is visited by tens of thousands each year, including heads of foreign governments.

Visitors are given a self-guided tour brochure. The tour begins in the exhibition hall, where memorabilia of King and the civil rights movement are displayed. Here you can see his Bible and clerical robe, a handwritten sermon, a photographic essay on his life and work and, on a grim note, the suit he was wearing when a deranged woman stabbed him in New York City, as well as the key to his room at the Lorraine Motel in Memphis, Tennessee, where he was assassinated. In an alcove off the main exhibit area is a video display on Martin Luther King's life and works. Additional exhibits—including a room honoring Rosa Parks and another honoring Gandhi—are in **Freedom Hall.**

Outside in Freedom Plaza, Dr. King's white marble crypt rests, surrounded by a five-tiered reflecting pool, a symbol of the life-giving nature of water. An eternal flame burns in a small circular pavilion directly fronting the crypt.

An important part of a visit is the **Screening Room,** where four excellent half-hour videos play continuously throughout the day. They show many of Dr. King's most stirring sermons and speeches, including "I've Been to the Mountaintop" and "I Have a Dream"—speeches that are as much a part of America's heritage as the Gettysburg Address.

449 Auburn Ave. (between Boulevard and Jackson sts.). ℘ **404/524-1956.** www.thekingcenter.org. Free admission. Daily 9am–5pm. Closed Thanksgiving, Christmas, and New Year's Day. MARTA: Five Points, then bus 3.

**Ebenezer Baptist Church** From 1960 to 1968, this Gothic Revival–style church, founded in 1886 and completed in 1922, became a center of world attention. Martin Luther King, Jr., served as co-pastor of the church during the civil rights struggle. Martin Luther King, Sr., a civil rights leader before his son, was also a pastor here. In early 1999, the National Park Service assumed a 99-year lease on the church and will oversee it as a living museum, with guided weekday tours, periodic church services, and a monthly choir performance.

400–407 Auburn Ave. ✆ **404/688-7263.** Free admission, but donations welcomed. Mon–Sat 9am–6pm; Sun only for services, at 7:45am and 11am. MARTA: King Memorial; then a long 8-block walk. Bus: 3 from Peachtree St.

**Birth Home of Martin Luther King, Jr.** ✦ This Queen Anne–style house is where Martin Luther King, Jr., was born on January 15, 1929. He was the oldest son of a Baptist minister and a music teacher. King lived at this modest house until he was 12. It has been restored to its appearance when young Martin lived here. Even the linoleum is an authentic reproduction, and a good deal of King memorabilia is displayed. Be warned that in summer, tickets to the house often run out because of the crowds.

501 Auburn Ave. (at Hogue St.). ✆ **404/331-3920.** Free admission (obtain tickets at 449 Auburn Ave.). Daily 9am–5pm. Closed major holidays. MARTA: Five Points; then bus 3.

## MUSEUMS

**Atlanta History Center** ✦✦ From the Civil War and the burning of Atlanta to the civil rights movement of Martin Luther King, Jr., it's all here in vivid display in this vast museum. There's even a collection of memorabilia from Margaret Mitchell. There are frequently changing exhibits as well—everything from *Gone With the Wind* to Atlanta's first black millionaire.

On the grounds is **Swan House and Gardens,** the finest residential design of architect Philip Trammell Schutze. This classical home was constructed in 1928 by the Edward H. Inman family, heirs to a cotton fortune. It's listed on the National Register of Historic Places. Also on the grounds is a "plantation plain" home (ca. 1840), the **Tullie Smith Farm.** Here you can see how Georgia farmers lived in the mid-1800s right before the Civil War.

130 W. Paces Ferry Rd. (at Slaton Dr.). ✆ **404/814-4000.** www.atlantahistorycenter.com. Admission $12 adults, $10 seniors and students 13 and up, $7 children 4–12, free for children 3 and under. Mon–Sat 10am–5:30pm; Sun noon–5:30pm. MARTA: Lenox; then bus 23 to Peachtree St. and W. Paces Ferry Rd., then a 3-block walk.

**Cyclorama** For a panorama of the Battle of Atlanta, see this 42-foot-high, 356-foot-circumference, 1880s painting with a three-dimensional foreground and special lighting, music, and sound effects. When you see the monumental work, you'll know why Sherman said, "War is hell." One of only three cycloramas in the United States, it has recently been fully restored—an artistic and historical treasure that many visitors to Atlanta miss, erroneously thinking it "strictly for kids." There are 15 shows daily.

800 Cherokee Ave., in Grant Park. ✆ **404/624-1071.** Admission $7 adults, $6 seniors, $5 children 6–12, free for children 5 and under. Daily 8:50am–4:30pm. Closed major holidays. MARTA: Five Points; then bus 97 (Georgia Ave.).

**High Museum of Art** ✦ This little gem of a museum is one of the finest in Georgia, but sensitive Atlantans warn that it shouldn't be oversold to visitors. It's not the Louvre, the Prado, or the Metropolitan. The building itself, designed in 1983 by Richard Meier at a cost of $20 million, has been called an "architectural masterpiece." Its exterior is coated with white enamel tiles, and the central atrium is flooded with natural light. You'll find first-rate traveling exhibitions along with the museum's permanent collection. Part of the Woodruff Arts Complex, the museum houses some 10,000 works, including a painting by one of our favorites, John Singer Sargent. Many are by artists like Mattie Lou O'Kelley and Howard Finster, with roots in Georgia. There's also an extensive sub-Saharan African art collection. We visit at times just to view the Virginia Carroll Crawford Collection of American Decorative Arts, covering changing tastes from 1825 to 1917.

The museum's downtown branch, the **High Museum of Art Folk Art and Photography Galleries,** is located at 133 Peachtree St. in the Georgia-Pacific Center. It's open Monday through Saturday from 10am to 5pm (© **404/577-6940;** admission free).

In the Woodruff Arts Center, 1280 Peachtree St. NE. © **404/733-4200** or 404/733-HIGH for 24-hr. information. www.high.org. Admission $10 adults, $8 seniors and students, $6 children 6–17, free for children 5 and under. Tues–Sat 10am–5pm (1st Thurs of each month 10am–9pm); Sun noon–5pm. Closed major holidays. MARTA: Arts Center.

**Margaret Mitchell House**    Margaret Mitchell was the author of *Gone With the Wind,* the best-selling book in the world next to the Bible, and this is her former home. A suspicious fire damaged the house in 1994, and on May 12, 1996, just 40 days before its scheduled reopening, arson struck again. Daimler-Benz, Germany's largest industrial group, came to the rescue and the property was rebuilt and opened to the public. Although Margaret Mitchell hated the place and called it "The Dump," her turn-of-the-20th-century house is once again a major tourist attraction. The author would probably have been horrified to see millions of people traipsing through the place where she lived and wrote and created characters like Scarlett O'Hara and Rhett Butler.

Atlanta's first city landmark and listed on the National Register of Historic Places, the house was dedicated on May 16, 1997, exactly 1 year after the second fire on the property. You can experience a 40-minute anecdotal guided tour that shares the life story of this amazing author and the impact her book and the movie made upon the world. A new *Gone With the Wind* Museum opened here in late 1999, exhibiting the Herb Bridges collection of *Gone With the Wind* movie memorabilia, to coincide with the 60th anniversary of the movie's premiere in 1939. You can see props, scripts, posters, and even seats from the Loew's Grand Theatre, the Atlanta theater where the movie premiered. More people have seen *Gone With the Wind* than any other motion picture ever produced.

The house and adjacent visitor center contain exclusive photographs and archival exhibits, including the original typewriter on which she crafted her novel, the 1937 Pulitzer Prize, original movie posters from around the world, and other exhibits. Mitchell lived here in this small apartment from 1925 to 1932.

990 Peachtree St. (at 10th St.). © **404/249-7015.** www.gwtw.org. Admission $12 adults, $9 students and seniors, $5 children 7–17, free for 6 and under. Public tours daily 9:30am–5pm (last tour begins at 4pm). MARTA: Midtown.

**Michael C. Carlos Museum of Emory University**    Only a tenth of its holdings are ever on display, so Atlantans return again and again. As an out-of-towner, you can count on something interesting even if it's only a small piece of the Carlos pie. Beautiful objects from the ancient Mediterranean, stunning art from Africa, and pre-Columbian art are among its rich collections. There are also special shows mounted from the museum's vast holdings, including exquisite drawings—some as old as the 1600s. There's nothing in Georgia to equal this collection. The 1916 Beaux Arts building housing the museum is listed on the National Register of Historic Places.

Kilgo St. (near the junction of Oxford and N. Decatur roads on the Main Quadrangle of the Emory campus). © 404/727-4282. $3 donation recommended. Tues–Wed and Fri–Sat 10am–5pm; Thurs 10am–9pm; Sun noon–5pm. Closed major holidays. Bus: 6 or 36.

**SciTrek** ⭐ *Kids*    This interactive museum provides an entertaining hands-on immersion in the wonders of science for the entire family. Among the permanent exhibits are the Cyber Playground, a display of computer games through the years; the Color Factory, where you literally play with color; and KidSpace, a gallery specially designed to entertain small children with interactive exhibits.

397 Piedmont Ave. NE (adjacent to the Civic Center). © 404/522-5500. www.scitrek.org. Admission $9.50 adults; $7.50 children 3–12, college students, and seniors; free for children under 3. Mon–Sat 10am–5pm; Sun noon–5pm. Closed major holidays. MARTA: Civic Center.

**Fernbank Museum of Natural History** ⭐    This is the largest museum of the natural sciences in the Southeast, a $43-million complex that abuts 65 acres of virgin forest. Opened in 1992, it has a permanent exhibition, "A Walk Through Time in Georgia," taking visitors through more than a dozen galleries that explore Georgia's scenic wonders. "Spectrum of the Senses" comprises some 65 displays shown on a rotating basis. Adventures here include stepping inside a life-size kaleidoscope, and IMAX Theater films on a six-story screen.

767 Clifton Rd. (off Ponce de Leon Ave.). © 404/378-0127. www.fernbank.edu/museum. Museum $12 adults, $11 students and seniors, $10 children, free for kids 11 and under; IMAX $10 adults, $9 seniors and students, $8 children. Combination museum and IMAX $17 adults, $15 seniors and students, $13 children. Mon–Sat 10am–5pm; Sun noon–5pm. MARTA: North Ave.; then bus 2 to Clifton Rd.

**Fernbank Science Center**    This is a planetarium, observatory, and museum all rolled into one. Next to the 65-acre Fernbank Forest, it's a branch of the Fernbank Museum of Natural History (see above). Many visitors who've seen all the exhibits come for the 1.5-mile forest trail, showcasing some of the state's most popular trees such as magnolias and dogwoods. Inside, you can see the original Apollo 6 space capsule and a spacesuit, as well as a replica of the Okefenokee Swamp (see chapter 21 for details on the real one). The greenhouse, 2.5 miles from the center, is open only on Sunday, and presents changing workshops and lectures.

156 Heaton Park Dr. NE (at Artwood Rd., off Ponce de Leon Ave.). © 678/874-7102. http://fsc.fernbank.edu. Center free admission; planetarium shows, $4 adults, $3 students, free for seniors (children 4 and under not admitted). Museum: Mon 8:30am–5pm; Tues–Fri 8:30am–10pm; Sat 10am–5pm; Sun 1–5pm. Planetarium shows: Tues–Fri at 8pm; Wed, Fri, Sat, Sun 3:30 and 8pm. Observatory: Thurs–Fri at 8:30pm (or dusk–10:30pm). Forest trails: Sun 2–5pm; Mon–Fri 9am–5pm; Sat 10am–5pm. Closed major holidays. Take North Ave. east and make a left onto Piedmont. Make a right onto Ponce De Leon Ave. and follow this road for 4½ miles. Take a left onto Artwood Rd. and then a right on Heaton Park Dr.

**William Breman Jewish Heritage Museum**    An unusual museum for the South, this is the most expansive museum of its type in the entire Southeast. It focuses on the Jewish heritage but places a spotlight on the Jewish experience in Atlanta itself. Its permanent exhibit, "Creating Community: the Jews of Atlanta from 1845 to the Present," shows how Jews not only settled into Atlanta but contributed to the community. Some of the exhibits tell sad tales such as the 1913 Leo Frank case. Frank was wrongfully accused of murder, and was lynched by a mob although his sentence was commuted by Georgia's governor. Exhibits also document anti-Semitic attacks in Atlanta, such as the 1958 bombing of the Temple on Peachtree Street. Documents, photographs, and memorabilia re-create the Jewish saga. There are programs with hands-on activities for younger children.

1440 Spring St. NW, in the Selig Center at 18th St. (C) 678/222-3700. www.thebreman.org. Admission $6 adults, $4 seniors and students, free for children 6 and under. Mon–Thurs 10am–5pm; Fri 10am–3pm; Sun 1–5pm. Closed major holidays. MARTA: Arts Center.

## A FASCINATING CEMETERY

**Oakland Cemetery** 𝕩 Margaret Mitchell, the most famous author ever to emerge from the Deep South, is buried here. Many other famous personages are also here, including golfing great Bobby Jones. The cemetery is an 88-acre Victorian site founded 10 years before the Civil War. It later became the burial place for nearly 50,000 soldiers, both Confederate and Union. This is actually an outdoor museum of funerary architecture, including both classic and Gothic Revival mausoleums. People often bring a picnic lunch and eat ham sandwiches among the dead. The visitor center distributes a self-guided walking-tour map and brochure for $2.

248 Oakland Ave. SE (main entrance at Oakland Ave. and Martin Luther King, Jr., Dr.). (C) 404/688-2107. www.historicoakland.com. Free admission. Summer daily sunrise–7pm; off season daily sunrise–6pm. Visitor center Mon–Fri 9am–5pm; Sat 9am–8pm; Sun 1–5pm. Guided tours are offered Sat 10am, 2pm, and 7pm; Sun 2pm. The tour costs $10 adults, $5 children and students, $3 seniors. MARTA: King Memorial.

## A HISTORIC HOME

**Alonzo F. Herndon Home** 𝕩 *Finds* Although born into slavery in 1858, only 2 years before the Civil War, Herndon was an industrious man. By 1895 he was the richest black man in Atlanta and had founded the Atlanta Life Insurance Company, the nation's largest black-owned insurer. With his newly acquired wealth, he built this lavish mansion in the Beaux Arts neoclassical style, complete with a colonnaded entrance, and furnished it with antiques and art he'd amassed over a lifetime. The building stands at the Vine Street edge of the Morris Brown campus.

587 University Place (between Vine and Walnut sts.). (C) 404/581-9813. Free admission. Tours $5 adults; $3 students, seniors, and children. Tues–Sat 10am–4pm (tours on the hour). Closed major holidays. MARTA: Vine City.

## PARKS & GARDENS

Encompassing 21 acres of downtown Atlanta real estate, **Centennial Olympic Park** 𝕩 ((C) **404/223-4412** or 404/222-PARK), built for the 1996 Olympics, is at the junction of International Boulevard, Techwood Drive, and Baker and Marietta streets. It was designed as a "landscape quilt," and creates a green "lung" in the center of one of Atlanta's most congested neighborhoods. The energy present during the Games has long since subsided, but Atlantans still frequent the park with its outdoor amphitheater, reflecting pool, and the Olympic rings fountain. A marker notes the site of the bomb blast that claimed two lives in July 1996. Undaunted by the bombing, people were waiting in line for the park to reopen after the mishap, and that spirit still holds true today. You can stroll among the gardens or put on your bathing suit and jump into the geyser-like fountains—an activity for which they were designed. Twice daily, the fountains spurt water in synchronized patterns, arching gracefully in time to the marching tunes that were played during the 1996 Olympics. Hours of these water spectaculars vary—call the park number listed above for exact show times. Admission to the park is free; it is open from 7am to 11pm.

Another highlight is **Atlanta Botanical Garden,** at Piedmont Avenue and the Prado, in Piedmont Park (© **404/876-5859**). Sprawling across 30 acres, this garden is Atlanta's most tranquil urban retreat, embracing a 15-acre hardwood forest. A highlight is the glass-walled Dorothy Chapman Fuqua Conservatory, which opened in 1989. Admission is $12 for adults, $9 for seniors, $7 for students, and free for children 3 and under. It's open Tuesday 9am to 9pm and Wednesday to Sunday 9am to 7pm (to 6pm off season).

## 6 Especially for Kids

The Botanical Garden (see above) has added a children's garden loaded with child-friendly instructions about plants and other data.

**Zoo Atlanta** ★★ *Kids*   This absolutely delightful 40-acre zoo is an exciting and creatively run facility, with animals housed in large, open enclosures that simulate their natural habitats. The zoo gained new prestige in 1999 when it became the home of a pair of giant pandas, Lun Lun and Yang Yang, both on loan from China for the next 10 years. **Flamingo Plaza** is the first habitat you'll see upon entering the zoo. Farther on, **Masai Mara** houses rhinos, lions, and African elephants. The lushly landscaped **Ford African Rain Forest** centers on four vast gorilla habitats separated by moats. Sumatran tigers (a highly endangered species) and orangutans live in the **Asian Forest** section, an Indonesian tropical rainforest with clusters of bamboo and a waterfall. A zoo train travels through the **Children's Zoo** area, a peaceful enclave with a playground and children's petting zoo. There are shops and snack bars throughout the zoo, and tree-shaded picnic areas in Grant Park. Free animal shows in the Kroger Wildlife Theater are presented daily at 11:30am, 1:30pm, and 3:30pm May through September.

800 Cherokee Ave. (in Grant Park). © 404/624-5600. www.zooatlanta.org. Admission $17 adults, $13 seniors, $12 children 3–11, free for children 2 and under. Daily 9:30am–5:30pm. The admission booth closes an hour before zoo closing. Closed holidays. Take I-75 S. to I-20 E. Get off at the Boulevard exit and follow the signs to Grant Park. MARTA: Five Points, then bus 97. A MARTA bus labeled "Zoo Shuttle" runs from Five Points June–Sept.

**Center for Puppetry Arts** *Kids*   Don't miss this place even if you're not traveling with the kids. It offers puppet shows, workshops, and a museum containing puppets from all around the world. A video with the late Jim Henson as host provides an overview of puppetry and takes visitors around the world to meet masters of the art. The puppet shows are sophisticated and riveting, full-stage productions with elaborate scenery. Some are family oriented; others, with nighttime showings, are geared toward adults. Call ahead to find out what's on; reservations are essential.

1404 Spring St. NW (at 18th St.). © 404/873-3089 or 404/873-3391 for the box office. Museum $5 adults; $4 children 13 and under, students, and seniors. Combination ticket for the museum, show, and workshop $12 ages 2 and up. Tues–Fri 9am–5pm. Closed holidays. MARTA: Arts Center.

**Six Flags Over Georgia** *Kids*   This theme park is one of the best of its kind in the country. Set on 88 fun-filled acres, it incorporates more than 100 rides, a multitude of shows, and several restaurants. Hours and prices are subject to change, so it's a good idea to call to check.

7561 Six Flags Pkwy. © 770/739-3400. Admission $43 for 1 day, $26 seniors and children 48 in. tall and under. Admission covers all rides and all shows except for amphitheater concerts. Late May to Labor Day Sun–Fri 10am–6pm, Sat 10am–8pm; Apr to late May and Labor Day to Oct Sat–Sun only. Closed Nov–Mar. Take I-20 W. for 12 miles; it's just off the highway.

## 7 Organized Tours

**American Coach Gray Line of Atlanta,** 50 Upper Alabama (© **800/965-6665,** 404/767-0594, or 770/449-1806), offers three tours of Atlanta that will take you to most of the sites you want to see in the city. *Atlanta's Past and Present* is a tour of historical attractions, or what's left of them. You'll see Peachtree Street proper, the Woodruff Arts Center, Margaret Mitchell's house, the World of Coca-Cola, Centennial Park and other related Olympic sites, CNN, and the Cyclorama. The 3½-hour tour departs at 9am and is priced at $40 for adults, $36 for seniors, and $32 for children 6 to 12. The *All Around Atlanta* tour takes you to many of the same sites, but includes a stop at the Martin Luther King, Jr., sites, the Jimmy Carter Museum, and the Governor's Mansion. Departing at 1:30pm, this 4-hour tour costs $42 for adults, $38 for seniors, and $34 for children 6 to 12. The *Black Heritage Tour* covers "Sweet Auburn" and sites associated with the birthplace of the modern civil rights movement. You'll tour the Atlanta University Complex (Morehouse College, Spelman College, and Clark-Atlanta University) and the home of Alonzo F. Herndon, Atlanta's first black millionaire. The tour lasts 4 hours and is priced at $45 for adults, $41 for seniors, and $35 for children 6 to 12. You can combine the two tours leaving at 9am as listed, returning for a lunch break and departing again at 1:30pm as listed.

The most intriguing tours in Atlanta are those found at the **Atlanta Preservation Center,** 156 7th St. NE, Suite 3 (© **404/876-2040;** www.preserve atlanta.com). The center offers seven 1½- to 2-hour guided walking tours, each costing $10 for adults, $5 for seniors and students, free for children 4 and under. Most tours are offered only from February to November and many are specialized; call for details. For example, the *Historic Downtown Tour* surveys the city's architecture; the *Inman Park Tour* visits the city's first garden suburb; the *Sweet Auburn Tour* surveys the stomping grounds of Martin Luther King, Jr.; *Walking Miss Daisy's Druid Hills* explores the neighborhood of the film *Driving Miss Daisy.*

## 8 Outdoor Pursuits

**BIKING**    Although it may be a bit crowded, **Piedmont Park** is best for biking because it's closed to traffic. Enter the park on Piedmont Avenue between 10th and 14th streets. Bikes can be rented at **Skate Escape,** across the park at 1086 Piedmont Ave. (© **404/892-1292**). It rents single-speed bikes for $6 per hour or $25 per day, with mountain bikes going for $40 per day or $125 a week, including a helmet. A Georgia license or a major credit or charge card is required as a deposit. Skate Escape is open daily from 11am to 7pm.

**BOATING**    **Lake Lanier Islands Beach and Water Park,** 7000 Holiday Rd., Lake Lanier Islands (© **770/932-7200**), includes in its entry fee use of canoes, paddleboats, and sailboats. To reach it from Atlanta, a distance of 45 miles, take I-85 North to I-985 (exit 45); get off I-985 at exit 1 and turn left at the end of the ramp, following the signs. This family retreat is part of a larger resort complex with golf courses, homes, campgrounds, and freshwater marinas. It contains more than half a dozen water slides, a wave pool, and a tropical lagoon designed exclusively for children. Open Memorial Day to Labor Day, Sunday to Thursday from 10am to 6pm and Friday and Saturday from 10am to 7pm. Admission is $27 for adults, $17 for children and seniors 55 and over, and free for children 2 and under.

**CAMPING**    **The Family Campground,** P.O. Box 778, at Stone Mountain, GA 30086 (© **770/498-5600**), about 16 miles from Atlanta, has 400 wooded sites for RVs and tents. There are full hookups for RVs, LP gas, showers, a laundry area, a supply store, and a restaurant. There's also minigolf, swimming, boating, fishing, and other recreational activities. Rates for two campers at tent sites begin at $23, plus $2 for each additional person. Full hookup costs $30 to $45. Take I-285 to the Stone Mountain exit, then drive 7½ miles east on Ga. 78 to Stone Mountain Park.

**"CANOEING THE HOOCH"** This is one of the city's favorite outdoor adventures. At the **Chattahoochee Nature Center,** 1990 Island Ford Pkwy., in Dunwoody (© **770/992-2055**), you can take canal trips Thursday to Sunday from June to August at 6pm. The trips cost $25 per person for ages 6 and up. The sunset trip goes on a 2½-hour educational adventure led by an experienced naturalist, who will point out beavers, otters, herons, ospreys, wildflowers, and a variety of wetland plants. No prior canoeing experience is necessary, and life jackets (furnished on-site) are required. The center is open Monday to Saturday 9am to 5pm, Sunday noon to 5pm. It's closed New Year's Day, Thanksgiving, and Christmas.

**FISHING** **The Fish Hawk,** 279 Buckhead Ave. NE, between Peachtree and Piedmont roads (© **404/237-3473**), sells Georgia fishing licenses costing $24 for the season. Seasonal trout stamps are $13. After supplying you with quality tackle and other gear, it will direct you to the best places to fish along the Chattahoochee River, in the North Georgia mountains, or at Lake Lanier with its 38,000-acre reservoir. The store is open Monday to Friday from 9am to 6pm and on Saturday from 9:30am to 5pm. Other information can be supplied by the **Georgia Department of Natural Resources,** Wildlife Resources Division, 2023 U.S. 278 SE, Social Circle, GA 30025 (© **770/918-6418**).

**GOLF** The best course is Georgia's **Stone Mountain Park Golf Course,** in Stone Mountain Park (© **770/498-5690**), with its 36-hole greens designed by Robert Trent Jones. This challenging course is 16 miles east of the center of Atlanta. Greens fees are $36 to $60, including use of the cart. Open daily from 7:30am to dusk.

**JOGGING** Most joggers prefer Piedmont Park in spite of its overcrowding, although the Chattahoochee National Recreation Area is more scenic. Serious joggers should contact the **Atlanta Track Club,** 3097 Shadowlawn Ave. (© **404/231-9064**).

**SWIMMING** Dozens of Atlanta hotels have their own swimming pools. Public swimming is available at **Piedmont Park.** If you'd like to swim in climate-controlled conditions, contact **Martin Luther King, Jr., Natatorium,** 70 Boulevard Dr. (© **404/658-7330**), open Monday to Friday from 6:30am to 7:45pm and on Saturday from 9am to 4:45pm. Admission is $2 for adults, $1 for children under 17.

**TENNIS** The best courts are those at the **Bitsy Grant Tennis Center,** 2125 Northside Dr., between I-75 and Peachtree Battle Avenue (© **404/609-7193**), leased from the Atlanta Parks and Recreation Department. Offered are six outdoor clay courts plus 10 outdoor hard courts, all of which are lighted. No reservations are accepted—it's strictly first come, first play. Facilities include a pro shop, showers, and lockers. The cost is $4 per person per hour for the clay courts, or $2.50 per person per hour for the hard courts. Hours are Monday to Friday from 9am to 9pm, and Saturday and Sunday from 9am to 6pm.

## 9 Shopping

Think of Atlanta as a great shopping bazaar. There's nothing in the American Southeast to equal it. It consists of mall after endless mall—each packed with goodies.

If you're downtown and looking for a souvenir, head for **Underground Atlanta,** but if your tastes are more refined, it's the mall for you. For high fashion—and high prices too—head for **Buckhead,** 8 miles north of the center. Here the main shopping district centers around Lenox Square Mall and Phipps Plaza, and there are at least 200 specialty stores in the Greater Buckhead area. In Buckhead seek out **Bennett Street,** a 2-block strip off Peachtree on the southern periphery. A warehouse district at the time of the Civil War, the street today is loaded with galleries and boutiques, selling art, antiques, decorative accessories, whatever. At the intersection of West Paces Ferry and Peachtree roads is **Buckhead West Village,** another healthy concentration of shops, ideal for strolls.

If you'd like something a little more imaginative, go to **Virginia-Highland,** which has been referred to as "New York's SoHo a decade ago." The neighborhood, near the junction of Highland Avenue at Virginia Avenue and Ponce de Leon Avenue, offers five different art galleries, at least 30 restaurants, a scattering of artsy cafes, and endless rows of stores devoted to clothing, flea-market junk, antiques, jewelry, and everything from high to low camp.

For "New York's downtown a decade ago," meander your way to **Little Five Points,** Atlanta's resident art community. Discover eclectic items from hard-to-find books to jazz vinyl records you thought were a part of the past, plus clothes and jewelry to adorn any aspiring rock star. Its mythical center is at the junction of North and Moreland avenues, just east of downtown Atlanta.

For the antiques buff, one of the densest concentrations of such stores is near the T-junction of Peachtree Road and Broad Street, in the northern suburb of **Chamblee,** 17 miles from central Atlanta.

If you're yearning for granite countertops in your kitchen, or access to some of the most prestigious designers and antiques dealers in Atlanta, chances are good that you'll find them within the cluster of entrepreneurs at **Miami Circle.** Set in the heart of Buckhead, off Piedmont Avenue, it's a premier resource for anyone buying or building a house in any of Atlanta's affluent neighborhoods

## ANTIQUES

Atlanta is home to several permanent antiques shop clusters that sell everything from arts and crafts to old and custom furniture. The vendors who peddle here are often from around the country and only appear once or twice a year—the result is a revolving roster of hawkers whose wares are always fresh, however often you shop here. Markets are usually held on weekends, and mostly only once a month, so call ahead for details.

---

*Finds* **Post-Olympic Shopping**

**Westside** is another one of those Atlanta areas that was deep in decay until its old warehouses were rediscovered, revamped, and turned into chic little shops. It's fun to come here to browse, especially on Howell Mill Road. Don't visit on a Sunday or Monday, however, when most places are closed.

Shopping here should be like any yard, garage, or stoop sale—the early bird gets the steal. Get here first—on Thursday during set-up—for the best finds. However, for the best deals, bargain on Sunday, usually the last day of the sale. Many dealers aren't interested in taking their things back home, so you may be able to bargain them down for a deal. The best streets for permanent year-round shopping for antiques and flea-market discoveries are **Bennett Street** and **Miami Circle** at Buckhead.

**Bittersweet Antiques**   One of Atlanta's better outlets, this store is the place to go for majolica, antique English sporting goods, and English bone china, including a beautiful collection of Blue Willow patterns. ✆ **404/351-6594**. Bus: 23.

**Lakewood Antiques Market**   Held at the Lakewood Fairgrounds on the second weekend of each month, this market is by far the largest and most diverse in the area. With more than 1,500 dealer spaces, you'll find something, ranging from old reproductions to books, cookware, linens, custom furniture, pottery, and sculpture. But this only scratches the surface. Hours on the second weekend of each month are Thursday to Saturday 10am to 6pm, and Sunday 10am to 5pm. Admission to the market is $3, except on Thursday ("early buyer day"), which is $5. At the Lakewood Fairgrounds, between downtown Atlanta and the airport. Take I-75/85 S. to exit 243. Go east to the fairgrounds. ✆ **404/622-4488**. Free parking.

**Pride of Dixie Antiques Market**   Some 600 dealers set up the fourth weekend of each month to peddle their wares. You'll find everything from dealers who make their own wares to vendors who have found things you surely thought extinct—items from Grandma's attic and estate sales that can date to the 19th century. And of course, there are many antiques to choose from. Open the fourth weekend of each month, Thursday to Saturday 9am to 6pm, Friday 9am to 5pm, Saturday 9am to 6pm, and Sunday 11am to 5pm. Admission is $4; children are admitted free. At the North Atlanta Trade Center, north of Atlanta. Take I-85 North to the Indian Trail exit (about 25 min. from downtown), then follow the signs. ✆ **770/279-9853**. Free parking.

**Rust & Dust Antiques**   This is one of the larger (and more interesting) stores along Antiques Row. The owners often volunteer to pick up patrons at the Chamblee MARTA station, which lies about three-quarters of a mile away. 5486-92 Peachtree Rd., Chamblee. ✆ **770/458-1614**. MARTA: Chamblee; then bus 132 (Tilly Mill).

## ART GALLERIES

**Art Station**   Established in 1985, this well-recommended art gallery occupies the premises of what was once a garage for trolley cars. It sells works by regional and some national and international artists. 5384 Manor Dr., Stone Mountain. ✆ **770/469-1105**. Bus: 120 to Manor Dr.

## BOOKS

**Barnes & Noble**   This popular flagship of seven Atlanta locations, south of the Lenox Square Mall, has everything. When you've chosen among the wealth of books, the cafe invites you to relax with your book or newspaper. Book signings and other events are frequent. 2900 Peachtree Rd., Buckhead. ✆ **404/261-7747**. MARTA: Lenox.

**Borders**   This upper-Buckhead location affords you the opportunity to sip a caffè latte while you peruse your next book. It's one of five Borders locations, whose late hours are a hit with the working reader. 3637 Peachtree Rd. NE, Buckhead. ✆ **404/237-0707**.

**Chapter 11 Books** ⓐ   Located in the upscale residential district of Buckhead, this is the largest independently owned bookstore in the Southeast. It's the site of a staggering number of books of every imaginable description, as well as periodicals from virtually everywhere. There's also sheet and recorded music, and book signings by widely read authors. Another branch of this store is located at 1544 Piedmont Ave. (ⓒ **404/872-7986**). In the Peachtree Battle Shopping Center, 2345 Peachtree Rd. NE, Buckhead. ⓒ **404/237-7199**. MARTA: Buckhead.

## DEPARTMENT STORES

**Parisian**   This is the local branch of an apparel chain that originated in Birmingham, Alabama, decades ago. Its prices are less elevated than those at Saks or Lord & Taylor. Brand-name fashions are available for men, women, and children, as well as a large line of cosmetics. In Phipps Plaza, 3500 Peachtree Rd. NE. ⓒ **404/814-3305**. MARTA: Lenox.

## DISCOUNT SHOPPING

**Tanger Factory Outlet** 𝘝𝘢𝘭𝘶𝘦   Located 60 miles north of Atlanta, on the highway leading to Greenville, South Carolina, this mall is a targeted destination for dozens of tour buses of shoppers from as far away as Macon. A destination in its own right, it contains 115 factory outlets for well-established manufacturers from around North America. Most merchandise is discounted at an average of 40%. 111 Tanger Dr., at exit 149 (U.S. 441) off I-85 N., in Commerce. ⓒ **706/335-4537**.

## FASHION

**Andrew Men Women & Home** ⓐ   It earned its fame in Buckhead, but this tasteful outlet is now at a bigger location in midtown. A leader in Atlanta in menswear, it also carries a fashionable line of Paul Smith women's clothing. Some beautiful items for the home are also sold, including Knoll chairs. 1545 Peachtree St. ⓒ **404/607-1747**. Bus: 23.

**Mitzi & Romano**   Local designers are showcased here in a series of sexy "cocktail dresses," as we used to call them back in the '50s. Their accessories are "of-the-moment," including Herve Chapelier bags, chunky leather belts, and Kate Spade handbags. 1038 N. Highland Ave. NE. ⓒ **404/876-7228**. Bus: 16.

**Mooncake Clothing Co.**   Like its whimsical name, this clothing outlet takes us back to the nostalgic '70s for its vintage jewelry, flowing scarves, and floppy hats. This retro-style clothing only looks old: It's actually new but based on vintage designs. 1019 Virginia Ave. NE. ⓒ **404/892-8043**.

**Susan Lee**   Its specialty is women's dresses, suitable for the office, eveningwear, or cocktail hour, and no matter how hard you look, you won't find a shred of sportswear. 56 E. Andrews Dr., Buckhead. ⓒ **404/365-0693**. MARTA: Buckhead.

**Versace**   It sells more of the garments by the house of Gianni Versace, for both men and women, than many of that designer's other outlets. It's unusual in enjoying exclusivity for all of Georgia, and for maintaining under one roof every line ever produced by the award-winning house. In Phipps Plaza, 3500 Peachtree Rd. NE. ⓒ **404/814-0664**. MARTA: Lenox.

## FOOD

**Atlanta State Farmer's Market** ⓐ   The largest food outlet in the Southeast, this market covers 146 acres. About half the vendors sell wholesale only; the other half sell to the public, purveying meats, poultry, plants, flowers, fruits, vegetables, and a staggering variety of home-canned jams, pickles, and relishes.

---

**Finds  A Little Bit of Italy in Atlanta**

Southerners and Italians are a lot alike in many ways. Both have a soulful approach to eating and both cherish good, earthy food that is lovingly prepared and convivially shared with family and friends. A local chef's love of all things Italian has resulted in one of the country's hottest gourmet food lines, already touted on the Food Channel and at international food fairs: **Bella Cucina Artful Food,** handmade pestos, fresh and chunky pasta sauces, coarse-grain and honey mustards, and fruit preserves prepared with farm produce and beautifully packaged right here in Hotlanta. Now you can buy the stuff at the company's first retail store, **Bella Cucina** (493 Peachtree St.; ℭ **800/580-5674;** www.bellacucina.com), a European-style spot with antique countertops and vintage light fixtures.

---

Most vendors don't accept credit cards. Open 24 hours daily. Closed Christmas Day. 16 Forest Pkwy., Forest Park. ℭ **404/675-1782.** Take I-75 S to exit 78, a 15-min. drive south of downtown Atlanta.

**Dekalb Farmer's Market**   Strictly speaking, because all the stalls are owned by the same entrepreneur, this is not a farmer's market at all. Instead, it's one of the largest, best-stocked, and most atmospheric grocery stores in Atlanta, rustically outfitted like your fantasy version of a country fair. 3000 E. Ponce de Leon Ave., Decatur. ℭ **404/377-6400.**

## GIFTS

**The Fickle Manor**   This boutique is filled with fun gifts, art, jewelry, accessories, and designer items created by such trendy fashionistas as Jill Stuart and David & Goliath. 1402 N. Highland Ave. NE, Suite 4, Atlanta. ℭ **404/541-0960.** Bus: 16.

## JEWELRY

**Richters**   Specializing in antique jewelry, this is one of the most unusual stores in town, a compendium of Grandmother's grandest things—don't expect the baroque jewels worn by the grand duchess of Austria. The owners stress that this is not a museum, and that almost everything displayed was made during the 20th century. Pieces incorporate Edwardian, Art Deco and the "retro" styles of the 1950s. 2300 Peachtree Rd., Buckhead. ℭ **404/355-4462.** MARTA: Lenox.

## MALLS & SHOPPING CENTERS

**Lenox Square Mall**   North of Atlanta's commercial core, near the upscale district of Buckhead, this began as a small cluster of merchants in 1959, but has been expanded at least four times since then. Today, it incorporates a modern hotel (the JW Marriott), half a dozen movie theaters, two dozen restaurants, and a bewildering array of at least 200 shops. 3393 Peachtree Rd. NE, at Lenox Rd. ℭ **800/344-5222** or 404/233-6767. MARTA: Lenox.

**Phipps Plaza** ★   This is the most upscale shopping mall in Atlanta. A short drive north of downtown in Buckhead, it was enlarged in 1992. Today its two largest tenants (Lord & Taylor and Saks) function as "anchors" at the opposite ends of passageways incorporating some of the most elegant boutiques in the Southeast. There's also a food court, a handful of tony restaurants, and a movie theater with more than a dozen screens. 3500 Peachtree Rd. NE, at the Buckhead Loop. ℭ **404/262-0992.** MARTA: Lenox.

**Underground Atlanta** Sunk partly underground, on the site of Atlanta's original antebellum core, this site manages to fulfill the roles of living-history museum, nightlife venue, and shopping mall all rolled into one ongoing carnival. (For more information on Underground Atlanta, refer to "Attractions," earlier in this chapter.) Alabama St., between Peachtree St. and Central Ave. ✆ 404/523-2311. MARTA: Five Points.

## 10 Atlanta After Dark

Most hotels and motels distribute free the publications *Where, Key: This Week in Atlanta,* or *After Hours.* The Saturday edition of the *Atlanta Constitution* has a "Weekend" section to fill you in further. Should you *still* be at a loss as to how to spend an evening, take yourself to Kenny's Alley at Underground Atlanta.

## THE PERFORMING ARTS

**CLASSICAL MUSIC** The **Atlanta Symphony Orchestra** ✮✮✮, performing in the Woodruff Arts Center, 1280 Peachtree St. NE, at 15th Street (✆ **404/733-4900** or 404/733-5000 for the box office), celebrated its 50th anniversary in 1995. Under the musical directorship of Yoel Levi, it's acclaimed especially for the 200-voice Atlanta Symphony Orchestra Chorus, formerly the Robert Shaw Chorus.

The season runs from September to May, and includes the master series and the light classics series. The master series features world-acclaimed guest artists. Light classics are likely to dip into such fun shows as "Broadway's Hottest Tickets." The **Chastain Summer Concerts** ✮ are held in 7,000-acre Chastain Park Amphitheater between June and August. It's the custom to bring an elaborate picnic to the event. Artists such as the Beach Boys perform here. Holiday concerts are also performed at Christmas and other times.

Ticket prices vary but are generally $25 to $50 for the master series, $20 to $45 for the light classics series, and $22 to $45 for the Chastain Summer Concerts. To reach the Woodruff Arts Center, take MARTA.

**OPERA** The **Atlanta Opera** ✮✮, performing in the Fox Theatre, 660 Peachtree St. NE, at Ponce de Leon Avenue (✆ **404/881-2000** box office or 404/817-8700), is under the artistic direction of William Fred Scott. Founded in 1979, the opera company has gone on to win national recognition. It presents a trio of fully staged productions each summer at the Fox Theatre, plus various productions at other venues. Tickets range from $20 to $125, with seniors and students granted 50% discounts on the day of the performance if any tickets are available (tickets are generally extremely difficult to obtain). The season lasts from late May to Labor Day. Take MARTA to North Avenue.

**BALLET** The **Atlanta Ballet** ✮ performs at the historic Fox Theatre, 660 Peachtree St. NE, at Ponce de Leon Avenue (✆ **404/817-8700** box office or 404/881-2000). The Atlanta Ballet, under artistic director John McFall, is the oldest in the nation, now into its 70th year. McFall creates excitement with new sets, costumes, and choreography. Ticket prices range from $25 to $55. Take MARTA to North Avenue.

**THEATER** **7 Stages,** 1105 Euclid Ave. (✆ **404/523-7647**), in the Little Five Points district, is the leading producer of new and contemporary plays in Atlanta. It's also a venue for performances by international touring theater companies. Performances run Wednesday to Sunday in the newly renovated theater.

Tickets cost $10 to $25 for most productions, with discounts offered to seniors and students. Take MARTA to Inman Park.

**Alliance Theatre Company,** at the Woodruff Arts Center, 1280 Peachtree St. NE (© **404/733-5000**), is the largest resident professional theater troupe in the Deep South. It produces about 10 plays a year, ranging from a musical of *The Color Purple* to love stories like the *Guardsmen.* Such famous actors as Jane Alexander often appear with this group. Ticket prices range from $20 to $55. The season runs September to May, with occasional productions staged in summer. Take MARTA to the Arts Center.

## THE CLUB & MUSIC SCENE
### COMEDY CLUBS

**Punchline Comedy Club**   Some of the best touring comics in America play here in the Balconies Shopping Center and have been doing so for the past 18 years. Jerry Seinfeld has appeared here. The club is small but most tables have a good view. Shows run Wednesday to Sunday. 280 Hildebrand Dr. NE. © **404/252-5233.** Cover $10–$30, higher for big-name acts.

### JAZZ & BLUES

**Blind Willie's Live Blues Club**   This is one of the best live blues clubs in Atlanta. Opened in 1986, it has a simple interior of old brick walls and wooden floors, and is dimly lighted. Sometimes nationally known acts are booked here, and Cajun entertainment is often featured. 828 N. Highland Ave. NE. © **404/873-2583.** Cover $5–$8 Sun–Thurs, $8–$10 Fri–Sat.

**Café 290**   Jazz and blues, along with some R&B, form the background in this club, drawing a crowd that ranges in age from 30 to 50. At the back is a sports bar with televised games and pool tables. But most patrons come here for the music. Reservations are needed on Friday and Saturday. Fine dancing is also a feature here, or you can enjoy intimate, candlelit dining. The cuisine is Continental, and a specialty is hand-carved steaks. Only fresh ingredients are used, and meals cost $12 to $25. The venue is suitable for unescorted women. 290 Hildebrand Dr. NE. © **404/256-3942.** Cover $5–$10 for those not dining at the restaurant.

**Dante's Down the Hatch**   Dante's design has created the illusion of a pirate ship tied up to an old Mediterranean wharf. In the wharf section there's jazz, classical, and flamenco guitar until 8pm nightly. As for the "crew," most have been aboard for a long time, and all really make you feel cared for. Dante himself is always on hand to see that you have a good time. This is really a jazz supper club, with many intimate seating areas, the most romantic being the semi-private cabins on the lower "deck." A trio plays traditional jazz later in the evening, and classical folk guitarists perform on weekend nights. Across from the Lenox Square Mall, 3380 Peachtree Rd., Buckhead. © **404/266-1600.** Cover $7 on the ship deck, none on the wharf.

### COUNTRY & ROCK

**Dark Horse Tavern**   Opened in 1989, this Virginia-Highland tavern is a tri-level venue. The top floor is for private parties. The second level has a restaurant and bar, with the original railing used on the set of *Gone With the Wind.* The tavern is decorated with hunter-green walls and an antique brass bar and grill with saddles and bridles. The music offers everything from jazz to rockabilly and pop; rock predominates. Both Atlanta and national bands perform in the downstairs bar. 816 N. Highland Ave. NE. © **404/873-3607.** Cover $3–$10 for bands, no cover to enter.

## DANCE CLUBS

**Johnny's Hideaway**   This ballroom, frequented by everybody ages 35 to 65, is just a local tavern during the day. The Big Band sounds of the 1940s, including Glenn Miller, live on here, as do the golden sounds of 1950s rock 'n' roll, including the music of Macon-born Little Richard. This is a good place for the single visitor, either male or female. Chances are, if you're lookin' good, you'll be asked to dance. A silver ball still rotates above the dance floor in the grand old tradition. Two big-screen TVs provide further *divertissement*. 3771 Roswell Rd. ℂ 404/233-8026. Cover varies, but is imposed only for special entertainment, when there's a 2-drink minimum.

**Masquerade**   This is primarily a dance club with live dance bands. On occasion it is a center for internationally known rock groups. The three-level club is housed in what was once the Excelsior paper mill. The bar downstairs is appropriately called Purgatory, complete with exposed pipes and video games. The effect is that of a dungeon. Hell is just across the way, complete with hanging chains—an appropriate venue for Wednesday's Club Fetish nights, when patrons can live out their S&M fantasies. Loud dance music fills Hell. Heaven, with a capacity of about 1,000 patrons, is painted blue with fluffy clouds. 695 North Ave. NE. ℂ 404/577-8178. Cover $6–$40, slightly higher for national acts.

## THE BAR SCENE

**Atkin's Park**   One of the most frequented Virginia-Highland taverns, this is called "the Cheers of the neighborhood." It attracts 25- to 35-year-olds. Photographs of the city's tumultuous history decorate the walls. The patio, with a decor of brick, brass, and wood floors, is a little small for dining, but it's extremely lively on weekends. Music is country, pop, Top-40, and rock—and is it ever loud. 794 N. Highland Ave. NE. ℂ 404/876-7249.

**Eddie's Attic**   Believe it or not, the once-sleepy Decatur area is becoming a magnet on the after-dark circuit. A favorite spot here, Eddie Attic showcases up-and-coming singer-songwriters as well as big names—the Indigo Girls got their start here. The attic is divided into a trio of sections, including the main bar for music lovers; the Billy Pilgrim of tomorrow may be appearing on the small stage here. Rowdier areas are the pool room and the covered patio. A pub menu is available for those with the munchies. 515B N. Mcdonough St., Decatur, next to the old courthouse on the square. ℂ 404/377-4976. Cover $4–$10. MARTA: Decatur.

**Halo Lounge**   Stylishly remodeled in the basement of the Biltmore Hotel, this bar is one of the most fashionable and beautiful in the city. Unusual for Atlanta, it draws a mixture of both gay and straight patrons (Thurs is the most popular night for the gay crowd). Candy-colored lawn furniture is spread around the interior. You'll see some of the city's sexiest people at the back-lit onyx bar, ordering one of the 17 single-malt scotches. Some of the coolest DJs in town spin tunes here. 817 W. Peachtree St. NW. ℂ 440/962-7333. MARTA: Midtown.

**Manuel's Tavern**   This is the hangout for local politicos. Jimmy Carter shows up every now and then, ordering a Moosehead, whereas his Secret Service boys order Atlanta's favorite hometown drink, Coca-Cola. Since 1956 the tavern has been serving its burgers, steaks, and hot dogs to the local gang. Dress is always casual. 602 N. Highland Ave. NE. ℂ 404/525-3447.

**Mo's & Joe's**   Offering a cool refuge from the blazing Atlanta heat, this is one of the most nostalgia-packed bars in Atlanta. Set at the street corner that gave Virginia-Highland its name, it has thrived here since 1947, amid a collection of sports memorabilia that grows every year. Lots of liquor has been swilled here since its debut (it sells more Pabst Blue Ribbon than any other bar in the South-east), and it's so genuinely friendly and indulgent that you might quickly adopt it as your local hangout. Menu items include a roster of predictable bar platters, including burgers and barbecued chicken wings. 1033 N. Highland Ave. at the corner of Virginia Ave. ✆ 404/873-6090.

**Park 75 Lounge** ★★ Sheathed in a zillion dollars' worth of russet-colored marble and richly figured mahogany, this is the most appealing and opulent hotel bar in Atlanta. A magnet for a clientele that includes lots of well-heeled residents of nearby homes and condominiums, it offers a staggering array of sin-gle-malt scotches, rare wines by the glass, vintage ports, and two-fisted cocktails that are poured tableside by a hip, well-trained, and endlessly indulgent staff. Light platters and desserts are served as well, in a setting that evokes the best aspects of a discreet but chic private club in London. In the Four Seasons Hotel Atlanta, 75 14th St. (between Peachtree and W. Peachtree sts.). ✆ 404/881-9898.

## GAY & LESBIAN BARS

**The Armory** ★ This is the largest gay dance club in town, with what some fans claim is Atlanta's finest sound system. A cavernous enclave with a 25-year history, it sports five different rooms (one of which is devoted to drag shows), an outdoor patio, hundreds of mirrors, and a "Robo-scan" lighting system that turns night into quasi-psychedelic day. 836 Juniper St. NE. ✆ 404/881-9280. Cover $5 Fri–Sat.

**Bulldog & Co.** Named after the canine pet of the entrepreneur who founded the place in 1978, it's a gay-lifestyle staple for men ages 30 and over who, while not addicted to leather, don't flinch at it, either. Inside, you'll find five or six bars, depending on the season, and a crowd that runs from the Marlboro Man to look-alikes for Denzel Washington and Billy Dee Williams. In fact, Bulldogs has been called the most harmonious and gregarious racially mixed bar in the South, with lots of successful dialogues and pairings between black and white men who enjoy one another's company. 893 Peachtree St. NE. ✆ 404/872-3025. Cover $2 for nonmembers.

**The Heretic** Come here for hot music, a big dance floor, and the close proxim-ity of hundreds of buff, well-muscled, and glistening men and men/boys fresh from the gym and/or the most recent circuit party. Most of the clients are under 35, and hail from virtually everywhere on the North American mainland. Time spent here will really convince you that Atlanta's populace comes from far, far beyond the bor-ders of Georgia. Depending on the night of your arrival, there might be a high per-centage of leather and uniforms, even a bit of latex, especially every Wednesday and Sunday after 10pm. 2069 Cheshire Bridge Rd. ✆ 404/325-3061. Cover $3 Fri–Sat after 11pm.

**Hoedowns** It's cited as the most fun and most charming gay bar in Atlanta. Here cowboys are dancing with cowboys, and the look is long-legged and lean and evokes home on the range within a very urban and very hip setting. There's virtually no attitude among the crowds of steer-busters who hang out here. Tight jeans, Stetsons, and boots are the preferred dress code, and no one will mind if you opt for chaps and spurs, too. 931 Monroe Dr. ✆ 404/876-0001.

**My Sister's Room** This lesbian club is in Decatur, about 4 miles east of mid-town. Its appealing setting is an old stable from the 1890s, with a landscaped garden and marble-floored terrace. Sandwiches and simple platters are available every day from 11am to 1am, priced from $4.95 to $11; wine costs from $3.50 to $5.50 a glass. The main attraction is the bar, where women from all walks of life gather for conversation. Well-behaved men who happen to wander in are welcome, or at least are tolerated. 222 E. Howard Ave. ✆ 404/370-1990. MARTA: Decatur.

# 17

# Athens, the Antebellum Trail & Augusta

If you looked for antebellum Georgia around Atlanta, you were in the right church but the wrong pew. The state's pre–Civil War moonlight-and-magnolias romance lives on, and you'll find it some 60 to 100 miles east of Atlanta in charming old towns with patriotic names like Madison and Milledgeville, two classic antebellum towns that Sherman didn't burn. And although the cities of central Georgia that lie along the Antebellum Trail are cut off from the mountains or the seashore,

they are at the doorstep of some of the state's most mammoth lakes.

This area also encompasses two of the most famous cities of Georgia, Athens and Augusta. Athens, called "The Classic City," is the home of the University of Georgia, and lies in a setting beside the Oconee River. Many of its restored and still occupied antebellum houses make it a worthwhile stopover. Augusta, founded in 1736, is today famed as the headquarters of the Masters Golf Tournament the first full week in April.

## 1 Athens ⟨★

85 miles NW of Augusta; 58 miles E of Atlanta

Just below the foothills of the Blue Ridge Mountains, near the confluence of the North and Middle Oconee rivers, lies the city of Athens amid the rolling red-clay hills of North Georgia.

Athens's fame grew because of the University of Georgia (www.uga.edu/visctr), which covers 605 acres and includes 313 buildings in the center. The university was incorporated in 1785, making it America's first state-chartered college. Abraham Baldwin, one of Georgia's four signers of the U.S. Constitution, was named president. Today, the University of Georgia is ranked among the nation's top research institutions, and boasts America's 19th-largest library and many nationally recognized programs of study, including pharmacy, business, and journalism. More than 28,000 students attend the university.

In the last 2 decades, Athens has gained national attention for its music scene as well. This was where R.E.M., the Indigo Girls, and the B-52s got their start. They occasionally return to Athens to play local clubs, but their presence is felt philanthropically through donations to local homeless shelters and AIDS organizations. The town continues to have a booming music scene; for the latest music news and concert information, see "Athens After Dark," below.

## ESSENTIALS

**GETTING THERE** From Atlanta, take I-85 northwest to Highway 316, which leads the rest of the way to Athens. From Augusta, take I-20 West to Atlanta, cutting northwest on Highway 78 into Athens via Washington.

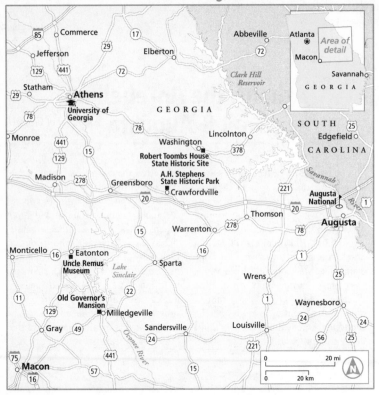

US Airways (© **800/428-4322** or 706/549-5783; www.usairways.com) offers flights only between Athens and Charlotte, North Carolina. Planes land at **Athens–Ben Epps Airport** (© **706/613-3420**).

**VISITOR INFORMATION** **Athens Welcome Center,** 280 E. Dougherty St. (© **706/353-1820;** www.visitathensga.com), is open from 10am to 5pm Monday to Saturday and from 2 to 5pm on Sunday.

**SPECIAL EVENTS** The best time to visit is during the **Historic Homes Tour,** the last weekend in April. Sponsored by the Athens-Clarke Heritage Foundation, this is one of the most attended events in East Georgia. For information, call © **706/353-1801.**

## SEEING THE SIGHTS

Athens begins Georgia's antebellum trail and showcases several buildings of note, many centered around the University of Georgia.

**Taylor-Grady House,** 634 Prince Ave. (© **706/549-8688**), a Greek Revival home constructed in the 1840s by Gen. Robert Taylor, planter and cotton merchant, is open year-round. Filled with period furniture, it has 13 columns said to symbolize the original 13 states. Henry W. Grady, a native of Athens, lived here from 1865 to 1868. As managing editor of the *Atlanta Constitution,* he became a spokesperson for the New South. Admission is $3. Hours are Monday to Thursday from 9am to 5pm; closed 1 to 2pm.

Athens's **Double Barreled Cannon** is the only one of its kind in the world, and is among the most unusual relics preserved from the Civil War. It was designed by John Gilleland and built at a local foundry in 1863. The concept was to load the cannon with two balls connected by a chain several feet in length. When fired, the balls and chain would whirl out, bola-style, and cut down the unfortunate enemy soldiers caught in the path of this murderous missile. It stands on the City Hall lawn at College and Hancock avenues.

**"The Tree That Owns Itself,"** at Dearing and Finley streets, is another Athens landmark. William H. Jackson, a professor at the University of Georgia, owned the land on which a large oak stood. He took such delight in the shade of the tree that he willed the tree 8 feet of land surrounding its trunk. The original tree blew down in a windstorm in 1942. The local garden club planted a sapling on the land in 1946, grown from one of the acorns from the original. Locals refer to the tree as "the world's most unusual heir and property owner."

The main campus of the **University of Georgia** ✮ extends 2 miles south from "The Arch" at College Avenue and Broad Street. For information, call ℂ **706/542-0842** or visit www.uga.edu/visctr. The current campus was established in 1801. John Milledge, late governor of the state, purchased and gave the board of trustees the chosen tract of 633 acres on the banks of the Oconee River. The view from the hill on which the 1832 Chapel now stands reminded Milledge of the Acropolis in Athens, and the hill was named after its Greek forebear, the classical center of learning. The school produced its first graduating class in 1804. Later funds were raised for the first permanent structure on campus, Old College (1806), which still stands today.

**The State Botanical Garden of Georgia** ✮, 2450 S. Milledge Ave. (ℂ **706/542-1244;** www.uga.edu/botgarden), encompassing 313 acres, is a "living laboratory" in teaching and research open to the public. Its three-story conservatory features a display of tropical and semitropical plants. Along the garden's 5 miles of nature trails are diverse ecosystems, with many plants labeled. There are nearly a dozen specialty gardens. The garden lies a mile from U.S. 441, about 3 miles from the university campus. Admission is free; it's open daily from 8am to sunset. A visitor center and the conservatory are open Tuesday to Saturday from 9am to 4:30pm and on Sunday from 11:30am to 4:30pm. Grounds open daily April to September 8am to 8pm, October to March 8am to 6pm.

The **Georgia Museum of Art,** 90 Carlton St. (ℂ **706/542-4662;** www.uga.edu/gamuseum), is the official state art museum, offering an extensive collection of American paintings, prints, and drawings in a new 52,000-square-foot facility. It is open Tuesday, Thursday, Friday, and Saturday from 10am to 5pm, Wednesday from 10am to 9pm, and Sunday from 1 to 5pm. Closed Monday. Admission is free.

**Founders Memorial Garden and Houses,** 325 S. Lumpkin St. on the University of Georgia campus (ℂ **706/542-4776;** www.uga.edu/gardenclub/founder.html), became the first garden club in the United States, founded in 1891 by 12 Athens women. Set on 2½ acres, it offers varying landscapes and the seasonal foliage of a Southern garden. Plantings range from the native to the exotic, and the gardens are a particular delight in spring when the azaleas burst into bloom. The boxwood garden evokes the formality of bygone ages, and the camellia walk is notable. Admission is free, and the garden is open during daylight hours.

## OUTDOOR PURSUITS

**Sandy Creek Nature Center,** half a mile north of the Athens bypass, off U.S. 441, offers some 200 acres of woodland and marshland, with a live animal exhibit. It has many nature trails for hikers, and on-site is a cabin nearly 2 centuries old. For more information, call ✆ **706/613-3615** or visit www.sandy creeknaturecenter.com.

Visitors can enjoy **Sandy Creek Park** (✆ **706/613-3631;** www.sandycreek park.com), north on U.S. 441 (signposted). It offers a beach, fishing, playgrounds for children, softball, volleyball, and shelters for picnics. Paddleboats and canoes can be rented. April to September, hours are Tuesday to Sunday 7am to 10pm. Off-season hours are Tuesday to Sunday 7am to 7pm.

Golf can be played at the **Green Hills Country Club** (✆ **706/548-6032**), an 18-hole, par-72 course at 4080 Barnett-Shoals Rd. Greens fees are $13 to $34, and hours are daily 7:15am to dusk.

## WHERE TO STAY

In addition to the listings below, there's a **Holiday Inn** at 197 E. Broad St. (✆ **800/ TO-ATHENS** or 706/549-4433; www.hi-athens.com).

**Magnolia Terrace**    In the Cobbham historic district, close to the center of town, this large 1912 house is one of the best B&Bs in the area. Each tastefully furnished guest room comes with a private bathroom with period claw-foot tubs and modern showers or whirlpools. It's a hospitable place, warm and gracious.

277 Hill St., Athens, GA 30601. ✆ **706/548-3860**. Fax 706/546-8040. www.bbonline.com/ga/magnoliaterrace. 8 units. $85–$150 double. Rates include continental breakfast on weekdays. MC, V. **Amenities:** Breakfast room; 2 lounges. *In room:* A/C, TV, dataport.

**Nicholson House** ★ *(Finds)*    On 34 tranquil acres of rolling hills, this property, run by Celeste and Harry Neeley, is a riot of magnolias and azaleas in the spring. Its history goes back to 1779, when land was granted to William Few, a signer of the U.S. Constitution. Now restored, the antebellum Georgian house has been decorated with museum-quality antiques from the early 19th century and offers eight large, elegant, and comfortable guest rooms. Each room has a private bathroom, central climate control, and a telephone. A big breakfast features fresh fruit and bread and a hearty entrée like caramel-apple French toast. Children under 17 are not welcome at this B&B. Smoking is only permitted outside the home.

6295 Jefferson Rd. (5 miles north of the UGA campus), Athens, GA 30607. ✆ **706/353-2200**. Fax 706/ 353-7799. www.bbonline.com/ga/nicholson. 8 units. $119–$149 double. Rates include full breakfast. DISC, MC, V. **Amenities:** Breakfast room; lounge. *In room:* A/C, TV, hair dryer, ceiling fan.

**Rivendell** ★★    Although it was only built in 1989, this inn contains many architectural features that make you think it's much older. Set on the Oconee River on 11 acres of forested private land, it's the finest inn in the area. It contains lofty beamed ceilings, two fireplaces crafted from large stones, antiques collected from around the world, and big windows opening onto views of the surrounding countryside. Each unit contains a well-kept bathroom with a tub/shower. There are walking paths for woodland strolls, with many nice places to stop for picnicking. Complimentary tea and sherry are provided in the afternoon. No smoking.

3581 S. Barnett Shoals Rd. (10 miles southeast of Athens), Watkinsville, GA 30677. ✆ **706/769-4522**. Fax 706/ 769-4393. www.negia.net/~rivendell. 4 units. $75–$90 double. Rates include full breakfast. MC, V. Drive 8 miles south on U.S. 441, then 5 miles west on Barnett Shoals Rd. No children under 11. **Amenities:** Breakfast room; lounge. *In room:* A/C.

## WHERE TO DINE

**East West Bistro** FUSION    This place, which opened in 1995 on the main street in Athens, is all the rage. Upstairs, dining is more formal, in a classically styled room where the fare of Northern Italy is sometimes prepared with zest and flavor, though the other dishes are uneven at best. Depending on the night, many dishes merit a rave, whereas others, such as shrimp and mussels tossed with spaghetti in a mild red-curry cream sauce, don't make it. Try fresh grilled yellowfin tuna with a parsley caper butter or chicken breast breaded with shaved ginger and orange instead. Downstairs is the largest selection of tapas in Athens, including carpaccio and a Thai ratatouille crepe. Main dishes range from jerk chicken to salmon in rice paper.

351 E. Broad St. © **706/546-9378**. Reservations recommended. Upstairs main courses $15–$22. Downstairs sandwiches and pizzas $6–$8, main courses $9–$13. AE, DISC, MC, V. Sun–Thurs 11am–10pm; Fri–Sat 11am–11pm.

**Five & Ten** ★★ SOUTHERN/CONTINENTAL   For the most imaginative food offered by any restaurant reviewed in this chapter, partake of the viands featured at Hugh Acheson's place. He calls his own food "contemporary American with inspirations from Italy and France." What he says it's *not* is fusion. A self-trained chef, Acheson has risen to the top of the list among the chefs of Athens. The location of his bright, contemporary restaurant is Five Points, 1 mile south of the University of Georgia. It has an enclosed patio for alfresco dining, plus a long metallic bar with wooden accents. We take delight in his specialty, Frogmore stew, a modern version of a Low Country "boil" with shrimp, sausage, potatoes, corn, and other vegetables. He calls it "a Southern version of bouillabaisse." Almost any dish you order at Five & Ten (so-called because the building used to be a five-and-dime store) is likely to be good. We've enjoyed the pork tenderloin with roasted pepper, asparagus, and potatoes, and especially the red grouper served with a scallion broth, braised endive, and leek-flecked mashed potatoes. The desserts are the best in town and include a delightful blueberry cinnamon tart with cinnamon ice cream and warm maple syrup.

1653 S. Lumpkin St. © **706/546-7300**. Reservations required. Main courses $18–$27. AE, DISC, MC, V. Daily 5:30–10pm; Sun brunch 10:30am–2:30pm.

**Harry Bissett's New Orleans Cafe & Oyster Bar** ★ CAJUN/SEAFOOD At the gates to the University of Georgia, this is one of the enduring favorites of locals, both students and faculty. Up front is a bar with tables, although a more formal dining room is found in the rear. This building used to be a bank, and the tin ceiling is still intact. A selection of meat dishes—certified Angus only—includes "carpetbagger steak," which is really filet mignon topped with fried oysters. Cajun dishes include crawfish tails, Louisiana oysters, and blackened fresh catch of the day seasoned liberally and seared in a black-iron skillet. You might also try grilled andouille sausage and Gulf shrimp tossed with pasta Alfredo. Dishes are generally reliable, some zesty and full of flavor.

279 E. Broad St. © **706/353-7065**. Reservations recommended. Main courses $13–$26. AE, DC, DISC, MC, V. Tues–Sun 11:30am–3pm; Mon–Sun 5:30–11pm.

**Last Resort Grill** MODERN SOUTHERN   This is the most artsy haunt in town, attracting a mostly young college crowd. Although its days as a center for avant-garde music are over, it's still a place to find out what's happening in town. We prefer the booths in the bar area, although others like the courtyard with its open end protected by ornate grillwork. In chilly weather, a gas heater blasts away. The chefs really try hard, and many of their dishes are among the best in town, but it's a hit-or-miss affair. Check out the blackboard specialties, or try your luck and sample grilled salmon with Charlestonian grits, chicken stuffed with cheese and covered with a honey-praline sauce, or chipotle pork chops grilled and marinated.

174–184 W. Clayton St. ℭ **706/549-0810**. Reservations not accepted. Main courses $7.95–$23. AE, MC, V. Daily 11am–3pm; Sun–Thurs 5–10pm; Fri–Sat 5–11pm.

## ATHENS AFTER DARK

To find out who's playing and what's on, pick up *Flagpole,* Athens's arts, entertainment, and events weekly, free at many shops, restaurants, bars, and clubs; or go online to **www.athensmusic.net** or **www.rockathens.com** for the latest band information. Another good barometer of what's happening is the UGA student newspaper, the *Red and Black.* Remember that this is a college town, so the nightlife scene is much hotter during the school year. Most of the music clubs and bars present nightly live bands September through June only, shrinking their offerings to just the weekends in the summer.

Make a pilgrimage to the famous **40 Watt Club,** 285 W. Washington St. (ℭ **706/549-7871;** www.40watt.com), the little joint that launched the B-52s and R.E.M. Although you can still hear up-and-coming local bands, these days the 40 Watt is more geared toward national bands, such as Luscious Jackson or the Lemonheads. They also run a late-night disco several times a week, as does the **Georgia Theatre,** 215 Lumpkin St., at the corner of Clayton Street (ℭ **706/ 549-9918;** www.georgiatheatre.com). A former movie theater, it gives local college-rock bands (along with a smattering of blues and Southern rock) the chance to jam long into the night. Oh, and that skinny guy standing in the corner may just be Michael Stipe.

**Boneshakers,** 433 E. Hancock Ave. (ℭ **706/543-1555**), has recorded techno and retro dance music (mostly disco and '80s). Doors open at 9pm and they stop serving drinks at 2am, but the dancing goes on much longer. This is also the gay-friendliest joint in town, and you can show up in anything from jeans and a T-shirt to drag.

Our favorite bar in town by far, however, is the **Globe,** 199 N. Lumpkin St. at Clayton Street (ℭ **706/353-4721**). The place seems more like a bar in New York's Greenwich Village than a watering hole in Athens. In the mix are students, an occasional filmmaker, and a cross-cultural selection of anyone from hip latter-day rebels to necktie-toting salesmen in town for a fling. It's like an English pub, with the largest selection of exotic beers in Athens—more than 150 brands. It also has a collection of 50 kinds of single-malt whiskies that would gladden the heart of any Scotsman. Try Laphroaig or Macallan. There's also wine, port, and sherry, served by the glass, and nine boutique bourbons. Oh, and that skinny guy reading alone at one of the tables? It just may be the ubiquitous Michael Stipe.

## 2 Madison ⟨★⟩

52 miles E of Atlanta; 73 miles W of Augusta; 21 miles N of Eatonton

Madison, off I-20, an hour's drive east from Atlanta, was once populated by wealthy merchants and cotton planters who erected houses that were fine examples of Federal and Greek Revival architecture. Antebellum travelers called it "the wealthiest and most aristocratic village between Charleston and New Orleans." Late in 1864, with Atlanta in flames, Gen. William T. Sherman's Union juggernaut reached Madison's outskirts. Happily for us, they were met by former U.S. senator Joshua Hill, a secession opponent who'd known Sherman in Washington. Old ties prevailed, and the town was spared.

Today, thousands of visitors come to see the oak-lined streets, historic homes, parks, gardens, churches, galleries, and antiques shops. The historic district encompasses most of the town and was recognized by the Department of the Interior as one of the finest such districts in the South.

## ESSENTIALS

**The Madison Chamber of Commerce,** P.O. Box 826, 115 E. Jefferson St. (© **706/342-4454;** www.madisonga.org), has information about the area. It's open Monday to Friday 8:30am to 5pm, Saturday 10am to 5pm, and Sunday 1 to 4pm.

## SEEING THE SIGHTS

Stop first at the **Madison-Morgan Cultural Center,** 434 S. Main St., U.S. 441 (© **706/342-4743**). The redbrick schoolhouse (ca. 1895) features a history museum on the Piedmont region of Georgia, an 1895 classroom museum, art galleries with changing exhibits, and an auditorium for presentations. Programs range from Shakespeare to chamber orchestras to gospel singing. Hours are Tuesday to Saturday 10am to 5pm, Sunday 2 to 5pm. Adults pay $3, children $2.

Pick up a self-guided walking-tour map and other information at the center and stroll past the majestic Greek Revival, Federal, Georgian, neoclassical, and Victorian homes lining Main Street, Academy Street, Old Post Road, and the courthouse square. You'll find plenty of places to buy antiques and handcrafts.

You can relax outdoors at **Hard Labor Creek State Park** (© **706/557-3001** or golf course 706/557-3006), near Madison. Leave town via I-20 West and take exit 49 into Rutledge, then drive 2 miles on Fairplay Road to the park. *Golf* magazine rates the park's 18-hole course as one of the finest public courses in America. You can also swim at a sand beach, fish for bass and catfish, and hike the 5,000 wooded acres. The park has 51 campsites with electricity, water, restrooms, and showers for $20 to $22 a night. There's also 20 fully furnished two-bedroom cottages at $70 (Sun–Thurs) and $100 (Fri–Sat) per night. A Michael J. Fox movie, *Poison Ivy*, was filmed here in the mid-1980s.

## WHERE TO STAY

**The Brady Inn** *Finds* These restored Victorian cottages lie in the center of the historic district (they were once two private homes linked by a walkway). Rooms are tastefully furnished, often with antiques, and the breakfast is most generous. All units also have well-kept bathrooms with tub/shower combinations. You get old-fashioned hospitality here, along with a good night's sleep.

250 N. Second St., Madison, GA 30650. © 706/342-4400. www.bradyinn.com. 8 units. $85 double; $150 suite. Rates include full breakfast. AE, DISC, MC, V. **Amenities:** Breakfast room; lounge. *In room:* A/C.

**Burnett Place** *Finds* This B&B (ca. 1830) is equally as good as its closest rival, the Brady Inn. It is a large two-story Federal home, one of the few in the area spared from Sherman's notorious march to the sea. It has been authentically maintained and is beautifully kept up. In the heart of the historic district of Madison, it rents only three attractively furnished and most comfortable guest rooms, all with good-size private bathrooms with both tubs and showers. We prefer the sky-lit bathroom in the Joshua Hill room, named for a Southern U.S. senator opposed to the war and a friend of General Sherman. Hill may have saved the town from being burned to the ground. Rooms are also named for both former president James Madison and Dolley Madison. Expect four-poster pine beds, longleaf pine floors, or late Victorian oak pieces.

317 Old Post Rd., 30650 Madison, GA. $(C)$ 706/342-4034. www.burnettplace.com. 3 units. $85 double. Rates include full breakfast. MC, V. **Amenities:** Breakfast room; sitting room; nonsmoking rooms. *In room:* A/C, TV, coffeemaker, fireplace (in some).

## WHERE TO DINE

**Old Colonial Restaurant** *Value* SOUTHERN   This is the busiest restaurant in Madison. The site it occupies, close to the town's main square, comprises an early-18th-century tavern that later functioned as a bank and a storefront. The staff manages to be friendly, helpful, and restrained all at the same time. Don't expect grand cuisine: Breakfast is served by the staff at your table; lunches and dinners are summer-camp cafeteria style, with copious portions of Southern vegetables and meat. The atmosphere's just as old-fashioned as the food. If you like candied yams, pork chops, and collard greens, come on in. Corn bread is served with everything.

108 E. Washington St. $(C)$ 706/342-2211. Full breakfasts $3.50–$5.75; main lunch and dinner courses $2.50–$3.95. DISC, MC, V. Mon–Sat 5:30am–8:30pm.

## 3 Eatonton

21 miles S of Madison; 22 miles N of Milledgeville; 47 miles NE of Macon; 75 miles SE of Atlanta

Home of Br'er Rabbit and the Uncle Remus Tales, this town, filled with antebellum architecture, is a sleepy old place of tree-lined streets and historic homes. Eatonton is not only the original home of Joel Chandler Harris, who created the Uncle Remus Tales, but also of Alice Walker, author and Pulitzer Prize winner for *The Color Purple.*

## ESSENTIALS

To get here from Madison, take Highway 441 South. The **Eatonton-Putnam Chamber of Commerce,** 105 Washington St. ($(C)$ **706/485-7701;** www.eatonton. com), dispenses information Monday to Friday 8:30am to 5pm.

## SEEING THE SIGHTS

**Uncle Remus Museum,** Highway 441 South ($(C)$ **706/485-6856**), lies in Turner Park, 3 blocks south of the courthouse. It has a kid-pleasing collection of memorabilia about Br'er Rabbit, Br'er Fox, and Harris's other storybook critters. The log cabin is the combination of two former slave cabins. In each window are scenes of a Southern plantation during the antebellum days. The museum is open Monday to Saturday 10am to 5pm (except 1 hr. for lunch), Sunday 1 to 5pm. Admission is 50¢. Closed Tuesday, September through May.

   **Bronson House,** 114 N. Madison Ave. ($(C)$ **706/485-6442**), is the home of the Eatonton/Putnam Historical Society. Constructed in 1822 by Thomas T. Napier, it was purchased in 1852 by Andrew Reid, who was the first patron of Joel Chandler Harris. The author lived with his mother in a tiny cottage in back of the mansion. Several rooms of the Greek Revival mansion have been restored, displaying local memorabilia. The house can be visited on Saturday and Sunday from 1 to 5pm, for a $2 admission charge.

   Two sights in the environs of Eatonton merit a visit, including **Lake Oconee,** east of Ga. 16 and north on Ga. 44. This 19,000-acre lake with 375 miles of shoreline was created when the Oconee River was impounded. You can camp, swim at the beach, fish, and boat (there's a marina). Because of a laissez-faire attitude from Georgia Power about shoreline restrictions, Lake Oconee has also been the site of golf community development. For more information, call $(C)$ **706/ 485-8704.**

**Rock Eagle Effigy** lies 7 miles north on U.S. 441, in the Rock Eagle 4-H Center. Shaped like a gigantic prone bird, the 8-foot-high mound of milky quartz has its head turned to the east with outspread wings. It measures more than 100 feet from wingtip to wingtip, the body rising about 10 feet above the ground. The monument may be 5,000 years old and was used, or so it's believed, by Native Americans as a part of religious rites. The monument may be viewed from an observation tower. For more information, call © **706/484-2800.**

## WHERE TO STAY

**The Ezell House Bed and Breakfast** 🌟 *Finds*   Opening for business in the summer of 2004, this is now the most desirable place to stay in town. Owner Shelagh Fagan purchased the Victorian house—formerly known as "The Pink Lady"—in 1997 and restored it. The house dates from 1887, when it was constructed by a local banker and plantation owner, Evan B. Ezell. Shelagh has decorated the midsize-to-spacious rooms with Victoriana. Each unit is exceedingly comfortable, with a well-maintained private bathroom with tub and shower. During restoration, a dark-green paint was discovered from the past, and that color was used in the repainting. A formal sit-down breakfast, and a good one at that, is offered every morning. Children 10 and older are welcome. All rooms are nonsmoking.

300 N. Madison Ave., Eatontown, GA 31204. © 706/923-0031. www.theezellhouse.com. 4 units. $65–$80. Rates include breakfast. No credit cards. **Amenities:** Breakfast room; afternoon wine and cheese. *In room:* A/C, fireplace, bathrobes, no phone.

## 4 Milledgeville

20 miles S of Eatonville; 30 miles NE of Macon; 90 miles SE of Atlanta

This town ranks along with Madison and Washington in historic sights. Locals will tell you that this is, in fact, "the antebellum capital" of Georgia. Carved from Native American territories in 1803, Milledgeville was the capital of Georgia until 1868, when the seat was moved to Atlanta. Like Madison, Milledgeville was miraculously spared by General Sherman, and today remains a treasure trove of antebellum architecture.

### ESSENTIALS

From Eatonton, follow U.S. 441 South into Milledgeville. The Welcome Center of the **Milledgeville-Baldwin County Convention & Visitors Bureau** is at 200 W. Hancock St. (© **478/452-4687;** www.milledgevillecvb.com). It's open Monday to Friday from 8:30am to 5pm and Saturday from 10am to 4pm.

### SEEING THE SIGHTS

**Old Governors Mansion,** 120 S. Clark St. (© **478/445-4545;** www.gcsu.edu/ mansion), a pink marble Palladian beauty, has been exquisitely restored and refurbished as the home of the president of Georgia College. You may tour the antiques-rich public rooms. The mansion was the home of Georgia's governors from 1839 to 1868. This National Historic Landmark house is an excellent example of Greek Revival architecture. Guided tours begin on the hour from Tuesday to Saturday 10am to 4pm and on Sunday 2 to 4pm. Admission is $5 for adults, $1 for children 12 to 17, and free for children 11 and under.

The mansion is on the campus of **Georgia College & State University,** 231 W. Hancock St. (© **478/454-2771**), a former women's college that dates from 1889 and today is home to some 5,500 students. The college occupies four 20-acre plots. You may want to stroll about the campus.

At the college's **Ina Dillard Russell Library** on Clark Street (✆ **478/ 445-0988**), you can visit the Flannery O'Connor Room, but check its status before coming here. It is currently closed for renovations. O'Connor, distinguished author of *The Violent Bear It Away* and *A Good Man Is Hard to Find,* lived in Milledgeville and received a bachelor of arts degree from Georgia College. You can also visit **Memory Hill Cemetery** (www.friendsofcems.org/ memoryhill), the oldest burial ground in the city, where the author is buried along with state legislators, Wild West outlaws, slaves, soldiers, and patriots.

O'Connor fans also visit **Andalusia—Flannery O'Connor's Farm** ⭐, Columbia Street/Highway 441 (✆ **478/454-4029;** www.andalusiafarm.org), outside of town. It is free and open to the public Tuesday and Saturday 10am to 4pm. The author lived at her family's farm from 1951 until her death from lupus in 1964. Andalusia was the source of many of the settings and characters of the O'Connor stories. While here, she completed two novels and two short-story collections. The location of the memorabilia-filled farmhouse is 4 miles northwest of Milledgeville on the west side of U.S. Highway 441. Visitors can see the 544-acre estate, complete with the main house, main barn, even smaller barns, three tenants' houses, and water tower, plus a man-made pond. The white, two-story, plantation-style main house (ca. 1850) is listed on the National Register of Historic Places.

The easiest way to see the town is to take a **Historic Guided Trolley Tour.** The 2-hour tour explores the major sights in the town, including the old governor's mansion and the former state capitol building (ca. 1807). Tours depart from the Visitors Bureau (see above) Monday to Friday at 10am, Saturday at 2pm. Cost of the tour is $10 for adults, $5 for children 6 to 16, and free for children 6 and under.

Nearby, you can visit **Lake Sinclair,** north on U.S. 441, a 15,330-acre lake with 417 miles of shoreline. It was created when the Oconee River was impounded, and is today a venue for fishing and boating. There's a marina, and camping is possible. Phone ✆ **706/485-8704** for more information.

## WHERE TO STAY

**Antebellum Inn** ⭐   Innkeepers Debbie and Hill Thompson welcome you to their well-restored 1890 Greek Revival home in the heart of the Antebellum Trail in the center of Milledgeville, just a block from the Georgia College & State University campus. The Old Governor's Mansion is just down the street. The inn has two old-fashioned parlors and five spacious guest rooms. Individually furnished guest rooms have beds covered with tasteful linens and down comforters. Several of the well-kept bathrooms have antique claw-foot tubs. The town's best B&B breakfast is served in an elegant dining room. If you'd like to recapture the feel of Georgia's former capital, find a rocking chair on the wraparound porch. The grounds are beautifully landscaped.

200 N. Columbia St., Milledgeville, GA 31061. ✆ 478/453-3993 or 478/454-5400. www.antebelluminn.com. 5 units. $79–$119 double. AE, DISC, MC, V. **Amenities:** Breakfast room; parlor; outdoor pool. *In room:* A/C, TV, dataport, hair dryer.

**Milledgeville Days Inn** *Value*   This modest motel is preferred over its major competitor, the 169-room Holiday Inn out on U.S. 441 North. Days Inn is a two-story inn filled with Southern comfort. Its guest rooms are strictly functional, but they're well maintained, with good beds and spacious bathtubs with tub/shower combinations.

2551 N. Columbia St., Milledgeville, GA 31061. ✆ 800/541-3268 or 478/453-8471. Fax 478/453-8482. www.daysinn.com. 91 units. $60 double; $100–$150 suite. Rates include continental breakfast. Children under 18 stay free in parent's room. AE, DC, DISC, MC, V. Pets allowed with $10 nonrefundable fee. **Amenities:** Breakfast room; lounge; outdoor pool; 2 tennis courts; basketball court; fitness center; Jacuzzi; sauna; limited room service; nonsmoking rooms; rooms for those w/limited mobility. *In room:* A/C, TV, fridge, hair dryer, microwave.

## WHERE TO DINE

**The Brick** PASTAS/PIZZAS/SANDWICHES   This local favorite was initially opened in 1993 with the object of becoming a bar and pizza joint. But what a difference a few years makes! The bar was successful and the restaurant even more so—so much that it had to move its location two doors down the street. Owners Frank Pendergast and Mitch Brooks have made the "new" Brick one of the more exciting dining experiences in a town not known for its dining. Exposed brick, an oak-and-walnut bar, and heart pine floors adorn a dining area that is not crowded and is conducive to family dining. The lunch and dinner menus offer a wide choice of pastas, calzones, sandwiches, and authentic brick-oven pizzas, with styles ranging from the all-meat "Cannibal" to the all-veggie "Environmentally Correct." This restaurant is a popular choice with the Milledgeville business community and with college students when parents are visiting. For a taste of the Milledgeville nightlife, the sibling bar, the **Tavern** (née Brick), 120 W. Hancock St., serves burgers and alcoholic drinks from 4pm to 2am.

136 W. Hancock St. ✆ 478/452-0089. Main courses $5.75–$7.95; pizzas $7.75–$18. AE, DC, DISC, MC, V. Mon–Sat 11am–11pm.

**Cafe South** SOUTHERN   About a quarter-mile south of the center in the hamlet of Hardwick, the cafe is in an old brick-fronted building, with an old-time decor. The format is cafeteria-style—but waitresses are on hand to bring drinks and difficult-to-carry items directly to your table. Serving hours are limited, but the place is an introduction to virtually everyone in town. Everybody seems to appreciate the simple Southern menu of creamed corn, turnip greens, fried chicken, roast beef, catfish, and—when available—tuna dumplings. A main platter comes with a choice of three vegetables. This is one authentic Southern meal to truly take in and enjoy.

132 Hardwick St., Hardwick. ✆ 478/452-3164. Lunch $6.15. AE, MC, V. Sun–Fri 11am–2pm.

## 5 Augusta ★

139 miles E of Atlanta; 122 miles N of Savannah

Home to one of the world's most prestigious men's professional golf tournaments, the Masters, Augusta is a Southern city of charm and grace. Lying along the banks of the Savannah River, it stands about halfway between Savannah and Atlanta, but bears little resemblance to either one.

Augusta is the state's second-oldest city, dating from 1736, when it was marked off for settlement by Gen. James E. Oglethorpe, founder of Georgia. Surprisingly, long before Florida became fashionable, it was a major winter resort, attracting the Yankee wealthy seeking to escape their own bitter winters. In time, tycoons such as John D. Rockefeller, who could afford to go anywhere, selected Augusta for extended winter stays on "The Hill," also known as Summerville. Except at the time of the Masters Tournament, Augusta doesn't attract vacationers like it did in its heyday, but that's beginning to change.

## ESSENTIALS

**GETTING THERE**   Augusta lies off I-20, the main route from Atlanta, on the west bank of the Savannah River.

**Bush Field Airport** lies just a 15-minute drive from the center of Augusta. Fifty commercial flights wing their way into the airport daily. Connections are possible via **Delta** (𝒞 **800/221-1212;** www.delta.com) or **US Airways** (𝒞 **800/ 428-4322;** www.usair.com) from both Atlanta and Charlotte.

**VISITOR INFORMATION**    The **Augusta Metropolitan Convention & Visitors Bureau,** 1450 Greene St. (𝒞 **800/726-0243** or 706/823-6600; www. augustaga.org), is open Monday to Friday 8:30am to 5pm.

**SPECIAL EVENTS**    It seems that half the world—at least the golfing half— focuses on Augusta the first full week in April for the nationally televised **Masters Golf Tournament** ✦✦✦, a tradition since 1934 and now the most prestigious golf tournament in the world. Hotel space is at a premium then, and prices for rooms soar to whatever the market will bear. Call 𝒞 **706/667-6000** or go to www.master.org for more information. Tickets are impossible to get, but you might be able to book a multiday package that includes tickets through **Best Golf Tours** (𝒞 **888/817-4653**). They're not cheap, but they're your best shot, and you probably have a better chance of being struck by lightning at that—unless, of course, you're willing to part with several thousand dollars.

## SEEING THE SIGHTS

The major attraction is **Riverwalk** ✦, the tree-lined paths at the edge of the Savannah River, between 5th and 10th streets, which are resplendent with greenery and seasonal flowers. Riverwalk includes 5 blocks of unique development, including a full-service, 67-slip marina. It boasts a 1,700-seat amphitheater that plays host to various performances throughout the year. It's perfect for a moonlit stroll, or an afternoon spent picnicking, shopping, and enjoying one of the city's many festivals. You can see the river from both bi-level and tri-level platforms, and historical markers along the way give you an insight into the city's history.

Although it's not a grand attraction, you can visit the **Boyhood Home of Woodrow Wilson,** 419 7th St. (𝒞 **706/722-9828;** www.wilsonboyhoodhome. org), which has been restored and opened to the public. The future president lived here from 1860 to 1870 during the years his father served as pastor of the First Presbyterian Church. Admission is $5 for adults and $3 for children, and hours are Tuesday to Saturday 10am to 5pm.

**Confederate Powderworks,** along the Augusta Canal on Goodrich Street, is a 168-foot-tall chimney, all that remains of the second-largest powder factory in the world, which operated between 1862 and 1865. It is the only permanent structure begun and completed by the Confederate government, and it once consisted of 26 buildings.

**Ezekiel Harris House**    Constructed by Ezekiel Harris, a leading Augusta tobacco merchant, this 1797 house re-creates the heyday of the late 18th century, when locals grew rich trading in tobacco. The planter's house is filled with period furnishings.

1840 Broad St. 𝒞 **706/724-0436.** Admission $2 adults, $1 seniors, 50¢ children under 18. Sat 10am–4pm; Mon–Fri 1–4pm.

**Gertrude Herbert Institute of Art**    This Federal-style house was built in 1818 for Augusta mayor Nicholas Ware at the cost of $40,000—a tidy sum back then. It now serves as an art institute, a center not only for art classes but for changing exhibitions open to the public.

506 Telfair St. 𝒞 **706/722-5495.** Free admission; donations accepted. Mon–Fri 8:30am–5pm.

**Meadow Garden**   This Sand Hill cottage (ca. 1791) was the home of George Walton, youngest original signer of the Declaration of Independence and twice Georgia governor. It is the oldest documented house in Augusta and the first historic preservation project in the state.

1320 Independence Dr. (near the intersection of 13th St. and Walton Way). © **706/724-4174.** Admission $4 adults, $3.50 seniors, $1 children. Mon–Fri 10am–4pm.

**Morris Museum of Art**   This museum features period galleries that display more than 2,000 works spanning 1790 to the present. The museum, which hosts changing exhibitions quarterly, also has a museum shop and a visitor-orientation gallery. Admission is free on Sunday.

Riverwalk and Tenth St. © **706/724-7501.** www.themorris.org. Admission $3 adults, $2 students and seniors, free for children 5 and under. Tues–Sat 10am–5:30pm; Sun 12:30–5:30pm.

**St. Paul's Episcopal Church**   The fourth structure on the site, the St. Paul's you see today, was built after a fire destroyed much of the downtown area in 1915. The first St. Paul's was constructed in 1750 as part of the site of the Fort Augusta constructed by the British in 1739. The Celtic Cross, used to designate the site, still stands. The cemetery next to the church was used during Colonial days up through 1819, and many notable Georgians are buried here.

605 Reynolds St. © **706/724-2485.** www.stpauls.org. Free admission. Tours by appointment only. Mon–Fri 9am–5pm; Sat 10am–noon. Regular worship service every Sun.

**TOURS**   The best way to introduce yourself to Augusta is to contact **Historic Augusta Tours** (© 706/724-4067), which conducts tours every Saturday from 10:30am to noon. The tour leaves from the Cotton Exchange Building at 32 Eighth St. on the Riverwalk. Reservations are required by noon the Friday before. Cost is $10 for adults, $5 for children.

## GOLF & OTHER OUTDOOR PURSUITS

Golf is king in Augusta, and though the famous tournament course at Augusta National isn't open to the public, we recommend **Goshen Plantation,** 1601 Goshen House Club Dr. (© **706/793-1168**), one of the most beautiful and challenging courses in the CSRA. Ellis Maples designed the course, which offers the largest green in Georgia. It has well-bunkered greens, demanding par 3s, 4s, and 5s, and requires you to use every club in your bag. It also has a fully stocked pro shop and an "On the Green" restaurant. Greens fees are $15 to $37, and hours are daily 7:30am to dusk.

**Augusta Canal** (© 706/823-0440; www.augustacanal.com), stretching across two counties from the center of Augusta to Evans-to-Locks Road in Columbia County, is the setting for an array of activities, including bicycling, fishing, canoeing, hiking, running, walks, and picnicking. Visit **Savannah Rapids Park** (© 706/868-3349) for easy access to the canal. For canoe rentals, call © 706/738-8500.

**Thurmond Lake,** north on Washington Road (about 20 miles from the center of Augusta), offers 1,200 miles of shoreline bordering Georgia and South Carolina. One of the largest inland bodies of water in the South, it has some of the best outdoor sports around, including swimming, sailing, water-skiing, fishing, hunting, or just plain sunbathing. The lake is surrounded by a 70,000-acre park. A Visitor and Information Center is located at the South Carolina end of the dam off Highway 221.

## WHERE TO STAY

If you can't get a room in town for the Masters, try for lodgings in Aiken, South Carolina (see chapter 14).

**The Azalea Inn** ★★ *Finds*   Just 3 blocks from the Riverwalk, on Greene Street, this Victorian inn dates back to 1895. Renovations in 1998 made it all the more desirable. David Tremaine and Andrew Harney, your innkeepers, go out of their way to ensure that your stay in Augusta is exactly what you expected. Twenty-one suites, most with 11-foot ceilings, are furnished with Victorian pieces; each unit's Jacuzzis and other present-day luxuries tastefully mesh with the past. All bathrooms have shower units as well. Several suites offer kitchenettes and glass sun porches. Packages are available for 4 nights year-round. The inn's location in Old Augusta offers a wealth of antiques shopping, historic sites, and the food and drink of the Riverwalk.

314–316 Greene St., Augusta, GA 30901. © 706/724-3454. Fax 706/724-3454. www.theazaleainn.com. 21 units. $109–$179 double. Rates include breakfast. AE, MC, V. **Amenities:** Breakfast room; lounge; Jacuzzi; sauna. *In room:* A/C, TV, hair dryer, iron/ironing board.

**The Partridge Inn** ★   During Augusta's heyday as a winter resort—roughly from 1889 to 1930—The Partridge Inn was known as the city's grande dame. The resort's fame faded when Henry Flagler extended the railroads to Florida and the Great Depression hit, and by the early 1980s the hotel was slated for demolition. Fortunately, it was saved, and in 1988, after a major restoration, it reopened.

Today's accommodations come in an almost dizzying array of combinations, from standard double to queen- and king-size beds, and some rooms offer views or kitchenettes. Furnishings are traditional, with quilted spreads, lots of ruffles, and matching draperies. All units have well-kept bathrooms with tub/shower combinations.

2110 Walton Way, Augusta, GA 30904. © 800/476-6888 or 706/737-8888. Fax 706/731-0826. www.partridge inn.com. 156 units. $79–$247 double; $89–$287 studio; $99–$397 suite. Rates include Southern buffet breakfast. AE, DC, DISC, MC, V. **Amenities:** 2 restaurants; bar; lounge; outdoor pool; fitness center; limited room service; babysitting; laundry service/dry cleaning; nonsmoking rooms; rooms for those w/limited mobility. *In room:* A/C, TV, dataport, kitchenette (in some), coffeemaker, hair dryer, iron/ironing board.

**Radisson Riverfront Hotel** ★   This chain hotel enjoys the best location in town; its well-furnished but standard rooms open onto the Savannah River and historic Riverwalk. Each unit has a well-kept bathroom with a tub/shower combination. Readers Michael Barnas and Phyllis Feingold-Barnas likened the spacious second-floor concourse of the hotel to a trip back to the "Castle of Versailles, with its sweeping marbled floor length, chandelier after chandelier ceiling, and profusion of flower-filled oversize vases." Augustino's serves only fair Italian dishes, and an adjoining lounge offers big-screen sports. The staff will direct guests to 19 premium golf courses in the area, challenges to both novices and pros alike.

2 Tenth St., Augusta, GA 30901. © 800/333-3333 or 706/722-8900. Fax 706/823-6513. www.radisson.com. 237 units. $118–$169 double; $189–$209 suite. Extra person $10. AE, DC, MC, V. **Amenities:** Restaurant; bar; 2 pools (1 indoor); fitness center; Jacuzzi; sauna; limited room service; massage; laundry service/dry cleaning; nonsmoking rooms; rooms for those w/limited mobility. *In room:* A/C, TV, kitchenette (in some), coffeemaker, hair dryer, iron/ironing board, safe.

**Rosemary Hall and Lookaway Halls** ★★   For the ultimate statement in luxury inns in the Greater Augusta area, you have to cross the border into North Augusta (which is actually in South Carolina, about a 10-min. drive from Hwy.

20). Rosemary Hall and Lookaway Hall are actually two properties, all with white columns and wraparound porches evoking Tara. Both former private homes were built in the early 1900s by the Jackson brothers, founders of North Augusta, and are located across the street from each other. These restored inns represent antebellum living at its best, recapturing the charm of an era gone with the wind. Each guest room has an individual character, with period antiques, fine artwork, and custom-made carpets. Several have their own Jacuzzis or private verandas. All have beautifully kept bathrooms with tub/shower combinations. Beautifully furnished public rooms are found on the ground floor of each inn. The entrance hall of Rosemary Hall has a stunning wood staircase, worthy of the one on which Scarlett killed that mean Yankee soldier. Breakfast is served on antique china. If you're considering this inn for Masters accommodations, think again: That week has already been booked for the next several years.

804 Carolina Ave., N. Augusta, SC 29841. © **803/278-6222.** Fax 803/278-4877. 23 units. $125–$250 double. Rates include breakfast and afternoon hors d'oeuvres. AE, DC, DISC, MC, V. **Amenities:** Breakfast room; lounge; laundry service/dry cleaning; nonsmoking rooms; rooms for those w/limited mobility. *In room:* A/C, TV, hair dryer.

## WHERE TO DINE

**Bambu** ★ FRENCH/ASIAN/FUSION/SUSHI   The modern world of dining has arrived at the time-honored landmark, the Partridge Inn. With its full bar, sushi bar, and elegant dining, this is one of the better choices for eating in Augusta. The setting is lush, with cascading water and tropical plants. Platters are a delight both to the palate and the eye, with rice bread delivered to your table on Chinese parasols. In addition to sushi and sashimi, the chef's specialties include a mustard-and-wasabi-crusted filet mignon served with a plum wine and shallot-laced reduction sauce. The tuna hand rolls come three ways: spicy tuna, tuna cucumber, and tuna avocado. The signature dessert is Bambrûlée, a trio of crème brûlée, fresh fruit, and coconut ginger sorbet. In addition, the Partridge Inn also shelters the **P. I. Bar & Grill,** an American cafe and steakhouse.

2110 Walton Way. © **706/737-8888.** Reservations recommended. Main courses $15–$26. AE, DC, DISC, MC, V. Tues–Thurs 6–10pm; Fri–Sat 6–11pm.

**French Market Grille** ★ LOUISIANA   In a faux French-market atmosphere located in a shopping center, this restaurant is often hailed as the best in Augusta. It's locally owned and operated by Chuck and Gail Baldwin. Po' boys are featured at lunch and might be stuffed with everything from spicy chicken to soft-shell crab. Recommended is the chef's crab chop a la Charles (crabmeat bound by white sauce, with the added flavors of green onions and other seasonings). Two other guests helped us devour our scallops maison, and the etouffée (choice of either shrimp or crawfish) was suitably spicy, Cajun style. The desserts, including pecan praline pie and New Orleans bread pudding, have been voted "best desserts in Augusta" by *Augusta Magazine* several years in a row.

425 Highland Ave. © **706/737-4865.** Reservations not accepted. Main courses $14–$24. AE, DISC, DC, MC, V. Mon–Thurs 11am–10pm; Fri–Sat 11am–11pm.

**La Maison on Telfair** ★ FRENCH/AMERICAN   In a Southern Revival home, this elegant choice for dining is perhaps the finest in Augusta in terms of cuisine, ambience, and service. Its special feature is a wine bar and tapas lounge, recognized by *Wine Spectator* for its excellence. This is the finest choice in Augusta for a romantic dinner. Appetizers are often typical, though excellent: French appetizers such as snails in garlic butter, and delightful surprises such as smoked ostrich carpaccio with arugula and vine-ripened tomatoes misted with truffle oil. Chef Heinz's signature dishes, and we endorse them with enthusiasm, include rack of lamb with fresh herbs and an apricot teriyaki glaze, and Dover sole sautéed in butter with grapes and almonds. The five-course light dinner is the best value in the city.

404 Telfair St. ℂ **706/722-4805.** Reservations required. Main courses $18–$28; 5-course dinner $25. AE, DC, DISC, MC, V. Mon–Sat 5–10pm.

**Le Café du Teau** FRENCH/CAJUN   In spite of its hard-to-find location, this place remains one of the most enduring and popular spots with discriminating diners in the Augusta area. As a very young man, Donn du Teau of Atlanta established this restaurant in what had once been a TV repair shop. The moldy-looking outside is unimpressive, but inside you'll find a long, corridor-like room filled with paddlewheel fans, watercolors, hanging plants, and even Gulf Coast driftwood paneling. A cocktail lounge is in back.

The waiters in white aprons are quite a hip bunch. Pay close attention to the daily specials, as they are often better than the regular offerings. Boudin blanc is a homemade seafood sausage, and you can order such Continental favorites as escargot shiitake ragout. A dinner guest's choice of jambalaya was a mistake (it needed far more spicing). Still, in spite of the uneven fare, some dishes are superb. Renovations to the restaurant added a new bar and kitchen, and the menu has an array of gourmet pizzas cooked on Augusta's only wood-fired stove. One diner said that their smoky taste "will spoil you."

1855 Central Ave. ℂ **706/733-3505.** Reservations recommended. Main courses $15–$24; gourmet pizzas $6.95–$9.95. AE, DISC, DC, MC, V. Tues–Thurs 5:30–10pm; Fri–Sun 5:30–10:30pm.

**Old McDonald Fish Camp, Inc.** ⭐ *Value* SEAFOOD   When locals from Augusta hanker for catfish and hush puppies and all those good things, they head right to this old fish camp. It's known for serving the best catfish in the area, although you can also order ocean perch, fried shrimp, scallops, crabs, oysters, and even fried gator. One feature is a Low Country boil, with shrimp, sausage, potatoes, corn, and coleslaw. The Thursday-night special is an all-you-can-eat fry of catfish, fish filet, and perch filet—a real bargain. It's a family favorite, even if the fish is often overcooked—that's the way the locals like it.

335 Currytown Rd., N. Augusta. ℂ **803/279-3305.** Main courses $7.95–$14. MC, V. Thurs 5–9pm; Fri 5–9:30pm; Sat 4–9:30pm. Take I-20 E. to exit 1 in South Carolina, turn left, and go 5 miles.

# 18

# North Georgia

Within 70 to 120 miles of Atlanta, North Georgia may be one of the Deep South's best-kept travel secrets. City dwellers can hike through national forests, scale Georgia's highest peak, canoe and swim in mountain lakes, and return home at dusk, or stay over in a comfortable lodging or campground.

Tennessee, Alabama, and Georgia meet in the "TAG Corner" on the Cumberland Plateau. "TAG" is a terrain of sheer-walled canyons, limestone caves, boulder-littered fields, streaming waterfalls, and mesa-topped mountains that has been compared to a landscape in the West. The first European visitors claimed they had rediscovered Eden when they first came upon the area. It's amazing how little-known these Georgia mountains are—as one visitor said, "I've heard of the Blue Ridge Mountains, but I had no idea they came into Georgia. In fact, I didn't realize Georgia had mountains at all." The mountain chain, occupying some two-thirds of

North Georgia, consists of the Blue Ridge Mountains frontal range to the east and the Cohutta Mountains to the west.

Northwest Georgia is also filled with remnants of the Civil War (called "The War of Northern Aggression" in these parts) and with artifacts left over from ancient aboriginal civilizations. Etowah Mounds, off I-75 outside Cartersville, is one of the most significant archaeological sites in North America, offering a view of life as lived some 4 centuries ago. You'll also be introduced to traditional Appalachian culture, Georgia style. Arts and crafts, including pottery making, basket weaving, and quilting, are still practiced in the region. And at all local festivals and even on the front porch on a Saturday night, the sound of bluegrass music still fills the air.

Dahlonega (later in this chapter) and its environs are the premier "gateways" to the area. The best parks to visit include Amicalola Falls, Unicoi, and Vogel.

## 1 The Great Outdoors in North Georgia

As one naturalist said of North Georgia, "Scenic touring is about any road you want to travel." Of course, some trails and scenic highways are more memorable than others. Just north of Helen and within easy reach of Blairsville, the **Richard Russell Scenic Highway** (Ga. 348) is one we always travel, with mountain vistas up to 3,644 feet.

If you don't like to hike, you can see much of the panorama of North Georgia from your car by taking Ga. 52, the highway between Chatsworth and Ellijay (the latter called the apple capital of the state). This road offers scenic previews of **Fort Mountain State Park,** about 7 miles east of Chatsworth (© **706/695-2621**) and the **Cohutta Wilderness.**

Much of North Georgia is encompassed by **Chattahoochee National Forest** ★★, a vast region of some 750,000 acres, including the Georgia Blue Ridge Mountains to the north. Elevations range from 1,000 to some 5,000 feet. It's a vacationer's paradise, with some two dozen picnic areas, the same number of campsites, six swimming beaches, and 10 protected wilderness areas. The forest takes in such natural attractions as **Anna Ruby Falls,** 6 miles north of Alpine Helen; the **Appalachian National Scenic Trail; Vogel State Park** south of Blairsville; and **Amicalola Falls State Park,** with the state's highest waterfall, outside Dahlonega.

For information about exploring this vast forest, write to the **U.S. Forest Service,** 1755 Cleveland Hwy., Gainesville, GA 30501 (© **770/297-3000**).

In contrast, the **Cohutta Wilderness** alone covers 37,000 acres or some 60 square miles spilling over into Tennessee. When an area called Hemp Top was added in 1986, the region became the third-largest mountain wilderness in the East. Fishers claim that the Cohuttas have the best trout streams in the south. Hikers and anglers alike are seen along the banks of the Conasauga River and Jack's River. Walking trails follow the old logging roads of the 1920s. Hikers and backpackers should take 17-mile Jack's River Trail, which virtually crosses the wilderness going northwest to southeast.

For detailed information about this vast wilderness, call © **706/695-6736** and speak to the U.S. Forest Service in advance of your trip. Always check road conditions before venturing into such wild terrain—roads may be closed in bad weather.

Of course, the most famous trail in the area—in fact, America's most fabled scenic trail—is the "A.T.," or the **Appalachian Trail** ★★★, beginning at Georgia's Springer Mountain and crossing 14 states until it finally comes to an end some 2,100 exhausting miles later in Katahdin, Maine. Hikers usually leave Georgia in April, arriving in Maine in September or even as late as October, when they earn the right to call themselves a "2,000 Miler." The trail runs across Georgia for 79 miles before reaching the border of North Carolina.

Among our favorite state parks in Georgia is **Cloudland Canyon State Park.** The terrain is rugged, but the park has modern outdoor amenities, such as a swimming pool and a tennis court. The 2,120-acre scenic park lies near the village of Rising Fawn, on the west side of Lookout Mountain. Gulch Creek, a deep gorge, slices through the park, with elevations ranging from 800 to 1,800 feet. It has some 75 camping sites and lots of ideal spots for a picnic.

The park lies on Ga. 136, 8 miles east of Trenton and I-59, and 18 miles northwest of La Fayette. It's open daily 7am to 10pm year-round. For additional information, contact **Cloudland Canyon State Park,** Department of Natural Resources, 122 Cloudland Canyon Rd., Rising Fawn, GA 30738 (© **706/657-4050;** fax 706/398-9748).

**Lookout Mountain** sprawls more than 100 miles, ignoring state lines and spilling into Tennessee, Alabama, and Georgia. The northern end overlooks the city of Chattanooga at the border of Tennessee and Georgia. Two towns—both named Lookout Mountain—lie on each side of the border. Lookout Mountain is accessible by I-24 from Chattanooga heading toward Georgia.

## 2 Chickamauga & Chattanooga National Military Park ★★

110 miles N of Atlanta

The country's oldest (1890) and biggest military park stretches across an 8,000-acre site 9 miles south of Chattanooga on U.S. 27. Ranking along with Gettysburg and Vicksburg, the national historic shrine consists of four different parks: Chickamauga, Point Park, Missionary Ridge, and Orchard Knob.

The park is a memorial to both Union and Confederate troops who fought one of the bloodiest battles of the Civil War here in 1862. The casualties were staggering, the battle called "a massive slaughterhouse." It was fought for control of not only Chattanooga but also Atlanta.

On September 19 and 20, a Confederate force of 66,000 men met by accident a Union force of 58,000. The 2-day battle left 36,000 casualties. It marked the greatest success of Confederate armies in the west, although the advantage was not seized.

Some 1,500 historical markers, tablets, artillery pieces, and monuments mark the movement of troops. At the **visitor center** (© **706/866-9241**), on the northern entrance to the battlefield, self-guided audiotape tours are available. A slide show recounts the battle hour by hour. For those who tire of all the carnage, some 80 miles of hiking trails are cut through the valley. The center is open daily from 8am to 5:45pm Memorial Day to Labor Day, shutting down for the rest of the year at 4:45pm. Admission is free to the park, but a multimedia program costs $3 for adults 17 or older, $1.50 for seniors, free for children 16 and under. To reach the park, exit I-75 at Ga. 2 and go west for 6 miles to Hwy. 27 (exit 141), at which point you head south to the park, which is a mile from the town of Fort Oglethorpe.

## WHERE TO STAY

Accommodations are available in Chattanooga, or else you can stay at the **Gordon-Lee Mansion** (see below) in Chickamauga, 2½ miles south of the battlefield.

**Gordon-Lee Mansion** ✦   This restored historic inn lies 2½ miles south of the park. Dating from 1840, it was the headquarters of Union Gen. William Rosecrans during September 1863. One double offers a four-poster bed, the others queen-size canopied beds. All rooms are furnished with antebellum-style antiques. The lone cabin has one king-size bed and two twin beds, gas and wood fireplaces, a refrigerator, a microwave, and two well-kept bathrooms. This is a dry county—no alcohol is sold, so if you want a drink, you must bring your own. There's no restaurant on the premises; most guests drive 15 miles north to Chattanooga for dinner. Children over 12 are welcome.

217 Cove Rd. (off Hwy. 27), Chickamauga, GA 30707. © **800/487-4728** or 706/375-4728. Fax 706/375-9499. www.gordon-leemansion.com. 5 units, 1 cabin. $75–$125 double; $100–$125 log cabin. Rates include full breakfast (not for cabin). AE, MC, V. Closed Dec–Jan. **Amenities:** Breakfast room; lounge; nonsmoking rooms. *In room:* A/C, TV, no phone.

## 3 Adairsville

60 miles N of Atlanta

An hour's drive north of Atlanta will deliver you to northwest Georgia's most romantic retreat. The Barnsley Gardens, which lay in ruins for half a century, are now restored and part of a luxury resort funded by Prince Hubertus Fugger of Babenhausen, Germany.

Before 1999, it was easy to skip Adairsville, until the German prince and his princess opened the sprawling 1,300-acre resort. It's nestled in the foothills of the Blue Ridge Mountains, and has a history filled with love, loss, and myth. Even if you're not a guest, you can dine at one of its restaurants, including a Bavarian beer garden, or else explore its 19th-century ruins, small museum, and 160-year-old formal gardens. Many Chattanooga residents also drive here, since the city lies only 52 miles west. For a full review of the resort, see below.

## ESSENTIALS

**GETTING THERE**  **By Car**  Take I-75 north from Atlanta for 60 miles, getting off at exit 306. Go west on Route 140 for 10 miles, following the signs to Barnsley Gardens.

## EXPLORING THE GARDENS

**Barnsley Gardens** ★★ are the only Andrew Jackson Downing–inspired gardens in the South. They were based on his designs. Downing, a renowned 19th-century architect, was the original designer of the White House grounds and the Washington Mall. He believed in fitting man-made elements naturally into their surroundings. The gardens themselves were planned in the late 19th century by Godfrey Barnsley, a cotton baron who built an Italian-style manor house and English gardens for his wife, Julia, in the foothills of the Blue Ridge Mountains.

The estate boasts the largest private collection of private conifers in the Southeast, with 88 species of pines and 16 acres of grounds where guests can wander. A museum in the manor's kitchen wing contains artifacts from the Civil War and memorabilia tracing the history of the ill-fated Barnsley family.

Nonguests are invited to explore the museum and garden daily. Hours for the museum are 9am to 5:30pm, for the garden 6am to 6pm. Admission is $10 for adults, $8 for seniors, and $5 for children.

**Barnsley Inn & Golf Resort** ★★★  Prince Fugger stated his goal at the very beginning to his architects. He wanted his future guests to feel as if they were visiting the country estate of a friend. He has succeeded admirably. The authentic-looking, 19th-century pedestrian village is in keeping with Godfrey Barnsley's original vision for the land. All 45 of the buildings on the estate, including 33 guest cottages, were based on architect Andrew Jackson Downing's drawings and principles.

Guests can stay in one-, two-, or four-bedroom cottages, each with a private porch with rocking chairs. Suites come with wood-burning fireplaces, heart-of-pine floors, 12-foot ceilings, and custom-made king-size sleigh or poster beds dressed in Egyptian linens. Bathrooms have period-inspired ball-and-claw cast-iron tubs with separate shower units.

Accommodations are decorated in a warm, homelike style with antiques, plus original prints by Princess Alexandra, once a noted botanical photographer for *National Geographic.* Dining is among the finest in the area, with chefs providing innovative interpretations of Southern classics. The German royals have also installed a Bavarian beer garden, where sausages are grilled over a bonfire pit. Barnsley also boasts one of the most spectacular spas in the state.

To add to the accolades, *Golf News* has proclaimed the **Barnsley Golf Course** the "Best Resort Course" in Georgia. The new par-72, 18-hole course was designed by Jim Fazio, with one of the most difficult par 3s in the country. A classical course, evocative of those designed at the turn of the 20th century, the Barnsley course offers a challenge to all levels of golfers. Fazio blended the course into its natural environment, following the principles of the 19th-century architect, Andrew Jackson Downing. The course stretches 5,450 yards (the red tees) to 7,200 yards (the pro tees) through the foothills of the Blue Ridge Mountains. Greens and cart fees are seasonal, varying from $55 to $100 per golfer.

597 Barnsley Gardens Rd., Adairsville, GA 30103. ⓒ **877/773-2447** or 770/773-7480. Fax 770/773-1779. www.barnsleyinn.com. 70 units. $385–$1,670 suite. Rates include breakfast. AE, DC, MC, V. **Amenities:** 3 restaurants; bar; outdoor pool; 2 clay tennis courts; fitness center; spa; fly-fishing; 4.5 miles of walking trails; children's programs; picnic lunches; clay shooting; horseback riding; business services; nonsmoking rooms; rooms for those w/limited mobility. *In room:* A/C, TV, dataport, minibar, coffeemaker, fireplace.

## Will the Real Scarlett O'Hara Please Stand Up?

Julia, the daughter of cotton baron Godfrey Barnsley, was named after her mother and is said to be the inspiration for Margaret Mitchell's tempestuous character Scarlett O'Hara in *Gone With the Wind*. Detailing her Reconstruction struggles to hold onto the Barnsley estate in a letter to a friend, Julia wrote, "With God as my witness, I will never go hungry again." Of course, that became one of the most famous lines in the film.

Mitchell had read a book called *St. Elmo*, which was written about Julia in the 1860s, and in the process of researching *Gone With the Wind*, the Atlanta novelist interviewed Julia's daughter, Addie. It turns out that Julia might not have gone hungry, but her family fortune didn't improve. In 1906, a tornado blew the roof off the manor, forcing the family to live in the kitchen wing. The final blow came in 1935, when Preston Saylor, great-grandson of Godfrey and a successful prizefighter, shot and killed his brother in the kitchen wing of the manor during a dispute over control of the property. He was convicted of murder and sent to prison. Preston had fought Jack Dempsey and other top boxers in the 1920s and 1930s.

Descendants of Godfrey and Julia continued to live on the estate until it was auctioned off in 1942. The manor fell into a state of disrepair, and it was in this ruinous state that Prince Hubertus Fugger of Bavaria and his wife, Princess Alexandra, found it when they decided to buy it in 1988.

## 4 Tate & Jasper

60 miles N of Atlanta

As Georgia towns go, even some state residents draw a blank at the mention of either of these towns that virtually adjoin one another. Tate, in fact, doesn't appear on most maps. Nevertheless, Tate and Jasper contain two of the most famous inns in the northern part of the state. Either town makes an ideal base for exploring the northwest corridor of Georgia, as all the major scenic attractions can easily be reached on day trips.

Jasper is one of the marble centers of Georgia—in fact, marble quarried here was used in the Lincoln Memorial and the Capitol in Washington, D.C. A Marble Festival in early October highlights tours of the quarries, with country music, food, and arts and crafts.

## ESSENTIALS

**GETTING THERE    By Car**    From Atlanta, take I-75 North to I-575, which turns into Highway 515 going north. Continue along Highway 515 North until you reach Highway 53 North, which will take you into the center of Jasper.

**VISITOR INFORMATION**    Contact the **Pickens Chamber of Commerce,** 500 Stegall Rd., Jasper, GA 30143 (© **706/692-5600**). The chamber distributes information about the Tate/Jasper area. Hours are Monday to Friday from 9am to 5pm.

## WHERE TO STAY & DINE

**Tate House** ⭐ *Finds*    This is the most unusual B&B in northeast Georgia. In 1926, the owner of the Georgia Marble Company, Colonel Sam Tate, ordered a palatial mansion to be built entirely out of a rare vein of rose-colored ("Etonah pink") marble. He died a decade later, but tales of his brutality circulated through the area. After the death of his last surviving relative, the empty house was subject to widespread vandalism and was supposedly haunted by legions of ghosts.

Today, innkeepers maintain an inn of aristocratic, European grandeur, richly furnished with taste and style. You can opt for one of the quintet of suites in the main house, which feature well-kept bathrooms with tub/shower combinations. Less formal, and more woodsy, are the nine log-sided cabins that lie in a grassy meadow a 5-minute walk from the main house. Cabins carry the advantage of having large Jacuzzis and overhead sleeping lofts.

The only major drawback to this property is its lack of a restaurant; clients must drive to inconvenient locations (especially on Sun) for a meal.

Hwy. 53 (P.O. Box 33), Tate, GA 30177. ✆ **770/735-3122.** www.tatehouse.com. 14 units. $145 cabin; $175 suite. AE, DISC, MC, V. Rates include breakfast. **Amenities:** Breakfast room; lounge; outdoor pool; tennis court; library. *In room:* A/C, TV.

**The Woodbridge Inn** ⭐⭐    Known for the quality of its food and lodging, this is the most famous inn in Northwest Georgia. It's in an antebellum setting with mountain vistas from all directions. The three-level lodge was designed to take in the views—patios and balconies open off the accommodations. Some of the upper-level rooms have spiral staircases leading to sleeping lofts. All units have well-maintained bathrooms with tub/shower. The lodge is completely modern, having been reconstructed after a fire. People drive from miles away, even from Atlanta, to sample the food here. Both European and American dishes are offered, everything from veal Oscar to oysters Rockefeller. All the food is fresh, and dishes are individually prepared. Save room for dessert, especially the lemon cream pie.

The place has a long history. It was once known as Ed Lenning's Inn. Ed fought as a Confederate soldier and founded the restaurant with money from a gold strike in California. In the old days, when the railroad used to stop out front, people from Florida came here to escape the summer heat. All rooms are nonsmoking.

44 Chambers St., Jasper, GA 30143. ✆ **706/253-6293.** Fax 706/253-9061. www.woodbridgeinn.net. 18 units. Sun–Thurs $65 double, Fri–Sat $75 double. AE, DC, DISC, MC, V. **Amenities:** Breakfast room; lounge; outdoor pool; 1 room for those w/limited mobility. *In room:* A/C, TV.

## 5 Dahlonega ⭐

70 miles NE of Atlanta

*Dahlonega* is a Cherokee word meaning "precious yellow." In 1828, according to legend, a trapper named Benjamin Parks stubbed his toe on a rock and uncovered a vein of gold here that quickly brought prospectors streaming into these hills. A town called "Dahlonega" suddenly appeared—America's first mining boomtown. The gold craze changed Cherokee culture forever.

Although prospecting hasn't been a major industry since the Civil War, enough gold is still around to periodically re-leaf the dome of Georgia's State Capitol, and to intrigue visitors who come here to pan for it (see below).

## ESSENTIALS

**GETTING THERE   By Car**   From Atlanta, take Highway 19/S.R. 400 North to S.R. 60, which you follow north for another 5 miles to reach Dahlonega.

**VISITOR INFORMATION**   The **Dahlonega Chamber of Commerce,** 13 S. Park St. (© **800/231-5543** or 706/864-3711; www.dahlonega.org), is open daily from 9am to 5:30pm. The staff distributes information about scenic attractions, state parks, and gold panning in the area.

## SEEING THE SIGHTS

**Dahlonega's Public Square** sports a rustic look. Old galleried buildings and stores have been turned into shops purveying gold-panning equipment, gold jewelry, mountain handcrafts, antiques, ice cream, and fudge. It's very touristy but preserves a quaint charm in spite of the hordes who sometimes descend on summer days, mostly families with lots of kids in tow.

Formerly the Lumpkin County Courthouse, the **Dahlonega Courthouse Gold Museum,** Public Square (© **706/864-2257**), is in the center of the town square. Artifacts, coins, and tools from the nation's first major gold rush are shown, and a 23-minute film chronologically documents the feverish era. Recently, the Gold Museum has added a gold coin exhibit displaying a variety of quarters, half dollars, and whole dollars minted at the Dahlonega Branch Mint from 1838 to 1861. Besides being a gold miners' haven, this old museum is the state's third-oldest standing courthouse. It's also the second most visited Georgia historical site. The hours of operation are Monday to Saturday 9am to 5pm, and Sunday 10am to 5pm. Admission is $3 for adults, $2.50 for seniors, $1.50 for children 6 to 18, and free for children 5 and under.

You can take a tour and pan for gold at **Consolidated Gold Mines,** 125 Consolidated Gold Mines Rd. (© **706/864-8473**). At the turn of the 20th century it boasted the largest and most advanced gold mine east of the Mississippi River, covering more than 7,000 acres, with some 200 tunnels. In 1 day it recovered about 55 pounds of gold. Tours into illuminated tunnels take about 40 minutes and are conducted by miners. Look for the 250-foot vertical shaft. The mine also offers a chance to pan for gold. It's open daily from 10am to 5pm. Admission is $11 adults, $7 children 4 to 14. To reach the mine from the center of Dahlonega, take Highway 400 North to Highway 60, turn left, and follow the signs.

## WHERE TO STAY

**The Smith House**   The owners, the Welch family, are known mainly for their restaurant (see below). With the Smith House, they offer plenty of mountain hospitality, if you don't mind staying at a place overrun with visitors. Originally built atop a rich vein of gold ore in 1884, it was turned into an inn in 1922, although the original owners wouldn't recognize today's bustling place. The inaugural $4.50-a-night rooms are long gone, too. Rooms are furnished in a cozy, 19th-century style, and all have been authentically remodeled. Each unit has a neatly kept bathroom with a tub/shower combination. One section of the little two-story hotel was originally a carriage house. This is very much a country inn, with rocking chairs on the front porch. A swimming pool was added in the 1980s, and guests can pan for gold on the premises for $3.

84 S. Chestatee St., Dahlonega, GA 30533. © **800/852-9577** or 706/867-7000. Fax 706/864-7564. www.smithhouse.com. 18 units. $89–$139 double. Rates include continental breakfast. AE, MC, V. **Amenities:** Restaurant; bar; lounge; outdoor pool; nonsmoking rooms. *In room:* A/C, TV, coffeemaker, hair dryer, iron/ironing board.

## STAYING NEARBY

**Forrest Hills Mountain Resort & Conference Center** ★ *(Finds)* Surrounded by the mountains of North Georgia, this adults-only retreat is a luxurious hideaway. It offers deluxe B&B rooms in the main lodge, and 12 bilevel luxury suites in the resort's Mountain Laurel Inn. But its special attraction is its rustic cottages, many ideal for a honeymoon with bedroom hot tubs and large canopied beds. Fireplaces and well-kept bathrooms with tub/shower combinations add to the allure. The cottages have a woodland setting best enjoyed from porch swings. The 140 wooded acres border Chattahoochee National Forest and are about 4 miles from Amicalola Falls State Park; there are many hiking and bridle trails. Make reservations as far in advance as possible.

135 Forrest Hills Rd. (P.O. Box 510), Dahlonega, GA 30533. © **800/654-6313** or 706/864-6456. Fax 706/ 864-0757. www.foresths.com. 45 units. $79–$129 B&B double; $150–$299 Mountain Laurel Inn suite; $139–$350 cabin . Room rates include full breakfast and candlelight dinner; no dinner Wed and Thurs. AE, DISC, MC, V. 10 miles west on Ga. 52, then right onto Wesley Chapel Rd. No children. **Amenities:** Restaurant; lounge; pool; Jacuzzi; horseback riding; nonsmoking rooms. *In room:* A/C, TV, no phone.

## WHERE TO DINE

**The Smith House** *(Value)* SOUTHERN    In North Georgia, this large family-style restaurant—a tradition since 1922—is called "pig-out heaven." A lavish array of Southern food, along with homemade Smith House rolls, relishes, and desserts, is served at shared tables. Some 2,000 meals are hauled out on Sunday alone. This is true mountain cookin'—and plenty of it, all you can eat. Many dishes are based on recipes 100 years old. Continuously replenished platters arrive, including angel biscuits, sweet-baked country-fried steak, and lots and lots of Southern fried chicken. Barbecue is a feature, and so is fried catfish (is there any other kind?). Everything tastes better with the homemade corn bread, especially the Southern-style vegetables that include fried okra, squash casserole, black-eyed peas, rice and gravy, stewed apples, and candied yams. No one saves room for dessert, but everyone eats it anyway—banana fritters, strawberry shortcake, fruit cobbler, whatever.

84 S. Chestatee St. © **706/867-7000.** www.smithhouse.com. Reservations not accepted. All-you-can-eat lunch and dinner Tues–Fri $12, Sat–Sun $16. AE, MC, V. Tues–Sat 11am–3pm; Tues–Fri 4–8pm; Sat 3–8:30pm; Sun 11am–8pm.

## 6 Blairsville

105 miles NE of Atlanta

You don't come here to visit this mountain town itself, but you can use it as a center for exploring—including Georgia's highest point, offering a panoramic view of the whole northern part of the state. Blairsville is set in a national forest.

A **Sorghum Festival** is held the first three weekends in October. Crafts are displayed, canned goods sold, and cane converted to sweet sorghum syrup before your eyes, with lots of free samples. Square dancing, greased pole climbing, and other contests typical of the mountain folk are followed by country music and more dancing.

## ESSENTIALS

**GETTING THERE    By Car**    From Atlanta, take I-75 North to I-575 and continue north on this highway until you reach Highway 515. Go north on Highway 515 to reach Blairsville.

**VISITOR INFORMATION**    The **Blairsville Chamber of Commerce,** 385 Welcome Center Lane, in Blairsville (© **877/745-5789** or 706/745-5789;

www.blairsvillechamber.com), is open Monday to Friday from 8:30am to 4:30pm and Saturday 10am to 1pm, distributing maps and brochures about the area.

## EXPLORING THE AREA

**Brasstown Bald** ✿✿, Georgia's highest mountain, is set in a national forest with an observation tower atop its 4,784-foot summit. Here you'll have a 360-degree view across ridges into four different states. After parking, you can walk up the half-mile paved road or else take a bus to the top. There is no steeper half-mile walk in all of Georgia! At the top you can see a video explaining the legend and lore of the mountain. There's access to four hiking trails ranging from a half-mile to 6 miles in length, and picnic tables are available. The surrounding area is home to a wide variety of plants and animals.

The park is open May to mid-November Monday to Friday 10am to 6pm and Saturday and Sunday 10am to 6:30pm. In April it is open only Saturday and Sunday. Admission is $3 for parking. The bus ride to the top and back costs $2 for all ages. For more information, write **Brasstown Ranger District,** 1881 Hwy. 515, Blairsville, GA 30512 (✆ **706/745-6928;** fax 706/745-7494). There is also a **Visitor Information Center** at the park (✆ **706/896-2555**).

To reach the mountain from Blairsville, take U.S. 19/129 South for 8 miles. Turn left or east onto Ga. 180 and go 12 miles to Ga. 180 Spur, where you turn left, or north. Another 3 miles leads to the Brasstown Bald parking lot.

**Vogel State Park** ✿ is Georgia's second-oldest state park and one of its most frequented. Located in the heart of the North Georgia mountains at the foot of Blood and Slaughter mountains, it sprawls across 240 acres cut through with nature trails. It has a 22-acre lake, Lake Trahlyta, named for a Cherokee princess. You can swim (there's a bathhouse) or fish for bass, trout, and bream. The park hosts festivals, like Old Timer's Day in August.

Campsites are available with power and water hookups, hot showers, and laundry facilities. A tent costs $12 Monday to Friday, $20 on weekends. Cottages, 36 in all, are comfortably furnished and have wood-burning fireplaces. Prices range from $65 to $70 for a one-bedroom, $75 to $90 for a two-bedroom, and $95 to $110 for a three-bedroom.

At an elevation of 2,500 feet, park temperatures are cool, even in July and August. The park is open year-round daily from 7am to 10pm. It's 11 miles from Blairsville on U.S. 19/129. For more information, write **Vogel State Park,** 7485 Vogel State Park Rd., Blairsville, GA 30512 (✆ **706/745-2628;** fax 706/745-3139).

**Richard Russell Scenic Highway** is south of Blairsville, via U.S. 19/129, and east on Ga. 180. This 14-mile scenic mountain drive, with elevations ranging from 1,600 to 3,000 feet, offers panoramic views at every turn. The drive is especially popular in fall, when hardwoods blaze with colors. At the 3,500-foot Tesnatee Gap, the highway crosses the Appalachian Trail. The road crosses the Blue Ridge and forms the northern perimeter of the eastern half of Raven Cliffs Wilderness.

## WHERE TO STAY

**Blood Mountain Cabins and Country Store** These cabins stand near the breezy top of Blood Mountain at a 3,000-foot elevation, and the Appalachian Trail crosses U.S. 19/129 only yards away. Summers here are the coolest in Georgia, especially if you're escaping that fiery cauldron known as Atlanta, but winter will send you seeking a seat close to the stove. The owners, Colley and

George Case, can be found in their general store, dispensing information on the area and selling freshly brewed coffee. Cabins are furnished in a rustic style and—at least in spring—don't match their natural setting when all the rhododendrons and azaleas burst into flame. Each cabin has a bedroom and an additional sleeping loft, plus a fireplace, ceiling fan, fully equipped kitchen, well-kept up-to-date bathroom with tub/shower combination, and spacious deck with country rockers for taking in that view of Blood Mountain. Weekly rates range from $389 to $469.

9894 Gainesville Hwy., Blairsville, GA 30512. 🅒/fax **800/284-6866** or 706/745-9454. www.bloodmountain. com. 12 units. $79–$99 cabin for 4. 2-night minimum. DISC, MC, V. 13 miles south of Blairsville along U.S. 19/129. **Amenities:** Lounge. *In room:* A/C, TV, no phone.

**Misty Mountain Inn and Cottages**   This Victorian-style farmhouse in a bucolic setting is both a B&B and an inn, offering rooms with private bathrooms, fireplaces, and balconies, plus a cottage cluster with wood-burning fireplaces and kitchenettes. A pet-friendly environment, it's where you can do nothing more than (at their suggestion) "smell the flowers or listen to the bullfrogs at the pond." Rooms are furnished in a country rustic style, and maintenance is high. Two cabins have whirlpool baths, and all have well-kept bathrooms with tub/shower combinations. Queen-size beds, fireplaces, and linens are furnished with each unit. Family cottages sleep five to eight, although two are suitable for only two guests. Hiking trails nearby include the Appalachian Trail; and Brasstown Bald Mountain is less than 10 miles away. White-water rafting is within a short drive, as are trout-filled mountain streams. Boating is possible on two lakes nearby.

4376 Misty Mountain Lane at Town Creek Rd., Blairsville, GA 30512. 🅒 **888/647-8966** or 706/745-4786. Fax 706/781-1002. www.jwww.com/misty. 10 units. $70–$85 B&B room; $85–$100 cottage. Rates include breakfast in B&B rooms. MC, V. **Amenities:** Breakfast room; lounge. *In room:* A/C, TV.

## 7 Alpine Helen ⊛

85 miles NE of Atlanta

Once a quiet Appalachian village, Helen has been turned into a bit of Bavaria in the Georgia hills. Main Street buildings have red roofs, flower boxes, balconies, and murals. You can shop for sweaters, porcelains, cuckoo clocks, and Christmas ornaments; enjoy wurst and beer to oompah music at an outdoor beer garden; and in September and October join the revelry of Oktoberfest. Numerous alpine-style hotels, with names that include the Heidi Motel, have comfortable accommodations and restaurants.

### ESSENTIALS

**GETTING THERE   By Car**   From Atlanta, head north on I-85 to exit 45 near Gainesville. From here, take Highway 985/365 North for some 20 miles to Highway 384. After that, go for another 20 miles to Highway 75, then turn right for the final 3 miles into Helen.

**VISITOR INFORMATION   Alpine Helen Convention and Visitors Bureau,** 726 Brucken St. (a half-mile from downtown), right off Main Street (🅒 **800/858-8027** or 706/878-2181; www.helenga.org), dispenses information and provides maps and brochures of attractions in the area. Hours are Monday to Saturday from 9am to 5pm and Sunday from 10am to 4pm.

### EXPLORING THE AREA

The best time to be here is for a special event, such as the Hot Air Balloon Festival, which kicks off the race to the Atlantic Ocean in late May (lasting until

June), and Oktoberfest, a pale imitation of the real one in Munich. This beer-drinking fest in alcohol-shy Georgia begins in mid-September and continues to mid-October. German bands from the U.S. and Europe perform nightly, and singalongs and the famous "Chicken Dance" are part of the fun. Show up in an authentic Bavarian costume.

After you've seen all the shows and bought all those beer mugs and lederhosen you don't really need, you can do some serious exploring in the environs of Helen, which many visitors find more alluring than the overly commercialized town itself, with its *faux* Bavarian everything.

## OUTDOOR PURSUITS

Alpine tubing is the most popular outdoor sport here. If the day is hot, more people can be seen tubing on the Chattahoochee River than buying beer steins. The river runs right through Helen, and tube-rental outfits abound all along the banks. There are some rapids here but they're rather brief, so even small children go tubing. We prefer **Cool River Tubing** (© **800/896-4595** or 706/878-2665), which will take you on a 2-hour float and bring you back to your starting point. The cost is $5 per person.

**Sunburst Stables,** 9 miles east of Helen on Ga. 255 in the Sautee Valley (© **800/806-1953** or 706/947-7433), offers 25 miles of scenic wooded trails year-round. You can even go riding in winter, perhaps spotting a deer cavorting through the forest. Various types of rides are offered, including a 2-day overnight ride and a 3-hour sunset ride. The stables are set on 60 acres and adjoin the Chattahoochee National Forest. The outfit also offers hayrides.

Advance reservations are required; the hourly rate is $25 per person. No children under 8 are allowed. When making a reservation and agreeing upon the time, give them your height, weight, and experience in riding. A major credit card (American Express, Discover, MasterCard, or Visa) is required to hold a reservation. Weight limits of 240 pounds for men or women are imposed.

## SHOPPING

**Betty's Country Store** It's the most folkloric large grocery store in Georgia, stocked with all the inventory you'd expect in a modern grocery chain, yet permeated with the old-time aura of an early-20th-century general store. Its central core was built in 1937, but even the more recent enlargements feature a decor as rough-hewn as a log cabin in the Georgia mountains, while the completely concealed amenities are as modern as the computer age. Overall, the place is a conversation piece and a bit of a tourist attraction in its own right, a setting right out of the *Old Farmer's Almanac.* N. Main St. (Hwy. 75). © **706/878-2943**. www.bettys countrystore.net.

**Nora Mill Granary** At first glance, you might bypass this rustic plank-sided building as little more than a battered tourist emporium, on the main road about 2 miles south of Helen. Actually, it's one of the most famous sites in the region, visited by schoolchildren as a slice of Americana, and sought after by engineers eager for a glimpse of its old-time grinding wheels. It was built in 1876 as a water-driven mill powered by the flowing waters of the Chattahoochee River. Today, you can sample grits and oatmeal, which bubble away on a massive antique stove, or buy burlap minibags of grits, stone-ground flour (buckwheat, rye, and whole wheat), pancake mix, and bread mix. A gift store next door sells cookbooks, candy, and crafts. Both enterprises are open daily from 9:30am to 5pm. 7107 S. Main St., Helen. © **800/927-2375** or 706/878-2375. www.noramill.com.

**The Old Sautee Store**    Four miles from Helen, this 128-year-old country store is as much a museum as it is a store. In fact, an antique museum can be found in a section of the store where the post office used to be. The Old Sautee Store has the largest collection of old-store memorabilia in all of Georgia, including items of merchandise not for sale. It's also a Scandinavian specialty shop: Astrid Fried still remembers her native Norway, and will show you her personally selected imports, including ski sweaters and hand-carved trolls; Scandinavian crystal and dinnerware; Norwegian pewter, gold, and enamel jewelry; and gourmet foods. The store is listed on the National Register of Historic Places. Admission is free. Hours are Monday to Saturday from 9:30am to 5:30pm and Sunday from noon to 5:30pm. Ga. 17 and Ga. 255, Sautee-Nachoochee. © 800/463-9853 or 706/878-2281. www.sauteestore.com.

## WHERE TO STAY

**Helendorf River Inn**    Tucked away on a side street, in the Teutonic-looking heart of the village, this hotel sports Bavarian-style frescoes on its stucco surfaces that look oddly incongruous in the Georgia heat. It's one of the town's enduring hotels, with one of the most central locations. Despite its folkloric exterior, it's remarkable for what this hotel doesn't offer: Its lobby is cramped and unimaginative and there's no bar. However, there is a small restaurant, the Wooden Shoe. You'll find an ersatz kind of folklore, a staff with a laconic mountain drawl, and a wide variety of accommodations. The most appealing overlook the Chattahoochee River, which runs against one foundation of the building. Some have hints of alpine coziness, and many have private balconies. Suites contain Jacuzzis and fireplaces. All units contain neatly kept bathrooms with tub/shower combinations.

33 Munichstrasse St., Helen, GA 30545. © 800/445-2271 or 706/878-2271. Fax 706/878-2271. www.helendorf. com. 99 units. $54–$104 double; $150–$170 suite. MC, V. **Amenities:** Restaurant; indoor pool; laundry service/dry cleaning; nonsmoking rooms; rooms for those w/limited mobility. In room: A/C, TV, kitchenette (in some), coffeemaker (in some), fireplace (in some).

**Hofbrau Riverfront Hotel**    This is a *faux* German-style guesthouse. At any minute you expect to see a ruby-cheeked innkeeper emerge to wish you *Guten Appetit*. Its restaurant, **The Hofbrauhaus,** is one of the best and most famous in Helen (see below). Families enjoy the shaded patio with its porch swings, and guests stroll down to watch the flow of the river. The guest rooms are simply furnished but comfortable, each well maintained, with a tub/shower combination in the private bathrooms. Couches and TVs are found in the lounge.

1 Main St., Helen, GA 30545. © 800/830-3977 or 706/878-2184. www.riverfronthotel.com. 38 units. $49–$79 double; $109–$175 suite. AE, DC, DISC, MC, V. Children under 12 stay free in parent's room. **Amenities:** Restaurant; bar; limited room service; nonsmoking rooms; fridge. In room: A/C, TV, hair dryer (available), iron/ironing board (available).

**The Lodge at Smithgall Woods** ⭐ *(Finds*    This elegant mountain retreat stands in the midst of a 5,555-acre conservation area, attracting a well-heeled clientele who enjoy its seclusion and the country charm of a private mountain estate. It also opens onto one of the finest trout streams in Georgia and, as such, often attracts the movers and shakers of industry who want to get away from it all. In peace and seclusion, the guest rooms are well furnished and exceedingly comfortable, all with private bathrooms with tub/shower combinations. Each of the five different guesthouses opens onto panoramic views. The accommodations are individually decorated with antiques, well-chosen fabrics, and Oriental rugs, the ambience both rustic yet elegant. The cuisine is another good reason to stay here. Naturally, the chef's specialty is mountain trout, as the nearby river is said to be one of the top 100 trout streams in the United States. You can order the fish smoked, grilled, or pan-sautéed, along with a small but excellent choice of other dishes nightly. In addition to fishing, activities include hiking, biking, birding, and nature walks.

61 Tsalaki Trail, Helen, GA 30545. (© **800/318-5248** or 706/878-3087. Fax 706/878-0301. www.smithgallwoods. com. 14 units. $289–$349 double. Rates include all meals on weekends. AE, DC, MC, V. **Amenities:** Dining area; lounge; nonsmoking rooms; rooms for those w/limited mobility. In room: A/C, TV.

**Stovall House**  Nestled amid a copse of trees at the summit of a hill, this veranda-ringed farmhouse was built in 1837 as the centerpiece of a 300-acre plantation. It was converted into a B&B in 1983 by Hamilton ("Ham") Schwartz, a hardworking schoolteacher and soccer coach from Philadelphia. Guest rooms are high ceilinged and outfitted with an eclectic mix of antiques. They include old-fashioned beds, which might not be as comfortable as the ones you're used to, but which compensate with their charm. Top-floor rooms have skylights. All units contain well-kept bathrooms with tub/shower combinations.

Dinner is a celebration of well-flavored food. Served Thursday to Saturday 5:30 to 8:30pm (Sun brunch 11am–2pm), menu items include a "phyllo of the day" (including a version filled with ham, broccoli, and cheddar), chicken stuffed with cream cheese and herbs, scaloppini of pork, and at least two versions of fresh mountain trout. Full dinners are a bargain, tending to range from $10 to $15 per person.

1526 Hwy. 255 N., Sautee, GA 30571. (© **706/878-3355.** www.stovallhouse.com. 5 units. $92 double. Rates include continental breakfast. Discounts of 10% Dec–Mar. AE, MC, V. 5 miles southeast of Helen on Hwy. 255. **Amenities:** Breakfast room; lounge; nonsmoking rooms. In room: A/C, no phone.

**Unicoi State Park and Lodge** *Value*  Set on a pristine lake in the midst of 1,063 acres of woodland, this state lodge, built in 1972, stands in the heart of the park. Warm and wood-beamed, it offers fully equipped and rather rustic cottages tucked into the wooded hillsides. The guest rooms we inspected needed refurbishing, but the price was right. The cottages lie along the lake and farther up Smith Creek. Each unit contains a neatly kept bathroom with a shower. The lodge has an excellent cafeteria-style dining room serving three meals a day at modest prices. Even if you're not staying here, consider a stopover for an all-you-can-eat buffet, costing $7.95 to $9.95 at lunch and $9.95 to $20. at dinner. All rooms are nonsmoking.

Unicoi State Park (P.O. Box 849), Helen, GA 30545. (© **800/573-9659** or 706/878-2201. Fax 706/878-1897. 100 units; 30 cottages. $99–$129 double; $99–$139 cottages. AE, DC, DISC, MC, V. **Amenities:** Restaurant; bar; outdoor pool; 4 tennis courts; fishing; biking. In room: A/C, TV, dataport, kitchenettes (in some), coffeemaker, hair dryer, iron/ironing board, fireplace (in some).

## WHERE TO DINE

**The Hofbrauhaus** INTERNATIONAL  By virtue of its name alone, this is the most famous restaurant in Helen, with a Teutonic-derived *schmaltz* that can be endearing in a rather corny way. It sits at the edge of the Chattahoochee, and caters to a hard-core battalion of serious beer drinkers, especially during Oktoberfest. Most of the time, however, the place is a family-trade enclave. The menu is divided into six categories that cover a wide cross section of the world's cuisines. There's Italian (chicken cacciatore); French (frogs' legs Provençale and steak au poivre); seafood (chargrilled swordfish); German/Bavarian (Wiener schnitzel); and American (fried Georgia mountain trout or prime rib of beef). All main courses include soup, salad, vegetable, roll, and butter.

9001 Main St. (© **706/878-2184.** Reservations recommended. Main courses $13–$29. AE, DC, DISC, MC, V. Bar/lounge daily 3pm–1am; restaurant daily 5–10pm.

## 8 Rabun County

In northeast Georgia, 2 hours north of Atlanta on Highway 444, Rabun County is one of the gems of the Deep South. From Atlanta take I-85 North to I-985, then continue to its end at Highway 441. Proceed 30 miles north into the heart of Rabun County, with its Blue Ridge Mountains scenery galore.

With cascading waterfalls, lakes, mountain vistas, and fish-filled streams, Rabun is one of the vacation meccas of Georgia. Bordering both Carolinas, it is filled with outdoor adventures—though not necessarily those depicted in the famous film *Deliverance* with Burt Reynolds, which was shot here.

The Chattahoochee National Forest covers more than 60% of the county, including wilderness areas like the Wild and Scenic Chattooga River, consistently rated among the top 10 white-river runs in America. Attractions range from Tallulah Gorge, called "the Grand Canyon of the South," to Rabun Bald with its panoramic vistas.

### TALLULAH FALLS & GORGE ⋆

This land of waterfalls and gorges was a fashionable resort with several upmarket hotels until 1913. But the construction of the Georgia Power Hydroelectric Dam changed the fate of the community, and the area became a bit of a ghost town.

At 600 feet, Tallulah Gorge is one of the deepest and most panoramic in the east. The Cherokees believed it was inhabited by a race of "little people," and that those who ventured inside never came out.

Hiking in the gorge is very strenuous. The recreational center is at the 300-acre **Terrora Park and Visitor Center** (© 706/754-7970), with picnic areas, 50 campsites with water and electrical hookups, a beach for swimming, a playground, a bathhouse, and tennis courts, along with several nature trails. Office hours are 8am to 5pm. Nightly campsite rentals cost $14 for campers with tents, $16 for those with RVs. **Terrora Park** is immediately north of the bridge over Tallulah Gorge on the west side of U.S. 441 in the town of Tallulah Falls.

### LAKE RABUN

About 5 miles from Tallulah Falls and some 20 miles from Alpine Helen, in Chattahoochee National Forest, **Lake Rabun Recreation Area** has camping sites, a fishing pier, a boat dock, hiking trails, a public beach, and picnic areas. For information about the area, call the **National Forest Tallulah Ranger District** at © 706/782-3320. The lake is also the site of one of the area's best-known hotels and many summer homes.

### WHERE TO STAY

**Lake Rabun Hotel** ⋆ *Finds*    This is a real, old-fashioned place. First built in 1922, it still has no room telephones, air-conditioning, or TVs. As a getaway it's been called "Georgia's sweetest secret garden." Some of the hotel's original furnishings of rhododendron and twisted laurel are still here, a little worse for wear, but mellow. Quilts on the beds and tiebacks holding the ruffled curtains add to the old-time charm. Most of the rooms have sinks, but outside bathrooms are shared. Guests gather informally around the big, old fireplace. The food is good and home-cooked. Canoes are available if you'd like a closer look at the lake. Management warns, "Nobody puts on fancy airs here." They're right!

Lake Rabun Rd. (P.O. Box 10), Lakemont, GA 30552. © **706/782-4946.** 16 units, some with bathroom. $69–$89 double. Rate includes continental breakfast. DISC, MC, V. Closed Dec–Mar. **Amenities:** Restaurant/bar; lounge; great room; nonsmoking rooms. *In room:* No phone.

# MOUNTAIN CITY

The mountain is Black Rock Mountain, setting of Black Rock Mountain State Park, so named for its dark granite cliffs. It's the highest state park in Georgia, at 3,640 feet in elevation, embracing some 1,500 acres. On a clear day, views extend for 80 miles. To reach the park, leave Mountain City and go 3 miles north of Clayton via U.S. 441. The park is open daily from 7am to 10pm year-round. It offers 48 tent and trailer sites, 11 walk-in campsites, and 10 rental cottages, plus a playground and a 17-acre lake. There are six scenic overlooks and a 10-mile trail system. For more information, contact **Black Rock Mountain State Park,** P.O. Box A, Mountain City, GA 30562 (② **706/746-2141**).

## WHERE TO STAY

**York House** ⑂   This is the oldest B&B in Georgia, once the accommodations for the man who built the Tallulah Railroad. Today, Victoria Phillips is the innkeeper with panache, maintaining the collections of oak, cherry, and pinewood furniture that have furnished the place since the early part of the century, and upgrading the accommodations with nostalgic charm and modern style. All units contain neatly kept bathrooms with tub/shower combinations. In 1903, scenes from *The Great Train Robbery* were filmed here, and the building is listed on the National Register of Historic Places. A kitchen is available in the main house for guest use. Call ahead to discuss the inn's children's policy.

P.O. Box 126, Mountain City, GA 30562. ② 800/231-YORK or 706/746-2068. Fax 706/746-0210. www.york houseinn.com. 13 units. $89–$109 double; $119 suite. Rates include country breakfast. MC, V. **Amenities:** Breakfast room; lounge; nonsmoking rooms. *In room:* A/C, TV, fireplace (in some), no phone.

# DILLARD

There's one good reason to come here: to eat. Dillard lies along Highway 441, 2 miles south of the North Carolina border, about a 2-hour drive north from Atlanta. It's Southern hospitality all the way here, especially at Dillard House.

## WHERE TO DINE

**Dillard House** ⑂ (Value) SOUTHERN   The family-style meals served here are famous all over Georgia. More than five million hungry eaters have devoured food at the Dillard House since 1915. Country-cured ham, Southern fried chicken, tons of fresh vegetables, old-fashioned corn bread, pan-fried trout, and all the relishes and desserts you could ever want burden the tables. No one in history has ever left here hungry. You can also lodge at **Dillard House Hotel,** which has been restored and furnished in part with antiques. It has 61 rooms, costing $59 to $129. Two suites with kitchenettes cost $99 to $159. Guests have use of a swimming pool and tennis courts, and can also go on horseback rides at the Dillard House Stables.

Old Dillard Rd., U.S. 441/23 (P.O. Box 10), Dillard, GA 30537. ② 800/541-0671 or 706/746-5348. www.dillard house.com. Reservations required for 15 or more. Lunch $15–$19; dinner $18–$20. AE, DC, DISC, MC, V. Daily 7:30–10:30am and 11:30am–8pm.

# 19

# Macon & the Southwest

Southwest Georgia is the land of peach orchards, pecan groves, and Jimmy Carter. It's also a land of giant textile mills, pulp and paper plants, and manufacturing centers for automobiles, metal, chemicals, and furniture that bear the definite stamp of the New South.

Macon, the cherry tree capital of Georgia, is only 84 miles southeast of Atlanta and might easily be your gateway to the state's southwest. Home of rock legend Little Richard and birthplace of Southern poet Sidney Lanier, Macon is filled with white-columned antebellum buildings on the National Register of Historic Places.

After visiting the historic heartland of Georgia, you can cut southwest through two very different tourist districts, which Georgia dubs "Presidential Pathways" and "Plantation Trace." The first honors two presidents: Franklin Roosevelt, who sometimes lived at Warm Springs, and Plains's own Jimmy Carter. Steeped in history, this land is one of rolling hills and green forests. It also encompasses Pine Mountain, the gateway to the 2,500-acre Callaway Gardens—the most beautiful natural setting in Georgia. Along Plantation Trace, Native Americans and frontier soldiers have given way to farmers and timber barons. Its pocket of posh is Thomasville, which in the 1880s became the center for winter sunshine for the wealthy from the North.

## 1 Macon (★)

### 84 miles SE of Atlanta

Only Savannah tops Macon for its striking old buildings. What comes as a huge surprise to visitors, though, is that Macon has 170,000 cherry trees—and they're a remarkable sight in late March when in bloom. Compare Washington, D.C.'s famous Cherry Blossom Festival (with a mere 3,000 trees), and you'll understand how perfumed that time of year is in Macon.

The original city planners designed Macon in 1823 as a "city in a park." Today that heritage has been preserved. Wide avenues are lined with grand, stately mansions, many built before the Civil War during the cotton boom. It's more than just a river town, with its many cultural offerings—such as the Georgia Music Hall of Fame, Georgia Sports Hall of Fame, and Grand Opera House—and educational institutions, such as Macon College, Mercer University, and Wesleyan College, the world's first college for women. Also, a $36-million revitalization project was launched in 1999. Through this expenditure, much of the original charm of Macon has been restored.

As you'll see below, Macon has a wealth of historic sites, a handful of delightful places to stay, and the hospitality for which the South is known.

## ESSENTIALS

**GETTING THERE**   Take I-75 South from Atlanta, exiting at the signposted exits.

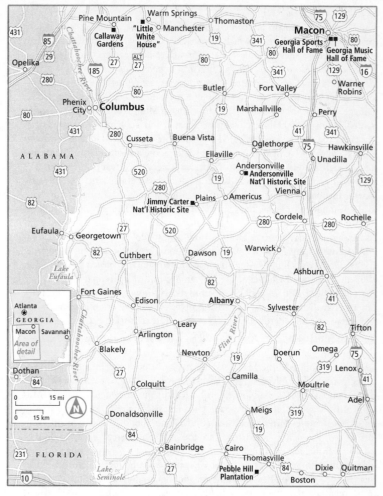

**VISITOR INFORMATION**   If you're traveling south toward Macon on I-75, there's a **welcome center** and rest area north of the city, open daily from 8:30am to 5:30pm. When you get into town, the **Downtown Macon Welcome Center,** 200 Cherry St., Macon, GA 31201 (© **800/768-3401** or 478/743-3401; www. maconga.org), at the foot of Cherry Street in the historic Macon Terminal Station, will provide you with information. It's open Monday to Saturday from 9am to 5pm.

**SPECIAL EVENTS**   The **Cherry Blossom Festival** ✿ is traditionally held around the last 10 days in March. During that time, 500 activities are planned around the city. You'll find everything from hot-air ballooning to a giant parade with marching bands and floats. Many events are held in the city parks. The residential areas are filled with thousands of Yoshino cherry trees. For more information, contact the Macon Cherry Blossom Festival, Inc., 794 Cherry St., Macon, GA 31201 (© **478/751-7429;** www.cherryblossom.com).

## SEEING THE SIGHTS

The **Downtown Macon Welcome Center** (see "Essentials," above) is located in the Macon Terminal Station, which dates back to 1916, when it hosted more than 100 trains a day. The Welcome Center offers three different discounted "Around Town" combination tickets, which admit you to several attractions in town. The **Historic Macon Combination Ticket** gives you free passage aboard the downtown trolley plus admission to the Cannonball House, Hay House, Sidney Lanier Cottage, St. Joseph's Catholic Church, Georgia Music Hall of Fame, Georgia Sports Hall of Fame, Historic Douglass Theatre, and Tubman African American Museum; the cost is $24 adults, $12 youth. The **Historic Macon Downtown Tour** includes the Georgia Music Hall of Fame, Georgia Sports Hall of Fame, Historic Douglass Theatre, and Tubman African American Museum; the cost is $15 adults, $8 youth. Almost 25 stops are listed in this walking tour. The **Historic Macon Intown Tour** gives you free passage on the intown trolley plus admission to the Cannonball House, the Hay House, the Sidney Lanier Cottage, and St. Joseph's Catholic Church; the cost is $14 adults, $8 youth. "Around Town" tickets are sold Monday through Saturday from 9am to 5:30pm.

At **Central City Park,** a 250-acre recreational area, you can enjoy ongoing events. Dr. Martin Luther King, Jr., made his only major speech in Georgia in 1957 at the **Steward Chapel of the African Methodist Episcopal Church,** 887 Forsyth St. (© **478/742-4922**). **Ocmulgee National Monument,** at 1207 Emery Hwy., is a memorial to native peoples on the site of an ancient Indian settlement and burial grounds. It's open daily, and admission is free.

**Georgia Music Hall of Fame** ⋆   When it comes to music, few states can lay claim to the number of influential acts that Georgia has produced. Opened in 1996, the Georgia Music Hall of Fame has since inducted into the hall such music greats as Ray Charles, Little Richard, Otis Redding, the Allman Brothers Band, James Brown, Lena Horne, Gladys Knight, Johnny Mercer, Ronnie Milsap, Curtis Mayfield, Issac Hayes, and Chet Atkins. The tradition of music continues with more current acts like R.E.M. and the B-52s, two bands who introduced the genre "alternative" to the music industry. The 12,000-foot exhibit hall includes a virtual Tune Town, re-creating a Georgia village at twilight, with such exhibits as a Gospel Chapel, a Soda Fountain, and the Skillet Licker Cafe. Music, photos, instruments, and memorabilia can be found at every turn, including the shoes that Otis Redding was wearing the day he died in a plane crash, as well as a classic James Brown costume. A delightful children's wing, the Billy Watson Music Factory, opened in late 1999, with interactive drums, keyboards, and the like.

200 Martin Luther King, Jr., Blvd. © **478/750-8555.** www.garocks.com. Admission $8 adults, $6 seniors, $3.50 children 4–16, free for children 3 and under. Mon–Sat 9am–5pm; Sun 1–5pm.

**Grand Opera House**   The Academy of Music was constructed in 1884 and later became known as the Grand Opera House. Such old-timers as Sarah Bernhardt, Will Rogers, the Gish sisters, Dorothy Lamour, and Burns and Allen have performed here. With seating for 1,057, it also boasts one of America's largest stages—big enough to accommodate a production of *Ben Hur* with its stage machinery and treadmills for the chariot races. Around Christmas each year, the Allman Brothers Band performs a homecoming concert for a small crowd of friends, family, and fans.

400 Poplar St. © **478/301-5470** for box office information. Tickets $25–$40. Box office Mon–Fri 10am–5pm.

**Tubman African American Museum**   This offbeat and unusual museum, dedicated to exploring the cultural heritage of African Americans, was named in honor of Harriet Tubman, a former slave who led some 300 people to freedom as a conductor on the Underground Railroad. It includes cultural artifacts, folk and African art, rotating exhibits, and a mural spanning two walls that took decades to complete and depicts African-American culture in the region. The museum will move to a new $15-million facility on Cherry Street in the summer of 2006.

340 Walnut St. (*C* 478/743-8544. www.tubmanmuseum.com. Admission $5 adults, $3 children 12 and under. Mon–Sat 9am–5pm; Sun 2–5pm.

**Hay House** ✶   If you see nothing else in Macon, see the Hay House. Built between 1855 and 1860 for the then-exorbitant cost of $100,000, this extravagant Italian Renaissance Revival home belonged to William Butler Johnston, the keeper of the Confederate treasury. The restored interiors here are nothing short of spectacular—stained glass, ornate period furnishings, Carrara marble, and *trompe l'oeil* wall paintings. Its infrastructure was ahead of its time as well, with a cleverly designed ventilation system, hot and cold running water, and central heating. An ongoing restoration is uncovering original hand-painted decorative walls. The house is a registered National Historic Landmark.

934 Georgia Ave. (*C* 478/742-8155. www.hayhouse.org. Admission $8 adults, $7 seniors, $4 students, free for children 6 and under. Mon–Sat 10am–5pm; Sun 1–5pm. Closed holidays.

**Rose Hill Cemetery**   This beautiful 68-acre cemetery alongside the Ocmulgee River was landscaped in 1840, making it one of the oldest surviving public cemeteries in the country. Terraced hills and cypress trees give it a grandeur not unlike that of the Forum in Rome. Among those buried here are Confederate generals, Georgia politicians and entrepreneurs, beloved pets, and two members of the Allman Brothers rock band, who died within a year of each other in motorcycle accidents at the same Napier Street intersection.

Riverside Dr. (*C* 478/751-9119. Free admission. Open daily until sundown.

**Sidney Lanier Cottage**   This 1842 Victorian cottage was the birthplace of Sidney Lanier, one of Georgia's most famous citizens, a poet who is best known for "The Marshes of Glynn." The wedding gown of Lanier's wife, Mary Day, is on display; Scarlett O'Hara would have been pea-green with envy over the bride's ultra-tiny waist. The house is outfitted in furnishings of the period and is home to the Middle Georgia Historical Society.

935 High St. (*C* 478/743-3851. www.historicmacon.org. Admission $5 adults, $3 students, free for children 5 and under. Mon–Fri 9am–5pm; Sat 10am–4pm. Closed holidays.

## TOURS

Stop at the Downtown Macon Welcome Center (see "Essentials," above) for a self-guided tour map, or download it yourself from the Welcome Center's website (www.maconga.org). You can also arrange, through the Welcome Center, **customized group tours** with professional guides; or you can buy an "Around Town" combination ticket. The ticket gives you admission to several attractions (see "Seeing the Sights," above).

Organized tours are offered by the popular **Around Town Tours,** Terminal Station Building, 200 Cherry St. (*C* 478/743-3401; www.maconga.org), which offers tours of three historic homes. The tour is given Monday to Saturday at 10am and 2pm and costs $15 for adults and $9 for children 5 to 18, including admission prices. It's advised that you arrive at least 15 minutes prior to tour departure.

## WHERE TO STAY

Along I-75 are many chain hotels and motels, including Howard Johnson, Comfort Inn, Holiday Inn, and Hampton Inn. Off I-475 are Ramada Inn, Travelodge, and Holiday Inn. The best chain choice is the **Courtyard by Marriott,** 3990 Sheraton Dr. (℄ **478/477-8899**).

**1842 Inn** ★★★    The 1842 Inn is reason enough to come to Macon. It's truly special, and is one of our favorite inns south of the Mason-Dixon Line. This inn is romantic, upscale, and charming. You're likely to find a working fireplace in your room, along with antiques, expensive fabrics, four-poster beds, and maybe even a whirlpool. But what turns this place into something truly memorable is the lovely staff, who have been here for years and who epitomize warm-as-toast Southern hospitality. JoAnne Dillard's specially made mint juleps are fashioned from mint fresh from the kitchen garden and served in elegant silver julep cups, along with evening hors d'oeuvres, in one of the parlor rooms. The inn has no restaurant (look for on-site dining facilities in the near future), but travelers arriving late can arrange to have a fine French meal from La Lavandier waiting for them on the candlelit patio. Across the courtyard is a 1900 Victorian cottage with equally elegant rooms. Come to Macon and add your name to the list of celebrities (including Dr. Ruth and Barbara Walters) who have stayed here. All rooms are nonsmoking.

353 College St., Macon, GA 31201. ℄ **800/336-1842** or 478/741-1842. Fax 478/741-1842. www.1842 inn.com. 19 units. $180–$230 double. AE, DC, MC, V. Take exit 52 off I-75, then go 4 blocks to the center of the historic district. **Amenities:** Breakfast room; lounge; rooms for those w/limited mobility. *In room:* A/C, TV, hair dryer.

## WHERE TO DINE

Macon has a growing number of upscale restaurants, but if it's down-home Southern cooking you want, you won't be disappointed. **Len Berg's Restaurant,** in Old Post Alley between Walnut and Mulberry streets (℄ **478/742-9255**), is a Macon institution, serving home cooking, pure and simple. Try the fried catfish filet or the grilled liver with onions, and finish with the cream-topped macaroon pie for dessert. Barbecue lovers can opt for **Satterfield's,** on 120 New St. (℄ **478/745-8342**), where you can snack on homemade boiled peanuts while you wait for your order of good barbecue, Brunswick stew, and long-cooked vegetables. (It even offers an all-you-can-eat Quail Night.) **Fincher's Barbecue,** 3947 Houston Ave. and three other locations (℄ **478/788-1900**), is another local institution. The family-run restaurant offers curb service at the Houston Avenue location and good, old-fashioned barbecued pork, ribs, and chicken.

**The Back Burner Restaurant** ★ NOUVELLE CONTINENTAL    Chef Christian Losito has brought serious food to Macon at this charming cottage off Ingleside Avenue. The Nice, France, native offers a changing menu that may include a Chilean halibut in a champagne-and-shallot sauce; rack of lamb in a Dijon-thyme sauce; or grilled shrimp over penne pasta in a mushroom-wine sauce. Lunchtime soups and salads are fresh and innovative. The restaurant is broken into intimate, low-ceilinged rooms, each painted a different, handsome color; nice linens and flowers complete the sunny picture.

2242 Ingleside Ave. ℄ **478/746-3336**. Main courses $10–$13 lunch, $17–$30 dinner. Tues–Sat 11:30am–2pm and 6–9:30pm. Closed Sun and Mon.

## 2 Callaway Gardens ★★★

70 miles S of Atlanta

One of the most beautiful spots in the South, Callaway Gardens embraces 14,000 acres of gardens, woodlands, and lakes, with wildlife and outdoor activities. Some 750,000 visitors are attracted to this site annually, especially in spring when its Azalea Trail displays some 700 colorful varieties. But every season brings something new into bloom, from rhododendron and holly trails to wildflowers.

Callaway Gardens at Pine Mountain was begun back in the 1930s. Cason Callaway, head of one of Georgia's most prosperous textile mills, once said, "All I've done is try to fix it so that anybody who came here would see something beautiful wherever he might look." He set about rebuilding the soil, nurturing and importing plant life, building the largest man-made inland beach in the world, and providing inn and cottage accommodations—and opened it all to citizens of modest means.

## ESSENTIALS

**GETTING THERE**   From Atlanta, take I-85 South to I-185, continue on I-185 South to exit 14, and then turn left on U.S. 27 and drive 11 miles to Callaway Gardens. Driving north on either I-185 or I-85, exit east on Ga. 18 to Pine Mountain, and then turn right on U.S. 27 and enter Callaway Gardens.

## SEEING THE GARDENS

**Callaway Gardens,** at Pine Mountain (© **706/663-2281;** www.callawayonline. com), include floral and hiking trails and acres of picnic grounds. Special events abound, particularly the Spring Celebration. In May, Callaway plays host to the Masters Waterski Tournament. July 4th is the occasion of the sunrise-to-sunset Surf and Sand Spectacular, giving way to the Sky High Balloon Festival over Labor Day weekend. The Fall Festival celebrates the beauty of the chrysanthemums, and Fantasy in Lights at Christmas is a brilliant ride through the gardens with a display of lights and music.

The park has many attractions. The **Cecil B. Day Butterfly Center** ★, a $5.3-million center, ranks with the world's foremost conservatories in London, Melbourne, and Tokyo. The octagonal conservatory houses more than 1,000 free-flying butterflies and numerous birds. The conservatory includes a 12-foot waterfall and lush tropical foliage.

**John A. Sibley Horticultural Center,** one of the most advanced garden and greenhouse complexes in the world, encompasses 5 acres with 20,200 square feet of indoor floral displays, plus 30,675 square feet of greenhouse space. Floral displays integrate indoor and outdoor settings.

**Mr. Cason's Vegetable Garden,** started in 1960, was the last major project initiated by Mr. Callaway. On 7½ acres, gardeners demonstrate scientific, educational, and practical applications of fruit and vegetable cultures. A trio of large terraces in a semicircular design, the vegetable garden produces more than 400 varieties of crops that range from traditional Southern fruits and vegetables to wildflower test plots. The PBS show *Victory Garden* films its Southern segments from here.

**Ida Cason Callaway Memorial Chapel,** in the English Gothic style, was built to honor Mr. Callaway's mother, Ida Cason. It was dedicated in 1962 by Dr. Norman Vincent Peale. It's patterned much like a rural wayside chapel of the 16th and 17th centuries.

The park is open daily from 9am to 5pm with extended summer hours. Admission is $13 for adults, $6.50 for children 6 to 12, and free for children 5 and under.

## OUTDOOR PURSUITS

**BEACH RESORT    Robin Lake Beach,** on a 65-acre lake, is the largest inland man-made white-sand beach anywhere in the world. It offers a center for children with a large outdoor playground, as well as miniature golf, badminton, and rides on a riverboat. In summer, a show is presented by Florida State University's Flying High Circus. A trail stretches nearly a mile around the lake with 20 fitness stations. Robin Lake Beach is a virtual miniresort, with sand, surf, and dozens of other activities. Admission is $13 for adults, $6.50 for children 6 to 12, free for children 5 and under. The beach is open daily from 9am to 6pm in summer. It is closed from Labor Day until the first of June.

**BIKING**    Callaway Gardens has 7½ paved miles for bikers who'd like to see the gardens up close instead of from a car. The Discovery Bicycle Trail is a family favorite. It begins at Bike Barn near the beach parking lot at Robin Lake, where you can rent bikes and helmets (some bikes are equipped with child safety seats). A ferry is available near the end of the trail at the boat dock to transport riders across Mountain Creek Lake back to their starting point. The Bike Barn rents bikes daily from 8am to 6pm, charging $12 for 2 hours, $18 for a half-day.

**FISHING**    Fishing is available on Mountain Creek Lake, where two persons can rent a boat for $40 per half-day or $55 per full day.

**GOLF**    Callaway's well-groomed courses, hailed by *Golf Digest* and *Golf* magazine, are set in the midst of clear lakes, lush landscaping, and wooded shores. **Mountain View,** designed by Dick Wilson, is viewed as the best by many golfers. Tight, tree-lined fairways are characteristic of this championship course. At hole no. 15 (par 5), the threat of water looms over both tee and approach shots. This hole is ranked as the fourth-most difficult par 5 on the tour by *USA Today.* **Lake View** was the original course, designed only in part by Dick Wilson. Mr. Callaway himself provided the inspiration for this course, whose challenge lies in its 9 water holes. The par-70 course is known for its no. 5 with its island tee and serpentine bridge over Mountain Creek Lake to the green in front of the Gardens Restaurant. **Mountain View** is the most expensive course to play, at a cost of $70, while Lake View costs $55. Finally, the 9-hole **Sky View** is a par-31 executive course ideal for an hour or two of fresh air and warm-up for 18 holes. Greens fees here are $35.

**TENNIS**    *Tennis* magazine awarded Callaway a "Top 50" national rating. Nine courts are hard surfaced, and eight have Rubico surfaces. Two glass-walled racquetball courts and a pro shop are also located in the complex.

## WHERE TO STAY

**Callaway Gardens Resort** ★★    In 1951, as the success of Callaway Gardens attracted visitors from around the country, Cason Callaway engaged Holiday Inn to build a motel on gently sloping terrain across the highway from the gardens. Eventually Callaway acquired the property and enlarged it. Despite the complete renovation, some units still evoke the Holiday Inn of old.

Set adjacent to the resort's freshwater beach, rustic two-bedroom cottages contain fireplaces, kitchens, and lots of modern luxuries. Popular with families, they're what you'd expect at an outdoor camping retreat, and seem to have endured their share of wear and tear. More stylish are the villas; all have kitchens, relatively formal furnishings, fireplaces, screened-in verandas, and a greater emphasis on style and comfort. Every unit has a well-maintained bathroom with a tub/shower combination.

U.S. 27, Pine Mountain, GA 31822. © **800/CALLAWAY** or 706/663-2281. Fax 706/663-5090. www.callaway online.com. 349 units, 155 1- and 2-bedroom cottages, 57 2- to 4-bedroom villas. $99–$139 double; $149–$264 suite; $129–$290 1- and 2-bedroom cottages; $242–$499 2- to 4-bedroom villas. Honeymoon, sports, and monthly packages available. AE, DC, DISC, MC, V. **Amenities:** 9 restaurants; 2 lounges; 3 pools (1 indoor); 2 18-hole golf courses; 10 tennis courts; fitness center; boutiques; limited room service; baby-sitting; laundry service/dry cleaning; nonsmoking rooms; rooms for those w/limited mobility. *In room:* A/C, TV, dataport, coffeemaker, hair dryer, iron/ironing board.

**Magnolia Hall B&B** *Finds*    Open year-round, this B&B lies 5 miles from the entrance to Callaway Gardens. An 1890s Victorian home, it's surrounded by an acre of land with azaleas, tea olives, camellias, and the namesake magnolias. Potted ferns and cushioned wicker evoke the Deep South. Antiques-filled rooms, a grand piano in the sitting room, and high ceilings add grace notes. Guest rooms are spacious and contain well-kept bathrooms with tub/shower combinations. This is not necessarily a place for kids and definitely not a place for smokers. All rooms are nonsmoking.

127 Barnes Mill Rd. (P.O. Box 326), Hamilton, GA 31811. © **706/628-4566.** Fax 706/628-5802. www.magnolia hallbb.com. 5 units. $105–$125 double. Extra person $25. Rates include breakfast. AE, MC, V. **Amenities:** Breakfast room; 2 lounges . *In room:* A/C, TV, hair dryer, no phone.

**Valley Inn Resort** *Kids*    There's nothing special here, but as motels go, it's one of the best of the lot. Families, especially in summer, like this small resort set on 52 acres near a lake. Bedrooms are comfortably furnished. Some units contain kitchens, and all units contain well-kept bathrooms with tub/shower combinations. You can bring your own RV to park in the Travel Trailer Park or rent a two-bedroom mobile home unit that sleeps up to six. All rooms are nonsmoking.

14420 Hwy. 27, Hamilton, GA 31811. © **800/944-9393** or 706/628-4454. www.valleyresort.com. 24 units. $79 double; $105 1-bedroom cottage; $120 2-bedroom cottage. AE, DC, DISC, MC, V. **Amenities:** Breakfast room; lounge; outdoor pool 1 room for those w/limited mobility. *In room:* A/C, TV, kitchenette (in some).

**White Columns Motel**    One mile to Callaway Gardens, this small family-owned and -operated white-columned motel is a favorite budget choice in the area. There's a large swing on the front lawn under an old magnolia tree, a great place to spend a lazy summer afternoon. Rooms are basic but clean and comfortable, and have been recently "fixed up." Each unit contains a neatly kept bathroom with shower. Pets are accepted. Within walking distance of the motel are two good and moderately priced restaurants.

Hwy. 27 S. (P.O. Box 531), Pine Mountain, GA 31822. © **800/722-5093** or 706/663-2312. 14 units. $55–$65 double. Rates include continental breakfast. MC, V. **Amenities:** Nonsmoking rooms; rooms for those w/limited mobility. *In room:* A/C, TV, kitchenette (in some), fridge, iron/ironing board, microwave (in some).

## WHERE TO DINE

**The Country Kitchen** SOUTHERN    First things first: Don't come here looking for health food. Despite that, its premises (a stone-built roadside country store about a mile south of the Callaway Gardens' entrance, near the top of Pine Mountain) are usually mobbed with families looking for a taste of wholesome country nostalgia. The setting is rustic and woodsy. Menu items include chicken or country ham with biscuits and gravy, an array of vegetables, burgers, and club sandwiches. Dessert might be a portion of muscadine ice cream. If you need grits to get your day started right, have them along with "Mama's pancakes" or a country omelet.

Hwy. 27, near Callaway Gardens. ⓒ 706/663-2281. Breakfast platters $6.25–$8.50; main courses $7–$11. AE, DISC, MC, V. Daily 7:30am–8pm.

**The Gardens** ITALIAN/INTERNATIONAL    The Gardens occupies a sprawling and immensely atmospheric building whose stout timbers and rambling verandas resemble a grange in eastern France or Germany. Our favorite tables are perched on a balcony overlooking a landscape of golf fairways and a pond that has a serpentine bridge zigzagging across its waters. The menu emphasizes grilled steaks, seafood, and chops, and the kitchen prepares this fare exceedingly well.

Hwy. 27, near Callaway Gardens. ⓒ 706/663-2281. Reservations recommended. Main courses $12–$19. Wed–Sun noon–9:30pm.

**The Plantation Room** *Value* SOUTHERN    The buffets here celebrate culinary traditions of the Old South. Vegetables are the freshest in summer, when they come to your table just hours after being picked from Mr. Cason's vegetable garden. If you've never eaten corn just pulled from the stalk, you'll find how different it is from store-bought corn pulled days before. It can get very crowded here, especially on Friday nights, when the theme is seafood.

At Callaway Gardens. ⓒ 706/663-2281. Breakfast buffet $8.75; lunch buffet $11; dinner buffet $18. AE, DISC, MC, V. Daily 6:30–10:30am, 11:30am–2pm, and 5:30–9pm.

## 3 Warm Springs & FDR's Little White House ★★

17 miles E of Callaway Gardens; 65 miles S of Atlanta

If you take Ga. 190 East and follow the signs, you'll be directed to Warm Springs, forever associated with the legacy of Franklin D. Roosevelt, who died here on April 12, 1945. Most visitors—some 110,000 a year—come to visit the "Little White House." Warm Springs village is also an attraction. After Roosevelt's death, it became a virtual ghost town, but today the village is alive with 65 shops selling antiques, crafts, and collectibles.

The **Franklin D. Roosevelt State Park,** off U.S. 27, is one of the largest in Georgia's state system, with many historic buildings, the King's Gap Indian Trail, a swimming pool, and fishing and camping facilities. For more information, contact the Superintendent, 2970 Ga. 190 E. (ⓒ 800/864-7275 or 706/663-4858; www.gastateparks.org).

### ESSENTIALS
**GETTING THERE**    Take I-85 South from Atlanta to Alt. U.S. 27 South, which you follow into Warm Springs.

To reach Warm Springs from Callaway Gardens, take U.S. 27 North into the town of Pine Mountain. At the intersection of U.S. 27 and Ga. 18, take Ga. 18 East to Ga. 194, and proceed on Ga. 194 East until it joins Alt. U.S. 27. Stay on Alt. U.S. 27/Ga. 194 South into Warm Springs.

**VISITOR INFORMATION    Warm Springs Welcome Center,** 1 Broad St. (P.O. Box 578), Warm Springs, GA 31830 (ⓒ 706/655-3322; www.warmsprings ga.ws), is open Monday to Saturday 10am to 5pm and Sunday 1 to 5pm, dispensing information and maps of the village.

### THE "LITTLE WHITE HOUSE"
This home, which came to be called the **"Little White House,"** a quarter of a mile south of Warm Springs on Ga. 85 West (ⓒ 706/655-5870; www.fdr-little whitehouse.org), was built in 1932 for $8,738—a modest outlay for a man of

Franklin Roosevelt's wealth. This tiny place was once the occasional nerve center of the commander-in-chief of the nation during the greatest war of all time.

FDR discovered Warm Springs in 1924. He contracted polio in 1921, and came here for the beneficial effect of swimming in its healing waters. Two years later he bought the springs, hotel, and some cottages and founded his Georgia Warm Springs Foundation to develop facilities for helping paralytic patients from all over the country. When he became president, this was the retreat he loved most. Today the house is much as he left it when he died here in 1945. At the time he was sitting for a portrait; the *Unfinished Portrait*, his wheelchair, ship models, sea paintings, Fala's dog chain, and gifts sent him by various citizens are preserved as he last saw them. The house is open daily from 9am to 4:45pm. Admission is $7 for adults, $6 for seniors, $4 for children 6 to 18, and free for children 5 and under.

On-site is the **FDR Memorial Museum** (© 706/655-5870), which opened in the spring of 2004, following a $5-million redevelopment. It has been the goal of the friends of Warm Springs for years to expand a tiny little museum onsite into a much larger space and a visitor center. Today, FDR memorabilia is displayed in a modern 12,000-square-foot museum constructed on one level, with special care taken to provide entry for persons who suffer disabilities (the four-time American Depression and wartime president himself was disabled with polio). Roosevelt wanted a place to make his records of the past available "for the use of men and women in the future." The unfinished portrait that Elizabeth Shoumatoff was painting on the day the president died is on display here (see "An Unfinished Portrait," below). Other artifacts and memorabilia document FDR's halcyon days in Georgia. The museum is open daily 9am to 4:45pm. Adults pay $7, seniors $6, children 6 to 18 $4.

## WHERE TO STAY

**Hotel Warm Springs Bed and Breakfast Inn** ⭐    This hotel, built in 1907, thrived when the region's economy boomed because of the presence of FDR

---

### An Unfinished Portrait

Although never completed, one of the world's most famous portraits rests in Warm Springs in FDR's "Little White House." He was posing for it shortly before he died on April 12, 1945. In some respects, Elizabeth Shoumatoff's portrait symbolizes Roosevelt's unfinished life, and his unfinished (and unprecedented) fourth term that was to be filled out by Harry S. Truman. Roosevelt, plagued by ill health, would have continued to face monumental decisions that year if he'd lived. He would have presided over the defeat of the Nazi armies, and been faced with the decision of whether or not to drop the atomic bomb (which he'd ordered built) on Japan. After that fateful spring day, Truman had to make those decisions in FDR's place.

The president's ashen pallor and his tired, drawn face are captured in the unfinished portrait, revealing the stress FDR felt at the end of the most destructive war in history. His wife, Eleanor, arrived in Warm Springs shortly after midnight on the day of his death. When she wrote about that night in *This I Remember*, Mrs. Roosevelt chose not to mention that Lucy Mercer Rutherford, FDR's sweetheart, was with him when he died. However, she later wrote: "All human beings have failings, and all human beings have needs and temptations and stresses." It is Roosevelt's humanity that we remember.

---

throughout the war years. Gerrie Thompson, its owner since 1988, can recite a guest list that includes the queen of Mexico (who came for the cure, and slept on the floor because of an injured spine); the king and queen of Spain; the president of the Philippines; armies of journalists, Cabinet members, and Secret Service agents—and a screen legend named Bette Davis.

Despite some half-hearted attempts at redecoration (new curtains, the installation of a heart-shaped Jacuzzi in the honeymoon suite), this artfully dowdy period piece from another age evokes the languor and sultriness of the 1940s in the Deep South. Some of the guest rooms contain old-fashioned oak furniture made in the factory Eleanor Roosevelt established in Val-Kill, New York, to relieve unemployment during the Great Depression. All units have well-kept bathrooms with showers and tubs. Sitting rooms and a high-ceilinged breakfast room are located on the second and third floors. Interestingly, this structure was the home of the first phone system in Warm Springs. All rooms are nonsmoking.

47 Broad St., Warm Springs, GA 31830. ℂ 800/366-7616 or 706/655-2114. Fax 706/655-2406. 14 units. $75–$125 double; $130–$190 suite. Rates include breakfast. AE, DISC, MC, V. **Amenities:** Breakfast room; lounge. *In room:* A/C, TV, hair dryer, iron/ironing board.

## WHERE TO DINE

**Bulloch House Restaurant** SOUTHERN   Set on a leafy hillside, a 10-minute walk from the center of town, the place occupies the genteel premises of a house originally built in 1892. Citizens from virtually every walk of life file by the buffets, plate in hand. There are five different homey, dowdy dining areas. One is a front porch overlooking the road, although most diners remain in the air-conditioned interior. Menu items celebrate deep-fried, local cookery, and always include fried green tomatoes, fried fish, fried chicken, fried okra, butterbeans, turnip greens, potatoes, biscuits, bread, and copious amounts of iced tea. No alcohol of any kind is served. It's very much a family-fry operation.

47 Bulloch St. ℂ 706/655-9068. Lunch buffet $6.95; dinner buffet $9.95. AE, DISC, MC, V. Daily 11am–2:30pm; Fri–Sat 5–8:30pm.

## 4 Plains: Jimmy Carter's Hometown

80 miles SE of Callaway Gardens; 85 miles SW of Macon; 10 miles W of Americus

More than any other president in recent years, Jimmy Carter is closely identified with his hometown—Plains, Georgia. The aptly named town of 716 is both plain and sited on the plains.

Humble though it is, Plains is where a young boy grew up to become the 39th president of the United States. If FDR was an American aristocrat, "Jimmy," as he is called locally, was—and still is—a man of the people, the most approachable president in recent history, and a Nobel prize winner to boot.

You'll know Plains by the little green-and-white train depot, its water tower brightly painted with the Stars and Stripes. Despite the fame of its most outstanding citizen, a small-town charm still clings to Plains and its people. The early-1900s buildings are much as they were before the Depression forced their closing (most were used as warehouses until Jimmy Carter's campaign brought business back to town).

## ESSENTIALS

**GETTING THERE**   From Macon, take I-75 South to Cordele; exit there onto U.S. 280 and head west through Americus to Plains. From Callaway Gardens, take U.S. 27 to Pine Mountain, turn left on Ga. 18 to I-185, and then take I-185 South through Columbus to U.S. 280; head south (or east) on U.S. 280 into Plains.

**VISITOR INFORMATION**   If you stand in the middle of the street, you can almost see the whole town, including Billy Carter's former service station, which used to sell beer to newspeople when Billy was alive. For a do-it-yourself walking or driving tour to points of interest, stop in at the **Georgia Visitor Center,** east of Plains at 1763 Hwy. 280 W. (© **229/824-7477;** www.plainsgeorgia.com), open daily from 8:30am to 5:30pm. The staff there will furnish maps and brochures.

## SEEING THE SIGHTS

**Jimmy Carter National Historic Site** ⭐ (© **229/824-3413;** www.nps.gov/jica) is 77 acres administered by the U.S. Department of the Interior. An old-fashioned railway depot from 1888 is the headquarters of the visitor center—it also served as Carter's campaign headquarters in 1976 and again in 1980 when he lost to Ronald Reagan. The depot is filled with campaign memorabilia, and is open daily (except Thanksgiving, Christmas, and New Year's Day) from 9am to 5pm. Admission is free. An information booklet costs $1.25.

The one-story, ranch-style brick **Carter home** is on Woodland Drive; when the Carters are in residence, there are Secret Service booths at this entrance and at the one on Paschal Street (you can get a pretty good look at it by walking and driving west on Church St.). Then there's the **Plains Methodist Church,** at the corner of Church and Thomas streets, where Jimmy asked Rosalynn for their first date. When he's in town, Jimmy teaches Sunday school at **Maranatha Baptist Church.** Visitors are invited—check the notice in the window of Hugh Carter's Antiques on Main Street. **Archery,** a 2½-mile drive west of town on U.S. 280, is where Jimmy Carter lived as a child when his father operated a country store. Anybody in Plains can give you explicit directions.

In 2001, the Depression-era **Jimmy Carter Boyhood Farm** signposted off Route 280 West (© **229/824-3413**) opened to the public. The last living occupant of the one-story, white-frame house, the former U.S. president himself, was an adviser to the restorers of the house. The former president took such an interest that he spent 2 days supervising the reconstruction of a privy in back of the house. He wanted it to be "authentic" as memory served him. The farm has been restored to its appearance in 1937 before electricity was put in.

Mr. Carter lived in the house from 1928 to 1942 until he went off to college. The historic site lies 2½ miles west of Plains and 120 miles south of Atlanta. Visitors can explore the former Carter home, a reconstructed barn, a small farm store, a windmill, a buggy shed, a pump house, and a blacksmith shop on 15 acres of what originally was a 360-acre farm.

There are several walking trails along the property. Hours are daily from 10am to 5pm, and admission is free.

## WHERE TO STAY

**Plains Bed and Breakfast Inn** ⭐ *Finds*   Painted in a stylish shade of dusty rose and built in 1910 by a Baptist preacher, this place provides the only conventional lodgings in Plains. It sits adjacent to the trailerlike building that houses the local sheriff, two doors away from a service station that proclaims its enduring association with Billy Carter. The inn is an odd mixture of small-town virtue and religious revivalism. Its best feature is the spacious veranda for porch swinging. Most of the inside, however, is old-fashioned. Each unit is well maintained and equipped with a tidily kept bathroom with a tub/shower combination. Miss Lillian and her new husband occupied one of the upstairs bedrooms around the time the future president was conceived. A sign in the upstairs hallway obliquely refers to this portentous event in ever-so-polite phrasing. During Carter's term, some of the most visible figures in American media slept here.

Main St., Plains, GA 31780. ⓒ 229/824-7252. 4 units. $80 double. Rate includes Southern breakfast. DC, MC, V. **Amenities:** Breakfast room; lounge. *In room:* A/C.

**Plains Historic Inn & Antiques** ★★★    After being the most powerful man in the world for years, what's left but to sit on a swing on the front porch and welcome visitors to Plains and your B&B? Assisted by his wife, Rosalyn, former president Jimmy Carter doesn't have to worry about controversies over the White House's Lincoln Bedroom. Now he's got his own bedrooms to fret about. When Rosalyn and the former president saw hundreds of tourists coming through each day, with no place to stay, the couple decided to convert the upstairs portions of two buildings into guest rooms, each themed to a specific decade. Naturally, the 1970s are represented with a presidential suite. Other rooms are authentically furnished from the 1920s to the 1980s—the latter "that dreadful decade" that brought in Reagan. "Every room is a history lesson," Carter explains. Accommodations are authentic to their era—Mrs. Carter actually furnished the rooms with magazine issues published in each period. All rooms are nonsmoking.

Carter himself helped with the carpentry, aided by a group of prison inmates in white uniforms. The inmates were even invited to the grand opening, a first for Georgia; prisoners don't usually get invited to such gala affairs.

Guests share a public room and a balcony overlooking the historic square where Carter once had his campaign headquarters. Below, two old storefronts have been converted into an antiques mall. Few guests miss the opportunity to have a cup of coffee and some boiled peanuts at the adjacent Plains Coffee Shop. And for the rarest treat documented in this entire guide, on some afternoons "Mister Jimmy and Miz Rosalyn" drop in to join guests on the front porch for afternoon tea and to discuss politics. Talk about being an eyewitness to history!

106 Main St., Plains, GA 31780. ⓒ 229/824-4517. www.plainsgeorgia.com/plainsinn.htm. 7 units. Sun–Thurs $85 double, Fri–Sat $95 double; Sun–Thurs $125 presidential suite, Fri–Sat $140 presidential suite. AE, MC, V. **Amenities:** "Common Room" (public lounge); nearby coffee shop; rooms for those w/limited mobility. *In room:* A/C, TV, dataport, hair dryer, iron/ironing board.

## WHERE TO DINE

Do as the Carters do and head for nearby Americus—notably the **Grand Dining Room at the Windsor Hotel,** 125 W. Lamar St. (ⓒ **888/297-9567**). This high-ceilinged, historic restaurant reigns in a town filled with rustic, down-home contenders. Expect the most generous luncheon buffet available. Dinners showcase upscale versions of Caesar salad garnished with shrimp or chicken; quail stuffed with rice and served with a brandy-cream sauce; and a delectable version of pork Normandy, stuffed with apples and served with an apple-brandy sauce.

## A SIDE TRIP TO ANDERSONVILLE

Just 21 miles northeast of Plains (take U.S. 280 to Americus, then Ga. 49 North) is the site of the most infamous of Confederate prison camps, Andersonville. It was built to hold 10,000 but at one time had a prisoner population of more than 32,000, struggling to survive on polluted water and starvation rations. Nearly 15,000 prisoners died here. The commander, Capt. Henry Wirtz, although powerless to help the situation, was tried and hanged after the

Civil War on charges of having conspired to murder Union prisoners. Today you can visit the **Drummer Boy Civil War Museum** (© **229/924-2558**), open Thursday to Saturday 10am to 5pm; Sunday 1 to 5pm. Admission is $2 for adults, $1 for children 6 to 12, and free for children 5 and under. You'll see slide shows of the camp's sad history, as well as the remains of wells and escape tunnels. Legend says that **Providence Springs** gushed up in answer to prayers of prisoners during the drought of 1864. **Andersonville National Historic Site** (© **229/924-0343**) is open daily from 8am to 5pm; admission is free.

After visiting the historic site, browse the antiques shops in the adjacent village of Andersonville. Stop by the **Andersonville Guild Welcome Center** (© **229/924-2558**) in the old train depot and meet Peggy Sheppard, a gregarious, transplanted New Yorker who spearheaded the village's rejuvenation. The center is open daily from 9am to 5pm.

If you're looking for a bite to eat, try the **Andersonville Restaurant,** 213 W. Church St. (© **229/928-8480**)—a real down-home establishment with a buffet groaning under the weight of Southern fried chicken, country ham and, in summer, fresh vegetables. Everybody orders second or even third helpings of biscuits to mop up the juices. Your $6 entitles you to one meat, three vegetables, biscuits, beverage, and dessert—a real bargain. Fresh catfish is fried up on Friday nights. Its can't-miss location is in the village center.

**Andersonville National Historic Site and National Prisoner of War Museum** ⭐    This museum was dedicated in April 1998 by a host of senators including John McCain, R-Arizona, a prisoner of war in Vietnam for 5 years; and Georgia governor Zell Miller. The museum is adjacent to the site of one of the two deadliest Civil War POW encampments, and its 10,000 square feet contain artifacts in tribute to the 800,000 soldiers who have suffered as POWs, from the American Revolution to the Persian Gulf conflict.

Housed within the museum are postcards from soldiers who hoped that their future brides had not assumed they were dead, letters to families who thought they would never see their sons again, pictures, and models of prison cells, including a Vietnamese bamboo cage. The $5.8-million structure was built from private funds raised by POW veterans, with $3.6 million coming from the State of Georgia and the federal government. The first museum of its kind in the United States, it touches on a subject long ignored by the American public, in large part due to veterans' reluctance to relive the horrors of imprisonment. There are stories of prisoners in Japanese camps who lost 55 pounds during their stay, and tales of brothers who were imprisoned together, with only one surviving.

Adjacent to the museum is the notorious Confederate POW camp, Andersonville (see above). When its inmate population was heaviest during the last 14 months of the Civil War, the mortality rate was 29%, partly because of the heat, since Northerners were not acclimated to the Southern weather. The camp's Union counterpart in Elmira, New York (known as "Hellmira") had a mortality rate of 24% during its lifetime, conversely because of the cold; many Southerners froze to death. Visitors are allowed to walk the grounds, and an audiocassette or CD tour of the grounds is available for $1.

Ga. 49, Andersonville. © 229/924-0343. www.nps.gov/ande. Free admission to museum and site; donations accepted. Museum daily 8:30am–5pm; site daily 8am–5pm. From I-75 North or South, take exit 127 at Montezuma/Hawkinsville. Travel west along Ga. 26, continuing south on Ga. 49. The park entrance will appear on your left just outside Andersonville.

## 5 Thomasville ★★

45 miles W of Valdosta; 35 miles NE of Tallahassee; 230 miles S of Atlanta

From the 1800s to the early 1900s, Thomasville was one of the world's most fashionable places, hailed by *Harper's Magazine* in 1887 as "the best winter resort on three continents." After the Civil War, when much of the South was embittered and in ruins, a remarkable and progressive group of civil leaders began building resorts that attracted the wintering wealthy. Few other places in the South wanted to encourage the "damn Yankees" at the time. Regrettably, every one of the grand hotels that once flourished here has disappeared, victims of fires, rot, termites, and the opening of nearby Florida as a holiday destination. Many of the Victorian homes of the town, however, remain intact, attracting architectural enthusiasts from around the state.

Considering that the wealth of North America's Gilded Age once disported itself here, Thomasville remains relatively obscure. Even in Georgia, its name sometimes draws a blank. Yet at various times, the world press has descended on the area, notably when President Eisenhower used to play golf here, and when Jacqueline Kennedy was discovered hiding out here to recuperate following the assassination of her husband.

Historic Thomasville remains unique in the South today as the centerpiece of a county containing approximately 70 enormous plantations encompassing some 300,000 acres. Only the post–Civil War prosperity of the town's 19th- and early-20th-century tourism allowed these estates to survive intact. Throughout the rest of the South, plantations were broken up, subdivided, sold for back taxes, allowed to fall into decay and, in a later age, turned into housing developments. Regrettably, of the many that survive, only one is open to the public.

### ESSENTIALS

**GETTING THERE** **By Car** From Tallahassee, head northeast along Highway 319. From Atlanta, take I-75 South to the junction with Route 122 to Tifton, exiting onto Highway 319 southwest into Thomasville.

**VISITOR INFORMATION** The welcome center for the **Thomasville Tourism Authority** at 401 S. Broad St. (© **229/227-7099;** www.thomasvillega.com) is one of the most helpful in Georgia. It's open Monday to Friday from 8am to 5pm and Saturday from 10am to 3pm. A genealogical library is also maintained by the city.

### SEEING THE SIGHTS

The town's mascot is **"The Big Oak,"** at the corner of North Crawford and East Monroe streets, in back of the Federal Courthouse and the post office. It's at least 3 centuries old and has been a respected member of the National Live Oak Society since 1936. If anyone attempted to cut it down or harm it in any way, the townspeople would rise up in revolt. The giant is 68 feet tall with a limb spread of 162 feet and a circumference of 24 feet.

**Thomas County Museum of History** This is the best place for learning about the extraordinary "Winter Resort Era" that began in Thomasville in the 1880s. Although all the grand Victorian hotels are gone, photographs on display show their remarkable architecture. Along with memorabilia of Thomasville from this era are exhibits of historic plantations, restored 19th-century buildings, antique women's dresses, and vintage automobiles. Out back is an antique bowling alley. The museum also offers guided hour-long bus tours of Thomasville for $50.

725 N. Dawson St. © **229/226-7664.** Admission $5 adults, $1 children. Mon–Sat 10am–noon and 2–5pm.

**Lapham-Patterson House** ★ This example of Victorian architecture, declared a National Historic Landmark in 1975, is known for its fish-scale shingles, Asian-style porch decorations, long-leaf pine inlaid floors, and double-flue chimney with walk-through stairway and cantilevered balcony. Built between 1884 and 1885, it was the winter cottage for a prosperous shoe merchant, C. W. Lapham of Chicago. As a survivor of the Great Chicago Fire, Lapham wanted to make his winter cottage as safe as possible. This explains why, in the 19 rooms in this cottage, there are 45 doors, 26 of them exterior. All of the 53 windows open from the bottom up and the top down.

626 N. Dawson St. ✆ 229/225-4004. Admission $4 adults, $2 ages 18 and under. Tues–Sat 9am–5pm; Sun 2–5:30pm.

**Pebble Hill Plantation** ★ *Finds* They called her "Miss Pansy," and she was a local legend, greatly admired by Jimmy Carter. Her name was Elisabeth Ireland Poe (1897–1978), and she was the last of the Hanna dynasty, which owned Pebble Hill. A sportswoman, she was also a patron of the arts, a grand hostess, and a collector, and upon her death she willed that her home should be open to the public for a glimpse into an elegant past. Hers is the only plantation home in Thomas County open to the public. Established in the 1820s, the house was almost destroyed by fire in the 1930s but was rebuilt under the direction of architect Abram Garfield, son of the nation's 20th president.

5 miles southwest of Thomasville via U.S. 319. ✆ 229/226-2344. www.pebblehill.com. Grounds $3 adults, $1.50 children under 12. Main house $7 adults, $3.50 children grades 1–6 (younger children not admitted). Tues–Sat 10am–5pm; Sun 1–5pm.

## WHERE TO STAY

**1884 Paxton House Inn** ★★ This is the finest, best-furnished, and most meticulously maintained bed-and-breakfast hotel in Thomasville, the one most often cited as a role model and learning forum for anyone considering going into the B&B trade. It's in a dignified Victorian house within an upper-class neighborhood, 4 blocks east of the town center. It contains a museum-quality collection of porcelain, acquired over many decades, which decorates virtually every corner of a tasteful and elegant decor, inspired by 18th- and early-19th-century models. Ms. Susie Sherrod is the innkeeper. All units are nonsmoking and have well-kept bathrooms with tub/shower combinations. Breakfasts are lavish affairs, featuring eggs Benedict or orange-flavored French toast, served with meticulous Southern charm.

445 Remington Ave., Thomasville, GA 31792. ✆ 229/226-5197. Fax 229/226-9905. www.1884paxtonhouse inn.com. 9 units. $165–$275 double; $195–$225 suite. Rates include breakfast. AE, MC, V. **Amenities:** Breakfast room; lounge; outdoor lap pool; 8 tennis courts; health club; Jacuzzi. *In room:* A/C, TV, dataport, hair dryer, iron/ironing board.

**Evans House Bed & Breakfast** This is an imposing, socially prominent, clapboard-sided house designed in the Colonial Revival style in 1898. Its owner, Gladys Veese, has refurbished the inn completely with Victorian pieces. Today, benign ghosts continue to inhabit the building, flushing toilets and pacing the floors at unexpected intervals. Rather than recoiling, many B&B guests enjoy the tales of hauntings, and sleep comfortably in the large bedrooms that are tastefully outfitted with mission oak and turn-of-the-20th-century antiques. The place has an unfussy kind of dignity. All units are nonsmoking and have neatly kept bathrooms with shower units.

725 S. Hansell St., Thomasville, GA 31792. ✆ 229/226-1343. Fax 229/226-0653. 4 units. $85–$96 double; $125 suite. Rates include breakfast. No credit cards. **Amenities:** Breakfast room; lounge. *In room:* A/C, TV, dataport, hair dryer.

---

(Fun Fact   **Where *Gone With the Wind* Was First Screened**

On the site of the elegant new resort Melhana—The Grand Plantation, in Thomasville, the first actual screening of *Gone With the Wind* was at the plantation's on-site theater, built in 1934. The Hanna family, who owned Melhana at the time, had built the theater to resemble a river showboat. John Whitney, a major investor in the film, was a neighbor of the Hannas. He obtained a copy of the film after its final editing in 1939, and asked the Hannas if it could be shown at their little theater at a private screening before the official Atlanta premiere. The theater has now been restored on the property of the new resort.

---

**Melhana—The Grand Plantation** ★★★   This small town has a major, full-fledged resort at last, and it's a honey. In a town noted for its B&Bs, this is a standout, with such services as bellhops and a concierge. Genteel yet elegant, it's a modern version of what an Old South plantation might have looked like (but never did). Surrounded by formal gardens, it lies in an oak and magnolia hammock, just like Tara or Twelve Oaks. Its Avenue of Magnolias is a frequent setting for weddings, and the "plantation" has both classical gardens and sunken gardens. You have a choice of beautifully furnished rooms, suites, or cottages. Each is nonsmoking and offers the best comfort in town, complete with state-of-the-art bathrooms with tub and shower. The cuisine in the Chapin Dining Rooms is the finest in the county.

301 Showboat Lane, Thomasville, GA 31792. © **888/920-3030** or 229/226-2290. Fax 229/226-4585. www. melhana.com. 38 units. $285–$650 double; $400–$1,000 suite. Rates include full breakfast. AE, DC, DISC, MC, V. **Amenities:** Restaurant; indoor pool; tennis; exercise equipment; lawn games; carriage rides; business center; 24-hr. room service; massage; babysitting; laundry service; 1 room for those w/limited mobility. *In room:* A/C, TV, dataport, minibar, fridge, hair dryer, iron/ironing board, whirlpools (in some).

**Serendipity Cottage** ★ *Finds*   Partly because of its isolation on a leafy residential street away from city traffic, the Serendipity is in some ways the least obvious B&B inn in town. It's also one of the most charming, a cozy "four-square cottage" that is a perfect example of its architectural style. It was built by a local lumber baron as his private home in 1906. Every board in the building was hand-picked—a source of pride (and an effective marketing tool for his business), until he lost his home and fortune during the stock market crash of 1929. The building's most recent incarnation came about when a couple from Virginia, Ed and Kathy Middleton, tastefully restored the place as a B&B. The house has a cool and airy sense of spaciousness, with many fine interior details inspired by the Arts and Crafts movement. All units are neatly maintained, are nonsmoking, and come equipped with well-kept bathrooms, most with tub/shower combinations. The signature breakfast usually includes apple-flavored French toast spiked with apple liqueur. Children over 12 are not welcome here.

339 E. Jefferson St., Thomasville, GA 31792. © **800/388-7377** or 229/226-8111. www.serendipitycottage. com. 4 units. $105–$135 double. Rates include breakfast. AE, DISC, MC, V. **Amenities:** Breakfast room; lounge; washer/dryer. *In room:* A/C, TV, hair dryer, ceiling fans.

## WHERE TO DINE

**Plaza Restaurant** *Value*   GREEK/AMERICAN   In the center of town, this well-established dining room is the place the local B&B ladies recommend when their guests ask for the best place to eat in town. Restaurants come and go around Thomasville, but this one has built a loyal clientele and makes new friends every year. Whether it's breakfast, lunch, or dinner, the Plaza is open to serve you—just don't expect innovative cuisine. What you get is good, solid fare. For lunch, we opt for the tantalizing Greek salad. Many guests come for the oyster sandwich, a Southern favorite. Dinners get more elaborate, including a succulent pasta with seafood. The usual array of steaks, chicken, and seafood is prepared well with fresh ingredients. Thursday night is Greek Night, when the national dish of that country, moussaka, is often featured.

217 S. Broad St. ⓒ **229/226-5153**. Breakfast $2.95–$8.95; lunch buffet $6; main courses $3.95–$6.95 lunch, $8.95–$30 dinner. AE, DISC, MC, V. Mon–Sat 6:30am–9:30pm; Sun 7am–2:15pm.

# 20

# Savannah

If you have time to visit only one city in Georgia, make it Savannah. It's that special.

The movie *Forrest Gump* may have put the city squarely on the tourist map, but nothing changed the face of Savannah more than the 1994 publication of John Berendt's *Midnight in the Garden of Good and Evil*. The impact has been unprecedented, bringing in countless millions in revenue as thousands flock to see the sights from the mega-bestseller. In fact, Savannah tourism has increased some 46% since publication of what's known locally as The Book. Even after all this time, many locals still earn their living off The Book's fallout, hawking postcards, walking tours, T-shirts and, in some cases, their own careers, as in the case of the Lady Chablis, the black drag queen depicted in The Book who played herself in the Eastwood film.

We asked an old-timer what made Savannah so special. "Why, here we even have water fountains for dogs," he replied.

The free spirit, the passion, and even the decadence of Savannah resembles that of Key West or New Orleans more than it does the Bible Belt, down-home interior of Georgia. In that sense, it's as different from the rest of the state as New York City is from upstate New York.

Savannah—pronounce it with a drawl—conjures up all the clichéd images of the Old South: live oaks dripping with Spanish moss, stately antebellum mansions, mint juleps sipped on the veranda, magnolia trees, peaceful marshes, horse-drawn carriages, ships sailing up the river (though no longer laden with cotton), and even General Sherman, no one's favorite military hero here.

Today, the economy and much of the city's day-to-day life still revolve around port activity. For the visitor, however, it's Old Savannah, a beautifully restored and maintained historic area, that's the big draw. For this we can thank seven Savannah ladies who, after watching mansion after mansion demolished in the name of progress, managed in 1954 to raise funds to buy the dilapidated Isaiah Davenport House—just hours before it was slated for demolition to make way for a parking lot. The women banded together as the Historic Savannah Foundation, then went to work buying up architecturally valuable buildings and reselling them to private owners who'd promise to restore them. As a result, more than 800 of Old Savannah's 1,100 historic buildings have been restored, using original paint colors—pinks and reds and blues and greens. This "living museum" is now the largest urban National Historic Landmark District in the country—some 2½ square miles, including 20 1-acre squares that still survive from Gen. James Oglethorpe's dream of a gracious city.

## 1 Orientation

### ARRIVING

**BY PLANE**    **Savannah Hilton Head International Airport** is about 8 miles west of downtown just off I-16. **American** (© **800/433-7300;** www.aa.com), **Delta** (© **800/221-1212;** www.delta.com), **United** (© **800/241/6522;** www. united.com), and **US Airways** (© **800/428-4322;** www.usairways.com) have flights from Atlanta and Charlotte, with connections from other points.

**BY CAR**    From the north or south, I-95 passes 10 miles west of Savannah, with several exits to the city, and U.S. 17 runs through the city. From the west, I-16 ends in downtown Savannah, and U.S. 80 also runs through the city from east to west. AAA services are available through the **AAA Auto Club South,** 712 Mall Blvd., Savannah, GA 31406 (© **912/352-8222;** www.aaa.com).

**BY TRAIN**    The **train station** is at 2611 Seaboard Coastline Dr. (© **912/ 234-2611**), some 4 miles southwest of downtown; cab fare into the city is around $5. For **Amtrak** schedule and fare information, contact © **800/USA-RAIL** (www.amtrak.com).

### VISITOR INFORMATION

The **Savannah Information Visitor Center,** 301 Martin Luther King, Jr., Blvd., Savannah, GA 31401 (© **912/944-0455**), is open Monday to Friday 8:30am to 5pm and Saturday and Sunday 9am to 5pm. The staff is friendly and efficient. The center offers an audiovisual presentation ($4 adults, $1 children), organized tours, and self-guided walking, driving, or bike tours with excellent maps, cassette tapes, and brochures.

Tourist information is also available from the **Savannah Area Convention & Visitors Bureau,** 101 E. Bay St., Savannah, GA 31402 (© **877/SAVANNAH** or 912/644-6401; www.savannahvisit.com).

For everything you might want to know about The Book, check out the Internet site **www.midnightinthegarden.com**.

### CITY LAYOUT

Every other street—north, south, west, and east—is punctuated by greenery. The grid of **21 scenic squares** was laid out in 1733 by Gen. James Oglethorpe, the founder of Georgia. The design—still in use—has been called "one of the world's most revered city plans." It's said that if Savannah didn't have its history and architecture, it would be worth a visit just to see the city layout.

**Bull Street** is the dividing line between east and west. On the south side are odd-numbered buildings, on the north side even street numbers.

### NEIGHBORHOODS IN BRIEF

**Historic District** The Historic District—the real reason to visit Savannah—takes in both the riverfront and the City Market, described below. It's bordered by the Savannah River and Forsyth Park at Gaston Street and Montgomery and Price streets. Within its borders are more than 2,350 architecturally and historically significant buildings in a 2½-square-mile area. About 75% of these buildings have been restored.

**Riverfront** In this popular tourist district, River Street borders the Savannah River. Once lined with warehouses holding King Cotton, it has been the subject of massive urban renewal, turning this strip into a row of restaurants, art galleries, shops, and bars. The source of the area's growth was the river, which offered a prime shipping avenue for New World goods bound for European ports. In 1818, about half of Savannah fell under quarantine during a yellow-fever epidemic. River Street never fully recovered and fell into disrepair until its rediscovery in the mid-1970s. The urban-renewal project stabilized the downtown and revitalized the Historic District. Stroll the bluffs along the river on the old passageway of alleys, cobblestone walkways, and bridges known as **Factor's Walk.**

**City Market** Two blocks from River Street and bordering the Savannah River, the City Market was the former social and business mecca of Savannah. Since the late 18th century, it has known fires and various devastations, including the threat of demolition. But in a major move, the city of Savannah decided to save the district. Today, former decaying warehouses are filled with restaurants and shops offering everything from antiques to collectibles, including many Savannah-made products. And everything from seafood and pizza to French and Italian cuisine is served here. Live music often fills the nighttime air. Some of the best jazz in the city is presented here in various clubs. The market lies at Jefferson and West Julian streets, bounded by Franklin Square on its western flank and Ellis Square on its eastern.

**Victorian District** The Victorian District, south of the Historic District, holds some of the finest examples of post–Civil War architecture in the Deep South. The district is bounded by Martin Luther King, Jr., Boulevard and by East Broad, Gwinnett, and Anderson streets. Houses in the district are characterized by gingerbread trim, stained-glass windows, and imaginative architectural details. In all, the district encompasses an area of nearly 50 blocks, spread across some 165 acres. The entire district was listed on the National Register of Historic Places in 1974. Most of the two-story homes are wood frame and were constructed in the late 1800s on brick foundations. The district, overflowing from the historic inner core, became the first suburb of Savannah.

## 2 Getting Around

The grid-shaped Historic District is best seen on foot—the real point of your visit is to take leisurely strolls with frequent stops in the many squares.

**BY CAR** Though you can reach many points of interest outside the Historic District by bus, your own wheels will be much more convenient, and they're absolutely essential for sightseeing outside the city proper.

All major car-rental firms have branches in Savannah and at the airport, including **Hertz** (© **800/654-3131** or 912/964-9595 at the airport); **Avis** (© **800/831-2847**), with locations at 422 Airways Ave. (© 912/964-1781) and at 2215 Travis Field Rd. (© 912/964-0234); and **Budget** (© **800/527-0700**), with offices at 7070 Abercorn St. (© 912/966-1771).

**BY BUS** You'll need exact change for the $1 fare, plus $1 for a transfer. For route and schedule information, call **Chatham Area Transit (CAT)** at © **912/233-5767.**

**BY TAXI** The base rate for taxis is 60¢, with a $1.20 additional charge for each mile. For 24-hour taxi service, call **Adam Cab Co.** at © **912/927-7466.**

## FAST FACTS: Savannah

*American Express*   The American Express office has closed, but cardholders can obtain assistance by calling ✆ 800/221-7282.

*Dentist*   Call **Abercorn South Side Dental,** 11139 Abercorn St. (✆ 912/925-9190), for complete dental care and emergencies, Monday to Friday 8:30am to 3pm.

*Drugstores*   Drugstores are scattered throughout Savannah. A good choice is **CVS,** 12012 Abercorn St. (✆ 912/925-5568), open Monday to Friday 8am to 10pm, Saturday 8am to 6pm, and Sunday 10am to 6pm.

*Emergencies*   Dial ✆ **911** for police, ambulance, or fire emergencies.

*Hospitals*   There are 24-hour emergency-room services at **Candler General Hospital,** 5353 Reynolds St. (✆ 912/819-6000); and at the **Memorial Medical Center,** 4700 Waters Ave. (✆ 912/350-8390).

*Newspapers*   The *Savannah Morning News* is a daily filled with information about local cultural and entertainment events. The *Savannah Tribune* and the *Herald of Savannah* are geared to the African-American community.

*Police*   In an emergency, call ✆ **911.**

*Post Office*   Post offices and sub-post offices are centrally located and open Monday to Friday 8am to 4:30pm. The main office is at 3601 Montgomery St. (✆ **912/234-8935**).

*Safety*   Although it's reasonably safe to explore the Historic and Victorian districts during the day, the situation changes at night. The clubs along the riverfront, both bars and restaurants, report very little crime. However, muggings and drug dealing are common in the poorer neighborhoods of Savannah.

*Taxes*   Savannah has a 6% sales tax. It tacks a 6% accommodations tax (room or occupancy tax) on your hotel bill.

*Transit Information*   Call **Chatham Area Transit** at ✆ 912/233-5767.

*Weather*   Call ✆ **912/964-1700.**

## 3 Where to Stay

The undisputed stars here are the small inns in the Historic District, most in restored old homes that have been renovated with modern conveniences while retaining every bit of their original charm.

*A note on rates:* Because many of Savannah's historic inns are in converted former residences, price ranges can vary greatly. A very expensive hotel might also have some smaller and more moderately priced units. So it pays to ask. Advance reservations are necessary in most cases, since many of the best properties are quite small.

By and large, the double rooms in the recommended hotels and inns below have private bathrooms with tub/shower combinations, unless otherwise noted.

### ALONG THE RIVERFRONT
#### EXPENSIVE

**Hyatt Regency Savannah** ★   There was an outcry from Savannah's historic preservation movement when this place went up in 1981. Boxy and massively

# Savannah Accommodations

The Azalea Inn **23**
Ballastone Inn **13**
Bed & Breakfast Inn **17**
Cathérine Ward House Inn **18**
Courtyard by Marriott **22**
East Bay Inn **7**
Eliza Thompson House **16**
Fairfield Inn by Marriott **22**
Foley House Inn **14**
Forsyth Park Inn **20**
Gaston Gallery
  Bed & Breakfast **24**
The Gastonian **25**
Hampton Inn Historic District **4**
Hilton Savannah DeSoto **15**
Hyatt Regency Savannah **1**
The Kehoe House **10**
Magnolia Place Inn **19**

Marriott Riverfront Hotel **8**
The Marshall House **6**
The Mulberry Inn **9**
Park Avenue Manor **21**
Planters Inn **5**
The President's Quarters
  Inn **12**
The River Street Inn **3**
17 Hundred 90 **11**
The Westin Savannah Harbor
  Golf Resort & Spa **2**

bulky, it stands in unpleasant contrast to the restored warehouses flanking it along the legendary banks of the Savannah River. Today it is grudgingly accepted as the biggest and flashiest hotel in town. It has a soaring atrium as well as glass-sided elevators. The comfortable rooms, often with paper-thin walls, are international and modern in their feel, all with good-size bathrooms and some with balconies overlooking the atrium. Room prices vary according to their views—units without a view are quite a bargain. Chances are you'll find better food by dining outside the hotel at one of the independent restaurants recommended.

2 W. Bay St., Savannah, GA 31401. ✆ **800/223-1234** or 912/238-1234. Fax 912/944-3678. www.hyatt.com. 347 units. $175–$265 double; $315–$665 suite. AE, DC, DISC, MC, V. Parking $15. **Amenities:** Restaurant; bar; indoor pool; fitness center; limited room service; laundry service/dry cleaning; nonsmoking rooms, rooms for those w/limited mobility. *In room:* A/C, TV, dataport, hair dryer, iron/ironing board, safe.

**Marriott Riverfront Hotel** ⍟   At least the massive modern bulk of this place is far enough from the 19th-century restored warehouses of River Street not to clash with them aesthetically. Towering eight stories, with an angular facade sheathed in orange and yellow brick, it doesn't quite succeed at being a top-rated luxury palace, but nonetheless it attracts lots of corporate business and conventions to its comfortable, modern units. The rooms aren't style-setters but are generous in space, with bathrooms containing tub/shower combinations that are large enough to store your stuff and a generous supply of towels.

100 General McIntosh Blvd., Savannah, GA 31401. ✆ **800/228-9290** or 912/233-7722. Fax 912/233-3765. www.marriott.com. 379 units. $160–$200 double; from $250 suite. Children 12 and under stay free in parent's room. AE, DC, DISC, MC, V. Parking $10. **Amenities:** Restaurant; bar; lounge; 2 pools (1 indoor); fitness center; Jacuzzi; limited room service; laundry service/dry cleaning; nonsmoking rooms; rooms for those w/limited mobility. *In room:* A/C, TV, dataport, coffeemaker, hair dryer, iron/ironing board.

**The Westin Savannah Harbor Golf Resort & Spa** ⍟   Savannah's largest hotel was opened late in 1999 in a 16-story blockbuster format that dwarfs the city's existing B&Bs. It rises somewhat jarringly from what were until the late 1990s sandy, scrub-covered flatlands on the swampy, rarely visited far side of the river from Savannah's historic core. Conceived as part of a massive resort development project, it derives the bulk of its business from corporate groups who arrive for large conventions throughout the year. It's the largest of the four large-scale hotels that dominate the city's convention business, yet despite a worthy collection (more than 250 pieces) of contemporary art that accents the labyrinth of high-ceilinged public rooms here, there's something just a bit sterile, even lifeless, about this relatively anonymous blockbuster hotel. Compounding the problem is its isolated position, both geographically and emotionally, from the bustle, grace, and charm of central Savannah—this in spite of cross-river shuttle ferries that deposit clients into the center of the River Street bar and restaurant frenzy. The most elaborate guest rooms are on the two top floors, and contain extras and comforts designated as Club Level. Otherwise, rooms are comfortable but bland, outfitted in pale colors and conservative furnishings.

1 Resort Dr. (P.O. Box 427), Savannah, GA 31421. ✆ **800/WESTIN-1** or 912/201-2000. Fax 912/201-2001. www.westinsavannah.com. 403 units. $239–$299 double; $325–$800 suite. AE, DC, DISC, MC, V. Water taxis (free for hotel guests, $1 round-trip for everyone else) shuttle you across the river to Rousakis Plaza on River St. at 15-min. intervals. From I-95 and Savannah International Airport, take exit 17A to I-16 toward Savannah. Follow sign for Rte. 17–Talmadge Bridge. Take the Hutchinson Island exit onto Resort Dr. **Amenities:** 2 restaurants; bar; 2 outdoor pools; 18-hole golf course; 4 tennis courts; fitness center; Jacuzzi; sauna; beauty treatments; 24-hr. room service; babysitting; laundry service/dry cleaning; nonsmoking rooms; rooms for those w/limited mobility. *In room:* A/C, TV, dataport, minibar, coffeemaker, hair dryer, iron/ironing board, safe.

## MODERATE

**The River Street Inn** ★★ *Kids*    When Liverpool-based ships were moored on the nearby river, this building stored massive amounts of cotton produced by upriver plantations. After the boll weevil decimated the cotton industry, it functioned as an icehouse, a storage area for fresh vegetables, and (at its lowest point) the headquarters of an insurance company. Its two lowest floors, built in 1817, were made of ballast stones carried in the holds of ships from faraway England.

In 1986, a group of investors poured millions into its development as one of the linchpins of Savannah's River District, adding a well-upholstered Colonial pizzazz to the public areas and converting the building's warren of brick-lined storerooms into some of the most comfortable and well-managed rooms in town.

124 E. Bay St., Savannah, GA 31401. ℂ 800/253-4229 or 912/234-6400. Fax 912/234-1478. www.riverstreet inn.com. 86 units. $159–$229 double; $275 suite. Children 13 and under stay free in parent's room. AE, DC, MC, V. Parking $6. **Amenities:** Restaurant; lounge; Jacuzzi; nonsmoking rooms. *In room:* A/C, TV, dataport, hair dryer.

# IN THE HISTORIC DISTRICT
## VERY EXPENSIVE

**Ballastone Inn** ★★    This glamorous inner-city B&B occupies a dignified 1838 building separated from the Juliette Gordon Low House (original home of the founder of the Girl Scouts of America) by a well-tended formal garden; it's richly decorated with all the hardwoods, elaborate draperies, and antique furniture you'd expect. For a brief period (only long enough to add a hint of spiciness), the place functioned as a bordello *and* a branch office for the Girl Scouts (now next door). It has an elevator, unusual for Savannah B&Bs, but no closets (they were taxed as extra rooms in the old days and so never added). It also has many truly unusual furnishings—cachepots filled with scented potpourri, and art objects that would thrill the heart of any decorator. A full-service bar is tucked into a corner of what was originally a double parlor. Each suite has a Jacuzzi tub as well as a private dressing area. All rooms are nonsmoking.

14 E. Oglethorpe Ave., Savannah, GA 31401. ℂ 800/822-4553 or 912/236-1484. Fax 912/236-4626. www. ballastone.com. 16 units. $215–$375 double; $395 suite. Rates include full breakfast, afternoon tea, and evening hors d'oeuvres. AE, MC, V. Free parking. No children. **Amenities:** Breakfast room; lounge; spa treatments. *In room:* A/C, TV, hair dryer, fireplace (in some).

**The Gastonian** ★    One of the two or three posh B&Bs in Savannah, the Gastonian incorporates a pair of Italianate Regency buildings constructed in 1868 by the same unknown architect. Hard times began with the 1929 stock market crash—the buildings were divided into apartments for the payment of back taxes. In 1984, the Lineberger family visiting from California saw the place, fell in love with it, and poured $2 million into restoring it. Today everything is a testimonial to Victorian charm, except for a skillfully crafted serpentine bridge connecting the two buildings and curving above a verdant semitropical garden. The rooms are appropriately plush, comfortable, cozy, and beautifully furnished.

220 E. Gaston St., Savannah, GA 31401. ℂ 800/322-6603 or 912/232-2869. Fax 912/232-0710. www. gastonian.com. 17 units. $195–$415 double; $395 suite. Rates include full breakfast. AE, DISC, MC, V. No children under 12. **Amenities:** Breakfast room; lounge; nonsmoking rooms. *In room:* A/C, TV, dataport, hair dryer.

**The Kehoe House** ★★★    The Kehoe was built in 1892. In the 1950s, after the place had been converted into a funeral parlor, its owners tried to tear down the nearby Davenport House (see "Exploring Savannah," later in this chapter) to build a parking lot. The resulting outrage led to the founding of the Historic Savannah Association and the salvation of most of the neighborhood's remaining historic buildings.

Today, the place functions as a spectacularly opulent B&B, with a collection of fabrics and furniture that's almost forbiddingly valuable. However, it lacks the warmth and welcome of the Ballastone. This isn't a place for children—the ideal guest will tread softly on floors that are considered models of historic authenticity and flawless taste. Breakfast and afternoon tea are part of the ritual that has seduced such former clients as Tom Hanks, who stayed in room no. 301 during the filming of parts of *Forrest Gump*. The rooms are spacious, with the typical 12-foot ceilings, and each is tastefully furnished with English period antiques. Each unit is equipped with a well-kept bathroom containing a tub/shower combination. Amenities include a concierge and twice-daily maid service with turndown. All rooms are nonsmoking.

123 Habersham St., Savannah, GA 31401. © **800/820-1020** or 912/232-1020. Fax 912/231-0208. www.kehoe house.com. 13 units. $179–$295 double; $275–$325 suite. Rates include full breakfast, evening tea, and hors d'oeuvres. AE, DISC, MC, V. **Amenities:** Breakfast room; lounge; rooms for those w/limited mobility. *In room:* A/C, TV, dataport, hair dryer.

**Magnolia Place Inn** ⭐ *Finds*    This building was begun in 1878 on a desirable plot overlooking Forsyth Square and completed 4 years later by a venerable family who'd been forced off their upriver plantation after the Civil War for nonpayment of taxes. A family ancestor had represented South Carolina at the signing of the Declaration of Independence, so this Second Empire ("steamboat Gothic") house was designed to be as grand as funds would allow. The result includes the most endearing front steps in town (Neiman Marcus asked to display them as a backdrop for one of its catalogs, but the negotiations broke down), verandas worthy of a Mississippi steamer, and an oval skylight (an "oculus") that illuminates a graceful staircase ascending to the dignified rooms. Some rooms contain Jacuzzis.

503 Whitaker St., Savannah, GA 31401. © **800/238-7674** outside Georgia or 912/236-7674. Fax 912/236-1145. www.magnoliaplaceinn.com. 13 units. $185–$295 double. Rates include full breakfast, afternoon tea, and evening hors d'oeuvres. AE, DC, DISC, MC, V. Free parking. No children under 12. **Amenities:** Breakfast room; lounge; Jacuzzi; breakfast-only room service. *In room:* A/C, TV, hair dryer.

## EXPENSIVE

**The Azalea Inn** ⭐ *Finds*    The furnishings of this B&B are a little richer, its colors a bit more evocative, and its decor more appealingly cluttered than those of many of its nearby competitors. The setting is an Italianate house (ca. 1889) set less than 2 blocks east of Forsyth Park, within a garden that has a swimming pool. It was originally built for Capt. Walter Coney, an army officer whose fortune derived from a then-flourishing maritime supply company. Rooms are furnished with period antiques, and each has its own distinctive Victorian-era decor. Especially appealing is the Gentleman's Parlor, a ground-floor room once dominated by men discussing manly things, which still carries a hint of the bourbon and cigars consumed liberally within its confines. More frilly and feminine is the Magnolia Room, where white walls offset a four-poster bed with upholsteries depicting—you guessed it—magnolia blossoms. Newest of all is the Captain's Room, with a massive four-poster and a deck overlooking the swimming pool. Some of the rooms have fireplaces, and all have private bathrooms, most of them with showers. A hand-painted mural on the wall of the dining room—site of morning breakfasts—depicts a version of the history of Savannah. Children under 12 are not welcome. There's usually someone on hand to deliver a cold or warm (nonalcoholic) drink, depending on the season, to clients whenever one is needed.

217 E. Huntingdon St., Savannah, GA 31401. © **800/582-3823** or 912/236-2707. www.azaleainn.com. 9 units. $160–$260 double. Rates include full breakfast. MC, V. **Amenities:** Outdoor pool; nonsmoking rooms. *In room:* A/C, TV, hair dryer, iron/ironing board.

**Catherine Ward House Inn** ✦ *Finds*   The restoration of this house has won several civic awards, and it's so evocative of Savannah's "carpenter Gothic" Victorian revival that Clint Eastwood inserted a long, graceful shot of its exterior in *Midnight in the Garden of Good and Evil.* Built by a sea captain for his wife (Catherine Ward) in 1886 in a location a short walk from Forsyth Park, it offers one of the most lavishly decorated interiors of any B&B in Savannah, but at prices that are significantly less than those offered at better-known B&Bs a few blocks away. Alan Williams, the owner and innkeeper, maintains a policy that discourages children under 16, and that stresses a gay-friendly but even-handed approach to a widely diverse clientele. Breakfast is relatively elaborate, served on fine porcelain in a grandly outfitted dining room. A garden in back encourages languid sun-dappled dialogues. Each midsize guest room is richly decorated.

118 E. Waldburg St., Savannah, GA 31401. (℅) **912/234-8564.** Fax 912/231-8007. www.catherinewardhouse inn.com. 10 units. $149–$335 double. Rates include full breakfast. DISC, MC, V. **Amenities:** Breakfast room; lounge; tennis courts (nearby); laundry service/dry cleaning; nonsmoking rooms. *In room:* A/C, TV, dataport, hair dryer.

**Hilton Savannah DeSoto** ✦   The name still evokes a bit of glamour—built in 1890, this hotel was for many generations the city's grandest. In 1967, thousands of wedding receptions, Kiwanis meetings, and debutante parties later, the building was demolished and rebuilt in a bland modern format. It's a well-managed commercial hotel, fully renovated by new owners in 1995. The guest rooms are conservatively modern and reached after you register in a stone-sheathed lobby whose decor was partly inspired by an 18th-century Colonial drawing room. Despite the absence of antique charm, many guests like this place for its polite efficiency and modernism.

15 E. Liberty St. (P.O. Box 8207), Savannah, GA 31412. (℅) **800/426-8483** or 912/232-9000. Fax 912/232-6018. www.hilton.com. 246 units. $99–$279 double. AE, DC, DISC, MC, V. **Amenities:** 2 restaurants; bar; pool; fitness center; limited room service; massage; babysitting; laundry service/dry cleaning; nonsmoking rooms; rooms for those w/limited mobility. *In room:* A/C, TV, dataport, hair dryer, iron/ironing board.

**Foley House Inn** ✦   Decorated with all the care of a private home, this small B&B occupies a brick-sided house built in 1896. Its owners doubled its size by acquiring the simpler white-fronted house next door, whose pedigree predates its neighbors by half a century. All rooms are neatly furnished. The staff will regale you with tales of the original residents of both houses—one was the site of a notorious turn-of-the-20th-century suicide. Breakfast and afternoon hors d'oeuvres, tea, and cordials are served in a large, verdant space formed by the two houses' connected gardens.

14 W. Hull St., Savannah, GA 31401. (℅) **800/647-3708** or 912/232-6622. Fax 912/231-1218. www.foleyinn.com. 18 units. $200–$345 double. Rates include full breakfast, afternoon hors d'oeuvres, tea, and cordials. AE, MC, V. No children under 12. **Amenities:** Breakfast room; laundry service; nonsmoking rooms. *In room:* A/C, TV, dataport, hair dryer, safe, Jacuzzi (in some).

**The Mulberry Inn** ✦ *Kids*   Locals point with pride to the Mulberry as a sophisticated adaptation of what might've been a derelict building into a surprisingly elegant hotel. Built in 1868 as a stable and cotton warehouse, it was converted in 1982 into a simple hotel, and in the 1990s it received a radical upgrade and a dash of decorator-inspired Chippendale glamour. Today, its lobby looks like that of a grand hotel in London, and the rooms, though small, have a formal decor (think English country-house look with a Southern accent). The hotel's brick-covered patio, with fountains, trailing ivy, and wrought-iron furniture, evokes the best aspects of New Orleans.

601 E. Bay St., Savannah, GA 31401. (C) **877/468-1200** or 912/238-1200. Fax 912/236-2184. www.savannah hotel.com. 145 units. $179–$269 double; $229–$269 suite. Children under 18 stay free in parent's room. AE, DC, DISC, MC, V. Parking $8. **Amenities:** Restaurant; lounge; outdoor pool; fitness center; Jacuzzi; limited room service; nonsmoking rooms; rooms for those w/limited mobility. *In room:* A/C, TV, dataport, fridge, hair dryer, iron/ironing board, microwave.

### The President's Quarters Inn ★★    This hotel has many appealing aspects. The guest rooms and bathrooms are among the largest and most comfortable of those of any inn in Savannah. It manages to combine the charm of a B&B with the efficiency of a much larger place. It has appealed to guests as diverse as the former president of Ireland and numbers of Hollywood actors. Each unit is named after a U.S. president who visited Savannah during his term in office.

225 E. President St., Savannah, GA 31401. (C) **888/592-1812** or 912/233-1600. Fax 912/238-0849. www. presidentsquarters.com. 19 units. $137–$167 double; $187–$235 suite. Rates include breakfast. AE, DISC, MC, V. Free parking on premises. **Amenities:** Lounge; limited room service. *In room:* A/C, TV, dataport, fridge, hair dryer, bathrobes, fireplace.

## MODERATE

### East Bay Inn    Though the views from its windows might be uninspired, the East Bay is conveniently located near the bars and attractions of the riverfront. It was built in 1853 as a cotton warehouse; green awnings and potted geraniums disguise the building's once-utilitarian design. A cozy lobby contains Chippendale furnishings and elaborate moldings. The rooms have queen-size four-poster beds and reproductions of antiques. The hotel frequently houses tour groups from Europe and South America. In the cellar is **Skyler's** ((C) **912/232-3955**), an independently managed restaurant specializing in European and Asian cuisine.

225 E. Bay St., Savannah, GA 31401. (C) **800/500-1225** or 912/238-1225. Fax 912/232-2709. www.eastbay inn.com. 28 units. $149–$210 double. Rates include continental breakfast. AE, DC, DISC, MC, V. **Amenities:** Breakfast room; nonsmoking rooms. *In room:* A/C, TV, dataport, coffeemaker, hair dryer, iron/ironing board, safe, bathrobes.

### Eliza Thompson House ★★    Many newer B&Bs try mightily to re-create this inn's (ca. 1847) patina of historicity, but it's hard to beat the real thing. It's set on a distinguished tree-lined street whose weatherbeaten cobblestones demonstrate their craftsmanship of very long ago. The wrought-iron accents and meticulously maintained details of its shutter-accented facade imply enormous care on the part of its owners. Inside, high ceilings, elaborate cove moldings, and well-chosen antiques reveal a mixture of genteel propriety and rivers of (discreetly understated) romantic potential. Historical references abound in rich but understated interiors. About half the rooms in this stately-looking inn are inside the main house; the remainder lie within a much-restored and very tasteful building in back that was originally conceived as a stable and carriage house. Linking the two buildings is one of the largest and most lavishly landscaped courtyards in the city's historic core. In the words of a writer from *Georgia Magazine*, "Like its namesake, the Eliza Thompson House is a hospitable hostess."

5 W. Jones St., Savannah, GA 31401. (C) **912/236-3620.** Fax 912/238-1920. www.elizathompsonhouse.com. 25 units. $149–$269 double. Rates include continental breakfast. AE, DC, DISC, MC, V. **Amenities:** Breakfast room; lounge; nonsmoking rooms. *In room:* A/C, TV, dataport, hair dryer, iron/ironing board, bathrobes.

### Forsyth Park Inn ★    One of the grandest houses on the western flank of Forsyth Park is this yellow frame place built in the 1890s by a sea captain (Aaron Flynt, aka Rudder Churchill). A richly detailed staircase winds upstairs from a paneled vestibule, and the Queen Anne decor of the formal robin's-egg-blue salon extends through the rest of the house. Guest rooms have oak paneling and

oversize doors that are testimonials to turn-of-the-20th-century craftsmanship. The more expensive guest rooms, including one in what used to be the dining room, are among the largest in town. Home-baked breads and pastries are a staple of the breakfasts. Don't expect frivolity: The inn is just a bit staid.

102 W. Hall St., Savannah, GA 31401. © **912/233-6800.** Fax 912/233-6804. www.forsythparkinn.com. 11 units, 1 cottage with kitchenette. $130–$225 double; $185 cottage. Rates include full breakfast. AE, DISC, MC, V. **Amenities:** Breakfast room; lounge; nonsmoking rooms. *In room:* A/C, TV, bathrobes.

**Gaston Gallery Bed & Breakfast**   This major investment in period restoration was built as two separate houses sharing an Italianate facade. In 1997 a lavish reunification of the two houses was undertaken. Today, the unified building bears the distinction of having the city's longest and most stately front porch (called a gallery in Savannah) and inner ceilings that are almost dizzyingly high. Each unit is beautifully furnished, and most are equipped with a well-maintained bathroom containing a tub/shower combination. The breakfasts are social events, each featuring a different dish, like curried eggs or Southern grits casserole. Wine and cheese are served daily at 5pm or upon your arrival, according to your wishes.

211 E. Gaston St., Savannah, GA 31401. © **800/671-0716** or 912/238-3294. Fax 912/238-4064. www.gaston gallery.com. 15 units. $90–$175 double. AE, DISC, MC, V. **Amenities:** Breakfast room; lounge; nonsmoking rooms; 1 room for those w/limited mobility. *In room:* TV, ceiling fans, fireplace (in some).

**Hampton Inn Historic District** *Kids*   This is the most appealing of the city's middle-bracket large-scale hotels. Opened in 1997, it rises seven redbrick stories above the busy traffic of historic Bay Street, across from Savannah's Riverwalk and some of the city's most animated nightclubs. Its big-windowed lobby was designed to mimic an 18th-century Savannah salon, thanks to the recycling of heart pine flooring from an old sawmill in central Georgia and the use of antique Savannah bricks. Comfortably formal seating arrangements, a blazing fireplace, and an antique bar add cozy touches. The guest rooms are simple and comfortable, with wall-to-wall carpeting, midsize tiled bathrooms, and flowered upholstery. On the roof are a small pool and a sun deck supplemented by an exercise room on the seventh floor. There's no restaurant, but many eateries are a short walk away.

201 E. Bay St., Savannah, GA. © **800/426-7866** or 912/232-9700. Fax 912/231-0440. www.hampton-inn. com. 144 units. $140–$210 double. AE, DC, DISC, MC, V. Parking $8. **Amenities:** Breakfast room; lounge; rooftop pool; laundry service/dry cleaning; nonsmoking rooms; rooms for those w/limited mobility. *In room:* A/C, TV, dataport, coffeemaker, hair dryer, iron/ironing board.

**The Marshall House**   Some aspects of this hotel—especially the second-story cast-iron veranda that juts above the sidewalk—might remind you of a 19th-century hotel in the French Quarter of New Orleans. It originally opened in 1851 as the then-finest hotel in Savannah. In 1864 and 1865, it functioned as a Union Army hospital, before housing such luminaries as Conrad Aiken and Joel Chandler Harris, author of *Stories of Uncle Remus.* After a ratty-looking decline, it closed—some people thought permanently—in 1957. In 1999, it reopened as a "boutique-style" inn. Despite the fact that this place has some of the trappings of an upscale B&B, don't think that it will provide the intimacy or exclusivity of, say, the Foley House. There's something a bit superficial about the glamour here, and some aspects evoke a busy motel, albeit with a more-elegant-than-usual set of Colonial-era reproductions in the public areas. Guest rooms succeed at being mass-production-style cozy without being particularly opulent. Each is sheathed in one of three standardized possibilities: yellow with pinewood furniture, green with wrought-iron furniture, and blue with white-painted furniture. Seven of the largest and most historically evocative rooms in the hotel are on the second floor, overlooking noisy Broughton Street, and are prefaced with wrought-iron verandas with wrought-iron furniture. All units contain neatly kept bathrooms with showers. The bar has exposed brick, a very Southern clientele, and green leather upholstery. The **45 Bistro,** set beneath the glassed-in roof of what used to be the hotel's rear stable yard, is a restaurant serving Southern and international cuisine.

123 E. Broughton St., Savannah, GA 31401. (℃) **800/589-6304** or 912/644-7896. Fax 912/234-3334. www. marshallhouse.com. 68 units. $169–$189 double; $199–$219 suite. AE, DC, DISC, MC, V. Rates include continental breakfast at 45 Bistro. **Amenities:** Restaurant; bar; nonsmoking rooms. *In room:* A/C, TV, hair dryer.

**Park Avenue Manor**   Historic and cozy, this is Savannah's premier gay-friendly guesthouse. An 1897 Victorian B&B, it has an old-fashioned charm with antiques, double staircases, two formal parlors, and angel ceiling borders. Accommodations include four-poster beds with antiques, silk carpets, porcelains, working fireplaces, and period prints. All units contain neatly kept bathrooms with showers. The small-scale inn has a well-rehearsed management style and an emphasis on irreverently offbeat Savannah. Many straight clients also book here, as the place is noted not only for its comfort but for its warm welcome and one of the best Southern breakfasts served in town. The guesthouse was created in 1997, when a pair of Victorian houses were "sewn" together into a tasteful whole. A favorite is the Robert E. Lee Room with a large bay window.

107–109 W. Park Ave., Savannah, GA 31401. (℃) **912/233-0352.** 4 units. $99–$125 double; $170 suite. MC, V. **Amenities:** Breakfast room; lounge; tennis courts (nearby); nonsmoking rooms. *In room:* A/C, TV, hair dryer, no phone.

**Planters Inn**   This small European-style inn is more businesslike than the average Savannah B&B. Built adjacent to Reynolds Square in 1912 as a seven-story brown brick tower, it boasts a lobby with elaborate millwork and a scattering of Chippendale reproductions. The guest rooms are comfortably outfitted with four-poster beds and flowery fabrics; they're rather dignified and formal. Each unit contains a neatly kept bathroom with a tub/shower combination. The Planters Inn isn't associated with the well-recommended Planters Tavern (which stands next door and is separate).

29 Abercorn St., Savannah, GA 31401. (℃) **800/554-1187** or 912/232-5678. Fax 912/232-8893. www.planters innsavannah.com. 59 units. $115–$195 double. Rates include continental breakfast. AE, DC, MC, V. Parking $6.95. **Amenities:** Breakfast room; lounge; nonsmoking rooms. *In room:* A/C, TV, dataport, coffeemaker, hair dryer.

**17 Hundred 90** ✺   The oldest inn in Savannah is located in a small but dignified clapboard-sided house that was built in the year that gave the establishment its name. Reminiscent of the kind of sea captain's house you might see in New England, this cozy, personalized, and charming inn is decorated in ways that emulate a well-appointed private home. Eleven of the 13 smallish but charming guest rooms have fireplaces. Conversations and occasional sounds of laughter come from a basement-level restaurant with a beamed ceiling and exposed original brickwork where locals come to eat and drink. The staff isn't shy about referring to a resident ghost, the unhappy victim of an early-19th-century love affair that ended in suicide. Rich in associations of both requited and unrequited love, this is the kind of place that encourages romantic fancies and attachments, hopefully to the person you brought with you. The inn is run by the Presidents Quarters, to which all calls are directed.

307 E. President St., Savannah, GA 31401. (℃) **877/468-1200** or 912/238-1200. Fax 912/236-2184. www.17 hundred90.com. 14 units. $129–$169 double. Rates include full breakfast. AE, MC, V. **Amenities:** Restaurant; bar; limited room service; nonsmoking rooms. *In room:* A/C, TV, dataport, minibar, coffeemaker, hair dryer.

## INEXPENSIVE

**Bed & Breakfast Inn** ⭐ (*Value*)　Adjacent to Chatham Square, in the oldest part of historic Savannah, this is a dignified stone-fronted town house built in 1853. You climb a gracefully curved front stoop to reach the cool, high-ceilinged interior, outfitted with a combination of antique and reproduction furniture. The accommodations are good-size, comfortable, and tastefully furnished.

117 W. Gordon St. (at Chatham Sq.), Savannah, GA 31401. ℭ **888/238-0518** or 912/238-0518. Fax 912/233-2537. www.savannahbnb.com. 18 units. $89–$169 double. Rates include full breakfast. AE, DISC, MC, V. **Amenities:** Breakfast room; lounge; nonsmoking rooms. *In room:* A/C, TV, hair dryer, iron/ironing board, fireplaces (in some).

**Courtyard by Marriott**　Built around a landscaped courtyard, this is one of the more recommendable motels bordering the Historic District. Many Savannah motels, though cheap, are quite tacky, but this one has renovated suites with separate seating areas, oversize desks, and private patios. The restaurant serves a la carte and buffet breakfasts.

6703 Abercorn St., Savannah, GA 31405. ℭ **800/321-2211** or 912/354-7878. Fax 912/354-1432. www.marriott.com. 144 units. $99–$102 double; from $129–$149 suite. Children 15 and under stay free in parent's room. Senior discounts available. AE, DC, DISC, MC, V. Free parking. From I-16, take exit 164A to I-516 East and turn right on Abercorn St. **Amenities:** Breakfast room; bar; lounge; outdoor pool; exercise room; laundry service/dry cleaning; nonsmoking rooms; rooms for those w/limited mobility. *In room:* A/C, TV, dataport, hair dryer.

**Fairfield Inn by Marriott**　Not quite as good as Marriott's other recommended motel (above), this reliable budget hotel offers standard but comfortably appointed guest rooms with large, well-lighted desks and well-kept bathrooms. Health-club privileges are available nearby, as are several good, moderately priced restaurants.

2 Lee Blvd. (at Abercorn Rd.), Savannah, GA 31405. ℭ **800/228-2800** or 912/353-7100. www.marriott.com. 135 units. $59–$109 double. Rates include continental breakfast. Children 17 and under stay free in parent's room. AE, DC, DISC, MC, V. Free parking. From I-16, take exit 34A to I-516 East, then turn right on Abercorn St. and go right again on Lee Blvd. **Amenities:** Breakfast room; lounge; outdoor pool; nonsmoking rooms; rooms for those w/limited mobility. *In room:* A/C, TV, dataport, coffeemaker, hair dryer, iron/ironing board.

## 4 Where to Dine

Savannah is known for the excellence of its seafood restaurants. They're among the best in Georgia, rivaled only by those in Atlanta. The best dining is in the Historic District, along River Street, bordering the water. However, locals also like to escape the city and head for the seafood places on Tybee and other offshore islands.

Some of Savannah's restaurants, like Elizabeth on 37th, are ranked among the finest in the entire South. And others, like Mrs. Wilkes' Dining Room, are places to go for real Southern fare—from collard greens and fried okra to fried chicken, corn bread, and hot biscuits.

## ALONG OR NEAR THE WATERFRONT
### EXPENSIVE

**The Chart House** ⭐ STEAK/SEAFOOD　Overlooking the Savannah River and Riverfront Plaza, "the home of the mud pie" is part of a nationwide chain—and one of the better ones. It's housed in a building that predates 1790, reputed to be the oldest masonry structure in Georgia and once a sugar-and-cotton warehouse. You can enjoy a view of passing ships on the outside deck, perhaps ordering an appetizer and a drink before dinner. The bar is one of the most atmospheric along the riverfront. As in all Chart Houses, the prime rib is slow-roasted and served au jus. The steaks from corn-fed beef are aged and hand-cut on the premises before

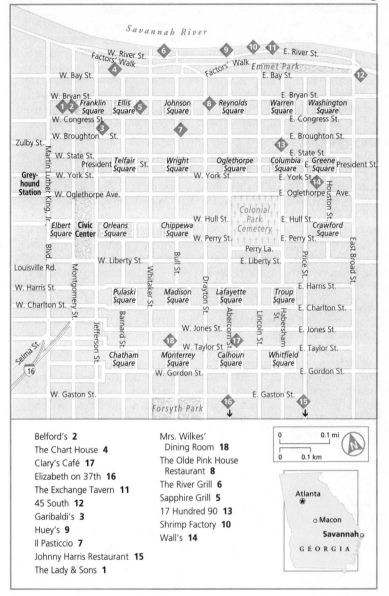

Belford's **2**
The Chart House **4**
Clary's Café **17**
Elizabeth on 37th **16**
The Exchange Tavern **11**
45 South **12**
Garibaldi's **3**
Huey's **9**
Il Pasticcio **7**
Johnny Harris Restaurant **15**
The Lady & Sons **1**

Mrs. Wilkes'
  Dining Room **18**
The Olde Pink House
  Restaurant **8**
The River Grill **6**
Sapphire Grill **5**
17 Hundred 90 **13**
Shrimp Factory **10**
Wall's **14**

being chargrilled. The most expensive item is lobster. You may prefer one of the fresh catches of the day, which can be grilled to your specifications.

202 W. Bay St. ℂ **912/234-6686.** Reservations recommended. Main courses $22–$40. AE, DC, DISC, MC, V. Mon–Fri 5–10pm; Sat 5–10:30pm; Sun 5–9pm.

## MODERATE

**Huey's** ⌖ CAJUN/CREOLE   At first glance, this casual place overlooking the Savannah River seems little different from the other restored warehouses. The chef even manages to please visitors from New Orleans—and that's saying a lot. The place is often packed. Breakfast begins with such dishes as a Creole omelet, followed by an oyster "po' boy" for lunch. It's at dinner, however, that the kitchen really shines, producing jambalaya with andouille sausage, crayfish étouffée, and crab-and-shrimp au gratin (with Louisiana crabmeat and Georgia shrimp). The soups are homemade and the appetizers distinctive. Breakfast can be ordered from 7am to 3pm daily. The bar next door offers live entertainment.

In the River Street Inn, 115 E. River St. ℂ 912/234-7385. Reservations recommended. Main courses $12–$22; sandwiches $6–$10. AE, DISC, MC, V. Mon–Thurs 7am–10pm; Fri 7am–11pm; Sat 8am–11pm; Sun 8am–10pm.

## INEXPENSIVE

**The Exchange Tavern** SEAFOOD/LOW COUNTRY   A local favorite, this tavern is in a 1790s former cotton warehouse that opens onto the riverfront. The chefs make no pretense about their food. Everything is hale and hearty rather than gourmet. Your best bet is the ocean-fresh seafood, served grilled, broiled, or fried. Hand-cut grilled rib-eye steaks are a specialty, along with Buffalo-style wings, shrimp, oysters, and well-stuffed sandwiches served throughout the day. This place has been dispensing its shish kabobs, fresh salads, and homemade soups since 1971. It's also a good place for a drink.

201 E. River St. (east of Bull St.). ℂ **912/232-7088.** Main courses $11–$23. AE, DC, MC, V. Sun–Thurs 11am–11pm; Fri–Sat 11am–midnight.

**The Lady & Sons** ★★ Finds SOUTHERN   Paula Deen started this place in 1989 with $200, the help of her sons, and a 1910 structure. Today, she runs one of Savannah's most celebrated restaurants. Her first cookbook, *The Lady & Sons Savannah Country Cookbook* (Random House), is in its second printing (John Berendt wrote the introduction); and her second, *The Lady & Sons Too,* was published in 2000. Paula has yet a third best-selling cookbook and also hosts a top-rated cooking show, *Paula's Home Cooking,* on the Food Network. One taste of the food and you'll understand the roots of her success. Menu items like crab cakes (one Maryland visitor claimed they were the best he'd ever eaten), crab burgers, and several creative varieties of shrimp best exhibit her style. The locals love her buffets, which are very Southern. With fried chicken, meatloaf, collard greens, beef stew, "creamed" potatoes, or macaroni and cheese, this buffet is more aptly described as "more-than-you-can-eat."

Lunches are busy with a loyal following; dinners are casual and inventive. The aphrodisiac dish has to be the oyster shooters—half a dozen raw oysters, each served in a shot glass ("It's like killing two birds with one stone"). Paula's signature dish, chicken potpie topped with puff pastry, looks so attractive you'll have reservations about eating it: Maybe that's why *Southern Living* used a picture of it in their magazine. Be careful not to fill up on the cheese biscuits and hoecakes that constantly land on your table. If for some reason you don't want a glorious glass of syrup-sweet tea, you'd better ask for unsweetened. But why rob yourself of the complete experience?

120 W. Congress St. ℂ **912/233-2600.** www.ladyandsons.com. Reservations recommended for dinner. Main courses $6–$13 lunch, $18–$24 dinner. All-you-can-eat buffet $13 lunch, $17 dinner. Sun buffet $15. AE, DISC, MC, V. Mon–Sat 11am–3pm; Mon–Thurs 5–9pm; Fri–Sat 5–10pm; Sun 11am–5pm (buffet only).

**The River Grill** SEAFOOD   Its decor was modeled after a barn somewhere on the panhandle of Texas; the recorded music might remind you of the country-western tunes they play at this place's namesake in Houston. The seafood here is fresh and tender—try the fresh stuffed flounder topped with a lobster brandy sauce or the delicious homemade crab cakes. Appetizers feature a warm crab-and-artichoke dip and oysters Rockefeller, and steaks and seafood include grilled swordfish, battered shrimp platters, and at least five kinds of Angus beef.

21 E. River St. $C$ 912/234-5588. Main courses $7.95–$30. AE, DISC, MC, V. Sun–Thurs 11am–10pm; Fri–Sat 11am–11pm.

**Shrimp Factory** *Value* SEAFOOD    The exposed old brick and wooden plank floors form a setting for harborside dining in a cotton warehouse (ca. 1850). Lots of folks drop in before dinner to watch the boats pass by, perhaps enjoying a Chatham Artillery punch in a souvenir snifter. Yes, the place is touristy, never more so than when it welcomes tour buses. A salad bar rests next to a miniature shrimp boat, and fresh seafood comes from local waters. A specialty, pine bark stew, is served in a little iron pot with a bottle of sherry on the side; it's a potage of five seafoods simmered with fresh herbs but minus the pine bark. Other dishes include peeled shrimp, shucked oysters, live Maine lobsters, sirloin steaks, and various fish filets.

313 E. River St. (2 blocks east of the Hyatt). $C$ 912/236-4229. Reservations not accepted. Main courses $6.25–$15 lunch, $19–$28 dinner. AE, DC, DISC, MC, V. Mon–Thurs 11am–10pm; Fri–Sat 11am–11pm; Sun noon–10pm.

## IN THE HISTORIC DISTRICT
### VERY EXPENSIVE

**45 South** ✷✷ INTERNATIONAL    Recommended by such magazines as *Food & Wine, Southern Living,* and even *Playboy,* this ritzy restaurant offers a cuisine that has been called "gourmet Southern." Its ever-changing menu is likely to feature smoked North Carolina trout, rack of lamb flavored with crushed sesame seeds, grilled venison with au gratin of sweet potatoes, chicken breast with truffled pâté, or sliced breast of pheasant with foie gras. Appetizers might include anything from South Carolina quail to crab cakes. Among the most expensive restaurants in Savannah, it's softly lighted with elegantly set tables and a cozy bar. The service is impeccable.

20 E. Broad St. $C$ 912/233-1881. Reservations suggested. Jackets advised. Main courses $26–$45. AE, MC, V. Mon–Thurs 6–9pm; Fri–Sat 6–9:30pm.

**Sapphire Grill** ✷ AMERICAN/LOW COUNTRY    One of the city's most consistently stylish restaurants evokes a low-key, counterculture bistro, but its cuisine is grander and more cutting-edge than its industrial-looking decor and its level of hipness would imply. Christopher Nason is the owner and the most talked-about chef of the moment in Savannah, preparing what he defines as a "coastal cuisine" based on seafood hauled in, usually on the day of its preparation, from nearby waters. If you opt for a table here, you won't be alone: Scads of media and cinematic personalities will have preceded you. Collectively, they add an urban gloss of the type you might expect to see in Los Angeles. Launch your repast with a "firecracker salad"—that is, roasted red peppers and a red chile and shallot vinaigrette—or crisp fried green tomatoes, perhaps tuna medallions, and even James Island littleneck clams tossed in a foie gras butter, each beginning course a delectable choice. The chef is justifiably proud of such signature dishes as duck served with a roasted tomato cannelloni or grilled prime tenderloin of beef with dauphinoise potatoes. The local black grouper is flavored with lemon coriander, and a double-cut pork loin chop is one of the most elegant versions of this dish in Savannah. Each day the chef serves a tasting menu—based on the market price—that includes an appetizer, salad, main course, and confections. Ask about it, as it might be your best dining bet.

110 W. Congress St. ℂ **912/443-9962.** Reservations recommended. Main courses $19–$28. AE, DC, MC, V. Sun–Thurs 6–10:30pm; Fri–Sat 5:30–11:30pm.

## EXPENSIVE

**The Olde Pink House Restaurant** ✦✦ SEAFOOD/SOUTHERN    Built in 1771 and glowing pink (its antique bricks show through a protective covering of stucco), this house has functioned as a private home, a bank, a tearoom, and headquarters for one of Sherman's generals. Today, its interior is severe and dignified, with stiff-backed chairs, bare wooden floors, and an 18th-century aura similar to what you'd find in Williamsburg, Virginia. The cuisine is richly steeped in the traditions of the Low Country and includes crispy scored flounder with apricot sauce, steak au poivre, black grouper stuffed with blue crab and drenched in Vidalia onion sauce, and grilled tenderloin of pork crusted with almonds and molasses. You can enjoy your meal in the candlelit dining rooms or in the Planters Tavern.

23 Abercorn St. ℂ **912/232-4286.** Reservations recommended. Main courses $15–$30. AE, MC, V. Sun–Thurs 5:30–10:30pm; Fri–Sat 5:30–11pm.

**17 Hundred 90** ✦ INTERNATIONAL    In the brick-lined cellar of Savannah's oldest inn (see "Where to Stay," earlier in this chapter), this place evokes a seafaring tavern along the coast of New England. Many visitors opt for a drink at the woodsy-looking bar in a separate back room before heading down the slightly claustrophobic corridor to the nautically inspired dining room. Students of paranormal psychology remain alert to the ghost rumored to wander through this place, site of Savannah's most famous 18th-century suicide. Lunch might include the quiche of the day, Southern-style crab cakes, and a choice of salads and sandwiches. Dinners are more formal, featuring crab bisque, snapper Parmesan, steaks, and bourbon-flavored chicken. The cooking is of a high standard.

307 E. President St. ℂ **912/236-7122.** Reservations recommended. Main courses $20–$27. AE, DISC, MC, V. Mon–Fri 11:30am–2pm; daily 6–10pm.

## MODERATE

**Il Pasticcio** NORTHERN ITALIAN    This restaurant is one of the city's most popular dining spots. In a postmodern style, with big windows and a high ceiling, it has a definite big-city style. A rotisserie turns out specialties. Many locals come here just for the pasta dishes, all homemade and served with savory sauces. Begin with carpaccio (thinly sliced beef tenderloin) or a tricolor salad of radicchio, endive, and arugula. Main dishes are likely to feature a mixed-grill seafood platter or grilled fish steak with tricolor roasted sweet peppers.

2 E. Broughton St. (corner of Bull and Broughton sts.). ℂ **912/231-8888.** Main courses $15–$28. AE, DC, DISC, M, V. Mon–Thurs 5:30–10pm; Fri–Sat 5:30-11:30pm.

## INEXPENSIVE

**Clary's Café** ✦ *Value* AMERICAN    Clary's Café has been a Savannah tradition since 1903, though the ambience today, under the devilish direction of Michael Faber, is decidedly 1950s. The place was famous long before it was featured in *Midnight in the Garden of Good and Evil* in its former role as Clary's drugstore, where regulars like eccentric flea-collar inventor Luther Driggers breakfasted and lunched. John Berendt is still a frequent patron, as is the fabled Lady Chablis. Begin your day with the classic Hoppel Poppel (scrambled eggs with chunks of kosher salami, potatoes, onions, and green peppers) and go on from there. Fresh salads, New York–style sandwiches, and stir-fries, along with Grandmother's homemade chicken soup and flame-broiled burgers, are served throughout the day, giving way in the evening to chicken potpie, stuffed pork loin, or planked fish (a fresh filet of red snapper—broiled, grilled, or blackened).

404 Abercorn St. (at Jones St.). ✆ **912/233-0402.** Breakfast $3.95–$7.95; main courses $5.95–$7.95. AE, DC, DISC, MC, V. Daily 8am–4pm.

**Mrs. Wilkes' Dining Room** ⚘ *Kids* SOUTHERN   Remember the days of the boardinghouse, when everybody sat together, and belly-busting food was served in big dishes in the center of the table? Before her death in late 2002 at the age of 95, Sema Wilkes had served breakfast and lunch to locals and travelers in just that manner since the 1940s. Bruce Willis, Demi Moore, and Clint Eastwood are on the long list of celebrities who've dined here. The tradition continues. Expect to find a line of people patiently waiting for a seat at one of the long tables in the basement dining room of this 1870 brick house with curving steps and cast-iron trim.

Mrs. Wilkes believed in freshness and planned her daily menu around the seasons. Your food will be a reflection of the cuisine Savannah residents have enjoyed for generations—fried or barbecued chicken, red rice and sausage, black-eyed peas, corn on the cob, squash and yams, okra, corn bread, and collard greens.

107 W. Jones St. (west of Bull St.). ✆ **912/232-5997.** www.mrswilkes.com. Lunch $13. No credit cards. Mon–Fri 11:30am–2pm.

**Wall's** *Kids* BARBECUE   This is the first choice for anyone seeking the best barbecue in Savannah. Southern barbecue aficionados have built-in radar to find a place like this. Once they see the plastic booths, bibs, Styrofoam cartons, and canned drinks from a fridge, they'll know they've found home. Like all barbecue joints, the place is aggressively casual. Spareribs and barbecue sandwiches star on the menu. Deviled crabs are the only non-barbecue item, though a vegetable plate of four nonmeat items is also served.

515 E. York Lane (between York St. and Oglethorpe Ave.). ✆ **912/232-9754.** Main courses $6.50–$10. No credit cards. Wed 11am–5pm; Thurs–Sat 11am–9pm.

## IN & AROUND THE CITY MARKET
### EXPENSIVE

**Belford's** ⚘ LOW COUNTRY   This restaurant keeps alive the tradition of offering good food in the area of the old city market. The setting is nostalgic, with hardwood floors, dark-wood paneling, glass-topped tables, black-and-white tablecloths, high ceilings, and a patio. The cooks prepare a daily crab stew that is excellent, along with such other favorites as fried calamari or crab cakes, the latter served with a spicy tomato jam and lemon aioli. A trio of pastas is featured daily, our favorite being the lobster and wild mushroom ravioli served with a spicy calamari salad and a balsamic brown butter sauce.

For your main course, the array of delights may include herb-encrusted sea bass with fresh herbs, pan sautéed and finished off with a savory crab beurre blanc. It's served with buttermilk mashed potatoes. The hazelnut red snapper is also a temptation, served with prawns and lump crabmeat in a hazelnut-liqueur sauce and a side of apple chutney. Shrimp, greens, 'n grits is a favorite, with smoked bacon, green onions, and a chardonnay butter sauce.

315 W. St. Julian St. ✆ **912/233-2626.** Reservations recommended. Breakfast buffet $5.95–$13; lunch $6.95–$11; Sun brunch $7–$13; main courses $17–$33. AE, DC, DISC, MC, V. Mon–Sat 8am–11am; daily 11:30am–3pm and 6–10pm. Closed Thanksgiving, Christmas Eve (night), and Christmas Day.

### MODERATE

**Garibaldi's** SEAFOOD/ITALIAN   Many of the city's art-conscious students appreciate this Italian cafe because of the fanciful murals adorning its walls.

(Painted by the owner's daughter, their theme is "The Jungles of Italy.") If you're looking for a quiet, contemplative evening, we advise you to go elsewhere—the setting is loud and convivial during the early evening and even louder later at night. Designed as a fire station in 1871, it boasts the original pressed-tin ceiling.

Menu items include roasted red peppers with goat-cheese croutons on a bed of wild lettuces; crispy calamari; artichoke hearts with aioli; about a dozen kinds of pasta; and a repertoire of Italian-inspired chicken, veal, and seafood dishes. Daily specials change frequently but sometimes include duck Garibaldi, king-crab fettuccine, and a choice of lusciously fattening desserts.

315 W. Congress St. ✆ 912/232-7118. Reservations recommended. Main courses $12–$28. AE, MC, V. Sun–Thurs 5:30–10:30pm; Fri–Sat 5:30–11pm.

## IN THE VICTORIAN DISTRICT
### VERY EXPENSIVE

**Elizabeth on 37th** ★★ MODERN SOUTHERN   This restaurant is frequently cited as the most glamorous and upscale in town. It's housed in a palatial neoclassical-style 1900 villa ringed with semitropical landscaping and cascades of Spanish moss. The menu items change with the seasons and manage to retain their gutsy originality despite an elegant presentation. They may include roast quail with mustard-and-pepper sauce and apricot-pecan chutney, herb-seasoned rack of lamb, or broiled salmon with mustard-garlic glaze. You might begin with grilled-eggplant soup, a culinary first for many diners. There's also an impressive wine list. The desserts are the best in Savannah.

105 E. 37th St. ✆ 912/236-5547. www.elizabethon37th.com. Reservations required. Main courses $23–$36. AE, DC, DISC, MC, V. Daily 6–10pm.

## DINING NEARBY

**Johnny Harris Restaurant** AMERICAN   Started as a roadside diner in 1924, Johnny Harris is Savannah's oldest continuously operated restaurant. The place has a lingering aura of the 1950s and features all that great food so beloved back in the days of Elvis and Marilyn: barbecue, charbroiled steaks, and seafood. The barbecued pork is especially savory, and the prime rib is tender. Colonel Sanders never came anywhere close to equaling the fried chicken here. Guests can dine in the "kitchen" or in the main dining room, where you can dance under the "stars." The place will make you nostalgic.

1651 E. Victory Dr. (Hwy. 80). ✆ 912/354-7810. Reservations recommended. Lunch items $8–$10; dinner main courses $11–$26. AE, DC, DISC, MC, V. Mon–Thurs 11:30am–9:30pm; Fri–Sat 11:30am–10:30pm.

## 5 Exploring Savannah

Most likely, the first sights you'll want to see in Savannah are those mentioned in *Midnight in the Garden of Good and Evil*. So if that's your wish, see "Organized Tours," below.

## HISTORIC HOMES

**Davenport House Museum**   This is where seven determined women started the whole Savannah restoration movement in 1954. They raised $22,500, a tidy sum back then, and purchased the house, saving it from demolition and a future as a parking lot. They established the Historic Savannah Foundation, and the whole city was spared. Constructed between 1815 and 1820 by master builder Isaiah Davenport, this is one of the truly great Federal-style houses in the United States, with delicate ironwork and a handsome elliptical stairway.

# Downtown Savannah Sights

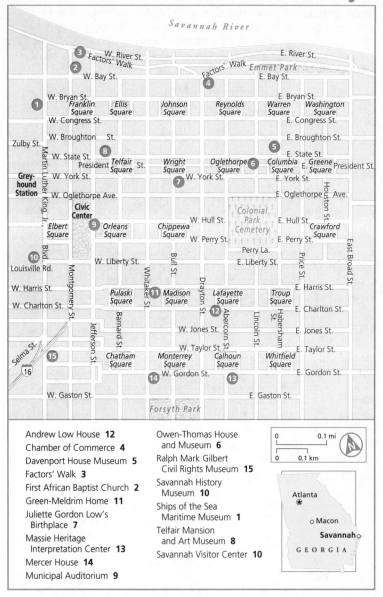

*Savannah River*

W. River St. — E. River St.
**3** Factors' Walk
**2**
W. Bay St. — Factors' Walk — Emmet Park — E. Bay St.
**4**

**1**

W. Bryan St. — E. Bryan St.
*Franklin* *Ellis* *Johnson* *Reynolds* *Warren* *Washington*
*Square* *Square* *Square* *Square* *Square* *Square*
W. Congress St. — E. Congress St.

W. Broughton St. — E. Broughton St.
Zulby St. — **5**
W. State St. — E. State St.
**8** President *Telfair* St. *Wright* *Oglethorpe* **6** *Columbia* E. *Greene* President St.
*Square* *Square* *Square* **6** *Square* *Square*
**Grey-** W. York St. — **7** W. York St. — E. York St.
**hound**
**Station** W. Oglethorpe Ave. — E. Oglethorpe Ave.

**Civic** *Colonial*
**Center** *Park*
**9** *Elbert* *Orleans* *Chippewa* *Cemetery* *Crawford*
*Square* *Square* *Square* W. Hull St. — E. Hull St. *Square*
W. Perry St. — E. Perry St.
**10** Perry La.
Louisville Rd. — W. Liberty St. — E. Liberty St.

W. Harris St. — E. Harris St.
*Pulaski* **11** *Madison* *Lafayette* *Troup*
W. Charlton St. — *Square* *Square* *Square* *Square* — E. Charlton St.
**12**
W. Jones St. — E. Jones St.
W. Taylor St. — E. Taylor St.
Selma St. **15** *Chatham* *Monterrey* *Calhoun* *Whitfield*
*Square* *Square* *Square* *Square*
**16** **14** W. Gordon St. **13** — E. Gordon St.
W. Gaston St. — E. Gaston St.
*Forsyth Park*

Andrew Low House **12**
Chamber of Commerce **4**
Davenport House Museum **5**
Factors' Walk **3**
First African Baptist Church **2**
Green-Meldrim Home **11**
Juliette Gordon Low's
   Birthplace **7**
Massie Heritage
   Interpretation Center **13**
Mercer House **14**
Municipal Auditorium **9**

Owen-Thomas House
   and Museum **6**
Ralph Mark Gilbert
   Civil Rights Museum **15**
Savannah History
   Museum **10**
Ships of the Sea
   Maritime Museum **1**
Telfair Mansion
   and Art Museum **8**
Savannah Visitor Center **10**

0                0.1 mi
0                0.1 km

Atlanta
o Macon
**Savannah** o
GEORGIA

324 E. State St. ✆ **912/236-8097**. Admission $7 adults, $3.50 children 6–18, free for children 5 and under. Mon–Sat 10am–4pm; Sun 1–4pm. Closed major holidays.

**Green-Meldrim Home**    This impressive house was built on Madison Square for cotton merchant Charleston Green, but its moment in history arrived when it became the Savannah headquarters of Gen. William Tecumseh Sherman at the end of his 1864 "March to the Sea." It was from this Gothic-style house that the general sent his now infamous (at least in Savannah) Christmas telegram to President

Lincoln, offering him the city as a Christmas gift. Now the Parish House for St. John's Episcopal Church, the house is open to the public. The former kitchen, servants' quarters, and stable are used as a rectory for the church.

14 W. Macon St. ✆ **912/233-3845**. Admission $5 adults, $3 children. Tues and Thurs–Fri 10am–4pm; Sat 10am–1pm.

**Juliette Gordon Low's Birthplace**   Juliette Gordon Low—the founder of the Girl Scouts—lived in this Regency-style house. It's now maintained both as a memorial to her and as a National Program Center. The Victorian additions to the 1818–21 house were made in 1886, just before Juliette Gordon married William Mackay Low.

142 Bull St. (at Oglethorpe Ave.). ✆ **912/233-4501**. Admission $8 adults, $6 children 18 and under. Mon–Tues and Thurs–Sat 10am–4pm; Sun 12:30–4:30pm. Closed major holidays and some Sun Dec–Jan.

**Andrew Low House**   After her marriage, Juliette Low (see above) lived in this 1848 house, and it was here where she actually founded the Girl Scouts. She died on the premises in 1927. The classic mid-19th-century house facing Lafayette Square is of stucco over brick with elaborate ironwork, shuttered piazzas, carved woodwork, and crystal chandeliers. William Makepeace Thackeray visited here twice (the desk at which he worked is in one bedroom), and Robert E. Lee was entertained at a gala reception in the double parlors in 1870.

329 Abercorn St. ✆ **912/233-6854**. Admission $7 adults; $4 students, children 6–12, and Girl Scouts; free for children 5 and under. Mon–Wed and Fri–Sat 10am–4pm; Sun noon–4pm. Closed major holidays.

**Telfair Mansion and Art Museum** ✮   The oldest public art museum in the South, housing a collection of both American and European paintings, was designed and built by William Jay in 1818. He was a young English architect noted for introducing the Regency style to America. The house was built for Alexander Telfair, son of Edward Telfair, the governor of Georgia. A sculpture gallery and rotunda were added in 1883, and Jefferson Davis attended the formal opening in 1886. William Jay's period rooms have been restored, and the Octagon Room and Dining Room are particularly outstanding.

121 Bernard St. ✆ **912/232-1177**. Admission $8 adults, $2 students, $1 children 6–12, free for children 5 and under. Mon noon–5pm; Tues–Sat 10am–5pm; Sun 1–5pm.

**Owen-Thomas House and Museum** ✮   Famed as a place where Lafayette spent the night in 1825, this house evokes the heyday of Savannah's golden age. It was designed in 1816 by English architect William Jay, who captured the grace of Georgian Bath in England and the splendor of Regency London. The place has been called a "jewel box." You can visit not only the bedchambers and kitchen but also the garden and the drawing and dining rooms. Adapted from the original slave quarters and stable, the Carriage House Visitors' Center opened in 1995.

124 Abercorn St. ✆ **912/233-9743**. Admission $8 adults, $4 students, $2 children 6–12, free for children 5 and under. Mon noon–5pm; Tues–Sat 10am–5pm; Sun 1–5pm.

## MUSEUMS

**Savannah History Museum**   Housed in the restored train shed of the old Central Georgia Railway station, this museum is a good introduction to the city. In the theater, *The Siege of Savannah* is replayed. An exhibition hall displays memorabilia from every era of Savannah's history.

303 Martin Luther King, Jr., Blvd. ✆ **912/238-1779**. Admission $4 adults, $3.50 seniors and students, $3 children ages 6-11, free for children under 6. Mon–Fri 8:30am–5pm; Sat–Sun 9am–5pm.

## *Moments* Martinis in the Cemetery

All fans of *Midnight in the Garden of Good and Evil* must pay a visit to the now world-famous **Bonaventure Cemetery,** filled with obelisks and columns and dense shrubbery and moss-draped trees. Bonaventure is open daily 8am to 5pm. You get there by taking Wheaton Street east out of downtown to Skidaway to Bonaventure Road. (You don't want to approach it by boat like Minerva the "voodoo priestess" and John Berendt did—and certainly not anywhere near midnight.)

This cemetery lies on the grounds of what was once a great oak-shaded plantation, built by Colonel John Mulryne. In the late 1700s, the mansion caught fire during a formal dinner party; reportedly, the host quite calmly led his guests from the dining room and into the garden, where they settled in to finish eating while the house burned to the ground in front of them. At the end, the host and the guests threw their crystal glasses against the trunk of an old oak tree. It's said that on still nights you can hear the laughter and the crashing of the crystal. In The Book, Mary Harty called the ruins the "scene of the Eternal Party. What better place, in Savannah, to rest in peace for all time—where the party goes on and on."

It was at the cemetery that John Berendt had martinis in silver goblets with Miss Harty, while they sat on the bench-gravestone of poet **Conrad Aiken.** She pointed out to the writer the double gravestone bearing the names of Dr. William F. Aiken and his wife, Anna, parents of Conrad. They both died on February 27, 1901, when Dr. Aiken killed his wife and then himself. The Aikens are buried in Lot #78H. Songwriter **Johnny Mercer** is also buried in Lot #49H.

But not **Danny Hansford,** the blond hustler of the book. You can find his grave at plot Lot #6, Block: G-8 in the Greenwich Cemetery, next to Bonaventure. After entering Bonaventure, turn left immediately and take the straight path to Greenwich. Eventually you'll see a small granite tile:

DANNY LEWIS HANSFORD
MARCH 1, 1960
MAY 2, 1981

Incidentally, **Jim Williams** is buried in Gordon, Georgia, a 3½-hour drive northwest of Savannah.

**Ships of the Sea Maritime Museum**    This museum has intricately constructed models of seagoing vessels, from Viking warships to nuclear-powered ships. In models ranging from the size of your fist to 8 feet in length, you can see such famous ships as the *Mayflower* and the *Savannah,* the first steamship to cross the Atlantic. More than 75 ships are in the museum's ship-in-a-bottle collection, most of them constructed by Peter Barlow, a retired British Royal Naval commander.

41 Martin Luther King, Jr., Blvd. Ⓒ 912/232-1511. www.shipsofthesea.org. Admission $7 adults, $5 children 8–12, free for children 7 and under. Tues–Sun 10am–5pm. Closed major holidays.

## LITERARY LANDMARKS

Long before John Berendt's *Midnight in the Garden of Good and Evil,* there were other writers who were associated with Savannah.

Chief of these was **Flannery O'Connor** (1924–64), one of the South's greatest writers, author of *Wise Blood* (1952) and *The Violent Bear It Away* (1960). She was also known for her short stories, including the collection *A Good Man Is Hard to Find* (1955). She won the O. Henry Award three times. Between October and May, an association dedicated to her holds readings, films, and lectures about her and other Southern writers. You can visit the **Flannery O'Connor Childhood Home,** 207 E. Charlton St. (℃ 912/233-6014). The house is open only Saturday and Sunday from 1 to 4pm. Admission is free.

**Conrad Aiken** (1889–1973), the American poet, critic, writer, and Pulitzer Prize winner, was also born in Savannah. He lived at 228 (for the first 11 years of his life) and also at 230 E. Oglethorpe Ave. (for the last 11 years of his life). In *Midnight in the Garden of Good and Evil,* Mary Harty and the author sipped martinis at the bench-shaped tombstone of Aiken in Bonaventure Cemetery (see "Martinis in the Cemetery," above).

The **Mercer House,** 429 Bull St., featured in The Book, has been restored and is now open to the public as the **Mercer House Williams Museum** (℃ 877/430-6352; www.mercerhouse.com; Mon–Tues and Thurs–Sat 10:30am–3:40pm, Sun 12:30–4pm; closed Wed and off-season; $12.50 per person) (it's the primary residence of Jim Williams's sister Dorothy Kingery and her family). Although many of its most elegant contents were auctioned off at Sotheby's in October 2000 for $1 million—including the Anatolian carpet upon which the hapless Danny Hansford is reputed to have fallen after being shot—furniture and art from the private collection of Jim Williams are on display.

Visitors can also shop for books, decorative accessories, and antiques (some from Willams's antiques store and country home) at the **Carriage House Shop,** located directly behind the Mercer House at 430 Whitaker St. (Mon–Fri 10am–4:30pm, Sat 10am–5pm, Sun 10:30am–4pm).

## BLACK HISTORY SIGHTS

Savannah boasts the **First African Baptist Church,** 23 Montgomery St., Franklin Square (℃ 912/233-6597), the first such church in North America. It was established by George Leile, a slave whose master allowed him to preach to other slaves when they made visits to plantations along the Savannah River. Leile was granted his freedom in 1777 and later raised some $1,500 to purchase the present church from a white congregation. The black congregation rebuilt the church brick by brick, and it became the first brick building in Georgia to be owned by African Americans. The pews on either side of the organ are the work of African slaves. Sunday-morning worship is at 8:30am and 11:30am.

**Ralph Mark Gilbert Civil Rights Museum,** 460 Martin Luther King, Jr., Blvd. (℃ 912/231-8900), close to the Savannah Visitors Center, opened in 1996. It's dedicated to the lives and services of African Americans and their contributions to the civil rights movements in Savannah. Dr. Gilbert died in 1956 but was a leader in early efforts to gain educational, social, and political equity for African Americans in Savannah. Hours are Monday to Saturday 9am to 5pm. Admission is $4 for adults, $3 for seniors, and $2 for children.

## NEARBY FORTS

About 2½ miles east of the center of Savannah via the Islands Expressway stands **Old Fort Jackson,** 1 Fort Jackson Rd. (℃ 912/232-3945), Georgia's oldest standing fort, with a 9-foot-deep tidal moat around its brick walls. In 1775, an earthen battery was built here. The original brick fort was begun in 1808 and manned during the War of 1812. It was enlarged and strengthened between 1845 and 1860 and saw its greatest use as headquarters for the Confederate river defenses during the Civil War. Its arched rooms, designed to support the weight of heavy cannons mounted above, hold 13 exhibit areas. The fort is open daily 9am to 5pm, charging $4 for adults, $3 for seniors and children 6 to 18; admission is free for children 5 and under.

**Fort McAllister,** Richmond Hill, 10 miles southwest on U.S. 17 (© **912/727-2339**), on the banks of the Great Ogeechee River, was a Confederate earthwork fortification. Constructed in 1861–62, it withstood nearly 2 years of bombardments before it finally fell on December 13, 1864, in a bayonet charge that ended General Sherman's infamous "March to the Sea." There's a visitor center with historic exhibits and also walking trails and campsites. It's open daily 8am to 5pm. Admission is $2.50 for adults, $1.50 for children over 5, and $2 for seniors.

**Fort Pulaski** (© **912/786-5787**), a national monument, is 15 miles east of Savannah off U.S. 80 on Cockspur and McQueen islands at the very mouth of the Savannah River. It cost $1 million and took 25 tons of brick and 18 years of toil to finish. Yet it was captured in just 30 hours by Union forces. Completed in 1847 with walls 7½ feet thick, it was taken by Georgia forces at the beginning of the war. However, on April 11, 1862, defense strategy changed worldwide when Union cannons, firing from more than a mile away on Tybee Island, overcame the masonry fortification. The effectiveness of rifled artillery (firing a bullet-shaped projectile with great accuracy at long range) was clearly demonstrated. The new Union weapon marked the end of the era of masonry fortifications. The fort was pentagonally shaped, with galleries and drawbridges crossing the moat. You can still find shells from 1862 imbedded in the walls. There are exhibits of the fort's history in the visitor center. It's open daily (except Christmas) from 9am to 7pm. Admission is $3 for adults and free for those 16 and under.

## ESPECIALLY FOR KIDS

**Massie Heritage Interpretation Center**    Here's a stop in the Historic District for the kids. Geared to school-age children, the center features various exhibits about Savannah, including such subjects as the city's Greek, Roman, and Gothic architecture; the Victorian era; and a history of public education. Other exhibits include a period costume room and a 19th-century classroom, where children can experience a classroom environment from days gone by.
207 E. Gordon St. © 912/201-5070. Admission $3 for all ages. Mon–Fri 9am–4pm.

## 6 Organized Tours

If it's a *Midnight in the Garden of Good and Evil* tour you seek, then you've obviously come to the right place. Virtually every tour group in town offers tours of the *Midnight* sites, many of which are included on their regular agenda. Ask any of the tour groups. Note that some tour outfits will accommodate only groups, so if you're traveling alone or as a pair, be sure to make that known when you make your tour reservations.

A delightful way to see Savannah is by horse-drawn carriage. An authentic antique carriage carries you over cobblestone streets as the coachman spins a tale of the town's history. The 1-hour tour ($19 for adults, $8 for children 5–11) covers 15 of the 20 squares. Reservations are required, so contact **Carriage Tours of Savannah** at © **912/236-6756.**

**Old Town Trolley Tours** (℃ 912/233-0083) operates tours of the Historic District, with pickups at most downtown inns and hotels ($20 for adults, $10 for children 4–12), as well as a 1-hour **Haunted History** tour detailing Savannah's ghostly past (and present). Call to reserve for all tours.

**Gray Line Savannah Tours** (℃ 912/236-9604) has joined forces with **Historic Savannah Foundation Tours** to feature narrated bus tours of museums, squares, parks, and homes. Reservations must be made for all tours, and most have starting points at the visitor center and pickup points at various hotels. Tours cost $19 for adults and $8 for children 11 and under.

**Savannah Riverboat Cruises** are offered aboard the *Savannah River Queen,* operated by the River Street Riverboat Co., 9 E. River St. (℃ **800/786-6404** or 912/232-6404). You get a glimpse of Savannah as Oglethorpe saw it back in 1733. You'll see the historic cotton warehouses lining River Street and the statue of the *Waving Girl* as the huge modern freighters see it when they arrive daily at Savannah. Lunch and bar service are available. Adults pay $28, and children 12 and under are charged $17.

**Ghost Talk Ghost Walk** takes you through colonial Savannah on a journey filled with stories and legends based on Margaret Debolt's book *Savannah Spectres and Other Strange Tales.* If you're not a believer at the beginning of the guided tour, you may be at the end. The tour starts at Reynolds Square. For information, call ℃ **912/233-3896.** Hours for tour departures can vary. The cost is $10 for adults and $5 for children 12 and under.

**Low Country River Excursions,** a narrated nature cruise, leaves from the Bull River Marina, 8005 Old Tybee Rd. (U.S. 80 E.). Call ℃ **912/898-9222** for information. Passengers are taken on a 1993 38-foot pontoon boat, *Natures Way,* for an encounter with the friendly bottle-nosed dolphin. Both scenery and wildlife unfold during the 90-minute cruise down the Bull River. Trips are possible daily at 2pm, 4pm, and sunset, spring through fall, weather permitting. Adults pay $15, seniors $12, and children 11 and under $10. There's a 30-passenger limit.

## 7 Outdoor Pursuits

**BIKING**    Savannah doesn't usually have a lot of heavy traffic except during rush hours, so you can bicycle up and down the streets of the Historic District, visiting as many of the green squares as you wish. There's no greater city bicycle ride in all the state of Georgia. In lieu of a local bike-rental shop, many inns and hotels will provide bikes for their guests.

**CAMPING**    The **Bellaire Woods Campground,** 805 Fort Argyle Rd. (℃ **912/ 748-4000**), is 2½ miles west of I-95, 4½ miles west of U.S. 17, and 12 miles from the Savannah Historic District on the banks of the Ogeechee River. Facilities include full hookups, LP gas service, a store, self-service gas and diesel fuel, a dump station, hot showers, laundry facilities, and a pool. Rates are $30 to $35 for tents or RV hookups.

Open year-round, **Skidaway Island State Park** (℃ 912/598-2300) offers 88 camping sites with full hookups, costing $24. On arrival, you purchase a $2 parking pass valid for your entire stay. The grounds include 1- and 3-mile nature trails, grills, picnic tables, a pool, a bathhouse, and laundry facilities. Also open year-round, the **River's End Campground and RV Park,** Polk Street, Tybee Island (℃ **912/786-5518**), consists of 128 sites featuring full hookups, with groceries and a beach nearby. Tent sites cost $27 to $30 per day and RV sites $34 per day.

**DIVING**   The **Diving Locker-Ski Chalet,** 74 W. Montgomery Cross Rd. (© **912/927-6604**), offers a wide selection of equipment and services for various watersports. Scuba classes cost $230 for a series of weekday evening lessons and $245 for a series of lessons beginning on Friday evening. A full scuba-gear package, including buoyancy-control device, tank, and wet suit, is included. You must provide your own snorkel, mask, fins, and booties. It's open Monday to Friday 10am to 6pm and Saturday 10am to 5pm.

**FISHING**   **Amicks Deep Sea Fishing,** 6902 Sand Nettles Dr. (© **912/897-6759**), offers daily charters featuring a 41-foot 1993 custom-built boat. The rate is $95 per person and includes rod, reel, bait, and tackle. Bring your own lunch, though beer and soda are sold on board. Reservations are recommended, but if you show up 30 minutes before the scheduled departure, there may be space available. The boat departs at 7am and returns at 6pm.

**GOLF**   **Bacon Park,** Shorty Cooper Drive (© **912/354-2625**), is a 27-hole course with greens fees of $25 for an 18-hole round including carts. Golf facilities include a lighted driving range, putting greens, and a pro shop. It's open daily dawn to dusk.

Or **Henderson Golf Club,** 1 Henderson Dr. (© **912/920-4653**), includes an 18-hole championship course, a lighted driving range, a PGA professional staff, and golf instruction and schools. The greens fees are $40 Monday to Friday and $44 Saturday and Sunday. It's open daily 7:30am to 10pm.

Or try the 9-hole **Mary Calder,** West Congress Street (© **912/238-7100**), where the greens fees are $15 per day Monday to Friday and $17 per day Saturday and Sunday. It's open daily 7:30am to 7pm (to 5:30pm in winter).

**JOGGING**   "The most beautiful city to jog in"—that's how the president of the Savannah Striders Club characterizes Savannah. He's correct. The historic avenues provide an exceptional setting for your run. The Convention & Visitors Bureau can provide you with a map outlining three of the Striders Club's routes: Heart of Savannah YMCA Course, 3.1 miles; Symphony Race Course, 5 miles; and Children's Run Course, 5 miles. .

**NATURE WATCHES**   Explore the wetlands with **Palmetto Coast Charters,** Lazaretto Creek Marina, Tybee Island (© **912/786-5403**). Charters include trips to the Barrier Islands for shell collecting and watching for otter, mink, birds, and other wildlife. The captain is a naturalist and a professor, so he can answer your questions. Palmetto also features a dolphin watch usually conducted daily 4:30 to 6:30pm, when the shrimp boats come in with dolphins following behind. The cost is $125 for up to six people for a minimum of 2 hours, plus $50 for each extra hour.

**RECREATIONAL PARKS**   **Bacon Park** (see "Golf," above and "Tennis," below) includes 1,021 acres with archery, golf, tennis, and baseball fields. **Daffin Park,** 1500 E. Victory Dr. (© **912/351-3851**), features playgrounds, tennis, basketball, baseball, a pool, a lake pavilion, and picnic grounds. Both parks are open daily: May to September 8am to 11pm and October to April 8am to 10pm.

Located at Montgomery Cross Road and Sallie Mood Drive, **Lake Mayer Park** (© **912/652-6780**) consists of 75 acres featuring a multitude of activities, such as public fishing and boating, lighted jogging and bicycle trails, a playground, and pedal-boat rentals.

**SAILING**   **Sail Harbor,** 618 Wilmington Island Rd. (© **912/897-2896**), features the Catalina 25 boat, costing $150 per full day, with an extra day costing $100. It's open Tuesday to Saturday 10am to 6pm and Sunday 12:30 to 5:30pm.

**TENNIS**   **Bacon Park** (see "Golf," above; (C) **912/351-3850**) offers 16 lighted courts open Monday to Thursday 9am to 9pm, Friday 9am to 4pm and 5 to 8pm, and Saturday 9am to 1am. **Forsyth Park,** at Drayton and Gaston streets ((C) **912/351-3850**), has four courts open daily 7am to 9pm. Both parks charge $3 per hour. The use of the eight lighted courts at **Lake Mayer Park,** Montgomery Cross Road, costs nothing. They are open daily 8am to 11pm.

## 8 Shopping

**River Street** is a shopper's delight, with some 9 blocks (including Riverfront Plaza) of interesting shops, offering everything from crafts to clothing to souvenirs. The **City Market,** between Ellis and Franklin squares on West St. Julian Street, boasts art galleries, boutiques, and sidewalk cafes along with a horse-and-carriage ride. Bookstores, boutiques, and antiques shops are located between Wright Square and Forsyth Park.

  **Oglethorpe Mall,** at 7804 Abercorn St., has more than 100 specialty shops and four major department stores, as well as restaurants and fast-food outlets. The **Savannah Mall,** 14045 Abercorn St., is Savannah's newest shopping center, with two floors of shopping, plus a food court with its own carousel. The anchor stores are Dillard's, Parisian, and Belk.

### ANTIQUES

**Alex Raskin Antiques**   This shop offers a wide array of antiques of varying ages. The selection includes everything from accessories to furniture, rugs, and paintings. 441 Bull St. (in the Noble Hardee Mansion), Monterey Sq. (C) **912/232-8205.**

**J. D. Weed & Co.**   This shop prides itself on providing "that wonderful treasure that combines history and personal satisfaction with rarity and value." If you're looking for a particular item, just let the staff know and they'll try to find it for you.102 W. Victory Dr. (C) **912/234-8540.**

**Memory Lane**   More than 8,000 square feet of collectibles can be found here. The specialty of the house is a collection of German sleds and wagons. You'll also find glassware, furniture, and pottery. 230 W. Bay St. (C) **912/232-0975.**

### ART & SCULPTURE

**Gallery 209**   Housed in an 1820s cotton warehouse, this gallery displays two floors of original paintings by local artists, sculpture, woodworking, fiber art, gold and silver jewelry, enamels, photography, batiks, pottery, and stained glass. You'll also find a wide selection of limited-edition reproductions and notecards of local scenes. 209 E. River St. (C) **912/236-4583.**

**John Tucker Fine Arts**   This gallery offers museum-quality pieces by local artists as well as those from around the world, including Haitian and Mexican craftspeople. In a restored 1800s home, the gallery features 19th- and 20th-century landscapes, marine-art painting, portraits, folk art, and still life. 5 W. Charlton St. (C) **912/231-8161.**

**Morning Star Gallery**   This gallery features the works of more than 80 artists. Pieces include hand-thrown pottery, metalwork, paintings, prints, woodworks, jewelry, and glass (hand-blown and leaded). 8 E. Liberty St. (C) **912/233-4307.**

**Village Craftsmen**   This collection of artisans offers a wide array of handmade crafts, including hand-blown glass, needlework, folk art, prints, restored photographs, and hand-thrown pottery. 223 W. River St. (C) **912/236-7280.**

# BLACKSMITH

**Walsh Mountain Ironworks** This is the sales outlet of the most successful and high-profile blacksmith in Savannah. Inventories include house, kitchen, and garden ornaments, many of which have modern, but vaguely Gothic, designs. You can buy headboards for beds, garden arbors, trellises, tables, chairs, wine racks, CD racks, and ornamental screens. Prices range from $4 to $1,600, and in some cases require several weeks of waiting time. 427 Whitaker St. ✆ 912/239-9818.

# BOOKS

**Book Warehouse** This store offers more than 75,000 titles, including fiction, cookbooks, children's books, computer manuals, and religious tomes. Prices begin at less than a dollar, and all proceeds are donated to Emory University for cancer research. 11 Gateway Blvd. ✆ 912/927-0824.

**E. Shaver, Bookseller** Housed on the ground floor of a Greek Revival mansion, E. Shaver features 12 rooms of tomes. Specialties include architecture, decorative arts, regional history, and children's books as well as 17th-, 18th-, and 19th-century maps. 326 Bull St. ✆ 912/234-7257.

# CANDY & OTHER FOODS

**Plantation Sweets Vidalia Onions** Outside Savannah, check out the Vidalia onion specialties offered by the Collins family for more than 50 years. Sample one of the relishes, dressings, or gift items as well. Call for directions. Rte. 2, Cobbtown. ✆ 800/541-2272.

**River Street Sweets** Begun more than 20 years ago as part of the River Street restoration project, this store offers a wide selection of candies, including pralines, bear claws, fudge, and chocolates. Included among the specialties are more than 30 flavors of taffy made on a machine from the early 1900s. 13 E. River St. ✆ 800/627-6175 or 912/234-4608.

**Savannah's Candy Kitchen** Chocolate-dipped Oreos, glazed pecans, pralines, and fudge are only a few of the delectables at this confectionery. Staff members are so sure you'll be delighted with their offerings that they offer a full money-back guarantee if you're not satisfied. 225 E. River St. ✆ 800/242-7919 or 912/233-8411.

# GIFTS & COLLECTIBLES

**Charlotte's Corner** Featuring local items, this shop offers a wide array of gifts and souvenirs. The selection encompasses children's clothing, a few food items, Sheila houses, and Savannah-related books, including guidebooks and Southern cookbooks. 1 W. Liberty St. (at Bull St.). ✆ 912/233-8061.

**The Christmas Shop** This shop keeps the Christmas spirit alive all year with a large selection of ornaments, Santas, nutcrackers, and collectibles. Collectors will appreciate the various featured lines, including Dept 56, Polonaise, Christina's World, and Patricia Breen. 307 Bull St. ✆ 912/234-5343.

**Enchantments** If you collect bears and dolls, this store has a pet for you. Among its other selections is an array of quality toys and collector's pieces. 407 E. Montgomery Cross Rd. ✆ 912/651-9035.

# JEWELRY & SILVER

**Levy Jewelers** Located downtown, this boutique deals mainly in antique jewelry. It offers a large selection of gold, silver, gems, and watches. Among its other items are crystal, china, and gift items. 101 E. Broughton St. ✆ 912/233-1163.

**Simply Silver**    The specialty here is sterling flatware, ranging from today's designs to discontinued items of yesteryear. The inventory includes new and estate pieces along with an array of gift items. 236 Bull St. ✆ **912/238-3652.**

## 9 Savannah After Dark

**River Street,** along the Savannah River, is the major after-dark venue. Many night owls stroll the waterfront until they hear the sound of music they like, then follow their ears inside. In summer, concerts of jazz, Big Band, and Dixieland music fill downtown **Johnson Square** with lots of foot-tapping sounds that thrill both locals and visitors. Some of Savannah's finest musicians perform regularly on this historic site.

### THE PERFORMING ARTS

**Savannah Symphony Orchestra** has city-sponsored concerts in addition to its regular ticketed events. Spread a blanket in Forsyth Park and listen to the symphony perform beneath the stars; or be on River Street on the Fourth of July when the group sends rousing strains echoing across the river.

The orchestra is one of two fully professional orchestras in the state of Georgia, and its regular nine-concert masterworks series is presented in the Savannah Civic Center's **Johnny Mercer Theater,** Orleans Square (✆ **912/236-9536**), which is also home to ballet, musicals, and Broadway shows. Call to find out what's being presented at the time of your visit. Tickets range from $25 to $50.

**Savannah Theater,** Chippewa Square (✆ **912/233-7764**), presents contemporary plays. Tickets are usually $32 for regular admission, $30 for seniors or students, $15 for ages 12 to 16, and $10 for children 11 and under.

Late September brings the 5-day **Savannah Jazz Festival** (✆ **912/232-2222**), with nationally known musicians appearing around the city.

### LIVE-MUSIC CLUBS

**Monkey Bar**    This is a "high octane" bar in the Fusion Restaurant, with a self-proclaimed "martini chic" atmosphere and a sort of West Indies decor. Longtime restaurateur and club owner Wendy Snowden is the host, welcoming all for a good time. The live music agenda changes every night, ranging from piano music to soul. The hottest bands in Savannah can often be found rocking away the night here. Drink specials have names like "Jungle Mai-tai" and "Monkey Shot," and Monkey Hour with reduced drink prices is from 4 to 7pm. The club opens at 4pm Tuesday through Saturday and closes at 2am. 8 E. Broughton St. ✆ **912/232-0755.**

**Planters Tavern**    This is Savannah's most beloved tavern, graced with a sprawling and convivial bar, a pair of fireplaces, and a decor of antique bricks and carefully polished hardwoods. Because it's in the cellar of the Olde Pink House, many guests ask that platters of food be served at their tables. Otherwise, you can sit, drink in hand, listening to the melodies emanating from the sadder-but-wiser pianist. Foremost among the divas who perform is the endearingly elegant Gail Thurmond, one of Savannah's most legendary songstresses, who weaves her enchantment Tuesday to Sunday. In the Olde Pink House Restaurant, 23 Abercorn St. ✆ **912/232-4286.**

### BARS & PUBS

**Bernies**    This bar and grill, conveniently located on the riverfront, lies in one of the city's pre–Civil War cotton warehouses and has the ambience of an old portside pub. The bar offers live music, televised sports, and extended late weekend hours. The bartenders claim their Bloody Mary is the best on River Street, and it's presented in a Mason jar and topped with pickled okra. If you're hungry, a light menu features seafood, burgers, and sandwiches. It's open Monday through Thursday 11am to midnight, Friday to Saturday 11am to 3am, and Sunday noon to midnight. No cover. 115 E. River St. ✆ **912/236-1827.** www.berniesriverstreet.com/index.html.

**Kevin Barry's Irish Pub**    The place to be on St. Patrick's Day, this waterfront pub rocks all year. Irish folk music will entertain you as you choose from a menu featuring such Irish fare as beef stew, shepherd's pie, and corned beef and cabbage. Many folks come here just to drink, often making a night of it in the convivial atmosphere. It's open Monday to Friday 4pm to 3am and Saturday and Sunday 11am to 3am. 117 W. River St. ✆ **912/233-9626.**

**Mellow Mushroom**    Don't expect grandeur here. A member of a Georgia-based restaurant chain, it appeals to a funky, irreverent, and sometimes raucous crowd of college students and faded counter-culture aficionados from yesterday. Decor includes rambling murals painted with an individualized—and subjective—iconography that might require an explanation from a member of the cheerful waitstaff. There's the cut-off front end of a VW Beetle near the entrance; a limited menu that focuses almost exclusively on pizzas, salads, and calzones; and a die-hard emphasis on cheap beer, especially Pabst, which sells by the pitcher. Expect lots of SCAD (Savannah College of Art & Design) students, a battered and dimly lighted interior, recorded (not live) music, and a vague allegiance to the hard rock, hard drugs, and hard sex fantasies of the early 1970s. Open daily 11am to midnight. 11 W. Liberty St. ✆ **912/495-0705.**

**Mercury Lounge**    The venue is as hip, counterculture, and artfully kitsch as anything you might have expected in Manhattan, with the added benefit of a reputation for the biggest martinis (10 oz.) in town. You'll find the most comfortable barstools anywhere (they're covered in faux leopard or zebra), live music most nights and, when a band is not performing, a jukebox. Everything is congenially battered, with enough rock and musical memorabilia to please the curators of a rock-'n'-roll hall of fame. It's open daily from 3pm to 3am. 125 W. Congress St. ✆ **912/447-6952.**

**Savannah Smiles**    Near River Street and in back of the Quality Inn, this piano bar not only encourages audience participation, it requires it. A pair of talented musicians duels for the audience's attention as they play old-time favorites. Request a song, and the musicians will do the rest. Savannah Smiles won city awards for best new bar in 2001 and best overall bar in 2002. There are several shows of the "dueling pianos" every night, and an "open mic" night on Sunday. The bar is open Wednesday through Saturday 6pm to 3am, Sunday 6pm to 2am. Cover varies from $3 to $5 (on some nights, ladies and/or service members get in free). 314 Williamson St. ✆ **912/527-6453.**

**17 Hundred 90 Lounge**    This is Savannah's haunted pub. The ghost of Anna Powers, who killed herself by jumping out of the third-floor window onto a brick courtyard, has been spotted wandering about at night. She committed suicide after falling in love with a married sea captain who sailed away. If you don't mind ghosts, this is a cozy bar attached to one of Savannah's most acclaimed restaurants. Happy hour with hors d'oeuvres lasts from 4:30 to 7pm nightly. It's open Monday through Friday 11am to closing, and weekends from 6 to 10pm. 307 E. President St. ✆ **912/236-7122.**

**Six Pence Pub** You can drop into this authentic-looking English pub for pub grub along with homemade soups, salads, and sandwiches. On Sunday an ale-and-mushroom pie is featured. Drinks are discounted during happy hour Monday through Friday 5 to 7pm. It's open Sunday through Thursday 11:30am to midnight, Friday and Saturday 11:30am to 2am. 245 Bull St. © **912/233-3156.**

**The Rail** Not as aggressively noisy as Club One (see below), the Rail manages to be sophisticated and welcoming of divergent lifestyles. Its name acknowledges the 19th-century day laborers who used to congregate nearby every morning in hopes of being hired for a job on the local railway. Today you can "work the rail" in much more comfortable circumstances among some of Savannah's most engaging writers, artists, and eccentrics. Tavern-meisters Trina Marie Brown (from Los Angeles) and Melissa Swanson (from Connecticut) serve snack-style food, but most folks just drink and chat. 405 W. Congress St. © **912/238-1311.**

## GAY & LESBIAN BARS

**Chuck's Bar** Most of the bars along Savannah's River Street are mainstream affairs, attracting goodly numbers of tourists, some of whom drink staggering amounts of booze and who seem almost proud of how rowdy they can get. In deliberate contrast, Chuck's usually attracts local members of Savannah's counterculture, including lots of gay folk, who rub elbows in a tucked-away corner of a neighborhood rarely visited by locals. The setting is a dark and shadowy 19th-century warehouse, lined with bricks, just a few steps from the Jefferson Street ramp leading down to the riverfront. Hours are Monday to Saturday from 6pm to 3am. 305 Wet River St. © **912/232-1005.**

---

### ⟨ Finds ⟩ Strolling Around Isle of Hope

About 10 miles south of downtown Savannah is the charming community of **Isle of Hope** ⋒. First settled in the 1840s as a summer resort for the wealthy, it's now a showcase of rural antebellum life. To reach Parkersburg (as it was called in those days), citizens traveled by steamer down the Wilmington River or by a network of suburban trains. Today you can reach Isle of Hope by driving east from Savannah along Victory Drive to Skidaway Road. At Skidaway, go right and follow it to LaRoche Avenue. Take a left and follow LaRoche until it dead-ends on Bluff Drive.

This is the perfect place for a lazy afternoon stroll. The short path is home to authentically restored cottages and beautiful homes, most enshrouded with Spanish moss cascading from the majestic oaks lining the bluff. A favorite of many local landscape artists and Hollywood directors, Bluff Drive affords the best views of the Wilmington River.

As you head back toward Savannah, drive down Skidaway Road. On your left is **Wormsloe Plantation,** 7601 Skidaway Rd. (© **912/353-3023**). Wormsloe, the home of Noble Jones, isn't much more than a ruin. After you enter the gates, you proceed down an unpaved oak-lined drive, and the ruins lie less than half a mile off the road. Dr. Jones was one of Georgia's leading Colonial citizens and a representative to the Continental Congress. Wormsloe has also been home to forts and garrisons during the Civil and Spanish-American wars. It's open Tuesday to Saturday 9am to 5pm and Sunday 2 to 5:30pm. Admission is $2.50 for adults and $1.50 for students 6 to 18; children 5 and under are admitted free.

**Club One** ★★    Club One defines itself as the premier gay bar in a town priding itself on a level of decadence that falls somewhere between New Orleans's and Key West's, and it's the hottest and most amusing spot in town. Patrons include lesbians and gays from the coastal islands; visiting urbanites; and cast and crew of whatever film is being shot in Savannah at the time (Demi Moore and Bruce Willis showed up here in happier times). There's also likely to be a healthy helping of voyeurs who've read *Midnight in the Garden of Good and Evil.*

You pay your admission at the door, showing ID if the attendant asks for it. Wander through the street-level dance bar, trek down to the basement-level video bar for a (less noisy) change of venue, and (if your timing is right) climb one floor above street level for a view of the drag shows. There, a bevy of black and white *artistes* lip-synch the hits of Tina Turner, Gladys Knight, and Bette Midler. The bar is open Monday to Saturday 5pm to 3am and Sunday 5pm to 2am. Shows are nightly at 10:30pm and 12:30am. 1 Jefferson St. © **912/232-0200.** Cover (after 9:30pm) $10 for those 18–20, $5 for those 21 and older.

## DINNER CRUISES

The *Savannah River Queen,* a replica of the boats that once plied this waterway, is a 350-passenger vessel operated by the River Street Riverboat Co., 9 E. River St. (© **912/232-6404;** www.savannah-riverboat.com). It offers a 2-hour cruise with a prime rib or fish dinner and live entertainment. Reservations are necessary. The fare is $42 for adults and $27 for children 11 and under. Departures are usually daily at 6pm, but the schedule might be curtailed in the colder months.

# 21

# The Golden Isles & the Okefenokee Swamp

Georgia's barrier islands extend along the Atlantic coast from Ossabaw Island near Savannah all the way down to Cumberland Island, near Florida. Although some have been developed, others, such as Cumberland and Little St. Simons, still linger in the 19th century. Some of the islands are accessible only by boat.

This 150-mile-long stretch of Georgia coast is semitropical and richly historic. The scenic Georgia portion of U.S. 17 goes past broad sandy beaches, creeks and rivers, and the ruins of antebellum plantations. The major highlights are the "Golden Isles"—principally Jekyll Island, Sea Island, and St. Simons Island. Cumberland Island, the newest National Seashore, is still under development.

Brunswick is the gateway to the Golden Isles. Sea Island and St. Simons are just across the F. J. Torras Causeway (which passes over the famous Marshes of Glynn, immortalized by local poet Sidney Lanier). Jekyll Island is south of town, across the Lanier Bridge then south on Ga. 520 (large signs point the way). Together, they form one of the prime resort areas along the Atlantic coast.

The islands became world-famous for their Sea Island cotton, grown on huge plantations supported mainly by slave labor. The last slaver, the *Wanderer,* landed its cargo of Africans on Jekyll Island as late as 1858. The importing of slaves was by that time illegal and the crew was promptly arrested. Without a large labor force, the plantations languished and finally disappeared in the post–Civil War period.

In the late 1880s the Golden Isles got into the resort business when a group of Yankee millionaires discovered Jekyll Island. They bought it for $125,000 and built "cottages" here with anywhere from 15 to 25 rooms and a clubhouse large enough to accommodate up to 100 members. Until 1947, when second-generation members of the Jekyll Island Club sold the property to the state of Georgia for $675,000, the Millionaires' Village was so exclusive that no uninvited guests ever set foot on the place—even invited guests were limited to visits of no more than 2 weeks. Many of the cottages are open to visitors today, and all the attractions that drew the wealthy are now public property.

Sea Island was purchased back in 1927 by Howard Coffin (he already owned another "golden isle," Sapelo Island), who built a causeway from St. Simons to reach the 5-mile-long barrier island. Then he set about developing what has become a world-famous resort, The Cloister, which opened in October 1928.

The Golden Isles are ideal for naturalists, with miles and miles of private secluded beaches, plus acres of ancient forests. More than 200 species of birds are sighted locally, so birders flock here, especially to Little St. Simons. Many islands conduct year-round guided nature walks, where locals explain the coastal environment and you can see salt marshes and wildlife.

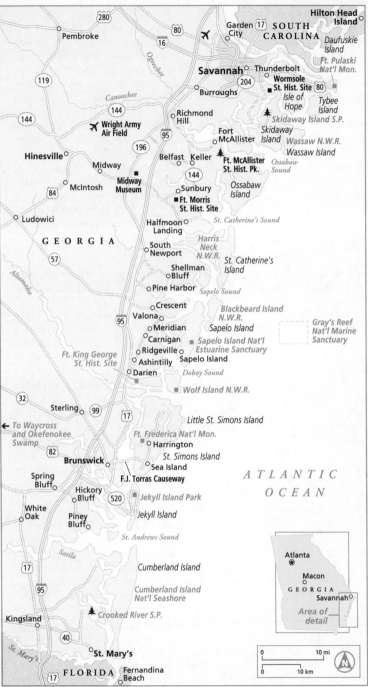

# The Golden Isles

**Hilton Head Island**

Pembroke

SOUTH CAROLINA

Garden City

Daufuskie Island

Ft. Pulaski Nat'l Mon.

Savannah
Thunderbolt
Wormsole St. Hist. Site
Burroughs
Isle of Hope
Tybee Island

Skidaway Island S.P.

Richmond Hill

Wright Army Air Field

Fort McAllister
Skidaway Island
Wassaw N.W.R.
Wassaw Island

Hinesville
Belfast
Keller
Ft. McAllister St. Hist. Pk.
Ossabaw Sound

Midway
Midway Museum
Sunbury
Ossabaw Island

McIntosh
Ft. Morris St. Hist. Site

Ludowici
Halfmoon Landing
St. Catherine's Sound

GEORGIA
South Newport
Harris Neck N.W.R.
St. Catherine's Island

Shellman Bluff
Pine Harbor
Sapelo Sound

Crescent
Valona
Blackbeard Island N.W.R.

Meridian
Sapelo Island
Gray's Reef Nat'l Marine Sanctuary

Carnigan
Ridgeville
Sapelo Island Nat'l Estuarine Sanctuary
Ashintilly
Sapelo Island
Ft. King George St. Hist. Site
Darien
Doboy Sound

Sterling
Wolf Island N.W.R.

To Waycross and Okefenokee Swamp

Little St. Simons Island

Ft. Frederica Nat'l Mon.
Harrington
St. Simons Island

Brunswick
Sea Island
F.J. Torras Causeway

Spring Bluff
Hickory Bluff
Jekyll Island Park

White Oak
Piney Bluff
Jekyll Island

St. Andrews Sound

ATLANTIC OCEAN

Cumberland Island

Cumberland Island Nat'l Seashore

Crooked River S.P.

Kingsland

St. Mary's

FLORIDA
Fernandina Beach

Atlanta

Macon

GEORGIA
Savannah

Area of detail

0        10 mi
0        10 km

Temperature and climate make the islands a year-round destination. Spring arrives early in March, with air temperatures ranging from 50° to 80°F (10°–27°C) and water temperatures at 66°F (19°C). Summer is hot, although the heat and humidity are moderated by coastal breezes. Temperatures range from 72° to 90°F (22°–32°C), with water temperatures at 80°F (27°C)— ideal beach weather. Fall arrives in mid-October and is marked by clear days and low humidity, with temperatures averaging 68°F (20°C). Winter is brief and mild, with daytime highs in the 60s (teens Celsius), lows in the 40s (single digits Celsius), and water temperatures averaging 50°F (10°C).

If all this weren't enticement enough, the Golden Islands are also the gateway to the Okefenokee Swamp Park, an hour's drive to the west. Called the "land of trembling earth," this swamp is one of the most forbidding yet one of the loveliest places in America, covering some 412,000 acres. Boating excursions into the swamp allow close encounters with alligators. The centerpiece is a 111-acre lake that attracts water-skiers, anglers, and boaters. On the west side of the swamp is the Stephen C. Foster State Park, offering cabins and campsites along with signposted nature trails and canoe rentals.

## 1 Sapelo Island ⟨★⟩

The fourth largest of Georgia's barrier islands, Sapelo Island is filled with the diverse wildlife of the forested uplands as well as a salt marsh and a complex beach and dunes system. The island is reached from the Sapelo ferry dock, 8 miles northeast of Darien off Ga. 99. Educational tours of this undeveloped barrier island are conducted year-round by the Georgia Department of Natural Resources.

Taking in everything from maritime forests to marshes, the **R. J. Reynolds State Wildlife Refuge** encompasses 8,240 acres. Some 5,900 of these acres have been designated as the **Sapelo Island National Estuarine Research Reserve.**

Guale Indians, Spanish missionaries, English freebooters, and French royalists called this island home before Thomas Spalding purchased the south end of the island in 1802. In the antebellum years, Spalding (1802–51) refined the Georgia Sea Island cotton and sugar industries and designed and constructed an octagonal tabby sugar mill in 1809. (Tabby is a mixture of equal parts of oyster shell, sand, water, and lime.)

In 1912, Howard E. Coffin purchased the island from Spalding's heirs. Coffin undertook a complete rebuilding of **South End House,** Spalding's plantation mansion, which dated from 1810. By 1928 the house was ready to entertain President and Mrs. Coolidge and later President and Mrs. Hoover in 1932. In February 1929, Charles A. Lindbergh landed on the island and visited the Coffins. The house was purchased in 1934 by the tobacco heir Richard J. Reynolds. Twenty years later Reynolds donated the dairy complex of the farm to the University of Georgia for use as a marine research laboratory. Jimmy Carter used the mansion during his administration in 1980.

Today, the island has some 400 acres of private property, concentrated in a hamlet known as Hog Hammock, whose residents are descended from slaves from Spalding's plantation days. Interpretive programs include marsh and beach walks, bird and wildlife observation, and special historic tours. Salt-marsh vegetation includes needlerush, sea oxeye, salt grass, glasswort, and cordgrass. You'll see osprey feeding in the Duplin River and hear the call of the clapper rail, a marsh bird. The island is inhabited by such species as raccoons, feral cows, white-tailed deer, and a variety of snakes, including the eastern diamondback rattler and the cottonmouth. Chachalacas, a Mexican species of bird introduced to the island as a game bird, might also be spotted.

A 30-minute ferryboat ride from the mainland aboard the *Sapelo Queen* takes visitors to the island. Guides accompany guests on the half-day bus tour, including a marsh walk. The ferry leaves Wednesdays and Fridays at 8:30am, returning at 12:30pm; and Saturdays at 9am, returning at 1pm. An extended tour is conducted the last Tuesday of each month March through October from 8:30am to 2:30pm. Reservations are required, costing $10 for adults, $6 for children 6 to 18, including the boat ride. To book tours, contact the **Sapelo Visitors Center** (© **912/437-3224**), Landing Road, in Meridian, Georgia, just outside of Darien, Georgia.

## 2 Brunswick

75 miles S of Savannah; 15 miles S of Darien

The gateway to the Golden Isles is a sleepy town not quite awake to the tourism potential of its antique houses, palms, flowering shrubs, and moss-draped live oaks. Brunswick has always been an important port, with a natural harbor that can handle oceangoing ships. In World War II, with Nazi U-boats prowling the Atlantic, Brunswick's shipyard began to construct "Liberty Ships," the name for a stronger, larger cargo vessel. Beginning in 1943, these 447-foot vessels slipped down the ways at the feverish rate of some four a month. Today, instead of Liberty Ships you'll find a large fleet of shrimp boats—the town bills itself as the "shrimp capital of the world."

At some point you'll want to sample **Brunswick stew** in the town of its origin (although the citizens of Brunswick County, Virginia, would beg to differ). It is made basically with a combination of meats, and flavored with an array of vegetables such as tomatoes, potatoes, okra, lima beans, and corn. In old days cooks would make it with squirrel, rabbit, or what virtually amounted to road kill ("or anything else you could catch in the woods," as one local diner told us), all simmering in the same pot—but preparations are less exotic today. A good time to sample the versions is during the **Brunswick Stewbilee,** a Brunswick stew cook-off held here the second Saturday in October from 11:30am to 3pm.

### ESSENTIALS

**GETTING THERE**    From Savannah, head west, following the signs to I-95; you'll take the highway south until the Brunswick turnoff.

Six miles north of Brunswick, **Glynco Jetport** (© **912/264-9200**) is served by **Delta ASA** (© **800/221-1212** or 912/267-1325; www.delta.com), an affiliate of Delta. It offers flights to the Brunswick area from Atlanta. At the small airport, car rentals are available, including **Avis** (© **912/638-2232**) and **Hertz** (© **912/265-3645**).

**VISITOR INFORMATION**    The **Brunswick-Golden Isles Visitors Bureau** (www.bgivb.com) operates a welcome center located at I-95 southbound, between exits 42 and 38 (© **912/264-0202**), and two visitor centers: one on U.S. 17 at the F. J. Torras Causeway in Brunswick (© **912/264-5337**), and another in the Old Casino Building on St. Simons Island (© **912/638-9014**). The friendly staff of each can give you area information. If you come without reservations, they can book a room for you at one of more than 20 nearby hotels and motels. Hours are daily 9am to 5pm.

## SEEING THE SIGHTS

The welcome center will provide you with a free map indicating the main points of interest, which include the waterfront off Bay Street, with its bustling docks and fleet of shrimp boats. Oceangoing freighters are often seen here.

The **Lanier Oak,** along U.S. 17, off Lanier Boulevard, is said to be the tree where the Georgia poet, Sidney Lanier, was inspired to write *The Marshes of Glynn.* Another tree, the 9-centuries-old **Lover's Oak,** at Albany and Prince streets, is also a source of pride for the town.

After dark, the big attractions are the dinner and casino cruises aboard the *Emerald Princess* (© **800/842-0115**). Bookings can be made at the **Golden Isles Cruise Lines,** 1 St. Andrews Court in Brunswick (© **912/265-3558**). This 200-foot luxury cruiser offers dining, dancing, and live entertainment on one level, and a full casino with slot machines, poker, blackjack, craps, and roulette on another level. After departure, the ship sails out past the 3-mile limit, where the casino then opens for business. Cruises depart from Golden Isles Cruise Lines docks at the Brunswick Landing Marina (Newcastle and K sts.).

Reservations are not required, but you should make them anyway just to be on the safe side. Monday to Thursday, the rate is $10 per person, going up to $20 on Friday, Saturday, and Sunday. Cruise hours are Monday to Thursday 7pm to midnight, Friday and Saturday 7pm to 1am, and Sunday 1 to 6pm. A special Saturday-morning departure leaves at 11am and returns at 4pm, at a cost of $20. All cruises offer a full meal at sea, with music, dancing, and games such as scavenger hunts. Call ahead for special summer deals.

## WHERE TO STAY

**Brunswick Manor** 🎔🎔   This is the most imposing, most impressive, and most elegant B&B in Brunswick. It was built in 1886 by an entrepreneur from Ohio who moved, carpetbagger-style, to manage the local bank and establish a nearby cooperage. The house is an eclectic and rather masculine brick-sided Victorian, with many Eastlake features and the most elaborate Corinthian portico (a later addition) of any house in Brunswick. Inside, a collection of Empire and Federal furniture, a greenhouse-style hot tub, and a collection of miniature electric trains demonstrate the personal flair of the owners, Harry and Claudia Tzucanow. Guest rooms are tastefully outfitted, especially the nautically stylish "Romance of the Seas" room. The least expensive rooms are in the clapboard-sided Victorian house next door. All units are nonsmoking and have neatly kept bathrooms with tub/shower combinations.

825 Egmont St., Brunswick, GA 31520. © **912/265-6889.** Fax 912/265-7879. 9 units. $80–$90 double; $90–$100 suite. Rates include full breakfast and afternoon tea. MC, V. **Amenities:** Breakfast room; lounge; Jacuzzi; library . *In room:* A/C, TV, fridge, hair dryer, ceiling fan.

**WatersHill Bed & Breakfast** 🎔   Some of the most old-fashioned hospitality in Brunswick is found at this restored 1860s Victorian house. It's an exceedingly comfortable place, with guest rooms named after the mothers and grandmothers of the present owners. The B&B is among the most conveniently located in town, right in the center of the historic old section. Each of the guest rooms is nonsmoking and has a private bathroom equipped with a tub/shower combination. Breakfast is one of the best in the area. Each afternoon, as a quaint old touch, tea or wine with cheese is served in the parlor.

728 Union St., Brunswick, GA 315210. © **912/264-4262.** Fax 912/265-6326. www.watershill.com. 5 units. $85–$115 double. Rates include breakfast. AE, DISC, MC, V. **Amenities:** Breakfast room; lounge . *In room:* A/C, TV.

## WHERE TO DINE

**Mack's Barbecue Place** ★ Ⓥ*alue* BARBECUE    Mack's occupies a 1960s building of no architectural charm, and lies beside the grimy commercial edges of Highway 17, on the heavily trafficked outskirts of town. Despite its lack of visual appeal, the place serves the best barbecue in the Golden Isles. Notice the neatly arranged cords of oak firewood stacked in the parking lot. The domain is maintained with an iron grip by members of the Wilson family. The interior resembles that of an uninspired steakhouse beside a thruway, enhanced with a smoking chamber that gobbles firewood and looks like a hybrid between a blast furnace and a locomotive. The menu is limited to fabulous sandwiches or platters of barbecued pork, beef, chicken, turkey, ribs, and hamburgers, accompanied by salad, coleslaw, fried mushrooms, onion rings, and corn. And you've got to have Brunswick stew on the side. No alcohol is served.

2809 Glynn Ave. Ⓒ **912/264-0605.** Sandwiches $3.15–$3.55; main courses $4.95–$7.95. AE, DISC, MC, V. Mon–Sat 10:30am–8:30pm.

**Spanky's** SEAFOOD/AMERICAN    Set between the coastal highway and the sea, this place is like a sprawling, clapboard-sided seafood restaurant and saloon in New England. It's rather chaotic, but it's always buzzing with locals. Avoid the place during peak dinner hours on Friday and Saturday, when you might not get a seat. The food is delicious: a wide selection of seafood, burgers, Mexican platters, and steaks, including an especially tasty chicken Reuben sandwich. Seafood platters are served with hush puppies, of course, and there's a superb version of Brunswick stew, which a chef obviously labors over.

1200 Glynn Ave. Ⓒ **912/267-6100.** Burgers, salads, and sandwiches $6–$7.95; platters $16–$18. AE, DISC, MC, V. Sun–Thurs 10am–9:30pm; Fri–Sat 11am–11pm.

## 3 St. Simons Island ★ ★

80 miles S of Savannah; 10 miles E of Brunswick

The largest of the Golden Isles, St. Simons is also the most popular for its beaches, golf courses, scenery, and numerous tennis courts. Through tunnels of ancient oaks, you can bike and drive the length of St. Simons, finding treasures at every turn. It's very much a vacation haven for families.

## ESSENTIALS

**GETTING THERE**    Take I-95 to Ga. 25 (the Island Pkwy.) or U.S. 17 to Brunswick, where signs direct visitors across the F. J. Torras Causeway to St. Simons Island.

**VISITOR INFORMATION**    The **St. Simons Island Visitors Center & Chamber of Commerce,** 530 Beachview Dr. W. (Ⓒ **912/638-9014**), offers maps and information, particularly on beaches. It's open daily 9am to 5pm.

## SEEING THE ISLAND

The best way to introduce yourself to the island is via **St. Simons Trolley Island Tours** (Ⓒ **912/638-8954**), which acquaint you with 400 years of history and folklore, taking 1½ hours and costing $18 for adults and $10 for children 10 and under. Tours depart March 15 to Labor Day, daily at 11am and 1pm; off season, daily at 11am.

The island's chief attraction is **Fort Frederica National Monument** (Ⓒ **912/638-3639;** www.nps.gov/fofr), on the northwest end of the island (signposted). Go first to the National Park Service Visitor Center, where a film and displays explain the role of the fort. There isn't much left; about all you'll see of the original construction is a small portion of the king's magazine and the barracks tower, but archaeological excavations have unearthed many foundations. The fort was constructed in 1736 by Gen. James Oglethorpe. On the grounds is a gift shop, and walking tours can be arranged. Admission is $5 per car. It's open from 9am to 5pm daily.

The **Museum of Coastal History,** 101 12th St. (© **912/638-4666**), is in a restored lighthouse-keeper's house next to St. Simons Light. A gallery dispenses information about the coastal region on the ground floor. Hardy souls can climb the lighthouse's 129 steps for a panoramic view of the Golden Isles, which is far more intriguing than any of the museum's exhibits. Adults pay $5 and children 6 to 12 are charged $2.50 (children 5 and under enter free). It's open Monday to Saturday from 10am to 5pm and on Sunday from 1:30 to 5pm.

**Christ Church,** 6329 Frederica Rd., at the north end of the island, was built in 1820. It was virtually destroyed when Union troops camped here during the Civil War, burning the pews for firewood and butchering cattle in the chapel. In 1886 Anson Greene Phelps Dodge, Jr., restored the church as a memorial to his first wife, who had died on their honeymoon. The serene white building nestled under huge old oaks is open every day from 2 to 5pm during daylight saving time, 1 to 4pm at other times. There's no admission charge.

Scattered from end to end on St. Simons are ruins of the plantation era: the **Hampton Plantation** (where Aaron Burr spent a month after his duel with Alexander Hamilton) and **Cannon's Point** on the north; **West Point, Pines Bluff,** and **Hamilton Plantations** on the west along the Frederica River; **Harrington Hall** and **Mulberry Grove** in the interior; **Lawrence, St. Clair, Black Banks, The Village,** and **Kelvyn Grove** on the east; and the **Retreat Plantation** on the south end. There's a restored chapel on West Point Plantation made of tabby, with mortar turned pink from an unusual lichen. Locals say it reflects blood on the hands of Dr. Thomas Hazzard, who killed a neighbor in a land dispute and built the chapel after being so ostracized that he would not attend Christ Church.

## BEACHES, GOLF & OTHER OUTDOOR PURSUITS

St. Simons not only attracts families looking for a beach, it's also heaven for golfers, with 99 holes. One golfer we met who's played every hole said that each one presents a worthy challenge. Other sports are boating, inshore and offshore fishing, and water-skiing. Jet-skiing, parasailing, charter fishing, scuba diving, and cruising can also be arranged at **Golden Isles Marina Docks,** 206 Marina Dr. (© **912/634-1128**), on the F. J. Torras Causeway.

**Neptune Park,** at the island's south end, has miniature golf, a kids' playground, picnics under the oaks, and pier fishing. There's beach access from the park.

**BEACHES** You'll find two white-sand public beaches here, foremost of which is the **Massingale Park Beach,** Ocean Boulevard. It has a county-maintained beach with a picnic area and a bathhouse. It's open with a lifeguard on duty June 1 to Labor Day, daily from 8am to 4pm. Parking is free in designated areas, and drinking is allowed on the beach but only from plastic containers (no glasses). Fishing is free from the beach but allowed only from 4 to 11pm.

Another public beach is the **Coast Guard Station Beach,** East Beach Causeway, again family-oriented, with a bathhouse and showers. Lifeguards are on duty from June 1 to the Labor Day weekend, daily from 10am to 4pm. Parking is free in designated areas, and fishing is permitted during nonswimming hours from 4:30 to 11pm. Drinking is allowed on the beach from plastic containers only.

Further information about beaches can be obtained from the **Glynn County Recreation Department** (☏ 912/554-7780).

**BIKE RENTALS** **Ocean Motion,** 1300 Ocean Blvd. (☏ **800/669-5215** or 912/638-5225), suggests that you explore St. Simons by bike, and will provide detailed instructions about the best routes. The island is relatively flat, so biking is easy. Beach cruisers are available for men, women, and kids, with infant seats and helmets. Bike rentals cost $9 for 4 hours or $14 for a full day.

**FISHING** Your best bet is **Golden Isles Charter Fishing,** 104 Marina Dr., Golden Isles Marina Village (☏ **912/638-7673**), which offers deep-sea fishing and both offshore and inshore fishing. Captain Mark Noble is your guide.

**GOLF** It's golf—not tennis—that makes St. Simons Island a star attraction. Foremost among the courses is the **Sea Island Golf Club** ★★★, 100 Retreat Ave. (☏ **912/638-5118**), owned by the Cloister of Sea Island. At the end of the "Avenue of Oaks" at historic Retreat Plantation, the club consists of a number of courses: the Retreat Course (9 holes, 3,260 yd., par 36), the Plantation Course (18 holes, 6,549 yd., par 72), the Seaside Course (9 holes, 3,185 yd., par 36), and the Ocean Forest (18 holes, 7,011 yd., par 72).

The club opened in 1927, and offers dramatic ocean views adding a measure of excitement to the game. The state-of-the-art Golf Learning Center on the grounds can help improve even an experienced golfer's game. Its greatest fans mention it with the same reverence as St. Andrews, Pebble Beach, or Ballybunion. Former president George H. W. Bush liked the courses so much that he played 36 holes a day. Seaside and Retreat are the most requested 9s, with Seaside definitely the most famous of all—known for the 414-yard no. 7. *Golf Digest* has called this hole one of the best in golf and among the toughest in Georgia. A drive has to clear a marsh-lined stream and avoid a gaping fairway bunker.

Greens fees for hotel guests only are $135 to $230, with cart included. Clubs rent for $40, and professional instruction is available for $100 to $230 per half-hour. Caddies cost $29 plus tip. On the grounds are a pro shop, clubhouse, and restaurant. The course is open daily from 7am to 7pm.

**St. Simons Island Club,** 100 Kings Way (☏ 912/638-3611), is an 18-hole, par-72 course of 6,200 yards. Known for its Low Country architecture, it hosts several popular tournaments every year. The demanding course, designed by Joe Lee, features narrow fairways lined by lagoons and towering pines. Greens fees for Cloister guests are $105 to $135; cottage guests at Sea Island pay the same. Professional instruction is available at $95 to $250 per hour through arrangements made at the clubhouse and pro shop. There's also a restaurant on the premises. Play is available daily from 7am to 7pm.

**Sea Palms Golf & Tennis Resort,** 5445 Frederica Rd. (☏ **912/638-3351**), offers outstanding golf on its Tall Pines/Great Oaks (18 holes, 6,500 yd., par 72), Great Oaks/Sea Palms West (18 holes, 6,200 yd., par 72), and Sea Palms West/Tall Pines (9 holes, 2,500 yd., par 72) courses. Some holes nestle alongside scenic marshes and meandering tidal creeks. Reserved tee times are recommended, and cart use is required. The courses are open daily from 7am to 7pm, charging greens fees of $69 for hotel guests and $84 for nonguests, with cart rentals included. Professional instruction costs $30 for a 30-minute session, $50 for an hour.

**NATURE TOURS** The **Ocean Motion Surf Co.,** 1300 Ocean Blvd. (☏ **912/ 638-5225**), offers nature tours by kayak of the island's marsh creeks and secluded beaches. Featured is either a 2-hour dolphin nature tour at $39 or a 4-hour wildlife tour, by request only, at $75.

**SAILBOAT RENTALS** **Barry's Beach Service, Inc.,** at the King and Prince Beach Hotel, 420 Arnold Rd. (© **912/638-8053**), arranges hourly, half-day, or full-day sailboat rentals, along with sailing lessons (by experienced instructors) and sailboat rides. Kayak rentals, tours, and instruction are also available.

**TENNIS** There are two public tennis courts on the island. The **Mallory Park Courts,** Mallory Street, has two lighted courts open year-round, and admission is free. **Epworth Park,** on Lady Huntington Drive, has two courts open 24 hours but not equipped with lights; it, too, is free.

## WHERE TO STAY

In addition to the accommodations listed below, private cottages are available for weekly or monthly rental on St. Simons. You can get an illustrated brochure with rates and availability information from **Parker-Kaufman Realtors,** 1699 Frederica Rd., St. Simons Island, GA 31522 (© **912/638-3368**). The office is open Monday to Friday 9am to 5pm and on Saturday 9am to 1pm. Vacation rental cottages can range from one to four bedrooms. Rentals begin at $550 per week in summer, lowered to as little as $450 per week off season.

**Best Western Island Inn** This unassuming, brick-sided motel was built in the late 1980s, about 2½ miles from the nearest beach. The efficiencies have a kitchenette, and the bedrooms are no-nonsense, unfrilly, and economical. All units have well-kept bathrooms with tub/shower combinations. About a dozen of them can be connected with adjoining rooms to allow families to create their own live-in arrangements.

301 Main St., St. Simons Island, GA 31522. © **800/937-8376** or 912/638-7805. Fax 912/694-4720. www. bestwestern.com. 61 units. $75–$96 double; $108–$135 suite. Rates include continental breakfast. AE, DC, DISC, MC, V. **Amenities:** Breakfast room; lounge; outdoor pool; health club privileges; Jacuzzi; playground; business services; nonsmoking rooms; rooms for those w/limited mobility. *In room:* A/C, TV, dataport, hair dryer.

**King and Prince Beach Resort** This is a midsize oceanfront resort founded in 1932 by partners who were evicted from the Jekyll Island Club. Today's reincarnation of five Spanish-style buildings is a venue for frequent corporate conventions. Frankly, it seems devoid of any real pizzazz; Hugh Hefner hasn't visited since the 1950s. Don't expect continuous access to a beach: During high tide, the beach completely disappears. The condo apartments have kitchenettes. All units have neatly kept bathrooms with tub/shower combinations.

201 Arnold Rd., St. Simons Island, GA 31522. © **800/342-0212** or 912/638-3631. Fax 912/634-1720. www. kingandprince.com. 187 units. $119–$269 double; $249–$469 villa. AE, DC, MC, V. **Amenities:** Restaurant; bar; 5 pools (1 indoor); 4 tennis courts; exercise room; Jacuzzi; limited room service; massage; babysitting; laundry service/dry cleaning; nonsmoking rooms; rooms for those w/limited mobility. *In room:* A/C, TV, kitchenette (in some), hair dryer, safe.

**The Lodge at Sea Island Golf Club** ★★ Golfers who have stayed at some of the greatest resorts in California and the Carolinas justifiably rave about this resort. A great golfing experience and first-rate accommodations combine to form this smoothly operating lodge. It doesn't pretend to have the grandeur of its sibling, The Cloister on Sea Island (see below), but for a luxurious, casual retreat, it's hard to beat, attracting not only golfers but small corporate groups. Attached to one of America's premier golf clubs, the lodge has been created in the spirit of one of those private clubs in Newport or the Hamptons. Set on beautiful grounds, it overlooks Rees Jones's Plantation Golf Course, often from a private balcony with views of the fairways and ocean. An English manor house decor prevails throughout. The guest rooms are spacious and beautifully furnished, with deluxe bathrooms with tub/shower combos. The inn's premier restaurant, Colt & Alison's, specializes in steaks, chops, and live Maine lobster. Guests of the lodge have full access to all of the amenities of the Cloister.

100 Retreat Ave., St. Simons Island, GA 31522. © **866/GOLF-LODGE** or 912/634-4300. Fax 912/634-3909. www.golflodge.com. $300–$700 double; $450–$900 suite. AE, DISC, DC, MC, V. **Amenities:** 4 restaurants; 2 bars; 3 18-hole golf courses; exercise room; spa; Jacuzzi; sauna; game room, 24-hr. room service; babysitting; laundry service/dry cleaning; nonsmoking rooms; rooms for those w/limited mobility. *In room:* A/C, TV, dataport, minibar, hair dryer, safe, 24-hr. butler service (lodge only).

**Sea Gate Inn**   Its charms and advantages are often underestimated because of its low-rise format, unpretentious entrance, and location near other, much larger hotels. Despite that, this is a clean, respectable hotel whose accommodations are divided into two buildings separated from one another by a quiet road that runs parallel to the sea. The more desirable (and expensive) of the two is the Ocean House, a 1985 annex built on stilts. The less expensive, and less desirable, lodgings are clustered around a swimming pool, roadside-motel style. All units contain well-kept bathrooms with tub/shower combinations. Some units contain modest kitchenettes. The hotel, incidentally, was named after an old-fashioned ferryboat that used to ply the waters between Brunswick and St. Simons Island.

1014 Ocean Blvd., St. Simons Island, GA 31522. © **800/562-8812** or 912/638-8661. Fax 912/638-4932. www.seagateinn.com. 48 units. $75–$110 double; $93–$155 suite. DISC, MC, V. **Amenities:** Lounge; outdoor pool. *In room:* A/C, TV, kitchenette (in some).

**Sea Palms Golf & Tennis Resort** ★★   This place imitates the older and more upscale resorts nearby. Sprawled over 800 landscaped acres, it combines aspects of a retirement community with a family-friendly resort. Most people stay 3 to 5 days.

After registering in a woodsy bungalow near the entrance, you'll be waved off towards your accommodations, to which you carry your own bags. If you're looking for maximum isolation, this place might be appropriate; otherwise, you might feel it's too anonymous. All guest rooms contain well-maintained bathrooms with tub/shower combinations. Each suite contains a kitchenette. There's a golf course on the premises, and views over some beautiful marshland from many of the simply furnished units. The nearest good beach is about 4 miles away.

5445 Frederica Rd., St. Simons Island, GA 31522. © **800/841-6268** or 912/638-3351. Fax 912/634-8029. www.seapalms.com. 154 units. $119–$169 double; $169–$289 1– or 2–bedroom suite. Children 17 and under stay free in parent's room. Golf, tennis, and honeymoon packages available. AE, DC, MC, V. **Amenities:** Restaurant; bar; 2 outdoor pools; 27-hole golf course; 12 tennis courts; fitness center; sauna; babysitting; laundry service/dry cleaning; nonsmoking rooms; rooms for those w/limited mobility. *In room:* A/C, TV, dataport, hair dryer.

# WHERE TO DINE
## EXPENSIVE

**The Restaurant at the Sea Island Golf Club** ★ INTERNATIONAL Despite the name, this place stands firmly on St. Simons Island. It was built on the ruins of a cow barn of a plantation great house that long ago burned to the ground. The restaurant occupies a simple square dining room in back of the golf course's clubhouse, and has big windows extending out over the landscape of trees and lawns. Uniformed staff members give the impression of being old family retainers as they serve a luncheon menu of burgers, salads, club sandwiches, and fresh fish. Dinner is more formal, offering worthy but not particularly experimental dishes that include boned and browned Blue Ridge salmon trout, seafood fettuccine, seafood crepes, and grilled steaks.

100 Retreat Ave. © **912/638-5154.** Reservations recommended for dinner. Main courses $27–$40. AE, DC, MC, V. Tues–Sun noon–3:30pm and 6:30–9pm.

## MODERATE

**Chelsea's** INTERNATIONAL    Set close to the road, a few steps from the larger and more visible King and Prince Hotel, this well-known restaurant combines aspects of a singles bar with a relaxed, unpretentious dining room. It's in a long, low-rise building trimmed with ferns, lattices, and wine racks. You never know who you might meet at the bar. The menu includes steaks, salads, pastas, lobster-tail fingers, chicken breasts encrusted in Romano cheese, and roast lamb. A menu like that offers few surprises—but few disappointments, either.

1226 Ocean Blvd. ② 912/638-2047. Reservations recommended. Main courses $12–$32. AE, DISC, MC, V. Daily 5:30–10pm.

## INEXPENSIVE

**Bennie's Red Barn** *Value* STEAKS/SEAFOOD    Established in 1954, the place has a Southern folksiness, almost a hillbilly kind of charm. Menu items include an uncomplicated medley of food to please everyone's Southern grandmother, including fried or broiled fish, chicken, and shrimp. Steaks are sizable slabs, woodfire-grilled and appropriately seasoned. Dinners include house salad, potato, rolls, and tea or coffee. If you're a biscuit-and-gravy kind of diner, you've arrived.

5514 Frederica Rd. ② **912/638-2844.** Reservations recommended Sat–Sun. Main courses $9.75–$20. DISC, MC, V. Daily 6–10pm.

**Blue Water Bistro** AMERICAN    Set in the island's most congested neighborhood a few steps from the waterfront, this place is New South all the way. It also knows how to throw a good party. Look for the bronze bank-deposit vault piercing its facade, a hint of the building's original role as a commercial landmark. Inside you'll find a cozy nautical decor, an antique Wurlitzer jukebox, and an Atlanta brand of hip. Dishes reflect the region's party ethic with names that include Mardi Gras pasta (with shellfish and andouille sausage). Also available are uptown, urban dishes such as Mediterranean chicken, *pescado veracruzano*, and a stew of deep-sea scallops with green-lip mussels. But for dessert, there's Southern-style bread pudding like Mother used to make.

115 Mallory St. ② **912/638-7007.** Reservations recommended. Main courses $6.95–$15. AE, DISC, MC, V. Mon–Sat 11am–10pm.

**The Crab Trap** *Kids* SEAFOOD    For the family in pursuit of coleslaw, hush puppies, and fried shrimp, the Crab Trap is the island's most popular seafood restaurant and a good buy. Forget fancy trappings—the place is downright plain. Fresh seafood is offered daily, and you can order it fried, broiled, blackened, or grilled. Appetizers include oysters on the half shell and crab soup. Boiled crab is the chef's specialty, and the seafood platter is big enough for three. For those who aren't turned on by crabs and shrimp, steaks in various cuts are also available. Heaps of battered fries come with most dishes. That hole in the middle of your table is for depositing shrimp shells and corncobs. Dress as if you're going on a summer fishing trip.

1209 Ocean Blvd. ② **912/638-3552.** Main courses $8.95–$19. AE, MC, V. Mon–Thurs 5–10pm; Fri–Sat 5–10:30pm; Sun 5–10pm. Closed Thanksgiving and Christmas.

**Delaney's Bistro** AMERICAN    Local chef Tom Delaney's loyal following includes both islanders and visitors. He aims to appeal to a wide culinary taste, and in general succeeds. In his low-rise building, Delaney offers an array of food ranging from fresh seafood to certified Black Angus beef. The menu at lunch is light, including the usual pastas, sandwiches, and salads, as well as grilled shrimp salad or sautéed crab cakes. Tom is more ambitious at night. You might begin with a pâté of foie gras or baked goat cheese before selecting a main course such as a mixed grill (beef, veal, and lamb chop in a cabernet sauce) or veal Hannah (a scaloppini topped with wild mushrooms and crab). Desserts are made fresh daily.

3415 Frederica Rd. © **912/638-1330.** Reservations recommended. Main courses $7.95–$13 lunch, $17–$35 dinner. AE, DC, DISC, MC, V. Tues–Sat 11am–2:30pm and 6–10pm.

**Frannie's Place on St. Simons** ★ *Finds* SOUTHERN   Chef-owners Lisa Cook (an appropriate last name) and Fran Kelly win many awards for making the "Best Brunswick Stew" in the Golden Isles. They are the "Stewbilee" champs. Cook makes 20 gallons of the stew every day, and Kelly estimates that some 95% of diners order the signature soup either as a main dish or an appetizer. Most customers request a big steaming bowl with homemade corn bread and "sweet tea" on the side. It's topped off with a generous slice of pecan pie or Key lime pie. Of course, you can order other items here, including sandwiches, salads, and even vegetarian dishes. We like the crab cakes and shrimp salad.

318 Mallory St. © **912/638-1001.** Breakfast specials $4.95–$5.95; lunch $4.95–$8.95; bowl of Brunswick stew $3.95. No credit cards. Wed–Sun 11am–2:30pm.

## 4 Little St. Simons Island ★

20-min. boat ride from St. Simons Island

The ideal place to savor the wild beauty of Georgia's coast is still untouched by commercial development. Reached only by boat, Little St. Simons Island—6 miles long and 2 to 3 miles wide—remains one of the last privately owned islands off the Georgia coast. The current owners have welcomed family and friends since the early 1900s, but in 1978 it was opened to the general public, with accommodations limited to 24.

The island is a haven for naturalists and for those seeking a secluded getaway. (But be warned that mosquitoes are a serious problem in summer.) Activities on Little St. Simons include shelling, swimming, and sunbathing along 7 miles of secluded beaches; and hiking (watch out for snakes) and horseback riding through acres of ancient forest. There are also canoeing and fishing in the island's many rivers and creeks, plus bird-watching of at least 200 species. Guests can learn about the local ecosystems by joining naturalists on explorations. In all, 10,000 acres of secluded wilderness have been left virtually untouched for more than a century.

### ESSENTIALS

**GETTING THERE**   Take I-95 to Ga. 25 (the Island Pkwy.) or U.S. 17 to Brunswick, where signs direct visitors across the F. J. Torras Causeway to St. Simons Island. Once on the island, follow the signs to the Hampton River Club Marina. At the marina, on the north end of St. Simons, a ferryboat departs daily at 10:30am and again at 4:30pm, taking visitors to Little St. Simons. It's privately owned, so unless you're a guest you are not even allowed to ride the ferry, which will immediately turn around.

**VISITOR INFORMATION**   All information is supplied directly by the lodge (see below).

### WHERE TO STAY & DINE

**The Lodge on Little St. Simons Island** ★ *Finds*   The lodge is for those seeking a Robinson Crusoe–type of vacation. It's surprisingly exclusive, but unlike luxury resorts such as Fripp Island, it doesn't have plush upholstery and dramatic architecture. If you like life summer-camp style, this is for you. Accommodations, in simple bedrooms cooled by ceiling fans, include the 1917 Hunting Lodge in the main house (which contains the dining room); the 1930s Michael Cottage (a two-bedroom cottage at the forest's edge); and the 1980s Cedar Lodge and River Lodge, each a cottage with four private guest rooms sharing a sitting room with a fireplace and screened porch. All units are nonsmoking and have neatly kept bathrooms with tub/shower combinations.

You pour your own drinks at a makeshift bar in the corner of a communal living room with hunting trophies from another era. Hearty, homey meals are served family style in the main dining room, and the staff will be happy to prepare a picnic lunch for you. The menu features locally caught seafood and such Southern staples as fried chicken and barbecue.

P.O. Box 21078, Little St. Simons Island, GA 31522. ℂ **888/733-5774** or 912/638-7472. Fax 912/634-1811. www.littlestsimonsisland.com. 15 units. $600–$675 double; 2-, 3-, and 4-bedroom accommodations $1,100–$2,400 year-round; full island rental for up to 30 persons $7,700–$8,000 year-round. Rates include full board. Additional person in room $225–$250 extra. AE, DISC, MC, V. **Amenities:** Restaurant; bar; outdoor pool; biking; boating; fishing; hiking; horseback riding; bird-watching. *In room:* A/C, ceiling fans, no phone.

## 5 Sea Island ★★

11 miles E of Brunswick

Since 1928 this has been the domain of the Cloister hotel (see below). Today, in addition to the hotel, it's home to some of the most elegant villas and mansions in the Southeast. Most of Sea Island's homes—many in the Spanish-Mediterranean style—are second homes to CEOs and other rich folk. Some can be rented if you can afford it. Call **Sea Island Cottage Rentals** (ℂ **912/638-5112;** www.seaislandcottages.com) and be prepared for some higher mathematics.

The island was acquired by Ohio-based Howard Earle Coffin, an automobile executive, in 1925. Still owned by Coffin's descendants, The Cloister combines 10,000 acres of forest, lawn, and marshland, plus 5 miles of beachfront. The island has impressed everybody from Margaret Thatcher to Queen Juliana of the Netherlands, plus four U.S. presidents, including George H. W. Bush, who honeymooned here with his wife Barbara in the 1940s. Many day visitors who can't afford the high prices of the Cloister come over for a scenic drive along Sea Island Drive, called "Millionaire's Row"—there's no tollgate. ·

### ESSENTIALS

**GETTING THERE**    From Brunswick, take the F. J. Torras Causeway to St. Simons Island and follow Sea Island Road to Sea Island.

**VISITOR INFORMATION**    There is no welcome center. Information is provided by the Cloister, but the staff prefers to cater to registered guests.

### WHERE TO STAY & DINE

**The Cloister** ★★★    Georgia's poshest hotel retreat, set amid the most elaborate landscaping on the coast, is a vast compound between the Atlantic Ocean and the Black Banks River. It takes in about 50 carefully maintained buildings, some of them massive and others on neighboring St. Simon's Island. Most replicate the Iberian–Moorish Revival style of the resort's original architect, Addison Mizner.

Everyone from honeymooners to golfers checks in here, with the family trade predominating in July and August. Traditionalists prefer a room in the main building, with twin, double, or king-size beds, often with a private balcony or patio, too. These rooms tend to be smaller than the newer units. The secluded cottages and beach houses also offer additional accommodations. The ocean-front rooms are in contemporary buildings with sumptuous modern furnishings, lacking tradition but offering greater comfort and more room to breathe. All units have well-kept bathrooms with tub/shower combinations.

Full American Plan (lodging with three meals included) is required of all guests at the Cloister. The Main Dining Room is the most lavish restaurant in the region, with sumptuous buffets and vestiges of the 1940s apparent in the uniformed service and the hushed, very polite tones of both staff and guests.

Sea Island, GA 31561. © 800/732-4752 or 912/638-3611. Fax 912/638-5159. www.seaisland.com. $250–$700 double; $1,200 suite. Meals are $35 per day. Children 18 and under stay free in parent's room. Golf, tennis, or honeymoon packages available. AE, DC, DISC, MC, V. **Amenities:** 4 restaurants; 2 bars; 3 outdoor pools; 3 18-hole golf courses; 10 tennis courts; fitness center; spa; boutiques; salon; beach club; limited room service; massage; babysitting; laundry service/dry cleaning; nonsmoking rooms; rooms for those w/limited mobility. *In room:* A/C, TV, dataport, minibar (in some), hair dryer.

## 6 Jekyll Island ★★★

9 miles S of Brunswick

Once a winter playground for the Rockefellers, Pulitzers, Goulds, Morgans, and Cranes, Jekyll Island is the smallest of the state's coastal islands, with 5,600 acres of highlands and 10,000 acres of marshlands. Today it's no longer the exclusive enclave it once was, and is open to all those attracted by its miles of beautiful, white-sand Atlantic beaches and holes of championship golf. It also has far better tennis complexes than St. Simons Island. Families come here for a wealth of outdoor activities.

The word "wealth" had another meaning on the island, at least from 1886 to 1942. The Jekyll Island Club, which owned the then-private island, was reputed to represent more than one-sixth of the world's wealth. A 1904 edition of *Munsey's Magazine* referred to the Jekyll Island Club as the "richest, the most exclusive, and most inaccessible club in the world."

## ESSENTIALS

**GETTING THERE**    From Brunswick, take U.S. 17 South to the turnoff for Jekyll Island. Head east across the Jekyll Island Causeway, paying a daily parking rate of $3 per vehicle to enter the island.

**VISITOR INFORMATION**    The **Jekyll Island Visitors Center,** 901 Jekyll Island Causeway (© 912/635-3636), is open daily from 9am to 5pm, dispensing maps, brochures, and other helpful information.

## SEEING THE SIGHTS

The best way to see the **historic district** ★★—the former enclave of the millionaires of America's Gilded Age, who built what they called "cottages" here—is to take a guided historic tour departing daily on the hour from 10am to 3pm from the **Museum Orientation Center** (© 912/635-4036) on Stable Road. The tour lasts 1½ hours, costing $18 for adults, $8.75 for children 6 to 18, and free for children 5 and under. Highlights of the tour include **Indian Mound** (or Rockefeller) **Cottage** from 1892, and the **du Bignon Cottage** from 1884.

On your own, you can view the Goodyear Cottage in the district, housing the **Jekyll Island Arts Association** (© 912/635-3920)—with a gift shop and a free monthly exhibition. Admission is free, and it's open daily from noon to 4pm. Also in the district, **Mistletoe Cottage** (© 912/635-4092) showcases the work of the nationally renowned, late Jekyll Island sculptor, Rosario Fiore, and is open Saturday and Sunday 2 to 4pm.

Last, Jekyll Island is also the site of **Horton's Brewery Site,** Georgia's first brewery, signposted on the northwest end of the island. It was started by General Oglethorpe, who evidently knew how to put first things first for his settlers. This two-story ruin, dating from 1742, is one of the oldest standing structures in the state. It was mainly constructed of tabby, a building material made of crushed oyster shells that is native to coastal Georgia. Very near the brewery stand the ruins of a home built in 1738 by William Horton, one of Oglethorpe's captains.

## OUTDOOR PURSUITS

If you have a car, take the South Jekyll Loop to survey the scene before concentrating on specifics. Drive south on North Beachview Drive to view some of the island's 10 miles of public beaches with public bathhouses and picnic areas. Your loop around the island's southern end will include the **South Dunes Picnic Area.** Continue around onto South Riverview Drive, passing **Summer Waves** and the **Jekyll Harbor Marina,** until you return to Fortson Parkway.

**BEACHES**    There are three public beaches on the island, all open daily around the clock and free to the public. Those choosing to swim on Jekyll Island do so at their own risk, as there are no lifeguards on duty. The **St. Andrew Picnic Area,** reached beyond Summer Waves, the water park along South Riverview Drive, is one of the best beaches at the southeastern tip of the island. It has an adjacent picnic area, but no bathhouse or showers available. **South Dunes Beach,** with a picnic area and showers, is north of St. Andrew and is reached along South Beach Drive. Farther along, **Central Dunes** has showers but no picnic area. Saltwater fishing is allowed on the public beaches, and no license is required.

**BIKING**    Because of its flatness, Jekyll Island is relatively easy to explore by bike. Rentals are available from **Barry's Beach Service** (✆ 912/638-8053), at the Villas by the Sea (see the address below under "Where to Stay"). Bikes (including lock and helmet) rent for $9 for 4 hours, $14 for a full day, $39 for 1 week.

**FISHING**    Freshwater fishing is allowed with a Georgia license, which costs $3 and is available at most hardware or sporting-goods stores. No license is required for saltwater fishing.

**GOLF**    Three championship 18-hole courses await golfers on Jekyll Island, plus one historic 9-hole course. The **Great Dunes Golf Course,** Beach View Drive (✆ 912/635-2170), is a small 9-hole course patterned after the course at St. Andrews, Scotland. It offers some holes that were part of the original course laid out in 1898 when only millionaires played golf here. The course was remodeled as an authentic links course in the 1920s by Walter J. Travis. A 3,023-yard, par-36 course, it's open daily from 7am to 6pm. There are a small pro shop and clubhouse on the grounds. Greens fees are $19, with electric carts renting for $8. No professional instruction is available.

**Jekyll Island Golf Courses,** 322 Captain Wylly Dr. (✆ 912/635-2368), consists of three separate courses: **Oleander** (18 holes, 6,241 yd., par 72), **Pine Lake** (18 holes, 6,379 yd., par 72), and **Indian Mound** (18 holes, 6,282 yd., par 72). Dick Wilson's Oleander is consistently ranked among the state's best courses, and the *Atlanta Constitution* called its 12th hole "the most demanding par 4 of any daily fee course in the state." Pine Lakes was also designed by Wilson and is the longest and tightest layout on Jekyll Island. Tree-lined fairways dogleg both left and right as they wind through the island's interior. Indian

Mound was designed by Joe Lee with wide fairways and large, sloping greens. All courses prefer that you reserve tee times, and charge $40 for greens fees. Mobile carts can be rented for $17 for 18 holes, and clubs are available for $7 to $15. Play is daily from 7am to 6pm for all three courses. A clubhouse, restaurant, and pro shop are on the grounds. Professional instruction is available at the rate of $60 to $180 per hour.

**TENNIS Jekyll Island Tennis Center** ★★, 400 Captain Wylly Dr. (© **912/ 635-3154**), was ranked by *Tennis* magazine as one of the nation's top municipal tennis complexes. Its 13 clay courts, seven of them lighted for night play, are favored because of low-impact conditions and cooler court temperatures. The center is open daily 9am to 6pm. Ball machines are rented for $18 per hour, and court fees are $18 per hour. Professional instruction is available for $30 to $40 per hour. There's a pro shop on the grounds, plus a restaurant and showers on location.

**WATERSPORTS Summer Waves,** 210 S. Riverview Dr. (© **912/635-2074**), offers 11 acres of watersports with more than a million gallons of water. It features rides and attractions ranging from a totally enclosed speed flume that jets riders over three breathtaking humps, to a ride over the rolling waves in the Frantic Atlantic wave pool. You can also hang on around the twisting turns of the Hurricane Tornado and Force 3 slides. For toddlers, there's the Pee Wee Puddle—fun in only a foot of water. Admission is $17 for those 48 inches or taller, and $15 for children. Children 3 and under enter free. Open the weekend before Memorial Day to September 7, Sunday to Thursday from 10am to 6pm and Friday and Saturday from 10am to 8pm.

## WHERE TO STAY

Jekyll Island cottage rentals are available through **Parker-Kaufman Realtors,** Beachview Drive (P.O. Box 13126), Jekyll Island, GA 31527 (© **888/453-5955** or 912/635-2512), whose staff will mail you a color brochure upon request. The realtor offers 105 individual properties ranging from a small one-bedroom apartment to a six-bedroom home. Rental prices start at $285 per week in winter, rising to $400 per week in the busy summer months. Reservations for summer rentals are accepted as early as December 1. The office is open Monday to Saturday 9am to 5pm.

Motel accommodations are available at **Ocean Side Inn and Suites,** 711 Beachview Dr. (© **912/635-2211**); and **Holiday Inn Beach Resort,** 200 S. Beachview Dr. (© **800/7-JEKYLL** or 912/635-3311).

**Jekyll Island Campground,** North Beachview Drive, Jekyll Island, GA 31527 (© **912/635-3021**), is managed by the Jekyll Island Authority and is the only island campground in the Golden Isles. On its 18 wooded acres are 220 sites, nestled among live oaks and pines. The facilities include bathhouses, showers, laundry facilities, camping equipment, pure tap water, a grocery store, garbage pickup, LP gas, and bike rentals. Tent sites cost $19. Stay 6 nights and get your 7th night free.

**Buccaneer Beach Resort** At a location directly on the beach, this hotel is set near the island's convention center. It consists of comfortably outfitted units scattered over a compound of half a dozen rather stylish three- and four-story buildings, some of which sport better views of the sea than others. All units contain well-kept bathrooms with tub/shower combinations. If cost is a factor, ask for a room outfitted with a kitchenette and a view over the forest. The price will be approximately the same as the price of a room without cooking facilities situated closer to the water. The compound, like many of its competitors nearby, is connected to the beach via an elaborate network of raised boardwalks. About a third of the accommodations contain kitchenettes.

85 S. Beachview Dr., Jekyll Island, GA 31527. © **912/635-2261.** Fax 912/635-3230. www.buccaneerbeachresort. com. 207 units. $129–$269 double; $149–$349 suite. Children 18 and under stay free in parent's room. Golf packages available. AE, DC, DISC, MC, V. **Amenities:** Restaurant; 2 bars; outdoor pool; golf privileges; tennis court; fitness center; Jacuzzi; business services; limited room service; babysitting; laundry service. *In room:* A/C, TV, dataport, kitchen (in some), hair dryer.

### Jekyll Island Club Hotel ★★★

This is the undisputed star of Jekyll Island accommodations, steeped in the history of the Gilded Age. A rambling, turreted 1880s monument, it was conceived as a private club for millionaires. In 1987, long after its decline during World War II, the property was restored to its deliberately understated turn-of-the-20th-century grandeur. The bedrooms are high ceilinged and outfitted in the garnet, sapphire, and emerald tones of the building's original construction. All units contain well-maintained bathrooms with tub/shower combinations. Some are awkwardly shaped, but all are very comfortable and nostalgic. Don't expect easy access to the beach.

371 Riverview Dr., Jekyll Island, GA 31527. © **800/535-9547** or 912/635-2600. Fax 912/635-2818. www.jekyll club.com. 157 units. $139–$299 double; $259–$329 suite. Discounts of around 25% Labor Day to early May. Children 17 and under stay free in parent's room. AE, DC, DISC, MC, V. **Amenities:** 2 restaurants; 2 bars; lounge; pool; 3 18-hole golf courses and 1 9-hole golf course; limited room service; babysitting; laundry service/dry cleaning; nonsmoking rooms; rooms for those w/limited mobility. *In room:* A/C, TV, dataport, minibar, hair dryer, iron/ironing board, safe.

### Jekyll Oceanfront Resort & Spa ★

This is the largest oceanfront hotel on Jekyll Island, set on about 15 flat, sandy acres whose focal point is a rectangular swimming pool. It sits near the island's northern tip and is designed in a vaguely Iberian motif of white walls and terra-cotta roofs rising amid pine trees. An expanse of lawn and a breakwater composed of a ribbon of massive boulders separate the compound from the sea. Guests walk over a raised boardwalk to reach the sands. The accommodations are furnished in a rather bland style. Each unit has a well-managed bathroom with a tub/shower combination. The management rather grandly refers to its units as "villas"; they're more like duplex-style town houses, each of which abuts similar units to the left and right. On the hotel premises is a bar and restaurant, the Italian Fisherman.

975 N. Beachview Dr., Jekyll Island, GA 31527. © **800/736-1046** or 912/635-2531. Fax 912/635-2332. www. jekyllinn.com. 260 units, 75 1- and 2-bedroom town houses. $99–$179 double; $139–$239 1- or 2-bedroom town house. AE, DC, DISC, MC, V. **Amenities:** Restaurant; 2 bars; outdoor pool; fitness center; spa; 24-hr. room service; laundry service/dry cleaning; nonsmoking rooms; rooms for those w/limited mobility. *In room:* A/C, TV, dataport, hair dryer.

### Villas by the Sea ★

This is the most northerly and, after the Jekyll Island Club Hotel, one of the most upscale accommodations on Jekyll Island. Not a conventional hotel, it's a compound of condominium-style apartments scattered among 10 two-story buildings in a 17-acre forest. The 2,000 feet of ocean frontage is longer than that of any other hotel on the island, but you'll have to cross a raised boardwalk bridging a lawn and a rocky breakwater to reach it. Each of the accommodations is individually owned by absentee investors and decorated in a taste you may or may not love. Each unit comes with a neatly kept bathroom with a tub/shower combination. Frankly, there are better-built condos and apartments in other parts of the Golden Isles, but still, this place is ideal for vacationers who want lots of space and a working kitchen. The public areas contain a country restaurant and deli, Crackers, plus a video bar.

1175 N. Beachview Dr., Jekyll Island, GA 31527. ✆ **800/841-6262** or 912/635-2521. Fax 912/635-2569. www.jekyllislandga.com. 170 apts. $104–$199 1-bedroom apt; $134–$249 2-bedroom apt; $164–$299 3-bedroom apt. Discounts offered for stays of a week or more. AE, DC, DISC, MC, V. **Amenities:** Restaurant; bar; outdoor pool; laundry service/dry cleaning; nonsmoking rooms; rooms for those w/limited mobility. *In room:* A/C, TV, dataport, kitchenette, hair dryer.

## WHERE TO DINE

**Blackbeard's** *Kids* SEAFOOD/AMERICAN   This restaurant occupies a large, modern building set on a sandy and barren stretch down the island's eastern coast. Its menu items include shrimp, oysters, deviled crabs, scallops, and such fish filets as flounder. Steak, grilled chicken, and burgers are staples around here, and your sandwich choice might be oysters on a hoagie roll, turkey, or "crabby crabmeat." The food is standard fare but rather tasty and sold at a fair price. The kitchen also offers a children's menu.

200 N. Beachview Dr. ✆ **912/635-3522.** Platters/main courses $14–$19. AE, DISC, MC, V. Daily 11am–3:30pm and 5–10:30pm. Closed Christmas.

**The Grand Dining Room** ★★ INTERNATIONAL   Graciously formal and steeped in nostalgia, this place reigns as one of the Golden Isles' most elegant. Its design incorporates a double row of columns, soaring windows, and furniture evocative of an English country house. Our preferred spot for a drink is on the cluster of sofas adjacent to a pianist, who performs highly digestible music throughout the dinner hour. Menu items include fresh catch of the day, prepared in any of five different ways; chicken Atlantis (sautéed with crabmeat, shrimp, and cream sauce); scaloppini of veal with sun-dried tomatoes and artichoke hearts; and grilled lamb chops. The cuisine is first-rate, using the finest ingredients of any restaurant on island, each dish deftly handled by a well-trained kitchen staff.

In the Jekyll Island Club Hotel, 371 Riverview Dr. ✆ **912/635-2600.** Reservations recommended. Jackets preferred for men. Main courses $25–$31. AE, DC, DISC, MC, V. Mon–Sat 7am–2pm and 6–10pm; Sun 10:45am–2pm (brunch) and 6–10pm; Victorian tea daily 4–5:30pm.

**Latitude 31** ★ SEAFOOD/INTERNATIONAL   The leading seafood restaurant on Jekyll Island occupies a clapboard-sided house built on stilts above the tidal flats, adjacent to the wharves servicing the Jekyll Island Club Hotel. J. P. Morgan used the site as a mooring for his yacht *The Corsair.* ("If you have to ask what it costs, you have no business owning a yacht," he is reported to have said.) At the time, the building was a warehouse for storing supplies and ice. Today it's evocative of a 19th-century seafront building in Scandinavia, with a pale and airy interior, and a simple decor that the Shakers would have appreciated. The bar, whose view extends over the mud flats, is appealing. Menu items include bacon-wrapped tenderloin of beef, catch of the day (served grilled, baked, broiled, sautéed, or blackened), seafood crepes, and several preparations of fresh-off-the-boat shrimp.

Jekyll Wharf. ✆ **912/635-3800.** Main courses $16–$27. MC, V. Tues–Sun 5:30–10pm.

**Morgan's Grill** AMERICAN   Golfers can lunch here daily in a bright, airy room overlooking the greens. Trimmed in oak, the large room with an adjoining bar recalls Florida in its decor. You won't find grand cuisine here, just salads, soups, and sandwiches. From the grill comes a half-pound burger prepared as you like it, and you can also order a grilled chicken-breast sandwich or a super sub served on a hoagie, including ham, turkey, salami, cheese, and other ingredients. In spite of the plastic plates and spoons, this is one of the most relaxing spots for lunch on the island.

Golf Clubhouse, Captain Wylly Rd. © **912/635-4103.** Fixed-price lunch $6.75. AE, DISC, MC, V. Daily 7:30am–5pm.

**Zachry's Seafood Restaurant** ★ *(Finds* SEAFOOD    This local favorite sits in the midst of a collection of launderettes, convenience stores, and gift shops, in a shopping center across the street from the convention center. Part of its success derives from the Zachry's ownership of their own shrimp boat (the *Miss Angie*), which guarantees an almost-constant supply of fresh seafood. Menu items include stuffed jalapeño peppers served with marinara sauce, deep-fried or boiled shrimp, trout, deviled crab, stuffed broiled flounder, and combination platters. This is real good, finger-lickin' coastal Georgia home cookery, with more authentic flavor than any other place on the island.

44 Beachview Dr. © **912/635-3128.** Platters $18; main courses $12–$18. AE, DISC, MC, V. Easter to late Aug Sun–Thurs 11am–9pm, Fri–Sat 11am–10pm; late Aug to Easter daily 11am–8pm. Closed 2 weeks at Christmas.

## 7 Cumberland Island ★

7 miles NE of St. Marys

Nowhere else on the East Coast are peace and unspoiled natural surroundings so perfectly preserved as at Cumberland Island. Since 1972, most of this island has been a National Seashore administered by the National Park Service.

Cumberland Island reached the peak of its prestige in the Gilded Age when Carnegie steel barons used the island as a retreat. Their uninhabited mansion, Plum Orchard, is still standing, although badly deteriorating. Not only the Carnegies wielded power here, but so did the Rockefellers and even the Candlers of Atlanta (founders of Coca-Cola). More recently, the island was the top-secret site of the 1996 wedding of John Kennedy, Jr., and Caroline Bessette.

To visit Cumberland Island, just 16 miles long and 3 miles across at its widest point, is to step into a wilderness of maritime forest (with tunnel-like roads canopied by live oaks, cabbage palms, magnolia, holly, red cedar, and pine), salt marshes alive with waving grasses, sand dunes arranged by wind and tide into a double line of defense against erosion, and gleaming sand beaches that measure a few hundred yards in width at low tide. It is to enter a world teeming with animal life, where alligators wallow in marshes, white-tailed deer bound through the trees, wild pigs snuffle in the undergrowth, armadillos and wild turkeys roam freely about, more than 300 species of birds wheel overhead, and wild horses canter in herds or pick their way peacefully to watering holes.

### ESSENTIALS

**GETTING THERE**    The only public transportation to the island is via the ferry from St. Marys on the mainland. (Get to St. Marys on Ga. 40 from I-95 or U.S. 17.) You must reserve passage on the ferry; contact the National Park Service, **Cumberland Island National Seashore,** P.O. Box 806, St. Marys, GA 31558 (© **912/882-4335**). There are two trips daily from March 1 to September 30 every day except Tuesday and Wednesday in winter. In summer, book as far in advance as possible. The fare is $16 for adults, $13 for seniors, and $11 for children under 12.

If you plan to stay overnight, the best way to reach Cumberland is by the inn's ferry, the *Lucy R. Ferguson,* which maintains a regular schedule to Fernandina Beach, Florida. Reservations are necessary, and must be made through the Greyfield Inn (see below). We strongly urge that you bring your bicycle, since there's no public transportation on the island. You can, however, safely leave your car in the Fernandina Beach parking lot across from the police station.

There's an airstrip for small planes near the Greyfield Inn (see "Where to Stay & Dine," below), and air-taxi arrangements can be made from Jacksonville or St. Simons Island (call the inn for details).

**VISITOR INFORMATION**    Information is available from the Greyfield Inn (see "Where to Stay & Dine," below).

## EXPLORING THE ISLAND

Don't look for a swimming pool, tennis courts, or a golf course—Cumberland's attractions are a different sort, straight out of *The Prince of Tides*. The inn is just a short walk from those high sand dunes and a wild, undeveloped beach. Beach-combing, swimming, shelling, fishing, and exploring the island are high on the list of activities.

No signs are left of the Native Americans who lived here beginning some 4,000 years ago, nor of the Franciscan missionaries who came to convert them during the 1500s. No ruins exist of the forts built at each end of the island by Gen. James Oglethorpe in the 1700s, and the only thing that remains of his hunting lodge is its name, Dungeness. What you will find as you poke around this island are the ruins of Andrew Carnegie's own massive mansion, **Dungeness** (which burned in 1959); the **Greene-Miller cemetery,** which still holds inhabitants from Revolutionary times through the Civil War era; and the **Stafford plantation house.** Down the lane a bit are **"The Chimneys,"** a melancholy post–Civil War ruin (ask at the inn for the full story); and **Plum Orchard,** another Carnegie mansion, fully furnished but unoccupied and now the property of the U.S. Park Service.

## WHERE TO STAY & DINE

**Greyfield Inn** ⭐⭐ *Finds*    Cumberland's one hotel is no less enchanting than the island itself. The only commercial building (if you can call it that) in the area is this three-story plantation mansion with a wide, inviting veranda set in a grove of live oaks. Built shortly after the turn of the 20th century as a summer retreat by Thomas Carnegie (Andrew's brother and partner), Greyfield has remained family property ever since. Guests today are treated very much as family visitors were in years past: The extensive and very valuable library is open; the furnishings are those the family has always used; the bar is an open one, operated on an honor system (you simply pour your own and note it on a pad); you dine at the long family table, adorned with heirloom silver candlesticks. You're at liberty to browse through old family photo albums, scrapbooks, and other memorabilia scattered about the large, paneled living room (if the weather is cool, a fire is lighted in the oversize fireplace). Soft chimes announce meals (dinnertime means "dress"—informal dresses and jackets, no shorts or jeans). If beachcombing or exploring is what you have in mind for the day, the inn will pack a picnic lunch for you. The guest rooms vary in size, but all are nonsmoking; some bathrooms are shared and still hold the original, old-fashioned massive fittings; all bathrooms have tub/shower combinations. The rooms are not air-conditioned but are cooled by ceiling fans. Reservations must be

---

*Tips*  **Picnic Fixins**

If you are a day-tripper who would prefer not to dine at Greyfield (see below), you can assemble the makings of a picnic at the **Riverside Café** in St. Marys (*©* **912/882-3466**). It lies directly across from the ferry terminal where boats depart for Cumberland, and you can't miss it.

made well in advance. Bring along your cellphone if you need to stay in touch with the outside world—the hotel has only a radio-telephone for emergencies.

Cumberland Island, GA. Mailing address: P.O. Box 900, Fernandina Beach, FL 32035. © **904/261-6408**. Fax 904/321-0666. www.greyfieldinn.com. 16 units, 6 with bathroom. $395–$575 double. Rates include full board. 50% deposit required; 18% service and 6% tax extra. DISC, MC, V. No children under 6. **Amenities:** Dining room; bar; laundry service. *In room:* A/C, hair dryer, no phone.

## 8 The Okefenokee Swamp ★★

8 miles S of Waycross

This swamp is one of the largest preserved freshwater wetlands in the United States. Naturalists have hailed the wetlands as "the most beautiful and fantastic landscape in the world." It's unique on earth—it was once part of the ocean floor—and encompasses some 650 square miles, measuring 40 miles in length and 20 miles in width. The Creek Indians called it "land of the trembling earth" because of its many floating islands.

Okefenokee is one of the most ecologically intact swamps in North America. It takes in everything from tupelo stands to vast open prairies. A few acres fall within the northeastern corner of Florida. Runoff is discharged into the Suwanee and St. Marys rivers.

The swamp was inhabited as early as 2000 B.C. Many Native Americans, displaced from their homelands, settled here in the 1700s and 1800s. Beginning in 1909, the Hebard Lumber Company harvested some half a billion cubic yards of timber—most of it cypress—from the land before they went out of business in 1927. Virgin tracts of cypress still remain, however, and some trees are 6 centuries old. Conservation-minded advocates persuaded Franklin Roosevelt to designate the swamp a refuge area in 1937. Further protection came in 1974 when Congress added Okefenokee to the National Wilderness Preservation System. This system occupies some 90% of the swamp, home to such wildlife as alligators, deer, and bobcats. The swamp's bay trees bloom from May to October, with a distinctive white flower.

### EXPLORING THE SWAMP

Before heading in, you can visit the **Okefenokee Heritage Center,** 2 miles west of Waycross (birthplace of actor Burt Reynolds) on U.S. 82 (© **912/285-4260**). Here you can see a restored 1912 steam locomotive and depot, an "operating" 1890 print shop, and the restored 1840 Gen. Thomas Hilliard House, plus exhibits on local history. The center is open Tuesday to Saturday 10am to 4:30pm. Admission is $3 for adults, and $2 for children 5 to 18.

At the same site, the **Southern Forest World** (© **912/285-4056**) is a museum depicting the development and history of the South's forest industry. The collection includes a logging train, tools and other artifacts, and forestry-related relics, as well as a variety of audiovisuals. Hours are the same as those of the Heritage Center. Admission is $2.50 for those ages 5 to 54, $1.50 for seniors, and free for children 4 and under.

**Okefenokee Swamp Park**　The park—at the swamp's northern perimeter, on Cowhouse Island—can occupy a day of your time. It offers boat tours (included with admission), canoe rentals, interpretive programs, an outdoor museum, marked trails, and even a serpentarium with reptile shows. Take a cypress boardwalk into the swamp to a 90-foot-high observation tower. You'll see lots of the swamp's most famous residents, a collection of cruising Georgia alligators. There are no overnight facilities, but food and beverages are sold.

Waycross, GA 31501. ✆ **912/283-0583**. Admission $12 adults, $11 seniors 62 and over and children 5–11, free for children 4 and under. Daily 9am–5:30pm. Take I-95 to exit 296 at Brunswick and then U.S. 82 West toward Waycross; at the intersection with Ga. 177, go left for 11 miles to the park entrance.

### Stephen C. Foster State Park ✶

On the western edge of Okefenokee, 18 miles from Fargo, this is an 80-acre island park with a sprawling forest of black gum and cypress. As a refuge, it forms one of the thickest terrains of vegetation in the Southeast. In the mirrorlike black waters live some 55 species of reptiles, 37 species of fish, more than 40 species of mammals, and some 225 species of birds. The park has a half-mile nature trail and some 25 miles of day-use waterways. Canoes and motorboats can be rented, or you can take boat tours lasting 1 to 1½ hours. Minnie's Lake and Big Water can also be visited. Picnicking and camping are permitted. Two-bedroom cabins are also available for rentals: $70 a night Sunday to Thursday, going up to $80 on Friday and Saturday. Campsites with running water and electricity, including showers, go for only $10 a night. (For reservations, contact the superintendent at the address and phone number below.) Park gates close between sunset and sunrise to discourage wildlife poachers. Groceries can be obtained at stores in Fargo.

Georgia Department of Natural Resources, Rte. 1, Fargo, GA 31631. ✆ **912/637-5274**. Admission $5 per car. Mar to Labor Day daily 6:30am–8:30pm; off season daily 7am–7pm. Take I-95 to exit 6 at Brunswick and then U.S. 82 West to Waycross; there, head west on U.S. 84 to Homerville, and turn left onto U.S. 441 South to Fargo; at the intersection with Ga. 177, go left and follow the signs to the park.

### Suwanee Canal Recreation Area ✶

Run by the U.S. Fish and Wildlife Service, this recreation area offers some of America's finest birding and freshwater fishing. The area provides entry to the prairies of Mizell, Chase, Grand, and Chesser, the last the site of a century-old farmstead. Small lakes and "gator holes" are sprinkled throughout the area. The visitor information center provides an orientation film and offers exhibits of the swamp's flora and fauna. Take a boardwalk over the water to a 40-foot observation tower. Several interpretive walking trails and picnic sites are available. The 12-mile-long canal results from a failed attempt in the 1880s to drain the swamp. The U.S. Fish and Wildlife Service provides overnight and 2- to 5-day canoe trips, but reservations are essential. Canoe rentals begin at $25 for day trips, $16 for the second day. The Canal Recreation Concession rents everything from canoes to boats, from sleeping bags and Coleman stoves to portable toilets. It also rents bicycles at $10 per day.

U.S. Fish and Wildlife Service, Okefenokee National Wildlife Refuge, Rte. 2, Box 3330, Folkston, GA 31537. ✆ **912/496-7156**. Admission $5 per car. 1-hr. tours $13 adults, $8 children 5–11, free for children 1–4; 2-hr. tours $21 adults, $13 children 5–11, free for children 1–4. Mar–Sept 10 daily 6am–7:30pm; off season daily 7am–5:30pm. Take I-95 to exit 2 and go west along Ga. 40 to Folkston; there, turn onto Ga. 23/121 South for 7 miles, then turn right onto Spur Ga. 121 and follow the signs for 4 miles to the recreation area.

### Laura S. Walker State Park

Offering activities from water-skiing to camping, this state park dates from the WPA days of the 1930s. It's named after Laura Singleton Walker, a conservationist long before the movement became fashionable. Swimming is permitted when the park's pool is open in summer, and fishing is possible all year. The park is located in the Dixon Memorial Forest, which provides access to Okefenokee Swamp Park some 9 miles distant. A 1.25-mile nature trail is accessible all year. Canoe rentals are available, as are picnic areas. Campsites cost $10 with electrical and water hookups.

Georgia Department of Natural Resources, 5653 Laura Walker Rd., Waycross, GA 31501. ✆ **912/287-4900**. Admission $2 per car, Wed free. Daily 7am–10pm. Take I-95 to exit 6 at Brunswick and then U.S. 82 West toward Waycross; at the intersection with Ga. 177, go south for 2 miles to the park entrance.

# Appendix:
# The Carolinas & Georgia in Depth

The Carolinas and Georgia have much in common—a similar historical background, shared social traditions, and cherished culinary customs—and as movers and shakers of the New South, the states share a dynamic future. Here is a comprehensive cultural, political, and social history of the tri-state region.

## 1 History 101

Although they have their own political pasts, the Carolinas and Georgia began life as one British colony and, in many other respects, they have a common history. The way that they were settled by Europeans during the 17th and 18th centuries gave the three states a similar character, which has lasted to this day.

**ONE BIG COLONY BECOMES THREE** When the first English settlers arrived, they found the region inhabited by bands of American Indians, many of them part of the greater Iroquois and Sioux families. Some native tribes cooperated with the settlers; others were hostile. Whatever their reactions to the newcomers, Indian tribes were decimated by European diseases, and the whites pushed the survivors off their land, either through trumped-up sales or by force. Only the Cherokees, an Iroquoian people in the foothills and mountains of the southern Appalachians, have survived as an organized Indian nation (see chapter 9).

The tribes in today's South Carolina were the first to encounter the Europeans, beginning in 1520, when a Spanish caravelle explored St. Helena Sound. Six years later, Lucas Vásquez de Ayllón tried to establish a Spanish colony, first near the mouth of the Cape Fear River in North Carolina and later on Winyah Bay, but disease, bad weather, and the Indians put an end to it after only a year.

### Dateline

- 1520–26 Spanish arrive in South Carolina.
- 1540 Spanish conquistador Hernando de Soto crosses Georgia and the Carolinas, bringing disease and death to the Cherokee Indians.
- 1587 Sir Walter Raleigh sends English to settle Roanoke Island; the "Lost Colony" disappears.
- mid-1600s Planters from Virginia settle in the Albemarle Sound region in northeastern North Carolina.
- 1663 King Charles II of England grants land between Virginia and Florida to eight Lords Proprietors, who name the region "Carolina" in his honor.
- 1670 South Carolina's first permanent settlement is established on Ashley River.
- 1710 Proprietors appoint Edward Hyde governor of North Carolina, separating its administration from that of South Carolina.
- 1718 British forces behead buccaneer Edward "Blackbeard" Teach during a bloody fight off Ocracoke Island, North Carolina.
- 1729 Lords Proprietors sell Carolina to the English crown; the colony officially divides into North and South.
- 1730s Ulster Scots, Quakers, and Germans migrate south from Pennsylvania into the Piedmont regions of the Carolinas and Georgia.
- 1732 James Edward Oglethorpe founds Georgia in the southern part of the Lords Proprietors' grant.
- 1750 Slavery is introduced in Georgia, spurring production of rice, indigo, and cotton on large plantations.

In search of gold rather than colonies, Spanish conquistador Hernando de Soto explored the area's interior in 1540, crossing from Georgia through South Carolina to the mountains of western North Carolina. French Huguenots arrived in 1563 and built Fort Charles at South Carolina's Port Royal Sound, but they pulled up stakes when fire destroyed their supplies. A Spanish contingent from Florida came to the same site in 1566 and built Fort San Filipe; they stayed 20 years but abandoned the colony when English buccaneer Sir Francis Drake raided St. Augustine. (The Fort Charles/Fort San Filipe site is on the U.S. Marine Corps training center's golf course at Parris Island, S.C.)

**A COLONY LOST**   England fared no better in its first attempt to establish a colony. In 1584, Walter Raleigh, a soldier and courtier to Queen Elizabeth I, sent an expedition to search out a suitable site. The expedition returned with glorious tales of an island named Roanoke—inside what we know as North Carolina's Outer Banks—and with two Indians named Manteo and Wanchese. A year later, Raleigh sent Manteo, Wanchese, and 108 Englishmen (but no women) to colonize Roanoke Island. Rather than planting crops, they spent much of their time searching for gold and a passage to the Pacific Ocean. When Sir Francis Drake fortuitously showed up within the year, they hitched a ride with him back to England.

In June 1587, Raleigh's second attempt at colonization—this time with about 120 men, women, and children—arrived at Roanoke Island under the leadership of John White. It was too late in the year to plant crops, and White left for England at the end of August to secure fresh stores. War was on with Spain, however, preventing White's return. When he did sail back 3 years later, he found only the word *Croatoan*—the name of a nearby

- 1752 Moravians from Pennsylvania settle in northwestern North Carolina and found Salem (now part of Winston-Salem).
- 1774 Women in Edenton, North Carolina, protest the British tax on tea by refusing to brew English leaves.
- 1775 Patriots sign the Mecklenburg Declaration in Charlotte, declaring independence from Great Britain.
- 1776 North Carolina revolutionaries pass the Halifax Resolves, authorizing their delegates to the Continental Congress to vote for independence. The British attack Charleston and are repulsed.
- 1779 Gold is discovered near Charlotte, North Carolina, setting off the nation's first gold rush.
- 1780–81 Lord Cornwallis occupies Charleston and is defeated at the Battle of Kings Mountain near Gaffney, South Carolina.
- 1782 The British evacuate Charleston, the last city that they held south of Canada.
- 1793 Eli Whitney's cotton gin leads to an explosion of cotton production throughout the South.
- 1800 The nation's second federal canal (after the Erie) is dug to move cotton from inland South Carolina to Charleston.
- 1819 Northern opposition to the admission of Missouri as a slave state stirs talk of secession below the Mason-Dixon Line.
- 1822 The slave Denmark Vesey leads an insurrection and attempts to capture Charleston. The revolt is put down, and Vesey and 36 others are executed. Southern planters blame "outside agitators" and institute tighter controls on slaves.
- 1830s The abolitionist movement gains strength in the North. Extremists advocate the secession of the South from the North.
- 1830 The South Carolina legislature adopts the "Doctrine of Nullification" of federal laws by the states and threatens to leave the Union. Congress compromises by lowering the export tariff on cotton.

*continues*

Indian tribe—carved on a tree. The settlers had disappeared. Among them was White's granddaughter, Virginia Dare, the first child born in America of English parents. Not a trace of the legendary "Lost Colony" was ever found (see "The Lost Colony," in chapter 4).

**THE LORDS PROPRIETORS GET THEIRS** The English had better luck at Jamestown, Virginia, in 1607. By the mid-1600s, tobacco farmers had drifted south into the Albemarle Sound region of northeastern North Carolina, around Elizabeth City and Edenton. They were the first permanent European settlers in the Carolinas and Georgia.

But real colonization began after the restoration of King Charles II in England. In 1663, strapped for funds and owing financial and political debts to those who had supported his return to the throne, King Charles granted to eight Lords Proprietors all of North America between 31 degrees and 36 degrees North latitude—that's all of the Carolinas and Georgia. The grant was later extended north to 36½ degrees, to make sure that the Albemarle Sound area wasn't in Virginia, and south to 29 degrees. This extension infuriated the Spanish, because it encompassed nearly half of their colony in Florida.

The proprietors named their possession Carolina, in the king's honor. You'll see these men's names on places throughout the Carolinas: George Monck, duke of Albemarle; Edward Hyde, earl of Clarendon; William, earl of Craven; brothers Lord John Berkeley and Sir William Berkeley (the latter was then governor of Virginia); Sir George Carteret; Anthony Ashley-Cooper, later the first earl of Shaftesbury; and Sir John Colleton.

The proprietors soon recruited rice farmers from Barbados, who arrived on the banks of South Carolina's Ashley River in 1670 and planted their

- **1833** Great Britain emancipates all slaves in its colonies.
- **1835** The federal government orders the Cherokee Indians west to Oklahoma Territory. Thousands die on the Trail of Tears; others hide in the mountains and later form the Eastern Band of the Cherokee Nation.
- **1839** A young slave accidentally overheats a North Carolina tobacco barn, baking the drying leaves golden and creating the smooth-tasting Bright Leaf used in cigarettes.
- **1849** South Carolina objects to the admission of California as a free state. The legislature considers secession but backs off when other Southern states refuse.
- **1854** The Republican Party is formed, nominating John C. Fremont for president and adopting an antislavery platform. Democrat James Buchanan is elected president, however.
- **1858** Republicans gain the majority in Congress on a pro-business, antislavery platform.
- **1859** John Brown's aborted raid at Harpers Ferry (then in Virginia) alarms the South.
- **1860** A split at the Democratic National Convention in Charleston over a pro-slavery platform plank helps elect Republican Abraham Lincoln. South Carolina secedes.
- **1861** Georgia secedes on January 19. North Carolina waits until South Carolina forces attack Fort Sumter on April 15, launching the Civil War.
- **1864** Union Gen. William Tecumseh Sherman drives to the sea through Georgia, leaving a trail of destruction behind.
- **1865** The blockade-running port of Wilmington, North Carolina, falls to a Union amphibious assault in January. Sherman burns 80 square blocks of Columbia, South Carolina, in February. Confederate Gen. Joseph Johnston surrenders to Sherman in April at Durham, North Carolina
- **1865–67** White-dominated state legislatures pass "Black Code" laws, giving newly freed slaves some rights, but not the vote.
- **1867** Congress passes the Reconstruction Act, dividing the South into five military districts.

first crops 2 years later. Within a decade, they had established Charles Town on the point where the Ashley and Cooper rivers meet. With slaves producing bumper rice and indigo crops, and with one of the colonies' finest natural harbors at Charles Town, South Carolina soon became the wealthiest of England's American colonies. Indeed, Charles Town (its name was changed to Charleston in 1783) was America's busiest port until well into the 19th century.

The proprietors appointed a Colonial governor to sit in Charles Town, with authority to appoint a deputy for northern Carolina. The great distances involved made this plan unworkable, however, so in 1710 Edward Hyde (a cousin of Queen Anne, who was then on the throne) was named governor of the north. This arrangement lasted until the proprietors sold their possession to the British crown in 1729, whereupon North Carolina and South Carolina became separate British crown colonies.

**CONVICTS & CATHOLICS NEED NOT APPLY** Partially to create a buffer between the Spanish in Florida and flourishing South Carolina, the British crown in 1731 granted a charter to a group of investors, headed by Gen. James Edward Oglethorpe, to establish a colony in the southern part of the original Lords Proprietors grant.

Oglethorpe's utopian goal was to create a microcosm of England—but without land ownership, slaves, hard liquor, and Catholicism. Contrary to popular belief, he did not recruit convicts for this enterprise; instead, he sought industrious tradesmen, small-business owners, and laborers with promises of free passage, land to farm, and supplies. The first of the settlers arrived in the new colony of Georgia in 1732.

Without slaves (and also without liquor, some wags say), the settlers had a rough go of it initially. Only after

- **1870s** The Ku Klux Klan becomes active in the South.
- **1876** Reconstruction officially ends. Whites return to power and adopt "Jim Crow" laws to keep African Americans from voting.
- **1880s** Cotton, tobacco, and furniture factories in the Piedmont give the three states major industries for the first time.
- **1896** The U.S. Supreme Court's *Plessy v. Ferguson* decision legalizes separate-but-equal segregation laws.
- **1901–04** North Carolina builds 1,100 schools, bringing public education to all Tarheels.
- **1903** The Wright Brothers fly the first airplane at Kill Devil Hills on North Carolina's Outer Banks.
- **1911** A hurricane devastates the South Carolina coastal area, ending large-scale rice production.
- **1915** The Ku Klux Klan is reborn in a huge cross-burning atop Stone Mountain, Georgia. A mob enters a Georgia state penitentiary at Milledgeville and lynches Leo Frank, a northern-born Jew convicted of murdering 14-year-old Mary Phagan, a white girl, in an Atlanta pencil factory.
- **1922** Georgian feminist Rebecca Lattimer Felton, then 87, is appointed as the first female U.S. senator.
- **1934** Georgia Gov. Eugene Talmadge declares martial law and uses National Guard troops to break a statewide textile strike.
- **1940** Great Smoky Mountains National Park is dedicated by Pres. Franklin D. Roosevelt.
- **1942** Military bases in the Carolinas and Georgia make the area one of the nation's primary troop-training centers during World War II.
- **1945** President Roosevelt dies of a cerebral hemorrhage at Warm Springs, Georgia.
- **1954** The U.S. Supreme Court declares segregated schools unconstitutional in *Brown v. Board of Education.*
- **1960** A lunch-counter sit-in at Greensboro, North Carolina, launches similar civil-rights protests across the South.

*continues*

Georgia's first African slaves arrived in 1750 did rice, indigo, and cotton make the colony economically viable. As in South Carolina, the owners of the large plantations dotting the coastal plain grew rich, as did their merchant friends in the ports of Charles Town and Savannah.

## UP COUNTRY, LOW COUNTRY

The rich Easterners of the Carolinas and Georgia looked down on the poor, non-slave-owning farmers who settled the inland hills. In South Carolina, these farmers were called Up Country folk by the Low Country folk. In Georgia, the coastal crowd pejoratively referred to their country cousins as "crackers"—from the practice of cracking corn to make meal.

The rivers in the Piedmont tend to flow from northwest to southeast. South Carolina and Georgia are laid out in these directions, but the rivers took settlers in the hill country of North Carolina to South Carolina ports instead of east to their own state's coastal plain, further adding to the division between east and west.

Beginning in the 1730s, another type of settler arrived in the Piedmont area of all three colonies: Scots-Irish, Germans, and other Europeans who migrated overland into the Carolina and Georgia hills from Pennsylvania by way of the great valleys of Virginia. Most of them were self-sufficient yeoman farmers who built their houses of stone rather than wood. They had no use for slaves and even less for the rich folks down along the coast who didn't work with their hands. Instead of Anglican churches, they worshiped at Presbyterian, Quaker, and Moravian churches.

Thus developed a cultural, economic, and political schism between the lowlanders and the highlanders in all three colonies. Carolinians built their state capitals at Raleigh and Columbia on the boundary between the two groups—the fall line where the rivers rush out of the hills onto the

- **1964** Georgians cast the majority vote for Barry Goldwater as president—the first time that a Southern state goes Republican since Reconstruction.
- **1965** Congress passes the Voting Rights Act, enfranchising Southern African Americans for the first time since Reconstruction. Blacks are elected to Congress, local offices, and state legislatures.
- **1966** Segregationist restaurateur Lester "Ax Handle" Maddox is elected governor of Georgia.
- **1968** State police open fire during student protests at a bowling alley in Orangeburg, South Carolina, killing three and wounding 27.
- **1970** Courting Maddox voters, peanut farmer Jimmy Carter is elected governor of Georgia, promising to end racial discrimination.
- **1972** North Carolinians elect conservative Republican television commentator Jesse Helms to the U.S. Senate.
- **1973** U.S. Sen. Sam J. Ervin, Jr., of North Carolina leads the Senate Watergate hearings.
- **1976** Jimmy Carter becomes the first Southerner to be elected president of the United States since before the Civil War.
- **1989** South Carolina legislators are charged with taking bribes to vote for legalized horse-race betting in the FBI sting "Operation Lost Trust."
- **1994** African-American Ernest Finney is elected chief justice of the South Carolina Supreme Court.
- **1995** A federal court orders the Citadel in Charleston to admit the first female cadets.
- **1996** Atlanta hosts the Summer Olympic Games.
- **2000** The South experiences dramatic increases in population, largely in the suburbs. South Carolina's Confederate flag over the State Capitol stirs nationwide protest.
- **2003** After 48 years and 15,000 votes, South Carolina Sen. Strom Thurmond retires from the U.S. Senate and turns 100 years of age. He dies on June 26.

flat coastal plain. Although Piedmont industrial growth reversed the economic situation beginning in the 1880s, and although more recent migration from other states has changed the equation somewhat, this

■ 2004 U.S. Sen. John Edwards of North Carolina gives up his seat to run as the Democratic Party's nominee for Vice President on a ticket with U.S. Sen. John Kerry. They lose to incumbent George W. Bush.

division has survived to a large extent. Some people in the Charlotte and Atlanta areas still look down their noses at their "hick" kin in rural eastern North Carolina and South Georgia, and the Low Country–Up Country split is still very much alive in South Carolina.

**GIVING CORNWALLIS FITS**  People in the Carolinas and Georgia had mixed feelings about independence from Great Britain. Being largely of Scots-Irish or other European origins, the hill folk weren't particularly enamored of the English crown, but they also hesitated to endorse a war. Down in the lowlands, the rich planters and merchants saw themselves as being English, but they also chafed at the British import and export taxes, which hurt their businesses.

There were enough go-for-it patriots around, however, to throw things toward the side of freedom. To protest the English tax on tea, the women of Edenton, North Carolina, held a tea party in 1774 and promised never again to brew leaves from England. In 1775, a group of revolutionaries met in Charlotte and passed the Mecklenburg Resolves, declaring themselves to be independent of Britain. The same year, a group of patriots tarred and feathered British loyalists in Charleston, and shortly after the Battle of Bunker Hill in Massachusetts, patriots captured Fort Charlotte in South Carolina. In 1776, delegates from all three colonies endorsed the Declaration of Independence at Philadelphia.

When the British attacked Charleston in 1776, Revolutionary soldiers quickly built Fort Moultrie at the mouth of Charleston Harbor. They used palmetto logs, which proved to be impervious to cannon fire. The fort held out for 4 years, and the palmetto became the new state's symbol.

Lord Cornwallis, the British commander, decided in 1780 to launch a Southern strategy against George Washington's Continental Army. His plan was to take Charleston; march overland through the Carolinas, picking up Loyalist volunteers as he went; and attack Washington in Virginia. It took him 14 battles to finally capture Charleston, but Francis Marion (nicknamed "The Swamp Fox") escaped into the Low Country marshes and organized a series of successful guerrilla raids on the British forces.

The support of loyalist hill folk, which Cornwallis had counted on, disappeared when his forces massacred a group of rebels who were trying to surrender near Lancaster, South Carolina. The locals then pitched in with the patriots to defeat the British army at the Battle of Kings Mountain, near Gaffney. As a result, Cornwallis was forced to send half his men back to Charleston, thus weakening his forces and significantly contributing to his decisive defeat at Yorktown, Virginia, the following year.

Despite the defeat, Cornwallis marched north and captured Charlotte. A 14-pound nugget had been discovered near Charlotte a year earlier, setting off America's first gold rush. Cornwallis found more patriots than gold, causing him to describe the town as a "Hornet's Nest."

Cornwallis advanced through North Carolina to meet defeat at Washington's hands at Yorktown in 1781. The troops he had sent back to Charleston held out for a year, but they evacuated when Gen. Nathaniel Greene's army advanced to within 14 miles of the city. Charleston was the last British-held city south of Canada.

**KING COTTON & THE "PECULIAR INSTITUTION"**   Along with rice, indigo, and tobacco, cotton was important in the region's early history. But it was a labor-intensive crop. Growing and picking cotton was backbreaking work in itself, and after the fiber balls were harvested, someone had to tediously pick out the multitudinous seeds by hand. Thanks to the South's "peculiar institution," slaves did most of the work.

Slavery not only exploited those who were held in bondage, but it also was an inefficient use of human resources. Granted, labor was relatively cheap for the planters, whose major cost (after buying a human being) was keeping a slave alive. But because slaves had no realistic chance of ever gaining their freedom, they had little incentive to work any harder than was necessary to avoid the overseer's whip.

Most slaves were confined to the large coastal plantations during Colonial times. Then, in 1793, Eli Whitney invented the mechanical cotton gin on a Savannah River plantation in Georgia. That meant that a small farmer could buy a slave or two, plant his land with cotton, and not have to worry about extracting the seeds. Life in the South would never be the same.

With people in Great Britain and elsewhere beginning to prefer cotton garments to those made of wool and linen, the price of the fluffy white fibers went through the roof. More and more land was devoted to cotton, and production soared, especially in South Carolina and Georgia. (Although it produced substantial amounts of cotton, North Carolina remained primarily a tobacco state, like Virginia.) By 1850, cotton accounted for two-thirds of American exports.

But threatening clouds began to gather during the 1830s, with the growth of the abolitionist movement in the North. Some abolitionists were moderates, advocating that slave owners be compensated for the value of their freed slaves, as Britain did in 1833, when it abolished slavery in its colonies. Others were extremists, such as newspaper editor William Lloyd Garrison, who at one point advocated the secession of the North from the South.

**JOHN C. CALHOUN & THE DOCTRINE OF NULLIFICATION**
Secession wasn't a new idea, and soon its chief proponent would be a brilliant South Carolina lawyer named John C. Calhoun.

A chief spokesman for the Low Country planter class, Calhoun served as a U.S. senator, as secretary of war and secretary of state under Pres. James Monroe, and as U.S. vice president under Andrew Jackson in 1828. He was a nationalist in his early days. As a senator, he joined with Kentuckian Henry Clay to advocate a system of national laws and the building of federal roads and canals to bind the states of the rapidly expanding new nation.

Beginning in 1816, Calhoun supported a series of tariffs designed to protect America's emerging industries from inexpensive manufactured goods imported from overseas. He and other South Carolinians reasoned that their state had both water power and cotton, so they could build textile mills to manufacture cloth rather than import it.

But mills in New England profited from the tariffs, which drove up the price of consumer goods. At the same time, expanding production depressed the price of Southern cotton. Compounding the problem, much of South Carolina's land became worn out from overplanting with a single crop, causing some of its best planters to move to the rich black soil of Alabama and Mississippi. Many South Carolinians believed that textile interests up North were getting rich at their expense, and they started blaming their problems on the federal government (a feeling that persisted through the civil rights movement of the 1960s).

With the tariffs hurting his home state, and with the system of national laws that he had once advocated beginning to threaten slavery, Calhoun came up with the Doctrine of Nullification. According to this doctrine, because the U.S. Constitution was merely a compact among 13 sovereign nations, a single state could nullify laws passed by the federal government. By implication, any state was as free to secede from the Union as it was to join.

When Congress passed another, higher tariff in 1830, the South Carolina legislature declared it to be "null, void, and no law," and promised to secede from the Union if the federal government attempted to use force to collect the money. President Jackson declared that the Union could not be dissolved and threatened to use federal force. South Carolina raised a voluntary military force but backed off when Congress reduced the levy.

Nullification was unpopular up in North Carolina, although the Tarheels didn't like Jackson's threat to use force against a "sovereign" state. Down in Georgia, the state legislature said that it "abhorred" the doctrine, but it also proposed a convention of the Southern states.

**SAYING GOODBYE TO OLD GLORY**   The issue of secession next came up in 1849, when South Carolina objected to the admission of California as a non-slave state and called for a Southern convention, which met in Nashville, Tennessee, the following year. Congress prevented a showdown, however, by passing the Compromise of 1850, which admitted California as a free state but also enacted stringent fugitive-slave laws. The latter was a key point for Southerners, who wanted their escaped "property" to be returned, even from free states.

From the Southern slave-owning perspective, events in the North over the next decade were most unsettling—especially the creation of the Republican Party in 1854. Two years later, this new antislavery party nominated John C. Fremont for president, and in 1858, it won a majority in Congress. One of the party's prominent members was Abraham Lincoln, a lanky congressman from Illinois.

The Democrats held their 1860 national convention in Charleston, South Carolina. When the delegates refused to adopt a pro-slavery platform plank, the eight cotton states walked out. The split helped elect Lincoln, the Republican nominee. Although he was running on a platform of leaving slavery alone in the Southern states, Lincoln nevertheless frightened the cotton growers.

South Carolina called a convention that adopted an Ordinance of Secession on December 20, and the convention sent delegations to the other Southern states to beseech them to do likewise.

Georgia wasted little time, seceding on January 19, 1861, but a majority of North Carolina voters rejected the idea in February. Only some 35,000 of the one million Tarheels owned slaves, and the rest weren't spoiling for what they saw as a "rich man's war and a poor man's fight." The North Carolinians didn't change their minds until April, when Lincoln requested that they send troops to fight against their neighbors.

**"THE WAR OF NORTHERN AGGRESSION"**   The American Civil War (which many Southerners still call the War of Northern Aggression) began at 4:30am on April 15, 1861, when South Carolina forces opened fire on Fort Sumter in Charleston's harbor. Lincoln immediately called for volunteers to put down the rebellion. Within a few months, federal troops occupied much of the coastal lowlands of the Carolinas and Georgia, leaving only the port cities of Wilmington, Charleston, and Savannah in Confederate hands, albeit blockaded by the Union navy.

Except for a few skirmishes and the bombardment of Charleston in 1863, the Carolinas and Georgia escaped heavy fighting until May 1864, when Union Gen. Ulysses S. Grant told Gen. William Tecumseh Sherman to "get into the interior of the enemy's country as far as you can, inflicting all the damage you can against their war resources." Thus began Sherman's famous March to the Sea, the world's first modern example of total war waged against a civilian population.

Sherman fought his way south from Chattanooga, Tennessee, to Atlanta, a key railroad junction, which the Confederates evacuated on September 1. Leaving Atlanta burning, he departed for the sea on October 17, cutting a 60-mile path of destruction across central and eastern Georgia. "We have devoured the land, and our animals eat up the wheat and corn fields close," Sherman reported. "All the people retire before us, and desolation is behind. To realize what war is, one should follow our tracks."

Despite his orders to the contrary, looting and pillaging were rampant, especially by hangers-on and newly freed slaves, but there were few attacks on civilians and none against women.

Sherman arrived at Savannah on December 10, in time to make the port city a Christmas present to Lincoln. (Fortunately, he did not burn the city.) In January 1865, he turned his war machine northward into South Carolina. He torched 80 square blocks of Columbia in February. Confederate Gen. Joseph E. Johnston made several attempts to slow Sherman's advance. One such attempt was the Battle of Rivers Bridge, between Allendale and Erhardt, South Carolina, in February; the last was the Battle of Bentonville, near Durham in central North Carolina, in March. On April 26, 2 weeks after Gen. Robert E. Lee surrendered to Grant at Appomattox Courthouse in Virginia, Johnston met Sherman at Durham and handed over his sword. The war in the Carolinas and Georgia was over.

The conflict was monstrously costly to the region—particularly to North Carolina, which had joined the fray only reluctantly in the first place. Of the 125,000 Tarheels who served, 40,000 died in battle or of disease, more than from any other Southern state. Those who fought earned their "Tarheel" moniker because of their tenacious refusal to yield ground during battle.

**SCALAWAGS, CARPETBAGGERS & JIM CROW**    The Civil War survivors straggled home to face Reconstruction. At first, Confederate war veterans dominated the state legislatures in the Carolinas and Georgia. They enacted so-called Black Code laws, which gave some rights to the newly freed slaves but denied them the vote. This and other actions infuriated the radical Republicans who controlled the U.S. Congress and wanted to see the South punished for its rebellion. In 1867, Congress passed the Reconstruction Act, which gave blacks the right to vote and divided the South into five districts, each under a military governor who had near-dictatorial powers. Approximately 20,000 federal troops were sent South to enforce the act.

Recalcitrant white officials were removed from state office, and with their new vote, the ex-slaves helped elect Republican legislatures in all three states. Many blacks won seats for themselves. Despite doing some good work, these legislatures were corrupt (a free legislators-only restaurant and bar in South Carolina was a minor example). They also enacted high taxes to pay for rebuilding and social programs, further alienating the struggling white population.

White Carolinians and Georgians also complained bitterly about "scalawags" (local whites who joined the Republican Party) and "carpetbaggers" (Northerners who came South carrying all their possessions in bags made of carpet). The animosity led to the formation of two secret white organizations—the Knights of the Camilla and the Knights of the Ku Klux Klan—that undertook terrorism to keep blacks from voting or exercising their other new rights. The former slaves also were disappointed with the radical Republicans when it became obvious that they wouldn't receive their promised "40 acres and a mule." Those who did vote began to cast their votes for their former masters. Factions also developed between the local scalawags and the Northern carpetbaggers.

All this set the stage for whites to regain control of North Carolina and Georgia in 1871. By January 1877, only South Carolina still had a carpetbagger regime, and when the new president, Rutherford B. Hayes, a Republican, withdrew federal troops from Charleston in April, former Confederate Gen. Wade Hampton became governor. Reconstruction was over.

During the next 20 years, white governments enacted the Jim Crow laws, which imposed poll taxes, literacy tests, and other requirements intended to prevent African Americans from voting. Whites flocked to the Democratic Party, which restricted its primaries—which were tantamount to elections throughout the South—to white voters. Blacks who did try to vote faced having the Ku Klux Klan burn crosses on their lawns, if not being lynched. Indeed, "strange fruit" hung from many Southern trees during this period.

Racial segregation became a legal fact of life in the region, from public drinking fountains to public schools. The U.S. Supreme Court ratified the scheme in its 1896 *Plessy v. Ferguson* decision, declaring "separate but equal" public schools to be constitutional. Black schools in the South were hardly equal, but they surely were separate.

**LINTHEADS & BRIGHT LEAF**   Economically, the Carolinas and Georgia changed drastically during the 1880s. With slaves turned into sharecroppers and tenant farmers, the region went back to growing cotton after the Civil War—so much of it that the price dropped drastically. Taking advantage of the cheap raw material and free power provided by rushing rivers, enterprising industrialists soon built cotton mills throughout the Piedmont area. Instead of scratching a living out of their hardscrabble land, the Piedmont's farmers flocked to the new factory jobs. These low-paid workers, who worked long hours and included many women and children, became known pejoratively as "lintheads." But at long last, the region had the textile industry that John C. Calhoun had dreamed of.

The Civil War ended for General Sherman's troops at Durham, the heart of North Carolina's tobacco-producing region. The soldiers took home a taste for the smooth-tasting Bright Leaf (the result of a curing process discovered when a slave accidentally overheated a tobacco barn in 1839). Smokers had to roll their own in those days, but the invention of the cigarette-rolling machine in 1881 changed all that. Cigarette factories soon dotted central North Carolina, making fortunes for men such as James B. Duke and R. J. Reynolds.

The Piedmont rivers also powered new furniture factories, especially in North Carolina and northern Georgia.

**SIT-INS AT LUNCH COUNTERS**   For the first half of the 20th century, whites were firmly in control in the Carolinas and Georgia. The Democratic Party reigned supreme, and racial segregation was a way of life. For the most part, politics in the three states followed the old Low Country, Up Country split, but with the Piedmont's wealthy industrialists playing an increasingly important role.

From the beginning, the textile-mill owners fought any effort to unionize their predominately white workers, often threatening to replace them with blacks if they voted to join a union. In 1934, Georgia Gov. Eugene Talmadge went so far as to call out the state's National Guard to put down a strike. To this day, the Carolinas and Georgia are anti-union, "right to work" states.

The state legislatures tended to switch between progressive and conservative Democrats, often following hard-fought primary campaigns. The favorite progressive platform called for increased spending for public education. North Carolina built some 1,100 public schools between 1901 and 1904. But as late as 1942, conservative Governor Talmadge of Georgia claimed that "education ain't never taught a man to plant cotton" (or to mill it, some would say). Accordingly, the three states lagged far behind the nation in education. (To their credit, however, the industrialists did contribute to the region's institutions of higher learning; tobacco interests turned little Trinity College in Durham, N.C., into prestigious Duke University.)

Even after the U.S Supreme Court declared in its 1954 *Brown v. Board of Education* decision that segregated public schools were unconstitutional, division of the races continued. Nearly 10 years went by before the first black student enrolled in a South Carolina public school.

But all that began to change with the advent of the civil rights movement. In 1960, black college students in Greensboro, North Carolina, held the first sit-in at a Woolworth lunch counter. This action launched similar protests across the region. Unlike the violent scenes that erupted in Alabama and Mississippi, most civil rights demonstrations in the Carolinas and Georgia were peaceful. One exception was a 1962 rock-throwing incident in Albany, Georgia (a demonstration that set the precedent for the later protests of Dr. Martin Luther King, Jr.). Another exception occurred in 1968, when state police opened fire on black students at a bowling alley in Orangeburg, South Carolina.

Although the law was strenuously opposed by powerful U.S. Senators Richard B. Russell of Georgia, Strom Thurmond of South Carolina, and Sam J. Ervin, Jr., of North Carolina, Congress enacted the Voting Rights Act in 1965. No other result of the civil rights movement has changed the South more. Today, blacks represent several Carolina and Georgia districts in the U.S. House of Representatives; others hold many seats in the state legislatures; and African-American local officials number in the hundreds.

In 1966, Georgia Democrats nominated for governor a man named Lester Maddox, who had waved an ax handle to keep civil rights protesters out of his whites-only Atlanta restaurant. His Republican opponent actually won a plurality, but the Democratic legislature put Maddox in office. Four years later, a peanut farmer from Plains, Georgia, courted Maddox's segregationist voters, but at his inauguration as governor in 1971, Jimmy Carter promised to end the racial divide. In 1976, Carter became the first Georgian, and the first Southerner since before the Civil War, to be elected president of the United States.

The 1980s and 1990s saw many changes in the region. High-tech and other modern industries set up shop, especially in the Raleigh-Durham area in North Carolina, along the I-85 corridor in South Carolina, and in the burgeoning Atlanta suburbs. With them came a migration of people from the North, many bringing Republican leanings. Today, the Carolinas and Georgia are politically competitive, usually voting Republican in presidential elections but splitting their votes at the statehouse level. The old one-party South is a thing of the past.

Senator Strom Thurmond (1902–2003) died on June 26, 2003. The longest-serving senator in American history, Ol' Strom was completely senile at the end of a notorious political career. A bigot, segregationalist, and homophobe, among other credentials, he was also the master Southern politician and a war hero.

Elected governor of South Carolina in 1946, he later ran as a segregationalist Dixiecrat candidate for president in 1948. He was a study in contradictions, once proclaiming there were "not enough troops in the Army" to end segregation in the South, while at the same time providing support for his secret black daughter in college. His political legacy today rests on his reshaping of the Republican Party (the South used to be solidly Democratic) and re-establishing a two-party system in the Southeast.

As the South has moved into the 21st century, more and more urban planners have noted some astonishing trends. For example, since 1970 the suburbs around Atlanta have expanded dramatically and produced entire centers of population. The city of Atlanta, however, has grown less densely populated. At the end of the 20th century, the 10-county region around Atlanta grew by nearly 100,000 people, the second-largest annual population increase in its history. But the city of Atlanta itself grew by only 900 people. It is estimated that by the year 2025 another one million people will live in Greater Atlanta. Most of these, it is predicted, will reside in the suburbs and, by necessity, will be driving cars.

## 2 Southern Living Today

The late historian C. Vann Woodward once labeled the New South "the Second Reconstruction." As the millennium approached, he noted that Yankees were coming South, rural life was diminishing, and urbanization was ongoing. "Let's call it the 'Bulldozer Revolution,'" he said, adding that nonetheless, "I don't think it has demolished the South."

This fast-growing region remains one of the most changing and versatile in the country, and yet it still evokes stereotypes, caricatures, and images, some of them still there to be seen: corrupt potbellied sheriffs, crooked Southern judges, country politicians, demure belles, and hell-raisin' preachers. Parts of the backward South are notorious for its "redneck juries," insanely awarding millions upon millions of dollars' worth of damages in civil cases if the defendants are perceived as coming from Yankeeland. But it would be wrong to confuse the South with its caricatures or to fail to understand how rapidly the states of North Carolina, South Carolina, and Georgia are changing. Believe it or not, all Southerners do not eat grits, listen to country music, vote with the religious right, or have a crazy aunt or a football-playing brother with three first names.

The New South is meeting resistance, however. In some respects, the battles of the South no longer center on the age-old conflicts between blacks and whites. As if establishing a last stand in the Old South, the hard-right wing of the Republican Party and the religious right are engaging in a cultural war. Rather bizarrely, homosexuality is often the issue today that provokes the most moral outrage, with some Southern preachers ranting against it as a "sin against God," whereas more progressive elements in the South (sometimes from the pulpit but more often from the business world) preach tolerance and understanding, with respect for individual rights regardless of sexual preference.

A dramatic case highlighting this occurred in September 2000 when the Atlanta Gas Light Company, one of the biggest utilities in the South, announced that it would be offering domestic partner benefits as an option for its employees, including same-sex couples. The company said that it was inaugurating this change in its policy in order to attract the brightest and best employees in the future. Georgia Equality Project, the statewide gay political group, immediately hailed the move as a major breakthrough.

GEP is continuing to target other major companies in the state to offer the same benefits, and some of these companies are responding. But in other cases, the proposal is met with a "wall of silence." For the GEP, it's an uphill fight.

On the other hand, the New South has prevailed in other areas. Witness the removal of the Confederate flag from the dome of the South Carolina State Capitol. It had been flying since 1962, when it was raised in honor of the 100-year anniversary of the Civil War; in the ensuing years, repeated calls to remove it were rejected. This time, it was a fight to the finish: Election-year presidential hopefuls and media pundits from all over the globe weighed in, and 50,000 protesters marched in Columbia on Martin Luther King, Jr.'s birthday. In the glare of the national spotlight, the opposition agreed to a compromise. On July 1, 2000, the flag went down, only to have a shiny replica—said to be more "accurate" than the one that had flown for 38 years—hoisted on a 30-foot pole in front of the Capitol.

Cultural conflicts seem to be inevitable, given the rate of growth and the population shift. The South can boast the fastest-expanding economy in the industrialized world. Each day, the ever-changing population, attracted to the tri-state region by industry and technology, grows larger, wealthier, and better educated. Today, instead of magnolia-lined plantations or outhouse-dotted backwoods, you see a soccer-mom subculture in the southern suburbs of Atlanta and Charlotte, complete with minivans, malls, glass office towers, well-manicured subdivisions, and traffic jams. You'd think that you were in a suburb of Cleveland. Some tourist areas, such as Hilton Head, are flourishing and are filled with Northern transplants.

By contrast, income and population in "Black Belt" counties are shrinking. Ironically, the South also contains some of America's poorest regions, the home of millions who are mired in ignorance and poverty. The *Tobacco Road* image lingers in remote counties where young people often grow up but don't stick around. Problems are on the horizon, as automation and global trade promise to wipe out many of the remaining rural textile jobs. Welfare reform will eliminate the money needed to keep some small towns alive.

But there is reason for optimism and hope here, too. From elegant ballets to symphonies set in the refurbished concert halls of days gone by, Southern tradition is being redefined. Yes, a slow-paced way of life still holds in many small towns, but the cities of the New South are on the move. People have flocked to the cities from all areas of the world—Northerners seeking a milder climate; rural Southerners bored with small-town life; African Americans overcoming years of segregation; Asian immigrants seeking a new life in America; and gays and lesbians, who finally can taste liberation in a region where they were once shunned or which they once fled to escape the prevailing prejudices. People from all these diverse cultures can be seen sipping espresso in coffee shops, reading the *Wall Street Journal* on street corners, and turning once-lethargic areas into fast-paced international business complexes.

But time simply can't take away from the true Southerner his small pleasures: fresh-picked butterbeans in the summer, crisp iced sweet tea in the afternoon, a Saturday-morning golf game, sunset cocktails on the porch, church on Sunday, and a generally prevailing politeness and civility. Scarlett O'Hara would be proud that Atlanta has grown into one of the strongest industrial capitals in the world. As the home of some of the best-known companies in the nation (including Coca-Cola, BellSouth, and Delta), the city has become a transportation hub and has been highly praised for its capability to adapt to a rapidly changing environment.

From Savannah to Charlotte, Southern cities are sprucing up and replacing eyesores with colorful floral gardens and newly designed roadways. Visitors no longer have to restrict themselves to a strictly Southern cuisine, as world-class food marts and restaurants spring up all across the tri-state area. The land of hospitality has opened its arms even wider.

## 3 What's Cookin' in Dixie

A Southern-style breakfast may consist of the following: homemade biscuits, country (very salty) ham, red-eye gravy, and grits swimming in butter. If a fellow were still hungry, he might cook up some Jimmy Dean sausage, toss a few buckwheat pancakes with cane syrup (or molasses), and fry a mess o' eggs with the yolk cooked hard. Healthy? Hardly. But truth be told: It's easy to eat very well (and very nutritiously) in the South, given the region's bounty of local vegetables and fruits, farm-raised meats, and fresh-off-the-boat seafood.

Southern cuisine is a blend of the Old World (meaning Europe) and the New World (meaning North America). Necessity forced early settlers to find ways to integrate New World foods, like wild turkey and corn, into their bland diet of dumplings and boiled chicken. Many of the most important elements of the cuisine came from African slaves, who championed such exotica as okra and peanuts, and who turned the vitamin-rich black-eyed peas, used by plantation owners to fertilize fields, into a Southern classic. These influences came together to create Southern cuisine, an amalgam that embraces such favorites as sweet-potato pie, pecan pie, buttermilk biscuits, sweetened iced tea, long-cooked greens, sweet creek shrimp, fried green tomatoes, pan gravy, and peanuts (preferably boiled). But eating in the South is not just about good food: It's about community. Southerners love their hoppin' John and grits, but most of all, Southerners love setting a table and breaking bread with friends and family.

Virtual culinary wars have broken out over how to make **Southern fried chicken.** Even Colonel Sanders once denounced the way that his chain franchise fried chicken. In the old days, when company was coming, Ma Kettle would rush out into the backyard, grab a chicken, wring its neck, defeather it, and slice it up, tossing the entrails to the hound dogs. She then fried it in lard, sizzling-hot but not smoking. One old-time cook who had a reputation for serving the best fried chicken in Georgia confided that her secret was bacon grease and a heavy black skillet that was 50 years old. "Somehow, that skillet mysteriously flavors my chicken," she told us. "The skillet was given to me by my mother, who'd gotten it from her mother. None of us ever washed that skillet."

If you travel the hidden back roads of the tri-state area, you can still find a granny cooking country delicacies. To enjoy these offerings, you have to have been born in Dixie "one frosty morn." The most famous dish she's likely to offer is **chitlins** (chitterlings). This backwoods plate is more for Rhett Butler than for faint-hearted Melanie. These pig intestines are turned inside out and then braised, boiled, and deep-fried to a crispy brown. **Crackling bread** is corn bread with crispy leftovers from the renderings of pork fat at slaughter time. Granny is also the one smelling up the house cooking **collard greens,** prepared the long-simmered way and seasoned with ham hocks.

What lobster is to Maine, **catfish** is to the Southern palate. Fried catfish and **hush puppies** reign supreme. With a sweet, mild flavor and a firm texture, catfish (now commercially raised in ponds) is one of the most delectable of freshwater fish, despite its ugly appearance. The traditional way to cook it is in grease—a whole lot of grease. Cooks today, having been warned about the health dangers of eating so much fat, have created entire cookbooks about more delicate ways to cook catfish, serving it with such dainty preparations as lime-and-mustard sauce.

Low Country specialties in the Charleston area include such dishes as **shrimp 'n grits** and **she-crab soup. Oyster roasts** are popular in the late fall, when the bivalves grow big and plump. **Confederate bean soup** is made with onion, celery, bacon, sausage, ham stock, brown sugar, baked beans, and heavy cream. "No wonder our boys in gray lost the war," one diner told us.

In a bow to Southern heritage, **wild game** is featured on many a menu. Around October or November, hunters in the South, dressed in blaze orange, set out in the forests to stalk deer. The venison may be eaten right away or frozen for later use in the winter, when a steak might appear on your plate with grits and gravy. In the Carolinas, quail sautéed in butter is a tasty delicacy. More modern cooks season it with wine or sherry. Wild duck—brought down by hunters in blinds on the scenic coastal marshes—may be roasted and stuffed with potato-and-apple dressing (winning such noted gourmands as former President Bill Clinton).

Eventually, all talk of Southern cooking comes down to **barbecue.** People in Georgia, for example, have strong opinions about the barbecue that they're served in North Carolina—and take our word for it, those views are never favorable. And what Carolinians think about Georgia barbecue is best left unprinted. Unlike Texans, who prefer beef-based barbecue, Southern barbecue artists prefer a slab of pork ribs or pork shoulders. If you use beef brisket or lamb, members of your dinner party might get up and excuse themselves, never to darken your door again.

Some cooks slow-roast the pork shoulder for 12 hours or so. Traditionalists prefer smoking it with hickory wood, although some use charcoal. No one agrees on the sauce. Will it be a pepper-and-vinegar sauce (eastern North Carolina), a pepper, vinegar, and catsup sauce (western North Carolina), or a sweet mustard sauce (South Carolina)? Surely barbecue—regardless of how it's made—has entered Dixie's Hall of Culinary Fame.

In summer, the fruit pickings are plenty, with local **strawberries, blueberries, cantaloupes,** and **plums** ripening at dusty farm stands. Georgia **peaches** are legendarily sweet and fragrant. The melon of choice is the **watermelon.** You'll find the best ones in your own garden or a farm stand. Test for ripeness by giving the melon the thump test (it should have a hollow reverberation), then take the watermelon out on your back porch and slice it. Southerners bring salt shakers to a melonfest. No utensils should be used in eating the melon—only hands and mouth. Southerners suggest that you merely spit out the seeds that you encounter.

One piece of advice comes from Patsy Winton, who calls herself "South Carolina's literary sweetheart," even though her romantic purple poetry has never been published. She gave us this tip on eating watermelon: "Be sure to remove your shoes before you begin slurping, smacking, and finger-licking. No use to ruin a good pair of shoes. Whatever you do, don't scoop the delicious red flesh out with a melon baller. That will get you kicked out of the best Southern homes and invited never to return. Southern tradition must be maintained at all costs."

**Potlikker** (aka pot liquor) is the tasty water left in the pot after the greens, beans, or whatever have been long-cooked, usually in the company of bacon grease, a ham hock, or fatback. Potlikker sounds like something from an old *Hee Haw* routine, with Grandpa Jones smacking his lips, but it's delicious.

Many Southerners point with pride to the fact that you can get Continental dishes, French-influenced cuisine, and sushi throughout the South today. But visitors to the region deliberately seek out down-home Southern food—and, unfortunately, it's harder to come by than ever. You *can* find Old South cooking, however, by visiting a Southern bookstore. Look for any cookbook published by a local civic or church group. Sure, you'll probably find recipes that advise you to pour a can of Campbell's mushroom soup over your chicken, but you'll also discover priceless treasures of Americana. Where else can you find a good recipe for blackbird pie?

# Index

## NORTH CAROLINA

### A
AA (American Automobile Association), 17
Accommodations, 8–10, 18, 37
Active vacations, 33–36
African American Arts Festival, 29
AIDSinfo, 13
Airlie Gardens, 66
Airlines, 17, 37, 39
  from overseas, 16–17
Allanstand Craft Shop, 155–156
American Automobile Association (AAA), 17
American Dance Festival, 31, 98
American Express, 39
*The Andy Griffith Show,* 115
Annual Mountain Dance and Folk Festival, 142
Annual Star Fiddlers Convention, 30
Appalachian Ski Mountain, 164
Appalachian Trail, 146
Arts Center (Chapel Hill), 113
Asheboro, 135–136
Asheville, 1–2, 7, 26, 29, 141–156
  accommodations, 148–152
  attractions, 142–145
  nightlife, 155
  outdoor activities, 145–146
  restaurants, 152–155
  shopping, 146–148
  side trips from, 155–156
  traveling to, 141
  visitor information, 141
Atlantic Beach, 80
ATMs (automated-teller machines), 14

### B
Backpacking, 35, 179–180
Bald Head Island, 73
Balsam, 185
Banner Elk, 159–162
Bath, 85–86
Beaches, 46, 47, 55–56, 67
Bear Island, 81
Beaufort, 6, 74–77
Beaufort Historic Site, 75
Beech Mountain, 162–163
Bele Chere, 32, 142
Belvedere Country Club, 68
Bethabara Park, Historic, 117
Bicycling, 33–34, 91, 126, 132, 145, 180
Big Rock Blue Marlin Tournament, 77–78
Biltmore Estate, 32–33, 144, 145
Biltmore Village, 142–143, 147
Birding, 34, 56, 62, 126, 171, 180
The Birthplace of Pepsi-Cola Store, 83–84
Blowing Rock, 164–166
Blue Ridge Parkway, 5, 25, 139, 167–168
Blue Spiral 1, 147
Blumenthal Performing Arts Center, 129
Boat tours and cruises, Wilmington, 66
Bodie Island Lighthouse, 56
The Bogue Banks (the Crystal Coast), 80
Bonner House, 86
The Bookshop (Chapel Hill), 107
Boone, 156–159
Botanical gardens, 105–106, 124, 157
Brevard Music Center, 142

### C
Brevard Music Festival, 32
British Graveyard, 59
Bryson City, 183–185, 188
Burgwin-Wright House, 66
Business hours, 19
Bus travel, 18, 38

Cades Cove, 179
Calendar of events, 29–33
Cameron, 138
Cameron Indoor Stadium, 98–99
Campbell House, 136
Camping, 34, 68, 91, 182–183
Camp Lejeune, 82
Canadian Hole, 56
Cape Fear, 63, 65, 66, 68
Cape Fear Museum, 66–67
Cape Fear River, 66, 68
Cape Hatteras Lighthouse, 56
Cape Hatteras National Seashore, 8, 55–57
Capital Area Visitor Center, 88
Carolina Beach State Park, 68
The Carolina Carriage Classic in the Pines, 136
The Carolina Hotel golf courses, 7, 132
Carolina Panthers, 129
Car rentals, 18–19, 39
Car travel, 17, 37, 38–39
Cedar Island, 55, 61–62
Chapel Hill, 104–113
Charge cards, 15
Charlotte, 26, 123–129
Charlotte Bobcats, 1, 129
Charlotte Symphony Orchestra, 129
Cherokee, 26, 171–176
Cheviot Hills Golf Course, 90–91

Chimney Rock Park, 156
Chimney Tops, 179
The Chocolate Fetish, 147
Christmas at the Biltmore Estate, 32–33
Chrysler Classic of Greensboro, 32
Climate, 28
Clingmans Dome, 178
The Club at Longleaf, 132
Club Odyssey, 122
Coca-Cola 600, 30–31, 124
The Coffee Cup, 127
Coker Arboretum, 105
Connemara Farms, 156
Consulates, 19–20
Coon Dog Day, 31
Coquina Beach, 55–56
Corolla, 41, 42, 44
Cotton Exchange, 66
Credit cards, 15
Croatan National Forest, 83
The Crystal Coast (the Bogue Banks), 80
Currency and currency exchange, 14
Currituck Beach Lighthouse, 44
Customs requirements, 13–14

**D** aniel Boone Native Gardens, 157
Daniel Boone Theatre, 159
Daylight saving time, 23–24
Dillsboro, 185–186, 188
Disabilities, travelers with, 36–37
Discovery Place & the Nature Museum, 124, 126
Dixon-Stevenson House, 83
Downtown Southern Pines, 136
Drinking laws, 19
Driver's licenses, foreign, 15
Driving safety, 15–16
Drugstores, 39
Duck, 48–49, 53
Duke Chapel, 98
Duke Homestead State Historic Site, 98
Duke University, 98–99
Duke University Jazz Series, 30
Durham, 97–104
Durham Bulls, 99

**E** arthbound Arts (Gifts from Nature), 118
Easter Sunrise Service (Winston-Salem), 30
Edenton, 7, 46, 49–50
Electricity, 19
Elizabethan Gardens, 45
Embassies and consulates, 19–20
Emergencies, 39
Entry requirements, 12–13
Environmental Habitat, 160
Estes-Winn Memorial Automobile Museum, 145

**F** alls Lake State Recreational Area, 91
Fax machines, 23
Ferries, 39
Festival in the Park (Charlotte), 32
Festival of Flowers (Asheville), 30
Festival of Lights, 33
Festival of the Arts (Brevard), 31
First Flight Centennial, 42
Fish House and Blue Moon Gallery, 135
Fishing, 34–35, 46, 68, 77–78, 126, 141, 145–146, 162
Cherokee Indian Reservation, 173–174
Great Smoky Mountains National Park, 180
Flat Rock Playhouse, 156
Folk Art Center, 142, 155
Folkmoot USA (North Carolina International Folk Festival), 31, 142
Fontana Dam, 186
Fort Fisher State Historic Site, 67
Fort Macon, 80
Fort Raleigh National Historic Site, 45, 48
Fowler's, 103
Friends of the North Carolina Pottery Center, 135
Full Frame Documentary Film Festival, 30

**G** asoline, 20
Gay and lesbian travelers
Chapel Hill, 107
Charlotte, 129

Raleigh, 37, 96
resources, 37
Wilmington, 71
Winston-Salem, 122
Gay Men's Health Crisis, 13
Germanton Art Gallery and Winery, 118–119
Glebe House, 86
Golf, 35
Asheville, 146
Banner Elk, 160
Boone, 157–158
Chapel Hill, 106
Charlotte, 126
Great Smoky Mountains National Park, 180
the Outer Banks, 47
Pinehurst, 132, 133
Raleigh, 90–91
near Wilmington, 68
Winston-Salem, 117
Grandfather Mountain, 25, 139, 160
Grandfather Mountain Highland Games and Gathering of the Scottish Clans, 31, 160
Great Smoky Mountains National Park, 5, 34, 169–171, 176–189
access points and orientation, 176
accommodations, 183–187
avoiding the crowds, 177
fees, regulations and permits, 176–177
ranger programs, 178
restaurants, 188–189
seasons, 177–178
seeing the highlights, 178–179
sports and outdoor pursuits, 179–182
traveling to, 176
visitor centers, 176
Great Smoky Mountains Railroad, 185
Grove Arcade Public Market, 146–147
Grove Park Inn Resort, golf course at, 146
Grovewood Gallery, 144
Grovewood Studios, 144–145

**H** ammocks Beach State Park, 81
Hang gliding, 44
Harding's Landing, 86

Harkers Island, 77
Harrah's Cherokee Casino, 176
Hatteras, 56
Hatteras Island Fishing Pier, 56
Hawksnest Golf & Ski Resort, 160
Haywood County Apple Harvest Festival, 167
Henry, O., 144
Herb Day, 31
Herbert C. Bonner Bridge, 56
Hickory Ridge Homestead Museum, 157
High Country, 139–141
Hiking, 35, 68, 90, 126, 163
    Appalachian Trail, 146
    Great Smoky Mountains National Park, 180–181
    High Country, 139
Hillsborough Hog Day, 31
Historic Bethabara Park, 117
Historic Edenton Visitor Center, 46
Historic Old Salem, 114
History, 472–483
HIV-positive visitors, 13
Holiday Festival, Raleigh, 33
Holidays, 20
Home, Garden and Flower Show, 29–30
Home and Garden Show (Raleigh), 88
Home Moravian Church, 114–115
Horn in the West, 159
Horseback riding, 35, 146, 164, 181
Hunting, 35

I nsurance, 14
International Driving Permit, 18
Internationalist Book & Magazine Cooperative, 107

J acksonville, 82
Jockey's Ridge State Park, 44, 47
John Wright Stanly House, 83
Jugtown Pottery, 135
Julian, Lake, 145

K ill Devil Hills, 44, 50, 53–54
Kitty Hawk Watersports Sailing Site, 47

The Kress Emporium, 147–148
Kure Beach, 68

L atta Plantation Park, 126
Legacy Golf Links, 132
Legal aid, 20–21
Lexington Park, 143
Linville Caverns, 168
Linville Falls Visitor Center, 168
Linville Gorge Wilderness Area, 168
Liquor laws, 39
The Lost Colony, 31, 42, 48
Lure, Lake, 145–146

M cDowell Park and Nature Preserve, 126
Maggie Valley, 186–188
Maggie Valley Golf Course, 180
Mail, 21
Malaprop's Bookstore/Cafe, 147
Manteo, 45, 51, 54
Market-Firehouse, 114
Mast General Store, 148, 158
Mayberry Days, 32, 115
Meadowmont Village, 107
Measures, 21
Medical emergencies, 21
Medical requirements for entry, 13
Memorial Auditorium, 96
MESDA (Museum of Early Southern Decorative Arts), 115–116
Methodist Church, 179
Midland Road, 130
Mile High Swinging Bridge, 160
Mingus Mill, 178
Mint Museum of Art, 124
Missionary Baptist Church, 179
Mitchell, Mount, 156
MONEYGRAM, 23
Money matters, 14–15, 28–29
Montford Historic District, 143
Morehead City, 77–82
Morehead-Patterson Bell Tower, 105
Morehead Planetarium, 105
Moses Cone Memorial Park, 139

Mountain Dance & Folk Festival, 32
Mountainside Theater, 174
Mount Airy, 115
Mount Mitchell State Park, 25, 156
Mullet Festival, 82
MUMfest, 32
Museum of Early Southern Decorative Arts (MESDA), 115–116
Museum of Life and Science, 98
The Museum of the Cherokee Indian, 172–173
Mystery Hill, 164

N ags Head, 26, 42, 44, 46–48, 52–54
Nags Head Fishing Pier, 46
Nags Head Golf Links, 47
Nags Head Woods Preserve, 47
National Black Theatre Festival, 31–32
National Hollerin' Contest, 31
Nature walks and trails, 47, 182. See also Hiking
New Bern, 82–85
New Bern Firemen's Museum, 83
Newfound Gap, 178–179
New Morning Gallery, 142–143
Newspapers and magazines, 21, 39–40
North Carolina, USS, 66, 67
North Carolina Apple Festival, 32
North Carolina Aquarium, 45, 80
North Carolina Azalea Festival, 30, 65
North Carolina Botanical Garden, 105–106
North Carolina Homespun Museum, 145
North Carolina International Folk Festival (Folkmoot USA), 31, 142
North Carolina Maritime Museum, 75
North Carolina Museum of Art, 90
North Carolina Museum of History, 90
North Carolina Museum of Natural Sciences, 89–90

North Carolina State Fair, 32, 88
North Carolina Zoological Park, 135–136

**O**cean Edge Golf Course, 47
Oconaluftee Indian Village, 173
Oconaluftee Mountain Farm Museum, 178
Ocracoke Island, 26, 28, 55, 57–61
Ocracoke Pony Pens, 58
Old Boone Mercantile, 158
Old Burying Ground, 75
Old Europe, 148
Old Salem Christmas and Candle Teas, 33
Old Well, 105
Ole Time Fiddlers & Blue-grass Festival, 30
Opera Carolina, 129
Orchard at Altapass, 165
Oregon Inlet, 56
Orton Plantation Gardens, 67
The Outer Banks, 1, 5, 41–62

**P**ackage tours, 38
Palmer-Marsh House, 86
Pea Island Wildlife Refuge, 56
Petrol, 20
Pets, traveling with, 40
The Piedmont, 1, 26, 33, 36, 87–129
Piedmont Craftsmen, 118
Pinehurst, 130, 131–136
Pinehurst Harness Track Matinee Races, 136
Pine Needles Lodge golf course, 7, 132
Pond Creek Trail, 163
Ponies, wild, 57–58
Poplar Grove Plantation, 67
Portsmouth, 61
Powhatan, Lake, 145
Primitive Baptist Church, 179

**Q**ualla Arts and Crafts Mutual, 173
Qualla Boundary (Cherokee Indian Reservation), 172–173

**R**adio stations, 21–22
Raleigh, 29, 87–97
Raleigh/Durham/Chapel Hill area (Research Triangle), 26
Raven Rock State Park, 91
Regions in brief, 25–28
Restaurants, best, 10
Reynolda House Museum of American Art, 116
Riverside Cemetery, 144
Roanoke Island, 45–46
Roanoke Island Festival Park, 46
Roast Grill, 96

**S**afety, 15–16
St. Thomas Church, 86
Sandhills Community College, 135
Sandhills Theater Company, 138
Sarah P. Duke Gardens, 99
SAS Championship, 32
Scuba diving, 68, 75
Seagrove, 135
Seasons, 28
SECCA (Southeastern Center for Contemporary Art), 117
Senior travel, 37
Shaw House, 136
Shindig on the Green, 31, 142
Single Brothers House, 114
Single Sisters House, 114
Skiing, 36, 141, 160–164
Sneads Ferry, 82
Southeastern Center for Contemporary Art (SECCA), 117
Southern Pines, 136–138
Southern Pines Horse Trials, 136
A Southern Season, 106–107
South Main Building (Chapel Hill), 105
Springfest (Charlotte), 124
Spring Garden Tour (Winston-Salem), 30
Spring Historic Homes and Gardens Tour (New Bern), 30, 83
The State Capitol, 89
State Legislative Building, 90
Stoneybrook Steeple-chase, 30
Sugarlands Visitor Center, 176, 179

Sugar Mountain Resort, 160–161
Swansboro, 81–82
Swindell's Store, 86

**T**anglewood Park, 117
The Tavern (Winston-Salem), 114
Taxes, 22, 40
Teach, Edward "Blackbeard," 58
Telegraph and telex services, 23
Telephone, 22–23
Television channels, 21
Tennis, 36, 91, 126, 131, 132, 146
The Thalian Hall Theater, 74
Thomas Wolfe Memorial, 143–144
Time zones, 23–24, 40
Tipping, 24
Tour de Moore, 132
Tourist information, 28
Train travel, 17–18, 37–38
Transportation, 38–39
Travel Assistance International (TAI), 14
Traveler's Aid Society, 20
Traveler's checks, 14–15
Traveling
  around the U.S., 17–18
  to the U.S., 16–17
Traveling to North Carolina, 37–38
Tryon Palace Historic Sites & Gardens, 83
Tweetsie Railroad Theme Park, 157

**U**niversity of North Carolina (Chapel Hill), 104–105
University of North Carolina at Charlotte, 124
*Unto These Hills,* 174

**V**anderbilt, George Washington, 144
Van Der Veer House, 86
Village of Sugar Mountain Golf Course, 160
Virginia Dare Memorial Bridge, 42
Visas, 12–13
Visitor information, 28

**W**atersports, 47
Weather, 28, 29
Weaver Street Market, 107
Weymouth Woods-Sandhills
　Nature Preserve, 136
Wheeler, Lake, 90
White-water rafting, 35–36,
　146, 158, 182
Wildlife viewing, 56, 62,
　182. *See also* Birding
William B. Umstead State
　Park, 90
Wilmington, 1, 26, 63–74
Windsurfing, 47, 56
Wing Haven Gardens & Bird
　Sanctuary, 126
Winkler Bakery, 114
Winston-Salem, 26, 113–123
Wolfe, Thomas, 143–144
Woolworth Walk, 148
Wright Brothers National
　Memorial, 45
Wrightsville Beach, 8, 67–68

**Z**iggy's, 122–123

## SOUTH CAROLINA

**A**A (American Automo-
　bile Association), 17
Accommodations, 8–10, 18,
　37
Active vacations, 198–199
Africa Alive, 194
AIDSinfo, 13
Aiken, 301–304
Aiken Community Playhouse,
　304
Aiken County Historical
　Museum, 302
Aiken-Rhett House, 224
Aiken Triple Crown, 302
Airlines, 17, 199–200
　from overseas, 16–17
The Alabama Theatre, 279
Alder Lane, 245
American Automobile Asso-
　ciation (AAA), 17
American Express, 201, 205
Antiques, 234, 235, 284
Area codes, 201
Art galleries, Charleston,
　234
Arts Center of Coastal Car-
　olina, 259
ATMs (automated-teller
　machines), 14
Audubon-Newhall Preserve,
　248

Audubon Swamp Garden,
　227
Auto racing, 195, 196–197,
　266, 300
Avenue of Oaks, 227

**B**arefoot Landing, 280
The Battery (White Point
　Gardens), 223
Beaches, 198, 232
　Charleston, 232
　Hilton Head, 245
　Myrtle Beach/the Grand
　　Strand, 266–267, 282
Beachwalker County Park,
　232
Beaufort, 6, 192
Bicycling, 198, 232, 246
Birding, 282
　Hilton Head, 248
Boating, 232
Boat tours and cruises
　Charleston, 224, 231
　Georgetown, 285–286
　Hilton Head, 246
Boone Hall Plantation &
　Gardens, 227–229
Broadway at the Beach, 269,
　280
Brookgreen Gardens, 281
Build a Bear Workshop, 269
Business hours, 19
Bus travel, 18, 200

**C**aledonia Golf & Fish
　Club, 283
Calendar of events, 194
Camden, 190, 299–300
Camping, 198
　Charleston area, 233
　Myrtle Beach, 275
　Pawleys Island/Litchfield,
　　282
Candlelight Tour of Homes &
　Gardens, 196
Canoeing, 198, 285
Carolina Cup, 194
Carolina Dodge Dealers 500,
　195
The Carolina Opry, 279
Car rentals, 18–19
Car travel, 17, 200, 201
Chamber Orchestra Associa-
　tion, 297
Charge cards, 15
Charleston, 2, 6, 192,
　202–242
　accommodations, 206–215
　arriving in, 202–203
　average temperatures and
　　rainfall, 193

　beaches and outdoor pur-
　　suits, 232–234
　for kids, 230–231
　layout of, 203
　neighborhoods in brief, 203
　nightlife, 237–239
　organized tours, 231
　restaurants, 215–223
　shopping, 234–237
　side trips from, 241–242
　sights and attractions,
　　223–231
　transportation, 204
　visitor information, 203
Charleston Ballet Theatre,
　237
The Charleston Museum, 228
Charleston Stage Company,
　237
Charleston Symphony
　Orchestra, 238
Charles Towne Landing,
　228–229
Christmas in Charleston,
　197–198
The Citadel, 229
Citadel Memorial Archives
　Museum, 229
Civil War, 235
Climate, 193
Coastal Discovery Museum,
　245
Coastal Grand, 2, 270
Coligny Beach, 245
Colonial Cup, Camden, 197,
　299
Columbia, 2, 190, 192, 193,
　288–298
Columbia Marionette
　Theatre, 297
Columbia Museum of Art,
　290–291
Columbiana Centre, 298
Congaree Vista, 289
Consulates, 19–20
Cooper River Bridge, 2
Cooper River Bridge Run,
　194–195
Credit cards, 15
Cruises and tours. *See* Boat
　tours and cruises
Currency and currency
　exchange, 14
Customs requirements,
　13–14
Cypress Gardens, 228

**D**arlington, 190, 300
Daylight saving time, 23–24
Dentists, 205
Diamond Hill Plywood 200,
　195

Disabilities, travelers with, 199
Dixie Stampede Dinner and Show, 279
Dock Street Theatre, 237
Doctors, 205
Drayton Hall, 227
Dreissen Beach Park, 245
Drinking laws, 19
Driver's licenses, foreign, 15
Driving safety, 15–16

**E** disto Beach State Park, 233, 240
Edisto Island, 240–241
Edisto Memorial Garden, 292
Edisto Riverfest, 195
Edmondston-Alston House, 224
Electricity, 19
Embassies and consulates, 19–20
Emergencies, 201, 205
Entry requirements, 12–13

**F** all Festival of Houses, 196
Fall for Greenville, 196
Families with children, 199
    Charleston attractions, 230–231
Family Circle Cup, 194
Fax machines, 23
Festival of Houses and Gardens, 194
Fishing, 198, 201, 298, 299
    Charleston, 232–233
    Darlington, 300
    Hilton Head, 246
    Myrtle Beach, 268–269
Five Points, 289
Florence, 190
Flowertown Festival, 194
Folly Beach, 232
Folly Beach County Park, 232
Folly Field Beach, 245
Fort Moultrie, 230
Fort Sumter National Monument, 223–224
Francis Marion National Forest, 233

**G** asoline, 20
Gay and lesbian travelers, 199
    Charleston, 239
    Columbia, 298
Gay Men's Health Crisis, 13
Georgetown, 6, 284–287

The Gibbes Museum of Art, 228
Golf, 194, 198
    Charleston, 233
    Columbia, 293
    Georgetown, 285
    Hilton Head, 246–247
    Myrtle Beach, 267–268
    Pawleys Island, 283
Goodale State Park, 299
Governor's Cup, 196
Governor's Mansion, 291
The Grand Strand, 8, 192, 263. *See also* Myrtle Beach
    nightlife, 279–280

**H** ampton-Preston Mansion, 290
Harold Kaminski House Museum, 284–285
The Heartland, 190
Heritage Passport ticket, 223
Heyward-Washington House, 226
Hiking, Charleston area, 233
Hilton Head, 2, 6, 8, 193, 243–259
    accommodations, 250–255
    nightlife, 259
    outdoor activities, 245–250
    restaurants, 255–259
    shopping, 250
    side trip to Beaufort, 259–262
    special events, 245
    transportation, 245
    traveling to, 243
    visitor information, 243
Historic Brattonsville, 301
Historic Camden, 299
Historic Charleston Reproductions, 236
Historic Columbia Foundation, 290
History, 472–483
Hitchcock Woods, 302
HIV-positive visitors, 13
*H.L. Hunley* Confederate Submarine, 2, 224
Holidays, 20
Hopeland Gardens, 302
Horseback riding, 198, 233, 247, 302
Horse racing, 194, 197, 302
Hospitals, 205
Hunting, 198
Huntington Beach State Park, 282

**I** nsurance, 14
International Driving Permit, 18
Iris Festival, 195
Irmo, 299
Isle of Palms, 232, 241–242

**J** ogging, Hilton Head, 247
Joggling boards, 237
John Mark Verdier House Museum, 260
Joseph Manigault House, 226
Jubilee: Harvest of the Arts, 196

**K** ayaking, 285
    Hilton Head, 247
Kiawah Island, 232, 241
Kings Mountain Military Park, 301
Kingstree, 190

**L** ake Murray's July 4th Celebration, 195
Lakes, 198
Legal aid, 20–21
Legends in Concert, 279
Lights Before Christmas, 197
Liquor laws, 201
Litchfield, 282, 283
Low-Country Oyster Festival, 194
Lucas Belgian Chocolate, 235

**M** agnolia Plantation, 227
Mail, 21
Manns-Simons Cottage, 290
Marion, Lake, 292–293
Maurice Bessenger's Piggie Park, 296
MCI Heritage, 194
McKissick Museum, 291
Measures, 21
Medical emergencies, 21
Medical requirements for entry, 13
Medieval Times & Dinner Show, 280
Merrily Myrtle—A Holiday Celebration, 197
Middleton Place, 226–227
Mikasa Factory Outlet Store, 235–236
MOJA Festival, 196
MONEYGRAM, 23

Money matters, for international visitors, 14–15
Moultrie, Lake, 292–293
Mountain Dew Southern 500, 196–197
Mount Pleasant, 204
Murray, Lake, 298–299
Murrells Inlet, 192, 281–282
Myrtle Beach, 2, 8, 192, 263–280
   accommodations, 270–275
   beaches and outdoor activities, 265–270
   nightlife, 279–280
   restaurants, 275–278
   shopping, 270
   side trips from, 281–287
   traveling to, 265
Myrtle Beach Pavilion Amusement Park, 265
Myrtle Beach State Park, 266–267
Myrtle Beach Waves Water Park, 265–266

**N** ASCAR Speed Park, 266
Nathaniel Russell House, 224, 226
Nature preserves, 248–249
Newberry Opera House, 297
Newspapers and magazines, 21, 201
NMPA Stock Car Hall of Fame/Joe Weatherly Museum, 300
North Charleston, 204, 215

**O** kra Strut, 299
Old Charleston Joggling Board Co., 237
Old Exchange and Provost Dungeon, 229
Old South Golf Links, 7

**P** ackage tours, 200
The Palace Theater, 280
Palmetto Dunes Resort golf course, 7
Pawleys Island, 282–284
Pendleton, 192
Performing arts, Charleston, 237
Petrol, 20
Pharmacies, 205
Plantations, 226–228
Pontiac GMC Freedom Weekend Aloft, 195
Post office, 205

Preservation Society of Charleston Bookstore, 235
Prince George Winyah Episcopal Church, 285
Provost Dungeon, 229, 230

**R** adio stations, 21–22
Regions in brief, 190–193
Restaurants, best, 10
Restrooms, 205
Rice Museum, 285
Ripley's Aquarium, 266
Riverbanks Zoo and Garden, 291–292
River cruises. *See* Boat tours and cruises
Robert Ivey Ballet, 237
Robert Mills Historic House & Park, 290

**S** afety, 15–16, 205
Sailing, 248–249, 269
St. Francis Festival of Trees, 197
St. Helena's Episcopal Church, 260
Sanctuary at Kiawah Island, 2, 241
The Santee Cooper Lakes, 292–293
Santee State Park, 293
Scottish Games and Highland Gathering, 196
Scuba diving, 232, 270
Sea Pines Forest Preserve, 248
Seasons, 193
Senior travel, 199
Shawfest, 195
South Carolina Aquarium, 230
South Carolina Philharmonic, 297
South Carolina's Largest Garage Sale, 196
South Carolina State Fair, 289
South Carolina State Museum, 291
Southeastern Wildlife Exposition, 194
Spoleto Festival U.S.A., 195
Spring Fling, 195
State Farmers' Market, 292
The State House, 289
State parks, 199
Sullivan's Island, 232
Summerfest, 195
Sumter Military Antiques & Museum, 235

**T** aste of Charleston, A, 196
Taxes, 22, 201, 205
Telegraph and telex services, 23
Telephone, 22–23
Television channels, 21
Tennis, 194, 233–234, 249–250, 270
Thoroughbred Racing Hall of Fame, 302
Time zones, 23–24, 201
Tipping, 24
Tourist information, 193
Train travel, 17–18, 200
Transportation, 200–201
Travel Assistance International (TAI), 14
Traveler's Aid Society, 20
Traveler's checks, 14–15
Traveling
   to South Carolina, 199–200
   to and around the U.S., 16–18
Trustus Theater, 297
Two Days, Round the Fourth, 195

**U** niversity of South Carolina, 291

**V** isas, 12–13
Visitor information, 193

**W** alking tours, Charleston, 231
Watersports, 270
Weather, 193, 201
Weather updates, 205
Wedgefield Plantation, 285
White Point Gardens (the Battery), 223
White-water rafting, 199
Wild Dunes Resort, 241–242
   golf courses, 233
Wildlife viewing, Hilton Head, 248–249
Windsurfing, 250, 269
Woodrow Wilson's Boyhood Home, 290
Workshop Theater of South Carolina, 297
World Grits Festival, 194

**Y** ork, 300–301
*Yorktown*, USS, 230

# GEORGIA

### A
AA (American Automobile Association), 17
Accommodations, 8–10, 18, 37
Active vacations, 312–313
Adairsville, 387–388
AIDSinfo, 13
Aiken, Conrad, 439, 440
Aiken-Augusta Spring Regatta, 309
Airlines, 16–17, 314
Alliance Theatre Company, 366
Alonzo F. Herndon Home, 357
Alpine Helen, 394–397
Alpine tubing, 395
American Automobile Association (AAA), 17
American Express, 315, 321, 421
Amicalola Falls State Park, 386
Andalusia, 378
Andersonville, 412–413
Andersonville National Historic Site, 413
Andersonville October Fair, 311
Andrew Low House, 438
Anna Ruby Falls, 386
Antebellum Plantation, 352
Antique Auto & Music Museum, 352
Antiques, 361–362, 444
Appalachian National Scenic Trail, 386
Appalachian Trail, 386
Archery, 411
Art galleries, 444
    Atlanta, 362
Arts Festival of Atlanta, 310
Athens, 369–374
Atlanta, 305, 316–368
    accommodations, 323–335
    attractions, 347–358
    average temperatures and rainfall, 308
    for kids, 358
    neighborhoods in brief, 318–319
    newspapers and magazines, 322
    nightlife, 365–368
    organized tours, 359
    outdoor activities, 359–360
    restaurants, 335–347
    safety, 322–323

shopping, 361–365
taxes, 323
transit information, 323
transportation, 319–321
traveling to, 318
visitor information, 318
what's new in, 2
Atlanta Ballet, 365
Atlanta Botanical Garden, 358
Atlanta Convention & Visitors Bureau (ACVB), 12
Atlanta Dogwood Festival, 310
The Atlanta Film Festival, 310
Atlanta History Center, 354
Atlanta Opera, 365
Atlanta State Farmer's Market, 363–364
Atlanta Symphony Orchestra, 365
ATMs (automated-teller machines), 14
Augusta, 379–384
Augusta Canal, 381
Augusta Cutting Horse Futurity, 308
Augusta Southern National Dragboat Races, 311

### B
Bacon Park, 443, 444
Barnsley Gardens, 388
Barnsley Inn & Golf Resort, 388
Beaches, 312
    Jekyll Island, 464
    St. Simons Island, 456–457
Bellaire Woods Campground, 442
Betty's Country Store, 395
Bicycling, 464
    Atlanta, 359
    Callaway Gardens, 406
    Savannah, 442
    St. Simons Island, 457
The Big Oak, 414
Big Pig Jig, 311–312
Black Rock Mountain State Park, 399
Blairsville, 392–394
Boating, Atlanta, 359
Boat tours and cruises, 442, 449, 454, 471
Bonaventure Cemetery, 439
Boyhood Home of Woodrow Wilson, 380
Brasstown Bald, 393
Braves Clubhouse Store, 349
Bronson House, 376
Brunswick, 453–455

Buckhead, 319
    restaurants, 340–345
    shopping, 361
Business hours, 19
Bus travel, 18, 315

### C
Calendar of events, 308–312
Callaway Gardens, 405–408
Camping, 312–313
    Atlanta, 359–360
    Blairsville, 393
    Savannah, 442
    Stephen C. Foster State Park, 471
    Terrora Park, 398
Candlelight Tours, 312
Candles and Carols of Christmases Past, 312
Canoeing, 313, 360, 381, 471
Car rentals, 18–19
Carriage House Shop, 440
Carter, Jimmy, 410
    Boyhood Farm, 411
    home, 411
    National Historic Site, 411
The Carter Center, 349
Car travel, 17, 314
Cecil B. Day Butterfly Center, 405
Centennial Olympic Park, 357
Center for Puppetry Arts, 358
Central City Park, 402
Central Dunes, 464
Charge cards, 15
Chastain Summer Concerts, 365
Chattahoochee National Forest, 5, 385
Chattanooga National Military Park, 386–387
Cherry Blossom Festival, 309, 401
Chickamauga, 386, 387
Christ Church, 456
Christmas 1864, 312
Climate, 308
Cloister, 307
Cloudland Canyon State Park, 386
CNN Center, 349
Coast Guard Station Beach, 456
Cohutta Wilderness, 385, 386
Confederate Powderworks, 380
Consolidated Gold Mines, 391

Consulates, 19–20
The Cotton Pickin' Fair, 310, 311
Crafts Festival and Cane Grinding, 312
Credit cards, 15
Cumberland Island, 468–470
Currency and currency exchange, 14
Customs requirements, 13–14
Cyclorama, 354

D affin Park, 443
Dahlonega, 390–392
Dahlonega Courthouse Gold Museum, 391
Dahlonega's Public Square, 391
Davenport House Museum, 436
Daylight saving time, 23–24
Decatur, 319
Dillard, 399
Disabilities, travelers with, 313–314
Double Barreled Cannon, 371
Downtown Macon Welcome Center, 402
Drinking laws, 19
Driver's licenses, foreign, 15
Driving safety, 15–16
Drummer Boy Civil War Museum, 413
Dungeness, 469

E atonton, 2–3, 376–377
Ebenezer Baptist Church, 353, 354
Electricity, 19
Embassies and consulates, 19–20
Emergencies, 315
Emory University
    accommodations, 334
    Michael C. Carlos Museum of, 355–356
Entry requirements, 12–13
Ezekiel Harris House, 380

F amilies with children, 314, 358
Fax machines, 23
FDR Memorial Museum (Warm Springs), 3, 409
Fernbank Museum of Natural History, 356

Fernbank Science Center, 356
First African Baptist Church, 440
Fishing, 313, 406, 457, 464
    Atlanta, 360
    Savannah, 443
Forsyth Park, 444
Fort Frederica National Monument, 455–456
Fort McAllister, 441
Fort Mountain State Park, 385
Fort Pulaski, 441
Founders Memorial Garden and Houses, 371
Fourth of July Fireworks and Laser Show, 311
Fox Theatre, 349, 351
Franklin D. Roosevelt State Park, 408

G asoline, 20
Gay and lesbian travelers, 314
    Atlanta, 368
    Savannah, 448
Gay Men's Health Crisis, 13
Georgia College & State University, 377–378
Georgia Mountain Fair, 311
Georgia Museum of Art, 371
Georgia Music Hall of Fame, 402
Georgia Renaissance Festival, 309–310
Georgia's Stone Mountain Park, 352
Georgia State Capitol, 351
Georgia State Fair, 311
Georgia State Museum of Science and Industry, 351
Gertrude Herbert Institute of Art, 380
Gold, panning for, 313
Golden Corral 500, 309
The Golden Isles, 6, 307, 450–470
Golf, 309, 313
    Athens, 372
    Atlanta, 360
    Augusta, 380, 381
    Barnsley Inn & Golf Resort, 388
    Callaway Gardens, 406
    Jekyll Island, 464–465
    Madison, 375
    Savannah, 443
    St. Simons Island, 457
Gone With the Wind, 389, 416

Goshen Plantation, 381
Grand Opera House, 402
Greene-Miller cemetery, 469
Green-Meldrim Home, 437–438

H ampton Plantation, 456
Hard Labor Creek State Park, 375
Harris, Ezekiel, House, 380
Hay House, 403
Helen's Oktoberfest, 311
Herndon, Alonzo F., Home, 357
High Museum of Art, 354–355
High Museum of Art Folk Art and Photography Galleries, 355
Hiking, 313, 372, 398
Historic Guided Trolley Tour (Milledgeville), 378
Historic Homes Tour (Athens), 370
History, 472–483
HIV-positive visitors, 13
Holidays, 20
Holiday Tour of Homes, 312
Horseback riding, 395
Horton's Brewery Site, 464
Hunting, 313

I da Cason Callaway Memorial Chapel, 405–406
Ina Dillard Russell Library, 378
Insurance, 14
International Driving Permit, 18
Isle of Hope, 448

J asper, 389–390
Jekyll Island, 307, 463–468
Jekyll Island Arts Association, 463
Jimmy Carter National Historic Site, 411
Jogging
    Atlanta, 360
    Savannah, 443
John A. Sibley Horticultural Center, 405
Johnny Mercer Theater, 446
Juliette Gordon Low's Birthplace, 438
Juneteenth, 310

**K** ing, Martin Luther, Celebration, 308
King, Martin Luther, Jr.
  Birth Home of, 354
  National Historic Site, 353
The King Center, 353

**L** ake Lanier Islands Beach and Water Park, 359
Lake Mayer Park, 443, 444
Lake Rabun Recreation Area, 398
Lakes, 313
Lanier Oak, 454
Lapham-Patterson House, 415
Lasershow, 352
Laura S. Walker State Park, 471
Legal aid, 20–21
Liquor laws, 315
Little Five Points, 361
Little St. Simons Island, 461–462
Little White House, 408–409
Lookout Mountain, 386
Lover's Oak, 454

**M** acon, 7, 305, 400–404
Madison, 6, 374–376
Madison-Morgan Cultural Center, 375
Mail, 21
Malls and shopping centers, Atlanta, 364–365
Maranatha Baptist Church, 411
Margaret Mitchell House, 355
Martin Luther King, Jr., National Historic Site, 353
Martin Luther King Celebration, 308
Massie Heritage Interpretation Center, 441
Massingale Park Beach, 456
Masters Golf Tournament, 309, 380
Meadow Garden, 381
Measures, 21
Medical emergencies, 21
Medical requirements for entry, 13
Memorial Day at Old Fort Jackson, 310
Memory Hill Cemetery, 378
Mercer House Williams Museum, 440

Michael C. Carlos Museum of Emory University, 355–356
*Midnight in the Garden of Good and Evil*, 426, 434, 436, 439–441
Milledgeville, 377–379
Mistletoe Cottage, 463
Mitchell, Margaret, House, 355
MONEYGRAM, 23
Money matters, 14–15
Morris Museum of Art, 381
Mountain City, 399
Mountain Creek Lake, 406
Mr. Cason's Vegetable Garden, 405
Museum of Coastal History, 456

**N** ational Prisoner of War Museum, 413
Nature tours, St. Simons Island, 457
Neptune Park, 456
Newspapers and magazines, 21
Nora Mill Granary, 395
Northern Georgia, 305
North Georgia, 385–399

**O** akland Cemetery, 357
Ocmulgee National Monument, 402
Oconee, Lake, 376
O'Connor, Flannery, 378, 440
Okefenokee Swamp, 307, 470–471
Okefenokee Swamp Park, 470–471
Old Fort Jackson, 440–441
Old Governors Mansion, 377
The Old Sautee Store, 396
Owen-Thomas House and Museum, 438

**P** ebble Hill Plantation, 415
Petrol, 20
Piedmont Park, 359
Plains, 410–413
Plains Methodist Church, 411
Plum Orchard, 469
Providence Springs, 413

**R** abun, Lake, 398
Rabun County, 398–399
Radio stations, 21–22
Ralph Mark Gilbert Civil Rights Museum, 440
Rattlesnake Roundup, 308
Regions in brief, 305
Restaurants, best, 10–11
Richard Russell Scenic Highway, 385, 393
Riverfest Weekend, 310
Riverwalk, 380
R. J. Reynolds State Wildlife Refuge, 452
Robin Lake Beach, 406
Rock Eagle Effigy, 377
Roosevelt, Franklin D., 408–409
Rose Hill Cemetery, 403

**S** afety, 15–16
Sailing, 443, 458
St. Andrew Picnic Area, 464
St. Patrick's Day Celebration on the River, 309
St. Paul's Episcopal Church, 381
St. Simons Island, 455–461
Sandy Creek Nature Center, 371–372
Sandy Creek Park, 372
Sapelo Island, 452–453
Sapelo Island National Estuarine Research Reserve, 452
Savannah, 6, 305, 308, 418–449
  accommodations, 421–430
  arriving in, 419
  exploring, 436–441
  hospitals, 421
  layout of, 419
  neighborhoods in brief, 419–420
  nightlife, 446–449
  organized tours, 441–442
  post office, 421
  restaurants, 430–436
  safety, 421
  shopping, 444
  transportation, 420
  visitor information, 419
Savannah History Museum, 438
Savannah Irish Festival, 309
Savannah Jazz Festival, 311, 446
Savannah Rapids Park, 381

Savannah Symphony Duck Race, 310
Savannah Symphony Orchestra, 446
Savannah Theater, 446
The Savannah Tour of Homes & Gardens, 309
SciTrek, 356
Scuba diving, 443
Sea Island, 462–463
Sea Island Golf Club, 7–8, 457
Seasons, 308
7 Stages, 365–366
Ships of the Sea Maritime Museum, 439
Sidney Lanier Cottage, 403
Sinclair, Lake, 378
Six Flags Over Georgia, 358
Skidaway Island State Park, 442
Sorghum Festival, 392
South Dunes Beach, 464
South End House, 452
The State Botanical Garden of Georgia, 371
Stephen C. Foster State Park, 471
Steward Chapel of the African Methodist Episcopal Church, 402
Stone Mountain, accommodations, 334
Stone Mountain Park, 352
Stone Mountain Scenic Railroad, 352
Suwanee Canal Recreation Area, 471
Swan House and Gardens, 354

**T**allulah Falls and Gorge, 398
Tate, 389–390
Taxes, 22, 315
Taylor-Grady House, 370
Telegraph and telex services, 23
Telephone, 22–23
Television channels, 21
Telfair Mansion and Art Museum, 438
Tennis, 360, 406, 444, 458, 465
Terrora Park, 398
Thomas County Museum of History, 414
Thomasville, 7, 414–417
Thurmond Lake, 381
Time zones, 23–24, 315
Tipping, 24
Tourist information, 307
Train travel, 17–18, 314
Transportation, 315
Travel Assistance International (TAI), 14
Traveler's Aid Society, 20
Traveler's checks, 14–15
Traveling
    to Georgia, 314–315
    to and around the U.S., 16–18
"The Tree That Owns Itself," 371
Tubing, alpine, 395
Tubman African American Museum, 403
Tullie Smith Farm, 354
Turner Store, 349
Turner Studio, 349

**U**ncle Remus Museum, 376
Underground Atlanta, 351, 361, 365
*Unfinished Portrait,* 409
University of Georgia (Athens), 371

**V**isas, 12–13
Visitor information, 307
Vogel State Park, 386, 393

**W**arm Springs, 3, 408–410
Watersports, Jekyll Island, 465
Weather, 308
White-water rafting, 313
Wildlife viewing, 443, 471
William Breman Jewish Heritage Museum, 356–357
Wilson, Woodrow, Boyhood Home of, 380
The World of Coca-Cola, 351
Wormsloe Plantation, 448
Wormsloe's Colonial Faire and Muster, 308–309

**Y**ank/Reb Blues Festival, 312
Yellow Daisy Festival, 311

**Z**oo Atlanta, 358

# FROMMER'S® COMPLETE TRAVEL GUIDES

Alaska
Alaska Cruises & Ports of Call
American Southwest
Amsterdam
Argentina & Chile
Arizona
Atlanta
Australia
Austria
Bahamas
Barcelona, Madrid & Seville
Beijing
Belgium, Holland & Luxembourg
Bermuda
Boston
Brazil
British Columbia & the Canadian Rockies
Brussels & Bruges
Budapest & the Best of Hungary
Calgary
California
Canada
Cancún, Cozumel & the Yucatán
Cape Cod, Nantucket & Martha's Vineyard
Caribbean
Caribbean Ports of Call
Carolinas & Georgia
Chicago
China
Colorado
Costa Rica
Cruises & Ports of Call
Cuba
Denmark
Denver, Boulder & Colorado Springs
England
Europe
Europe by Rail
European Cruises & Ports of Call

Florence, Tuscany & Umbria
Florida
France
Germany
Great Britain
Greece
Greek Islands
Halifax
Hawaii
Hong Kong
Honolulu, Waikiki & Oahu
India
Ireland
Italy
Jamaica
Japan
Kauai
Las Vegas
London
Los Angeles
Maryland & Delaware
Maui
Mexico
Montana & Wyoming
Montréal & Québec City
Munich & the Bavarian Alps
Nashville & Memphis
New England
Newfoundland & Labrador
New Mexico
New Orleans
New York City
New York State
New Zealand
Northern Italy
Norway
Nova Scotia, New Brunswick & Prince Edward Island
Oregon
Ottawa
Paris
Peru

Philadelphia & the Amish Country
Portugal
Prague & the Best of the Czech Republic
Provence & the Riviera
Puerto Rico
Rome
San Antonio & Austin
San Diego
San Francisco
Santa Fe, Taos & Albuquerque
Scandinavia
Scotland
Seattle
Shanghai
Sicily
Singapore & Malaysia
South Africa
South America
South Florida
South Pacific
Southeast Asia
Spain
Sweden
Switzerland
Texas
Thailand
Tokyo
Toronto
Turkey
USA
Utah
Vancouver & Victoria
Vermont, New Hampshire & Maine
Vienna & the Danube Valley
Virgin Islands
Virginia
Walt Disney World® & Orlando
Washington, D.C.
Washington State

# FROMMER'S® DOLLAR-A-DAY GUIDES

Australia from $50 a Day
California from $70 a Day
England from $75 a Day
Europe from $85 a Day
Florida from $70 a Day
Hawaii from $80 a Day

Ireland from $80 a Day
Italy from $70 a Day
London from $90 a Day
New York City from $90 a Day
Paris from $90 a Day
San Francisco from $70 a Day

Washington, D.C. from $80 a Day
Portable London from $90 a Day
Portable New York City from $90 a Day
Portable Paris from $90 a Day

# FROMMER'S® PORTABLE GUIDES

Acapulco, Ixtapa & Zihuatanejo
Amsterdam
Aruba
Australia's Great Barrier Reef
Bahamas
Berlin
Big Island of Hawaii
Boston
California Wine Country
Cancún
Cayman Islands
Charleston
Chicago
Disneyland®
Dominican Republic
Dublin

Florence
Frankfurt
Hong Kong
Las Vegas
Las Vegas for Non-Gamblers
London
Los Angeles
Los Cabos & Baja
Maine Coast
Maui
Miami
Nantucket & Martha's Vineyard
New Orleans
New York City
Paris

Phoenix & Scottsdale
Portland
Puerto Rico
Puerto Vallarta, Manzanillo & Guadalajara
Rio de Janeiro
San Diego
San Francisco
Savannah
Vancouver
Vancouver Island
Venice
Virgin Islands
Washington, D.C.
Whistler

## FROMMER'S® NATIONAL PARK GUIDES

Algonquin Provincial Park
Banff & Jasper
Family Vacations in the National
  Parks

Grand Canyon
National Parks of the American
  West
Rocky Mountain

Yellowstone & Grand Teton
Yosemite & Sequoia/Kings
  Canyon
Zion & Bryce Canyon

## FROMMER'S® MEMORABLE WALKS

Chicago
London

New York
Paris

San Francisco

## FROMMER'S® WITH KIDS GUIDES

Chicago
Las Vegas
New York City

Ottawa
San Francisco
Toronto

Vancouver
Walt Disney World® & Orlando
Washington, D.C.

## SUZY GERSHMAN'S BORN TO SHOP GUIDES

Born to Shop: France
Born to Shop: Hong Kong,
  Shanghai & Beijing

Born to Shop: Italy
Born to Shop: London

Born to Shop: New York
Born to Shop: Paris

## FROMMER'S® IRREVERENT GUIDES

Amsterdam
Boston
Chicago
Las Vegas
London

Los Angeles
Manhattan
New Orleans
Paris
Rome

San Francisco
Seattle & Portland
Vancouver
Walt Disney World®
Washington, D.C.

## FROMMER'S® BEST-LOVED DRIVING TOURS

Austria
Britain
California
France

Germany
Ireland
Italy
New England

Northern Italy
Scotland
Spain
Tuscany & Umbria

## THE UNOFFICIAL GUIDES®

Beyond Disney
California with Kids
Central Italy
Chicago
Cruises
Disneyland®
England
Florida
Florida with Kids
Inside Disney

Hawaii
Las Vegas
London
Maui
Mexico's Best Beach Resorts
Mini Las Vegas
Mini Mickey
New Orleans
New York City
Paris

San Francisco
Skiing & Snowboarding in the
  West
South Florida including Miami &
  the Keys
Walt Disney World®
Walt Disney World® for
  Grown-ups
Walt Disney World® with Kids
Washington, D.C.

## SPECIAL-INTEREST TITLES

Athens Past & Present
Cities Ranked & Rated
Frommer's Best Day Trips from London
Frommer's Best RV & Tent Campgrounds
  in the U.S.A.
Frommer's Caribbean Hideaways
Frommer's China: The 50 Most Memorable Trips
Frommer's Exploring America by RV
Frommer's Gay & Lesbian Europe
Frommer's NYC Free & Dirt Cheap

Frommer's Road Atlas Europe
Frommer's Road Atlas France
Frommer's Road Atlas Ireland
Frommer's Wonderful Weekends from
  New York City
The New York Times' Guide to Unforgettable
  Weekends
Retirement Places Rated
Rome Past & Present

Travel Tip: He who finds the best hotel deal has more to spend on facials involving knobbly vegetables.

Hello, the Roaming Gnome here. I've been nabbed from the garden and taken round the world. The people who took me are so terribly clever. They find the best offerings on Travelocity. For very little cha-ching. And that means I get to be pampered and exfoliated till I'm pink as a bunny's doodah.

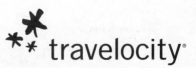

**travelocity**

1-888-TRAVELOCITY / travelocity.com / America Online Keyword: Travel

Travel Tip: Make sure there's customer service for any change of plans — involving friendly natives, for example.

One can plan and plan, but if you don't book with the right people you can't seize le moment and canoodle with the poodle named Pansy. I, for one, am all for fraternizing with the locals. Better yet, if I need to extend my stay and my gnome nappers are willing, it can all be arranged through the 800 number at, oh look, how convenient, the lovely company coat of arms.